The Public Domain

***

LAW AND CONTEMPORARY PROBLEMS

Volume 66 | Winter/Spring 2003 | Numbers 1 & 2

THE PUBLIC DOMAIN

James Boyle
Special Editor

LAW AND CONTEMPORARY PROBLEMS

Volume 66 | Winter/Spring 2003 | Numbers 1 & 2

FOREWORD: THE OPPOSITE OF PROPERTY?

JAMES BOYLE*

I
INTRODUCTION

In November of 2001, Duke University School of Law held a conference on the public domain; the "outside" of the intellectual property system, the material that is free for all to use and to build upon.[1] So far as we could tell, this was the first conference on the subject, which is surprising when one realizes the central role of the public domain in our traditions of speech, innovation and culture. In many ways, this imbalance—the hundreds of conferences, centers and initiatives that have intellectual property as their focus, and the comparative dearth of attention on the public domain—provided the best explanation for the event.

The conference was organized at Duke by my remarkable colleagues on the intellectual property faculty, Jerry Reichman and David Lange, and by me. The conference announcement set forth our goal:

> The last fifteen years has seen a rise in both the importance and the strength of intellectual property rights in the world economy; rights have expanded in areas ranging from the human genome to the Internet and have been strengthened with legally backed digital fences, lengthened copyright terms and increased penalties. Is this expansion of intellectual property necessary to respond to new copying technologies,

* Professor of Law, Duke University School of Law.

1 The Conference was generously supported by a major grant from the Center for the Public Domain.

> and desirable because it will produce investment and innovation? Must we privatize the public domain to avoid a "tragedy of the commons," or can the technologies of cheap copying and global networks actually make common pool management more efficient than legal monopolies? Questions such as these have thrown attention on the "other side" of intellectual property: the public domain. What does the public domain do? What is its importance, its history, its role in science, art, and in the building of the Internet? How is the public domain similar to and different from the idea of a commons? This conference, the first major meeting to focus squarely on the topic of the public domain, will try to answer some of these questions in areas ranging from the human genome to appropriationist art, from the production of scientific data to the architecture of our communications networks.[2]

To begin to answer these questions we brought together scientists and historians; environmental systems scholars and artists; lawyers and software engineers; film-makers, musicians and archivists. A number of framing papers were commissioned before the event to get the discussion going. The results were striking.

Running a conference is rather like organizing a dinner party. You are the person least likely to enjoy the food yourself. The fact that even *I* noticed the energy the conference unleashed was thus a testament to the cast of characters we had assembled. At first, I thought this was simple bias on my part. Media coverage of the event, however, confirmed the same impressions.[3] (The entire conference was webcast and has been archived so that anyone with an Internet connection can judge for themselves.[4]) The webcast, of course, cannot capture everything; my own favorite image from the conference was a moment of earnest methodological agreement between the Home Secretary of the National Academy of Sciences, Stephen Berry, Distinguished Professor of Chemistry at the University of Chicago, and Mark Hosler, a member of the appropriationist group, Negativland, who had just finished showing a video called "Free the Mermaid." Mertonian science and appropriationist art, it seemed, share something deeper than previously imagined.

The conference began with panels on the history and theory of the public domain and proceeded through a "state of the public domain" report in three subject areas—the digital realm, culture, and science. A more detailed analysis of each area was presented, followed by an examination of the "constitutionalization" of the public domain, and finally an open-ended discussion of future directions for scholarship, research, and action. With minor rearrangements and omissions,[5] that is the structure of the essays in this volume.

---

2. Conference on the Public Domain, About the Conference, *available at* http://law.duke.edu/pd/about.html (last visited February 3, 2003)

3. *See, e.g.*, Seth Shulman, *What Tree Huggers Can Teach us About the Public Domain of Ideas*, TECHNOLOGY REVIEW, March 2002, *at* http://www.technologyreview.com/articles/shulman0302.asp; Patti Waldmeir, *A Case of Creative Block*, FIN. TIMES, February 27 2002, at 16.

4. Conference on the Public Domain, *at* http://www.law.duke.edu/pd/realcast.htm (last visited February 3, 2003)

5. Most notably, three papers that were originally included in the conference materials are not included here, but luckily are not lost to the world. At our earnest pleading, Yochai Benkler graced us with not one, but two papers. The first, on the constitutionalization of the public domain appears in this volume, the second in the Yale Law Journal. *See* Yochai Benkler, *Through the Looking Glass:*

II

THE HISTORY AND THEORY OF THE PUBLIC DOMAIN

The first article, *The Second Enclosure Movement and the Construction of the Public Domain*, is a study of the theory and history of the public domain, which offers a framework for the themes of the volume.[6] Part I, *Enclosure*, traces the rationales behind the "second enclosure movement," recent expansions in intellectual property rights, and compares them to the rationales for the first enclosure movement—the enclosure of arable land. I conclude that the move to expand intellectual property rights is both empirically and theoretically questionable and quite possibly harmful to the very goals it attempts to serve. Interestingly, this conclusion is strengthened rather than weakened by the transformations wrought by the new digital media and the Internet.

Part II, *Against Enclosure*, offers an historical sketch of three types of 'resistance to enclosure' or skepticism about intellectual property: the anti-monopolist sentiments of the Framers of the U.S. Constitution, the emergence of affirmative arguments for the public domain, and the use of the language of the commons to defend the possibility of distributed methods of non-proprietary production (open source software being an obvious example). Apart from clarifying the relationship between the multiple definitions of the "public domain" and "the commons," the article offers a framework—built on the model of the environmental movement—within which to understand the various intellectual and political projects being pursued under the banner of the public domain.

Mark Rose is one of the foremost scholars of the history of literary property. His book, *Authors and Owners*, is a fascinating and deeply readable account of another period of ferment over intellectual property rights—the period immediately before and after the passage of the first true copyright statute, the Statute of Anne.[7] For this volume, we persuaded him to write about the other side of the coin. His essay here, *Nine-Tenths of the Law: The English Copyright Debates and the Rhetoric of the Public Domain*, presents a fascinating early history of the interaction between authorial property claims and those of

---

Alice and Constitutional Foundations of the Public Domain, 66 LAW & CONTEMP. PROBS. 173 (Winter/Spring 2003) [hereinafter Benkler, *Looking Glass*]; Yochai Benkler, *Coase's Penguin: Or Linux and the Nature of the Firm*, 112 YALE L.J. 369 (2002). An earlier version of Larry Lessig's article, *The Architecture of Innovation*, was delivered as the Frey Lecture at Duke University School of Law. *See* Lawrence Lessig, *The Architecture of Innovation*, 51 Duke L.J. 1783 (2002). The webcast is available at http://www.law.duke.edu/webcast/lessig.ram (last visited February 3, 2003). David Lange and Jennifer Lange Anderson's paper on fair use is being revised as David prepares a larger work on the constitution and the public domain. We do, however, have the pleasure of an essay from David. *See* David Lange, *Reimaging the Public Domain*, 66 LAW & CONTEMP. PROBS. 463 (Winter/Spring 2003) [hereinafter Lange, *Reimagining*]. The original papers can be found at http://www.law.duke.edu/pd/papers.html (last visited February 3, 2003).

6. James Boyle, *The Second Enclosure Movement*, 66 LAW & CONTEMP. PROBS. 33 (Winter/Spring 2003).

7. MARK ROSE, AUTHORS AND OWNERS: THE INVENTION OF COPYRIGHT (1993).

the public domain and of civil society.[8] Rose rightly reminds us that talk of an enclosure movement could conjure up an erroneous idyllic pre-history in which all literary property was held in common. This idyllic tale of the time before enclosure would be an inaccurate account even regarding the English "open fields" system. It most certainly does not apply to the world of copyright. The pre-history of copyright was not total freedom, but rather a set of guild publishing privileges that produced a framework of pervasive regulation. Instituting a copyright system with statutory time limits, particularly after the House of Lords rejected the author's claim of a perpetual common right, enabled a much freer and more open literary environment. It is only after the Statute of Anne, Rose points out, that certain classic works became available for any publisher to print in a competitive market.[9] Not only did copyright law make many works more freely available, its structure and rationale invited the first, albeit faint, reflections on the countervailing claims of civil society. In both practice and in rhetoric, as Rose puts it neatly, "[c]opyright and the public domain were born together."[10]

But if they were born together, Rose believes that one child was considerably healthier than the other. To paraphrase Rose, in the early debates over copyright we can see that the rhetoric of property is both familiar and powerful but that the affirmative case for the claims of civil society and the public domain is comparatively weak. There are certainly fascinating examples of writers who argue for the need to circumscribe copyright (including a little-known Memorandum from John Locke, whose theory is generally used to argue the countervailing view) but there are few freestanding defenses of the idea of a public domain.[11] (This is consistent with the pattern I describe in the first essay.) In fact, Rose suggests, this is a weakness that continues to the present day. What might such a defense look like?

Rose argues that a review of copyright's history suggests one important warning: The search for a rhetoric of the public domain is one that can too easily turn into the dead end of diatribes against the "meanness of writing for money," as in the case of Lord Camden's argument in *Donaldson v. Becket*.[12]

---

8. *See* Mark Rose, *Nine Tenths of the Law: The English Copyright Debates and the Rhetoric of the Public Domain*, 66 LAW & CONTEMP. PROBS. 75 (Winter/Spring 2003).

9. This is a point that cannot be made too often. Property regimes can feed the public domain as well as deplete it. The feudal practice of protecting systems of innovation by guild privileges and secrecy was hardly an open system marked by the free flow of information. Replacing guild secrecy with a statutory patent law system, in which disclosure of the invention is required and the term eventually expires, feeds the public domain in a way that the "intellectual property-less" system does not. Increasing the realm of property can sometimes expand the functional public domain; the relationship is a complex, multi-variant one, not a simple linear function.

10. *See* Mark Rose, *supra* note 8, at 76.

11. It is important to note, however, that Rose finds early analogues to the notion of the public domain in a combination of the free trader's anti-monopolistic language and the Enlightenment defense of the free circulation of ideas. Both this point, and Rose's broader argument are important correctives to the idea that the public domain was invented out of whole cloth in 1966 by the Supreme Court in the case of *Graham v. John Deere*, 383 U.S. 1 (1966).

12. 1 Eng. Rep. 837 (H.L. 1774).

But these diatribes fail to convey the importance or the function that the public domain has. What are the alternatives? In a conclusion that is, from my point of view, both encouraging and sobering, Rose discusses my proposal of an "environmentalist rhetoric" for the public domain.

> At the present moment, as we attempt to argue for the value of the public domain, we need to understand that we are fashioning a rhetoric as well as a politics of the public domain. Casting a defense of the public domain on the model of the environmental movement seems promising. As Boyle notes, before the movement, the environment was in effect invisible. Likewise, one element of the task today is to make the public domain visible—to develop an affirmative discourse that will make it a positive and prominent part of the social and cultural landscape. Part of the rhetorical strength of such an environmental model is that it draws on a metaphor that is already deeply embedded in copyright thought. Rhetoric is crucial. And the English copyright debates of the eighteenth century illuminate both the difficulties and the importance of the rhetorical task.[13]

Mark Rose's article is immediately followed by a piece from another Rose, Carol Rose, the distinguished property scholar from Yale Law School.

In *Romans, Roads, and Romantic Creators: Traditions of Public Property in the Information Age*, Carol Rose turns a new light on the question of the public domain by considering the arguments for common property in the material world; there the concept must swim against the tide of two powerful arguments in favor of exclusive rights: the danger of overuse and depletion, and the need to encourage investment and development.[14] In "Intellectual Space," by contrast, she believes the overuse argument is lacking.[15]

> The long and short of it, then, is that exclusive property rights come up long in Tangible Space but rather short in Intellectual Space. This means that although there is still a case for property in the intellectual realm, the commons or the public domain is relatively more thinkable.
>
> In this paper, I am going to leverage this point of the comparative advantage of

---

13. Mark Rose, *supra* note 8, at 87.

14. Carol Rose, *Romans, Roads, and Romantic Creators: Traditions of Public Property in the Information Age*, 66 LAW & CONTEMP. PROBS. 89 (Winter/Spring 2003).

15. Some intellectual property theorists would disagree. For example, one of the arguments supporting literary property (and trademark) is "stewardship"—that a single proprietor must police the meaning of the intellectual creation in order to maintain its integrity and meaning. If works or marks can be "played to death," diluted, tarnished or turned into clichés, then meaning can actually be depleted or destroyed. Signs lose their meaning, not from some post-modernist decay, but from inconsistent use, or simply overuse. Words can be overgrazed. This argument, however, is quite problematic, particularly for copyright cases. First, it is unclear how it fits into the American constitutional tradition, since both the Copyright Clause and the First Amendment seem opposed to the idea that, in the copyright context, Congress has a the power to police signs in order to preserve their meaning—even through a private party intermediary. "Promote semiotic stability" is not the same as "promote the progress of science," and claiming that works must be protected from others who attempt to transform their meaning obviously implicates the freedom of speech to which the First Amendment refers. The *Wind Done Gone* case is a nice example. *See* SunTrust Bank v. Houghton Mifflin Co., 268 F.3d 1257 (11th Cir. 2001); *cf.* San Francisco Arts & Athletics, Inc. v. U.S. Olympic Comm., 483 U.S. 522 (1987). Second, the semiotic stewardship claim is empirically questionable; would private property rights produce the desired result? Both sides use *It's a Wonderful Life* to support their arguments. One side suggests that the film gained its enormous contemporary popularity only when it fell (or so it seemed) into the public domain and was made widely available. The other side counters that, in the process, the film lost its meaning—becoming first a feel-good Christmas cliché and then simply a cliché. *See* IT'S A WONDERFUL LIFE (Liberty Films 1946).

> publicness in Intellectual Space. To do so, I will turn to the other side, to Tangible Space, to ask whether there is a case to be made even here for the public domain. One would think that if the public domain is at all attractive in Tangible Space, where there is such a strong argument to the contrary based on the potential waste of resources, then the arguments for the public domain should be even more compelling in Intellectual Space, where the counter-arguments for exclusivity are cut in half.[16]

Rose concludes that while there are arguments for common property even in Tangible Space, that they come with limitations and qualifications, some of which may also apply to Intellectual Space. In the most fascinating part of the article she notes the relative lack of interest in the concept of common property over the last three hundred years of the Anglo-American legal tradition. She turns instead to Roman law and its various categories of "public property": *res nullius, res communes, res publicae, res universatitis, and res divini juris*; respectively, things that are unowned and open to all by their nature, things that are publicly owned and made open to the public by law, things owned by a public group in its corporate capacity, and things "unownable" because of their divine or sacred status. Implicit in her remarks is that each of these categories reflects a consistently recurring pattern of empirical necessities and normative claims about the world. Each corresponds to a recurring pattern in human affairs, each suggests both potential solutions and problems, and each conjures up a characteristic set of claims about justice and utility. These patterns are not confined to the Institutes of Justinian, they are "paradigmatic" for certain situations in which norms of public property are likely to be deployed.

Rose offers some fascinating reflections on the possible applications of these notions to Intellectual Space. Intellectual property scholars, I think, will immediately see still others. For example, as Rose notes, the category of *res publicae* (things publicly owned and made open to the public by law) has interesting resonance for network protocols, which she analogizes to the Roman roads of the information age. Indeed, critics of Microsoft's monopoly on operating systems have sought to use antitrust law to impose *res publicae*-like openness on certain portions of the Windows Application Programming Interfaces, or API's,[17] while leaving the program itself as private property. This pattern is not an unusual one. As Rose notes, the goal of most of these categories of public property is not to undermine private property but to support it. Private land is worth more when served by public roads. Innovation on the Internet may flourish best when certain components of the communicative infrastructure are "open." The same point, of course, is repeatedly made about the public domain in intellectual space. In one sense it is intellectual property's antithesis, in another, its handmaid.

However, the categories of public property do not *always* serve those of private property. The category of *res divini juris* seems to demarcate the commodifiable, less to increase the efficiency of the property system than because "some

16. Carol Rose, *supra* note 14, at 90-91.

17. For a definition, see Windows API, *at* http://msdn.microsoft.com/en-us/vbdef98/html/vbdefwindowsapi.asp (last visited January 31, 2002).

things are sacred." For me, this section of *Roman Roads* conjured up the debates about ownership of the human genome, even more so than Rose's own example of the sanctity of Shakespeare, Mozart and—tongue-in-cheek—Mickey Mouse. Beyond the particular point-to-point comparisons, the most interesting aspect of the Roman categories is the subtle shading in the meaning of "publicness" or "openness" or "non-private-propertyness" each represents. As I argue in *The Second Enclosure Movement*, this is a subtlety and shading that we sorely need.

As the earlier articles point out, any discussion of intellectual property or the public domain proceeds in the shadow of the "the tragedy of the commons," the phrase coined in Garret Hardin's classic article on the environmental dysfunctions of overuse and underinvestment found in the absence of a private property regime.[18] Consequently, when organizing the conference we thought immediately to invite those who had advanced this debate since Hardin's article was first published. Carol Rose had done so through her work on "the comedy of the commons"—the occasions when collective management of a resource is socially more efficient than individual ownership.[19] No work, though, has brought more attention to the limitations and qualifications of the tragedy of the commons argument than Elinor Ostrom's classic book *Governing the Commons*.[20] Ostrom's work makes two vital points.

First, the absence of individualized legal control under a private property scheme is *not* the same as the absence of control altogether. When one actually looks at the practices of groups that "manage" a commons, one finds multiple informal and formal methods of regulation, many of which work to avoid the problems supposed to attend the commons.[21] In short, Hardin's schematic was too simplistic:

> The growing evidence from many field studies of common-pool resources conducted by anthropologists and historians called for a serious rethinking of the theoretical foundations for analysis of common-pool resources. The cumulative impact of the extensive empirical studies does not challenge the empirical validity of the conventional theory *where it is relevant*, but rather questions its presumed, universal generalizability.[22]

---

18. Garret Hardin, *The Tragedy of the Commons*, SCIENCE, Dec. 13, 1968 at 1243.

19. Carol Rose, *The Comedy of the Commons: Custom, Commerce, and Inherently Public Property*, 53 U. CHI. L. REV. 711 (1986).

20. ELINOR OSTROM, GOVERNING THE COMMONS: THE EVOLUTION OF INSTITUTIONS FOR COLLECTIVE ACTION (1990).

21. This work has been developed in very interesting ways by Margaret McKean and Bob Keohane, colleagues of mine at Duke. *See* Margaret McKean, *Management of Traditional Common Lands (Iriaichi) in Japan*, *in* MAKING THE COMMONS WORK: THEORETICAL, HISTORICAL, AND CONTEMPORARY STUDIES (Bromley et al. eds., 1992); LOCAL COMMONS AND GLOBAL INTERDEPENDENCE: HETEROGENEITY AND COOPERATION IN TWO DOMAINS (Elinor Ostrom & Robert Keohane eds. 1994). Robert Ellickson's classic work on the ranchers of Shasta County is the single best extended examination of the ways that informal methods of resource management work with, beside, and instead of legal rules. ROBERT C. ELLICKSON, ORDER WITHOUT LAW: HOW NEIGHBORS SETTLE DISPUTES (1991).

22. Charlotte Hess & Elinor Ostrom, *Ideas, Artifacts, and Facilities: Information as a Common-Pool Resource*, 66 LAW & CONTEMP. PROBS. 111, 118 (Winter/Spring 2003) (footnotes omitted).

Second, an empirical focus on the actual practices of successfully managed commons should not be a seen as a rejection of formal modeling; rather it points to a more nuanced set of categories in an analysis that tries to match the type of commons with the type of formal or informal, collective or individual regime that could manage it successfully. Since most of the major issues in environmental policy are built exactly around this question, it would be hard to imagine a more important set of theoretical tools.

Increasingly, intellectual property scholars and information economists have turned to the theorists of the commons in trying to understand innovation. In the process, as I point out in *The Second Enclosure Movement*, something very important happens. In the debates over intellectual property policy, we have been familiar with a conceptual scheme that portrays "intellectual property" as a monopoly,[23] and "the public domain," as its conceptual opposite—a realm of vaguely defined "freedom." In contrast, the commons literature gives us a conceptual scheme in which property, seen as a regime of individual, legal, market-based control is juxtaposed to its conceptual opposite—the well-run commons, a realm of collective, and sometimes informal, controls that avoids the tragedy of the commons without a need for single party ownership. The former juxtaposes monopolies against freedom, the latter juxtaposes individual formal controls against collective, and often informal, ones. Both give us a realm of property and a realm in which its opposite, or alternative, are offered. Despite these similarities, the two are by no means identical. Yet the two terms, public domain and commons, are often used as if they were interchangeable.

One of our goals in organizing the conference was to turn Ostrom and her distinguished collaborator Charlotte Hess loose on the intellectual commons with the goal of discussing the applicability of their ideas to this new realm, and perhaps of producing a similar matrix of types of commons and strategies of

23. Though this point is sometimes, appropriately, challenged: "Rights to exclude are not monopolies just because the property involved is an intangible rather than something you can walk across or hold in your hand." Frank H. Easterbrook, *Intellectual Property Is Still Property*, 13 HARV. J.L. & PUB. POL'Y 108, 118 (1990). The classic statement of this proposition was made by Edmund Kitch. *See* Edmund W. Kitch, Patents: Monopolies or Property Rights?, 8 RES. L. & ECON. 31, 33 (1986); Edmund W. Kitch, The Nature and Function of the Patent System, 20 J.L. & ECON. 265, 274-75 (1977). These articles make the point that the ability successfully to extract monopoly rents depends on market factors, not merely legal endowments, and that "substitute goods" may bring the price of a good protected by an intellectual property right below that of classic monopoly pricing. Both of those points are well taken. Still, no one may sell, copy or manufacture Viagra, Windows, or *Gone With the Wind* without the authorization of the owner of the respective intellectual property rights over those goods; but for those rights there would be competition in delivery of that good. Thus, the economic conditions under which these non-rival and largely non-excludable goods are distributed look considerably more similar to a monopoly than the economic conditions under which the owner of Blackacre sells his farm. Kitch and Easterbrook are right to stress that there are similarities between tangible and intangible property rights. There are. Both Gates and the farmer rely partly on their legal right to exclude to set a price. In one sense the farmer does have a monopoly over *that farm*. There are substitute operating systems just as there are substitute farms, and the existence of both may affect pricing. But there are also differences between the cases that I cite—differences rooted in the non-rival nature of the goods and the importance of the intellectual property right as opposed to other modes of exclusion. Both economists and lay people feel these differences are nicely grasped by the word "monopoly."

management. Could environmental policy in fact provide hints for the nurture and management of the public domain? Could the commoners of intellectual space ever successfully manage their open fields of the mind without the state coming in, turfing them off, and handing the resultant package over to a single landholder? If so, under what conditions?

Ostrom and Hess produced a *tour de force*. Focusing on the world of scholarly publishing and archives, they attempted to develop a clearer understanding of the language, methodology and outcomes of commons-based solutions.[24]

> To develop a broader and empirically verifiable theory that encompassed the dominant "tragedy of the commons" theory as a special case, scholars learned that they had to make some key distinctions between concepts that had previously and casually been treated as the same. Because we feel that a similar effort is needed for the intellectual public domain, we will discuss these distinctions in some depth. There are four basic confusions that need to be untangled. The source of confusion relates to the differences between (1) the nature of the good (common-pool *resources*) and a property regime (common-property *regimes*), (2) resource systems and the flow of resource units, (3) common property and open-access regimes, and (4) the set of property rights involved in "ownership." All four sources of confusion reduce clarity in assigning meaning to terms and retard theoretical and empirical progress.[25]

Ostrom and Hess's account has the great virtue of being a view from the outside. Some distinctions they suggest that legal scholars might be slurring, such as those based on the "rivalrousness" or "subtractability" of a good versus the ease of "exclusion" are, in my view, fundamental to thinking about intellectual property and have been for some time.[26] Other lines in the common pool resource literature may be even more finely calibrated in the legal literature. For example, they say,

> In a now classic article, Ciriacy-Wantrup and Bishop clearly articulated the difference between property regimes that are *open-access*, where no one has the legal right to exclude anyone from using a resource, and *common property*, where members of a clearly defined group have a bundle of legal rights including the right to exclude nonmembers from using that resource. Legal doctrine has long considered open-access regimes (*res nullius*)—including the classic cases of the open seas and the atmosphere—to involve no limits on who has authorized use.[27]

To this analytic division, legal scholars would add another—regimes where the owner (individual or collective) has a right to receive a revenue stream from those who wish access, but cannot refuse access.[28] In some situations, this is

---

24. Given their background in the more formalized tradition of the study of common pool resources, it is unsurprising that they echo my comments about the looser and more inconsistent ways in which the terms commons and public domain are thrown around by legal scholars!

25. Hess and Ostrom, *supra* note 22, at 118-119 (emphasis added).

26. Harold Demsetz, *The Private Production of Public Goods*, 13 J.L. & ECON. 293 (1970).

27. Hess and Ostrom, *supra* note 22, at 121-122 (emphasis in original).

28. This point also comes up in Ostrom and Hess's categorization of the interests incident to property, where they stress the ability to alienate as the most fundamental stick in the property bundle. In the post-legal-realist world, it is not clear that legal thought recognizes any *sine qua non* of property rights, but after Calabresi and Melamed's article legal scholars have tended to associate a property rule regime with the right to name the price at which access will be granted, and thus to exclude if desired. Guido Calabresi & A. Douglas Melamed, *Property Rules, Liability Rules, and Inalienability: One View of the Cathedral*, 85 HARV. L. REV. 1089 (1972). Thus they may put more stress on the right of exclusion, rather than on alienation, in defining the central attributes of property.

referred to as a liability rule regime,[29] rather than a property rule regime. Depending on the particular vocabulary used by the scholar in question, this could describe a broad range of situations:

- The ability of a maker of compilation CD's to reproduce sound recordings produced by others under a compulsory license with statutory royalty fees.
- A cement company having a legally protected interest to continue polluting so long as it pays actual damages for the costs imposed on the neighboring landowners (as opposed to the injured party having an entitlement to an injunction to shut down the pollution).
- The right of an owner of an important standard or protocol to receive flat fees for usage if the standard is open to all to use.

Interestingly, it is exactly this separation of the right to withhold access at will, from the right to receive payment that undergirds Larry Lessig's work on the commons. If one is worried about monopolistic choke-holds on innovation, rather than concerned about the cost of access to the resource, this distinction is an important one.

In the second part of their article, Hess and Ostrom turn their analysis of common pool resources to the world of scholarly publishing. After an extensive review of the methods and institutions involved in the generation of scholarship, they conclude that the "research commons" can be continued only through the pursuit of collective strategies by scholars for the production of knowledge. Here, too, it seems a well-managed commons may be superior to a regime relying purely on private property.

III

SPECIFIC SUBJECT AREAS

Following the first four foundational articles on the history and theory of the ideas of the public domain and the commons, the symposium turns to particular subject areas where those issues are applied. The conference focused particularly on three realms: the digital (including the role of the public domain in the architecture of the Internet), art and culture, and scientific and technical data. At the same time, across all realms we considered the extent to which the public domain is constitutionally protected in the United States, either by the First Amendment or by the limitations imposed by Congress's copyright and patent power in Article 1, Section 8, Clause 8.

We begin with Pamela Samuelson's lucid and thoughtful mapping of the public domain in the digital realm. Next we consider the role of fair use in art and culture, with articles by David Nimmer on the application of the four factors of the fair use test in a wide range of recent cases, followed by a provocative essay by two members of the appropriationist group Negativland on the

---

29. *See id. See generally* J.H. Reichman, *Of Green Tulips and Legal Kudzu: Repackaging Rights in Subpatentable Innovation*, 53 VAND. L. REV. 1743 (2000) [hereinafter Reichman, *Green Tulips*].

intersection of music and technology, proposing the role that fair use should play in the process. In two fascinating articles, William Van Alstyne and Yochai Benkler use very different methods of constitutional interpretation to give us sharply contrasting ways to understand the constitutional limits around intellectual property legislation and the constitutional significance of the public domain. The final section of this volume focuses on the relevance of the public domain to science and technology. Arti Rai and Rebecca Eisenberg discuss the "increasingly proprietary" nature of university scientific research and propose a series of reforms of the Bayh-Dole Act to give agencies greater discretion in determining whether information should go into the public domain. Finally, Jerome Reichman and Paul Uhlir offer a sweeping account of current and looming problems in contemporary scientific and technical data collection and utilization. They then suggest public and private strategies to avoid what they see as a fundamental threat to the American system of science and innovation by creating a flourishing "e-commons" of scientific data. The volume ends with an essay from my colleague David Lange, which reflects on his own contributions to the field over the last twenty-five years.

A. The Digital Realm

Pamela Samuelson is one of the best-known scholars of digital intellectual property, a longstanding participant in public policy debates on the regulation of the Internet, and the founder of the Samuelson Law, Technology and Public Policy Clinic at Berkeley. We asked her to provide an overview of the digital public domain, and to highlight emerging issues. She provided a "map" of the public domain, defining it mainly in terms of the legal status of the digital material involved, while focusing heavily on factual accessibility. The result is a composite image of fact, law and technological feasibility:

> Although I define the public domain as a sphere in which contents are free from intellectual property rights, there is another murky terrain near the boundaries of the public domain consisting of some intellectual creations that courts have treated as in the public domain for some, but not all, purposes.
>
> Across the border from the public domain are several categories of content that are so widely usable that, for practical purposes, they seem to be part of the public domain. This includes, importantly, much content that is technically protected by copyright law but is widely available to the public, as when it is posted on publicly accessible websites available to all comers without fee or apparent restrictions on use. Also outside the public domain in theory, but seemingly inside in effect, are such things as open source software; a penumbra of privileged uses under fair use, experimental use, and other copyright rules that permit unlicensed uses and sharing of information to take place; and standards that are licensed without payment of royalties. Also at the perimeter of the public domain are works whose intellectual property rights are on the verge of expiring and, arguably, some creations that are about to be made—such as a new computer programming language or the solution to a long-standing mathematical problem—that, once they exist, will be part of the public domain.[30]

30. Pamela Samuelson, *Mapping the Digital Public Domain: Threats and Opportunities*, 66 LAW & CONTEMP. PROBS. 147, 149 (Winter/Spring 2003) (footnotes omitted). Even in this list of examples,

One of the most compelling aspects of Samuelson's article is its extremely measured tone. She remarks that neither intellectual property law nor access restrictions can correctly be seen as a necessary impoverishment of the public domain. The relationship between the public domain and the restrictions around it is a complex dynamic equilibrium, not a simplistic binary choice. She points out that, in many cases, it is the incentives provided by intellectual property that allow the material first to be created, and later to flow into the public domain.[31] She also discusses the multiple ways in which physical access restrictions can *aid* the effective availability of information. For example, without the effective ability to exclude, she argues, high-quality services such as LEXIS would probably not be available, even though the service includes considerable material already in the public domain. Finally, when she turns to existing and pending regulations of digital intellectual property, she offers a particularly nuanced account of their effects on the public domain. For example, the Digital Millennium Copyright Act ("DMCA"),[32] for many the "bête noir" of recent expansions of digital intellectual property, has comparatively little effect. Other laws, such as Uniform Computer Information Transactions Act ("UCITA"), which claims not to regulate intellectual property at all, could in many ways have more serious implications.[33] Partly because of the carefully measured tone of her analysis, Samuelson is particularly convincing in describing how the greatest dangers may lie, not in individual pieces of legislation, but in the conjunction of three different types: increased scope of intellectual property protections, such that provided by a "database right";[34] greater legal protection for technical protection measures, such as that provided by the DMCA and proposed by the Hollings Bill; and greater enforceability of shrinkwrap contracts, such as that provided by UCITA. The whole, in this case, is greater than the sum of its parts, and Samuelson's topological metaphor enables her to lay out with some precision the likely effects of this tripartite approach.[35]

---

the "effective access component" of the areas contiguous to the public domain would depend on the uses one was imagining. For example, if I posted an MP3 file of my song on my website with no indication as to its legal status or any desired restrictions on use, you would clearly think you had (and, because of implicit license, statutory exception, fair use, or estoppel, would legally enjoy) a privilege to make a copy for personal use. It is unlikely however that you would feel free, or would in fact be legally free, to make a commercially distributed derivative work from the music, to include it on a mass-market CD, or to turn it into a sound-track for a Disney movie.

31. *See id.* at 168; *supra* note 8.

32. Digital Millennium Copyright Act (DMCA), 17 U.S.C. §§ 512, 1201-1205, 1301-1332, 28 U.S.C. § 4001 (2000).

33. The Uniform Computer Information Transactions Act, creates a uniform commercial code for computer information transactions. The drafting body for UCITA, approved and recommended UCITA for enactment in all fifty states in July 1999. *See* UNIF. COMPUTER INFO. TRANSACTIONS ACT (UCITA) (2001), *available at* http://www.ucitaonline.com/ (last visited February 3, 2003).

34. See, for example, recent database bill proposals H.R. 354, 106th Cong. (1999); H.R. 1858, 106th Cong. (1999). *See also* EU Database Directive 96/9/EC, art. 4(1), 1996 O.J. (L 77) 20. For a thoughtful discussion of the issues, see J. H. Reichman & Pamela Samuelson, *Intellectual Property Rights in Data?*, 50 VAND. L. REV. 51 (1997). *See also* Reichman, *Green Tulips*, *supra* note 29.

35. In the conference itself, Samuelson's article was a perfect introduction to a fascinating panel, *From Anarchist Software to Peer2Peer Culture: the Public Domain in Bandwidth, Software and Content.* The panel dealt with the role of the public domain (and the commons) in the attributes of our commu-

After this careful review, Samuelson's conclusion is all the more powerful, and could serve as the conclusion for the conference itself:

> It is possible to construct a new politics of intellectual property that has regard for the public domain and fair uses. To be successful, a new public-regarding politics of intellectual property must have a positive agenda of its own. It cannot just oppose whatever legislative initiatives the major content industry organizations support (although it almost certainly will need to do this as well). It should be grounded on the realization that information is not only or mainly a commodity; it is also a critically important resource and input to learning, culture, competition, innovation, and democratic discourse. Intellectual property must find a home in a broader-based information policy, and be a servant, not a master, of the information society.[36]

B. Creativity, Appropriation, Culture and The Public Domain

Is copyright a cultural policy?[37] Does intellectual property involve or promote a particular aesthetic?[38] Does it exist as an aesthetic form itself, such that the modernist love of genre-trashing might portray the violation of intellectual property rights as a type of artistic activity in its own right?[39] Or is it simply that copyright is unnecessarily hostile to the appropriationist aesthetic and the technologies which enable it? Does the conjunction of the idea/expression distinction and the fair use privilege allow copyright to promote expression without restricting it? How does the fair use doctrine actually operate? Two papers presented here[40] approach these issues from very different perspectives, which nevertheless appear to have some interesting common points.

David Nimmer is one of the most distinguished copyright scholars in the United States, and author, with his late father, of one of the most authoritative treatises on the subject.[41] In his article, *"Fairest of Them All" and Other Fairy Tales of Fair Use*, he explores the actual operation of the fair use doctrine.[42] In theory, at least, the four factors laid out in section 107 play an important role in determining whether or not a use is "fair."[43] Superficially, judicial practice

---

nications networks, and in the types of creativity they make possible—or at least easier. It can be found at http://realserver.law.duke.edu/ramgen/publicdomain/public%20domain%20panel%205.rm

As I mentioned earlier, papers for that panel by Larry Lessig and Yochai Benkler can be found elsewhere. *See supra* note 5.

36. Samuelson, *supra* note 30, at 170-71.

37. *See* Neil Weinstock Netanel, *Market Hierarchy and Copyrights in Our System of Free Expression*, 53 VAND. L. REV. 1879 (2000) [hereinafter Netanel, *Market Hierarchy*]; J.H. Reichman, *The Duration and the Limits of Cultural Policy*, 14 CARDOZO ARTS & ENT. L.J. 625 (1996).

38. JAMES BOYLE, SHAMANS, SOFTWARE AND SPLEENS: LAW AND THE CONSTRUCTION OF THE INFORMATION SOCIETY (1996); *cf.* Alfred C. Yen, *Copyright Opinions and Aesthetic Theory*, 71 S. CAL. L. REV. 247 (1998).

39. Negativland, *Tenets of Free Expression*, *at* http://www.negativland.com/riaa/tenets.html (last visited February 3, 2003) [hereinafter Negativland, *Tenets*].

40. As noted earlier, because of timing, David Lange and Jennifer Lange Anderson chose not to include their framing paper within this volume. The original version can be found at http://www.law.duke.edu/pd/papers/ (last visited February 3, 2003).

41. MELVILLE B. NIMMER & DAVID NIMMER, NIMMER ON COPYRIGHT (1976).

42. David Nimmer, *"Fairest of Them All" and Other Fairy Tales of Fair Use Factors*, 66 LAW & CONTEMP. PROB. 263 (Winter/Spring 2003).

43. *See* 17 U.S.C. § 107 (2000).

seems to support this. As Nimmer points out, courts that find a use to be fair normally find three or more of the factors in favor of the alleged offender, while courts that find against fair use do the reverse. When Nimmer revisited the fifty-nine cases decided since the Supreme Court's last major fair use decision and assessed each independently, however, he found a very different pattern. The overall correlation of a positive or negative decision on the four factors to a corresponding decision on fair use was 52.1%:[44]

> Basically, had Congress legislated a dartboard rather than the particular four fair use factors embodied in the Copyright Act, it appears that the upshot would be the same.
>
> This conclusion is not to say that judges enter findings as to the four factors in support of their ultimate fair use determination only half the time. Perusal of fair use cases would reveal that the figure actually approaches ninety percent. In other words, judges who uphold fair use almost always find that three, if not four, of the factors incline in its favor; judges who deny the fair use defense almost always find that three, if not four, of the factors incline against it. The difference between the chart's figure, showing virtually a dead heat, and the actual figure pushing ninety percent, stems from the malleability of the fair use factors.[45]

He concludes, in classically legal realist fashion, that judges' findings on the factors are the result of, not the reason for, their findings on the merits.

> In the ultimate analysis, my review of the cases convinces me that the high correspondence in judicial opinions between the individual fair use factors and courts' ultimate disposition, as opposed to the absence of any meaningful correspondence in the chart, reflects an important insight into how judges actually resolve fair use cases: Courts tend first to make a judgment that the ultimate disposition is fair use or unfair use, and then align the four factors to fit that result as best they can. At base, therefore, the four factors fail to drive the analysis, but rather serve as convenient pegs on which to hang antecedent conclusions.
>
> . . . .
>
> By now, we have come far enough to realize that, pious words notwithstanding, it is largely a fairy tale to conclude that the four factors determine resolution of concrete fair use cases.[46]

Interestingly, Nimmer concludes that this result was foreordained when Congress injected "such a high degree of subjectivity and imprecision into each factor and into their cumulative application."[47] Of course, there are other areas of law—antitrust, for example—in which apparently subjective and imprecise statutory injunctions, based on older common law tests, nevertheless become

44. Nimmer, *supra* note 42, at 280. To be sure, it must be stressed that this is based on Professor Nimmer's rating of the factors in the cases, and not that found by the courts. Still, given the role that Professor Nimmer's treatise plays in copyright litigation, and his influence as a scholar, this fact is a fairly significant one. At the very least, it suggests that well-regarded members of the relevant interpretive community find a very high degree of interpretive "openness" in the application of section 107.

45. *Id.*

46. *Id.* at 281-282. Nimmer concludes that the openness is so great that it is possible to fail to have fair use even when all four factors, correctly interpreted, point in your favor and vice versa. He uses a number of cases to illustrate this point including a fascinating discussion of the reproduction of a card written by Anne Frank.

47. *Id.* at 281.

court-interpreted schemes that are from year-to-year, *relatively* coherent and predictable. So perhaps the problem, if problem it is, lies deeper. Perhaps it is that fair use continues unabashedly to serve multiple and potentially contradictory goals—from encouraging transformational reworkings of original materials, to securing raw material for future creators, to reducing transaction costs, to avoiding network effects with strong negative externalities, to policing the boundaries of exclusive rights when equitable intuitions suggest that those would convey unduly great monopoly power in economic or expressive terms. Under the promptings of a number of commentators,[48] antitrust's original diverse goals have been "rationalized" into the injunction to serve the overriding goal of maximizing consumer welfare. No such rationalization has yet taken place in copyright law. Though some have suggested "master narratives" for fair use, none has yet come close to securing overwhelming acceptance. For many of us, this has seemed like a good thing. It is hard to see how a rationalized, limited fair use doctrine would have been able to deal with decompilation, and parody, and classroom copying, and sampling, and search engine thumbnail pictures, and so forth and so on. Indeed, judges have sometimes pointed out that in the changing economic conditions of network economics, the limitations on intellectual property law may need to evolve and perhaps increase still further.[49] The price of fair use's protean ability to reassess and readapt to a changing world has been a certain fuzziness around the edges. But is that an acceptable price?

At the end of his article, Nimmer offers an interesting, and perhaps optimistic conclusion. He quotes Harper and Row, where the Supreme Court is in turn quoting his late father:

> Professor [Melville] Nimmer notes: Perhaps no more precise guide can be stated than Joseph McDonald's clever paraphrase of the Golden Rule: Take not from others to such an extent and in such a manner that you would be resentful if they so took from you. This equitable rule of reason permits courts to avoid rigid application of the copyright statute when, on occasion, it would stifle the very creativity which that law is designed to foster.[50]

David Nimmer concludes his article thus: "Father knows best. More exacting explanations for the four factors seem, in the end, to be naught but fairy tales." Now if this quotation is meant to remind us not to rely mechanically on the four factors, or to point out that moral intuitions of the "do as you would be done by" variety, are often important in fair use cases, then it is a point well taken. But if it is supposed to represent an actual "equitable rule of reason" that will allow citizens and lawyers to "know fair use when they see it" then it, too, seems nothing but a fairy tale, and a deeply misleading one at that. My guess is that had one gone to Nimmer *père* or *fils*, presented the fifty-nine cases in the

48. *See, e.g.*, ROBERT H. BORK, THE ANTITRUST PARADOX (1978).

49. See the concurring opinion of Judge Boudin in *Lotus Development Corp. v. Borland International, Inc.*, 49 F.3d 807, 815 (1st Cir. 1995)(Boudin, J concurring).

50. Harper & Row, Publ'rs, Inc. v. Nation Enters, 471 U.S. 539 (1985). Quoted in Nimmer, *supra* note 42, at 287 (alteration in original).

table and asked for a prediction in each case *based on this paraphrase of the Golden Rule*, the results would not have been *that* much better than the performance of the four factors. Better, perhaps, because the very amorphousness of the "rule" would allow full scope to the intuition and gestalt pattern-recognition of a brilliant lawyer, well-versed in the assumptions of his own professional speech community, to predict the behavior of his colleagues on the bench. But how much better? Certainly Professor Nimmer's tone in his discussion of several of the cases suggests that he finds little equity, or reason, in their result. The "surprises" seem relatively frequent.

Is that good enough? That is a question Nimmer does not answer for us. But as I read his article, my faith in the protean power of fair use took a beating, even though I cling to it still. When copying and distribution were hard, the entities directly affected by copyright law were mainly firms who were well represented, and who had fairly consistent experience as repeat players in a familiar legal terrain. The global network changes that fact, completing a change begun with the photocopier, video-recorder and cassette tape recorder. Now anyone connected to the network is directly affected by copyright every day. It is wound into their daily acts of consumption, creation, distribution, and communication. These new citizen-subjects of copyright—the amateur film-makers and web site operators and backroom musicians and open source programmers and bloggers—these folk are not well-versed in copyright law, nor can they afford to hire David Nimmer. If the four factors perform in the way Nimmer's chart suggests, is fair use "working" for them? Can they know the limits on the exclusive rights of copyright holders? Can they create and consume and rework, and educate in the free space that section 107 is supposed to grant them?[51] Does the "equitable rule of reason" do any better? Would or should we trade some of fair use's protean quality, its attempt to serve many goals at once, for some more definite boundaries on exclusive rights? My answer in the past has been "no." Paradoxically, David Nimmer's relatively optimistic conclusion, implicitly supporting my preference for the equitable openness of the fair use doctrine, made me wonder if I was the one spinning fairy tales. Is fair use working adequately for the citizen-publishers, the consumer-artists of cyberspace?

A partial answer to that question may be given by Negativland's article in this volume, *Two Relationships to a Cultural Public Domain*.[52] I first encountered members of the appropriationist group Negativland about ten years ago. I was fascinated by the legal struggles within which they were embroiled, interested by their extremely readable manifestoes,[53] and enlightened by their book *Fair Use*.[54] I also really liked their music.[55] More importantly, I got the strong

51. For a wonderful organization that tries to make sure that they can, see http://www.chillingeffects.org (last visited February 4, 2003).

52. Negativland, *Two Relationships to a Cultural Public Domain*, 66 LAW AND CONTEMP. PROBS. 239 (Winter/Spring 2003) [hereinafter Negativland, *Two Relationships*].

53. Negativland, *Tenets*, *supra* note 39.

54. Negativland, Fair Use: The Story of the Letter "U" and the Numeral "2" 1995 (including a Negativland CD) (1995); James Boyle, *A Sense of Belonging*, Times Literary Supplement, July 4, 1997,

sense that *they did too*. They weren't doing this just because it was the today's station on the grand railway line of avant garde art, or because it was supposed to be a vital blow against world capitalism—even if they had a strong sense of their work's place in a rich history of collage art, and strong opinions about the role of intellectual property in inhibiting criticism of mass corporate culture. They were doing it because they enjoyed it, because they loved the music. The conceptual schema did not subsume the art:

> We've continued to work this way because we like the sound of it. We like the results. We get inspired by what we find out there, it's simply *fun* to do, and we sense we are not alone in these perceptions. In continuing to pursue collage and found-sound as elements in our music, we have set our work out as public examples of how appropriation from our media surroundings is neither culturally harmful nor dangerous to anyone else's business. Instead, it hopefully does represent some interesting art perspectives, as well as cultural commentary and criticism which are well worth having around whether or not our work happens to be "authorized" by our subjects and sources. We consider it to be a matter of free speech.[56]

Negativland see the technologies of digital reproduction giving new life to the old concept of the public domain. While they are perfectly willing to criticize commercial, wholesale, unauthorized reproduction of complete songs, and are skeptical about the harm caused by non-commercial digital "file sharing" on sales in other media, they believe that the technologies and art of partial appropriation and reworking need encouragement and legal support. Where some see the aesthetic of appropriation as somehow new—spawned by postmodernism or digital technology—Negativland see it as part of a much longer tradition. For most of history, they write:

> [T]he natural human approach to our own culture was to participate in it by not only absorbing it as an individual, but also by remaking it—adding to it, removing from it, recombining it with other elements, reshaping it to our own tastes—and then redistributing the adjusted results ourselves. Virtually the whole history of human culture consisted of altering, reusing, and copying from the universal public domain in various re-imagined ways . . . until copyright came along.[57]

This tendency of remaking can be found in everything from folk music and folktales to the early history of musical forms such as blues and jazz. To Negativland, the advent of copyright is also the advent of closed, frozen, culturally stabilized art—art that it was illegal to rework, to add to, to subvert, to modify. It is almost as though intellectual property is a layer of shellac over expressive content, sealing it off and separating the world into active artists (or content companies) on one side and passive consumers on the other. In their view, the Internet allows and dramatically encourages resistance to this dichotomy, promoting instead a cultural "public domain," a domain where the recipients of cultural material can also rework that material. They do not want, however, to

---

reviewing PAUL GOLDSTEIN, COPYRIGHT'S HIGHWAY (1996) *available at* http://www.law.duke.edu/boylesite/tlscopy.htm .

55. *See, e.g.*, (or in this case, *listen to, e.g.*) *The Letter U and the Numeral 2*, on U2 (1995) *available at* http://www.negativland.com/audio/tlutn2-2-cd.ra (last visited February 4, 2003).

56. Negativland, *Two Relationships*, *supra* note 52, at 240 (emphasis in original).

57. *Id.* at 242.

confine this idea to the post-Internet world:

> But the human urge towards a public domain is nothing new. Long before, and still continuing outside the Internet, this philosophical ideal concerning our cultural environment has been evident in the evolution of modern art. And that can form a historical basis from which to consider the desirability of all of today's forms of free cultural reuse in general.[58]

They argue for an understanding of fair use that would stretch expansively to cover most uses other than complete, verbatim copying. In a passage that I found quite striking, they note the spread of their term "culture jamming" and the reality that it represents in both mainstream and independent media:

> Observing this now generally culture-wide acceptance of collage's appropriation methodologies, one would think that sympathetic laws of allowance would also emerge to encourage the practice and assure that it is able to proceed legally. But that has not yet happened. What's wrong with this picture?[59]

C. The Constitutional Status of the Public Domain

When we organized the conference, we did not set out to demonstrate the range of interpretive approaches in constitutional thought. Indirectly, we did so anyway. In *Through the Looking Glass: Alice and the Constitutional Foundations of the Public Domain*, Yochai Benkler offers an holistic interpretation of two provisions of the U.S. Constitution relevant to the constitutional status of the public domain: the "Exclusive Rights Clause," his preferred appellation for Article 1, Section 8, Clause 8 of the U.S. Constitution; and the First Amendment.[60] He begins by illustrating the stakes involved in the public domain's status, and elucidating current judicial attitudes:

> Alice Randall, an African-American woman, was ordered by a government official not to publish her criticism of the romanticization of the Old South, at least not in the words she wanted to use. The official was not one of the many in Congress and the Administration who share a romantic view of the Confederacy. It was a federal judge in Atlanta who told Randall that she could not write her critique in the words she wanted to use—a judge enforcing copyright law.[61]

Through this example, and the stories of Dmitri Sklyarov, the Russian programmer prosecuted under the DMCA "because he wrote software that lets people read books that they are not allowed to read,"[62] and of Edward Felten, the Princeton computer scientist who after writing a paper on encryption schemes "received a threatening letter from the Recording Industry Association of America ("RIAA"),"[63] Benkler offers some deliberately stark portrayals of the potential speech-restricting effects of intellectual property rights. He does so, at least in part, because in the eyes of a number of scholars, the courts have not given adequate attention to the constitutional issues presented by

---

58. *Id.* at 250.
59. *Id.* at 240.
60. Benkler, *Looking Glass*, *supra* note 5.
61. *Id.* at 173. The Court of Appeals subsequently overturned the injunction as a prior restraint.
62. *Id.*
63. *Id.*

intellectual property rules.[64] Some, in fact, liken the treatment of intellectual property to the handling of free speech issues posed by libel before *New York Times v. Sullivan*.[65]

Benkler argues that the Exclusive Rights Clause, as interpreted by the Court in cases such as *Graham v. John Deere*[66] and *Feist Publications v. Rural Telephone Service Co.*,[67] imposes substantial restrictions on congressional power. Among other restrictions it provides that an exclusive right must at least plausibly encourage information production and free access to materials already in the public domain. What's more, according to Benkler, these restrictions extend beyond the boundaries of the exclusive rights clause to burden congressional power whenever Congress attempts to enact exclusive rights to information, whatever the ostensible source of its authority.[68]

The First Amendment poses additional limitations on congressional power, beyond those imposed by the exclusive rights clause. Benkler posits that the First Amendment "requires that the government justify its regulation of the use of information and cultural goods in terms that are largely understood to be the 'intermediate' level of scrutiny applied in *Turner Broadcasting System v. FCC*."[69] There is, in other words, no copyright exemption to the First Amendment.

While this is a somewhat breathless summary of an already compressed version of a much broader body of work (both by Benkler and others), it suffices to give a broad sense of the analysis. The argument given this far is in one way completely internal to the constitutional materials. Benkler considers the two constitutional provisions, the Supreme Court decisions interpreting them, the First Amendment doctrine represented by *Turner*, and the Court's communications law decisions, and from all of this argues that there is a two-part constitutional filter through which "exclusive rights in information" must pass. But in another sense this, like any legal argument, has an irreducible external, normative dimension. The political experience and normative aspirations from which the constitutional provisions arose, the cases which interpret those provisions, the rationales supporting those interpretations, and the dystopias and utopias conjured up in Congressional Hearings and court decisions—all have complex historical and political provenances from which they can never be fully insulated. Norms seep both ways. Differences of opinion exist over how much

64 Yochai Benkler, *Free as the Air to Common Use: First Amendment Constraints on Enclosure of the Public Domain*, 74 N.Y.U.L. REV. 354 (1999); BOYLE, SHAMANS, *supra* note 38; Lawrence Lessig, *Copyright's & First Amendment*, 48 UCLA L. REV. 1057 (2001); Neil Weinstock Netanel, *Locating Copyright Within the First Amendment Skein*, 54 STAN. L. REV. 1 (2001).

65 James Boyle, *The First Amendment in Cyberspace: The Clinton Years*, 63 LAW & CONTEMP. PROBS. 337 (Winter/Spring 2000), *available at* http://www.law.duke.edu/journals/63LCPBoyle.

66 383 U.S. 1 (1966).

67 499 U.S. 340 (1991).

68. *Id.*; *see also*, Yochai Benkler, *Constitutional Bounds of Database Protection: The Role of Judicial Review in the Creation and Definition of Private Rights in Information*, 15 BERKLEY L. & TECH J. 535 (2000).

69 Benkler, *Looking Glass*, *supra* note 5, at 178 (footnotes omitted).

seepage is inevitable, necessary, or desirable. Differences of opinion also arise over which "contexts" should legitimately be part of our interpretive practice. What is relevant to interpreting the Exclusive Rights Clause, or the First Amendment? The beliefs of the framers? The historically contemporaneous definitions of words used in legal documents? Supreme Court cases that are analogous, whether on semantic, structural or instrumental grounds? An economic analysis of information or innovation? The current political economy of cultural industries, or factual characteristics of modern communications media? Philosophical teachings about normative claims underlying the value of self-expression? These questions of method are generally answered only implicitly by the pattern of selections, and unexplained absences, in a constitutional argument.

Benkler takes a different approach. While his legal argument can presumably stand alone as an interpretation integral in the legal materials, he also offers an explicit political and normative grounding. My sense is that this argument is not intended to *prove* his constitutional interpretation correct, but rather to render it more plausible by showing the political ideals to which it gives effect. He describes this portion of his work as an attempt to explain "abstractly how one might understand the implications of exclusive private rights in information on democracy and autonomy—values at the core not only of the U.S. constitutional protection of freedom of expression, but of expressive freedom in modern liberal democracies more generally."[70] Dealing first with democracy, Benkler argues that intellectual property rights benefit certain organizations and groups, while disfavoring others. More generally, intellectual property rights tilt in favor of a particular industrial organization of information production:

> The conflict seen today regarding the scope of the public domain and the extent of exclusive private rights in information is a battle over the shape of the institutional ecology in which two very different modes of information production compete. The first mode is the increasingly industrial model of production that one sees in mass-mediated culture. Disney, AOL Time-Warner, Viacom, and News Corporation are some of the most visible examples. These are increasingly large organizations that control ever-larger inventories and integrate new production with reutilization and recycling of inventory. They aim to capture ever-larger audiences both nationally and internationally. Less well known, and quite poorly understood, is the emergence on the Internet of nonproprietary production as an increasingly important source of information and cultural materials. Over the past decade, with the widescale use of the Internet, the reach and scope of nonproprietary information production by nonprofit actors or by individuals—both amateur and professional—has expanded dramatically.[71]

The question for Benkler then becomes: "What can democratic theory tell us about the choice between commercial proprietary production, increasingly organized in large enterprises and whose products are sold as finished goods, and nonproprietary production, both peer-production and professional produc-

70. *Id.* at 180.
71. *Id.* at 181.

tion on a traditional nonprofit model?"[72] Benkler considers a number of arguments on these issues, including the very interesting reflections of Neil Netanel on the importance of copyright in encouraging and maintaining large, powerful and wealthy press organizations to act as a counterweight to other powerful groups in society.[73] He concludes nonetheless that "[t]o the extent one values active, engaged individual participation in defining and expressing political values in a polity as central to the democratic enterprise, one should strengthen peer-based models of information production and exchange, even if this requires policies that weaken proprietary production based on a sale of goods model."[74] The constitutional significance of this preference is obviously subject to debate, but for Benkler it is a considerable one.

The autonomy section, with its strong resonance in the Millian tradition of free expression, should be even more familiar to First Amendment thinkers. To the extent that human beings need access to certain information both to form and to exercise autonomous decisions, autonomy mandates the free flow of information. Again Benkler suggests that a widely dispersed information economy promotes autonomy in a way that has considerable normative significance, and should be considered as we structure the information environment through the rules of intellectual property law. Given the contours of the legislative process and the boundaries imposed by the double constitutional filter on exclusive rights, Benkler argues that traditional notions of institutional competence make it particularly appropriate for the courts to exercise their constitutional authority in ways that promote, rather than detract from, the values of democracy and autonomy.

Benkler concludes with a review of six pressure points on the constitutional framework. I shall not attempt to summarize the entire discussion here. Suffice it to say that I believe that, out of those points, the possible objections he raises to his claims about constitutional limitations from the First Amendment, and his discussion of "neo-Lochnerism and the Moral Inversion of the First Amendment" present some of the strongest reasons to believe that the constitution both does and should exercise significant control over the creation of private exclusive rights in information. Indeed the "six pressure points" section of the piece makes a fascinating freestanding article in its own right.[75]

My colleague William Van Alstyne is both one of the nation's leading First Amendment scholars and a constitutional thinker whose readings of Article 1, Section 8 have transformed academic thinking on the powers of Congress. It is hard to imagine a more appropriate person to comment on the extent to which the First Amendment limits the power of the federal government to create exclusive rights to authors' writings.

Interestingly, Van Alstyne does not begin by arguing that the First Amend-

72. *Id.* at 182.
73. Netanel, *Market Hierarchy*, *supra* note 37.
74. Benkler, *Looking Glass*, *supra* note 5, at 187.
75. *See id.* at 197-222.

ment, as an amendment, clearly limits the power of Congress under the copyright Clause. "Of course, the First Amendment is later in time. But nothing on the face of the First Amendment purports to affect the power granted to Congress pursuant to the Copyright Clause. So, again, one may say that whatever is *properly* done by Congress within the permission of the Copyright Clause ought not be said at the same time to be *forbidden* by some other part of the Constitution, at least unless that 'other part' so declares, or unless its express provisions are simply incompatible with an earlier part it necessarily displaces and amends."[76]

He begins his argument instead from an interpretive stance that seems almost to equate the two provisions, as if they were simply two simultaneously passed statutory provisions with an apparent tension between them. In fact, at the beginning of his argument, the Copyright Clause is almost given precedence because of its more specific nature. "It would seem again, on this basis as well, puzzling to declare that the First Amendment may forbid something the more specifically 'targeted' clause empowers Congress to do. One may well suggest that this is another clear case where the useful maxim, *expressio unius, exclusio alterius est*, appropriately applies."[77] This is a provocative interpretive approach. If the question is 1) historical and 2) all-or-nothing—Was the First Amendment understood at the time of its adoption to preclude Congress completely from securing exclusive rights to authors?—then surely this answer is correct. If the question is instead historical and more nuanced—Given the type and extent and duration of exclusive rights for authors handed out by the Congress in the early years of the Republic, and the contemporary understanding of the First Amendment, was anyone likely to have considered whether portions of statutes passed by Congress in the future under the copyright power could run afoul of the First Amendment?—then the answer is harder to discern. If the question is a-historical, merely a matter of dueling interpretive maxims and devoid of a particular interpretive context, then it is hard to know why the jurisprudential maxim "*expressio unius*," would trump the jurisprudential assumption that later in time is greater in effect: amendments amend. If the question is: How has the First Amendment been interpreted by the courts to limit certain exercises of the copyright power? or, Which theory of the relationship between the Copyright Clause and the First Amendment best expresses the political projects that structure the U.S. Constitution?, then, again, the answer is a very different one.

These interpretive options are not mere fancies; they are real ones, among and between which courts will begin to select. Benkler seeks answers by turning first to the Court's jurisprudence in copyright and communications law cases, then attempting to "confirm" the structure he unearths by examining its relationship on the political values of democracy, and autonomy as realized in the media economy of the Internet. Van Alstyne proceeds in the grand struc-

---

76. William W. Van Alstyne, *Reconciling What the First Amendment Forbids With What the Copyright Clause Permits*, 66 LAW & CONTEMP. PROBS. 225, 226 (Winter/Spring 2003).

77. *Id.* at 226.

tural tradition: He looks abstractly at the structure of the clauses and attempts to define a coherent interpretive perspective by proposing and rejecting different relationships between them. The history of the clauses, or the question of how they have been interpreted by the courts, is thus of subordinate importance to his argument. Other approaches make history,[78] or the likely dysfunctions of interest group politics,[79] considerably more relevant to the analysis.

Given this disparity of interpretive style, it is particularly interesting that Benkler and Van Alstyne agree on a number of points. Most importantly, they both believe that Article I, Section 8, Clause 8 provides no exception to, sanctuary from, or preemption of the First Amendment. Despite his skeptical interpretive baseline, Van Alstyne concludes that the Copyright Clause "'pre-empts' nothing within the protection of the First Amendment... and any feature of any portion of any act Congress has, or may in the future, provide under sanction of this clause, may always be brought into question respecting whether, on its face or as applied, it offends against the larger freedom of speech and of the press provided constitutional sanctuary in the First Amendment still unfolding in the United States."[80] This is a vital point and should be an obvious one, though the DC Circuit, at least, has held otherwise.[81]

But though they agree on this point, Benkler and Van Alstyne seem to disagree, at least in emphasis, on a number of others, both in substance and methodology. Benkler sees the "Exclusive Rights Clause" as providing boundaries on congressional power. By contrast, Van Alstyne sees the clause largely as one designed to ensure uniformity across the United States, replacing the patchwork of state schemes offering varying degrees of protection with a single Federal scheme. This does, indeed, seem to have been one justification for the clause (though from my point of view, only one of many), and one that also lies behind the first Copyright Act.[82] Seeing the clause largely as an attempt to ensure Federal uniformity, Van Alstyne believes that it should be read generously. A Federal law, for example, which contained no exceptions for fair use, would not on that ground be outside the boundaries of congressional power. However, the First Amendment would "shield" a critic who chose to copy a portion of a copyrighted work in a critical review. So far so good. Any differences here are largely in the reach of the First Amendment, rather than in the choice of the First Amendment over the copyright clause as being the relevant constitutional provision. Most scholars, I believe, would say that it is the First

---

78. Tyler T. Ochoa, *Patent and Copyright Term Extension and the Constitution: A Historical Perspective*, 49 J. COPYRIGHT SOC'Y U.S.A 19 (2002); Malla Pollack, *Purveyance and Power, or Over-Priced Free Lunch: The Intellectual Property Clause as an Ally of the Takings Clause in the Public's Control of Government*, 30 SW. U. L. REV. 1 (2000).

79 *See* Pollack, *supra* note 78.

80. Van Alstyne, *supra* note 76, at 238.

81 *See* Eldred v. Reno, 239 F.3d 372, (D.C. Cir. 2001). Sadly this misimpression was only partially corrected by the Supreme Court. Eldred v. Ashcroft, 123 S. Ct. 769, 789-90 (2003).

82. Ochoa, supra note 78, at 28; Edward C. Walterscheid, *To Promote the Progress of Science and Useful Arts: The Background and Origin of the Intellectual Property Clause of the United States Constitution*, 2 J. INTELL. PROP. L. 1, 1 (1994).

Amendment that would make a copyright statute lacking fair use unconstitutional, not the Copyright Clause. Van Alstyne would say that the First Amendment at least offers a constitutional defense to an alleged "infringer" who was making a "fair use." Difference of emphasis and reach arise, but not differences about the relevant clause or amendment.

It would be very interesting to know how far this logic takes Van Alstyne when considering other issues. Was the Supreme Court correct to interpolate the requirement of originality into the copyright clause, or to say in the context of the patent power, that Congress may not remove articles from the public domain or impede access thereto? A "thin" account of the clause, which sees it largely as a device to promote federal uniformity and believes that the powers it gives Congress should be read generously, does not necessarily take one to that position. Leaving aside any First Amendment limitation, would Congress have the power to create exclusive rights over unoriginal compilations of factual material, by recourse to the Commerce Clause? In other words, would the Copyright Clause have any negative precatory power, as Benkler and others have suggested? To the extent that there was any negative pregnant in limiting Congress's power under other clauses, the court in *United States v. Moghadam*[83] suggested that such a limitation would be restricted to those portions of the Copyright Clause that were fundamental, and suggested that the fixation requirement, for example, was not. But to have some sense about which limitations are "fundamental" and which not, one must have a theory about the substantive goals of the Copyright Clause that goes beyond the achievement of uniformity. Again, under the Copyright Clause, could Congress continually retrospectively extend copyright terms, without offering any plausible account of how this would aid in the production of original works? Are the "promote the progress" and "limited times" portions of the clause any kind of limitation on congressional power? Does the First Amendment inflect our reading of the copyright clause so that certain provisions have greater importance and weight?

Whatever the answer to these questions, it is both instructive, and important, to see the unequivocal rejection of the idea that copyright is somehow immune from or above the First Amendment. That notion of "copyright immunity" had a powerful opponent in Melville Nimmer,[84] but his arguments, as well as the other powerful criticisms of such a notion, have been trivialized in recent years so that they barely seem to have relevance beyond a ritualistic invocation of the idea-expression distinction.[85] It will be interesting to see

83. 175 F.3d 1269 (11th Cir. 1999).

84. Melville B. Nimmer, *Does Copyright Abridge The First Amendment Guarantees Of Free Speech and Press?*, 17 UCLA L. REV. 1180 (1970); *see also* Lawrence Lessig, *Copyright's First Amendment*, 48 UCLA L. REV. 1057 (2001).

85. Indeed, as noted earlier, the D.C. Circuit in *Eldred* appeared to go still further, suggesting that copyright was categorically immune from First Amendment scrutiny.

whether the Supreme Court, in *Eldred v. Ashcroft*,[86] revitalizes Nimmer's line of reasoning and, if so, whether it portrays the First Amendment as having any power beyond ensuring that the idea-expression distinction and the fair use privilege stay in the statutory scheme.

D. The Public Domain in Scientific Research and Discovery

There is no area in which public concern about intellectual property and the public domain has been greater than in scientific and technical research. Whether it is the controversy over the patenting of and access to the human genome, or pluripotent stem cell lines, the appropriate role of intellectual property in university research, or the use of ethno-botany and traditional herbal knowledge in pharmaceutical patenting, the coexistence of science and property rights has been a fairly constant concern over the last fifteen years. There have been important studies on access to scientific and technical information, such as the National Academies of Science's *Bits of Power*,[87] and proposals for a dramatic reshaping of the intellectual property environment surrounding scientific research—including a so-called "database right" that allows ownership of unoriginal compilations of factual data.[88] For these reasons we expected, and received, a particularly thought-provoking pair of papers from our two sets of authors.

Rebecca Eisenberg and Arti Rai are two of the most thoughtful scholarly commentators on the intellectual property issues involved in genetic research and innovation. For those interested in the interplay between the public domain and intellectual property protection, few subjects could be more appropriate. The sequencing of the human genome started as a government-funded basic science project, and gained impetus (and competition) from privately funded efforts, partly fueled by the prospect of expansive gene patents. The subject matter, the institutional settings where research was pursued, the attempt to move from fundamental scientific discovery to useful medical treatment, the questions of the appropriate thresholds for, and exceptions to, exclusive rights, each presented a series of conflicts between the norms of public science and private property. It is on the specific institutional manifestations of that tension, and their implications for the public domain that we asked these authors to write:

> Although the development of pharmaceutical end products has long been a proprietary enterprise, biomedical research comes from a very different tradition of open science. Within this tradition, longstanding norms call for relatively unfettered access to fundamental knowledge developed by prior researchers. The tradition of open science has eroded considerably over the past quarter century as proprietary claims have

86. *Eldred v. Ashcroft*, 123 S. Ct. 769 (2003), was handed down as this issue went to press. The answer to my questions was a partial "yes" (copyright is not somehow above the First Amendment) and a partial "no"(but normally all First Amendment issues are dealt with through fair use, etc.).

87. NATIONAL RESEARCH COUNCIL, BITS OF POWER: ISSUES IN GLOBAL ACCESS TO SCIENTIFIC DATA, COMMITTEE ON ISSUES IN THE TRANSBORDER FLOW OF SCIENTIFIC DATA (1997), *available at* http://www.nap.edu/readingroom/books/BitsOfPower/.

88. *See* Samuelson, *supra* note 30.

> reached further upstream from end products to cover fundamental discoveries that provide the knowledge base for future product development.[89]

In this context, Rai and Eisenberg address the operation of Bayh-Dole,[90] and Stevenson-Wydler,[91] the Federal laws designed to make sure that publicly funded discoveries are converted into commercially viable products. These Acts did not deal with the classic public goods problem of intellectual property policy, in which the inability to exclude others from valuable innovations leads to inadequate returns on research and development, and fails to encourage research in the first place. Instead these Acts address the fear that promising publicly funded research would never be converted into useful finished products. The market dysfunction these acts sought to correct was the uncertainty of entrepreneurs about whether they could recover their investments if their innovations built upon publicly funded, and thus potentially public domain, science. While both Rai and Eisenberg are supportive of many of the features of the statutory structure, they feel that its operation in the current world of intellectual property policy leaves some things to be desired.

As a number of the articles in the Symposium note, innovation can suffer both from leaving too little and from leaving too much in the public domain. The hard question, obviously, is deciding which aspects of science, culture and technology should be controlled through intellectual property rights and which should be open to all. Rai and Eisenberg's approach is to attempt to identify the body or entity that can best make that decision, rather than to identify a particular subject matter and argue that it is appropriately in one sphere or another:

> Although intellectual property rights may sometimes be necessary to motivate private firms to develop and disseminate university-based discoveries, the trend towards assertions of intellectual property rights by universities might also impede the progress of science. The challenge lies in distinguishing discoveries that are better developed and disseminated through open access from discoveries that are better developed and disseminated under the protection of intellectual property rights. Under the Bayh-Dole Act, institutions that perform funded research enjoy largely unfettered discretion to determine when intellectual property rights are appropriate. We argue, however, that it is the funding agencies that will often have a more appropriate combination of knowledge and incentives to make these determinations in furtherance of the overall public interest in research and product development. The Bayh-Dole Act should therefore be reformed to give funding agencies greater discretion to determine when to require that publicly-funded research discoveries be dedicated to the public domain.[92]

In reaching this conclusion, Rai and Eisenberg discuss a number of recent cases, including the controversy over pluripotent primate stem-cell lines, and the NF-kB cell-signaling pathway. In each case, patent rights were given over funda-

---

89. Arti K. Rai & Rebecca S. Eisenberg, *Bayh-Dole Reform and the Progress of Biomedicine*, 66 LAW & CONTEMP. PROBS. 289, 289 (Winter/Spring 2003) (footnotes omitted).

90. Act of Dec. 12, 1980, Pub. L. No. 96-517, § 6(a), 94 Stat. 3015, 3019-28 (1980) (codified as amended at 35 U.S.C. §§ 200-212 (2000)).

91. Stevenson-Wydler Technology Innovation Act of 1980, Pub. L. No. 96-480, 94 Stat. 2311-2320 (codified as amended at 15 U.S.C. §§ 3701-3714).

92. Rai & Eisenberg, *supra* note 89, at 291 (footnotes omitted).

mental discoveries relatively far upstream in a field of science with little prior art, and with low possibility of "workarounds" for biological reasons; the human genome, is after all, the *human* genome. Thus, they present a more significant danger of blocking or impeding future innovation. The standard response to such a danger is to assume that it will be resolved by licensing. But as Rai and Eisenberg note, the patent literature is replete with examples of patent holders in new areas of technology bargaining to impasse or otherwise delaying innovation, or other examples, such as the early history of the aircraft industry, in which only government intervention allowed the technology to develop.

There are a number of possible responses to this kind of danger. The requirements for patentable subject matter can be applied more strictly, or the crabbed U.S. research exemption—one that the Court of Appeals for the Federal Circuit has recently limited still further[93]—could be expanded. Rai and Eisenberg believe that there is merit in these approaches. Their paper, however, focus on Bayh-Dole, arguing that when the statute was passed, university attitudes and patenting and licensing strategies were very different. The norms of "open science" predominated, perhaps to the extent that they hampered the development of commercially viable products by outside entities. In that world, they argue, it may have made sense to give discretion on patenting to the entities that were performing the funded research. Nowadays, however, with university "Transfer of Technology Offices" carefully managing the university's patent portfolio, the universities have strong incentives to extract rent from their discoveries and much weaker ones to keep certain fundamental scientific advances in the public domain, even if that would be socially beneficial in the long run. Hence Rai and Eisenberg argue for a revision of Bayh-Dole that gives a much greater role in the patenting decision to the funding agency, which has an interest in the development of the field as a whole, rather than to a university involved in one particular piece of funded research.

Rai and Eisenberg's theme is echoed in the final article in this volume. My colleague Jerry Reichman, and Paul Uhlir of the National Academy of Sciences, have together authored a mammoth work—effectively a book—on threats to the dissemination of scientific and technical data. We are proud to publish such a piece as part of this symposium and believe that it will come to be seen as the seminal statement of both the current problems in access to scientific data, and the possible avenues for preserving and enhancing the public domain in science while maintaining the system of incentives which intellectual property is designed to provide. The article was finished too late for this introduction to provide a proper summary, but the following snapshot attempts to lay out some of the key points from earlier drafts.

In *A Contractually Reconstructed Commons for Scientific Data in a Highly Protectionist Intellectual Property Environment*, Reichman and Uhlir argue that

93. Madey v. Duke Univ., 307 F.3d 1351 (Fed. Cir. 2002).

there are a number of present and impending threats to the free public exchange of scientific information.[94] These include: underfunding of public data collection and distribution; increasing use of private patent rights to drive fundamental research; the move of universities further into the world of commerce; the rise of legally validated contracts of adhesion; the broadening and deepening of conventional intellectual property rights; and, above all, the threat (in the United States) and the reality (in the European Union) of a "database right" that covers unoriginal compilations of fact. Reichman and Uhlir have sympathy for some of these developments, such as the inducements provided by Bayh-Dole for universities to commercialize the output of their research. They believe, however, that the pendulum has swung too far, and that these developments will likely produce a series of undesirable social outcomes that risk upsetting a fragile and imperfectly understood ecology of information exchange.

One possible solution is legal reform of various kinds: the rejection or weakening of the database regimes,[95] the tightening of subject matter requirements for patentability, the rejection of contracts of adhesion as "privately legislated intellectual property rights,"[96] and the use of alternative intellectual property regimes which rely on "liability rules" rather than property rules.[97] In this article, however, Reichman and Uhlir lay great stress on "private" solutions aimed at reconstructing a commons of scientific information and avoiding the downward spiral of excessive protectionism. Through a variety of contractually constructed "commons'" of scientific information, each aimed at a different type of public goods problem, and an electronic architecture of peer-to-peer data systems, Reichman and Uhlir believe that the worst effects of balkanization and overprotection can be avoided.

At the end of the collection, David Lange provides a fascinating afterword in which he reconceives the public domain as a status, something like citizenship.[98] That article, too, arrived too late for me to incorporate fully in this foreword, but, in any case, David's mellifluous prose is always best experienced first hand.

IV

CONCLUSION

The remarkable essays gathered here cover topics ranging from the history and theory of the public domain; to its role in culture, in science, and in the

94. J.H. Reichman & Paul Uhlir, *A Contractually Reconstructed Research Commons for Scientific Data in a Highly Protectionist Intellectual Property Environment*, 66 LAW & CONTEMP. PROBS. 315 (Winter/Spring 2003).

95. Reichman & Samuelson, *supra* note 34.

96. J.H. Reichman & Jonathan A. Franklin, *Privately Legislated Intellectual Property Rights: Reconciling Freedom of Contract with Public Good Uses of Information*, 147 U. PA. L. REV. 875, 967 (1999).

97. Reichman, *Green Tulips*, *supra* note 29.

98. Lange, *Reimagining*, *supra* note 5.

structure of the digital environment; to the constitutional status of the public domain, and the possible interpretive approaches through which that question could be addressed. It would be impossible to tie all of those threads together here.

It is possible, however, to draw a few terminological and analytical conclusions, some of which I will develop in the next essay and others of which might point the way towards future research.

1. The terms "public domain" and "commons" are used widely, enthusiastically, and inconsistently.
2. In the context of innovation policy, they are generally used to refer to the "outside" or the "opposite" of intellectual property, in two broad ways—each with a number of sub-varieties. The most useful way to understand these terms and the ways they are used, I believe, is in relationship to the implicit fear or concern about intellectual property that each attempts to alleviate and the implicit ideal of the information ecology that each attempts to instantiate. For example, we might have as our principal concern that intellectual property rights raise the cost of access to some informational resource, with the public domain correspondingly a realm of costless access traced tightly around the limits, in duration, extent, and scope, of the minimum intellectual property rights necessary to provide incentives. Alternatively, our concerns might center not on price but on single-entity control—choke points on innovation created by intellectual property rights, particularly when those are in the hands of an entity controlling a vital resource, such as a dominant operating system, or a fundamental genetic technology with no easy "work arounds." We might believe that intellectual property rights themselves could, in certain conditions, be used to create a distributed, decentralized and non-commodified form of innovation that was both efficient and democratically desirable. Here, the emphasis is not on whether there is control, but on the type of control exercised. More interestingly, we might share all of these concerns and hopes, but with greater emphasis on one or other. It is the varied form and proportion of these concerns and aspirations that explains the marked differences in usage and definition. Why does Jessica Litman say the public domain is a commons? Why does Larry Lessig use the term commons to refer to any resource protected by a liability rule rather than a property rule? Why does he refer to open source software as a commons, though it is in fact protected by a property rule? Why do some scholars stress that open source software is not in the public domain, others refer to it as "a commons," while Pamela Samuelson calls it something that is outside the public domain in theory but seemingly inside it in effect? The answer, I argue in the next essay, lies in the particular functions and dysfunctions of property on which the theorist is implicitly concentrating while creating their image of property's outside, property's antonym. This is all to the good, but surely the various projects need to be better labeled, analyzed,

distinguished.

3. The term "public domain" is generally used to refer to material that is unprotected by intellectual property rights, either as a whole or in a particular context, and is thus "free" for all to use—a term that is itself susceptible to multiple meanings in this context, ranging from costless access, through political liberty, to free trade. The key axes of variation here are the granularity of the definition on the one hand and the extent to which the "freedom" referred to is formal or substantive on the other. By granularity, I mean the scope of the legal freedom required; do we only refer to complete works which are completely free as constituting the public domain, or is our definition more granular, including aspects of works and particular types of privileged usages, such as the fair use privilege to criticize or parody, as constituting part of the public domain? By formal or substantive freedom, I mean whether the definition of the public domain focuses on actual ability to obtain access, or on formal legal status under intellectual property laws. Definitions can vary between those that have a low degree of granularity (only complete works, completely free) and a high degree of concern with form (legal status is determinative, whatever the practical difficulties of access), to the reverse, where usages protected by fair use are in the public domain and practical access is a necessary precondition, whatever the formal legal status. Intermediate combinations are also possible. These definitions are often bandied around with only implicit suggestions as to the criteria being applied, let alone the reasons for adopting those criteria. When one reads that this work of art is not *really* in the public domain one must guess that the author believes that the difficulties of physical access to it preclude such a label. If one is told that fair use rights are not *really* part of the public domain, one must guess that the public domain consists only of complete works, completely free—more granular privileges do not qualify. And even after these guesses, *one must then intuit the intellectual project in the context of which such a definition makes sense.*
4. As the foregoing paragraph indicates, while the term "property" has largely lost its conceptualist and essentialist connotations in the richly pragmatist and legal realist tradition of contemporary American culture, the same is not necessarily true of the "public domain." The legal scholar will likely use the term "property" in four or five distinct and well-understood ways, depending on the context: a property interest as any legally cognizable condition of market advantage; those rights protected by a "property rule" rather than a "liability rule"; a variable bundle of rights of interest in things (and a bundle subject to almost unlimited state regulation and reformulation); any collection of privileges that includes market alienability, "sole, absolute and despotic dominion" and so on. Yet the same scholar is unlikely to have easy access to similarly varied, and contextually well understood conceptions of the public domain. One conclusion of my essay, and the collection as a whole, is that we need a "legal realism for the public

domain" to juxtapose to our legal realism about property. A second conclusion is that we need a better analytic process of definition—not to determine whether one definition is the essential, true public domain, but the reverse—to focus on whether each is well-suited for the tasks for which it was created. This point holds true as we turn to the next term.

5. "The commons" is *generally* used in the intellectual property literature to refer to material that is not subject to individual control; rather it is controlled, if at all, by some larger group. The articles by Carol Rose, and Ostrom and Hess, in this volume, and by Larry Lessig elsewhere, show how broad and variegated a terrain this term can cover. The axis of variation here is *not* the "owned" versus the "free," as it was in the discussion of the public domain. Rather, it is individual versus collective control or sometimes, more confusingly, the presence or absence of an individual right to *exclude*. If there is a single trend in the contemporary intellectual property literature, it is to replace the ubiquitous image of Hardin's tragic commons with the possibility of various comedic commons. Since the key to the well-run commons is frequently that it has informal systems of collective control that mitigate the inevitability of Hardin's tragedy, those who use the term "commons" are more likely to celebrate forms of control than those who write about the public domain. The point is perhaps clearest in writing about open source software development. It is both the fact that the creativity is exercised collectively on a resource workable by all *and* the fact that the GPL does not allow those who modify the software to conceal the source code or to restrict reproduction that causes theorists such as Lessig to refer to this as a "commons."
6. The various projects carried on under the banner of 'the public domain' or 'the commons' do not always run in parallel, any more than the various projects carried on under the banner of "nature" or "the environment." The person who is worried about the negative effects of monopolistic control over choke points of innovation may well settle for a "commons" built around non-discriminatory access for a fee under liability rules or compulsory licenses. The person who wishes to encourage peer-to-peer production over a distributed network will often insist that resources need to be both free of control and free of cost. Nevertheless, both concerns and resultant definitions overlap substantially, so that it is understandable to find them conflated.
7. From my biased perspective, at least, this volume presents an extraordinarily rich range of offerings—from the essays on the history of the public domain, and the types of public property, through musings on the need for a cultural public domain and a reconstructed commons of scientific and technical data. If there is a thread that links this work together it is this: Property is important. Our analytically rich and historically variegated love affair with the concept demonstrates just why it is important. Yet "the opposite of property"—its outside, its limitations, negations, inversions and

correctives—this is important too. If the papers in this collection can spur us to look at the opposite of property with the same historical care, analytical precision, and occasional utopian romanticism that we display when looking at property, they will have accomplished all that we could have hoped.

ENVOI

As this volume went to press, the Supreme Court handed down its decision in *Eldred v. Ashcroft*,[99] a challenge to the Copyright Term Extension Act ("CTEA").[100] Over two strong dissents, the Court upheld the constitutionality of the Act against both First Amendment and Copyright Clause challenges. The dead can have their copyrights extended yet again. Expect a surge of creativity from Hollywood's graveyards. The greatest legal restriction of speech in the history of the Republic—putting off-limits every book, poem, film, song and sculpture for another twenty years—can proceed without significant First Amendment review. Does this decision mean the task this symposium undertakes—to take seriously the contributions of the public domain to innovation, culture and speech—is ultimately one which, whatever its intellectual merits, is doomed to face a hostile or uncomprehending audience? Even though *Eldred* was focused specifically on two particular constitutional claims, the attitude of the majority towards the importance of the public domain—whether in the textual limitations on Congress's power, or in application of the First Amendment—can hardly be cause for optimism. And yet. . . . The media reaction was remarkable. *The New York Times* declared that the "decision makes it likely that we are seeing the beginning of the end of public domain and the birth of copyright perpetuity."[101] *The Washington Post*, though more inclined to agree that retrospective extension might be constitutional, declared the copyright system to be "broken"—in that it "effectively and perpetually protects nearly all material that anyone would want to cite or use. That's not what the framers envisioned, and it's not in the public interest."[102] The protection of the public domain, a topic that was culturally invisible when the CTEA was passed, and which even attracted incomprehension from some non-lawyers when we circulated the invitation to our conference, is now on the editorial pages of the nation's newspapers of record. It is hard to think of a more timely moment for the publication of this symposium.

---

99. 123 S. Ct. 769 (2003).

100. Pub. L. No. 105-298, 112 Stat. 2827 (1998) (codified as amended in scattered sections of 17 U.S.C.).

101. Editorial, *The Supreme Court Docket; The Coming of Copyright Perpetuity*, N.Y. TIMES, Jan. 16, 2003, at A28.

102. Editorial, *Free Mickey Mouse*, WASH. POST, Jan. 21, 2003, at A16 .

THE SECOND ENCLOSURE MOVEMENT AND THE CONSTRUCTION OF THE PUBLIC DOMAIN

JAMES BOYLE*

The law locks up the man or woman
Who steals the goose from off the common
But leaves the greater villain loose
Who steals the common from off the goose.

The law demands that we atone
When we take things we do not own
But leaves the lords and ladies fine
Who take things that are yours and mine.

The poor and wretched don't escape
If they conspire the law to break;
This must be so but they endure
Those who conspire to make the law.

The law locks up the man or woman
Who steals the goose from off the common
And geese will still a common lack
Till they go and steal it back.

Anonymous

PART ONE: ENCLOSURE

I

THE FIRST ENCLOSURE MOVEMENT

This poem[1] is one of the pithiest condemnations of the English enclosure movement, the process of fencing off common land and turning it into private

* Professor of Law, Duke University.

An earlier and considerably shorter version of this article appeared as *Fencing off Ideas*, DAEDALUS, Spring 2002, at 13. I wish to thank Yochai Benkler and Larry Lessig for comments, and Matt Jones, Greg Manter, and Victoria Von Portatius for their research.

1. Apart from being anonymous, the poem is extremely hard to date. It probably comes from the enclosure controversies of the eighteenth century. However, the earliest reference to it that I have been able to discover is from 1821. Edward Birch was moved to compose some (fairly poor) verses in response when he reported "seeing the following jeu d'esprit in a Handbill posted up in Plaistow, as a 'CAUTION' to prevent persons from supporting the intended inclosure of Hainault or Waltham Forest." He then quotes a version of the poem. Edward Birch, TICKLER MAG., Feb. 1821, at 45. In 1860,

property.[2] In a few lines, the poem manages to criticize double standards, expose the artificial and controversial nature of property rights, and take a slap at the legitimacy of state power. And it does this all with humor, without jargon, and in rhyming couplets. Academics (including this one) should take note. Like most of the criticisms of the enclosure movement, the poem depicts a world of rapacious, state-aided "privatization," a conversion into private property of something that had formerly been common property or, perhaps, had been outside of the property system altogether. Sir Thomas More went further, though he used sheep rather than geese to make his point. He argued that enclosure was not merely unjust in itself, but harmful in its consequences—a cause of economic inequality, crime, and social dislocation:

> But yet this is not only the necessary cause of stealing. There is another, which, as I suppose, is proper and peculiar to you Englishmen alone. What is that, quoth the Cardinal? Forsooth my lord (quoth I) your sheep that were wont to be so meek and tame, and so small eaters, now, as I hear say, be become so great devourers and so wild, that they eat up, and swallow down the very men themselves. They consume, destroy, and devour whole fields, houses, and cities. For look in what parts of the realm doth grow the finest and therefore dearest wool, there noblemen and gentlemen . . . leave no ground for tillage, they enclose all into pastures; they throw down houses; they pluck down towns, and leave nothing standing, but only the church to be made a sheep-house. . . . Therefore that one covetous and insatiable cormorant and very plague of his native country may compass about and enclose many thousand acres of ground together within one pale or hedge, the husbandmen be thrust out of their own.[3]

The enclosure movement continues to draw our attention. It offers irresistible ironies about the two-edged sword of "respect for property," and lessons about the way in which the state defines and enforces property rights to pro-

---

a staff writer for the journal *Notes and Queries* declares that "the animosity excited against the Inclosure Acts and their authors . . . was almost without precedent: though fifty years and more have passed, the subject is still a sore one in many parishes. . . . I remember some years ago, in hunting over an old library discovering a box full of printed squibs, satires and ballads of the time against the acts and those who were supposed to favour them,—the library having belonged to a gentleman who played an active part on the opposition side." The author then quotes the first verse as a "naive epigram . . . which forcibly impressed itself on my memory." *"Exon" Ballads Against Inclosures*, 9 NOTES AND QUERIES, at 130-131 (2nd ser., Feb. 1860). The context makes it appear that the poem itself must date from the late 18th century. In other sources, the poem is sometimes dated at 1764 and said to be in response to Sir Charles Pratt's fencing of common land. *See, e.g.*, Dana A. Freiburger, John Thompson, English Philomath—A Question of Land Surveying and Astronomy, poster paper submitted to the History of Astronomy Workshop University of Notre Dame, (July 1-4, 1999), note 15, *available at* http://www.nd.edu/ ~histast4/exhibits/papers/Freiburger/index.html (last visited Dec. 19, 2002). This attribution is widespread and may well be true, but I have been able to discover no contemporary source material that sustains it. By the end of the nineteenth century, the poem was being quoted, sometimes with amusement and sometimes with agreement, on both sides of the Atlantic. *See* Ezra S. Carr, *Aids and Obstacles to Agriculture on the Pacific-Coast*, in THE PATRONS OF HUSBANDRY ON THE PACIFIC COAST 290, 291 (San Francisco, A.L. Bancroft and Co. 1875); EDWARD P. CHEYNEY, AN INTRODUCTION TO THE INDUSTRIAL AND SOCIAL HISTORY OF ENGLAND 219 (1901).

2. Although we refer to it as "*the* enclosure movement," it was actually a series of enclosures that started in the fifteenth century and went on, with differing means, ends, and varieties of state involvement, until the nineteenth century. *See, e.g.*, J.A. YELLING, COMMON FIELD AND ENCLOSURE IN ENGLAND, 1450-1850 (1977).

3. THOMAS MORE, UTOPIA 32 (Alfred A. Knopf 1992) (1947).

mote controversial social goals. The most strident critics of the enclosure movement argue that it imposed devastating costs on one segment of society.

> Enclosures have appropriately been called a revolution of the rich against the poor. The lords and nobles were upsetting the social order, breaking down ancient law and custom, sometimes by means of violence, often by pressure and intimidation. They were literally robbing the poor of their share in the common, tearing down the houses which, by the hitherto unbreakable force of custom, the poor had long regarded as theirs and their heirs'. The fabric of society was being disrupted. Desolate villages and the ruins of human dwellings testified to the fierceness with which the revolution raged, endangering the defences of the country, wasting its towns, decimating its population, turning its overburdened soil into dust, harassing its people and turning them from decent husbandmen into a mob of beggars and thieves. Though this happened only in patches, the black spots threatened to melt into a uniform catastrophe.[4]

Some of these costs were brutally and relentlessly "material"—for example, the conversion of crofters and freeholders into debt-peons, seasonal wage-laborers, or simply, as More argued in *Utopia*, and Polanyi argues 400 years later, into beggars and thieves.[5] But other harms are harder to classify: the loss of a form of life; the relentless power of market logic to migrate to new areas, disrupting traditional social relationships and perhaps even views of the self or the relationship of human beings to the environment.

So much for the bad side of the enclosure movement. For many economic historians, everything I have said up to now is the worst kind of sentimental bunk, romanticizing a form of life that was neither comfortable nor noble, and certainly not very egalitarian. The big point about the enclosure movement is that it *worked*; this innovation in property systems allowed an unparalleled expansion of productive possibilities.[6] By transferring inefficiently managed common land into the hands of a single owner, enclosure escaped the aptly named "tragedy of the commons." It gave incentives for large-scale investment, allowed control over exploitation, and, in general, ensured that resources could be put to their most efficient use. Before the enclosure movement, the feudal lord would not invest in drainage systems, sheep purchases, or crop rotation that might increase yields from the common—he knew all too well that the fruits of his labor could be appropriated by others. The strong private property rights and single entity control that were introduced in the enclosure movement avoid the tragedies of overuse and underinvestment:[7] More grain will be grown, more sheep raised; consumers will benefit; and fewer people will starve in the long run. If the price of this social gain is a greater concentration of economic power, or the introduction of market forces into areas where they previously had not been so obvious, or the disruption of a *modus vivendi* with the envi-

---

4. KARL POLANYI, THE GREAT TRANSFORMATION: THE POLITICAL AND ECONOMIC ORIGINS OF OUR TIME 35 (1957); *see also* E.P. THOMPSON, THE MAKING OF THE ENGLISH WORKING CLASS 218 (1963).

5. POLANYI, *supra* note 4 at 35.

6. *See generally* LORD ERNLE, ENGLISH FARMING PAST AND PRESENT (1961).

7. For an excellent summary of the views of Hobbes, Locke and Blackstone on these points, see Hannibal Travis, *Pirates of the Information Infrastructure: Blackstonian Copyright and the First Amendment*, 15 BERKELEY TECH. L.J. 777, 789-803 (2000).

ronment—then, enclosure's defenders say, so be it. In their view, the agricultural surplus produced by enclosure helped to save a society devastated by the mass deaths of the sixteenth century. Those who weep tears about the terrible effects of private property should realize that it literally saves lives.

I am not going to concentrate on the first enclosure movement here. It is worth noting, however, that while earlier scholarship extolled enclosure's beneficial effects,[8] some more recent empirical work has indicated that it had few, if any, effects in increasing agricultural production.[9] The tragedies predicted in articles such as Hardin's *Tragedy of the Commons* did not occur.[10] In fact, the commons frequently may have been well-run, though the restraints on its depletion and the incentives for investment in it may have been "softer" than the hard-edged norms of private property.[11] Thus, while enclosure produced significant distributional changes of the kind that so incensed an earlier generation of critical historians, there are significant questions about whether it led to greater efficiency or innovation. These results are little known, however, outside of the world of economic historians. "Everyone" knows that a commons is by definition tragic, and that the logic of enclosure is as true today as it was in the fifteenth century. Private property saves lives.

---

8. *See* ERNLE, *supra* note 6.

9. The most notable work is that of Robert Allen. *See* Robert C. Allen, *The Efficiency and Distributional Consequences of Eighteenth Century Enclosures*, 92 ECON. J. 937 (1982) [hereinafter Allen, *Efficiency*]; ROBERT C. ALLEN, ENCLOSURE AND THE YEOMAN (1994). Allen argues that the enclosure movement produced major distributional consequences, but little observable efficiency gain. The pie was carved up differently, to the advantage of the landlords, but made no larger. In contrast, Michael Turner sees enclosure as one possible, though not necessary, route to productivity gains. *See* Michael Turner, *English Open Fields and Enclosures: Retardation or Productivity Improvements*, 46 J. ECON. HIST. 669, 688 (1986). Donald McCloskey's work also argues for efficiency gains from enclosure, largely from the evidence provided by rent increases. *See* Donald N. McCloskey, *The Enclosure of Open Fields: Preface to a Study of Its Impact on the Efficiency of English Agriculture in the Eighteenth Century*, 32 J. ECON. HIST. 15 (1972); Donald N. McCloskey, *The Prudent Peasant: New Findings on Open Fields*, 51 J. ECON. HIST. 343 (1991). In Allen's view, however, the change in rents was largely a measure of the way that changes in legal rights affected the bargaining power of the parties and the cultural context of rent negotiations; enclosure allowed landlords to capture more of the existing surplus produced by the land, rather than dramatically expanding it. "[T]he enclosure movement itself might be regarded as the first state sponsored land reform. Like so many since, it was justified with efficiency arguments, while its main effect (according to the data analyzed here) was to redistribute income to already rich landowners." Allen, *Efficiency*, *supra* at 950-51. Those contemporary accounts which argue that enclosure led to productivity gains tend to be more qualified in their praise. Compare Turner, *supra*, ("Enclosure cannot be seen as the automatic open door to this cycle of agricultural improvement, but the foregoing estimates do suggest that perhaps it was a door which opened frequently, and with profit.") with the more positive account given in ERNLE, *supra* note 6.

10. Garrett Hardin, *The Tragedy of the Commons*, SCIENCE, Dec. 13, 1968, at 1243.

11. The possibility of producing "order without law" and, thus, sometimes governing the commons without tragedy, has also fascinated scholars of contemporary land use. *See* ROBERT C. ELLICKSON, ORDER WITHOUT LAW: HOW NEIGHBORS SETTLE DISPUTES (1991); ELINOR OSTROM, GOVERNING THE COMMONS: THE EVOLUTION OF INSTITUTIONS FOR COLLECTIVE ACTION (1991).

II

THE SECOND ENCLOSURE MOVEMENT

This is all very well, but what does it have to do with intellectual property? We are in the middle of a second enclosure movement. It sounds grandiloquent to call it "the enclosure of the intangible commons of the mind," but in a very real sense that is just what it is.[12] True, the new state-created property rights may be "intellectual" rather than "real," but once again things that were formerly thought of as either common property or uncommodifiable are being covered with new, or newly extended, property rights.

Take the human genome as an example. Again, the supporters of enclosure have argued that the state was right to step in and extend the reach of property rights; that only in this way could we guarantee the kind of investment of time, ingenuity, and capital necessary to produce new drugs and gene therapies.[13] To the question, "Should there be patents over human genes?," the supporters of enclosure would answer that private property saves lives.[14] The opponents of enclosure have claimed that the human genome belongs to everyone, that it is literally the common heritage of humankind, that it should not and perhaps in some sense *cannot* be owned, and that the consequences of turning over the human genome to private property rights will be dreadful, as market logic invades areas which should be the farthest from the market. In stories about stem cell and gene sequence patents, critics have mused darkly about the way in which the state is handing over monopoly power to a few individuals and corporations, potentially introducing bottlenecks and coordination costs that slow down innovation.[15]

Alongside these accounts of the beneficiaries of the new property scheme run news stories about those who were not so fortunate, the commoners of the genetic enclosure. Law students across America read *Moore v. Regents of University of California*, a California Supreme Court case deciding that Mr. Moore had no property interest in the cells derived from his spleen.[16] The court tells us that giving private property rights to "sources" would slow the free-wheeling

---

12. The analogy to the enclosure movement has been too succulent to resist. To my knowledge, Ben Kaplan, Pamela Samuelson, Yochai Benkler, David Lange, Chrisopher May, David Bollier and Keith Aoki have all employed the trope, as I myself have on previous occasions. For a particularly thoughtful and careful development of the parallel between the two enclosure movements, see generally Travis, *supra* note 7.

13. *See, e.g.*, William A. Haseltine, *The Case for Gene Patents*, TECH. REV., Sept./Oct. 2000, *available at* http://www.technologyreview.com/articles/haseltine0900.asp (last visited Dec. 19, 2002); *cf.* Alexander K. Haas, *The Wellcome Trust's Disclosures of Gene Sequence Data into the Public Domain & the Potential for Proprietary Rights in the Human Genome*, 16 BERKELEY TECH. L.J. 145 (2001).

14. *See, e.g.*, Haseltine, *supra* note 13; Press Release, Biotechnology Industry Association, Genentech, Incyte Genomics Tell House Subcommittee Gene Patents Essential For Medical Progress (July 13, 2000), *available at* http://www.bio.org/genomics/genetech.html.

15. *See, e.g.*, Howard Markel, *Patents Could Block the Way to a Cure*, N.Y. TIMES, Aug. 24, 2001, at A19. For the general background to these arguments, see Rebecca S. Eisenberg, *Patenting the Human Genome*, 39 EMORY L.J. 721, 740-44 (1990).

16. 793 P.2d 479, 488-97 (Cal. 1990).

practice researchers have of sharing their cell lines with all and sundry.[17] The doctors whose inventive genius created a billion-dollar cell line from Mr. Moore's "naturally occurring raw material," by contrast, are granted a patent. Private property rights here, by contrast, are a necessary incentive to research.[18] Economists on both sides of the enclosure debate concentrate on the efficient allocation of rights. Popular discussion, on the other hand, doubtless demonstrating a reprehensible lack of rigor, returns again and again to more naturalistic assumptions such as the "commonness" of the property involved or the idea that one owns one's own body.[19]

The genome is not the only area to be partially "enclosed" during this second enclosure movement. The expansion of intellectual property rights has been remarkable—from business method patents,[20] to the Digital Millennium Copyright Act,[21] to trademark antidilution rulings,[22] to the European Database Protection Directive.[23] The old limits to intellectual property rights—the anti-erosion walls around the public domain—are also under attack. The annual process of updating my syllabus for a basic Intellectual Property course provides a nice snapshot of what is going on. I can wax nostalgic looking back to a five-year-old text, with its confident list of subject matter that intellectual property rights *couldn't* cover, the privileges that circumscribed the rights that did exist, and the length of time before a work falls into the public domain. In each case, the limits have been eaten away.

To be sure, there is a danger of overstatement. The very fact that the changes have been so one-sided makes it hard to resist exaggerating their impact. In 1918, Brandeis confidently claimed that "[t]he general rule of law is,

---

17. *Id.* at 493-94. One imagines Styrofoam coolers criss-crossing the country by FedEx in an orgy of communistic flesh swapping.

18. *Id.* at 493.

19. I might be suspected of anti-economist irony here. In truth, neither side's arguments are fully satisfying. It is easy to agree with Richard Posner that the language of economics offers a "thin and unsatisfactory epistemology" through which to understand the world. RICHARD POSNER, THE PROBLEMS OF JURISPRUDENCE xiv (1990) (citing the words of Paul Bator). On the other hand, explaining what it means to "own one's own body," or specifying the non-commodifiable limits on the market turns out to be a remarkably tricky business, as Margaret Jane Radin has shown with great elegance. *See* MARGARET JANE RADIN, CONTESTED COMMODITIES (1996).

20. *See* State St. Bank & Trust Co. v. Signature Fin. Group, 149 F.3d 1368, 1373 (D.C. Cir. 1998)

21. Pub. L. No. 105-304, 112 Stat. 2860 (1998) (codified as amended in scattered sections of 5, 17, 28 and 35 U.S.C.).

22. *See, e.g.*, Mead Data Central, Inc. v. Toyota Motor Sales, U.S.A., Inc., 875 F.2d 1026, 1030 (2d Cir. 1989); Mutual of Omaha Insurance Co. v. Novak, 836 F. 2d 397 (8th Cir. 1987), *cert. denied* 109 S. Ct. 326 (1987); American Express Co. v. Vibra Approved Laboratories Corp., 10 U.S.P.Q. 2d (BNA) 2006 (S.D.N.Y. Apr. 17, 1989); Jordache Enters., Inc. v. Hogg Wyld, Ltd., 625 F. Supp. 48, 56 (D.N.M. 1985), *aff'd*, 828 F.2d 1482 (10th Cir. 1987); Pillsbury Co. v. Milky Way Prod., Inc., 215 U.S.P.Q. (BNA) 124 (N.D. Ga. Dec. 24, 1981); General Electric Co. v. Almpa Coal Co., 205 U.S.P.Q. (BNA) 1036 (D.Mass. Oct. 12, 1979); Reddy Communications, Inc. v. Environmental Action Found., Inc., 199 U.S.P.Q. (BNA) 630 (D.D.C. Nov. 11, 1977); Coca-Cola Co. v. Gemini Rising Inc., 346 F. Supp. 1183 (E.D.N.Y. 1972).

23. Directive 96/9/EC of the European Parliament and of the Council of 11 March 1996 on the Legal Protection of Databases, 1996 O.J. (L 77) 20, *available at* http://europa.eu.int/ISPO/infosoc/legreg/ docs/969ec.html [hereinafter Directive] (last visited Dec. 19, 2002).

that the noblest of human productions—knowledge, truths ascertained, conceptions, and ideas—become, after voluntary communication to others, free as the air to common use."[24] That baseline—intellectual property rights are the exception rather than the norm; ideas and facts must always remain in the public domain—is still supposed to be our starting point.[25] It is, however, under attack. Both overtly and covertly, the commons of facts and ideas is being enclosed. Patents are increasingly stretched out to cover "ideas" that twenty years ago all scholars would have agreed were unpatentable.[26] Most troubling of all are the attempts to introduce intellectual property rights over mere compilations of facts.[27] If Anglo-American intellectual property law had an article of faith it was that unoriginal compilations of facts would remain in the public domain, that this protection of the raw material of science and speech was as important to the next generation of innovation as the intellectual property rights themselves.[28] The system would hand out monopolies in inventions and in original expression, while the facts below (and ideas above) would remain free for all to build upon. But this premise is being undermined. Some of the challenges are subtle: In patent law, stretched interpretations of novelty and non-obviousness allow intellectual property rights to move closer and closer to the underlying datalayer; gene sequence patents come very close to being rights over a particular discovered arrangement of data—Cs, Gs, As, and Ts.[29] Other challenges are overt: The European Database Directive does (and the various proposed bills in the United States would) create proprietary rights over compilations of facts, often without even the carefully framed exceptions of the copyright scheme, such as the usefully protean category of fair use.[30]

The older strategy of intellectual property law was a "braided" one: Thread a thin layer of intellectual property rights around a commons of material from which future creators would draw. Even that thin layer of intellectual property rights was limited to allow access to the material when the private property owner might charge too much. Fair use allows for parody, commentary and criticism, and also for "decompilation" of computer programs so that, for example, Microsoft's competitors can reverse engineer Word's features to make

24. Int'l News Serv. v. Associated Press, 248 U.S. 215, 250 (1918) (Brandeis, J., dissenting).

25. Yochai Benkler, *Free as the Air to Common Use: First Amendment Constraints on Enclosure of the Public Domain*, 74 N.Y.U. L. REV. 354, 361, 424 (1999) [hereinafter Benkler, *Free as the Air*].

26. The so-called "business method" patents, which cover such "inventions" as auctions or accounting methods, are an obvious example. *See, e.g.*, State St. Bank & Trust Co. v. Signature Fin. Group, Inc., 149 F.3d 1368, 1373 (Fed. Cir. 1998).

27. Collection of Information Antipiracy Act, S. 2291, 105th Cong. (1998); Database Investment and Intellectual Property Antipiracy Act of 1996, H.R. 3531, 104th Cong. (1996).

28. *See, e.g.*, Feist Publ'ns v. Rural Tel. Serv. Co., 499 U.S. 340, 350, 354 (1991) ("Copyright treats facts and factual compilations in a wholly consistent manner. Facts, whether alone or as part of a compilation, are not original and therefore may not be copyrighted." To hold otherwise would "'distort[]' basic copyright principles in that it creates a monopoly in public domain materials without the necessary justification of protecting and encouraging the creation of 'writings' by 'authors.'").

29. *See* Eisenberg, *supra* note 15; Haas, *supra* note 13.

30. *See* Directive, *supra* note 23.

sure that their program can convert Word files.[31] It may sound paradoxical, but in a very real sense protection of the commons was one of the fundamental goals of intellectual property law. In the new vision of intellectual property, however, property should be extended everywhere—more is better. Expanding patentable and copyrightable subject matter, lengthening the copyright term, giving legal protection to "digital barbed wire" even if it is used in part to protect against fair use: Each of these can be understood as a vote of no-confidence in the productive powers of the commons. We seem to be shifting from Brandeis's assumption that the "noblest of human productions are free as the air to common use" to the assumption that any commons is inefficient, if not tragic.

The expansion is more than a formal one. It used to be relatively *hard* to violate an intellectual property right. The technologies of reproduction or the activities necessary to infringe were largely, though not entirely, industrial. The person with the printing press who chooses to reproduce a book is a lot different from the person who lends the book to a friend or takes a chapter into class. The photocopier makes that distinction fuzzy, and the networked computer erases it altogether. In a networked society, copying is not only easy, it is a *sine qua non* of transmission, storage, caching, and, some would claim, even reading.[32] As bioinformatics blurs the line between computer modeling and biological research, digital production techniques blur the line between listening, editing, and recreating. "Rip, mix, and burn," says the Apple advertisement. It marks a world in which the old regime of intellectual property, operating upstream as a form of industrial unfair competition policy, has been replaced. Intellectual property is now in and on the desktop and is implicated in routine creative, communicative, and just plain consumptive acts that each of us performs every day. The reach of the rights has been expanded at the same moment that their practical effect has been transformed.

III

HOW MUCH OF THE INTANGIBLE COMMONS MUST WE ENCLOSE?

So far I have argued that there are profound similarities between the first enclosure movement and the contemporary expansion of intellectual property, which I call the second enclosure movement. Once again, the critics and proponents of enclosure are locked in battle, hurling at each other incommensurable claims about innovation, efficiency, traditional values, the boundaries of the market, the saving of lives, the loss of familiar liberties. Once again, opposition to enclosure is portrayed as economically illiterate; the beneficiaries of enclo-

31. Those who prefer topographical metaphors might imagine a quilted pattern of public and private land, with legal rules specifying that certain areas, beaches for example, can never be privately owned, and with accompanying rules giving public rights of way through private land if there is a danger that access to the commons might otherwise be blocked.

32. *See* JAMES BOYLE, SHAMANS, SOFTWARE, & SPLEENS: LAW AND THE CONSTRUCTION OF THE INFORMATION SOCIETY 135 (1996) [hereinafter BOYLE, SHAMANS]; JESSICA LITMAN, DIGITAL COPYRIGHT 91 (2001).

sure telling us that an expansion of property rights is needed in order to fuel progress. Indeed, the post-Cold War "Washington Consensus" is invoked to claim history teaches the only way one gets growth and efficiency is through markets; property rights, surely, are the *sine que non* of markets.[33]

But if there are similarities between our two enclosures, there are also profound dissimilarities; the networked commons of the mind has many different characteristics from the grassy commons of Old England.[34] I want to concentrate here on two key differences between the intellectual commons and the commons of the first enclosure movement: differences that should lead us to question whether this commons is truly tragic and to ask whether stronger intellectual property rights really are the solution to our problems. These differences are well known; indeed, they are the starting point for most intellectual property law. Nevertheless, reflection on them might help to explain both the problems and the stakes in the current wave of expansion.

Unlike the earthy commons, the commons of the mind is generally "nonrival." Many uses of land are mutually exclusive. If I am using the field for grazing, it may interfere with your plans to use it for growing crops. By contrast, a gene sequence, an MP3 file, or an image may be used by multiple parties; my use does not interfere with yours. To simplify a complicated analysis, this means that the threat of overuse of fields and fisheries is generally not a problem with the informational or innovational commons.[35] Thus, one type of tragedy of the commons is avoided. The concerns in the informational commons have to do with a different kind of collective action problem: the problem

---

33. The phrase "Washington Consensus" originated in John Williamson, *What Washington Means by Policy Reform*, *in* LATIN AMERICAN ADJUSTMENT: HOW MUCH HAS HAPPENED? 7-38 (John Williamson ed., 1990). Over time, it has come to be used as shorthand for a neo-liberal view of economic policy that puts its faith in deregulation, privatization, and the creation and defense of secure property rights as the cure for all ills. *See* Joseph Stiglitz, *The World Bank at the Millennium*, 109 ECON. J. 577, 577-97 (1999). It has thus become linked to the triumphalist neo-liberal account of the end of history and the victory of unregulated markets. *See* FRANCIS FUKUYAMA, THE END OF HISTORY AND THE LAST MAN (1992). Neither of these two results are, to be fair, what its creator intended. *See* John Williamson, *What Should The Bank Think About The Washington Consensus?*, Institute for International Economics, *available at* http://www.iie.com/papers/williamson0799.htm (last visited Sept. 20, 2002).

34. The differences are particularly strong in the arguments over "desert:" Are these property rights deserved or are they simply violations of the public trust and privatizations of the commons? For example, some would say that we never had the same *traditional* claims over the genetic commons that the victims of the first enclosure movement had over their commons; this is more like newly discovered frontier land, or perhaps even privately drained marshland, than it is like well-known common land that all have traditionally used. In this case, the enclosers can claim (though their claims are disputed) that they discovered or perhaps simply made usable the territory they seek to own. The opponents of gene patenting, on the other hand, turn to religious and ethical arguments about the sanctity of life and the incompatibility of property with living systems even more frequently than the farmers of the eighteenth century. These arguments, and the appeals to free speech that dominate debates over digital intellectual property, have no precise analogue in debates over hunting or pasturage, although there are common themes. For example, we are already seeing nostalgic laments of the loss of the immemorial rights of Internet users. At the same time, the old language of property law is turned to this more evanescent subject matter; my favorite title is *The Ancient Doctrine of Trespass to Web Sites*. I. Trotter Hardy, *The Ancient Doctrine of Trespass to Web Sites*, 1996 J. ONLINE L. art. 7, *available at* http://www.wm.edu/law/publications/jol/95_96/hardy.html (last visited Dec. 19, 2002).

35. The exceptions to this statement turn out to be fascinating. In the interest of brevity, however, I will ignore them entirely.

of incentives to create the resource in the first place. The difficulty comes because of the idea that information goods are not only non-rival (uses do not interfere with each other), they are also assumed to be non-excludable (it is impossible, or at least hard, to stop one unit of the good from satisfying an infinite number of users at zero marginal cost). Pirates will copy the song, the mousetrap, the drug formula. The rest of the argument is well known. Lacking an ability to exclude, creators will be unable to charge for their creations; there will be inadequate incentives to create. Thus, the law must step in and create a limited monopoly called an intellectual property right.

This is a well known argument, but it has recently acquired an historical dimension, a teleology of intellectual property maximalism. If the reason for intellectual property rights is the non-rival and non-excludable nature of the goods they protect, then surely the lowering of copying and transmission costs implies a corresponding need to *increase* the strength of intellectual property rights. Imagine a line. At one end sits a monk painstakingly transcribing Aristotle's *Poetics*. In the middle lies the Gutenberg printing press. Three-quarters of the way along the line is a photocopying machine. At the far end lies the Internet and the online version of the human genome. At each stage, copying costs are lowered and goods become both less rival and less excludable. My MP3 files are available to anyone in the world running Napster. Songs can be found and copied with ease. The symbolic end of rivalry comes when I am playing the song in Chapel Hill, North Carolina at the very moment that you are both downloading and listening to it in Kazakhstan—now *that's* non-rival. My point is that there seems to be an assumption that the strength of intellectual property rights must vary inversely with the cost of copying. To deal with the monk-copyist, we need no intellectual property right because physical control of the manuscript is enough. To deal with the Gutenberg press, we need the Statute of Anne.[36] To deal with the Internet, we need the Digital Millennium Copyright Act,[37] the No Electronic Theft Act,[38] the Sonny Bono Term Extension Act,[39] and perhaps even the Collections of Information Antipiracy Act.[40] As copying costs approach zero asymptotically, intellectual property rights must approach perfect control. If a greater proportion of product value and gross national product is now in the form of value-added information, then we have still another reason to need strengthened protection. A five-dollar padlock would do for a garden shed, but not for a vault.

Like any attractive but misleading argument, this one has a lot of truth. The Internet does lower the cost of copying and, thus, the cost of illicit copying. Of

36. 13 Ann., c. 15 (Eng.).

37. Pub. L. No. 105-304, 112 Stat. 2860 (1998) (codified as amended in scattered sections of 5, 17, 28, and 35 U.S.C.).

38. Pub. L. No. 105-147, 111 Stat. 2678 (1997) (codified as amended in scattered sections of 17 and 18 U.S.C.).

39. Pub. L. No. 105-298, 112 Stat. 2827 (1998) (codified as amended in scattered sections of 17 U.S.C.).

40. S. 2291, 105th Cong. (1998).

course, it also lowers the costs of production, distribution, and advertising, and dramatically increases the size of the potential market. Is the net result, then, a loss to rights-holders such that we need to increase protection to maintain a constant level of incentives? A large, leaky market may actually provide more revenue than a small one over which one's control is much stronger. What's more, the same technologies that allow for cheap copying also allow for swift and encyclopedic search engines—the best devices ever invented for detecting illicit copying. It would be impossible to say, on the basis of the evidence we have, that owners of protected content are better or worse off as a result of the Internet.[41] Thus, the idea that we must inevitably strengthen rights as copying costs decline doesn't hold water. And given the known static and dynamic costs of monopolies, and the constitutional injunction to encourage the progress of science and the useful arts,[42] the burden of proof should be on those requesting new rights to prove their necessity.

How about the argument that the increasing importance of information-value-added and information-intensive products to the world economy means that protection must increase? Must the information commons be enclosed because it is now a more important sector of economic activity?[43] This was certainly one of the arguments for the first enclosure movement. For example, during the Napoleonic War, enclosure was defended as a necessary method of increasing the efficiency of agricultural production, now a vital sector of a war-time economy. Here, we come to another big difference between the commons of the mind and the earthy commons. As has frequently been pointed out, information products are often made up of fragments of other information products; your information output is someone else's information input.[44] These inputs may be snippets of code, discoveries, prior research, images, genres of work, cultural references, or databases of single nucleotide polymorphisms—each is raw material for future innovation. Every potential increase of protection, however, also raises the cost of, or reduces access to, the raw material from which you might have built those products. The balance is a delicate one; one Nobel Prize-winning economist has claimed that it is actually impossible to strike that balance so as to produce an informationally efficient market.[45] Whether or not it is impossible in theory, it is surely a difficult

41. My intuitions—and historical experience with prior "dangerous" copying technologies such as the VCR—point strongly to the position that owners of protected content are better off; but there really isn't enough evidence either way.

42. U.S. CONST. art. I, § 8, cl. 8.

43. Remember, I am talking here about *increases* in the level of rights: protecting new subject matter for longer periods of time, criminalizing certain technologies, making it illegal to cut through digital fences even if they have the effect of foreclosing previously lawful uses, and so on. Each of these has the effect of diminishing the public domain in the name of national economic policy.

44. *E.g.*, BOYLE, SHAMANS, *supra* note 32; William M. Landes & Richard A. Posner, *An Economic Analysis of Copyright Law*, 18 J. LEGAL STUD. 325, 348 (1989); Jessica Litman, *The Public Domain*, 39 EMORY L.J. 965, 1010-11 (1990); Pamela Samuelson & Suzanne Scotchmer, *The Law & Economics of Reverse Engineering*, 111 YALE L.J. 1575 (2002).

45. Sanford J. Grossman & Joseph E. Stiglitz, *On the Impossibility of Informationally Efficient Markets*, 70 AM. ECON. REV. 393, 404 (1980).

problem in practice. In other words, even if enclosure of the arable commons always produced gains (itself a subject of debate), enclosure of the information commons clearly has the potential to harm innovation as well as to support it.[46] More property rights, even though they supposedly offer greater incentives, do not necessarily make for more and better production and innovation—sometimes just the opposite is true. It may be that intellectual property rights *slow down* innovation, by putting multiple roadblocks, multiple necessary licenses, in the way of subsequent innovation.[47] Using a nice inversion of the idea of the tragedy of the commons, Heller and Eisenberg referred to these effects—the transaction costs caused by myriad property rights over the necessary components of some subsequent innovation—as "The Tragedy of the Anticommons."[48]

IV

INTELLECTUAL PROPERTY AND DISTRIBUTED CREATIVITY

My arguments so far have taken as a given the incentives/collective action problems to which intellectual property is a response. I have discussed the extent to which the logic of enclosure works for the commons of the mind as well as it did for the arable commons, taking into account the effects of an information society and a global Internet. What I have not done is asked whether a global network actually *transforms* our assumptions about creativity and innovation so as to reshape the debate about the need for incentives, at least in certain areas. This, however, is exactly the question that needs to be asked.

For anyone interested in the way that networks can enable new collaborative methods of production, the free software movement, or the broader but less vociferous movement that goes under the name of open-source software, provide interesting case studies.[49] Open-source software is released under a

---

46. For a more technical account, see James Boyle, *Cruel, Mean, or Lavish?: Economic Analysis, Price Discrimination and Digital Intellectual Property*, 53 VAND. L. REV. 2007 (2000) [hereinafter Boyle, *Cruel*].

47. The most recent example of this phenomenon is the multiple legal roadblocks to bringing "Golden Rice" to market. For a fascinating study of the various issues involved and the strategies for working around them, see R. David Kryder et al., *The Intellectual and Technical Property Components of Pro-Vitamin A Rice (Golden Rice): A Preliminary Freedom-to-Operate Review*, *available at* http://www.isaaa.org/publications/briefs/Brief_20.htm (last visited Apr. 9, 2002). In assessing the economic effects of patents, one has to balance the delays and increased costs caused by the web of property rights against the benefits to society of the incentives to innovation, the requirement of disclosure, and the eventual access to the patented subject matter. When the qualification levels for patents are set too low, the benefits are minuscule and the costs very high—the web of property rights is particularly tangled, complicating follow-on innovation, the monopoly goes to "buy" a very low level of inventiveness, and the disclosure is of little value.

48. Michael A. Heller & Rebecca S. Eisenberg, *Can Patents Deter Innovation? The Anticommons in Biomedical Research*, SCIENCE, May 1, 1998, at 698.

49. *See* GLYN MOODY, REBEL CODE: LINUX AND THE OPEN SOURCE REVOLUTION (2001); PETER WAYNER, FREE FOR ALL: HOW LINUX AND THE FREE SOFTWARE MOVEMENT UNDERCUT THE HIGH-TECH-TITANS (2000); Eben Moglen, *Anarchism Triumphant: Free Software and the Death of*

series of licenses, the most important being the General Public License ("GPL"). The GPL specifies that anyone may copy the software, provided the license remains attached and the source code for the software always remains available.[50] Users may add to or modify the code, may build on it and incorporate it into their own work, but if they do so, then the new program created is also covered by the GPL. Some people refer to this as the "viral" nature of the license; others find the term offensive.[51] The point, however, is that the open quality of the creative enterprise spreads. It is not simply a donation of a program or a work to the public domain, but a continual accretion in which all gain the benefits of the program on pain of agreeing to give their additions and innovations back to the communal project.

The free software and open-source software movements have produced software that rivals and, many would say, exceeds the capabilities of conventional proprietary, binary-only software.[52] Its adoption on the "enterprise level" is impressive, as is the number and enthusiasm of the various technical encomia to its strengths. The remarkable thing is not merely that the software works technically, but that it is an example of widespread, continued, high-quality innovation. The remarkable thing is that it works socially, as a continuing system, sustained only by a network consisting largely of volunteers. Here, it seems, we have a classic public good: code that can be copied freely and sold or redistributed without paying the creator or creators. This sounds like a tragedy of the commons of the kind that I described in the first section. Obviously, with a non-rival, non-excludable good like software, this method of production cannot be sustained; there are inadequate incentives to ensure continued production. *E pur si muove*, as Galileo is reputed to have said in the face of Cardinal Bellarmine's certainties, "And yet it moves."[53]

There is a broad debate on the reasons that the system works. Are the motivations those of the gift economy? Is this actually a form of potlatch, in which one gains prestige by the extravagance of the resources one "wastes?" Is open-source an implicit résumé builder that pays off in other ways? Is it driven by the species-being, the innate human love of creation that continually drives

Copyright, 4 FIRST MONDAY 8 (Aug. 2, 1999), *at* http://firstmonday.org/issues/issue4_8/moglen/index.html.

50. Proprietary, or "binary only," software is generally released only after the source code has been compiled into machine-readable object code, a form that is impenetrable to the user. Even if you were a master programmer, and the provisions of the Copyright Act, the appropriate licenses, and the DMCA did not forbid you from doing so, you would be unable to modify commercial proprietary software to customize it for your needs, remove a bug, or add a feature. Open source programmers say, disdainfully, that it is like buying a car with the hood welded shut. *See, e.g.*, WAYNER, *supra* note 49, at 264.

51. *See* Brian Behlendorf, *Open Source as a Business Strategy*, *in* OPEN SOURCES: VOICES FROM THE OPEN SOURCE REVOLUTION, 149, 163 (Chris Dibona et al. eds., 1999).

52. *See* Bruce Brown, *Enterprise-Level Security Made Easy*, PC MAG., Jan. 15, 2002, at 28; Jim Rapoza, *Open-Source Fever Spreads*, PC WEEK, Dec. 13, 1999, at 1.

53. E. COBHAM BREWER, THE DICTIONARY OF PHRASE AND FABLE, 1111-12 (1894).

us to create new things even when *homo economicus* would be at home in bed, mumbling about public goods problems?[54]

Yochai Benkler and I would argue that these questions are fun to debate but ultimately irrelevant.[55] Assume a random distribution of incentive structures in different people, a global network: transmission, information sharing and copying costs that approach zero, and a modular creation process. With these assumptions, it just does not matter why they do it. In lots of cases, they *will* do it. One person works for love of the species, another in the hope of a better job, a third for the joy of solving puzzles, and so on. Each person has his own reserve price, the point at which he says, "Now I will turn off *Survivor* and go and create something." But on a global network, there are a *lot* of people, and with numbers that big and information overhead that small, even relatively hard projects will attract motivated and skilled people whose particular reserve price has been crossed. For the whole structure to work without large-scale centralized coordination, the creation process has to be modular, with units of different sizes and complexities, each requiring slightly different expertise, all of which can be added together to make a grand whole. I can work on the sendmail program; you on the search algorithms. More likely, *lots* of people try, their efforts are judged by the community, and the best ones are adopted. Under these conditions, this curious mix of Kropotkin and Adam Smith, Richard Dawkins and Richard Stallman, we *will* get distributed production without having to rely on the proprietary/exclusion model. The whole enterprise will be much, much, much greater than the sum of the parts.

What's more, and this is a truly fascinating twist, when the production process does need more centralized coordination, some governance that guides how the sticky modular bits are put together, it is at least theoretically possible that we can come up with the control system *in exactly the same way*. In this sense, distributed production is potentially recursive. Governance processes, too, can

---

54. For a seminal statement, see Moglen, *supra* note 49:

> "[I]ncentives" is merely a metaphor, and as a metaphor to describe human creative activity it's pretty crummy. I have said this before, but the better metaphor arose on the day Michael Faraday first noticed what happened when he wrapped a coil of wire around a magnet and spun the magnet. Current flows in such a wire, but we don't ask what the incentive is for the electrons to leave home. We say that the current results from an emergent property of the system, which we call induction. The question we ask is "what's the resistance of the wire?" So Moglen's Metaphorical Corollary to Faraday's Law says that if you wrap the Internet around every person on the planet and spin the planet, software flows in the network. It's an emergent property of connected human minds that they create things for one another's pleasure and to conquer their uneasy sense of being too alone. The only question to ask is, what's the resistance of the network? Moglen's Metaphorical Corollary to Ohm's Law states that the resistance of the network is directly proportional to the field strength of the "intellectual property" system. So the right answer to the econodwarf is, resist the resistance.

Id.

55. Benkler's explanation is characteristically elegant, even formal in its precision, while mine is clunkier. *See* Yochai Benkler, *Coase's Penguin, or, Linux and the Nature of the Firm*, 111 YALE L.J. 369 (2002) [hereinafter Benkler, *Coase's Penguin*].

be assembled through distributed methods on a global network, by people with widely varying motivations, skills, and reserve prices.[56]

But in the language of computer programmers, does it "scale?" Can we generalize anything from this limited example? How many types of production, innovation, and research fit into the model I have just described? After all, for most innovations and inventions one needs hardware, capital investment, and large-scale real-world data collection—*stuff*, in its infinite recalcitrance and facticity. Maybe the open-source model has solved the individual incentives problem, but that's not the *only* problem. And how many types of innovation or cultural production are as modular as software? Is open-source software a paradigm case of collective innovation that helps us to understand open-source software and not much else?

Again, I think this is a good question, but it may be the wrong one. My own guess is that an open-source method of production is far more common than we realize. "Even before the Internet" (as some of my students have taken to saying portentously), science, law, education, and musical genres all developed in ways that are markedly similar to the model I have described. The marketplace of ideas, the continuous roiling development in thought and norm that our political culture spawns, is itself an idea that owes much more to the distributed, non-proprietary model than it does to the special case of commodified innovation that we think about in copyright and patent. Not that copyright and patent are unimportant in the process, but they may well be the exception rather than the norm. Commons-based production of ideas is hardly unfamiliar, after all.

In fact, all the mottoes of free software development have their counterparts in the theory of democracy and open society; "with enough eyeballs, all bugs are shallow" is merely the most obvious example. Karl Popper would have cheered.[57] The importance of open-source software is not that it introduces us to a wholly new idea; it is that it makes us see clearly a very old idea. With open source the technology was novel, the production process was transparent, and the result of that process was a "product" which out-competed other products in the marketplace. "How can this have happened? What about the tragedy of the commons?" we asked in puzzlement, coming only slowly to the realization that other examples of commons-based, non-proprietary production were all around us.

Still, this does not answer the question of whether the model can scale further. To answer that question we would need to think more about the modularity of other types of inventions—can they be broken down into chunks suitable for distribution among a widespread community? Which forms of innovation have some irreducible need for high capital investment in distinctly

56. One organization theorist to whom I mentioned the idea said, "Ugh, governance by food fight." Anyone who has ever been on an organizational listserv, a global production process run by people who are long on brains and short on social skills, knows how accurate that description is. *E pur si muove*.

57. *See* KARL POPPER, THE OPEN SOCIETY AND ITS ENEMIES (1945).

non-virtual components—a particle accelerator or a Phase III drug trial? Again, my guess is that the increasing migration of the sciences towards data- and processing-rich models makes more innovations and discoveries potential candidates for the distributed model. Bio-informatics and computational biology, the open-source genomics project,[58] the possibility of distributed data scrutiny by lay volunteers[59]—all of these offer intriguing glances into the potential for the future. Finally, of course, the Internet is one big experiment in, as Benkler puts it, peer-to-peer cultural production.[60]

If these questions are good ones, why are they also the wrong ones? I have given my guesses about the future of the distributed model of innovation; my own utopia has it flourishing alongside a scaled-down, but still powerful, intellectual property regime. Equally plausible scenarios see it as a dead end, or as the inevitable victor in the war of productive processes. These are all guesses, however. At the very least, there is some possibility, even hope, that we could have a world in which much more of intellectual and inventive production is free. "'Free' as in 'free speech,'" Richard Stallman says, not "'free' as in 'free beer.'"[61] But we could hope that much of it would be *both* free of centralized control *and* low cost or no cost. When the marginal cost of production is zero, the marginal cost of transmission and storage approaches zero, the process of creation is additive, and much of the labor doesn't charge—well, the world looks a little different.[62] This is at least a *possible* future, or part of a possible future, and one that we should not foreclose without thinking twice. Yet that is what we are doing. The Database Protection Bills and Directives, which extend intellectual property rights to the layer of facts;[63] the efflorescence of software patents;[64] the UCITA-led validation of shrinkwrap licenses that bind third parties;[65] the Digital Millennium Copyright Act's anti-circumvention provisions[66]—the point of all of these developments is not merely that they make the peer-to-peer model difficult, but that in many cases they rule it out altogether. I will

58. *See* http://www.ensembl.org (last visited Sept. 18, 2002)

59. For example, NASA's "Clickworkers" experiment, which used public volunteers to analyze Mars landing data. *See* http://clickworkers.arc.nasa.gov/top (last visited September 30, 2002).

60. Benkler, *Coase's Penguin*, *supra* note 55 *at* 397.

61. Stallman, founder of the Free Software Foundation, describes this distinction at Website of the Free Software Foundation, *at* http://www.gnu.ai.mit.edu/philosophy/free-sw. html (last visited Dec. 19, 2002).

62. Exhibit A: the Internet—from the software and protocols on which it runs to the multiple volunteer sources of content and information.

63. *See, e.g.*, The Consumer and Investor Access to Information Act of 1999, H.R. 1858, 106th Cong., § 101(1) (1999); Database Investment and Intellectual Property Antipiracy Act of 1996, H.R. 3531, 104th Cong. (1996); *see also* Directive, *supra* note 23.

64. *See generally* Julie E. Cohen & Mark A. Lemley, *Patent Scope and Innovation in the Software Industry*, 89 CAL. L. REV. 1 (2001). *See also* Pamela Samuelson et al., *A Manifesto Concerning the Legal Protection of Computer Programs*, 94 COLUM. L. REV. 2308 (1994).

65. UNIF. COMPUTER INFO. TRANSACTIONS ACT (UCITA) (2001), a*vailable at* http://www.ucitaonline.com/ (last visited May 13, 2002).

66. 17 U.S.C. § 1201 (2002).

assert this point here, rather than argue for it, but I think it can be (and has been) demonstrated quite convincingly.[67]

The point is, then, that there is a chance that a new (or old, but under-recognized) method of production could flourish in ways that seem truly valuable—valuable to free speech, innovation, scientific discovery, the wallets of consumers, what William Fisher calls "semiotic democracy,"[68] and perhaps, valuable to the balance between joyful creation and drudgery for hire. True, it is only a chance. True, this theory's ambit of operation and its sustainability are uncertain. But why would we want to foreclose it? That is what the recent expansions of intellectual property threaten to do. And remember, these expansions were dubious even in a world where we saw little or no possibility of the distributed production model I have described, where discussion of network effects had yet to reach the pages of the *New Yorker*,[69] and where our concerns about the excesses of intellectual property were simply the ones that Jefferson, Madison, and Macaulay gave us so long ago.

V

BEYOND ENCLOSURE?

Thus, we have come full circle. Is this the second enclosure movement? As I have tried to show, in many ways it is. The opponents and proponents of enclosure remain locked in battle, each appealing to conflicting and sometimes incommensurable claims about efficiency, innovation, justice, and the limits of the market. But *should it be* the second enclosure movement? Do we know that property rights in this sphere will yield the same surge of productive energy that is claimed for the enclosure of arable land?[70] There, I think the answer is a resounding "No." We rush to enclose ever-larger stretches of the commons of the mind without convincing economic evidence that it will help our processes

---

67 This point has been ably made, *inter alia*, by Pamela Samuelson, Jessica Litman, Jerry Reichman, Larry Lessig, and Yochai Benkler. *See* LITMAN, *supra* note 32; Benkler, *Free as the Air*, *supra* note 25; Pamela Samuelson, *Intellectual Property and the Digital Economy: Why the Anti-Circumvention Regulations Need to be Revised*, 14 BERKELEY TECH. L.J. 519, 566 (1999); J.H. Reichman & Paul F. Uhlir, *Database Protection at the Crossroads: Recent Developments and Their Impact on Science and Technology*, 14 BERKELEY TECH. L.J. 793 (1999); Lawrence Lessig, *Jail Time in the Digital Age*, N.Y. TIMES, July 30, 2001, at A17. Each has a slightly different focus and emphasis on the problem, but each has pointed out the impediments now being erected to distributed, non-proprietary solutions. *See also* Boyle, *Cruel*, *supra* note 46.

68. William W. Fisher III, *Property and Contract on the Internet*, 73 CHI.-KENT L. REV. 1203, 1217-18 (1998).

69. *See* James Boyle, *Missing the Point on Microsoft*, SALON.COM, Apr. 7, 2000, *at* http://www.salon.com/tech/feature/2000/04/07/greenspan/index.html. [hereinafter Boyle, *Missing the Point*].

70. That is assuming that enclosure really *did* produce efficiency gains for arable land, though as I pointed out earlier, economic historians are now divided about that issue. *See* Allen, *Efficiency*, *supra* note 9. At best, one could say that the empirical evidence is equivocal. There are certainly reasons to believe that the commons, far from being tragic, was often relatively well managed. But the case for enclosure is at its strongest with arable land; even if one gives no weight at all to the contrary evidence there, the commons of the mind is very different and most of the differences cut strongly against the logic of enclosure—at least without considerably more evidence than we currently possess.

of innovation and with very good reason to believe it will actually hurt them.[71] As I have argued elsewhere, this second enclosure movement should bother people across the ideological spectrum, from civil libertarians to free marketeers; the world of the arts and sciences should be particularly interested in the process. The American system of science, for all its flaws, has worked astoundingly well. Changing some of its fundamental premises, such as by moving property rights into the data layer, is something not to be done lightly.

The dangers are particularly important at the moment for three reasons. First, propertization is a vicious circle. The argument is a little complex to lay out here,[72] but in essence the position is this: Once a new intellectual property right has been created over some informational good, the only way to ensure efficient allocation of that good is to give the rights holder still greater control over the user or consumer in the aftermarket so as to allow for price discrimination, since the only efficient monopoly is a monopoly with perfect price discrimination.[73] Yet, to achieve perfect price discrimination with digital intellectual property goods, whose marginal cost is zero, the rights holders will argue that they need even *more* changes of the rules in their favor: relaxed privacy standards so they can know more about our price points; enforceable shrinkwrap or clickwrap contracts of adhesion so that we can be held to the terms of our particular license, no matter how restrictive; and changes in antitrust rules to allow for a variety of practices that are currently illegal, such as resale price maintenance and various forms of tying. Rights holders will also claim that they need technical changes with legal backing, such as the creation of personalized digital objects surrounded by state-backed digital fences, objects that are tied to particular users and particular computers, so that reading my e-book on your machine is either technically impossible, a crime, or a tort—or possibly all three. The point of all this is that it is a slope that is much easier to go down than to come up. Thus, we ought to think clearly about the consequences of the decisions now being made in such a rush.

Second, in order to create the conditions for the kinds of price discrimination described above, the characteristics of the Internet that make it so attractive to civil libertarians—its distributed, anonymous character, its resistance to control or filtering by public or private entities, and its global nature—start to seem like bugs rather than features. The process of trying to make the Net safe for the price discrimination project has already begun; this, as Larry Lessig teaches us, is a fundamental public choice that ought to be made deliberately

---

71. Some of the legislation involved is also constitutionally dubious under the First Amendment and Copyright Clause. *See* Yochai Benkler, *Through the Looking Glass: Alice and the Constitutional Foundations of the Public Domain*, 66 LAW & CONTEMP. PROBS. 173 (Winter/Spring 2003). This is particularly strange at a time when other government subsidies are subjected to relentless skepticism and demands for empirical support. Is it *really* worthwhile teaching poor pre-schoolers to read? Where is the data?

72. The full version is given in Boyle, *Cruel*, *supra* note 46.

73. Perfect price discrimination is the ability to charge every user the exact maximum of their ability and willingness to pay, so that the market can be perfectly segregated by price.

and openly, not brought about imperceptibly as a side-effect of an economically dubious digital enclosure movement.[74] Because of threats such as terrorism, we might choose to live in a pervasively monitored electronic environment in which identity, geography, and thus regulability, have been reintroduced, though in my own view the price would not be worth paying. But to do so on the basis of some bad microeconomic arguments about the needs of the entertainment industry, in the absence of good empirical evidence, and to foreclose some of the most interesting new productive possibilities in the process? Well, that would be really sad.

Third, the arguments in favor of the new enclosure movement depend heavily on the intellectually complacent, analytically unsound assumptions of the "neo-liberal orthodoxy," the "Washington Consensus."[75] The world of the Washington Consensus is divided into two parts. In one, growing smaller by the minute, are those portions of the economy where the government plays a major regulatory role. The job of neo-liberal economic thought is to push us toward the privatization of the few areas that remain; after all, we know that "state intervention in the economy" is a recipe for disaster. The second area of the Washington Consensus is an altogether happier place. This is the realm of well-functioning free markets, where the state does not regulate, subsidize, or franchise, but instead defines and protects property rights. While unintended consequences are rife in the world of government regulation, no such dangers should be feared if the government is simply handing over a patent on gene sequences or stem cell lines, or creating a property right over compilations of facts. Property is good, and more property is better.[76] It would be ironic, to say the least, to maintain this view in the *information* commons, the one area where the delicate balance of the property system should be clearest and the political choices involved most obvious. It is doubly ironic to do so at a time when there are examples of modes of distributed production that stretch our sense of the economically possible, and that upset our complacency about the limited ways in which innovation and production can be managed.

But what is the alternative to the second enclosure movement? It is one thing to say, as I do, that we need more and better empirical information, and that our intellectual property system should be audited like any other government subsidy to make sure that we are getting what we pay for, and not paying too much for what we get. But the process I have described here is not entirely rational. In some cases, it is driven by industry capture of the levers of state power; in others, by a variety of alluring beliefs that dominate thought on the subject. The logic of enclosure ("Property saves lives! More incentives mean more production!") is the one I have concentrated on here. In other works, I have explored the impact of the ideal of original creation, creation *ex nihilo*, on

---

74. *See* LAWRENCE LESSIG, THE FUTURE OF IDEAS: THE FATE OF THE COMMONS IN A NETWORKED WORLD (2001).

75. *See supra* note 33.

76. *See* Boyle, *Missing the Point*, *supra* note 69.

our assumptions about the need to protect the public domain.[77] Who needs a public domain if you can create out of nothing? The point of this essay is that it is not enough merely to offer criticisms of the logic of enclosure. What is needed is deeper. We need a change in the way that these issues are understood, a change that transforms even our perceptions of self-interest, making possible coalitions where none existed before.

***

In the second half of this article, I try to develop the vocabulary and the analytic tools necessary to turn the tide of enclosure. I offer an historical sketch of various types of skepticism about intellectual property, from the anti-monopolist criticisms of the Framers of the U.S. Constitution, through the emergence of affirmative arguments for the public domain, to the use of the language of the commons to defend the possibility of distributed methods of non-proprietary production. In many ways, it turns out, concepts of the public domain show the same variation in assumptions, and the same analytic differences, as the concept of property itself. I conclude by arguing that, for a number of reasons, the appropriate model for the change in thinking which I argue for comes from the history of the environmental movement. The invention of the concept of "the environment" pulls together a string of otherwise disconnected issues, offers analytical insight into the blindness implicit in prior ways of thinking, and leads to perception of common interest where none was seen before. Like the environment, the public domain must be "invented" before it is saved. Like the environment, like "nature," the public domain turns out to be a concept that is considerably more slippery than many of us realize. And, like the environment, the public domain nevertheless turns out to be useful, perhaps even necessary.

77. BOYLE, SHAMANS, *supra* note 32; James Boyle, *A Theory of Law and Information: Copyright, Spleens, Blackmail, and Insider Trading*, 80 CAL. L. REV. 1413 (1992) [hereinafter Boyle, *Theory*].

PART TWO: AGAINST ENCLOSURE

VI

ANTI-MONOPOLY AND A TAX ON READING

Intellectual property has always had its critics—brilliant ones, at that, whose writing puts contemporary academics to shame.[78] Thomas Jefferson leads off the list for American audiences. Writers from justices of the Supreme Court of the United States to John Perry Barlow quote Jefferson's 1813 letter to Isaac McPherson:

> If nature has made any one thing less susceptible than all others of exclusive property, it is the action of the thinking power called an idea, which an individual may exclusively possess as long as he keeps it to himself; but the moment it is divulged, it forces itself into the possession of every one, and the receiver cannot dispossess himself of it. Its peculiar character, too, is that no one possesses the less, because every other possesses the whole of it. He who receives an idea from me, receives instruction himself without lessening mine; as he who lights his taper at mine, receives light without darkening me. That ideas should freely spread from one to another over the globe, for the moral and mutual instruction of man, and improvement of his condition, seems to have been peculiarly and benevolently designed by nature, when she made them, like fire, expansible over all space, without lessening their density in any point, and like the air in which we breathe, move, and have our physical being, incapable of confinement or exclusive appropriation. Inventions then cannot, in nature, be a subject of property.[79]

Those who quote the passage sometimes stop here, which is a shame, because it leaves the impression that Jefferson was unequivocally against intellectual property rights. But that would be an overstatement. When Jefferson said that invention can never be a subject of property, he meant a permanent and exclusive property right which, as a matter of natural right, no just government could abridge. "Stable ownership is the gift of social law, and is given late in the progress of society. It would be curious then, if an idea, the fugitive fermentation of an individual brain, could, of natural right, be claimed in exclusive and stable property."[80] This did not mean, however, that inventions could not be covered by temporary state-created monopolies, instituted for the common good. In the lines immediately following the popularly quoted excerpt, Jefferson goes on:

> Society may give an exclusive right to the profits arising from [inventions], as an encouragement to men to pursue ideas which may produce utility, but this may or may not be done, according to the will and convenience of the society, without claim or complaint from any body. Accordingly, it is a fact, as far as I am informed, that England was, until we copied her, the only country on earth which ever, by a general law, gave a legal right to the exclusive use of an idea. In some other countries it is sometimes done, in a great case, and by a special and personal act, but, generally speaking, other nations have thought that these monopolies produce more embarrassment than

---

78. To be fair, this is not hard to do.

79. Letter from Thomas Jefferson to Isaac McPherson (Aug. 13, 1813), *in* 13 THE WRITINGS OF THOMAS JEFFERSON 326, 333-34 (Albert Ellery Bergh ed., 1907) [hereinafter Jefferson/McPherson Letter].

80. *Id.* at 333.

> advantage to society; and it may be observed that the nations which refuse monopolies of invention, are as fruitful as England in new and useful devices.[81]

Jefferson's message was a skeptical recognition that intellectual property rights *might* be necessary, a careful explanation that they should not be treated as natural rights, and a warning of the monopolistic dangers that they pose. This message was famously echoed thirty years later in Britain by Thomas Babington Macaulay. Macaulay's speeches to the British Parliament in 1841 on the subject of copyright term extension still express better than anything else the position that intellectual property rights are necessary evils which must be carefully circumscribed by law. In order for the supply of valuable books to be maintained, authors "must be remunerated for their literary labor. And there are only two ways in which they can be remunerated. One of those ways is patronage; the other is copyright."[82] Patronage is rejected out of hand:

> I can conceive no system more fatal to the integrity and independence of literary men than one under which they should be taught to look for their daily bread to the favour of ministers and nobles. . . . We have, then, only one resource left. We must betake ourselves to copyright, be the inconveniences of copyright what they may. Those inconveniences, in truth, are neither few nor small. Copyright is monopoly, and produces all the effects which the general voice of mankind attributes to monopoly. My honourable and learned friend talks very contemptuously of those who are led away by the theory that monopoly makes things dear. That monopoly makes things dear is certainly a theory, as all the great truths which have been established by the experience of all ages and nations, and which are taken for granted in all reasonings, may be said to be theories. It is a theory in the same sense in which it is a theory that day and night follow each other, that lead is heavier than water, that bread nourishes, that arsenic poisons, that alcohol intoxicates. If, as my honourable and learned friend seems to think, the whole world is in the wrong on this point, if the real effect of monopoly is to make articles good and cheap, why does he stop short in his career of change? Why does he limit the operation of so salutary a principle to sixty years? Why does he consent to anything short of a perpetuity? He told us that in consenting to anything short of a perpetuity he was making a compromise between extreme right and expediency. But if his opinion about monopoly be correct, extreme right and expediency would coincide. Or rather, why should we not restore the monopoly of the East India trade to the East India Company? Why should we not revive all those old monopolies which, in Elizabeth's reign, galled our fathers so severely that, maddened by intolerable wrong, they opposed to their sovereign a resistance before which her haughty spirit quailed for the first and for the last time? Was it the cheapness and excellence of commodities that then so violently stirred the indignation of the English people? I believe, Sir, that I may with safety take it for granted that the effect of monopoly generally is to make articles scarce, to make them dear, and to make them bad. And I may with equal safety challenge my honourable friend to find out any distinction between copyright and other privileges of the same kind; any reason why a monopoly of books should produce an effect directly the reverse of that which was produced by the East India Company's monopoly of tea, or by Lord Essex's monopoly of sweet wines. Thus, then, stands the case. It is good that authors should be remunerated; and the least exceptionable way of remunerating them is by a monopoly. Yet monopoly is an evil. For the sake of the good we must submit to the evil; but the evil ought not to last a day longer than is necessary for the purpose of securing the good.[83]

---

81. *Id.* at 334.

82. Thomas B. Macaulay, A Speech Delivered in the House of Commons (Feb. 5, 1841), *in* VIII THE LIFE AND WORKS OF LORD MACAULAY 201 (London, Longmans, Green, and Co. 1897).

83. *Id.*

These words from Jefferson and Macaulay encapsulate an eighteenth and nineteenth century free-trade skepticism about intellectual property. Jefferson himself believed that the Constitution should have definite limits on both the term and the scope of intellectual property rights[84] and spoke of the difficulty of "drawing a line between the things which are worth to the public the embarrassment of an exclusive patent, and those which are not."[85] Madison, too, stressed the costs of any intellectual property right and the need to limit its term,[86] as did Adam Smith.[87] Their key concern was an anti-monopolistic one, though we should remember that for these men the concept of monopoly was a much richer one than the impoverished neo-classical economic concept we employ today. For them, monopoly involved not simply economic loss, though they certainly cared about that, but also the tendencies towards "corruption" that monopolies introduced. This corruption included the harm to the fabric of the republic caused by great concentrations of wealth and power as well as the perverse incentives given to the beneficiaries of state-granted monopolies to spend resources suborning the legislature on which their monopoly rent depended. Today, we call those incentives "campaign finance," "the participation of stakeholders in the legislative process," or just "business as usual."

The intellectual property skeptics had other concerns. Macaulay was particularly worried about the *power* that went with a transferable and inheritable monopoly.[88] It is not only that the effect of monopoly is "to make articles

---

84. For example, in a letter to Madison commenting on the draft of the Constitution:

> I like it, as far as it goes; but I should have been for going further. For instance, the following alterations and additions would have pleased me . . . Article 9. Monopolies may be allowed to persons for their own productions in literature, and their own inventions in the arts, for a term not exceeding ____ years, but for no longer term, and no other purpose.

Letter from Thomas Jefferson to James Madison (Aug. 28, 1789), *in* 7 THE WRITINGS OF THOMAS JEFFERSON 444, 450-51 (Albert Ellery Bergh ed., 1907).

85. Jefferson/McPherson Letter, *supra* note 79, at 355.

86. James Madison, *Monopolies, Perpetuities, Corporations, Ecclesiastical Endowments*, *in Aspects of Monopoly One Hundred Years Ago*, HARPER'S MAG., Mar. 1914, at 489-90.

87. Smith says:

> When a company of merchants undertake, at their own risk and expense, to establish a new trade with some remote and barbarous nation, it may not be unreasonable to incorporate them into a joint-stock company, and to grant them, in case of their success, a monopoly of the trade for a certain number of years. It is the easiest and most natural way in which the state can recompense them for hazarding a dangerous and expensive experiment, of which the public is afterwards to reap the benefit. A temporary monopoly of this kind may be vindicated, upon the same principles upon which a like monopoly of a new machine is granted to its inventor, and that of a new book to its author. But upon the expiration of the term, the monopoly ought certainly to determine; the forts and garrisons, if it was found necessary to establish any, to be taken into the hands of government, their value to be paid to the company, and the trade to be laid open to all the subjects of the state. By a perpetual monopoly, all the other subjects of the state are taxed very absurdly in two different ways: first, by the high price of goods, which, in the case of a free trade, they could buy much cheaper; and, secondly, by their total exclusion from a branch of business which it might be both convenient and profitable for many of them to carry on.

Adam Smith, *Of the expenses of public works and public institutions*, *in* III THE WEALTH OF NATIONS, 339 (London, Dent 1937) (1880).

88. Macaulay, *supra* note 82.

scarce, to make them dear, and to make them bad."[89] Macaulay also pointed out that those who controlled the monopoly, particularly after the death of the original author, might be given too great a control over our collective culture. Censorious heirs or purchasers of the copyright might prevent the reprinting of a great work because they disagreed with its morals.[90] From more recent examples, we can also see that heirs may keep policing the boundaries of the work, attempting to prevent parody or tarnishment, long after the original author is dead. One wonders what Macaulay would have thought about the attempt by Margaret Mitchell's estate to prevent the publication of *The Wind Done Gone*.[91]

There were certainly other concerns raised about intellectual property in the eighteenth and nineteenth centuries. For example, while Macaulay is the best remembered critic of copyright in the debates of the 1840s, there were other more radical opponents who saw copyright primarily as a "tax on literacy," identical in its effect to the newspaper stamp taxes.[92] At a time when mass literacy and mass education were the hotly debated corollaries to the enlargement of the franchise, reformers looked with hostility on anything that seemed likely to raise the cost of reading and thus continue to restrict political and social debate to the wealthier classes.[93]

Patent law, too, attracted its share of attacks in the mid-nineteenth century. A fusillade of criticism, often delivered by economists and cast in the language of free trade, portrayed the patent system as actively harmful.

> At the annual meeting of the Kongress deutscher Volkswirthe held in Dresden, September 1863, the following resolution was adopted "by an overwhelming majority:" "Considering that patents hinder rather than further the progress of invention; that they hamper the prompt general utilisation of useful inventions; that on balance they cause more harm than benefit to the inventors themselves and, thus, are a highly deceptive form of compensation; the Congress of German Economists resolves: that patents of invention are injurious to common welfare."[94]

---

89. *Id.*

90. In a speech to the house of commons, Macaulay said:

> These are strong cases. I have shown you that, if the law had been what you are now going to make it, the finest prose work of fiction in the language, the finest biographical work in the language, would very probably have been suppressed. But I have stated my case weakly. The books which I have mentioned are singularly inoffensive books, books not touching on any of those questions which drive even wise men beyond the bounds of wisdom. There are books of a very different kind, books which are the rallying points of great political and religious parties. What is likely to happen if the copyright of one of these books should by descent or transfer come into the possession of some hostile zealot?

Id.

91. The Mitchell estate attempted to block publication of *The Wind Done Gone* by Alice Randall, a work which retold *Gone With the Wind* from the slaves' perspective. The Eleventh Circuit reversed a preliminary injunction blocking publication. SunTrust Bank v. Houghton Mifflin Co., 268 F.3d 1257 (11th Cir. 2001).

92. *See* CATHERINE SEVILLE, LITERARY COPYRIGHT REFORM IN EARLY VICTORIAN ENGLAND: THE FRAMING OF THE 1842 COPYRIGHT ACT 46-48 (1999).

93. *Id.* at 48.

94. Fritz Machlup & Edith Penrose, *The Patent Controversy in the Nineteenth Century*, 10 J. ECON. HIST. 1, 4 n.8 (1950).

In the Netherlands, the patent system was actually abolished in 1869 as a result of such criticisms.[95] Observers in a number of other countries, including Britain, concluded that their national patent systems were doomed.[96] Various proposals were made to replace patent, with state-provided prizes or bounties to particularly useful inventions being the most popular.[97]

These snippets are hardly sufficient to constitute any kind of a survey of critical reactions to intellectual property systems, but I believe that nevertheless they give a relatively fair sense of the debate. Three points could be made.

First, from the early days of intellectual property as we now know it, the main objections raised against it were framed in the language of free trade and anti-monopoly. In the United States, the founding generation of intellectuals had been nurtured on the philosophy of the Scottish Enlightenment and the history of the struggle against royal monopolies. They were not immune to the arguments in favor of intellectual property, but they repeatedly warned of the need to circumscribe both its term and its scope. What were their concerns? They worried about intellectual property producing artificial scarcity, high prices, and low quality. They worried about its justice; given that we all learn from and build on the past, do we have a right to carve out our own incremental innovations and protect them by intellectual property rights?[98] Price aside, they also worried that intellectual property (especially with a lengthy term) might give too much control to a single individual or corporation over some vital aspect of science and culture. In more muted fashion, they discussed the possible effects that intellectual property might have on future innovation. But the overwhelming theme was the promotion of free trade and a corresponding opposition to monopolies.

Second, it is important to look at the structure of these comments by Jefferson, Macaulay, and others; they are framed as criticisms of intellectual property rather than defenses of the public domain or the commons, terms that appear rarely, if at all, in the debates. There is no real discussion of the world *outside* of intellectual property, its opposite, whether in conceptual or economic terms.

Third, a linked point: Most of these critics take as their goal the prevention or limitation of an "artificial" monopoly. Without this monopoly, our goal is to

---

95. *Id.* at 5.

96. *Id.* at 1.

97. CHRISTINE MACLEOD, INVENTING THE INDUSTRIAL REVOLUTION 191-96 (1988). Ironically, contemporary economists are rediscovering the attraction of patent alternatives. *See* Steven Shavell & Tanguy Van Ypersele, Rewards versus Intellectual Property Rights, Working Paper 6956, *available at* http://www.nber.org/papers/w6956 (last visited Jan. 14, 2003).

98. Benjamin Franklin recalled that:

> Gov'r. Thomas was so pleas'd with the construction of this stove . . . that he offered to give me a patent for the sole vending of them for a term of years; but I declin'd it from a principle which has ever weighed with me on such occasions, viz.: *That, as we enjoy great advantages from the inventions of others, we should be glad of an opportunity to serve others by any invention of ours; and this we should do freely and generously.*

Benjamin Franklin, *Autobiography* (1771), *in* THE WORKS OF BENJAMIN FRANKLIN 1, 237-238 (John Bigelow ed., 1904).

have a world of . . . what? The assumption is that we will return to a norm of freedom, but of what kind? Free trade in expression and innovation, as opposed to monopoly? Free access to innovation and expression, as opposed to access for pay? Or free access to innovation and expression in the sense of not being subject to the right of another person to pick and choose who is given access, even if all have to pay some flat fee? Or is it common ownership and control that we seek, including the communal right to forbid certain kinds of uses of the shared resource? The eighteenth and nineteenth century critics brushed over these points, but to be fair, we continue to do so today.

VII

RECOGNIZING THE PUBLIC DOMAIN

In the last section, I discussed the anti-monopolist criticisms of intellectual property law, criticisms that were heard from the beginning of intellectual property in its modern form and which continue to the present day. At what point does the negative account of the ills of intellectual property turn into, or get added to, a defense of something called "the public domain?"

By a defense of the public domain, I do not mean mere usage of the word. Though "public domain" was a term widely used to describe public lands in the United States, the intellectual property usage of the term comes to us from the French *domaine public* which made its way into American law in the late nineteenth century via the language of the Berne Convention.[99] But at what point do we find a defense of the public domain, rather than merely a criticism of the costs of intellectual property?

Many different starting points are defensible. In the United States, the work of Ralph Brown and Ben Kaplan is sometimes mentioned as initiating this way of looking at things.[100] The Supreme Court itself can plausibly be given some credit.[101] In a 1966 patent case, repeatedly citing the work of Jefferson, the Court made it clear that the public domain has a constitutional dimension:

> The Congress in the exercise of the patent power may not overreach the restraints imposed by the stated constitutional purpose. Nor may it enlarge the patent monopoly without regard to the innovation, advancement or social benefit gained thereby. Moreover, Congress may not authorize the issuance of patents whose effects are to remove existent knowledge from the public domain, or to restrict free access to materials already available.[102]

This is a remarkable statement. It goes beyond a mere recitation of the Framers' attitude toward the dangers posed by monopoly, and makes an affirmative defense of the public domain. Notice how the limitations are stated

---

99. *See* Litman, *supra* note 44. The process is somewhat ironic, since the French copyright law, with its focus on author's rights, is in many ways among the least solicitous and protective of the public domain.

100. *See* LITMAN, *supra* note 32; Edward Samuels, *The Public Domain in Copyright Law*, 41 J. COPYRIGHT SOC. 137, 150 (1993).

101. I admit this is an unusual admission from a legal academic.

102. Graham v. John Deere Co., 383 U.S. 1, 5-6 (1966).

as additive and not as mutually equivalent, or even as mere corollaries; the Court does not say that "the enlargement of the patent monopoly must promote innovation and *this limits* Congress's power to remove material from the public domain." Instead, it postulates an existent public domain and makes it unconstitutional under the patent clause for Congress to privatize any portion of that domain. There are echoes here of the "public trust doctrine," which restricts the state's ability to privatize public resources or waterways and turn them over to private parties.[103] Notice also that the Court gives the public domain both direct and indirect protection: Protection from measures which formally create patent rights over portions of the public domain, but also from those which merely "restrict free access to materials already available."[104]

Thus, there are a number of possible places where one could say, "the defense of the public domain begins here." But, like most people, I attribute central importance to the writing of my friend and colleague David Lange, whose article *Recognizing the Public Domain* really initiated contemporary study of the subject.[105] Lange's article was driven by indignation about, indeed eloquently sarcastic ridicule of, expansions of intellectual property protection in the 1960s and 1970s.[106] Lange claims that one major cause of this expansion was that intellectual property rights are intangible, abstract, and thus, imprecise.[107] He argues, in a way that would have been familiar to Macaulay or Jefferson, that we should cease the reckless expansion.[108] But he also argues that "recognition of new intellectual property interests should be offset today by equally deliberate recognition of individual rights in the public domain."[109]

Lange is not arguing:

> that intellectual property is undeserving of protection, but rather that such protection as it gets ought to reflect its unique susceptibility to conceptual imprecision and to infinite replication. These attributes seem to me to require the recognition of two fundamental principles. One is that intellectual property theory must always accept something akin to a "no-man's land" at the boundaries; doubtful cases of infringement ought always to be resolved in favor of the defendant. The other is that no exclusive interest should ever have affirmative recognition unless its conceptual opposite is also recognized. Each right ought to be marked off clearly against the public domain.[110]

But what does this *mean*? What is the nature of these "individual rights in the public domain?" Who holds them? Indeed, what *is* the public domain? Does it consist only of works that are completely unprotected, say books whose copy-

---

103. Carol Rose, *The Comedy of the Commons: Custom, Commerce, and Inherently Public Property*, 53 U. CHI. L. REV. 711, 727-28 (1986).

104. *Graham*, 383 U.S. at 6.

105. David Lange, *Recognizing the Public Domain*, 44 LAW & CONTEMP. PROBS. 147 (Autumn 1981).

106. *Id.* at 151-71.

107. For example, in one memorable discussion of a hypothetical drawn from Tom Wolfe: "I think it is useful to remember, however, that what we are talking about, insofar as our senses can perceive it, is still a wet spot on the dead wino's napkin. Everything else is hypothesis." *Id.* at 149.

108. *Id.* at 147.

109. *Id.*

110. *Id.*

right term has lapsed? Does it include *aspects* of works that are unprotectable, such as the ideas or the facts on which an argument is based, even if the expression of that argument is protected? What about limitations on exclusive rights, privileges of users, or affirmative defenses—are those part of the public domain too? Is the parody-able aspect of your novel in the public domain? What about the short quote on which a critical argument is mounted? Earlier in this article, I discussed the "commons of the mind."[111] What is the relationship between the public domain—however defined—and the commons?[112] If the public domain is so great, why? What does it do for us? What is its role? These questions can be reduced to two: (1) What is the public domain?, and (2) Why should we focus on it? In the following pages, I will argue that the answer to the first question depends on the answer to the second.

Work that followed Lange's article offered various answers to the questions he had posed. For example, Lindberg and Patterson's book *The Nature of Copyright* reverses the polarity from the normal depiction, and portrays copyright as a law of users' rights.[113] The public domain is the figure and copyright the ground. The various privileges and defenses are not exceptions, they are at the heart of copyright, correctly understood. Copyright is, in fact, a system designed to feed the public domain providing temporary and narrowly limited rights, themselves subject to considerable restrictions even during their existence—all with the ultimate goal of promoting free access.

Jessica Litman's fine 1990 article, *The Public Domain*, portrays the public domain's primary function as allowing copyright law to continue to work notwithstanding the unrealistic, individualistic idea of creativity it depends on:

> The public domain rescues us from this dilemma. It permits us to continue to exalt originality without acknowledging that our claims to take originality seriously are mostly pretense. It furnishes a crucial device to an otherwise unworkable system by reserving the raw material of authorship to the commons, thus leaving that raw material available for other authors to use. The public domain thus permits the law of

---

111. *See supra* Part II.

112. Non-lawyers, who are (rightly) skeptical of definitional inquiries and doubly skeptical of lawyers engaged in definitional inquiries, might believe these points are at best semantic and at worst essentialist. They could be right. We might take what Felix Cohen said about definitions of law and apply them to definitions of the public domain.

> A definition of [the public domain] is useful or useless. It is not true or false, any more than a New Year's resolution or an insurance policy. A definition is in fact a type of insurance against certain risks of confusion. It cannot, any more than can a commercial insurance policy, eliminate all risks.

Felix Cohen, *Transcendental Nonsense and the Functional Approach*, 35 COLUM. L. REV. 809, 835-36 (1935). Wittgenstein is equally eloquent in pointing out the dangers of seeking the one true definition:

> Naming appears as a queer connexion of a word with an object.—And you really get such a queer connexion when the philosopher tries to bring out the relation between name and thing by staring at an object in front of him and repeating a name or even the word "this" innumerable times. For philosophical problems arise when language goes on holiday.

LUDWIG WITTGENSTEIN, PHILOSOPHICAL INVESTIGATIONS 19 (1958). I am asking for a ten-page suspension of disbelief while I pursue the question.

113. L. RAY PATTERSON & STANLEY W. LINDBERG, THE NATURE OF COPYRIGHT: A LAW OF USERS' RIGHTS (1991).

> copyright to avoid a confrontation with the poverty of some of the assumptions on which it is based.[114]

Litman's definition of the public domain is both clear and terse: "[A] commons that includes those aspects of copyrighted works which copyright does not protect."[115] Precisely because she sees the function of the public domain as allowing the kinds of additive and interstitial creation that the language of individual originality fails to capture, her *definition* of the public domain includes the recyclable, unprotected elements in existing copyrighted works as well as those works that are not protected at all. Form follows function.

Yochai Benkler takes a slightly different approach. He follows Litman in rejecting the traditional, absolutist conception of the public domain, a conception which included only those things that are totally unprotected by copyright:

> The particular weakness of the traditional definition of the public domain is that it evokes an intuition about the baseline, while not in fact completely describing it. When one calls certain information "in the public domain," one means that it is information whose use, absent special reasons to think otherwise, is permissible to anyone. When information is properly subject to copyright, the assumption (again absent specific facts to the contrary) is that its use is not similarly allowed to anyone but the owner and his or her licensees. The limited, term-of-art "public domain" does not include some important instances that, as a descriptive matter, are assumed generally to be permissible. For example, the traditional definition of public domain would treat short quotes for purposes of critical review as a fair use—hence as an affirmative defense—and not as a use in the public domain. It would be odd, however, to describe our system of copyright law as one in which users assume that they may not include a brief quotation in a critical review of its source. I venture that the opposite is true: Such use generally is considered permissible, absent peculiar facts to the contrary.[116]

Benkler's alternative definition, however, does not include every privileged use—such as, for example, the fair use privilege that I am able to vindicate only after litigating an intensely complicated case that involves highly specific factual inquiries.

> The functional definition therefore would be: The public domain is the range of uses of information that any person is privileged to make absent individualized facts that make a particular use by a particular person unprivileged. Conversely, [t]he enclosed domain is the range of uses of information as to which someone has an exclusive right, and that no other person may make absent individualized facts that indicate permission from the holder of the right, or otherwise privilege the specific use under the stated facts. These definitions add to the legal rules traditionally thought of as the public domain, the range of privileged uses that are "easy cases."[117]

The key to Benkler's analysis is his focus on the public domain's role in information production and use by all of us in our roles as consumers, citizens, and future creators. We need to focus on those works, and aspects of works, that the public can know to be free without having to go through a highly individualized factual inquiry. "Free" meaning what? Earlier in this essay, I asked what we mean when we speak of the freedom that the public domain will

114. Litman, *supra* note 44, at 1023.
115. *Id.* at 968.
116. Benkler, *Free as the Air*, *supra* note 25, at 361-62.
117. *Id.*

allow.[118] Free trade in expression and innovation, as opposed to monopoly? Free access to expression and innovation, as opposed to access for pay? Or free access to innovation and expression, in the sense of not being subject to the right of another person to pick and choose who is given access, even if all have to pay some flat fee? Or is it common ownership and control that we seek, including the communal right to forbid certain kinds of uses of the shared resources? I *think* that Benkler is arguing that the most important question here is whether lay people would know that a particular piece or aspect of information is free—in the sense of being *both* uncontrolled by anyone else and costless.

The test case is simple to imagine: Do we count as part of the public domain songs that can be "covered" by subsequent artists upon payment of a defined fee under a compulsory license? To put it in the language of legal theory, is content that is covered only by "liability rules"[119] actually part of the public domain? Well, of course that depends on why we care about the public domain, on what vision of freedom or creativity we think the public domain stands for, and what danger it protects against. The public domain will change its shape according to the hopes it embodies, the fears it tries to lay to rest, and the implicit vision of creativity on which it rests. There is not one public domain, but many.

What is true for the public domain turns out to be true also for the third and final language that seeks to circumscribe and offer limits to the enclosure movement: the language of the commons. The "commons" is a term that has come to be used increasingly often over the last five years to refer to wellsprings of creation that are outside of, or different from, the world of intellectual property. The Internet was seen as such a commons. The Internet expanded so rapidly precisely because its core protocols, TCP/IP and HTML, are open; like languages, these systems allowed all to create by offering a common framework owned by no one. And that insight, coupled with the positive images of communal production that the Net offered and the negative images of network-effect leveraged monopolies that the Net also offered galvanized a related but different type of interest in "the outside of property." It is to the commons that I will now turn.

VIII

DISCOVERING THE E-COMMONS

Let us start with Larry Lessig's definition of a commons:

> It is commonplace to think about the Internet as a kind of commons. It is less commonplace to actually have an idea what a commons is. By a commons I mean a resource that is free. *Not necessarily zero cost, but if there is a cost, it is a neutrally imposed, or equally imposed cost.* Central Park is a commons: an extraordinary resource of peacefulness in the center of a city that is anything but; an escape and

118. *See supra* Part VI.

119. In particular, I refer to statutory liability rules with pre-specified payments.

refuge, that anyone can take and use without the permission of anyone else. The public streets are a commons: on no one's schedule but your own, you enter the public streets, and go any direction you wish. You can turn off of Broadway onto Fifty-second Street at any time, without a certificate or authorization from the government. Fermat's last theorem is a commons: a challenge that anyone could pick up; and complete, as Andrew Wiles, after a lifetime of struggle, did. Open source, or free software, is a commons: the source code of Linux, for example, lies available for anyone to take, to use, to improve, to advance. No permission is necessary; no authorization may be required. These are commons because they are within the reach of members of the relevant community without the permission of anyone else. They are resources that are protected by a liability rule rather than a property rule. Professor Reichman, for example, has suggested that some innovation be protected by a liability rule rather than a property rule. The point is not that no control is present; but rather that the kind of control is different from the control we grant to property.[120]

Note the difference in focus between Lessig and Benkler. If our concern is monopolistic control over choke-points imposed by the will of others, freedom from others "telling us what we can do," then the norm of freedom we will seek to instantiate in property's outside, whether we describe it as a public domain or a commons, is a norm of non-discriminatory access. Freedom in one powerful liberal tradition means freedom *from the will of another*, not freedom from the background constraints of the economic system.[121] Why pick this vision of freedom instead of the vision provided by Benkler's account of the public domain—content that is literally "free," both free from exclusive rights, and available at zero cost?[122] There are lots of reasons. In the world of "network effects," an intellectual property right over a widely used standard or network protocol can give an unprecedented amount of power to the rightholder; the power might even include the ability to leverage one's rights to stifle innovation that threatens one's business. The Microsoft case is an obvious example.[123] The complaint against the Microsofts of the world is not so much that they keep their prices high—though that is sometimes alleged. Instead it is the claim that their intellectual property rights over fundamental standards with strong positive network effects give them too much power to control the course of innovation.

As the dysfunctional side of property/monopoly comes to be seen as a restraint on innovation rather than a problem of price gouging, correspondingly, property's outside—"not property"—shifts its core characteristics. If one's main concern is maintaining innovation, one might think that the danger

120. Larry Lessig, *The Architecture of Innovation*, 51 DUKE L. J. 1783, 1788 (2002).

121. Which is not to say that this is Lessig's only concern. *See* LAWRENCE LESSIG, CODE AND OTHER LAWS OF CYBERSPACE (1999) (focusing particularly on "material," code-based restraints imposed by the architecture of communications networks, and arguing that choices within and among different potential architectures should be subject to more democratic and constitutional scrutiny); *see also* James Boyle, *Foucault in Cyberspace: Surveillance, Sovereignty and Hard-Wired Censors*, 66 U. CIN. L. REV. 177 (1997) [hereinafter Boyle, *Foucault*].

122. *See supra* Part VII.

123. It is only fair to point out, however, that both the particular claims and the general economic observations about strong network effects and "path dependency" have been hotly disputed by Microsoft and independent academics. For a marvelously readable example, see Stephan E. Margolis & Stan Liebovitz, We Don't Know Why She Swallowed The Fly: Policy and Path Dependence, *at* http://www.utdallas.edu/~liebowit/regulatn.html (last visited Jan. 14, 2003).

of monopoly here is not higher prices, but rather the power of control itself; access to the intellectual property in question on payment of a flat fee might seem to avoid those dangers and to allow for free competition in follow-on innovation. The world of monopoly and property comes to be seen as a world of restraint on innovation, more than a world of restricted output and high prices. In technical terms, an imagined commons of pure Hohfeldian privileges gives way to a commons partly constituted of resources protected by liability rules.[124] The "opposite of property" comes to be defined as "that which will cure monopoly control of standards with strong network effects" rather than that which is not owned, or is owned by all. In describing the possibility of open standards with which all can work, the language of the commons apparently resonates better than the language of the public domain.

But I suspect that there is a second reason for the way in which "commons" and "public domain" now jockey for position as the instantiation of intellectual property's "outside." Although we present our reasoning on these matters in neat chains of apparently logical argument, our doing so conceals the power of "the paradigm case,"[125] the core example, or irresistible counter-example, in shaping our ideas.

As I argued in the first part of this essay, most recent theorists of the public domain start with the irresistible example of the free and open-source software movements before their eyes.[126] Here was a real-world spur to rethink the public goods problem, the tragedy of the commons, on which the economic rationale for intellectual property rights was based. Here was a "comedy of the commons."[127] To be sure, the claim was not that open-source or free software would provide a model that rendered all intellectual property unnecessary. There would still be an enclosed domain; the open source model would not work everywhere.[128] *But now, the placement of the line between the two domains was everywhere up for grabs.* This is a point that cannot be stressed enough. There was one small problem, however. Though open-source software is of particular interest to those concerned about the worldwide expansion of intellectual property rights, it is by no means clear how it fits into the binary opposition between intellectual property on the one hand and the public domain on the other.

---

124. For the most important statement of the value of liability rules in promoting follow-on innovation, see J.H. Reichman, *Of Green Tulips and Legal Kudzu: Repackaging Rights in Subpatentable Innovation*, 53 VAND. L. REV. 1743 (2000). Reichman does not, however, take a position on whether to define the information goods protected by liability rules as part of the commons.

125. I owe this insight to Jed Rubenfeld, *The First Amendment's Purpose*, 53 STAN. L. REV. 767 (2001).

126. *See supra* Part IV.

127. I borrow the phrase from the title of Carol Rose's magnificently prescient article which discusses the occasional superiority of common property regimes to individual private property rights. *See* Rose, *supra* note 103; *see also* Carol Rose, *The Several Futures of Property: Of Cyberspace and Folk Tales, Emission Trades and Ecosystems*, 83 MINN. L. REV. 129, 155-56 (1998).

128. *See supra* Part IV.

Though journalists frequently and mistakenly claim otherwise, neither "free software," nor most "open-source software" is in the public domain. After all, the thing that makes open-source software work is the General Public License.[129] All the things that seem so interesting about open-source—its model of distributed production, the way it grows, binding future innovators who make use of it to add to the store themselves—are built on this license.[130] That license, in turn, rests on an intellectual property right, the copyrights held by the Free Software Foundation and other entities.[131] The GPL says, in effect: Here is this copyrighted body of work; you may use it, add to it, modify it, or copy it—all of these uses are legal, but *only* if you comply with the terms of the GPL. Otherwise, your actions are infringements of the exclusive rights conferred by section 106 of the Copyright Act.[132] If, for example, you take the Linux kernel, fiddle with it, add your own material, and attempt to sell the result as proprietary, binary-only software, you have violated the GPL license which gives you permission to reproduce this copyrighted material in the first place. In legal terms, at least, the free software movement stands squarely on intellectual property.

Given that free software stands as the kind of "irresistible example" around which theories tend to form, how is it to be assimilated into the older criticisms of intellectual property and defenses of the public domain? The free software movement, at least, was formed explicitly around criticisms of the effects of intellectual property that would have been familiar to Jefferson and Macaulay.[133] The answer to the perceived negative effects of strong intellectual property rights on innovation and freedom, however, was not to write a lot of code and release it unprotected by copyright. Instead, the free software movement attempted to build a living ecology of open code, where the price for admission was your commitment to make your own incremental innovation part of the ecology.[134] On the one hand, this fit poorly into the old model of the "total freedom" public domain; there were, after all, significant restraints on use of the software, restraints that were vital to the project. On the other hand, however, it fit very well into a new literature on governing the commons from Elinor Ostrom, Robert Keohane, Margaret McKean, and many others.[135] This litera-

---

129. GNU Library General Public License, *available at* http://www.gnu.org/copyleft/library.txt (last visited Jan. 14, 2003).

130. *Id.*

131. *Id.*

132. 17 U.S.C. § 106 (1994).

133. *See supra* Part VI.

134. An alternative approach, the Free BSD License, is closer to a mainstream understanding of public domain software. BSD License, *available at* http://www.opensource.org/licenses/bsd-license.html (last visited Jan. 14, 2003). The user is free to do anything with software covered by this license, including adding to it and selling the resultant program in a proprietary, binary-only format.

135. *See, e.g.*, SUSAN BUCK & ELINOR OSTROM, THE GLOBAL COMMONS (1998); LOCAL COMMONS AND GLOBAL INTERDEPENDENCE: HETEROGENEITY AND COOPERATION IN TWO DOMAINS (Elinor Ostrom & Robert Keohane eds., 1994); MARGARET MCKEAN, MAKING THE COMMONS WORK: THEORETICAL, HISTORICAL, AND CONTEMPORARY STUDIES (David Bromley et al. eds., 1992); ELINOR OSTROM, GOVERNING THE COMMONS: THE EVOLUTION OF INSTITUTIONS FOR COLLECTIVE ACTION (1991); Margaret McKean, *Success on the Commons: A Comparative*

ture was able to show that not every commons was a tragedy. But the literature also showed that successful commons were not *entirely* "free"—they ran on layers of norms that were frequently invisible to the legal system, but which nevertheless served to avoid the various paradoxes of collective action. Whether the examples were Japanese herdsmen or Silicon Valley programmers, the literature seeks to show just how the commons was, and should be, governed.[136]

Notice the differences in approach. The old dividing line in the literature on the public domain had been between the realm of property and the realm of the free.[137] The new dividing line, drawn on the palimpsest of the old, is between the realm of individual control and the realm of distributed creation, management, and enterprise. To be sure, the two projects share a great deal, but they are also different in important ways. To put it bluntly, some of the theorists of the e-commons do not see restraints on use as anathematic to the goal of freedom; indeed, they may see the successful commons as defined by its restraints.[138] Those restraints may be legal—Lessig's liability rules—or they may be built on community norms and prestige networks of various kinds. The point is that "property's outside," property's antonym, was now being conceived of differently, though frequently, and somewhat confusingly, using the same words and many of the same arguments.

Examination of Institutions for Common Property Resource Management, 4 J. OF THEORETICAL POL. 247 (1992); Elinor Ostrom, *Reformulating the Commons*, 6 SWISS POL. SCI. REV., Apr. 15, 1999, at 29.

136. One of the most interesting attempts to revive the notion of the commons and apply it to contemporary intellectual property policy issues comes from David Bollier. Bollier's concerns go well beyond using intellectual property to deal with many different types of public assets. *See, e.g.*, David Bollier, Public Assets, Private Profits, *available at* http://www.bollier.org/pdf/PA_Report.pdf (last visited Feb. 13, 2003). Nevertheless he also places a very strong emphasis on the public domain and the information commons. *See* David Bollier, Recent Works, *available at* http://www.bollier.org/recent.htm (last visited Feb. 13, 2003).

137. *See supra* Part VI, recognizing a lot of ambiguities in the term "free."

138. Yochai Benkler wrote:

> [B]y limiting implementation of information policy to focus on two institutional devices, privatization and direct regulation, we have limited the potential for decentralization of information production in our society. Introducing a third institutional device, the commons, is likely to increase the degree of decentralization that can be sustained within the institutional constraints our society imposes on information production and exchange. Two efforts are necessary in order to introduce commons as a stable element in our information environment. First, it is necessary to identify information and communications inputs that, like radio frequency spectrum and some information, can be used without being subject to the exclusive control of any governmental or non-governmental organization. *Second, it is necessary to undertake the design of the institutional constraints necessary to take advantage of the economic or technological attributes that make these inputs susceptible to being used on a commons model.* These tasks are important avenues to serving two commitments our society has traditionally located in the first amendment.

Yochai Benkler, The Commons As A Neglected Factor of Information Policy (1998), *available at* http:// www.law.nyu.edu/benklery/commons.pdf (last visited Dec. 19, 2002) (emphasis added).

IX

DISAGGREGATING FREEDOM: A LEGAL REALISM FOR THE PUBLIC DOMAIN

This has been very long way of answering a short question. (I am an academic after all.) What are the alternatives to, and the critiques of, the second enclosure movement? I have sketched out three projects here: an anti-monopolistic critique of intellectual property, a defense of "a free public domain," and an attempt to outline the rules for a commons of the mind on the global net. These three projects overlap, draw from similar philosophical and economic sources, and use the same vocabulary. They are also not necessarily consistent with each other, and each may use the same term in different ways. "Free," "public domain," "commons," "enclosure"—each term shifts its meaning as we move from one intellectual project to the next, in part because each project is built around a different set of hopes and fears.

The first stage of the story I outlined here was the attempt by Jefferson, Madison, Macaulay, and others to balance the arguments in favor of intellectual property with criticism of its monopolistic costs and dangers; the goal was to build an awareness of the need for limitations *into the grant itself*. The second stage was a little more complex. Here, an affirmative argument for the public domain was put forward, rather than a mere criticism of intellectual property. There was an existent public domain, whose value we should recognize and which should have protection—perhaps even constitutional protection—against the danger that knowledge would be removed from it, or access to existing material impeded. Fine and dandy, but what *was* this public domain that we were to protect? There the answers were less clear. What norm of freedom did the public domain instantiate? Free trade? Free beer? Freedom from monopolistic control? Free communal production? The early public domain theorists were enigmatic on this point; the later ones vocal, but not necessarily consistent. The final panel in my triptych still relies on the criticisms of enclosure and monopoly, but in the place of the public domain, we find the rhetoric of the commons, a commons that in some conceptions one might have to pay to use.

At first sight, this may all seem distressingly messy. Surely, conceptions of the public domain, or the commons, should be more consistent. Why so much variation, such different definitions? Look at the question from the other side of the looking glass. Is this little potted history so very different from the history of the concept of property? We know very well that concepts of property have varied enormously over time and that the assumptions of the legal system about the analytical details of property have also varied enormously. Does property include notions that we might describe as human rights, or individual liberty, as it probably did for Locke?[139] Is property the sole, absolute, and des-

139. My colleague Laura Underkuffler has been particularly insightful in showing how Locke, or for that matter Madison, used "property" in ways that are unfamiliar to modern eyes. Laura Underkuffler, *On Property: An Essay*, 100 YALE L.J. 127, 132-139 (1990).

potic dominion that Blackstone wrote about (even though that did not match the reality in his own legal system)?[140] Are property rights the impermeable wall conjured up by the majority in the *Leroy Fibre* case, inside which we can do what we will without having to think about the possible conduct of others?[141] Is property the bundle of rights that first year law students learn about—more accurately a grab bag of rights, powers, privileges and immunities held together by nothing stronger than nominalism? (We choose to call these things "property," and so they are.)

Each of these conceptions of property is linked in a complicated way to the structure of belief in the larger society and in the legal system from which the property right came. Some of these conceptions are Sunday suits, smart clothing for external consumption, while others are working clothes, the day-to-day approximations used by legal practitioners to solve the problems before them. Our conceptions of property and sovereignty overlap, as the legal realists famously taught us, and the ideas of property taught in a law school classroom are markedly different from the same concept in ordinary language. We do not generally, however, throw up our hands and conclude that the whole concept should be jettisoned.

And what is true for property is true for the public domain. Just as there are many "properties," so too there are many "public domains." To the simple vision of property rights as consisting only of the state of absolute, perfect dominion can be counterposed the simple vision of the public domain as that which exists only where total freedom reigns. Here the "public domain" consists only of complete works that are completely free: free for appropriation, transfer, redistribution, copying, performance, and even rebundling into a new creation, itself covered by intellectual property.[142] To the "bundle of rights" conception of property, on the other hand, can be counterposed the "bundle of privileges" vision of the public domain, where we assume, for example, that fair use over a copyrighted work is part of the public domain. And to the predictive, legal realist vision of property, "predictions of what the courts will protect in fact," to paraphrase Holmes,[143] can be counterposed a predictive, critical conception of the public domain, "predictions of what the public can do freely and nothing more pretentious," to paraphrase Benkler.[144] Lessig's vision of the commons even includes works for which one has to pay, so long as the legal interest is protected merely by a liability rule and the payment is non-discriminatory.[145]

---

140. 2 WILLIAM BLACKSTONE, COMMENTARIES *233.

141. Leroy Fibre Co. v. Chicago Milwaukee & St. Paul Ry., 232 U.S. 340, 350 (1914).

142. It is no surprise to find this vision of the public domain flourishing at the times and in the places where the concept of property is hailed as being absolute—even if that is far from the actual truth.

143. *See* Oliver Wendell Holmes, Jr., *The Path of the Law*, 10 HARV. L. REV. 457, 461 (1897)

144. Benkler, *Free as the Air*, *supra* note 25, at 361.

145. It is not exactly clear how Lessig uses the term "liability rule." He uses free software as an example, but under the classic definition, software under the GPL is actually protected by a property rule backed by injunctive remedies. Under a liability rule, you could incorporate free software into a

Each of these definitions is driven by an explicit or implicit goal. It may be that the public domain consists of those aspects of works which must remain outside of property if copyright's misleading presumptions about creation are to be squared with reality. It may be that the commons is constructed around the twin notions of preventing monopoly control over network protocols in order to preserve innovation, while still allowing for the type of collective management that will avoid a tragedy of the commons. We have not one public domain, not one theory of the public domain, but many. My own point of view is that this is all to the good, though a little clarity is certainly in order. But not everyone agrees.

X

CONCLUSION: REIFYING THE NEGATIVE?

What is gained by reifying the negative and imaging a "theory" of the public domain?
Edward Samuels.[146]

The process I have described was a gradual one. From having been the invisible Other, the unquestioned margin of intellectual property, the public domain began to attract increasing attention. (Some of it, I must admit, from me, though I have wisely omitted that work from the history in this essay, out of self-preservation if nothing else.)[147] Soon, this body of work began to receive

---

proprietary, closed-source, program (itself not subject to the GPL) provided you paid the appropriate level of damages, normally set at "actual harm." This is not the interpretation of the GPL, or the Copyright Act, that the Free Software Foundation supports, and I would have to agree with them. Leaving aside the question of whether or not a commons that includes content protected by liability rules includes free software, is this a useful definition of the commons? The non-discriminatory liability rule does deal with certain problems of open access to networks, protocols, or choke points for innovation. Under a liability rule regime, payment would be disaggregated from control. The Internet Service Provider would, on payment of a fee, get access to the cable company's network to provide competition with the cable company itself. The researchers would be entitled to access the stem cell lines, on payment of a flat statutory access fee to the patent-holder. But some of the types of distributed innovation described later will flourish only under a system where material is available free—meaning at zero cost. *The Wind Done Gone* might get published under a liability rule regime; Margaret Mitchell's estate could not say "No." They could merely demand a fee, and the potential profits might more than justify the payment. But a system which required *pervasive* paying of license fees (the Copyright Clearance Center generalized to all forms of data) would surely fail to live up to the appellation of a "commons." It would deter both collective creation by the poor, and complicated, multi-source, incremental innovation even by relatively wealthy institutions. Personally, I would reserve the label "commons" for something closer to Benkler's definition of the public domain—material that an individual is legally privileged to use, absent a showing of individualized facts to the contrary. Nevertheless, Lessig has an important point. The successful commons will often have some form of governance, and liability rules have extraordinary advantages, mitigating one of the largest potential dangers of the intellectual property system. I am probably reading too much into all of this because Lessig's remarkable new book avoids the liability rule definition altogether, simply saying that resources can be "free even though a price must be paid (a park is 'free' in the sense that I mean even if an access fee is required—so long as the access fee is neutrally and consistently applied)." LESSIG, *supra* note 74 at 20.

146. Edward Samuels, *The Public Domain in Copyright Law*, 41 J. COPYRIGHT SOC'Y U.S.A. 137, 150 (1993).

147. *See* BOYLE, SHAMANS, *supra* note 32; Boyle, *Cruel*, *supra* note 46; James Boyle, *The First Amendment and Cyberspace: The Clinton Years*, 63 LAW & CONTEMP. PROBS. 337 (Winter/Spring 2000); Boyle, *Foucault*, *supra* note 121; James Boyle, *Intellectual Property Online, A Young Person's Guide*, 10 HARV. J. L. & TECH. 47 (1997); Boyle, *Missing the Point*, *supra* note 69; James Boyle, *A*

the ultimate intellectual compliment—thoughtful skepticism from others about whether there was any *there*, there:

> After reviewing the various proposed arguments supporting a general theory of the public domain, by Patterson and Lindberg or by other authors, it would appear that there simply is no such general theory. Instead, there are several discrete contexts in which arguments about the public domain are encountered, each context raising different considerations that may have little or nothing to do with each other, and that cumulatively constitute what remains after one examines all possible sources of legal protection for works of authorship .... *What is gained by reifying the negative, and imagining a "theory" of the public domain*? If one wants to encourage a presumption against new forms or areas of protection, then one can do so without having to invoke a magical "public domain." There are dozens of battlegrounds between those who want to expand intellectual property protection and those who want to limit it or narrow it in any given context. The arguments in each context should be kept separate, since they raise different policy issues. Nevertheless, the individual issues sometimes tend to be elusive, and one's attitude toward them tends to be flavored as often as not by one's general attitude toward copyright law. If those who find themselves continually on the side arguing for a limitation of protection need a rallying cry, perhaps it can be "the public domain." The invocation may seem to add a moral overtone to the argument, to counterbalance the morally charged principles invoked time and again by the protectionists. In the final analysis, however, "such vague rhetoric does little more than adorn the stage on which actual choices must be played out."[148]

What is gained by reifying the negative? Professor Samuels' question is a good one. He supplies part of the answer with his thought that perhaps the language of the public domain will be used to counter the language of sacred property. This is, indeed, an important point—*language matters*, and not just as rhetoric. Even if the limits of my language are not the limits of my world,[149] the limits of my language certainly influence my world in a deeper way than as "vague rhetoric" adorning a stage, "on which actual choices must be played out."

The analogy I have tried to develop in my writing is that of the environmental movement.[150] Why talk of "an environment" or "environmental harm?" Why not simply list the pros and cons of each particular piece of development, type of technology, aspect of land use? In each case, there will be issues to be thought about: clean water, beautiful vistas, biodiversity, raised sea levels, the morals of species preservation, skin cancers from thinned ozone layers, carbon sequestration, responsibilities to future generations, and so on. It is not clear that there is any Ariadne's thread that links these issues together. What's more, it is fairly clear that there is no coherent or consistent definition of "nature" or

---

Politics of Intellectual Property: Environmentalism for the Net?, 47 DUKE L.J. 87 (1997) [hereinafter Boyle, *Politics*]; Boyle, *Theory*, *supra* note 77.

148. Samuels, *supra* note 146.

149. LUDWIG WITTGENSTEIN, TRACTATUS LOGICUS PHILOSOPHICUS §5.6 ("*The limits of my language* mean the limits of my world. . . . We cannot think what we cannot think; so what we cannot think we cannot say either.") Gibbon made a simpler but related point in describing the role of language in politics: "Augustus was sensible that mankind is governed by names; nor was he deceived in his expectation that the senate and people would submit to slavery, provided they were respectfully assured that they still enjoyed their ancient freedom." THE PORTABLE GIBBON: THE DECLINE AND FALL OF THE ROMAN EMPIRE 99 (D. Saunders ed., Viking Press 1952) (1782).

150. Boyle, *Politics*, *supra* note 147.

"the environment."[151] There are certainly lots of discrete contexts in which the idea of nature or the environment is raised, and many different arguments for and against a particular type of development or technology. Why not simply deal case-by-case with the harms to this river, that wetland, this species, or that way of life? Why reify these individual loci of potential harm into a single entity called "the environment?" Part of the answer, of course, *is* rhetorical. The idea of the environment seems to add a moral overtone to the discussion, to counterbalance the arguments about "progress" and "growth" and "modernity." And this is hardly an unimportant function.

But that is not all there is to it. The environmental movement also gained much of its persuasive power by pointing out that there were structural reasons for bad environmental decisions—a legal system based on a particular notion of what "private property" entailed, and a scientific system that treated the world as a simple, linearly-related set of causes and effects. In both of these conceptual systems, the environment actually disappeared; there was no place for it in the analysis. Small surprise, then, that we did not preserve it very well. In other work, I have argued that the same is true about the public domain.[152] The fundamental tensions in the economic analysis of information issues, the source-blindness of an original author-centered model of property rights, and the political blindness to the importance of the public domain as a whole (not "my lake," but "The Environment") all come together to make the public domain disappear, first in concept and then, increasingly, as a reality.[153]

Of equal importance is the power of a concept like the environment both to clarify and to reshape perceptions of self-interest. When we are talking about the particular costs of this development proposal or that, the duck hunter is less

151. As I put it in a previous work:

> [S]mall wonder, then, that faith in Nature is hard to reconcile with the rationalist philosophers' critique of the naturalistic fallacy. Environmental ideas of Nature are often based on a skepticism about the power of reason, and a willingness to put faith in spontaneous order precisely because one knows the limits of one's own knowledge about the working of the system. We reify and anthropomorphize Nature in part to express this "faith in the system." But if we would be suspicious of this anthropomorphism when it is applied to "the Market" or to "national tradition," shouldn't we try to apply the same skepticism and feeling for nuance to "Nature"? Which system, which Nature, is being venerated? Are we humans in it? In medicine, does anything organic count as Natural? Do we let aconite and malaria have their way, smiling indulgently? Or is it merely any plant or mineral "traditionally" used as medicine? In environmental terms, is it some imaginary world without the impact of human history, without landscapes transformed, species eradicated, plant varieties cultivated? Is it "Nature as scenery;" the world with the human interventions we like, whether they are English hedgerows, drystane dykes, the bleak beauty of a Scottish moor, deforested before Dr. Johnson passed it by? The trouble with declaring one's reverence for a system, be it a market, a culture or an ecosystem, is that people actually disagree strongly about what the "natural" state of that system is. Then they disagree further about the normative implications of that natural state. Both sets of disagreements could often benefit from some old-fashioned rationalist skepticism.

James Boyle, *Against Nature*, TIMES LITERARY SUPPLEMENT, July 24, 1998 (reviewing Phil Macnaghten & John Urry, *Contested Natures* (1998)), *available at* http://www.law.duke.edu/boylesite/tls98na1.htm. What all of this *doesn't* mean, of course, is that the concept of Nature, or the Environment, is useless.

152. Boyle, *Politics*, *supra* note 147.

153. *Id.*

likely to make common cause with the bird-watcher in another region, let alone the person worried about genetic drift in salmon populations or the effect of CFCs on the ozone layer. The idea that there is "an environment" allows a coalition to be built around a reframed conception of common interest. In the narrowest sense, that common interest might be the realization, spurred by greater attention to environmental interrelationships, that wetlands are important to both the duck hunter and the bird-watcher, and that they provide all kinds of ecosystem services. Naming encourages study.

In the broader sense, though, it is not merely the word "environment" that catalyses attention. Rather, there were two very important ideas behind the environmental movement. The first was the idea of ecology—the fragile, complex, and unpredictable interconnections between living systems.[154] The second was the idea of welfare economics—the ways in which markets can fail to make activities internalize their full costs.[155] The combination of the two ideas yielded a powerful and disturbing conclusion: Markets would *routinely* fail to make activities internalize their own costs, particularly their environmental costs. This failure would routinely disrupt or destroy fragile ecological systems, with unpredictable, ugly, dangerous, and possibly irreparable consequences.

These two types of analysis pointed to a general interest in environmental protection, and thus helped to build a large constituency which supported governmental efforts to that end. They were coupled with a simple point from public choice theory—public decisions are particularly likely to be bad when concentrated and well-organized groups with stable, substantial, and well-identified interests face off against diffuse groups with high information costs whose interests, while enormous in the aggregate, are individually small. There are lots of people who might be affected by a decision to rely on a particular power source, say, a coal-burning power plant in the Northeast. There are people who see acid rain killing off the fish in their lake, there are others who worry about particulate emissions, and there are those whose houses will be swallowed up by the sea if global warming lives up to its billing. But in the decisions about energy purchase and planning, they are neither as well-informed, nor is it easy for them to be as well-organized, as the company which proposes to run the particular plant. The notion of "an environmental movement" helps to sustain a coalition that people join, give money to, and so forth, even when the particular issue being lobbied over *affects them not at all*. By coming to be convinced that they should give loyalty to "the protection of the environment" rather than "oppose the stuff that affects me badly," the diffuse group was able to overcome some collective action problems. Specialized organizations fitting particular niches in the movement (Greenpeace, the Audubon Society, the Environmental Defense Fund, the Nature Conservancy) fulfilled a variety of roles and allowed

154. *See id.*

155. *See* PETER BOHM, SOCIAL EFFICIENCY: A CONCISE INTRODUCTION TO WELFARE ECONOMICS (1973); *see also* Boyle, *Politics*, *supra* note 147.

people to "subcontract" their information-gathering to experts whose norms and pedigree they trusted.[156]

And, what is true for the environment is—to a striking degree, though not completely—true for the public domain and for the commons. The idea of the public domain takes to a higher level of abstraction a set of individual fights—over this chunk of the genome, that aspect of computer programs, this claim about the meaning of parody, or the ownership of facts. Just as the duck hunter finds common cause with the bird-watcher and the salmon geneticist by coming to think about "the environment," so an emergent concept of the public domain could tie together the interests of groups currently engaged in individual struggles with no sense of the larger context. This notion, in turn, allows people to solve collective action problems in a number of different ways, including the creation of specialized organizations whose technical expertise and lobbying proficiency allows the diffuse interests of a wider public to be better articulated. Here, too, we can learn. The public domain should have its Greenpeace, its Environmental Defense Fund, its Nature Conservancy, its Environmentally Concerned Scientists. In fact, organizations paralleling each of these functions are currently being created.[157]

The analogy goes further. Just as "the environment," or "nature," takes on multiple shadings of meaning to respond to different hopes and fears—biodiversity, the preservation of beauty, a particular relationship between human beings and the planet—so, too, the various images of the public domain and the commons each expresses a specific set of fears about the dangers of property and hopes about the creative process. Frequently, the concept is constructed as an antonym—mirroring the analytic structure of the dominant idea of property to which it is counterposed. Samuels' skepticism is useful here; more clarity about the contents of the public domain and the relationship between the concept of the commons and of the public domain would indeed be useful. The literature on governing the commons promises to be exceptionally useful here,[158] as does the sadly neglected tradition of Hohfeldian legal analysis.[159] Each can offer a different kind of clarity. But just as with the environment, with nature, we do not respond to the revelation that these words are used in multiple and overlapping ways with the conclusion that we should

156. Once I decide that the Environmental Defense Fund does good science and good legal research, I rely on their opinion—leveling the playing field a bit between the power company, with its hired scientists and lawyers, and me.

157. *See, e.g.*, Public Knowledge, http://www.publicknowledge.org (last visited Jan. 14, 2003); Electronic Frontier Foundation's Campaign for Audio Visual Free Expression, http://www.eff.org/cafe (last visited Jan. 14, 2003); Creative Commons, http://www.creativecommons.org (last visited Jan. 14, 2003); Duke Law School's Center for the Study of the Public Domain, http://www.law.duke.edu/news/current/20020905pdic.html (last visited Jan. 14, 2003). There are, of course, other efforts along these lines. Honesty requires the confession that I am involved with several of these organizations as progenitor, advisor, or board member, which doubtless prejudices my selection.

158. *See supra* Parts I-III.

159. *See supra* Part VII.

simply abandon them and deal individually with the pluses and minuses of each development proposal, each dam, each CFC emission. The concept of the environment allows, at its best, a kind of generalized reflection on the otherwise unquestionable presuppositions of a particular mode of life, economy, and industrial organization. At their best, the commons and the public domain can do the same in helping us to reimagine creation, innovation, and speech on a global network. And this seems particularly important today.

The poem with which I began this essay told us: "And geese will still a common lack / Till they go and steal it back." I can't match the terseness or the rhyme, but if we assume that the second enclosure movement will have the benign effects claimed for the first, well, we will look like very silly geese indeed.

NINE-TENTHS OF THE LAW: THE ENGLISH COPYRIGHT DEBATES AND THE RHETORIC OF THE PUBLIC DOMAIN

MARK ROSE*

I
INTRODUCTION

To compare the present moment in the history of intellectual property to the English enclosure movements of the early modern period, as James Boyle and others do, is to employ a version of a metaphor that reaches back to the early history of copyright in the late seventeenth and early eighteenth centuries—the literary work as a kind of landed estate.[1] Embedded in this metaphor is an implicit narrative about the origin of copyright, a version of the familiar Enlightenment narrative about the origin of landed property in general. In the beginning, so the story goes, all the literary world lay free and open, but then various parts were settled and enclosed and literary property came into being. The story implies that the public domain, the literary commons, precedes copyright. But this is not quite the case. By 1557, when the Stationers' Company was chartered, printing and publishing had already become a highly regulated activity in which rights to print books of all kinds, both new and old, were either assigned directly by the crown or managed by the Stationers' Company.[2] True, many aspects of writing lay open in the pre-copyright period. Shakespeare, for example, had no hesitation about appropriating others' works in ways that would clearly constitute infringement today. So far as printers and booksellers were concerned, however, the book trade was regulated in all its dimensions, including such matters as the number of presses a printer might own and the number of apprentices and journeymen he might keep. Thus, even such Latin

---

This article is also available at http://www.law.duke.edu/journals/66LCPMarkRose.

* Professor of English, University of California, Santa Barbara.

1. James Boyle, *The Second Enclosure Movement and the Construction of the Public Domain*, 66 LAW & CONTEMP. PROBS. 33 (Winter/Spring 2003). On the landed estate metaphor, see Mark Rose, *Copyright and Its Metaphors*, 50 UCLA L. REV. 1 (2002).

2. *See generally* CYPRIAN BLAGDEN, THE STATIONERS' COMPANY: A HISTORY, 1403-1959 (1960). Whether printing was open or regulated in the early period of printing in England was the subject of intense debate in the seventeenth and eighteenth centuries. One party insisted that printing was originally common, while another argued that it was part of the royal prerogative and the personal dominion of the king. *See* ADRIAN JOHNS, THE NATURE OF THE BOOK: PRINT AND KNOWLEDGE IN THE MAKING 324-79 (1998). I am grateful to David Lange for raising questions about the status of printing in England in the earliest period.

and Greek classics as Aesop, Cicero, Ovid, Terence, and Virgil were protected titles, the property of the Stationers' Company itself, which could assign individual books to whichever guild members it chose for printing.[3] We must be cautious, therefore, about projecting into the past an idyll of communality from which we have supposedly declined. The absolutist regimes of the Tudor and Stuart monarchs were characterized by pervasive regulation, and they were very different from the post-revolutionary civic society in which copyright law emerged.

II

CIVIL SOCIETY AND THE BIRTH OF THE PUBLIC DOMAIN

Copyright and the public domain were born together. They were formed in the course of the long social process that Jürgen Habermas identifies as the emergence of the "public sphere."[4] This process involves the circulation of cultural products as commodities rather than as displays of aristocratic magnificence, and it involves a sense of civil society as a collectivity distinct from either the private realm of the family or the public realm of the state. The emergent sense of civil society was crucial to the transformation of the old regime of royally chartered regulation into the new regime of property rights defined by the legislature and the courts. It was also an important rationale for the limited term of copyright, a limitation that brought the public domain into being. As Samuel Johnson remarked in conversation in 1773:

> There seems . . . to be in authours a stronger right of property than that by occupancy; a metaphysical right, a right, as it were, of creation, which should from its nature be perpetual; but the consent of nations is against it, and indeed reason and the interests of learning are against it; for were it to be perpetual, no book, however useful, could be universally diffused amongst mankind, should the proprietor take it into his head to restrain its circulation. No book could have the advantage of being edited with notes, however necessary to its elucidation, should the proprietor perversely oppose it. For the general good of the world, therefore, whatever valuable work has once been created by an authour, and issued out by him, should be understood as no longer in his power, but as belonging to the publick; at the same time the authour is entitled to an adequate reward. This he should have by an exclusive right to his work for a considerable number of years.[5]

Thus, the establishment of the author as an owner and the establishment of the rights of the public at large were both Enlightenment products, embedded in Enlightenment modes of thought.

---

3. *See* BLAGDEN, *supra* note 2, at 243 fig. XII (reprinting a broadside of 1766 listing some of the titles that were part of the company monopoly).

4. JÜRGEN HABERMAS, THE STRUCTURAL TRANSFORMATION OF THE PUBLIC SPHERE: AN INQUIRY INTO A CATEGORY OF BOURGEOIS SOCIETY 57-67 (Thomas Burger trans., 1991).

5. JAMES BOSWELL, BOSWELL'S LIFE OF JOHNSON 546-47 (R.W. Chapman ed., Oxford Univ. Press 1953) (1791).

The 1709 Statute of Anne[6] recognized authors as owners and also provided for term limits—twenty-one years for books already in print and fourteen years for new books, with the possibility of a second fourteen-year term if the author were still living at the end of the first term. But even after the passage of the Statute, the major London booksellers continued to treat literary property—including works by such classic English writers as Shakespeare and Milton—as perpetual properties, and they regularly secured chancery injunctions against those who would reprint such classic texts. In practice, then, the public domain did not exist even after the passage of the Statute of Anne. The London booksellers' claims were based on the theory that an author enjoyed a perpetual common-law right of property in his or her work, and that this property right was transferred to the bookseller by deed when the work was sold. The statutory right, the booksellers argued, was merely a supplement to the common-law right, and that right lasted forever. These claims led to six decades of legal struggle over the question of literary property, as it was called, and to two great cases in which the matter was resolved.

First, in the King's Bench case of *Millar v. Taylor*[7] a divided court upheld the author's common-law right and the perpetuity. Then, in *Donaldson v. Becket*,[8] the House of Lords overturned *Millar* and declared that literary property was limited to the terms specified in the Statute. For the first time, classic works became free for anyone to print. Soon after the *Donaldson* decision, booksellers in Edinburgh and London issued multi-volume collections of classic British works under titles that emphasized the national character of the publications. The Edinburgh bookseller John Bell, for example, introduced a multi-volume Shakespeare even as *Donaldson* was pending, and then, after the decision, went on to publish *Bell's British Theatre* in twenty-one volumes (1776-80) and the monumental *Poets of Great Britain* in one hundred and nine volumes (1776-82).

III

THE DISCOURSE OF THE PUBLIC DOMAIN

We need to distinguish, however, between the fact of the public domain and what might be called the discourse of the public domain—that is, the construction of a legal language to talk about public rights in writings. One component in the development of this discourse was the strong anti-monopoly sentiment that reached back to the days of Queen Elizabeth and came to a head in the Jacobean Statute of Monopolies in 1623.[9] Although this act abolished most existing monopolies and established limited terms for the grants of monopoly rights in inventions, it explicitly excluded printing privileges from these limita-

6. Statute of Anne, 1709, 8 Ann., c. 19 (Eng.). On the Statute and for fuller discussion of the literary property struggle, see generally MARK ROSE, AUTHORS AND OWNERS: THE INVENTION OF COPYRIGHT (1993).

7. 98 Eng. Rep. 201 (K.B. 1769).

8. 1 Eng. Rep. 837 (H.L. 1774).

9. Statute of Monopolies, 1623, 21 Jac. 1, c.3 (Eng.).

tions. By the late seventeenth and early eighteenth centuries, the great London booksellers had become wealthy and important men in large part as a consequence of their monopolies of ancient and modern classics. There was considerable resentment against what was known as the "trade."

One of the earliest writers to agitate against the booksellers' perpetual monopolies was John Locke. In 1693, the Licensing Act,[10] the instrument through which the Stationers' Company was empowered to regulate the trade, faced renewal. Concerned particularly with the guild's monopolies in Latin writers, Locke wrote to his friend, Edward Clarke, a Member of Parliament, urging him to speak in Parliament for the interests of the educated public at large:

> I wish you would have some care of book-buyers as well as all of booksellers and the company of stationers, who having got a patent for all or most of the ancient Latin authors (by what right or pretense I know not) claim the text to be theirs, and so will not suffer fairer or more correct editions than any they print here, or with new comments to be imported without compounding with them, whereby these most useful books are excessively dear to scholars, and a monopoly is put into the hands of ignorant and lazy stationers.[11]

One year later, when the Licensing Act was again being considered, Locke drafted a formal *Memorandum* for Clarke in which he repeated his objection to the guild's monopolies in the Latin classics and argued that copyrights in contemporary authors should also be limited in term:

> That any person or company should have patents for the sole printing of ancient authors is very unreasonable and injurious to learning; and for those who purchase copies from authors that now live and write, it may be reasonable to limit their property to a certain number of years after the death of the author, or the first printing of the book, as, suppose, fifty or seventy years.[12]

Locke's comments blend traditional anti-monopoly sentiment with the Enlightenment commitment to the circulation of knowledge, a view he shared with other members of the recently founded Royal Society. His *Memorandum* was influential in securing the lapse of licensing in 1695, but it remained unpublished until the early nineteenth century.

Whether Locke's *Memorandum* was known to the drafters of the Statute of Anne is unclear, but the Statute shows both the influence of anti-monopoly sentiment and of the Enlightenment commitment to the circulation of knowledge. The title emphasizes the encouragement of learning: "An act for the encouragement of learning, by vesting the copies of printed books in the authors or publishers of such copies, during the times therein mentioned."[13] And, although the preamble opens by addressing the need to protect literary property, it goes

---

10. Licensing Act, 1662, 14 Car. II, c. 33 (Eng.).

11. Letter from John Locke to Edward Clarke (Jan. 2, 1693), *in* THE CORRESPONDENCE OF JOHN LOCKE AND EDWARD CLARKE 366 (Benjamin Rand ed., 1927).

12. LORD PETER KING, THE LIFE OF JOHN LOCKE 208 (London, Henry Colburn 1829). On Locke's role in securing the end of licensing, see Raymond Astbury, *The Renewal of the Licensing Act in 1693 and its Lapse in 1695*, 33 LIBR. 296-322 (1978).

13. Statute of Anne, 1709, 8 Ann., c. 19 (Eng.).

on to say that the purpose of the Act is also "the encouragement of learned men to compose and write useful books."[14] In this way, the Statute aligns itself with broad civic purposes as well as with private property.[15] As originally introduced in Parliament, the booksellers' bill said nothing about term limits. These, along with the provision for authors, were added in the legislative process, probably because of the suspicion about booksellers' monopolies, as is suggested by the fact that the terms of protection are modeled on those of the Jacobean Statute of Monopolies.[16] Nonetheless, although the influence of anti-monopoly and Enlightenment ideas on the Statute of Anne is clear, the Statute is a sketchy document that did not in itself directly contribute much to the development of a discourse of the public domain.

What the Statute did, however, was set the stage for the legal debate over the booksellers' claims about perpetual copyright. The single most influential figure in this struggle, and the one who more than any other determined the frame in which the debate took place, was Lord Mansfield, the great Chief Justice of the Court of King's Bench. Mansfield certainly appreciated the progress of knowledge, but he saw the copyright question primarily as a matter of property rights, and in his opinion in *Millar* he formulated the classic statement of the author's natural right: Upon what basis was the author's common-law right founded?

> From this argument—because it is just, that an author should reap the pecuniary profits of his own ingenuity and labour. It is just, that another should not use his name, without his consent. It is fit that he should judge when to publish, or whether he ever will publish. It is fit he should not only choose the time, but the manner of publication; how many; what volume; what print. It is fit, he should choose to whose care he will trust the accuracy and correctness of the impression; in whose honesty he will confide, not to foist in additions: with other reasonings of the same effect.[17]

Mansfield concluded that perpetual copyright followed as a matter of course from these fundamental principles. He had nothing to say about the kinds of issues John Locke had raised seventy years earlier, and most likely he knew nothing of Locke's *Memorandum*.

The most prominent opponent of the common-law right was Justice Joseph Yates, who cast the sole dissenting vote in *Millar* and who maintained that by their very nature writings, being immaterial, were incapable of being regarded as property. An author had a property in his manuscripts, of course, but the act of publication necessarily constituted a gift to the public. A published work was "like land thrown into the highway."[18] The legislature might create a limited

14. *Id.*

15. Ronan Deazley has recently emphasized the civic purposes of the Statute of Anne, arguing that the statute incorporates an exchange between the author and society in which the author receives a limited monopoly in return for making the work public. Ronan Deazley, On the Origin of the Right to Copy: Charting the Movement of Copyright Law in Eighteenth Century Britain (1695-1775) at 81 (2001) (unpublished Ph.D. dissertation, Queen's University of Belfast) (on file with author).

16. Statute of Monopolies, 1623, 21 Jac. 1, c. 3 (Eng.).

17. Millar v. Taylor, 98 Eng. Rep. 201, 252 (K.B. 1769).

18. Tonson v. Collins, 96 Eng. Rep. 180, 185 (K.B. 1761). In this case, Yates was counsel for the defense. Yates later used a similar phrase in his minority opinion in *Millar*: "[W]hen an author prints

privilege as it had done in the Statute, but there could be no common-law right. Yates touched upon some of the arguments drawn from anti-monopoly and Enlightenment thought, noting that, if copyright were determined to be perpetual, works might be priced at exorbitant rates or arbitrarily withdrawn from circulation. Moreover, he invoked the concept of dedication to the public and, in speaking about land thrown into the highway, he even came close to the trope of a literary commons. Nevertheless, the heart of his position was a scholastic point about the nature of property. How could ideas, which have no bounds or marks or anything that is capable of visible possession, give rise to a common-law right of property?

> Their whole existence is in the mind alone; incapable of any other modes of acquisition or enjoyment, than by mental possession or apprehension; safe and invulnerable, from their own immateriality: no trespass can reach them; no tort affect them; no fraud or violence diminish or damage them. Yet these are the phantoms which the author would grasp and confine to himself . . . .[19]

The legal struggle in which Mansfield and Yates were antagonists was thus only indirectly a struggle over knowledge and the public domain. It was essentially an argument over the theory of property. Moreover, in terms of logic and rhetorical power, Mansfield got the better of the day, for his argument not only invoked high-minded principles of fitness and justice but also implied a forward-looking theory of property. Yates's position, on the other hand, implied a rigid conception of property of a kind that would soon become outmoded.

Donaldson overturned *Millar*, but this climactic case, too, was framed in terms of property theory. Was there a common-law right of literary property? Did it survive publication? Was it taken away by the Statute? Before voting on whether to sustain the chancery injunction on which the case turned, the lords solicited the opinions of the twelve common-law judges on these questions. The judges were divided in their opinions, but it appears that a majority maintained that there was a common-law right, that it survived publication, and that it was not taken away by the Statute. In overturning *Millar*, then, the lords were probably going against the majority opinion of the judges. But on what grounds did they do so? What, in other words, was the rationale through which the public domain was finally confirmed? Given the nature of the process—the matter appears to have been decided by a simple voice vote—it is of course impossible to say. The major statement of the day, however, came from Mansfield's old political and legal antagonist Lord Camden, who delivered a long address to the House after the judges had spoken.

Camden began by tracing the legal record and explaining his specifically legal reasons for rejecting the common-law right. But then he moved to the broader grounds of public policy:

> If there be any thing in the world common to all mankind, science and learning are in their nature *publici juris*, and they ought to be as free and general as air or water.

---

and publishes his work, he lays it entirely open to the public, as much as when an owner of a piece of land lays it open into the highway." *Millar*, 98 Eng. Rep. at 234 (Yates, J., dissenting).

19. *Millar*, 98 Eng. Rep. at 233 (Yates, J., dissenting).

> They forget their Creator, as well as their fellow creatures, who wish to monopolize his noblest gifts and greatest benefits. Why did we enter into society at all, but to enlighten one another's minds, and improve our faculties, for the common welfare of the species? Those great men, those favoured mortals, those sublime spirits, who share that ray of divinity which we call genius, are intrusted by Providence with the delegated power of imparting to their fellow-creatures that instruction which heaven meant for universal benefit; they must not be niggards to the world, or hoard up for themselves the common stock.[20]

In this passage, Camden was perhaps echoing the distinguished Scottish jurist and author Lord Kames, who had recently published a speech delivered in a Scottish case in which he countered Lord Mansfield's opinion on the common-law right.[21] Whereas Mansfield had grounded his opinion in the fundamental principle of the individual's right to property, Kames grounded his in "the first principles of society." "Why," he asked, "was man made a social being, but to benefit by society, and to partake of all the improvements of society in its progress toward perfection?"[22] He went on to contend that the limited term was useful because it provided an incentive for authors at the same time that it avoided the evils of a perpetual monopoly which would raise the price of books and limit their sale to the rich. As a result, commerce would decline and fewer books would be written. Thus, Kames said, "a perpetual monopoly of books would prove more destructive to learning, and even to authors, than a second irruption of Goths and Vandals."[23]

Likewise, Camden asked rhetorically about the social nature of mankind. "Why did we enter into society at all, but to enlighten one another's minds, and improve our faculties, for the common welfare of the species?"[24] Camden, too, touched upon anti-monopoly and Enlightenment themes. But Camden's speech did not emphasize the destructive potential of a perpetual monopoly; instead he focused on the meanness of writing for money. The climax of his speech would be much quoted in later years:

> Glory is the reward of science, and those who deserve it, scorn all meaner views: I speak not of scribblers for bread, who teaze the press with their wretched productions; fourteen years is too long a privilege for their perishable trash. It was not for gain, that Bacon, Newton, Milton, Locke, instructed and delighted the world; it would be unworthy such men to traffic with a dirty bookseller for so much a sheet of a letter press. When the bookseller offered Milton five pound for his Paradise Lost, he did not reject it, and commit his poem to the flames, nor did he accept the miserable pit-

---

20. WILLIAM COBBETT, XVII THE PARLIAMENTARY HISTORY OF ENGLAND col. 999 (London, R. Bragshaw 1813).

21. The case was *Hinton v. Donaldson*, in which the Scottish Court of Session decided that, despite the King's Bench decision in *Millar*, so far as Scotland was concerned, there was no common-law right of literary property. 1 Hailes Dec. 535 (Sess. Cas. 1773). It was reported by Boswell in *The Decision of the Court of Session upon the Question of Literary Property*, and issued while *Donaldson* was pending so that the Scottish case might be taken into account in the lords' decision. *See* JAMES BOSWELL, THE DECISION OF THE COURT OF SESSION UPON THE QUESTION OF LITERARY PROPERTY (Edinburgh, James Donaldson 1774).

22. BOSWELL, *supra* note 21, at 19.

23. *Id.* at 20.

24. COBBETT, *supra* note 20.

> tance as the reward of his labour; he knew that the real price of his work was immortality, and that posterity would pay it.[25]

If copyright were confirmed as perpetual, Camden said:

> All our learning will be locked up in the hands of the Tonsons and the Lintons of the age, who will set what price upon it their avarice chuses to demand, till the public become as much their slaves, as their own hackney compilers are . . . . [E]very valuable author will be as much monopolized by them as Shakespeare is at present . . . .[26]

Thus, Camden combined a denunciation of the very idea of professional authorship with a derisive swipe at "dirty" booksellers.

Camden's speech was widely circulated in newspapers and magazines, and it was generally regarded as a key factor in the lords' vote against perpetual copyright. But the extravagance of his rhetoric and anachronistic contempt for literary commerce made him an easy target for, among others, the republican historian Catharine Macaulay. She responded immediately with a pamphlet in which she heaped sarcasm on the notion that worthy authors ought not to be concerned with money:

> There are some low-minded geniusses, who will be apt to think they may, with as little degradation to character, traffic with a bookseller for the purchase of their mental harvest, as opulent landholders may traffic with monopolizers in grain and cattle for the sale of the more substantial product of their lands. They will be apt to consider, that literary merit will not purchase a shoulder of mutton, or prevail with sordid butchers and bakers to abate one farthing in the pound of the exorbitant price which meat and bread at this time bear . . . .[27]

The reverberations of his speech continued to be heard for many years with the arguments for the author's common-law right—now, typically, coming from authors themselves—often being fashioned as responses to Camden.

The poet Robert Southey, for example, who agitated for new copyright legislation in the early nineteenth century, singled out Camden's fervid passage about glory as the reward of science:

> Is it possible that this declamation should impose upon any man? The question is simply this: upon what principle, with what justice, or under what pretext of public good, are men of letters deprived of a perpetual property in the produce of their own labours, when all other persons enjoy it as their indefeasible right—a right beyond the power of any earthly authority to take away? Is it because their labour is so light,—the endowments which it requires so common,—the attainments so cheaply and easily acquired, and the present remuneration so adequate, so ample, and so certain?[28]

Whereas Camden had cited Milton and Shakespeare as examples of authors who did not care about money, Southey noted that Milton's descendants had died in poverty and that Shakespeare's were still living in poverty. Many books of the highest merit achieved recognition slowly and therefore permanent copy-

---

25. *Id.* col. 1000.

26. *Id.* Kames had also mentioned that the "best authors write for fame." BOSWELL, *supra* note 21, at 21. Camden, however, was much more dismissive of professional writers than was Kames.

27. CATHARINE MACAULAY, A MODEST PLEA FOR THE PROPERTY OF COPY RIGHT 14-15 (Bath, R. Cruttwell 1774).

28. *Inquiry in the Copyright Act*, 21 Q. REV. 211-12 (1819) (attributed without evidence to Robert Southey in *Quarterly Review* Index).

right was a necessity if the "reward of literary labour" was to be "in just proportion to its deserts."[29]

The reaction continued in the late 1830s and early 1840s in the movement for copyright reform led by Thomas Noon Talfourd in collaboration with his friend William Wordsworth. Talfourd, too, invoked Camden's remark about glory.

> When the opponents of literary property speak of glory as the reward of genius, they make an ungenerous use of the very nobleness of its impulses, and show how little they have profited by its high example .... The liberality of genius is surely ill urged as an excuse for our ungrateful denial of its rights .... Do we reward our heroes thus? Did we tell our Marlboroughs, our Nelsons, our Wellingtons, that glory was their reward, that they fought for posterity, and that posterity would pay them? We leave them to no such cold and uncertain requital; we do not even leave them merely to enjoy the spoils of their victories, which we deny to the authour; we concentrate a nation's honest feeling of gratitude and pride into the form of an endowment, and teach other ages what we thought, and what they ought to think, of their deed, by the substantial memorials of our praise. Were our Shakespeare and Milton less the ornaments of their country, less the benefactors of mankind?[30]

Thus, the language of civil society—or rather the language of nationalism into which it had by this point mutated—could be deployed against the limited term as well as against the perpetuity.

Talfourd and Wordsworth both believed that copyright was a natural right of authors and should last forever, but they were willing to compromise on an extended term of sixty years to be computed from the death of the author. Their reform movement led to the Copyright Act of 1842, which extended the term to the life of the author plus seven years or a total of forty-two years, whichever was longer.[31] The pivotal figure in defeating Talfourd's movement for a greatly extended term was Thomas Babington Macaulay, whose speech to the House of Commons in 1841 has become a standard point of reference in discussions of the history of copyright, one often quoted for his epigrammatic description of copyright as "a tax on readers for the purpose of giving a bounty to writers."[32] Macaulay refused to be drawn into theoretical discussion of the nature of property—the subject that had dominated the copyright debates in the courts—and he also avoided invoking Camden. Instead, he eloquently recapitulated the anti-monopoly tradition, combining it with a utilitarian calculus about the benefits to be derived from a limited monopoly. "Copyright is monopoly, and produces all the effects which the general voice attributes to monopoly," Macaulay said.[33] Considered in itself, therefore, copyright had to be regarded as an evil, but it was necessary to submit to this evil in order to pro-

---

29. *Id.* at 213.

30. THOMAS NOON TALFOURD, *Speech Delivered in the House of Commons* (May 18, 1837), *in* THREE SPEECHES DELIVERED IN THE HOUSE OF COMMONS IN FAVOUR OF A MEASURE FOR AN EXTENSION OF COPYRIGHT 16-18 (London, Edward Moxon 1840).

31. Copyright Act, 1842, 5 & 6 Vict., c. 45 (Eng.).

32. Thomas B. Macaulay, A Speech Delivered in the House of Commons (Feb. 5, 1841), *in* VIII THE LIFE AND WORKS OF LORD MACAULAY 201 (London, Longmans, Green, and Co. 1897).

33. *Id.* at 198.

vide for authors. But, he added, "the evil ought not to last a day longer than is necessary for the purpose of securing the good."[34]

The nineteenth century controversy over Talfourd's copyright campaign can be understood as a recapitulation of the eighteenth century literary property debates. Once again, the issue of perpetual copyright was raised, and once again the legislature rejected the idea of a perpetual monopoly. But the notion that an author really *should* have a perpetual copyright remained alive after 1842, as did the memory of Lord Camden's speech. Thus, in 1879, Eaton S. Drone, the author of a standard treatise on British and U.S. copyright, praised Lord Mansfield's argument for the author's common-law right as "one of the grandest judgments in English judicial literature,"[35]and argued that *Donaldson* was wrongly decided through the influence of Lord Camden's "specious harangue."[36]

> It would seem that this extravagant speech would have moved the peers only to disgust; that the highest judicial tribunal of England, deliberating on one of the greatest questions ever brought before it, would have been guided by the pure principles which had been so forcibly expounded by the Chief Justice and the profoundest jurists of England, rather than by the fallacious theories of Judge Yates and the Sophomoric rhetoric of Lord Camden. But it was not so.[37]

Drone was writing only a few years before the term "public domain" entered Anglo-American copyright discourse through the French of the Berne Convention.[38] This reminds us that, though one might speak with Yates of a published work as a "gift to the public" or as "land thrown into the highway," or one might, as Camden did, employ the Latin tag *publici juris*, there was, in the early period, no positive term in which to speak affirmatively about the public domain.

The one strong form of discourse that was available to counter the arguments for perpetual copyright was the anti-monopoly tradition. Although this tradition reached back to the sixteenth century, for various reasons it did not lead to an effective major statement until Macaulay's speech in 1841. Locke's *Memorandum* had, of course, invoked the old anti-monopoly feeling, but the *Memorandum* remained unpublished until the nineteenth century. Ironically, Locke was most often cited by the supporters of the perpetuity, who relied on his labor theory of property for the foundation of their claim, but who were

34. *Id.* at 199.

35. EATON S. DRONE, A TREATISE ON THE LAW OF PROPERTY IN INTELLECTUAL PRODUCTIONS IN GREAT BRITAIN AND THE UNITED STATES 37 (Boston, Little, Brown and Co. 1879).

36. *Id.* at 39.

37. *Id.* at 40. Drone also argued that *Wheaton v. Peters*, 33 U.S. 591 (1834), the foundational American case in which copyright was held to be limited in term, was of dubious authority. DRONE, *supra* note 35, at 43-49. It is worth noting that the line of Anglo-American copyright treatises from Robert Maugham to Drone strongly supported authors' rights and, among other reforms, the extensions championed by Sergeant Talfourd. *See id.*; ROBERT MAUGHAM, A TREATISE ON THE LAWS OF LITERARY PROPERTY (1828).

38. On the use of the term in Anglo-American discourse, see Jessica Litman, *The Public Domain*, 39 EMORY L. J. 965, 975 n.60 (1990).

unaware that he actually had opposed perpetual copyright. The sketchy and ambiguous Statute of Anne, clear though it was on the matter of the terms, was not an effective source of rationale for the defense of the general public interest either. Perhaps the most important early published statement in defense of the public interest was Lord Kames's speech, but, despite Kames's personal stature both as a jurist and an author, his speech was delivered in a comparatively marginal context and it was soon lost in the publicity that attended the *Donaldson* decision and Lord Camden's address to the House of Lords.

IV

THE WEAKNESS OF PUBLIC DOMAIN DISCOURSE IN THE LAW

James Boyle notes that the anti-monopoly position did not represent an affirmative defense of the public interest so much as it did a criticism of literary property.[39] Perhaps, when blended with Enlightenment ideas about the circulation of knowledge as it was by both Locke and Kames, the anti-monopoly position might be understood as having something of an affirmative dimension. Nonetheless, it is clear that such arguments were better suited to legislative deliberation than to common law debate. Indeed, every time the matter came before the legislature, the perpetuity was defeated.[40] Whenever it came before the English law courts, however, the issue was approached in terms of property theory. Samuel Johnson might speak eloquently about works belonging to the public for the general good of the world, but the lawyers had a harder time than Johnson in dismissing a property right that, as even Johnson said, "should from its nature be perpetual."[41] That the English lawyers were able to develop a strong discourse of property rights but not an equivalent discourse of public rights should not be very surprising. As the adage has it, possession is nine-tenths of the law—or, as I would like to understand it, the law is mostly about property. The eighteenth century common lawyers had a much easier time thinking about copyright in terms of property rights—either pro or con—than they did in thinking about how to formulate the claims of civil society. The conclusion that one is forced to reach, then, is that in the early period in which modern copyright was forming in England, the legal discourse related to the public domain was feeble when compared to the strong arguments for authors' property rights.

The comparative weakness of public domain discourse contributes to Eaton S. Drone's conviction that *Donaldson* was wrongly decided,[42] and the compara-

39. Boyle, *supra* note 1, at 120-125.

40. That is to say, in 1709, when the House of Commons limited the term in the Statute of Anne; in 1774, when the House of Lords refused to confirm the perpetuity in *Donaldson*; and in 1842, in the context of Talfourd's movement for an extended term, when Parliament limited the term to the author's life plus seven years. Although *Donaldson* was, of course, a legal decision, nonetheless, the act of overturning the chancery decree by a vote of the full House of Lords was in practice more like a legislative than a legal decision.

41. BOSWELL, *supra* note 5, at 546.

42. DRONE, *supra* note 35, at 40-42.

tive weakness of public domain discourse remains evident today. As Lawrence Lessig puts it, "to question the universality and inevitability of complete propertization is [today] to mark yourself as an outsider."[43] The two hundred years of progressive expansion of property rights that followed the resolution of the eighteenth century copyright debates resulted in the present state of copyright. In this period, protection has been systematically extended to cover a wider and wider range of materials for longer and longer periods of time. Macaulay's "tax on readers" speech, for example, was framed in opposition to Talfourd's proposal that the term of copyright be extended to the life of the author plus sixty years, but in both Britain and the United States, the basic copyright term is now longer than that which Macaulay opposed. True, Locke and Johnson both imagined copyright terms that were long and based on the author's life, but neither imagined anything like the depth of protection that modern copyright affords. In the early period, protection did not extend to abridgements or translations, and the right protected was specifically the right to print and publish. Today, protection extends to every kind of derivative that may be produced from a work, and the right protected is not merely the right to print but to make copies of any kind including photocopies for one's own use. Copyright has therefore ceased to be primarily a matter of concern to booksellers; or even a matter of concern to booksellers and authors. It has become a subject of general concern.

V

CONCLUSION

Habermas's study of the public sphere in connection with the dual emergence of copyright and the public domain in the eighteenth century also describes the structural transformation of the public sphere, the process that he describes as its "hollowing out" in the context of advanced capitalism in the nineteenth and twentieth centuries.[44] Just as the early history of copyright is embedded in the formation of the public sphere, so the later history is embedded in the structural transformation of the public sphere. Any detailed discussion of that history is beyond the scope of this discussion, but it is apparent that the eighteenth century debates did not produce a legal discourse of public rights strong enough to balance the discourse of property rights.[45] Perhaps the single

43. Lawrence Lessig, *The Architecture of Innovation*, 51 DUKE L. J. 1783, 1784 (2002).

44. HABERMAS, *supra* note 4, at 141-80.

45. My focus has been on the English copyright debates of the eighteenth century, but in revolutionary France and the republican United States the discussion was somewhat different from that in Britain. In late eighteenth century France, the author was represented in some quarters as a public servant with the nation as his or her heirs, but within a few decades authorial legal identity began its course toward reprivitization. *See* CARLA HESSE, PUBLISHING AND CULTURAL POLITICS IN REVOLUTIONARY PARIS, 1789-1810, at 83-124, 205-39 (1991). American discourse of the Federal period also emphasized the public nature of print. *See* Meredith L. McGill, *The Matter of the Text: Commerce, Print Culture, and the Authority of the State in American Copyright Law*, 9 AM. LITERARY HIST. 21 (1997). How do we get from the public concerns of the Federal period to the emphatically privatized position of Eaton S. Drone in 1879? One turning point is *Wheaton v. Peters*, 33 U.S. 591

most important moment in the establishment of the public domain was, as this article suggests, the foundational case of *Donaldson* in 1774, which confirmed that the term of protection was limited. But, at the same time, *Donaldson* appears in hindsight to have been, so far as the development of a discourse of the public domain is concerned, something of a rhetorical disaster. Lord Camden's famous speech to the House of Lords may have influenced the lords in their decision, but it also probably did long-term damage to the cause of the public domain.

At the present moment, as we attempt to argue for the value of the public domain, we need to understand that we are fashioning a rhetoric as well as a politics of the public domain. Casting a defense of the public domain on the model of the environmental movement seems promising. As Boyle notes, before the movement, the environment was in effect invisible.[46] Likewise, one element of the task today is to make the public domain visible—to develop an affirmative discourse that will make it a positive and prominent part of the social and cultural landscape. Part of the rhetorical strength of such an environmental model is that it draws on a metaphor that is already deeply embedded in copyright thought. Rhetoric is crucial. And the English copyright debates of the eighteenth century illuminate both the difficulties and the importance of the rhetorical task.

(1834), in which, as McGill notes, the U.S. Supreme Court emphasized the limited nature of U.S. copyright, but also, I would add, incorporated the property discourse of the English debates into American law. For an excellent comparative discussion of French and American copyright law in the early period, see Jane C. Ginsburg, *A Tale of Two Copyrights: Literary Property in Revolutionary France and America*, *in* OF AUTHORS AND ORIGINS: ESSAYS ON COPYRIGHT LAW 131 (Brad Sherman & Alain Strowel eds., 1994).

46. Boyle, *supra* note 1, at 69-74.

***

ROMANS, ROADS, AND ROMANTIC CREATORS: TRADITIONS OF PUBLIC PROPERTY IN THE INFORMATION AGE

CAROL M. ROSE*

I

INTRODUCTION

In a recent publication, the historian Paul Greenough addresses what he describes as the "standard environmental narrative" ("SEN") about the relationships between people and the forest in southern Asia—a narrative that casts the local forest-dwellers of the past as something akin to keepers or caretakers of the forest. Greenough observes that when he encounters this generic and romantic "SEN," he always wants to know where the wild animals are.[1] Wildlife may seem thrilling and attractive to those who do not have to contend with it, but in the nineteenth century colonial Indian subcontinent, the animals of the forest were in constant battle with the villagers. The villagers thrived when the tigers and elephants were at bay, and they were horrified and demoralized when these creatures flourished, trampling crops and devouring the village women who carried firewood home from the woods. Indeed, when the wildlife gained sufficient ground, the villagers sometimes abandoned their homes, which were reclaimed by the trees and vines and their animal inhabitants.[2]

One might surmise that people who hold intellectual property rights have much the same attitude about the public domain that South Asian villagers once had about the jungle: Like the jungle and its beasts, the public domain threatens to overrun them at every turn. Try as they might to cultivate their little properties, their patents and copyrights expire, their secrets get found out, their trademarks come into general usage, and all these erstwhile possessions return to the wild of the public domain, where the savage creatures indiscriminately gobble up everything. Incidentally, people who have carved

---

This article is also available at http://www.law.duke.edu/journals/66LCPCarolRose.

* Gordon Bradford Tweedy Professor of Law and Organization, Yale Law School.

For their very helpful comments on earlier drafts, I would like to thank James Boyle, Arthur Campbell, Rochelle Dreyfus, and Kenji Yoshino, as well as the participants at the law faculty workshops at New York University and California Western, and of course, the Duke Symposium on the Public Domain.

1. Paul Greenough, *Naturae Ferae: Wild Animals in South Asia and the Standard Environmental Narrative*, *in* AGARARIAN STUDIES: SYNTHETIC WORK AT THE CUTTING EDGE 141, 141-147 (James C. Scott & Nina Bhatt eds., 2001).

2. *Id.* at 12-20.

out niches in the public lands of the United States seem to have much the same attitude about the more tangible version of the public domain: They are always at risk of being gobbled up by its environmental laws, its threats of increased grazing fees, and its newly-declared National Monuments and Roadless Areas.[3]

Both in such tangible spaces and in the "spaces" of intellectual endeavor, it is intriguing that the raging wildness of the public domain has so many champions. Is this simply a matter of ignoring the cultivated spaces of the villagers and leaving them to their fate? Or is there something positive to be said for these wild spaces in their own right?

No doubt, one ground for a favorable view of the public domain in what I will call "Intellectual Space" is simply that the positive arguments for exclusive property rights are so much thinner here than they are in what I will call "Tangible Space." It is widely thought that, with respect to tangible matters, two forceful Utilitarian arguments support exclusive property. The first is that exclusive property rights prevent wasteful overuse of resources and stave off the much-discussed "Tragedy of the Commons" that often accompanies open access.[4] The second is that exclusive property encourages optimal investment in resource development, since the gains and losses from that investment come back to the owner.[5]

In Intellectual Space, the first of these familiar arguments falls away, since there is no physical resource to be ruined by overuse. Books, tapes, and words may be copied, inventions may be imitated, pictures may be reproduced—all without the slightest damage to the original. Hence the Utilitarian case for exclusive rights in Intellectual Space rests entirely on the second argument, that the grant of exclusive property encourages appropriate investment in creativity. To be sure, there are non-Utilitarian arguments for intellectual property rights too, particularly claims based on labor or personality, but these are shared to a large degree with property in tangible resources. The long and short of it, then, is that exclusive property rights come up long in Tangible Space but rather short in Intellectual Space. This means that although there is still a case for property in the intellectual realm, the commons or the public domain is relatively more thinkable.

In this paper, I am going to leverage this point of the comparative advantage of publicness in Intellectual Space. To do so, I will turn to the other side, to Tangible Space, to ask whether there is a case to be made *even here* for the public domain. One would think that if the public domain is at all attractive in

---

3. For a tempered but sympathetic view of related grievances, see A. Dan Tarlock, *Can Cowboys Become Indians? Protecting Western Communities as Endangered Cultural Remnants*, 31 ARIZ. ST. L.J. 539 (1999).

4. For both propositions, see 2 WILLIAM BLACKSTONE, COMMENTARIES *3-*8 (describing humanity's early use of resources in common, leading to waste, leading to the creation of property to encourage investment); for a more modern version, see RICHARD A. POSNER, ECONOMIC ANALYSIS OF LAW 30 (3d ed. 1986) (similar points but stressing investment, citing Blackstone). The tragedy derives from Garrett Hardin, *The Tragedy of the Commons*, SCI., Dec. 13, 1968 at 1243.

5. BLACKSTONE, *supra* note 4, at *7.

Tangible Space, where there is such a strong argument to the contrary based on the potential waste of resources, then the arguments for the public domain should be even more compelling in Intellectual Space, where the counter-arguments for exclusivity are cut in half.

Ultimately, I will conclude that to some degree this surmise is true—that the arguments for the public domain are more persuasive in Intellectual Space—but the examination of "publicness" in Tangible Space reveals a number of considerations and limitations, some of which carry over into Intellectual Space. I am going to work through those considerations by reflecting on a very old body of thought, namely the Roman law's categories of nonexclusive property.[6] Anything that I say here should be taken, as the Romans said, *cum grano salis*, because I am at best a novice both in Roman law and in matters of intellectual property. All the same, I will suggest that the Roman law's reasons for the "publicness" of some tangible property might carry some weight in the intellectual realm as well—but so do some of the Roman law's limitations and qualifications on the "publicness" of property.

Unfortunately for the public domain, much of the interest in nonexclusive property began to melt away from Western legal thinking by the seventeenth century, a phenomenon that the legal historian Daniel Coquilette has ascribed to the growing visibility of the enclosure movement.[7] As Coquillette points out, Grotius cast doubt on whether some of the older Roman legal categories of nonexclusive property could really be called property at all,[8] and two centuries later, the American James Kent could observe that what was called "common property" was rapidly vanishing from American law.[9]

These developments displaced an earlier tradition of legal thought about nonexclusive property in the Roman law, as it was compiled and interpreted through the centuries. To be sure, the surviving sources of the Roman law did not develop the various types of nonexclusive property at any great length.[10] Moreover, the distinctions in the classical texts themselves seem "rather fluid," as one Roman law scholar delicately put it.[11] Nevertheless, the range of the accepted Roman law categories of nonexclusive property do at least give us a glimpse of a variety of concerns—concerns that are often blithely lumped together as "the commons" in our own legal and economic thinking.

---

6. Some others have also turned to the Roman law in analyzing aspects of intellectual property, though in a somewhat different way. *See, e.g.*, Russ VerSteeg, *The Roman Law Roots of Copyright*, 59 MD. L. REV. 522 (2000) (finding Roman law doctrines implicit in the private property of copyright).

7. Daniel R. Coquillette, *Mosses from an Old Manse: Another Look at Some Historic Property Cases about the Environment*, 64 CORNELL. L. REV. 761, 807-809 (1979).

8. *Id.* at 807.

9. *Id.* at 807 n.223.

10. *Id.* at 801-803.

11. WILLIAM. W. BUCKLAND, A TEXT-BOOK OF ROMAN LAW FROM AUGUSTUS TO JUSTINIAN 184 (rev., 3d ed., 1963); *cf.* ROBERT W. LEE, THE ELEMENTS OF ROMAN LAW: WITH A TRANSLATION OF THE INSTITUTES OF JUSTINIAN 109 (4th ed. 1956) (remarking of the classical distinctions, "[a]ll this is very confused").

Because these categories seem "fluid" even to scholars who know much more than I do about these historical matters, I will give a somewhat stylized version of the Roman law classes of nonexclusive property, along with the reasons why that body of law treated different classes of property as open to the public. Although the Roman law itself appears to have been quite relentlessly concerned with tangible property and not at all with intellectual property,[12] I will try to tease out applications and analogies to arguments for the public domain in the intellectual realm.

What follows, then, is a rough typology of nonexclusive property under the Roman law—its applications and limitations in the realm of tangible things, and the analogies and contrasts that might be drawn in the realm of intellectual achievements.

II

RES NULLIUS: THINGS BELONGING TO NO ONE

Aside from religious objects (of which more later), this first category of *res nullius* consists of things that are not by their nature nonexclusive; they have simply not yet been appropriated by anyone.[13] Fish and game animals are frequent examples in the literature, as is abandoned property and, interestingly and perhaps horribly, enemy property. With all these resources, the reduction of the "thing" to exclusive property is simply a matter of human desire, time, and effort—and nonexclusive property simply results from the lack of those qualities with respect to the thing in question.[14] In the United States, a much larger example lies in the public lands of the West as they existed up until the closing of the range in 1934.[15] Although these lands officially belonged to the United States, until that time they were effectively open for the taking, aside from often ignored Indian claims. By 1934, the areas that people considered the most valuable for mines, agriculture, forestry, water development, and other uses had already been appropriated. What was left behind to the supervision of what became the vastly overextended Bureau of Land Management ("BLM") were those lands that the settlers considered worthless, or at least as more trouble than they were worth—*res nullius*, it seemed, and likely to stay that way.[16] By the present, of course, attitudes about BLM lands have changed dramatically, and people now want to use these often strikingly austere and beautiful lands for everything from grazing to mining to dune-buggying to white-water rafting. Controversies rage over whether parts or all of these lands should be appropriable, and for what. Indeed, they would be appropriable for

---

12. VerSteeg, *supra* note 6, at 523-24.

13. BUCKLAND, *supra* note 11 at 184; WILLIAM A. HUNTER, INTRODUCTION TO ROMAN LAW 59-60 (rev., 9th ed., 1934).

14. HUNTER, *supra* note 13, at 60.

15. GEORGE CAMERON COGGINS ET AL., FEDERAL PUBLIC LAND AND RESOURCES LAW 133-34 (4th ed. 2001).

16. *Id.* at 133-34, 139, 142-43.

almost anything, if we still considered them *res nullius*, and if we continued to ignore the prior claims of Native Americans.

What about ideas and expressions and inventions in their undiscovered or un-created state? Insofar as they are open to the public, might they be *res nullius*, things simply awaiting appropriation? To a degree, yes, insofar as someone might use secrecy to keep exclusive use of some invention or discovery. Secrecy, however, is difficult to maintain in many intellectual endeavors, and since one cannot "appropriate" intellectual matters in any other ways in the natural world, it is difficult to class them with the appropriable-but-not-yet-appropriated things of *res nullius*. Hence, one might more easily see most intellectual matters as falling within the next Roman law category, to wit:

III

RES COMMUNES: THINGS OPEN TO ALL BY THEIR NATURE

Res communes encapsulates what might be called the Impossibility Argument against private property: The character of some resources makes them incapable of "capture" or any other act of exclusive appropriation.

Before coming to intellectual matters, let us first consider *res communes* in tangible things, as the Roman lawyers did. The usual Roman law examples of *res communes* resources were the oceans and the air mantle, since they were impossible for anyone to own.[17] Though the Roman lawyers did not say much about them, modern environmentalists might add the stocks of wild animals and fish—that is, wildlife *stocks* as opposed to individual wild specimens, which of course can be captured. Some wild stocks are indeed small and localized enough to be susceptible to common ownership by fishing communities, as in the well-known lobster fishing grounds around Monhegan Island.[18] But taken as wholes, many wildlife and fishing stocks are like the air or the oceans, in that they seem too wide ranging and diffuse for exclusive possession—whale stocks span the oceans, butterflies and hummingbirds cross continents.

Like the air and the open waters, however, such large and dispersed stocks are ultimately finite, and their seeming limitlessness only makes them more vulnerable to overhunting, overfishing, or pollution.[19] The English common law, while much influenced by Roman law, may have been more sensitive to the potential congestibility and exhaustibility of running water and fish stocks and air. Hence the English did assert that there was a kind of ownership or at least general supervision of such things through larger political institutions. To use Blackstone's language, in order to avoid the "disturbances and quarrels [that] would frequently arise" about such matters, the common law "wisely cut up the

---

17. HUNTER, *supra* note 13, at 65.

18. *See generally* JAMES M. ACHESON, THE LOBSTER GANGS OF MAINE (1988) (describing island fishing grounds and their governance).

19. H. Scott Gordon, *The Economic Theory of a Common-Property Resource: The Fishery*, 62 J. POL. ECON. 124 (1954); *see also* JAMES R. MCGOODWIN, CRISIS IN THE WORLD'S FISHERIES 61-64 (1990) (describing heavy decimation of open access fish stocks in modern era).

root of dissension, by vesting the things themselves in the sovereign of the state."[20] In the twentieth century, some nation-states have extended this pattern, claiming the resources of the ocean waters at least out to a two-hundred-mile limit.

In the last decade, we have seen a much more dramatic turn in the "propertization" of what might seem to be "un-ownable" diffuse resources or *res communes* in the tangible world. Since 1990, the United States has treated the air itself as national property, capping the air's use for certain types of pollution and then granting individually-held Tradeable Environmental Allowances ("TEAs") for limited pollution rights. Other countries, notably Australia and New Zealand, have adopted similar programs for limited but tradeable individual rights in portions of certain fish stocks.[21] As with intellectual property rights, the major objective of TEAs appears to be the encouragement of appropriate levels and directions of investment. When polluters have to buy TEAs, they may think about investing in prevention instead, and when fishers must buy fishing allotments, they may think about using their boats for something other than fishing.[22]

Currently, TEAs are in force only in very limited spheres, despite the enormous theoretical interest in them. Putting aside the political problems, it is still too expensive and complicated to work out tradeable rights in most complex ecosystem resources.[23] But this does not prevent calls for more. Tradeable rights have been discussed for new types of fisheries, wildlife habitat, and air pollutants (notably greenhouse gases), despite thorny questions about whether the ecosystem services derived from one set of resources can make up for losses in another.

These developments in property rights suggest that while the "impossibility argument" for *res communes* still has some force in Tangible Space, innovations in the law are chipping away at it. Governmental advances in measurement, record-keeping, and legal enforcement have allowed things once thought incapable of ownership to become ownable after all.

Now, what about Intellectual Space? Even more than air, water, or fisheries, intellectual achievements seem closely aligned to the Roman law idea of *res communes* as things incapable of ownership. Some inventions, of course,

---

20. BLACKSTONE, *supra* note 4, at *14, *15. Blackstone mentioned here *inter alia* "waste" lands and game animals.

21. *See* Carol M. Rose, *Expanding the Choices for the Global Commons: Comparing Newfangled Tradable Allowance Schemes to Old-Fashioned Common Property Regimes*, 10 DUKE ENVTL. L. & POL'Y F. 45, 51 (1999) (comparing TEAs to community based property).

22. *Id.* at 60. Aside from payment, TEAs do little in themselves to induce their holders to avoid overuse, since the holders of TEAs still have incentives to cheat on their individual allotments. The policing of overuse instead generally falls on the governments that enforce and monitor the overall system of rights.

23. Thomas W. Merrill, *Explaining Market Mechanisms*, 2000 U. ILL. L. REV. 275, 285, 296-98 (2000) (describing the small number of market-based environmental programs, attributing this to combination of cost and political obstacles); James Salzman & J. B. Ruhl, *Currencies and the Commodification of Environmental Law*, 53 STAN. L. REV. 607, 622-27 (2000) (describing difficulties of "nonfungibilities" in ecosystem trades).

may be "owned" through secrecy, and indeed, one of the objects of intellectual property law is to induce inventors to disclose secrets so that others may build on their ideas. But inventive secrets, especially commercially valuable ones, have long been subject to the intense scrutiny of rivals, and every successful feat of reverse engineering makes the invention slip further away from the inventor's exclusive grasp.[24] Moreover, secrecy is particularly ill suited to another main preoccupation of intellectual property, the protection of expressions, since secrecy would generally defeat the expression itself.[25] It is in this sense that intellectual matters seem akin to *res communes*: The inventor, and even more the artist, may have only limited ability to keep exclusive control over her achievements.

But what can give her that control is intellectual property law itself. Hence, in intellectual matters as in environmental ones, advances in legal thought and governmental administration undermine the "impossibility argument" at the foundation of *res communes*. Preliminarily, one might even say that the function of intellectual property is to turn *res communes*, things by their nature incapable of ownership, into *res nullius*, things not yet owned but capable of appropriation.

Indeed, legal regimes go further than this: Appropriation via intellectual property presumably adds to social well-being by creating appropriate incentives to invest in creative ideas. But in a development worrisome to many, private parties now use law to go beyond the more constrained private rights of intellectual property. Instead, some have deployed contract law to erect more far-reaching property-like barriers on intellectual products, as in the shrink-wrap contracts of software packaging.[26]

What about cyberspace? Could the ease of copying on this medium set up a last holdout for *res communes*, an arena where exclusive property is truly impossible? Some scholars argue that it could, because cyberspace is supposedly too vast and diffuse for its information flows to yield even to government management, much less to private ownership.[27] Yet here too, *res communes* may be somewhat open to doubt. Other scholars of cyberspace argue that growing legal and governmental capacities will permit something like ownership in many areas.[28] Indeed, when some members of the Clinton

---

24. Pamela Samuelson & Susan Scotchmer, *The Law and Economics of Reverse Engineering*, 111 YALE L. J. 1575, 1577 (2002).

25. Some religious ceremonies and ceremonial arts, however, are kept secret because they can be undermined by publicity. *See* Christine Haight Farley, *Protecting Folklore of Indigenous Peoples: Is Intellectual Property the Answer?* 30 CONN. L. REV. 1, 14-15 (1997) (arguing that some indigenous peoples resist publicity for religious art).

26. Mark Lemley, *Beyond Preemption: The Law and Policy of Intellectual Property Licensing*, 87 CAL. L. REV. 111 (1999) (attacking current contract law as bypassing public rights that are embedded in intellectual property law). *See, e.g.*, ProCD v. Zeidenberg, 908 F.Supp. 640 (W.D. Wis. 1996).

27. *See* David R. Johnson & David Post, *Law and Borders—The Rise of Law in Cyberspace*, 48 STAN. L. REV. 1367, 1370-78, 1390-91 (1996) (arguing that governments cannot control cyberspace).

28. Lawrence Lessig, *The Zones of Cyberspace*, 48 STAN. L. REV. 1403, 1408-09 (1996) (disputing the argument that cyberspace cannot be controlled).

Administration proposed a number of extensions of intellectual property into cyberspace, the ensuing heated exchange suggested that, whatever the wisdom of the policy of propertization, it is at least possible that patent and copyright law can spread property well into the digital world.[29] Subsequent legislation has only made that fact more obvious.[30]

From all appearances, then, it seems that the impossibility argument behind *res communes* cannot be the only support for the public domain in intellectual matters. Hence, it should not be any surprise that the current arguments for the public domain in Intellectual Space necessarily go beyond the simply naturalistic and become normative as well. Are there analogies to such normative arguments in Tangible Space? Yes, there are, and once again they are reflected in another Roman law category of nonexclusive property—one that is particularly salient to modern questions of intellectual endeavor and hence meriting a somewhat lengthy treatment:

IV

RES PUBLICAE: THINGS BELONGING TO THE PUBLIC AND OPEN TO THE PUBLIC BY OPERATION OF LAW

A. *Res publicae* in Tangible Space

The classic examples of *res publicae* for Roman law were roads, harbors, ports, bridges, rivers that flowed year-round, and lands immediately adjacent thereto.[31] Apparently this category was frequently mixed up with *res communes*,[32] just as in more modern times we tend to mix up normative arguments for "publicness" with naturalistic arguments about the impossibility of owning certain resources. What is the normative case for holding such properties open to the public? As Richard Epstein has pointed out, the case for holding property open to the public is stronger where there is little danger of overuse and where little investment is required, as in ocean lanes.[33] Some examples of *res publicae* do seem to fall into this category, such as some waterways and their shorelines. Nevertheless, other examples of *res publicae*, such as roads, harbors, and bridges, are clearly subject to congestion and overuse and require investment.

Low levels of congestibility and modest needs for investment, then, cannot be the only explanation for *res publicae*. Moreover, this normative category of inherently public property was not just a quirk of Roman law, but a concept

29. *See* Pamela Samuelson, *The Copyright Grab*, WIRED MAG., Jan. 1996, at 134 (opposing copyright extensions in digital communications).

30. *See* Maureen Ryan, *Cyberspace as Public Space: A Public Trust Paradigm for Copyright in a Digital World*, 79 OR. L. REV. 647, 670-74 (2001) (describing recent intellectual property legislation).

31. BUCKLAND, *supra* note 11, at 183; HUNTER, *supra* note 13, at 65-66; ANDREW BORKOWSKI, TEXTBOOK ON ROMAN LAW 143 (1994).

32. *See* BORKOWSKI, *supra* note 31, at 144 (describing seashores).

33. Richard A. Epstein, *On the Optimal Mix of Private and Common Property*, *in* PROPERTY RIGHTS 17, 27-28 (Ellen Frankel Paul et al. eds., 1994).

with continuing vitality in Western law. If anything it became most firmly fixed in our own United States, this most commercial of all republics, where one would suppose that the arguments for publicness would be steadfastly rejected. Nevertheless, the normative claims of publicness run like a red thread (yes, that kind of red) through our law, most strikingly in the continuing idea of a "public trust" in resources that very closely resemble the major examples of *res publicae* in Roman law.[34] Those resources are overwhelmingly the physical spaces required for mobility—lanes for travel, transportation, navigation, and communication among distant locations.[35] For the Romans, such spaces were initially developed into *res publicae* primarily for military reasons,[36] but for Americans, they came to serve as the backbone of commerce itself.

What are the characteristics that call for publicly-protected open access to such spaces? In the past there were several, and at least in the American law of "inherently public" property, they have had to exist in combination. The first characteristic is what economists call "transaction costs." Travel lanes like roads and waterways are typically long and thin,[37] and hence they are vulnerable to many possibilities for obstruction and bottlenecks, where any one of multiple miscreants or opportunistic adjacent owners can effectively take control of the whole length of the road. If the public is to use such ways, they may well require the protection of public officers or judges against these multiple threats of obstruction.[38] In a way, the problem for *res publicae* in Tangible Space is not that its appropriation is impossible, but rather that it is all too easy to appropriate.

But why *should* the public have open access to these otherwise appropriable properties, particularly in light of the ever-lurking threat of congestion, overuse and underinvestment in tangible things that are open to the public? This brings in the second and especially critical factor—the presence of wide-ranging synergies, or what are now called network effects. Nineteenth century courts located the center of the "publicness" of travel lanes in their suitability for commerce, but commerce itself is endlessly synergistic. Commerce permits and encourages specialization, and in so doing, wider commerce exponentially enhances the value of all parties' property: One can invest in one's property not

34. The modern *locus classicus* for the public trust concept is Joseph L. Sax, *The Public Trust Doctrine in Natural Resource Law: Effective Judicial Intervention*, 68 MICH. L. REV. 471 (1970) (describing public trust doctrine in U.S. law). *See also* Coquillette, *supra* note 7, at 809-820.

35. Carol M. Rose, *The Comedy of the Commons: Custom, Commerce, and Inherently Public Property*, 53 U. CHI. L. REV. 711, 774 (1986) [hereinafter Rose, *Comedy*]; *see also* Carol M. Rose, *Joseph Sax and the Idea of the Public Trust*, 25 ECOLOGY L.Q. 351, 359-60 (1998) (describing centrality of commerce in public trust idea).

36. *See* T. W. POTTER, ROMAN ITALY 130 (1987) (describing Roman road system as having primarily military significance, though noting also commercial uses, as in the Via Salaria, an important route in the salt trade).

37. *See* Lakeside Park Co. v. Forsmark, 153 A.2d 486, 487 (Pa. 1959) (describing navigable and hence public water as a long, thin "roadway of water" that joins communities).

38. *See* Rose, *Comedy*, *supra* note 35, at 749-50 (noting that potential monopolization was one rationale for public claims to roads and waterways; noting also the similarity to eminent domain rationales).

only for one's own use, but for the use of the person in the trading community who most values it. The greater the network of trade, the larger the market, the greater the opportunities for specialization, and the better for all participants.[39]

Traders have typically needed physical routes for transportation, and even though there may be congestion costs to those routes, there are ever-larger offsetting gains. The costs of congestion and overuse increase only arithmetically as lanes of trade are more widely used. While these costs must indeed be managed (a point to which I will return), the social benefits from the ensuing trade are exponential, and thus on the routes of *res publicae*, the more the merrier. Communication is similar. Consider the telephone network: As with other communications networks, the larger this network is, the more valuable it is for all participants, and the more the cross-fertilization of ideas can lead to still more ideas.

A related synergistic factor has to be teased out of American public trust law. This factor derives from the idea that commerce can play an educative and civilizing role. Republican theory at least as far back as Montesquieu and the Scottish Enlightenment suggested that commerce is "gentle," softening manners that would be hardened by the aristocratic characteristics of honor and pride.[40] Commerce instead requires that the participants pay attention to the wants and desires of their counterparts, and in learning to do so, they perforce learn to work with others and become interested in and sympathetic to people whom they might otherwise disdain.[41] There is, indeed, a whole panoply of arguments that commerce constitutes the social glue of democratic self-governance—for example, that property and trade are a school for rights-consciousness, that commerce deflects people from ideological enmity, and that commerce teaches us to operate by consent rather than force.[42]

Some of these arguments are more convincing, some less so, and some may seem odd when we often hear the worst aristocratic vices—callousness, brutality, grandiosity—associated with business and its "robber barons." Nevertheless, there is evidence from modern historians and experimental psychologists, among others, that trading relations can indeed turn into philanthropy, mutual aid, and what is now sometimes called social capital.[43] If we think of commerce in this light—as contributing to the political synergies of democratic self-governance—then it is not an accident that public claims on tangible property spilled over from the roads of commerce to public squares

39. *Id.* at 769-771 (describing combination of holdout and interactivity as prerequisites for public trust claims, particularly with respect to commercial lanes).

40. ALBERT HIRSCHMAN, THE PASSIONS AND THE INTERESTS 55-60 (1977).

41. *Id.*; Rose, *Comedy*, *supra* note 35, at 775-76.

42. Carol M. Rose, *Property as the Keystone Right?*, 71 NOTRE DAME L. REV. 329, 348-51, 354-55 (1996).

43. *See* FRANCIS FUKUYAMA, TRUST: THE SOCIAL VIRTUES AND THE CREATION OF PROSPERITY (1995) (describing commercial relations in several countries, their influence on social capital); Peter Kollock, *The Emergence of Exchange Structures: An Experimental Study of Uncertainty, Commitment, and Trust*, 100 AM. J. SOC. 313, 337-39 (1994) (reporting positive mutual attitudes of subjects in successful simulated trade relations).

and to other places for public speech and political communication.[44] It is not an accident that the lanes of travel, transportation, communication, and commerce are called *res publicae*, the very root of the republic. And finally, perhaps it is not an accident that attacks on the transportation system seem to strike the republic at its core.

Two caveats are in order about *res publicae*, however. The first is that *res publicae* is far from an untamed place, where "anything goes." On the contrary, precisely because of the potential problems of congestion and underinvestment, the public in *res publicae* must behave in an orderly fashion. Nineteenth century case law gave a clear picture of a public that was subject to customary rules of usage, and today's users of roads, highways, and waterways on the whole continue to vindicate that picture. The expectation was, and is, that drivers would move to the right to avoid oncoming traffic; that sailors would try to avoid fishermen's nets; that travelers who had to leave the road to avoid obstructions would take the closest and least damaging route through the adjacent private property.[45] In short, one is expected to behave one's self in the spaces of *res publicae*.

On the whole, however, the customary norms relevant to *res publicae* are relatively thin, and they can suffice to keep order only at very minor levels of congestion. Greater congestion may require road signs, harbor development, traffic management, lighthouses, air traffic control, piracy policing—any of which may easily surpass the capacity of a public that governs itself by informal norms alone. For that reason, we have to call on organized government to keep the spaces of *res publicae* in order. This was true for the Romans as well; it is no wonder that the Roman law's examples of *res publicae* included a large number of goods supplied and financed by organized governments.[46] The vision of the public domain in *res publicae* is tame rather than wild, more like a park than a wilderness, a set of public spaces most often overseen by organized public institutions.

A second caveat: The concept of *res publicae* was by no means antagonistic to private property. The two combined elements in *res publicae* are synergistic effects, taken together with the possibility of monopoly. There are many arenas in which synergistic effects give rise to public concern—for example, in health and education—but in which no particular input resources might generate holdout or bottleneck, and hence little worry about monopolistic private ownership of the relevant inputs. Even where bottleneck or monopoly does loom, as in railroads or ferryboats or airlines, private entities may still own the relevant resources, subject to requirements of reasonable public access. Indeed, if the public is otherwise adequately served, the concept of *res publicae* may

---

44. Rose, *Comedy*, *supra* note 35, at 753, 778.

45. *Id.* at 744-45.

46. POTTER, *supra* note 36, at 134 (stating that road maintenance was primarily at public expense); *cf. id.* at 82-83 (describing private finance of municipal baths and theaters by wealthy persons vying for political office and influence).

present no obstacle to additional private properties of the same kind—toll roads and the like—without much additional governmental supervision.

The most important point, however, is that the idea of *res publicae* works hand in glove with a regime in which most resources are the subject of private property. Indeed, open public access to commercial lanes would make little sense without an underlying regime of private property and trade. The openness of trade routes presumes that the users of these routes have their own incentives to trade, and that those incentives come in large part from private ownership.

B. The Internet as *Res publicae*

All this brings me to the counterparts to *res publicae* in Intellectual Space. The closest analogies clearly lie in modern telecommunications, and perhaps especially in the Internet. The roads and waterways of the tangible and traditional *res publicae* allowed goods and information to flow freely, and the Internet does the same; here ideas can cross-fertilize one another in wonderful synergies of creativity.[47] Indeed, the Internet even has the name "information superhighway," though that moniker now sounds slightly dated.

Looking at the Internet as the most obvious example of *res publicae* in Intellectual Space, let us take up the first of the caveats about the traditional *res publicae*, namely the question of governance. The *res publicae* in tangible property is a park and not a wilderness; but what about the Internet? Clearly the Internet is also not an arena where "anything goes." It has its protocols, its webmasters, its internal governance to repress vandals and promote orderly flows of information. But need this governance come from *formal* government, or are informal or customary norms enough? Recall that in the traditional *res publicae*, the need for formal governance comes in large part because there may be physical congestion and physical overuse of resources; some organized body must put up the traffic light and fix the potholes. On the Internet, problems of physical infrastructure and overcrowding are less apparent. Even though one's email inbox can indeed be loaded with spam, voluntary efforts and thin norms may possibly suffice to provide whatever governance and investment we need to keep lanes more or less clear.[48]

If voluntary self-organization suffices, the Internet as *res publicae* may be more like the informal roads of the nineteenth century American countryside,

47. *See, e.g.*, Margaret Chon, *New Wine Bursting from Old Bottles: Collaborative Internet Art, Joint Works, and Entrepreneurship*, 75 OR . L. REV. 257, 274 (1996) (describing Internet's chain art).

48. Johnson & Post, *supra* note 27, at 1388-91 (arguing that cyberspace users can develop internal norms); *cf.* Llewellyn Joseph Gibbons, *No Regulation, Government Regulation, or Self-Regulation: Social Enforcement or Social Contracting of Governance in Cyberspace*, 6 CORNELL J. L. & PUB. POL'Y 475, 520-23 (1997) (noting lack of homogeneity and multi-dimensional contacts that might generate thick norms, but noting other technological and social factors in policing behavior); Margaret Jane Radin, *Property Evolving in Cyberspace*, 15 J.L. & COM. 509, 516 (1996) (suggesting that thicker norms might have been more characteristic of "early cyberspace" when users were less numerous and more homogeneous).

where customary practices seemed to be enough to enforce good behavior. Still, that story suggests that with more users, greater congestion, more vandalism and the like, more formal institutions might ultimately be required to take over what was formerly a "People's Park." And, as others have noted, more formal governance raises questions about the democratic character of the governmental institutions that might come to manage the Internet, for example what constraints they might put on information, or what issues of privacy they might encounter.[49] Many of the ancient Romans may not have had much to say about their government's management of *res publicae*, but we do about ours.[50]

The second caveat about the tangible *res publicae* concerned its relation to private property. The Internet as *res publicae*, like the transportation routes of old, has a more complicated relationship to private property than simply posing a public realm against a private one. In his article in this symposium, James Boyle describes the new efforts to expand intellectual property as a second enclosure movement.[51] It is important to point out, however, that the public domain—or *res publicae* itself, in the form of extended transportation—was critical to the *first* enclosure movement. Transportation improvements in the early modern period integrated England into a more unified market; this integration in turn fostered agricultural specialization and enclosure while undermining the older, more localized and mixed economies of the common fields.[52] Similarly today, the greater opportunities for copying and disseminating via the Internet—the new *res publicae*—may well have engendered the new efforts towards "enclosure." Many intellectual accomplishments once needed no "fences" because they were difficult to copy, but they are now available to the world through digital access and reproduction. It is this dramatically enhanced new *res publicae* of digital communication that raises the demand for a much-extended fencing in of intellectual property. Thus, if we are now seeing a second enclosure movement, we might think that, as in the first enclosure movement, the enhancement of the *public* domain of communications itself has been deeply implicated in the efforts toward *private* enclosure.

This is not to say that the new privatization efforts reflect sound policy; far from it, as many of the articles in this symposium illustrate. But the more general lesson is that it is a mistake to suppose that the public domain and

---

49. This is not to say that there are no issues of democratic governance in informal norms. *See infra* notes 73-75 and accompanying text (concerning problems of informal norms).

50. Democratic control of formal government could even make formal government more attractive than community customs. *See* Carol M. Rose, *Common Property, Regulatory Property and Environmental Protection*, in THE DRAMA OF THE COMMONS 233, 251-53 (Elinor Ostrom et al. eds., 2002) (noting antidemocratic characteristics of some community customs, rejection of customary law in United States in favor of formal laws passed by representative governments).

51. *See* James Boyle, *The Second Enclosure Movement and the Construction of the Public Domain*, 66 LAW & CONTEMP. PROBS. 33 (Winter/Spring 2003).

52. *See* CARL J. DAHLMAN, THE OPEN FIELD SYSTEM AND BEYOND: A PROPERTY RIGHTS ANALYSIS OF AN ECONOMIC INSTITUTION 106-108, 167-68 (1980) (noting poor transportation as a factor in older localized agriculture, improved transportation as part of economic integration and demise of common field system); *see also id.* at 145-59 (describing the importance of regional specialization in enclosure movement).

private property are independent realms. Instead, the two are intimately intertwined, both historically and economically.

C. Intellectual Space Generally as *Res publicae?*

Turning from the Internet itself as *res publicae*, what about the *content* of materials flowing over the Internet? Might the whole realm of intellectual endeavor be considered *res publicae*? If one looks to the most important feature of *res publicae*, the synergies that are fostered by openness to the public, the answer seems obvious: Of course there are synergies in the intellectual world. It is widely known that creators develop their ideas in part from perceiving the ideas of others. Several scholars have criticized intellectual property law for its "romantic" and unrealistic conception of the sole, heroic individual author or inventor.[53] Scientific innovators are often described as "standing on the shoulders of giants,"[54] and the point at which one inventor's ideas leave off and another's begin is often impossible to discern. But more than that, the *interactions* among creators can deliver something that is vastly more than the sum of their individual efforts. Scholars of literature even have a word for this (and one sometimes borrowed by intellectual property scholars): "intertextuality," where one literary text "converses" with others, and the conversation itself is more than the sum of the parts.[55] The same can be said for philosophic texts: Witness Kant's famous reaction to his unsettlement upon reading Hume's views on causation.[56] Thus the whole of Intellectual Space, in a sense, seems to be a candidate for treatment as *res publicae*, things open to the public by operation of law, because of the synergies among ideas.

Synergies alone, however, are not enough to make the case for *res publicae*. The other factor is transaction costs—the possibility of obstructions. If intellectual accomplishments are by their nature non-rivalrous and not easily possessed, there should be no obstruction or transaction costs to their synergistic exchange aside from the ability of creators to keep secrets, generally a doubtful proposition over the long run. Intellectual accomplishments could be safely left as *res communes* (things incapable of ownership); desirable synergies should occur without the legal protection supplied for *res publicae*.

---

53. *See* JAMES BOYLE, SHAMANS, SOFTWARE AND SPLEENS: LAW AND THE CONSTRUCTION OF THE INFORMATION SOCIETY 56-57 (1996); *see also* MARK ROSE, AUTHORS AND OWNERS: THE INVENTION OF COPYRIGHT, 125-28 (1993) (describing and criticizing the idea of creative genius); Rosemary J. Coombe, *Left Out on the Information Highway*, 75 OR. L. REV. 237, 246 (1996) (noting contributions in artwork of many unacknowledged persons).

54. Letter from Sir Issac Newton to Robert Hooke, Feb. 5, 1675 *in* 1 THE CORRESPONDENCE OF ISAAC NEWTON 416 (Herbert W. Turnbull ed., 1959).

55. *See* George Kamberelis, *Genre as Institutionally Informed Social Practice*, 6 J. CONTEMP. LEGAL ISSUES 115, 130-32 (1995) (describing literary theories of intertextuality). For Internet scholars' borrowing, see, for example, Chon, *supra* note 47, at 264-65 (applying idea of "intertext" to Internet).

56. IMMANUEL KANT, PROLEGOMENA TO ANY FUTURE METAPHYSICS 5-6 (Paul Carus trans., Bobbs-Merrill 1950) (1783).

Instead, such obstructions as exist seem to come from law itself, sometimes in the direct form of censorship, but much more pervasively in the indirect form of intellectual property law. If intellectual property rights always and ineluctably blocked other intellectual efforts, the answer would seem obvious: Call off intellectual property, allow the realm of ideas to return to a happy state in which the synergistic interactions of *res publicae* are married to the ungoverned *res communes*—ungoverned, because, by their nature, ideas and information are freely available to all.

The mere fact of private ownership, however, does not mean that interactions are blocked. On the contrary, in Tangible Space, it is generally thought that well-defined property rights make interactions *more* possible, through the vehicle of trade.[57] At least some of Intellectual Space looks the same. Clearly, people buy patent rights and pay copyright royalties all the time, and they have invented a variety of methods to reduce the transaction costs of doing so.[58] More importantly, property rights, taken together with trade, should result in an even greater spread of ideas than would occur if intellectual matters were *res communes*. In the very standard theory, property rights give people an incentive to create innovations in the first place, and then to offer them freely on the market instead of keeping them secret, since they know that they can take the proceeds from trade.

As in Tangible Space, this argument is subject to qualifications: Transaction costs may still arise, a matter very common in a regime of intellectual property. At the extreme, a proliferation of multiple intellectual property rights can cause an "anticommons," paralyzing further research or creative endeavors.[59] For such blockages, *res publicae* does apply, because here synergies are threatened by private appropriation; the *res publicae* analogy suggests such doctrines as mandatory licensing or "fair use," granting limited public access during the term of the intellectual property right.[60]

Nevertheless, it is important to recall that second caveat about *res publicae*: At least in its traditional domains, this is not a concept that is hostile to private property. Instead, the idea of the *res publicae* plays Tweedledum to the Tweedledee of private property, presupposing the private gains that induce people to go out and engage in trade. Intellectual achievements are not

57. Clifford Holderness, *A Legal Foundation for Exchange*, 14 J. LEGAL STUD. 321, 322-26 (1985).

58. Robert P. Merges, *Contracting Into Liability Rules: Intellectual Property Rights and Collective Rights Organizations*, 84 CAL. L. REV. 1293 (1996) (describing patent and copyright pools that lessen trading costs of intellectual property).

59. Michael A. Heller & Rebecca S. Eisenberg, *Can Patents Deter Innovation?* SCI., May 1, 1998, at 698-99 (arguing that excessive patents can cause an "anticommons" blocking research access to the genome); Richard Stallman, *Reevaluating Copyright: The Public Must Prevail*, 75 OR. L. REV. 291, 293-94 (1996) (arguing that the public has justifiably acquired the habit of copying). *See also* Carol M. Rose *The Several Futures of Property: Of Cyberspace and Folk Tales, Emission Trades and Ecosystems*, 83 MINN. L. REV. 129, 154 (1998) (describing blockages as a species of "too much property") [hereinafter Rose, *Several Futures*].

60. *See* Wendy J. Gordon, *Fair Use as Market Failure: A Structural and Economic Analysis of the Betamax Case and its Predecessors*, 82 COLUM. L. REV. 1600, 1614-24 (1982).

necessarily different; sometimes their creation and dissemination may depend on the inducements that property brings.

Thus, in the final analysis, the closest analogy to *res publicae* in intellectual space seems to be to the *lanes and means* of communication, rather than to the *content* of communication.

Having said that, however, it may be that the lanes of communication are not so easily separable from their content in Intellectual Space. This is most obvious with digital communication, where some form of copying is essential to communication itself. And this is true more generally in Intellectual Space; the intertextuality of creative endeavors means that, in Marshall McLuhan's famous phrase, the medium *is* the message.[61] Here one cannot so easily designate content for private property, and communication lanes for *res publicae*.

Perhaps this is why, in Intellectual Space, *res publicae* has a primarily temporal character rather than a geographic one. One of the most interesting features of intellectual property law is that over the longer run, it does turn all once-propertized intellectual achievements into *res publicae*. I mentioned earlier that intellectual property functions to turn *res communes*, things that cannot be owned, into *res nullius*, things that are unowned but are capable of appropriation. At the end of the day, however, when the patent expires and the copyright runs out, the encapsulated creations do not become *res nullius* again, open for new appropriation under the laws of intellectual property. Instead they become *res publicae*, wide open to the public forever, by operation of law. They are now "prior art" or "public domain," never to be appropriated again under intellectual property law. Indeed, for this very reason, some inventors might prefer secrecy to patents. The sometimes-criticized liberality of the U.S. Patent Office might appear different in this light: A patent does assure that after the appointed length of time, inventions do indeed become open to the public for all time.

The underlying idea of this mixed regime, where private property and *res publicae* are segregated only temporally, seems to be a differential weighting over time of the relative importance of investment on the one hand and synergies on the other. Inducements to invest weigh more heavily at the outset, but the synergies of free availability and free use weigh more heavily later on. Again, from the perspective of an outsider, it seems that this balance between early private property and later *res publicae* could be the subject of a very central debate in intellectual property law. The balance would mean that the questions of duration of rights are critical to intellectual property law.[62] It could also mean that private contractual circumventions of the legal time periods for intellectual property rights—the "shrink-wrap" contracts, the "rights management containers," and the statutes that protect such devices—are

61. *See* MARSHALL MCLUHAN, UNDERSTANDING MEDIA 7-21 (1964).

62. *See, e.g.*, Jonathan Zittrain, *The Un-Microsoft Un-Remedy: Law Can Prevent the Problem That It Can't Patch Later*, 31 CONN. L. REV. 1361, 1373 (1999) (proposing a five- or ten-year limit on software copyright).

matters of even more critical importance.[63] If the private property and *res publicae* components of intellectual property are indeed temporal, then these questions of time are the very fulcrum of the balance between the two.

All this leads to a further question: Are private property and public access the only possibilities? Are there instances in which investment incentives and intertextual synergies might be quite differently organized, coming out somewhere between the public domain and exclusive private property? A good deal of intellectual property scholarship suggests that this is indeed the case, and that much creative effort actually takes place within property regimes that are neither entirely exclusive nor completely open to the public.[64]

Readers by now should not be surprised to find that there is a Roman law category for such mixed types of property, though the category has certain limitations:

V

RES UNIVERSITATIS: PROPERTY BELONGING TO A (PUBLIC) GROUP IN ITS CORPORATE CAPACITY

The standard "owner" for the Roman *res universitatis* was a municipality, and its belongings were such public facilities as theaters and race-courses; but both private and public groups could own property in common, including lands or other income-producing property.[65] The chief limitation on *res universitatis* in Roman times was that, at least in theory, the relevant corporate bodies required the authorization of the state. Nevertheless, in post-Roman times, medieval and early modern central states were weak indeed, and their lacunae were filled with countless groups that had their own properties and that often enjoyed semi-governmental authority. Such corporate bodies included guilds, monasteries, merchant groups, common field communities, and so on. In a continuation of their practices, a corporate body even governed New York City in its early days, largely managing the city through judicious use of the corporate property.[66] Interestingly enough, *universitatis* gave its name to the modern "university," which in medieval times was a corporate body of students and teachers dedicated to education.[67]

---

63. Ryan, *supra* note 30, at 667-74 (criticizing extensions of time, rights-management containers, and statutory protections of these limitations on use of digital works).

64. For a summary of some of this scholarship and some of the issues, see Rose, *Several Futures*, *supra* note 59, at 155-62.

65. WILLIAM L. BURDICK, THE PRINCIPLES OF ROMAN LAW AND THEIR RELATION TO MODERN LAW, 280-88 (Wm. W. Gaunt 1989) (1938).

66. *See* HENDRIK HARTOG, PUBLIC PROPERTY AND PRIVATE POWER: THE CORPORATION OF THE CITY OF NEW YORK IN AMERICAN LAW, 1730-1870, at 32-68 (1983) (describing New York's governance through property). Hartzog's picture of New York is similar to early modern European "co-governing" corporate groups. *See* Carol M. Rose, *Public Property, Old and New*, 79 NW. U. L. REV. 216, 218-222 (1984).

67. BURDICK, *supra* note 65, at 283.

Given the widespread and long-lasting character of group-based, limited common property regimes in Tangible Space, it is all the more interesting that these very important forms of resource management have been so widely overlooked in modern economic thinking about the commons, at least until recently. Elinor Ostrom is one of the chief scholars who has changed that pattern, and as she and her colleagues point out, there is no reason to think that the only forms of resource governance must come from individual ownership on the one hand, or from central governmental management on the other. She and others have found numerous examples of informal group property of "common-pool resources" far beyond Europe, from irrigating communities in the Philippines, to livestock-raising communities in Japan, to fishing communities in Turkey.[68] Such communities clearly refute the idea that the commons is necessarily "tragic"; on the contrary, a number of these limited common property regimes have lasted in Tangible Space for centuries.

Such limited common property regimes may be commons on the inside, but they are property on the outside, that is, vis-a-vis non-members.[69] But why have such regimes at all? They typically exist where a resource is too large for individual ownership, but still sufficiently bounded that its exploitation is amenable to joint management by a limited group. In a sense, *res universitatis* is a bounded form of *res publicae*, lending the advantages of interaction and cooperative joint management to a resource that is ultimately finite, as exclusively held property is. Because such common property regimes are more limited in membership than the public at large, they may generate a quite dense set of norms and customary practices—much more so than on the wide open transport lanes of *res publicae*. These customary practices in turn can help to limit overuse of the common resource and prod the members to invest in the common infrastructure—for example, a fishing community may work out elaborate means of taking turns with nets, or a set of irrigating communities along a river may devise rewards and punishments that induce individual farmers to maintain their shares of the common channels.

Are there analogs to *res universitatis* in Intellectual Space, where there is little or no need to police resource decimation or to maintain a physical infrastructure? Robert Merges has argued that there are, though he does not use the Roman law name.[70] He argues that researchers are often quite willing to share information and ideas with others in the same intellectual pursuits, and that they enjoy substantial creative synergies thereby; but he also argues that they are very unwilling to share these same ideas with commercial entrepreneurs or others in the world at large, perhaps in part because of the lack of reciprocity. And scientists are not the only ones; the Internet has

68. ELINOR OSTROM, GOVERNING THE COMMONS: THE EVOLUTION OF INSTITUTIONS FOR COLLECTIVE ACTION 18-21, 65-69, 82-88 (1990).

69. Rose, *Several Futures*, *supra* note 59, at 144.

70. Robert P. Merges, *Property Rights Theory and the Commons: The Case of Scientific Research*, 13 SOC. PHIL. & POL'Y 145 (1996); *see also* Merges, *supra* note 58, at 1293-1330, 1355-58 (using Ostrom's work to support contractual regimes for common use of intellectual properties).

generated a considerable amount of collaborative creativity, from story trees to Chain Art.[71] But these collaborative efforts are not simply wide open; Internet groups have also developed methods for excluding disruptive interlopers.

Might such groups mesh together to turn *res universitatis* into *res publicae*, common spaces open to all who are interested? Ostrom's work on limited common properties has described the "nesting" of smaller common properties into larger scale non-state governance regimes, for example, in irrigation;[72] and her and Charlotte Hess' contribution to this symposium discusses similarly expanding networks for sharing digitized information.[73]

One might note, however, that such groups appear to move away from informal norms and instead to adopt self-conscious and detailed governance rules, making them less akin to norm-governed communities and rather more like the trade associations that Lisa Bernstein has so interestingly analyzed.[74] Indeed, this self-consciousness may be a good thing from the perspective of democratic governance. Tangible Space certainly presents a warning about common regimes governed only by custom and community norms: Their norms can be hierarchical, xenophobic, and backward-looking, to the point that some critics say that we need to theorize a more "liberal commons" that is organized under the auspices of more democratic laws.[75] Intellectual Space is not immune from these problems. Customary norms in the literary community, for example, have been notoriously inhospitable to women, even well into the twentieth century, and scientific communities too have sometimes been equally and unjustifiably dismissive of outsiders.[76]

In whatever ways creative communities may be organized, the point remains that in many intellectual and artistic endeavors, creativity may be synergistic less with the world at large than with communities of other artists, creators, and contributors. The university itself, sharing its root with the *res universitatis*, gives perhaps the quintessential example of the phenomenon: Creativity is exponentially enhanced by the free flow of ideas within a scholarly community. Here too there are opportunists, charlatans and zealots—and to some degree commercial users—who can disrupt the process, and thus universities try to

---

71. Chon, *supra* note 47, at 274 .

72. OSTROM, *supra* note 68, at 101-02.

73. Charlotte Hess & Elinor Ostrom, *Ideas, Artifacts, and Facilities: Information as a Common-Pool Resource*, 66 LAW & CONTEMP. PROBS. 111 (Winter/Spring 2003).

74. *See* Lisa E. Bernstein, *The Questionable Empirical Basis of Article 2's Incorporation Strategy: A Preliminary Study*, 66 U. CHI. L. REV. 710, 717-46 (1999) (analyzing trade rules of the National Hay Association, the National Feed & Grain Association, the textile industry rules, and others).

75. Hanoch Dagan & Michael Heller, *The Liberal Commons*, 110 YALE L. J. 549, 566 (2001); Carol M. Rose, *Left Brain, Right Brain and History in the New Law and Economics of Property*, 79 OR. L. REV. 479, 484-87 (2000).

76. *See generally* MARY ELLMAN, THINKING ABOUT WOMEN (1968) (very wittily discussing the pattern of dismissiveness and condescension to women authors); EVELYN FOX KELLER, A FEELING FOR THE ORGANISM: THE LIFE AND WORK OF BARBARA MCCLINTOCK (1983) (describing the life of a neglected biologist); DAVA SOBEL, LONGITUDE: THE TRUE STORY OF A LONE GENIUS WHO SOLVED THE GREATEST SCIENTIFIC PROBLEM OF HIS TIME (1995) (describing impediments to inventors outside scientific establishment).

keep them out of bounds, albeit sometimes very clumsily, through such measures as peer review.

Community-based creative products that emerge from less developed countries have often been depicted in intellectual property law as unowned things; thus folklore, religious artifacts, and agricultural strains are sometimes treated as *res nullius*, open to appropriation by others, because they were not created by a single "romantic" artist or adventurer. If this is true, however, then the same might also be said of the products of the Globe Theater or the Fermi Labs, since so much creative work mixes individual contributions with ideas that are "in the air" of the creative community. Citizens of less developed countries, faced with the argument that their artworks and agricultural products are "the common heritage of mankind," might instead hear an echo of the Romans' view that conquered territory was *res nullius*. Better that we devise ways to think of these endeavors as *res universitatis*, so that these communities of creators too can enjoy their fruits.

Res universitatis, then, is a type of property that is non-exclusive but also bounded. For intellectual matters, *res universitatis* is a rubric that does acknowledge the usefulness of property rights in creative accomplishments. But unlike individual intellectual property, *res universitatis* focuses attention, first, on encouraging the group interactions that greatly foster creativity, and second, on policing the boundary of behaviors that are disruptive to creative groups. Perhaps not much more is needed, given the capacity of limited groups to generate their own norms. Once again from an outsider's perspective on intellectual property, it appears that this limited community aspect of Intellectual Space is rather underdeveloped in the law, as it has been until recently in Tangible Space.

Going back to trace the life cycle of intellectual property, then, we might find that intellectual matters begin as *res communes* (things incapable of ownership), whereupon intellectual property law turns them into a kind of legal *res nullius* (things open to appropriation); but they may well become *res universitatis* (things belonging to creative communities) on their way to the final wide-open synergies of the legally protected *res publicae*—things open to all by operation of law, the public domain that reigns after property protection expires.

I cannot leave the Romans, however, without mentioning one concluding type of nonexclusive property:

VI

RES DIVINI JURIS: THINGS THAT ARE UNOWNED BY ANY HUMAN BEING BECAUSE THEY ARE SACRED, HOLY OR RELIGIOUS[77]

The things classed under this rubric in Roman law—temples, tombs, religious statuary—were considered to belong to no one because they were

77. BURDICK, *supra* note 65, at 308-309; HUNTER, *supra* note 13, at 66.

dedicated to the service of the gods, or because an offense to them was considered to be offensive to the gods.[78] Such things were a class of *res nullius* because although they are physically capable of appropriation, they are still unowned; the impediment to propertization is not natural but divine.

I must confess that I once thought there were no real analogs to this kind of property in the tangible public property of modern secular countries, but I now think I was mistaken. At least in the United States, the great wilderness parks, deserts and seashores, with their sense of the sublime and the vast, may in some ways fill the role of *res divini juris*. Such places suggest to the visitor the majesty of creation, the vastness of space, the untamed-ness of something outside human capacity to grasp. If there is a role for *res divini juris* as tangible public property in our modern jurisprudence, surely this is one place where it resides.

Of course, it is physically possible to cut down trees in such places or to drill for oil in them or to race around in noisy, wide-tire vehicles, but the argument against such behavior is chiefly one that sounds in the quasi-religious terms of travesty and sacrilege: Such lands should be open to all, but each visitor should treat them with the appropriate attitude of awe. No bolt from heaven, however, strikes down the logger, the oil well-driller, or the dune-buggy driver. The divine wildness of the wide-open spaces is in the end metaphoric; the organized public, after all, has to protect them and invest in them if these spaces are to last.[79]

There is clearly also an analog for the *res divini juris* in the intellectual world as well. It is the canon, the classics, the ancient works whose long life has contributed to their status as rare, extraordinary—and also a little wild, never quite capable of complete domestication even by the most erudite pedant. And lest we forget that all things godlike may be accompanied by lesser gods (or even false ones) and their representations, we might wish to include here too the iconography of modern commercial culture, the Mickeys and Minnies and Scarletts. To be sure, such symbolic creations might well deserve the protection of private ownership until the time they actually become iconic. But thereafter, though the point is controversial, the category *of res divini juris* could well embrace this iconography and dedicate it at least in some measure to the public, as in copyright law's exception for parody.[80] Why? Precisely because the

78. In a somewhat odd wrinkle, this included climbing over the city walls, which was an offense punishable by death, because one was supposed to enter and exit the city by the gates. BURDICK, *supra* note 65, at 309.

79. For an appropriately named commentary, see Joseph Sax, *Helpless Giants: The National Parks and the Regulation of Private Lands*, 75 MICH. L. REV. 239 (1976) (primarily describing external threats to the parks); *cf.* ALSTON CHASE, PLAYING GOD AT YELLOWSTONE: THE DESTRUCTION OF AMERICA'S FIRST NATIONAL PARK (1987) (detailing mismanagement by the Park Service itself).

80. A somewhat similar note is sounded in the law of historic preservation about tangible things; some buildings seem to become "public" or at least subject to public constraint by operation of the passage of time and by the public's embrace of them—including some quite odd buildings that the public grows to like. *See* Carol M. Rose, *Preservation and Community: New Directions in the Law of Historic Preservation*, 33 STAN. L. REV. 473, 497, 497 n.110 (1981).

continuing reconsideration and reworking of the icons is so enormously productive of new cultural insights. And of course, because it is fun.[81] After all, even the comic gods need to be served.[82]

Notice that unlike the tangible *res divini juris*, the canon (and even the iconography) does not really need much public protection; we can generally rely on the devotees, imitators and satirists to keep these works in the public eye unless they grow terminally old and tired. Indeed, one of the functions that the public domain serves is to open would-be classics to the withering fires of ridicule and repetition, thus vividly demonstrating which can withstand these tests of mockery and cliché. Almost by definition, there is little that can destroy the true gods of the canon, however much they may suffer periodic temporal eclipses and satiric insult. Bach has survived the Swingle Singers and the Moog machine. That is why Bach is Bach. The Mona Lisa survives her cartoon picture on the Chunky Beef Soup can. If anything, she is all the more enigmatic for it. Bach can eat the Swingle Singers for breakfast, the Mona Lisa can eat Chunky Beef Soup for lunch. It remains to be seen what Mickey can survive.

81. For a recent case of the parody example, see the controversies over the 2001 publication of *The Wind Done Gone* by Alice Randall. SunTrust Bank v. Houghton Mifflin Co., 268 F.3d 1257 (11th Cir. 2001) (reversing preliminary injunction against new novel on the ground that *Gone With the Wind* author Margaret Mitchell's estate had not shown a likelihood of prevailing on merits, particularly "fair use" as parody). *See also* Bill Rankin, *Mitchell Estate to Continue "Gone" Battle*, ATLANTA J. & CONS., Oct. 12, 2001 at 3E (reporting 11th Circuit victory for parodist, which gave the Mitchell estate the resolve to pursue the suit).

82. *See* ROBERT M. POLHEMUS, COMIC FAITH: THE GREAT COMIC TRADITION FROM AUSTEN TO JOYCE, 3-9 (1980) (arguing that comedy is linked to religious sensibility).

IDEAS, ARTIFACTS, AND FACILITIES: INFORMATION AS A COMMON-POOL RESOURCE

CHARLOTTE HESS* AND ELINOR OSTROM**

I

INTRODUCTION

There is an increasing concern about the implications of recent and impending legislation on the future of academic research, open science, traditional knowledge, and the intellectual public domain. The Duke Law School Conference on the Public Domain brought together, for the first time, an interdisciplinary group of leading scholars studying the increasing enclosure[1] of the global information commons. In the past five years, law review articles have described an information arms race from various perspectives, with multiple sides battling for larger shares of the global knowledge pool.[2]

This article is also available online at http://www.law.duke.edu/journals/66LCPHess.

* Director, Workshop Research Library; Information Officer, International Association for the Study of Common Property; Director, Digital Library of the Commons.

** Arthur F. Bentley Professor, Indiana University Department of Political Science; Co-Director, Workshop in Political Theory and Policy Analysis; Co-Director, Center for the Study of Institutions, Population, and Environmental Change ("CIPEC").

This paper was initially presented at the Conference on the Public Domain, held at the Duke University School of Law on November 9-11, 2001, and the Workshop in Political Theory and Policy Analysis, March 25, 2002.

We would like to thank Gerry Bernbom, James Boyle, Julie Cohen, John Daly, Laura Gassaway, Shubha Ghosh, James Hanley, Tobias Klaus, Harini Nagendra, Robert Najlis, Vincent Ostrom, Enrico Schaar, Peter Suber, James Walker, and Wang Jianxun for their helpful and insightful comments. We are eternally grateful to Patty Zielinski for her expert technological, editorial assistance as well as her perseverance and patience. We also wish to thank the Ford Foundation for its essential support.

1. *See* James Boyle, *The Second Enclosure Movement and the Construction of the Public Domain*, 66 LAW & CONTEMP. PROBS. 33 (Winter/Spring 2003).

2. There is a rapidly growing legal literature on the ramifications of recent intellectual property legislation and its impact on the intellectual public domain. Some of the works that seem particularly relevant to the question of the information commons are: JAMES BOYLE, SHAMANS, SOFTWARE, AND SPLEENS: LAW AND THE CONSTRUCTION OF THE INFORMATION SOCIETY (1996); Yochai Benkler, *Free as the Air to Common Use: First Amendment Constraints on Enclosure of the Public Domain*, 74 N.Y.U. L. REV. 354 (1999); Dan L. Burk, *Muddy Rules for Cyberspace*, 21 CARDOZO L. REV. 121 (1999); Julie E. Cohen, *Copyright and the Jurisprudence of Self-Help*, 13 BERKELEY TECH. L.J. 1089 (1998); Mark A. Lemley, *Beyond Preemption: The Law and Policy of Intellectual Property Licensing*, 87 CAL. L. REV. 111 (1999); Michael J. Madison, *Complexity and Copyright in Contradiction*, 18 CARDOZO ARTS & ENT. L.J. 125 (2000); Robert P. Merges, *Property Rights Theory and the Commons: The Case of Scientific Research*, 13 SOC. PHIL. & POL'Y 145 (1996); J.H. Reichman & Jonathan A. Franklin, *Privately Legislated Intellectual Property Rights: Reconciling Freedom of Contract with Public Good Uses of Information*, 147 U. PA. L. REV. 875 (1999); Carol M. Rose, *Expanding the Choices for the Global Commons: Comparing Newfangled Tradable Allowance Schemes to Old-Fashioned Common*

Information that used to be "free" is now increasingly being privatized, monitored, encrypted, and restricted. The enclosure is caused by the conflicts and contradictions between intellectual property laws and the expanded capacities of new technologies.[3] It leads to speculation that the records of scholarly communication, the foundations of an informed, democratic society, may be at risk.

This "intellectual land-grab"[4] is an outcome of new technologies and global markets. Distributed digital technologies have the dual capacity to increase access to information while in some instances restricting such access. These technologies have generated greater access to important information about history, science, art, literature, and current events, while at the same time enabling profit-oriented firms to extract value from resources previously held in common and to establish property rights.[5] Multiple forces are vying for capture and restriction of traditionally available knowledge: corporations versus indigenous peoples, such as Monsanto owning the patent on the genetic structure of the neem; federal and state governments versus citizens regarding balancing encryption and digital surveillance with individual privacy; universities versus professors as to whether institutions or individuals will own intellectual property; and publishers versus libraries in the ephemeralization of library collections through licensing, bundling, and withdrawal of information.

This competition for ownership of previously shared resources is not unique to the public domain of knowledge. Given the opening of vast markets for commodities of all kinds, many natural as well as human-made resources are under pressure. The world's fisheries, for instance, are fighting depletion because of the capture capabilities of larger trawlers, wider and finer nets, and larger fleets. Local control of forests throughout the world is being increasingly encroached upon by state and private interests, resulting in alarming rates of deforestation. Resultant forest burning is not only rapidly reducing primary growth forests but is also contributing to the degradation of the global atmosphere as well.[6] Commodification and privatization of natural resources is

---

Property Regimes, 10 DUKE ENVTL. L. & POL'Y F. 45 (Fall 1999); Paul A. David, A Tragedy of the Public Knowledge "Commons"? Global Science, Intellectual Property and the Digital Technology Boomerang (SIEPR Discussion Paper no. 00-02, Stanford Institute for Economic Policy Research, 2000), *available at* http://siepr.stanford.edu/papers/pdf/00-02.html (last visited Oct. 10, 2002); Lawrence Lessig, Reclaiming a Commons, Keynote Address at Harvard University (May 20, 1999), *available at* http:// cyber.law.harvard.edu/events/lessigkeynote.pdf [hereinafter Lessig, Harvard].

3. *See* BOYLE, *supra* note 2, at 6-7; Yochai Benkler, *Overcoming Agoraphobia: Building the Commons of the Digitally Networked Environment*, 11 HARV. J.L. & TECH. 287 (Winter 1998); Jane C. Ginsburg, *Copyright and Control of New Technologies of Dissemination*, 101 COLUM. L. REV. 1613 (2001).

4. Boyle, *supra* note 1, at __; James Boyle, *A Politics of Intellectual Property: Environmentalism for the Net?*, 47 DUKE L.J. 87, 94 (1997).

5. Many new common-pool resources have "remained unclaimed due to a lack of technology for extracting their value and for establishing and sustaining property rights." Elinor Ostrom, *Foreword*, *in* SUSAN J. BUCK, THE GLOBAL COMMONS: AN INTRODUCTION xiii (1998).

6. *See* J.E. Michael Arnold, *Devolution of Control of Common Pool Resources to Local Communities: Experiences in Forestry*, *in* ACCESS TO LAND, RURAL POVERTY, AND PUBLIC ACTION 163, 164-65 (Alain de Janvry et al. eds., 2001).

a trend with virtually all types of resources. And radical changes in the structure and process of all natural and human-constructed resources can occur through the development of new technologies.[7]

The problems are complex, multilayered, and of crucial importance. To direct attention to this evolving situation, James Boyle has called for the re-creation of the public domain, drawing from the intellectual construct of the environment. "Like the environment," he writes, "the public domain must be invented before it can be saved."[8] A greater depth of understanding of the public domain requires the concept to be more deeply analyzed and clarified. It is a logical step, therefore, to draw from the fruitful research and analytical methods applied to the study of common-pool resources ("CPRs") and natural resource management.

The goal of this article is to summarize the lessons learned from a large body of international, interdisciplinary research on common-pool resources in the past twenty-five years and consider its usefulness in the analysis of scholarly information as a resource. We will suggest ways in which the study of the governance and management of CPRs can be applied to the analysis of information and the "intellectual public domain." The complexity of the issues is enormous for many reasons: the vast number of players, multiple conflicting interests, rapid changes of technology, the general lack of understanding of digital technologies, local versus global arenas, and a chronic lack of precision about the information resource at hand. We suggest, in the tradition of Hayek, that the combination of time and place analysis with general scientific knowledge is necessary for sufficient understanding of policy and action.[9] In addition, the careful development of an unambiguous language and agreed-upon definitions is imperative.

We focus on the *language*, *methodology*, and *outcomes* of research on common-pool resources to better understand how various types of property regimes affect the provision, production, distribution, appropriation, and consumption of scholarly information. Our analysis will suggest that collective action and new institutional design play as large a part in the shaping of scholarly information as do legal restrictions and market forces.

In Part II we present a brief intellectual history of the commons and discuss the development of the understanding of the term. Part III discusses key concepts of the terms "commons," "common-pool resources," and "common property." Four frequent areas of confusion are identified and elucidated. Part IV presents a method of analyzing information as a commons. Part V illustrates the development and change of scholarly information as a shared resource. It focuses on collective action initiatives as a response to the dilemmas of new technological freedoms within an increasing amount of legal constraints.

7. *See, e.g.*, Stephen R. Palumbi, *Humans as the World's Greatest Evolutionary Force*, SCIENCE, Sept. 7, 2001, at 1786, *available at* http: www.sciencemag.org/cgi/content/full/293/5536/1786.

8. *See* Boyle, *supra* note 1, at 19.

9. F. A. Hayek, *The Use of Knowledge in Society*, 35 AM. ECON. REV. 519, 521 (1945).

II

WHAT IS A COMMONS?

A large body of international, interdisciplinary literature on the commons has grown in the past fifteen to twenty years.[10] It reflects concerted attempts to arrive at unified understandings of the definition of the commons. The recent law literature on the commons, however, presents various different concepts of the commons without reference to this literature. Lawrence Lessig's concept of the commons is one of a universal, open access: "The commons: There's a part of our world, here and now, that we all get to enjoy without the permission of any."[11] Yochai Benkler's concept involves legal constraints against controlling regimes: "The commons refers to institutional devices that entail government abstention from designating anyone as having primary decision-making power over use of a resource. A commons-based information policy relies on the observation that some resources that serve as inputs for information production and exchange have economic or technological characteristics that make them susceptible to be allocated without requiring that any single organization, regulatory agency, or property owner clear conflicting uses of the resource."[12] Litman equates the commons with the public domain: "The concept of the public domain is another import from the realm of real property. In the intellectual property context, the term describes a true commons comprising elements of intellectual property that are ineligible for private ownership. The contents of the public domain may be mined by any member of the public."[13]

Indeed, in the law literature cited throughout this article, a wide variety of concepts and definitions of the commons or public domain is used. We feel there needs to be clarity, shared meanings, and a common language to research this area better. In the legal arena, the term "commons" is often used synonymously with the term public domain. Is it a given right, a nonassigned right, an unclaimed right, an unmanaged resource, or something that should just be there in a democracy?[14] A survey of law dictionaries does not clear matters up. *Oran's Dictionary of the Law*, for instance, gives two definitions of public domain: "land owned by the government" and "something free for anyone to

10. *See* CHARLOTTE HESS, A COMPREHENSIVE BIBLIOGRAPHY OF COMMON-POOL RESOURCES (CD-ROM, 1999). This bibliography contains 22,500 citations of works on the commons. A searchable version of this bibliography is available at http://www.iascp.org/cprbibs.html (last updated Dec. 16, 1999). A new edition with 35,000 citations is forthcoming.

11. Lawrence Lessig, Code and the Commons, Keynote Address at the Conference on Media Convergence, held at Fordham University Law School (Feb. 9, 1999), *available at* http://cyber.law.harvard.edu/works/lessig/fordham.pdf (last visited Sept. 1, 2002).

12. Yochai Benkler, The Commons as a Neglected Factor of Information Policy, Remarks at the Telecommunications Policy Research Conference (Sept. 1998), *available at* http://www.law.nyu.edu/benklery/commons.pdf (last visited Sept. 1, 2002).

13. Jessica Litman, *The Public Domain*, 39 EMORY L.J. 965, 975 (1990).

14. BOYLE, *supra* note 2, at xiv (pointing out the institutional nature of a commons: "Even a conventional economic analysis supports the idea that it is in the interest of those who are exploiting a 'commons' to make sure that the commons continues to exist.").

use or something not protected by patent or copyright."[15] In the first definition, there is an owner—the government. In the second, there is *no* owner. Are scholars trying to protect a realm of government ownership or a realm of no ownership?

In relation to the intellectual public domain, the commons appears to be an idea about democratic processes, freedom of speech, and the free exchange of information. The term "commons," however, has various histories, from property to shared spaces to notions of democratic ideals. It refers to the house of British Parliament representing nontitled citizens, and agricultural fields in England and Europe prior to their enclosure. In the United States, commons refers to public spaces such as the New England town square, campus dining halls, and concepts of the "common" good.[16] In almost all uses, the term has been contested. In the realm of legal property rights, the publication of *Ancient Law* by Henry Sumner Maine[17] in 1861 set off a major debate about the origin of the very concept of property in ancient times.[18] Drawing on his own extensive research in India and the research of others on early European communities, Maine argued that joint ownership by families and groups of kin (in other words, common property) was more likely the initial property regime in most parts of the world than the notion of property owned by a single individual.[19] This great debate was not simply one between historians over whether common property or individual private property came first. Rather, the debate framed a perspective on whether landed proprietors have a special role in society that needed protection and the legitimacy of enclosing properties owned communally. The debate started long ago and is still not fully resolved. A major textbook on property law devotes the entire first chapter to *The Debate over Private Property* and the second chapter to *The Problem of the Commons*.[20]

Social scientists have had their own debates about the consequences of allowing multiple individuals or firms to use jointly a resource system. The debate was kicked off half a century ago by the path-breaking works of H. Scott Gordon in 1954 and Anthony Scott in 1955,[21] which introduced an economic analysis of a natural resource (fisheries) that had, prior to that time, been the

15. DANIEL ORAN, ORAN'S DICTIONARY OF THE LAW 392 (3d ed. 2000).

16. Charlotte Hess, Is There Anything New Under the Sun?: A Discussion and Survey of Studies on New Commons and the Internet, *presented at* Constituting the Commons: Crafting Sustainable Commons in the New Millennium, the eighth biennial conference of the International Association for the Study of Common Property (May 31-June 4, 2000), *available at* http://dlc.dlib.indiana.edu/documents/dir0/00/00/05/12/dlc-00000512-00/iascp2000.pdf (last visited Dec. 3, 2002)

17. HENRY SUMNER MAINE, ANCIENT LAW (Raymond Firth ed., Beacon Press 1963) (1861).

18. *See* PAOLO GROSSI, AN ALTERNATIVE TO PRIVATE PROPERTY: COLLECTIVE PROPERTY IN THE JURIDICAL CONSCIOUSNESS OF THE NINETEENTH CENTURY 15 (1981).

19. MAINE, *supra* note 17, at 252.

20. PERSPECTIVES ON PROPERTY LAW (Robert C. Ellickson et al. eds., 2d ed. 1995).

21. H. Scott Gordon, *The Economic Theory of a Common-Property Resource: The Fishery*, 62 J. POL. ECON. 124 (1954); Anthony D. Scott, *The Fishery: The Objectives of Sole Ownership*, 63 J. POL. ECON. 116 (1955).

domain of biologists. The two articles are credited with outlining the conventional theory of the commons.[22] Gordon and Scott demonstrated that when multiple individuals jointly harvested high-demand fish without a limit on the amount that any fisher could withdraw, the quantity harvested would exceed both the maximum sustainable yield and the maximum economic yield. At that time, the only solution they contemplated to this problem was ownership of the fishery by a single firm or by the government. In 1968, biologist Garrett Hardin crystallized the thinking of many social scientists and policy makers with his metaphoric analysis of the "tragedy of the commons."[23] Hardin argued that individuals who jointly use a commons are hopelessly trapped in an immutable tragedy.[24] Given this inevitable trap of overuse (or, for Hardin, overpopulation), the *only* solution Hardin envisioned was externally imposed government or private ownership.[25] Unfortunately for the development of rigorous thinking, Hardin casually used the example of a pasture "open to all" as if all jointly owned pastures would be "open to all."[26]

Since the work of Gordon, Scott, and Hardin, most theoretical studies by political economists have analyzed simple common-pool resource systems using relatively similar assumptions. In such systems, it is assumed that the resource generates a highly predictable, finite supply of one type of resource unit (one species, for example) in each relevant time period. Appropriators (those who harvest from a resource system, such as fishers and pastoralists) are assumed to be homogeneous in terms of their assets, skills, discount rates, and cultural views. They are also assumed to be short-term, profit-maximizing actors who possess complete information. In this theory, *anyone* can utilize the resource and appropriate resource units. Appropriators gain property rights only to what they harvest. The harvested resource units are then privately owned and can be sold in an open, competitive market. The open-access condition is a given and the appropriators make no effort to change it. Appropriators act independently and do not communicate or coordinate their activities in any way.[27]

Many current textbooks in resource economics and in law and economics still present this conventional theory of a simple common-pool resource as the

---

22. *See* David Feeny et al., *The Tragedy of the Commons: Twenty-Two Years Later*, 18 HUM. ECOLOGY 1, 2 (1990).

23. Garrett Hardin, *The Tragedy of the Commons*, SCIENCE, Dec. 13, 1968, at 1243.

24. *Id.* at 1244-45.

25. *Id.* at 1245.

26. *Id.* at 1244.

27. Commenting on Gordon and Scott's work, David Feeny says:

> In this setting, as the incisive analysis of Gordon and Scott demonstrates, each fisherman will take into account only his own marginal costs and revenues and ignores the fact that increases in his catch affect the returns to fishing effort for other fishermen as well as the health of future fish stocks. . . . [E]conomic rent is dissipated; economic overfishing, which may also lead to ecological overfishing, is the result.

David Feeny et al., *Questioning the Assumptions of the "Tragedy of the Commons" Model of Fisheries*, 72 LAND ECON. 187, 189 (1996).

only theory needed for achieving a more general understanding of common-pool resources.[28] With the growing use of game theory, appropriation from common-pool resources is frequently represented as a one-shot or finitely repeated Prisoner's Dilemma game.[29] These models formalize the problem differently, but do not change any of the basic theoretical assumptions about the finite and predictable supply of resource units, complete information, homogeneity of users, their maximization of expected profits, and their lack of interaction with one another or capacity to change their institutions.

A sufficient number of empirical examples exist where the absence of property rights and the independence of actors captures the essence of the problem facing appropriators that the broad empirical applicability of the conventional theory was not challenged until the mid-1980s. The massive deforestation in tropical countries and the collapse of the California sardine fishery and other ocean fisheries confirmed for many scholars the worst predictions to be derived from this theory.

Since appropriators are viewed as being trapped in these dilemmas, repeated recommendations were made that external authorities must impose a different set of political regimes and property rights. Some scholars recommended private property as the most efficient form of ownership.[30] Others, drawing on Hobbes, recommended government ownership and control.[31] Implicitly, theorists assumed that regulators will act in the public interest and understand how ecological systems work and how to change institutions to induce socially optimal behavior.[32]

The possibility that the appropriators would find ways to organize themselves was not considered seriously in the political-economy literature until recently. Organizing to create rules that specify rights and duties of participants creates a public good for those involved. Anyone who is included in the community of users benefits from this public good, whether they contribute or not. Thus, getting "out of the trap" of the free-rider problem is itself a second-level dilemma. Further, investing in monitoring and sanctioning activities to increase the likelihood that participants follow the agreements they have made also generates a public good. Such investments represent a third-level dilemma. Since much of the initial problem exists because individuals are stuck in a

28. *But see* JEAN-MARIE BALAND & JEAN-PHILIPPE PLATTEAU, HALTING DEGRADATION OF NATURAL RESOURCES: IS THERE A ROLE FOR RURAL COMMUNITIES? 25-35 (1996).

29. *See* PARTHA DASGUPTA & GEOFFREY M. HEAL, ECONOMIC THEORY AND EXHAUSTIBLE RESOURCES (1979); Robyn M. Dawes, *The Commons Dilemma Game: An N-Person Mixed-Motive Game With a Dominating Strategy for Defection*, 13 OR. RES. BULL. (1973).

30. *See* RICHARD A. POSNER, ECONOMIC ANALYSIS OF LAW 28-30 (2d ed. 1977); Harold Demsetz, *Toward a Theory of Property Rights*, 57 AM. ECON. REV. 347 (1967); Randy T. Simmons et al., The Tragedy of the Commons Revisited: Politics vs. Private Property (Center for Private Conservation, Competitive Enterprise Institute, Washington, D.C., 1996).

31. William Ophuls, *Leviathan or Oblivion?*, *in* TOWARD A STEADY STATE ECONOMY 214, 219 (Herman E. Daly ed., 1973) ("Hobbes's answer to the tragedy of the commons then is a benevolent form of autocracy . . . .").

32. Feeny et al., *supra* note 27, at 195.

setting where they generate negative externalities on one another, it is not consistent with the conventional theory that they solve a second- and third-level dilemma to address the first-level dilemma.

The work of the National Academy of Sciences' Panel on Common Property challenged the application of this conventional theory to all common-pool resources regardless of the capacity of appropriators to communicate, coordinate their activities, and create institutions to allocate property rights and make policies related to a jointly owned resource.[33] The growing evidence from many field studies of common-pool resources conducted by anthropologists[34] and historians[35] called for a serious rethinking of the theoretical foundations for analysis of common-pool resources.[36] The cumulative impact of the extensive empirical studies does not challenge the empirical validity of the conventional theory *where it is relevant*, but rather questions its presumed, universal generalizability.

III

CLARIFYING KEY CONCEPTS

To develop a broader and empirically verifiable theory that encompassed the dominant "tragedy of the commons" theory as a special case, scholars learned that they had to make some key distinctions between concepts that had previously and casually been treated as the same. Because we feel that a similar effort is needed for the intellectual public domain, we will discuss these distinctions in some depth. There are four basic confusions that need to be untangled. The source of confusion relates to the differences between (1) the nature of the good (common-pool *resources*) and a property regime (common-property *regimes*), (2) resource systems and the flow of resource units, (3) common property and open-access regimes, and (4) the set of property rights

---

33. *See* PROCEEDINGS OF THE CONFERENCE ON COMMON PROPERTY RESOURCE MANAGEMENT (National Research Council ed., 1986).

34. *See, e.g.*, ROBERT MCC. NETTING, BALANCING ON AN ALP: ECOLOGICAL CHANGE AND CONTINUITY IN A SWISS MOUNTAIN COMMUNITY (1981); THE QUESTION OF THE COMMONS: THE CULTURE AND ECOLOGY OF COMMUNAL RESOURCES (Bonnie J. McCay & James M. Acheson eds., 1987); Robert McC. Netting, *Territory, Property, and Tenure*, *in* BEHAVIORAL AND SOCIAL SCIENCE RESEARCH: A NATIONAL RESOURCE 446, 446 (R. McC. Adams et al. eds., 1982).

35. *See, e.g.*, THOMAS F. GLICK, IRRIGATION AND SOCIETY IN MEDIEVAL VALENCIA (1970) (focusing on the conflict arising from an irrigation system that necessitated cooperation); ARTHUR MAASS & RAYMOND L. ANDERSON, . . . AND THE DESERT SHALL REJOICE: CONFLICT, GROWTH, AND JUSTICE IN ARID ENVIRONMENTS (1986) (observing irrigation systems in a number of the world's deserts, including southeastern Spain and the Western United States).

36. *See* COMMON PROPERTY RESOURCES: ECOLOGY AND COMMUNITY-BASED SUSTAINABLE DEVELOPMENT, at ix, 2 (Fikret Berkes ed., 1989); MAKING THE COMMONS WORK: THEORY, PRACTICE, AND POLICY, at xi, 4 (Daniel W. Bromley et al. eds., 1992); ELINOR OSTROM, GOVERNING THE COMMONS 2 (1990); ROBERT WADE, VILLAGE REPUBLICS: ECONOMIC CONDITIONS FOR COLLECTIVE ACTION IN SOUTH INDIA xiv (1994). *See also generally* NIRMAL SENGUPTA, MANAGING COMMON PROPERTY: IRRIGATION IN INDIA AND THE PHILIPPINES (1991); A SEA OF SMALL BOATS (John C. Cordell ed., 1989); THE TRADITIONAL KNOWLEDGE AND MANAGEMENT OF COASTAL SYSTEMS IN ASIA AND THE PACIFIC (Kenneth Ruddle & Robert E. Johannes eds., 1985).

involved in "ownership." All four sources of confusion reduce clarity in assigning meaning to terms and retard theoretical and empirical progress.

A. The Confusion between the Nature of a Good and a Property Regime

The problems resulting from confusing concepts were particularly difficult to overcome given that the term "common-*property* resource" was frequently used to describe a type of economic good that is more appropriately referred to as a "common-*pool* resource." For many scholars, the concept of a property regime and the nature of a good were thus conflated.

One of the key problems in developing a good analytical approach to the effect of diverse institutional arrangements on the incentives, activities, and outcomes of the individuals involved is getting a clear conception of the structure of events involved. The political-economy literature usually refers to the structure of the biophysical events as the nature of the goods.[37] For some time, economists struggled with classifying goods as either private or public.[38] By labeling all goods as fitting this dichotomy, scholars talked about those things that the market could solve most efficiently and those that would require government provision and production.

In the 1970s, a major breakthrough came with clear identification that there were more than two types of goods.[39] Two attributes have been identified in the political-economy literature that help identify four broad classes of goods. The first attribute is that the benefits consumed by one individual subtract from the benefits available to others.[40] The second attribute is that it is very costly to exclude individuals from using the flow of benefits either through physical barriers or legal instruments. Both attributes vary across a range.

Recognizing a class of goods that shares these two attributes enables scholars to identify the core theoretical problems facing individuals, whenever more than one individual or a group utilizes resources for an extended period of time. Using "property" to refer to a type of good reinforces the impression that goods sharing these attributes tend to share uniformly the same property regime. This is certainly not the case.

---

37. *See* Paul Samuelson, *The Pure Theory of Public Expenditure*, 36 REV. ECON. & STAT. 387 (1954).

38. *See generally* RICHARD A. MUSGRAVE, THE THEORY OF PUBLIC FINANCE: A STUDY IN PUBLIC ECONOMY (1959).

39. Vincent Ostrom & Elinor Ostrom, *Public Goods and Public Choices*, *in* ALTERNATIVES FOR DELIVERING PUBLIC SERVICES: TOWARD IMPROVED PERFORMANCE 7, 9-14 (E. S. Savas ed., 1977).

40. *Id.* (describing this attribute as jointness of use or consumption); RULES, GAMES, AND COMMON-POOL RESOURCES 6 (Elinor Ostrom et al. eds., 1994) [hereinafter RULES].

FIGURE 1
TYPES OF GOODS

		SUBTRACTABILITY	
		Low	*High*
EXCLUSION	*Difficult*	**Public Goods** Sunset Common Knowledge	**Common-Pool Resources** Irrigation Systems Libraries
	Easy	**Roll or Club Goods** Day-Care Centers Country Clubs	**Private Goods** Doughnuts Personal Computers

As shown in Figure 1, common-pool resources share with what economists call "public goods" the difficulty of developing physical or institutional means of excluding beneficiaries. Unless means are devised to keep nonauthorized users from benefiting, a strong temptation to free ride on the efforts of others will lead to a suboptimal investment in improving the resource, monitoring use, and sanctioning rule-breaking behavior. Second, the products or resource units from common-pool resources share with what economists call "private goods" the attribute that one person's consumption subtracts from the quantity available to others. Thus, common-pool resources are subject to the problems of congestion, overuse, pollution, and potential destruction unless harvesting or use limits are devised and enforced. In addition to sharing these two attributes, particular common-pool resources differ in many other attributes that affect their economic usefulness including their extent, shape, and productivity, as well as the value, timing, and regularity of the resource units produced.[41]

Common-pool resources may be owned by national, regional, or local governments, by communal groups, by private individuals or corporations, or used as open-access resources by whomever can gain access. Each of the broad types of property regimes has different sets of advantages and disadvantages, but at times may rely upon similar bundles of operational rules.[42] Examples exist of both successful and unsuccessful efforts by governments, communal groups, cooperatives, voluntary associations, and private individuals or firms to govern and manage common-pool resources.[43] Thus, no automatic association

41. *See* Edella Schlager et al., *Mobile Flows, Storage, and Self-Organized Institutions for Governing Common-Pool Resources*, 70 LAND ECON. 294 (1994).

42. Feeny et al., *supra* note 22, at 5-9.

43. Bromley et al., *supra* note 36, at 4; KATAR SINGH, MANAGING COMMON POOL RESOURCES: PRINCIPLES AND CASE STUDIES 314-19 (1994).

exists between common-pool resources and common-property regimes—*or, any other particular type of property regime.*

B. The Confusion between a Resource System and the Flow of Resource Units

The second confusion is related to the relationships between resource systems and a flow of resource units or benefits from these systems.[44] In regard to common-pool resources, the resource system (or alternatively, the stock or the facility) is what generates a flow of resource units or benefits over time.[45] Examples of typical common-pool resource systems include lakes, rivers, irrigation systems, groundwater basins, forests, fishery stocks, and grazing areas. Common-pool resources may also be facilities that are constructed for joint use, such as mainframe computers and the Internet. Examples of resource units from a common-pool resource are water, timber, medicinal plants, fish, fodder, and central processing units. The resource units from a complex facility like the Internet may be the data packets or the computer files (information artifacts), depending upon whether it is being studied as an infrastructure resource or as an information resource.[46] Devising property regimes that effectively allow sustainable use of a common-pool resource requires one set of rules that limits access to the resource system and another set of rules that limits the amount, timing, and technology used to withdraw diverse resource units from the resource system. It is frequently the case that the resource system is jointly owned, while the resource units withdrawn from the system are individually owned by appropriators.

C. The Confusion between Common-Property and Open-Access Regimes

In a now classic article, Ciriacy-Wantrup and Bishop[47] clearly articulated the difference between property regimes that are *open-access*, where no one has the legal right to exclude anyone from using a resource, and *common property*, where members of a clearly defined group have a bundle of legal rights including the right to exclude nonmembers from using that resource.[48] Legal doctrine has long considered open-access regimes (*res nullius*)—including the

---

44. William Blomquist & Elinor Ostrom, *Institutional Capacity and the Resolution of a Commons Dilemma*, 5 POL'Y STUD. REV. 383, 383 (1985).

45. *See, e.g.*, Dean Lueck, *Property Rights and the Economic Logic of Wildlife Institutions*, 35 NAT. RESOURCES J. 625, 636 (1995).

46. *See* Gerald Bernbom, Analyzing the Internet as a Common Pool Resource: The Problem of Network Congestion, *presented at* Constituting the Commons: Crafting Sustainable Commons in the New Millennium, the eighth biennial conference of the International Association for the Study of Common Property (May 31-June 4, 2000), *available at* http://dlc.dlib.indiana.edu/documents/dir0/00/00/02/18/index.html.

47. Siegfried V. Ciriacy-Wantrup & Richard C. Bishop, *"Common Property" as a Concept in Natural Resource Policy*, 15 NAT. RESOURCES J. 713, 715 (1975).

48. *See* DANIEL W. BROMLEY, ENVIRONMENT AND ECONOMY: PROPERTY RIGHTS AND PUBLIC POLICY 22-23 (1991); Daniel W. Bromley, *The Commons, Property, and Common-Property Regimes*, *in* MAKING THE COMMONS WORK: THEORY, PRACTICE, AND POLICY 3, 3-4 (Daniel W. Bromley et al. eds., 1992).

classic cases of the open seas and the atmosphere—to involve no limits on who has authorized use. Thus, the work of Gordon, Scott, and Hardin focused on resources that were paired with open-access regimes.[49] If anyone can use a resource—the definition of an open-access resource—then no one has an incentive to conserve its use or to invest in its improvements.

Some open-access regimes lack effective rules defining property rights by default.[50] Either the resources affected by these open-access regimes are not contained within a nation-state or no entity has successfully laid claim to legitimate ownership. Other open-access regimes are the consequence of conscious public policies to guarantee the access of all citizens to use a resource within a political jurisdiction.[51] The concept of *jus publicum* applies to their formal status, but effectively these resources are open-access.[52] Still other open-access regimes result from the ineffective exclusion of nonowners by the entity assigned formal rights of ownership. In many developing countries, the earlier confusion between open-access and common-property regimes paradoxically led to an increase in the number and extent of local resources that are *de facto* open-access.[53] Common-property regimes controlling access to and harvesting from local streams, forests, grazing areas, and inshore fisheries had evolved

49. *See supra* text accompanying notes 21-27.

50. *See* JOHN H. DALES, POLLUTION, PROPERTY, AND PRICES: AN ESSAY IN POLICY-MAKING AND ECONOMICS (1968).

51. As is the case for works in the public domain, works that are uncopyrightable, unprotectable, or for which copyright has expired. *See* Litman, *supra* note 13, at 967.

52. This point is well illustrated in Robert Higgs, *Legally Induced Technical Regress in the Washington Salmon Fishery*, *in* EMPIRICAL STUDIES IN INSTITUTIONAL CHANGE 247, 251 (Lee J. Alston et al. eds., 1996). The article outlines the case where the state governments of Oregon and Washington intervened in the early twentieth century to prevent local salmon fishermen from devising rules that would have limited entry and established harvesting limits. Fishing unions along U.S. coastal areas tried to organize inshore fisheries to limit entry and establish harvesting limits during the 1950s. Even though their efforts could not have had a serious impact on prices due to the presence of an active international market for fish, the fishing unions were prosecuted by the U.S. Department of Justice and found in violation of the Sherman Antitrust Act. Ronald N. Johnson & Gary D. Libecap, *Contracting Problems and Regulation: The Case of the Fishery*, 72 AM. ECON. REV. 1005, 1007-08 (1982). Thus, U.S. inshore fisheries have effectively been open-access resources during much of the twentieth century as a result of governmental action to prevent local fishing groups from establishing forms of common-property regimes within those political jurisdictions. In more recent times, however, both the national and state governments have reversed their prior stands and have actively sought ways of creating forms of co-management in inshore fisheries. *See* Evelyn Pinkerton, *Where Do We Go From Here? The Future of Traditional Ecological Knowledge and Resource Management in Native Communities*, *in* TRADITIONAL ECOLOGICAL KNOWLEDGE AND MODERN ENVIRONMENTAL ASSESSMENT 51, 56-58 (P. Boothroyd & B. Sadler eds., 1994); Evelyn Pinkerton, *Local Fisheries Co-Management: A Review of International Experiences and Their Implications for Salmon Management in British Columbia*, 51 CANADIAN J. FISHERIES & AQUATIC SCI. 2363 (1994); James A. Wilson, When are Common Property Institutions Efficient? (working paper, Department of Agriculture and Resource Economics, University of Maine, Orono, 1995) (on file with authors).

53. J.E. Michael Arnold & J. Gabriel Campbell, *Collective Management of Hill Forests in Nepal: The Community Forestry Development Project*, *in* PROCEEDINGS OF THE CONFERENCE ON COMMON PROPERTY RESOURCE MANAGEMENT 425, 425 (National Research Council ed., 1986).

over long periods of time in all parts of the world, but were rarely given formal status in the legal codes of newly independent countries.[54]

Many common-property regimes do efficiently regulate the joint use and management of a resource. There is, however, nothing inherently efficient or inefficient about such regimes. A modern, private corporation is, after all, a common-property regime that has widespread use throughout the global economy—with both efficient and inefficient consequences. Common-property regimes are essentially share contracts.[55] As such, they face the potential of opportunistic behavior and moral hazard problems. Common-property regimes, however, are much more likely to have beneficial consequences for a resource system and its users than an open-access regime.

As concern for the protection of natural resources mounted during the second half of the last century, many developing countries nationalized all land and water resources that had not yet been recorded as private property.[56] The institutional arrangements that many local users had devised to limit entry and use frequently lost legal standing.[57] The national governments that declared ownership of these natural resources, however, frequently lacked monetary resources and personnel to exclude users or to monitor the harvesting activities of users.[58] Thus, resources that had been under a *de facto* common-property regime enforced by local users were converted to a *de jure* government-property regime, but reverted to a *de facto* open-access regime. When resources that were previously controlled by local participants have been nationalized, state control has usually proven to be less effective and efficient than control by those directly affected, if not disastrous in its consequences.[59]

---

54. Fikret Berkes & Carl Folke, *Linking Social and Ecological Systems for Resilience and Sustainability*, *in* LINKING SOCIAL AND ECOLOGICAL SYSTEMS: MANAGEMENT PRACTICES AND SOCIAL MECHANISMS FOR BUILDING RESILIENCE 1, 13-20 (Fikret Berkes & Carl Folke eds., 1998).

55. THRÁINN EGGERTSSON, ECONOMIC BEHAVIOR AND INSTITUTIONS 223-28 (1990); Thráinn Eggertsson, *The Economic Rationale for Communal Resources*, *in* I A CONFERENCE ON COMMON PROPERTY REGIMES: LAW AND MANAGEMENT OF NON-PRIVATE RESOURCES 41 (Erling Berge ed., 1993); Dean Lueck, *Common Property as an Egalitarian Share Contract*, 25 J. ECON. BEHAV. & ORG. 93, 93-108 (1994).

56. *See, e.g.*, CLARK C. GIBSON, POLITICIANS AND POACHERS: THE POLITICAL ECONOMY OF WILDLIFE POLICY IN AFRICA 153-63 (1999).

57. *See, e.g.*, MINOTI CHAKRAVARTY-KAUL, COMMON LANDS AND CUSTOMARY LAW: INSTITUTIONAL CHANGES IN NORTH INDIA OVER THE PAST TWO CENTURIES 12-15 (1996).

58. *See* William Ascher, *Coping with Complexity and Organizational Interests in Natural Resource Management*, 4 ECOSYSTEMS 742 (2001), *available at* http://www.fish.washington.edu/people/naiman/Watershed/readings/ascher.pdf (last visited Dec. 3, 2002-).

59. WILLIAM ASCHER, COMMUNITIES AND SUSTAINABLE FORESTRY IN DEVELOPING COUNTRIES 10-14 (1995); *see also* Rita Hilton, *Institutional Incentives for Resource Mobilization: An Analysis of Irrigation Schemes in Nepal*, 4 J. THEORETICAL POL. 283 (1992). The harmful effects of nationalizing forests that had earlier been governed by local user-groups have been well documented for Thailand, the Niger, Nepal, and India. Arnold, *supra* note 53, at 430-31; David Feeny, *Agricultural Expansion and Forest Depletion in Thailand, 1900-1975*, *in* WORLD DEFORESTATION IN THE TWENTIETH CENTURY 112, 125-26, 129 (John F. Richards & Richard P. Tucker eds., 1988); Madhav Gadgil & Prema Iyer, *On the Diversification of Common-Property Resource Use by Indian Society*, *in* COMMON PROPERTY RESOURCES: ECOLOGY AND COMMUNITY-BASED SUSTAINABLE DEVELOPMENT 240, 247-49 (Fikret Berkes ed., 1989); N.S. Jodha, *Depletion of Common Property Resources in India: Micro-Level Evidence*, *in* RURAL DEVELOPMENT AND POPULATION:

D. The Confusion Over What Rights Are Involved in "Ownership"

A property right is an enforceable authority to undertake particular actions in a specific domain.[60] Within the property regime, different kinds of rights define actions that individuals can take in relation to other individuals regarding some "thing." If one individual has a right, someone else has a commensurate duty to observe that right. Edella Schlager and Elinor Ostrom identify five major bundles of rights that are most relevant for the use of common-pool resources: access, extraction,[61] management, exclusion, and alienation. These are defined as:

Access	The right to enter a defined physical area and enjoy nonsubtractive benefits (for example, hike, canoe, enjoy nature);
Extraction	The right to obtain resource units or products of a resource system (for example, catch fish, divert water);
Management	The right to regulate internal use patterns and transform the resource by making improvements;
Exclusion	The right to determine who will have access rights and withdrawal rights, and how those rights may be transferred; and
Alienation	The right to sell or lease management and exclusion rights.

In much of the economics literature, as well as in legal literature, private property is defined as "holding the right of alienation." Property-rights systems that do not contain the right of alienation are considered by many scholars to be *ill defined*. Further, they are presumed to lead to inefficiency, since property-rights holders cannot trade their interest in an improved resource system for other resources, nor can someone who has a more efficient use of a resource

INSTITUTIONS AND POLICY 261, 270-78 (Geoffery McNicoll & Mead Cain eds., 1990); James T. Thomson et al., *Institutional Dynamics: The Evolution and Dissolution of Common-Property Resource Management*, *in* MAKING THE COMMONS WORK: THEORY, PRACTICE, AND POLICY 129, 154-55 (Daniel W. Bromley et al. eds., 1992); *see also* Donald A. Messerschmidt, *People and Resources in Nepal: Customary Resource Management Systems of the Upper Kali Gandaki*, *in* PROCEEDINGS OF THE CONFERENCE ON COMMON PROPERTY RESOURCE MANAGEMENT 455 (National Research Council ed., 1986). Similar results have occurred when inshore fisheries were taken over by state or national agencies from local control. *See* PARTHA DASGUPTA, THE CONTROL OF RESOURCES 13-40 (1982); Wilfrido D. Cruz, *Overfishing and Conflict in a Traditional Fishery: San Miguel Bay, Philippines*, *in* PROCEEDINGS OF THE CONFERENCE ON COMMON PROPERTY RESOURCE MANAGEMENT 115, 115 (National Research Council ed., 1986); *see also* John C. Cordell & Margaret A. McKean, *Sea Tenure in Bahia, Brazil*, *in* MAKING THE COMMONS WORK: THEORY, PRACTICE, AND POLICY 183 (Daniel W. Bromley et al. eds., 1992).

60. *See* JOHN R. COMMONS, LEGAL FOUNDATIONS OF CAPITALISM (1968).

61. In Schlager and Ostrom, the term used for *extraction* is *withdrawal*. Edella Schlager & Elinor Ostrom, *Property-Rights Regimes and Natural Resources: A Conceptual Analysis*, 68 LAND ECON. 249, 250 (1992).

system purchase that system in whole or in part.[62] Consequently, it is assumed that property-rights systems that include the right to alienation will result in the highest-valued use of the resource systems affected. Bruce Larson and Daniel Bromley[63] challenge this commonly held view and show that much more information must be known about the specific values of a large number of parameters before judgements can be made concerning the efficiency of a particular type of property right.

Scholars studying common-property systems have found that it is more useful to examine which of the five bundles of property rights are exercised in the field and what consequences result. In this view private individuals, private associations or firms, and governments may hold well-defined rights to a resource that include or do not include all five of the rights defined above. This approach separates the question of whether a particular right is well defined from the questions of which rights are possessed and who possesses them. While not the conventional view of lawyers, analysis of resources can benefit from viewing these rights bundles as diverse forms of property rights. In this respect, the analysis of distributed digital information would particularly benefit from a close examination of these bundles of rights.

"Authorized entrants" include most recreational users of national parks who purchase an operational right to enter and enjoy the natural beauty of the park, but do not have a right to harvest forest products. Those who have both entry and withdrawal use-right units are "authorized users." The contents of the bundle of rights of an authorized user may vary substantially in regard to the quantity, timing, location, and use of resource units appropriated from a resource system. The presence or absence of constraints upon the timing, technology used, purpose of use, and quantity of resource units harvested is usually determined by operational rules devised by those holding the collective-choice rights (or authority) of management and exclusion over the resource system.[64] An external authority, however, may mandate that the owner of a resource system must allow some access or withdrawal rights to another individual or group than the proprietor or owner of the resource system.

"Claimants" possess the operational rights of access and withdrawal plus a collective-choice right of managing a resource that includes decisions

---

62. *See* Demsetz, *supra* note 30.

63. Bruce A. Larson & Daniel W. Bromley, *Property Rights, Externalities, and Resource Degradation: Locating the Tragedy*, 33 J. DEV. ECON. 235 (1990).

64. The operational rights of entry and use may be finely divided into quite specific "tenure niches" that vary by season, by use, by technology, and by space. JOHN W. BRUCE, LEGAL BASES FOR THE MANAGEMENT OF FOREST RESOURCES AS COMMON PROPERTY 12-14 (1999). Tenure niches may overlap when one set of users owns the right to harvest fruits from trees, another set of users owns the right to the timber in these trees, and the trees may be located on land owned by still others. *See* John W. Bruce et al., *Tenures in Transition, Tenures in Conflict: Examples from the Zimbabwe Social Forest*, 58 RURAL SOC. 626 (1993). Operational rules may allow authorized users to transfer access and withdrawal rights either temporarily through a rental agreement, or permanently when these rights are assigned or sold to others. *See* Allen Adasiak, *Alaska's Experience with Limited Entry*, 36 J. FISHERIES RES. BOARD CAN. 770 (1979) (describing the rights of authorized users of the Alaskan salmon and herring fisheries).

concerning the construction and maintenance of facilities and the authority to devise limits on withdrawal rights. Fishing territories are a frequent form of property for indigenous, inshore fishers.[65] Farmers on large-scale government irrigation systems frequently devise rotation schemes for allocating water on a branch canal.[66]

"Proprietors" hold the same rights as claimants with the addition of the right to determine who may access and harvest from a resource. Most of the property systems that are called "common-property" regimes involve participants who are proprietors and have four of the above rights, but do not possess the right to sell their management and exclusion rights even though they most frequently have the right to bequeath it to members of their family and to earn income from the resource.

"Full owners" possess the right of alienation—the right to transfer a good in any way the owner wishes that does not harm the physical attributes or uses of other owners—in addition to the bundle of rights held by a proprietor. An individual, a private corporation, a government, or a communal group may possess full ownership rights to any kind of good including a common-pool resource.[67] The rights of owners, however, are never absolute. Even private owners have responsibilities not to generate particular kinds of harms to others.[68]

What is particularly important in the context of the intellectual public domain about this view of property rights is that property rights to the flow of units from a resource system are frequently held by different actors than those who hold rights related to the system itself. Further, empirical studies of common-property institutions have found that proprietors (as contrasted to full owners) have sufficient rights to make decisions that promote long-term investment in, and sustainable harvesting from, a resource.[69]

---

65. E. Paul Durrenberger & Gisli Palsson, *The Grass Roots and the State: Resource Management in Icelandic Fishing*, *in* THE QUESTION OF THE COMMONS: THE CULTURE AND ECOLOGY OF COMMUNAL RESOURCES 370, 374-75 (B. J. McCay and J. M. Acheson eds. 1987). Another example is the net fishers of Jambudwip, India, who annually regulate the positioning of nets to avoid interference, but do not have the right to determine who may fish along the coast. *See* BIKASH RAYCHAUDHURI, THE MOON AND NET: STUDY OF A TRANSIENT COMMUNITY OF FISHERMEN AT JAMBUDWIP (Government of India Press, Anthropological Survey of India 1980).

66. *See generally* PAUL BENJAMIN ET AL., INSTITUTIONS, INCENTIVES, AND IRRIGATION IN NEPAL (1994).

67. *See generally* ROBERT A. DAHL & CHARLES E. LINDBLOM, POLITICS, ECONOMICS AND WELFARE: PLANNING AND POLITICO-ECONOMIC SYSTEMS RESOLVED INTO BASIC SOCIAL PROCESSES (1963); JOHN MICHAEL MONTIAS, THE STRUCTURE OF ECONOMIC SYSTEMS (1976).

68. *See* Demsetz, *supra* note 30, at 355-57.

69. Frank Place and Peter Hazell conducted surveys in Ghana, Kenya, and Rwanda to ascertain if indigenous land-right systems were a constraint on agricultural productivity. They and others found that having the rights of a proprietor as contrasted to an owner in these settings did not affect investment decisions and productivity. *See* Frank Place & Peter Hazell, *Productivity Effects of Indigenous Land Tenure Systems in Sub-Saharan Africa*, 75 AM. J. AGRIC. ECON. 10 (1993). In densely settled regions, however, proprietorship over agricultural land may not be sufficient. *See* GERSHON FEDER ET AL., LAND POLICIES AND FARM PRODUCTIVITY IN THAILAND (1988); Terry L. Anderson & Dean Lueck, *Land Tenure and Agricultural Productivity on Indian Reservations*, 35 J.L. & ECON. 427 (1992). As land is densely settled, the absence of a title reduces the options for farmers to sell their land and

A key finding from multiple studies is that *no* set of property rights work equivalently in all types of settings. For private-property systems in land to make a difference in productivity gains, one needs (1) a somewhat dense population so competition for use is present and (2) the existence of effective markets related to credit, inputs, and the sale of commodities. In a series of studies of inshore fisheries, self-organized irrigation systems, forest user groups, and groundwater institutions, proprietors tended to develop strict boundary rules to exclude noncontributors, established authority rules to allocate withdrawal rights, devised methods for monitoring conformance, and used graduated sanctions against those who did not conform to these rules.[70]

The world of property rights is far more complex than simply government, private, and common property. These terms better reflect the status and organization of the *holder* of a particular bundle of rights. All of the above rights can be held by single individuals or by collectivities. Some communal fishing systems grant their members all five of the above rights, including the right of alienation.[71] Members in these communal fishing systems have full ownership rights. Similarly, farmer-managed irrigation systems in Nepal, the Philippines, and Spain have established transferable shares to the systems. Access, withdrawal, and maintenance responsibilities may be allocated by the amount of water shares owned rather than by the amount of land owned.[72] On the other hand, some proposals to "privatize" inshore fisheries through the device of an Individual Transferable Quota ("ITQ") allocate transferable use rights to authorized fishers, but do not allocate rights related to the management of the fisheries, the determination of who is a participant, nor the transfer of management and exclusion rights. Thus, proposals to establish ITQ systems, which are frequently referred to as forms of "privatization," do not involve full ownership.

Most of the CPR examples discussed so far have been natural resource systems and human-made resources, such as irrigation systems. In the past five years, interdisciplinary researchers are finding great benefit in applying CPR

---

reap a return on this asset. Without a title, farmers lack collateral to obtain credit to invest more intensively in the productive potential of their land. *See* Lee J. Alston et al., *The Determinants and Impact of Property Rights: Land Titles on the Brazilian Frontier*, 12 J.L. ECON. & ORG. 25 (1996).

70. *See generally* Arun Agrawal, *Rules, Rule Making, and Rule Breaking: Examining the Fit between Rule Systems and Resource Use*, *in* RULES, *supra* note 40, at 267; WILLIAM BLOMQUIST, DIVIDING THE WATERS: GOVERNING GROUNDWATER IN SOUTHERN CALIFORNIA (1992); WAI FUNG LAM, GOVERNING IRRIGATION SYSTEMS IN NEPAL: INSTITUTIONS, INFRASTRUCTURE, AND COLLECTIVE ACTION (1998); Edella Schlager, *Fishers' Institutional Responses to Common-Pool Resource Dilemmas*, *in* RULES, *supra* note 40 at 247; Shui-Yan Tang, *Building Community Organizations: Credible Commitment and the New Institutional Economics*, 13 HUMAN SYS. MGMT. 221 (1994).

71. David Miller, *The Evolution of Mexico's Caribbean Spiny Lobster Fishery*, *in* COMMON PROPERTY RESOURCES: ECOLOGY AND COMMUNITY-BASED SUSTAINABLE DEVELOPMENT 185 (Fikret Berkes ed., 1989).

72. *See* Robert Yoder & Edward Martin, *Water Rights and Equity Issue. A Case from Nepal*, *in* SEARCHING FOR EQUITY: CONCEPTIONS OF JUSTICE AND EQUITY IN PEASANT IRRIGATION 133 (R. Boelens & G. Dávila eds., 1998); *see also* ROBERT Y. SIY, JR., COMMUNITY RESOURCE MANAGEMENT: LESSONS FROM THE ZANJERA (1982); MAASS, *supra* note 35.

analysis to a number of new or previously ignored common-pool resources.[73] Studies that have been written to date on the Internet as a common-pool resource[74] tend to focus on the technology infrastructure and the social network issues rather than the institutions developed about the distributed information per se. Addressing scientific information, some of the most useful works in recent years have been those based on Michael Heller's groundbreaking work on anticommons.[75] Heller's work demonstrates that among the usual outcomes of a shared resource (particularly overuse,[76] but also depletion, congestion, pollution, etc.), the occurrence of "underprovision" of a traditionally available resource is not only possible, but of growing concern because of increasing commodification of information through new legislation, competing markets, and the recent run on patents.[77]

IV

IDEAS, ARTIFACTS, FACILITIES: THE ECOLOGICAL MAKEUP OF SCHOLARLY INFORMATION

In CPR research, the distinction between resource system and resource units has proved helpful in analyzing the impact of diverse property rights on the incentives of participants in regard to resource systems and resource units related to water, fisheries, and other natural resources. When water rights to a groundwater basin are adjudicated, litigants receive defined quantities or shares of the flow to the system. They are not receiving a portion of land that goes down below their surface land. That much earlier conception proved to be inadequate in the adjudication of groundwater rights. So, where water rights have been adjudicated and privatized, what has been privatized is the *flow*. The resource system itself is a *facility* that holds the flow and is not privately owned by a single person or organization unless there is a single overlying owner that owns all the surface land over a groundwater basin. Similarly, with individual

73. Some of these include studies of surfer's waves, sports, national budgets, public radio, traditional music, knowledge and information, air slots, campus commons, urban commons (apartment communities and residential community associations, streets, parking places, playgrounds, reclaimed buildings etc.), highways and transboundary transportation systems, the Internet (domain names, infrastructure, acceptable use policies), tourism landscapes, cultural treasures, car-sharing institutions, garbage, and sewage. For citations to these works, see Hess, *supra* note 16.

74. *See* P. Kollock & Marc Smith, *Managing the Virtual Commons: Cooperation and Conflict in Computer Communities*, *in* COMPUTER-MEDIATED COMMUNICATION: LINGUISTIC, SOCIAL AND CROSS-CULTURAL PERSPECTIVES 109 (S. C. Herring ed., 1996); Douglas S. Noonan, *Internet Decentralization, Feedback, and Self-Organization*, *in* MANAGING THE COMMONS 188 (John A. Baden & Douglas S. Noonan eds., 1998); B. A. Huberman & Rajan M. Lukose, *Social Dilemmas and Internet Congestion*, SCIENCE, Jul. 25, 1997, at 535.

75. Michael A. Heller, *The Tragedy of the Anticommons: Property in the Transition from Marx to Markets*, 111 HARV. L. REV. 621 (1998).

76. *See generally* Elinor Ostrom et al., *Revisiting the Commons: Local Lessons, Global Challenges*, SCIENCE, Apr. 9, 1999, at 278.

77. *See, e.g.*, Keith Aoki, *Neocolonialism, Anticommons Property, and Biopiracy in the (Not-So-Brave) New World Order of International Intellectual Property Protection*, 6 IND. J. GLOBAL LEGAL STUD. 11 (1998); Michael A. Heller, & Rebecca S. Eisenberg, *Can Patents Deter Innovation? The Anticommons in Biomedical Research*, SCIENCE, May 1, 1998, at 698.

transferable quota systems that are extensively used in regard to fisheries, what has been privatized is either a proportion of the estimated yield or an amount of fish that is assigned to each boat for a season.

In struggling with the application of the evolving theory of common-pool resources to the study of information and the intellectual public domain, we would like to pose that this two-way distinction is not as useful as a three-way distinction between the *artifact*, the *facility*, and *ideas*.

FIGURE 2
FORMS OF INFORMATION

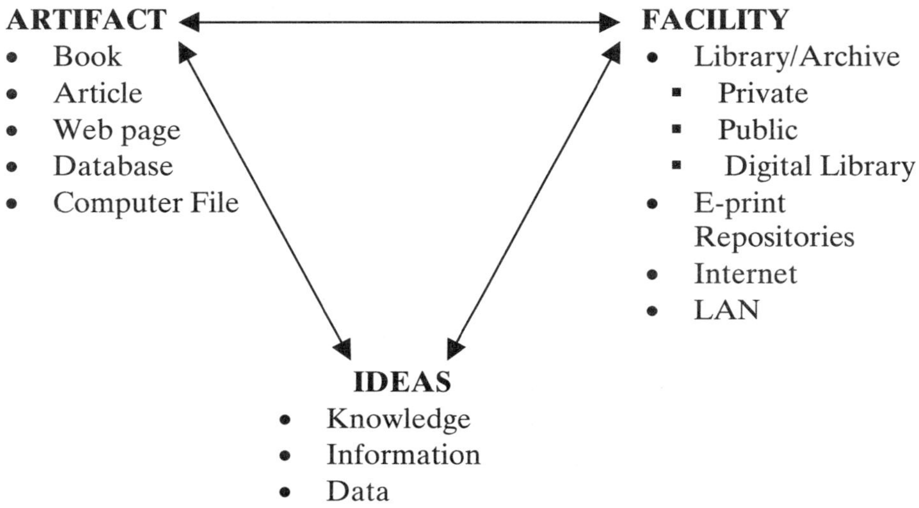

- An *artifact* is a discreet, observable, nameable representation of an idea or set of ideas. In regard to scholarly information, examples of artifacts include articles, research notes, books, databases, maps, computer files, and web pages. Artifacts vary in their durability. Physical artifacts can be used in a sequential fashion by multiple readers. Digital artifacts can be used concurrently by multiple users. Artifacts are the physical flow units from an information facility. Users can usually be excluded from using physical artifacts, but the process of excluding potential users has become more complex and less transparent with digital artifacts.
- A *facility* stores artifacts and makes them available. It is a resource system storing the artifacts and their ideas. Prior to the development of digital artifacts, traditional facilities were public and private libraries and archives that stored physical artifacts. A facility had a physical limit on the number and type of artifacts that could be stored. While the cost of excluding users was not usually extremely high, many libraries and archives did invest in the development of well-defined rules regarding who would be considered legitimate users, how long individuals could legally remove artifacts from the facilities, and the practices that were to

be followed within the facility (silence, no dancing) and in the use of the artifacts (no highlighting, tearing out pages, etc.) as well as guards for monitoring and enforcing these rules. The facilities themselves were subject to deterioration if a substantial investment was not made in their maintenance. Private collections were usually not open to the public.

- The *ideas* contained in an artifact can be understood to mean the creative vision, the intangible content, innovative information, and knowledge. Ideas are the nonphysical flow units contained in an artifact. This is the element that copyright does not protect.[78] Analytically, one person's use of an idea does not subtract from the corpus of that idea for use by others. It may, however, be possible to exclude others from knowing an idea by keeping it a secret.

It is our sense that in analyzing information in the public domain, developing a more careful understanding of the processes of providing and producing the information and artifacts, providing and producing information facilities, distributing artifacts to facilities and to users, and the various forms of consuming and using the information content of these artifacts is needed before one can begin to develop a better legal structure for these processes as they are challenged by new technologies in a global environment.

"Information" is a difficult term to define.[79] To economists, it can mean complete or incomplete knowledge, true or inaccurate knowledge; to governments, it can mean knowledge ranging from public to top-secret. In legal terms, it can mean that the conduit of information is currently owned, previously owned, or as yet unclaimed. Non-Governmental Organizations and donor agencies see access to information as the key ingredient for economic development. Referring to the multiple types of information issues, James Boyle has written: "Is there anything, apart from the *word* information, that holds these issues together? If there is some useful link, is it new to our society?"[80]

"Information" and "knowledge" as raw terms have been dissected and defined in several ways. Fritz Machlup introduced the division of data-information-knowledge, with data being raw bits of information; information as organized data in context; and knowledge as the assimilation of the information and understanding of how to use it.[81] Jerome Reichman and Jonathan Franklin

---

78. "The copyright will protect the expression in the work from being copied without permission, but will give *no protection whatsoever to the underlying ideas, facts, systems, procedures, methods of operation, principles, or discoveries.*" JESSICA LITMAN, DIGITAL COPYRIGHT 17 (2001) (emphasis added).

79. A recent *New York Times* article reported on an informal meeting of physicists and computer scientists to debate the meaning of the technology revolution. "[The scholars] found instead that they could not even agree on useful definitions of their field's most common terms, like 'information' and 'complexity,' let alone the meaning and future of this revolution." Dennis Overbye, *Time of Growing Pains for Information Age*, N.Y. TIMES, Aug. 7, 2001, at F3.

80. BOYLE, *supra* note 2, at 6 (emphasis added).

81. *See* Fritz Machlup, *Semantic Quirks in Studies of Information*, *in* THE STUDY OF INFORMATION: INTERDISCIPLINARY MESSAGES 641 (Fritz Machlup & Una Mansfield eds., 1983).

discuss the "dual function of information," which has high value as a commodity and as "the foundation of knowledge in the information economy."[82] Peter Lyman writes that the "the definition of the concept of information must be at the heart of any information policy."[83] Karl Popper earlier stressed that the knowledge contained in scientific reports, articles, and books comes to have an autonomous existence as it affects the thinking and research of the next generation of scientists.[84]

Sandra Braman presents a thorough survey of ways to look at information for policymakers, pointing out that the argument over how to define information is critical.[85] Examined are information as a commodity, as a perception of pattern, as a constitutive force in society.[86] Her analysis of information as a resource emphasizes how people *use* information rather than information's effect upon people.[87] For the purposes of our paper, Hayek's classic analysis of the two types of knowledge essential to bringing a clear understanding remains crucially relevant in the construction of scientific knowledge and information policy. He wrote in 1945 that while we are used to respecting scientific knowledge gathered by experts, it is only in combination with "local knowledge" that the knowledge takes on a real value. All of the valid research on common-pool resources involves this combination of scientific knowledge with time and place analysis, or as Hayek puts it, the "special knowledge of circumstances."[88]

In any discussion of information (including digital software) it is useful to remember that information is a human artifact, with agreements and rules, and strongly tied to the rules of language itself. [89] Thus, information has an important cultural component as well as intellectual, economic, and political functions. As such, it is a "flow resource" that must be passed from one individual to another to have any public value.[90]

---

82. Reichman & Franklin, *supra* note 2, at 884.

83. *See* Peter Lyman, *The Article 2B Debate and the Sociology of the Information Age*, 13 BERKELEY TECH. L.J. 1063, 1068 (1998).

84. "The world of language, of conjectures, theories, and arguments—in brief, the universe of objective knowledge—is one of the most important of these man-created, yet at the same time largely autonomous, universes." Karl Popper, *Epistemology Without a Knowing Subject*, *in* OBJECTIVE KNOWLEDGE: AN EVOLUTIONARY APPROACH 118 (1972).

85. Sandra Braman, *Defining Information: An Approach for Policymakers*, *in* THE ECONOMICS OF COMMUNICATION AND INFORMATION 3, 4 (D. M. Lamberton ed., 1989).

86. *Id.* at 6-11.

87. *Id.* at 6.

88. Hayek, *supra* note 9, at 521.

89. Vincent Ostrom has repeatedly emphasized the artifactual nature of knowledge and institutions:

> Every development—street sweeping, production of fertilizers, irrigation works, the development of new seed stocks—a component to it that is concerned with how the activities of people are organized in relation to one another.

Vincent Ostrom, Organization (working paper, Workshop in Political Theory and Policy Analysis, Indiana University, Bloomington, Indiana, 1969) (on file with authors).

90. *See* Mark Cooper, *Symposium Overview: Part II: Unbundling and Open Access Policies: Open Access to the Broadband Internet: Technical and Economic Discrimination in Closed, Proprietary Net-*

Intellectual property and contract laws are only a few of the complex issues facing scholarly communication. Current and future dilemmas extend much further than the legal questions of formal ownership and regulation. Other important areas include informal rights, agreements and standards, transaction costs, new user communities, globalization, growing international collaborative research, language, interdisciplinarity, interoperability, reliability, and accessibility.

But analyzing the whole ecosystem of scholarly information is much more tenuous than in *Governing the Commons*,[91] where (1) the boundaries were clear, (2) the resource systems studied were small and easy to observe, (3) solving problems was of high salience to appropriators, (4) institutions were long-enduring and had evolved over time, and (5) extensive field observation was available. The CPR resources were analyzed by examining the physical characteristics of that resource, the community of users and the actors involved in a situation, along with the rules in use that determine actions taken, the costs of those actions, the outcomes that can be achieved, how those actions are linked to outcomes, what information is available, how much control individuals can exercise, and what payoffs are to be assigned to particular combinations of actions and outcomes.[92]

Information, on the other hand, often has complex tangible and intangible attributes: fuzzy boundaries, a diverse community of users on local, regional, national, and international levels, and multiple layers of rule-making institutions. Until the invention of digital technologies, the flow of most scholarly information was easy to follow. One typical flow pattern was:

---

works, 71 U. COLO. L. REV. 1011, 1047-49 (2000) (discussing the problem of *flow control* or filtering the flow of distributed information).

91. OSTROM, *supra* note 36.

92. This methodological tool, called the *Institutional Analysis and Development (IAD) Framework*, is discussed at length in Chapter 2 of RULES, *supra* note 40, at 23-50.

FIGURE 3
TRADITIONAL FLOW PATTERN OF IDEAS → ARTIFACT → FACILITY → USER

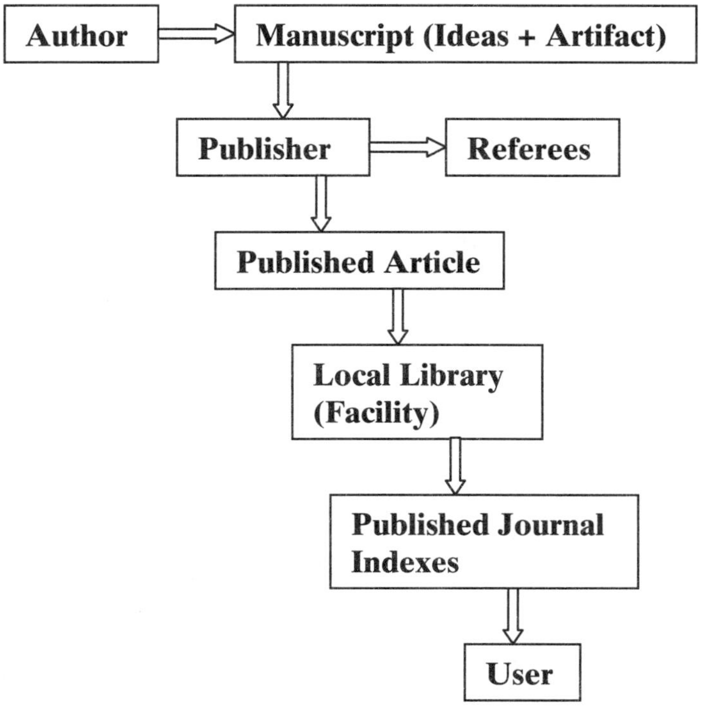

Each of the arrows in Figures 3 through 5 represents a transition where property rights may change in regard to the person or organization who holds the rights and/or in regard to the specific bundle of rights held. While the author retained copyright protection for her unique expression of ideas in a book or journal, the publishers, owned reproduction rights to the work, and sold copies of the artifacts to decentralized facilities (in this case, local libraries). The libraries owned their individual copies of the book, took responsibility for the organization, storage, preservation, and distribution of their "resource units." Working within the parameters of the formal rules of copyright, first sale, and fair use, the individual facilities designed the rules in use regarding the distribution and the qualified community of users.

The journal volumes, like books, are only temporarily subtractable, during one person's use, and are, thus, renewable resources over time. If the artifact is stolen or destroyed, replenishment is possible through re-purchase or through interlibrary loan. Journal articles are less subtractable because photocopying allowed through fair use lessens the competition for the resource. The ideas contained within the works are generally nonsubtractable.

The rules and flow patterns are different with digital information. John Perry Barlow pointed out several years ago that digitization, which converts information to ones and zeroes as a conduit of ideas, has obfuscated the "wine from the bottle";[93] that is, the physical characteristics and the boundaries of the resource are no longer clear. Digital artifacts are increasingly being licensed rather than sold, which means that publications are becoming more and more centralized. Centralization creates less stable and more "fugitive" artifacts, in that the publishers have the right of withdrawal. Libraries' distribution rights are increasingly limited by their contracts.

Distributed digitized information, such as that on the Internet, adds more layers of complexity to the flow. And, as with all common-pool resources, when technology changes the capture and use of the resource, the rules in use and the community of users will also change. On the other hand, digital information, though subject to congestion, is generally nonsubtractive; thus, the resource flow is not subject to erosion (deterioration) in that same way that physical information artifacts are (books, journals, newspapers, etc.).[94]

V

THE EVOLUTION OF SCHOLARLY INFORMATION

Prior to thirty years ago, the primary information facilities for scholarly information were public and academic libraries. These facilities were in charge of preserving "the scholarly record and the materials for future research"[95] by collecting, storing, preserving, and making available scholarly artifacts—primarily books and journal articles. Rules such as the fair use and first sale doctrines allowed libraries to provide access to the scholarly community.[96] Librarians consulted with university scholars and mainly purchased published scientific and academic books and journals. They made the distribution rules or lending policies and defined the eligible community of users. At that time, it was clear who was included in their community. For a state university library, for example, this usually included the faculty, students, and staff at that university, and any citizen of that state. The library owned its collection and was responsible for the storage, organization, and long-term preservation of the artifacts. The scholarly community sent their articles off for publication and depended on library personnel to meet their needs.

---

93. *See* John Perry Barlow, *The Economy of Ideas: Selling Wine Without Bottles: The Economy of Mind on the Global Net.*, WIRED, Mar. 1994, at 86, *available at* http://www.wired.com/wired/archive/2.03/economy.ideas_pr.html ("[T]he bottle was protected, not the wine."). In the same vein, Jessica Litman points out "copyright protects a painting or photograph of an automobile, but gives no protection to the automobile itself." LITMAN, *supra* note 78, at 18.

94. See Madison, *supra* note 2, for a discussion of the essential problems with the architecture and boundaries of digital information. "Digital computer network architecture, the substrate of cyberspace, has physical, virtual, and conceptual embodiments." *Id.* at 133.

95. Clifford A. Lynch, *The Transformation of Scholarly Communication and the Role of the Library in the Age of Network Information*, SERIALS LIBRARIAN, Summer 1993, at 5, 14.

96. *See* LITMAN, *supra* note 78, at 80, 81, 83.

Interlibrary Loan ("ILL")[97] was enhanced in the 1970s through the proliferation of new technology—the photocopy machine,[98] which allowed for duplication and easy lending of journal articles. It was further developed by the organization of the Online Computer Library Center ("OCLC"), the first electronic union catalog. ILL changed the user communities from local to local-regional-national (and later international) communities. With the costs of books and journals skyrocketing, the focus of library services changed from *owning collections* to serve present and future needs, to *accessing materials* for use upon demand.

Since 1995, the development of distributed digital information through network browsers has radically changed many of the traditional institutions of scholarly communication. Research information is moving much faster and much farther, often bypassing the normal publication process. While it is true that recent commodification and privatization of research information threatens the future of libraries' freedom to collect and distribute information, it is only one part of the story. Recent legislation, such as the Digital Millennium Copyright Act,[99] the Sonny Bono Copyright Term Extension Act,[100] the proposed legislation of the Uniform Computer Information Transactions Act ("UCITA"),[101] may all adversely affect the costs, access, and availability of scholarly information.[102] This focus of the intellectual public domain literature on commodification and privatization (along with issues of privacy and encryption) concentrates almost solely on the history, interpretation, and possible outcomes of such legislation on copyrighted works that have been *published.* But formal publication is only one type of scholarly communication.

With distributed digitized information, there are various flow patterns of the artifacts with varying property rights or contract arrangements at different points of the process. A sample flow pattern is shown in Figure 4:

97. Interlibrary Loan was formally proposed in the United States in 1898 by the University of California-Berkeley. The Library of Congress first began lending books in 1902. *See* http://www.loc.gov/rr/loan/ (last visited Oct. 17. 2002).

98. The first office copier was introduced in 1959. *See* Chip Holt, *Working Knowledge: Photocopiers*, SCI. AM., Oct. 1996, at 128.

99. 17 U.S.C. §§ 512, 1201-1205, 1301-1332; 28 U.S.C. § 4001 (1998).

100. Pub. L. No. 105-298, Title I, 112 Stat. 2827 (1998).

101. UNIF. COMPUTER INFO. TRANSACTIONS ACT (UCITA) (2001), *available at* http://www.law.upenn.edu/bll/ulc/ulc.htm. For discussions of "technological locks" for information proposed by UCITA, see Lyman, *supra* note 83 and Hannibal Travis, *Pirates of the Information Infrastructure*, 15 BERKELEY TECH. L.J. 777 (2000).

102. *See* Arnold Lutzker, *What the DMCA and the Copyright Term Extension Act Mean to the Library Community: Primer* (Mar. 8, 1999), *available at* http://www.ala.org/washoff/primer.html.

FIGURE 4
TRADITIONAL FLOW OF DIGITIZED INFORMATION TODAY

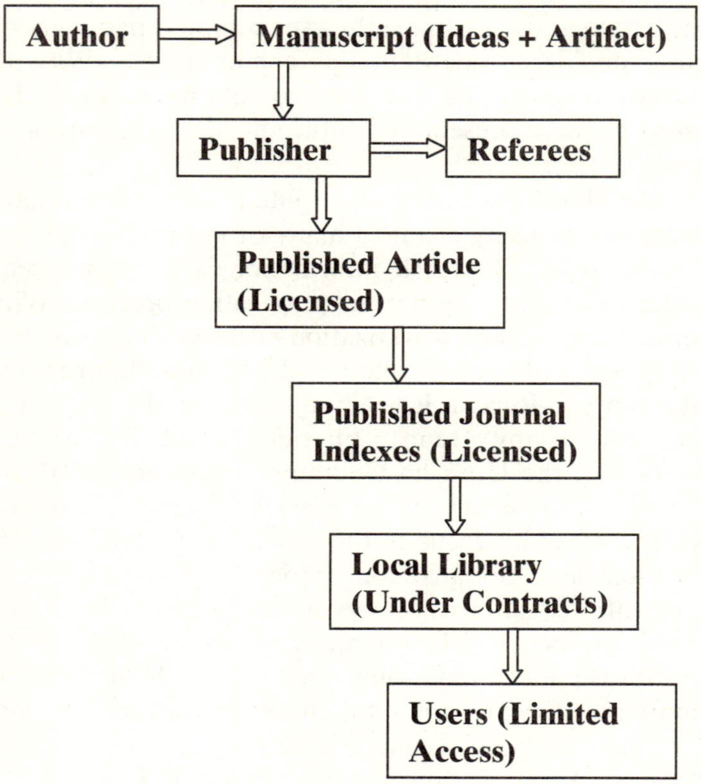

In this scenario, many of the rules in use are now determined by the publisher rather than the library. The facility, in other words, must now license access rights rather than purchase the artifacts. This change from property rights to contracts has multiple impacts on the distribution of scholarly information. The publisher may insist on a pay-per-view agreement, limiting the number of times the artifact can be accessed. Or, it may arbitrarily decide to withdraw certain journals that were formerly available. Frequently, publishers are "bundling" journals in a license package so that individual subscriptions cannot be cancelled by the libraries under that license agreement. At the same time, some contracts allow the publishers to makes changes to the bundles at their discretion.[103] Because of the enormous costs of these bundles, there is a growing inequity between the capacity of small versus large libraries

103. Kenneth Frazier gives as prime example Reed Elsevier, publishers of Lexis-Nexis, who have "both added and deleted content from their database at their discretion." Kenneth Frazier, *The Librarians' Dilemma: Contemplating the Costs of the "Big Deal"*, D-LIB MAG., Mar. 2001, *available at* http://www.dlib.org/dlib/march01/frazier/03frazier.html.

to participate in these deals. The license agreements also raise questions about the future of Interlibrary Loan (which would be a remedy for smaller libraries) since most of the licenses will not allow the copying of digital information.

A major spokesperson for the complexities of digital information for libraries, Clifford Lynch, noted in 1994 that if libraries did not make major changes in their collection practices, their role in store-housing scholarly information would be called into doubt.[104] One of the primary worries is the centralization of digital information:

> We have also yet to encounter the electronic analog of the burning of the great library at Alexandria (either due to natural disaster and inept off-site backup procedures or out of malice or cold, commercial calculation), which was so devastating precisely because in a pre-printing-press world there was such centralization of information at a single site. In a post-printing-press world, we run the danger of returning to the vulnerabilities inherent in such centralization. And it is not only publishers (both commercial and nonprofit) who are moving to centralized storage sites: government at all levels as well is exploiting the potential for low-cost distribution of information through computer networks.[105]

Libraries seem to be at the mercy of the publishers of scholarly digital information. They are dependent on digital publishers not only for the primary journals but also for the indexing and cataloging of scholarly journals. Because they add and delete journal titles from journal indexes, publishers have enormous power to shape the appearance and availability of research. Hence, libraries are able to provide only limited access, rather than the previous open access to journals in their collection. Even with the constraints of the new formal rules, however, library and information specialists are designing new institutions to deal with some of these problems. For instance, to tackle the problem of the precariousness or "fugitiveness" of digital information, one collective action initiative to counteract the loss of control over information is Lots of Copies Keep Stuff Safe ("LOCKSS"), which allows facilities to give permanence to the digital journals to which they subscribe.[106] If license agreements are cancelled, the libraries will still have digital copies of the journals to which they previously subscribed.

Public and academic libraries are also struggling with the possible ramifications of new intellectual property legislation, which more and more often contradicts the very nature of digital information.

---

104 Clifford A. Lynch, *Rethinking the Integrity of the Scholarly Record in the Networked Information Age*, EDUCOM REV. (1994) *at* http://www.educause.edu/pub/er/review/reviewArticles/29238.html; *see also* Pamela Samuelson & R. Davis, The Digital Dilemma: A Perspective on Intellectual Property in the Information Age, *presented at* the Telecommunications Policy Research Conference (2000), *available at* http://www.sims.berkeley.edu/~pam/papers/digdilsyn.pdf (last visited Oct. 11, 2002).

105 Lynch, *supra* note 104, at 39.

106. *See* http://lockss.stanford.edu/projectdescfaq.htm (last visited Oct. 10, 2002). This voluntary system developed at Stanford in 2000 "permits libraries to cache content they can access. If a library cancels a subscription and has not cached the content, they cannot get access to that content in the future. If a library caches content and then cancels their subscription, they continue to have access to the content they cached." *Id.* Over forty major libraries worldwide are now running the beta tests on this software. http://lockss.stanford.edu/projectstatus.htm (last visited Oct. 11, 2002).

> [C]opying occurs with all digital information. Use your computer to read a book, look at a picture, watch a movie, or listen to a song, and you inevitably make one or more copies. Contrast this with the use of traditional media: Reading a book does not involve making a copy of it, nor does watching a movie or listening to a song.
>
> This intimate connection between access and copying has considerable significance in the context of intellectual property protection. One of the essential elements of copyright—the right to control reproduction—works as expected in the world of traditional media, where there is an obvious distinction between access and reproduction and where the copyright owner's control of reproduction provides just that. But in the digital world, where no access is possible except by copying, complete control of copying would mean control of access as well. [107]

One type of action in response to the "digital dilemmas" is the increased monitoring, reporting, and educating to inform the public and information professionals about proposed legislation that may affect the access, costs, and distribution of scholarly information. Professional groups such as the American Library Association ("ALA"),[108] EDUCAUSE, and the Association of Research Libraries ("ARL") are taking on proactive roles to promote continued access to scholarly information. In ARL's May 2001 Membership Meeting Proceedings, Jean-Claude Guéédon stressed that "mapping effective counterattacks" against journal publishers who have transformed scholarly publication into big business "will require a fuller understanding of the situation and its roots."[109]

One of the most important sources of information on the developments of digital scholarly communication and research since December 2001 has been *The Free Online Scholarship (FOS) Newsletter*[110] written and compiled by Peter Suber, a professor of philosophy at Earhlam College. The newsletter presents a wide range of news and discussion on the migration of print scholarship to the Internet and efforts to make scholarly information available to readers free of charge. Its broader purpose is "to explore how the internet is transforming scholarly research and how researchers can realize its full potential."[111]

Libraries face many complex issues pertaining to the future of academic scholarly materials and its availability. Jessica Litman[112] and Lawrence Lessig,[113] among others, have discussed the precariousness of the fair use and first sale

---

107. COMMISSION ON PHYSICAL SCIENCES, MATHEMATICS, AND APPLICATIONS, THE DIGITAL DILEMMA: INTELLECTUAL PROPERTY IN THE INFORMATION AGE 31 (2000), *available at* http://www.nap.edu/html/digital_dilemma/index.html (last visited Sept. 6, 2002) [hereinafter DIGITAL DILEMMA].

108. *See, e.g.*, ALA's Washington Office homepage *at* http://www.ala.org/washoff/index.html (last visited Sept. 8, 2002); ARL's pages on its Scholarly Publishing and Academic Resources Coalition (SPARC) *at* http://www.arl.org/sparc/home/ (last visited Sept. 8, 2002); EDUCAUSE's Washington Office on information technology Policy Issues *at* http://www.educause.edu/policy/policy.html (last visited Sept. 8, 2002).

109. *See* Jean-Claude Guédon, *In Oldenburg's Long Shadow: Librarians, Research Scientists, Publishers, and the Control of Scientific Publishing*, *at* http://www.arl.org/arl/proceedings/138/guedon.html (last visited Sept. 8, 2002).

110. *See* http://www.earlham.edu/~peters/fos/index.html (last visited Sept. 8, 2002).

111. *Id.*

112. *See* LITMAN, *supra* note 78; Litman, *supra* note 13.

113. *See* LAWRENCE LESSIG, CODE AND OTHER LAWS OF CYBERSPACE 134 (1999).

doctrines as applied to licensed digital information.[114] As authors and information providers design new institutions to disseminate scholarly communication, library professionals must redefine many of their own institutions. Librarians can no longer build viable collections by selecting materials out of publishers' catalogs. They are becoming more actively involved in working with scholars, technologists, and policy makers to build trusted, reciprocal digital archive and repository systems.

The international e-prints "revolution" makes scholarly research freely available in unprecedented ways, in great contrast with the new legislation which increases copyright and patent restrictions, and encourages contract over property law through the constraints of embedded licensing agreements. The movement officially began with the mounting of arXiv.org at Los Alamos National Laboratory.[115] Developed in 1991 by physicist and information specialist Paul Ginsparg, arXiv.org was designed to serve as a repository for digital papers in physics and mathematics. By 1993, the site had received around 500 submissions. By September 24, 2002, the site had received 209,565 submitted papers.[116] Importantly, around 70% of the submissions came from outside of the United States.[117] The numbers reflect a better balance with much greater provision and access to international information, particularly in developing countries. The papers are free but unrefereed, requiring scholars to judge for themselves the accuracy and quality of the work. This archive is the first that actually changes the representation and visibility of the scholarly record.[118] The average number of site users range from 60,000 to 130,000 per day depending upon the day of the week.[119]

---

114. *See Individual Behavior, Private Use and Fair Use, and the System for Copyright*, DIGITAL DILEMMA, *supra* note 107 at 123-151.

115. The administration of arXiv.org was moved to the Cornell University Library site in September 2001; the main site hardware operations were transferred in December 2001. *See* http://arxiv.org/new (last visited Sept. 7, 2002).

116. *See* http://arxiv.org/show_monthly_submissions (last visited Sept. 7, 2002)

117. Figures from Paul Ginsparg, Creating a Global Knowledge Network, *presented at* UNESCO-HQ, Paris (Feb. 19-23, 2001), *available at* http://arXiv.org/blurb/pg01unesco.html.

118. A 1995 survey revealed that the main index of scientific journals, the *Science Citation Index*, indexes more than 3,300 journals of the roughly 70,000 that are published worldwide. *See* W. Wyat Gibbs, *Lost Science in the Third World*, SCI. AM., Aug. 1995, at 92, 92. A mere 2% of the journals indexed are written by authors from developing countries (with 80% of the world's population). *Id.* at 96. The author writes that the "near invisibility of less developed nations may reflect the economics and biases of science publishing as much as the actual quality of Third World research." *Id.* at 92. On the other hand, scientific research collaboration is rapidly increasing on an international scale. According to the National Science Board's *Science and Engineering Indicators*—2000, "growth in U.S. co-authorship reflects increases in international collaboration. By the mid-1990s, nearly one of every five U.S. articles had one or more international co-authors, up from 12 percent earlier in the decade." NATIONAL SCIENCE BOARD, SCIENCE AND ENGINEERING INDICATORS 2000 6-4, *available at* http://www.nsf.gov/sbe/srs/seind00/access/c6/c6h.htm (last visited Sept. 6, 2002).

119. *See* http://arxiv.org/show_weekdays_graph (last visited Sept. 6, 2002)

There are hundreds of other digital archives.[120] Some, like EconWPA,[121] are devoted to self-archiving and free distribution of working papers in economics. It is an impressive archive because of the number of other participating institutes. Others, like the Oxford Text Archive,[122] make available historical scholarly materials that are in the public domain and make the authorized, full-text versions universally available for free. BioMed Central[123] is the site of a commercial publisher that offers all its medicine and biology journal articles free of charge and provides a systematic pre-print service for research reports.[124] The Digital Library of the Commons[125] is both an e-print repository for self-archiving as well as a traditional/digital library.

An example of an effective grassroots initiative is that taken by the Public Library of Science ("PLS"), a nonprofit organization of scientists dedicated to making the world's scientific and medical literature freely accessible "for the benefit of scientific progress, education and the public good."[126] PLS has so far encouraged over 30,888 scientists from 182 countries to sign its open letter to publishers to make their publications freely available on the web site PubMed Central.[127] By September 2002, there were over eighty full-text journals available at this site.[128] Another new collective action initiative is the Creative Commons[129] founded by Lawrence Lessig, James Boyle, and others to promote "the innovative reuse of all sorts of intellectual works."[130] Their first project is to "offer the public a set of copyright licenses free of charge."[131]

A breakthrough for alternative publishing initiatives came only two years ago with the development of new technologies, data and metadata standards, and information provision communities. The Open Archives Initiative

---

120. For statistics on increased usage of electronic papers, journals, and citations, see Andrew Odlyzko, *The Rapid Evolution of Scholarly Communication*, LEARNED PUBLISHING, Jan. 2001, at 7, *available at* http://www.dtc.umn.edu/~odlyzko/doc/rapid.evolution.pdf (last visited Sept. 7, 2002).

121. *See* http://econwpa.wustl.edu/ (last visited Sept. 6, 2002).

122. *See* http://ota.ahds.ac.uk/ (last visited Sept. 6, 2002).

123. *See* http://www.biomedcentral.com (last visited Sept. 8, 2002).

124. Publisher Jan Velterop wrote in the online Free Online Scholarship Forum that BioMed Central differs from other, conventional, publishers, in that "authors are not 'giving' their article to us. They keep all the rights to their article, are not asked to transfer copyright, and are totally free to distribute their article in any way they like. What we provide, and what authors' institutions are paying for (a fraction, by the way, of what they collectively pay for articles published conventionally), is the service of organising and handling the process of having the article peer-reviewed, and, if accepted, published (given a unique bibliographic journal citation, DOI and URL) in open access, presented in various standardised formats (PDF and XML-generated HTML) and hotlinked (via CrossRef and others) and indexed (PubMed, Biosis and others) to enable optimum findability, citeability, dissemination, and 'embedding' in the network that science literature is." Posting of Jan Velterop to FOS Forum, http://www.topica.com/lists/fos-forum/index.html (Aug. 25, 2002) (copy on file with Law & Contemporary Problems).

125. *See* http://dlc.dlib.indiana.edu/index.html (last visited Sept. 6, 2002).

126. *See* http://www.publiclibraryofscience.org (last visited Oct. 29, 2002).

127. *Id.*

128. *See* http://www.pubmedcentral.nih.gov/index.html (last visited Oct. 29, 2002).

129. http://www.creativecommons.org/index.html (last visited Oct. 10, 2002).

130. *Id.*

131. *Id.*

("OAI") and the development of the free E-prints software[132] are already reshaping the direction of scholarly publication by establishing "low-barrier" interoperable standards.[133] OAI was established in October 1999 by an international group of information scholars to develop and promote interoperability standards that aim to facilitate the efficient dissemination of scholarly communication through the establishment of archives for e-prints and other digital materials. In OAI terminology the information artifact is a "record." The protocol developed by OAI provides access to the metadata of all OAI-compliant repositories by all networked servers (not limited to e-print servers).[134]

132. *See* http://www.eprints.org (last visited Sept. 7, 2002).

133. *See, e.g.*, Carl Lagoze & Herbert Van De Sempel, *The Open Archives Initiative: Building a Low-Barrier Interoperability Framework* (2001) *at* http://www.openarchives.org/documents/oai.pdf (last visited Sept. 6, 2002).

134. *See* Clifford A. Lynch, *Metadata Harvesting and the Open Archives Initiative*, ARL BIMONTHLY REPORT, Aug. 2001, at 217, *at* http://www.arl.org/newsltr/217/mhp.html (last visited Sept. 6, 2002).

FIGURE 5
SELF-ARCHIVING DIGITAL INFORMATION FLOW USING THE INTERNET

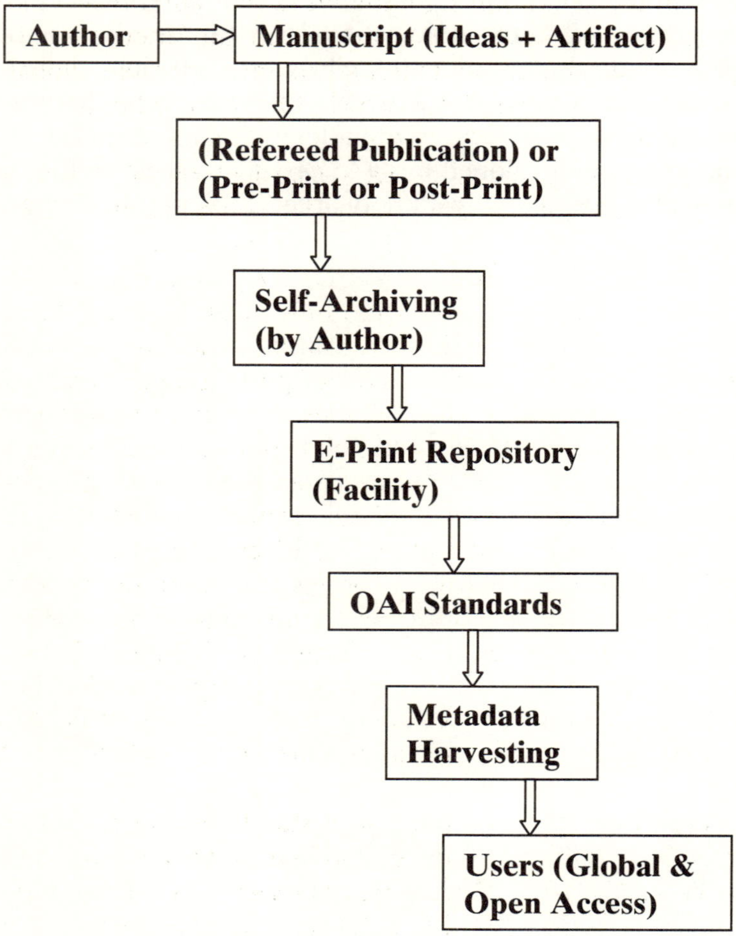

In this scenario, the author takes on a self-governing role in the distribution of scholarly information by submitting her digital file to an E-print repository (facility), such as CogPrints,[135] a repository for cognitive science, psychology, neuroscience, philosophy, linguistics, and biology. If the article has been, or is to be, published, she may get permission from the publisher,[136] amend the copyright transfer agreement with the publisher,[137] or submit the preprint (the

135. *See* http://cogprints.soton.ac.uk/ (last visited Sept. 7, 2002).

136. As happened with a published paper submitted to the Digital Library of the Commons ("DLC"), Jesse Ribot, *Theorizing Access: Forest Profits Along Senegal's Charcoal Commodity Chain*, 29 DEVELOPMENT AND CHANGE (1998), *available at* http://dlc.dlib.indiana.edu/documents/dir0/00/00/04/43/index.html. In this case the publisher granted the author the right to self-publish the paper on the DLC web site.

137. *See* Stevan Harnad, *For Whom the Gate Tolls? How and Why to Free the Refereed Research Literature Online Through Author/Institution Self-Archiving, Now*, *at* http://www.cogsci.soton.ac.uk/

refereed version) or a postscript (a subsequent revision to the published version).

What is new in the self-archiving initiative is that authors are participating, independently of governments and markets, in an international epistemic community that is committed to building an interoperable global scholarly library—a universal public good for which the more who have access, the greater the benefit for everyone.

Earlier we mentioned a prevalent view (particularly of Hardin advocates) that if anyone can use a resource, no one will have an incentive to conserve its use or to invest in improvements.[138] This does not seem to be the case for scholarly information. There are several incentives for taking an active role in these new information production institutions. Cost is one. Paul Ginsparg estimates the average cost per published journal article to be between $1000 and $2000, compared with the average cost of putting a self-archived paper on the web between $1 and $100.[139] Universities have incentives to support such self-archiving initiatives. Stevan Harnad points out that such action would free libraries from the increasing burden of their serials budgets. "This would be a small investment with an eventually huge return (reduction and eventual elimination of all annual Subscription/Site-License/Pay-Per-View ("S/L/P") expenditure)."[140] Rebecca Eisenberg points to scientific recognition and credibility that comes with public disclosure and increased visibility of information.[141] Global distribution of information facilitates better scholarly collaborative research. And, of course, a primary incentive is the sheer timeliness of distributed digital information with its ability to publish instantly and disseminate information, obviating the long delays of traditional publications.

A further development in building new standards, rules, and cooperative institutions to create resilience for the global knowledge resource is the growing movement to create Trusted Digital Repositories. A recent report by the Research Libraries Group and OCLC defines the required actions and rules for such systems as having: (1) audibility, security, and communication; (2) compliance and conscientiousness; (3) certification, copying controls, and following rules; (4) backup policies and avoiding, detecting, and restoring

~harnad/Tp/resolution.htm (last visited Sept. 4, 2002). Harnad, leader of the Self-Archiving Initiative, recommends that authors amend their copyright transfer agreements with their publishers as follows:

> I hereby transfer to [publisher or journal] all rights to sell or lease the text (on-paper and on-line) of my paper [paper-title]. I retain only the right to distribute it for free for scholarly/scientific purposes, in particular, the right to self-archive it publicly online on the Web.

Id.

138. *See supra* Part III.A.

139. *See* Ginsparg, *supra* note 117.

140. Stevan Harnad, *Free at Last: The Future of Peer-Reviewed Journals*, D-LIB MAG., Dec. 1999, *available at* http://www.dlib.org/dlib/december99/12harnad.html.

141. Rebecca S. Eisenberg, The Public Domain in Genomics (paper presented at New York University School of Law, Mar. 31–Apr. 2, 2000), *available at* http://www.law.nyu.edu/ili/conferences/freeinfo 2000/abstracts/eisengberg.html (last visited Dec. 3, 2002).

lost/corrupted information; (5) reputation and performance; (6) agreements between creators and providers; (7) open sharing of information about what it is preserving and for whom; (8) balanced risk, benefit, and cost; (9) complementarity, cost-effectiveness, scalability, and confidence; and (10) evaluation of system components.[142] These design principles point to the kinds of cooperative behaviors and system resilience that are needed to sustain scholarly information as a common-pool resource in an increasingly digital world.

The purpose of this section has been to give examples of collective action initiatives that create new institutions to manage and disseminate scholarly information. We have not discussed the risks and costs that may be involved. There are concerns among some academics that self-archiving may drive academic publishers out of business. Others question whether peer-review will be as respected and authoritative outside of commercial publications. There is also a delicate balance between a possible decline in the well-managed files that have been provided by library professionals in the past and the advantages of increased online accessibility. Confusion over versions and provenance of artifacts is inevitable without standards like the Machine-Readable Catalogue ("MARC")[143] record format. In addition, the fugitive nature of digital archives where authors usually have the right to submit *and* unsubmit is very different from traditional libraries where authors and editors are not permitted to remove their articles and books at whim.

VI

CONCLUSION

Governments, market forces, publishers, and traditional academic libraries can influence, but are not able to stop, the international movement of distributed information. The physical and virtual characteristics of distributed digital information have created a completely new type of information artifact.

The community of users—the international scholarly community—has grown increasingly aware that its shared resource of scholarly information is at risk. Growing international collaborative research necessitates immediate access and exchange of communication. Groups of scholars and information specialists have begun coordinating strategies to obtain higher joint benefits and to reduce their joint harm. Many of these collective-action initiatives are at the experimental stage, but the success of arXiv.org gives reason to believe in the success of other efforts to sustain the intellectual public domain.

We have described a gravitation of scholars' roles from passive *appropriator* of information to active *provider* of information by contributing directly into

---

142. Research Libraries Group, *Attributes of a Trusted Digital Repository: Meeting the Needs of Research Resources: An RLG-OCLC Report* (Aug. 2001), *at* http://www.rlg.org/longterm/attributes01.pdf (last visited Dec. 3, 2002).

143. *See* MARC Standards, http://www.loc.gov/marc/index.html (last visited Oct. 4, 2002).

the common pool. Their multiple goals include not only sustaining the resource (the intellectual public domain) but building equity of information access and provision, and creating more efficient methods of dissemination through informal, shared protocols, standards, and rules among the local and global scholarly community.

***

MAPPING THE DIGITAL PUBLIC DOMAIN: THREATS AND OPPORTUNITIES

PAMELA SAMUELSON*

I
INTRODUCTION

Whether the public domain is a virtual wasteland of undeserving detritus or the font of all new creation is the subject of some debate.[1] Those who adhere to the former perspective do not worry about "threats" to this domain any more than they would worry about scavengers who go to garbage dumps to look for abandoned property. Adherents of the latter view, interestingly enough, are not of one mind about "threats" to this domain. Some believe that propertizing value residing in the public domain will produce more social benefit than letting content languish there,[2] while others regard propertization itself as the main threat to the public domain.[3]

At the risk of seeming a contrarian, I concur with all three views: some of what is in the public domain is detritus; some of what is valuable in the public domain might be better utilized if propertized to some degree; other parts of the public domain need to remain open and unownable as sources for future creations. In the course of explaining why I embrace this seemingly contradic-

---

This article is also available at http://law.duke.edu/journals/66LCPSamuelson.

* Chancellor's Professor of Law and of Information Management, University of California at Berkeley.

This article is a derivative work of a paper presented at a conference on the public domain held at Duke University School of Law on November 9-10, 2001. My thanks to James Boyle, David Lange, and J. H. Reichman for convening this event and inviting me to participate in it, as well as for their many contributions to the literature on this subject. Research support for this paper was provided by NSF Grant No. SES 9979852.

1. Among those who seem to adhere to the former characterization are BENJAMIN KAPLAN, AN UNHURRIED VIEW OF COPYRIGHT 45-46 (1967) and Robert DeNicola, *Copyright in Collections of Facts: A Theory for the Protection of Nonfiction Literary Works*, 81 COLUM. L. REV. 516, 521-22 (1981). Among those who adhere to the latter are JAMES BOYLE, SHAMANS, SOFTWARE, & SPLEENS at x-xi (1998) and Jessica Litman, *The Public Domain*, 39 EMORY L.J. 965, 968 (1990).

2. *See, e.g.*, Eldred v. Reno, 239 F.3d 372, 379 (D.C. Cir. 2001), *cert. granted sub nom.* Eldred v. Ashcroft, 534 U.S. 1126 (2002), *and cert. amended*, 534 U.S. 1160 (2002) (suggesting that more works will be available if copyright terms are lengthened than if the works go into the public domain); JESSICA LITMAN, DIGITAL COPYRIGHT 77 (2001) (quoting Jack Valenti of the Motion Picture Association of America as saying that "[a] public domain work is an orphan," an observation that would seem to provide a rationale for perpetual protection for motion pictures).

3. *See, e.g.*, BOYLE, *supra* note 1, at 125-43; Yochai Benkler, *Free As the Air To Common Use: First Amendment Constraints on Enclosure of the Public Domain*, 74 N.Y.U. L. REV. 354, 397 (1999); David Lange, *Recognizing the Public Domain*, 44 LAW & CONTEMP. PROBS. 147, 147 (Autumn 1981).

tory perspective, I will offer a map of the public domain.[4] This map is a useful prelude to a discussion of possible impacts of various legal and policy developments affecting the digital public domain. Some initiatives would have adverse effects on the digital public domain, while others may not. This article will identify a number of threats to the public domain that deserve attention. It will also celebrate contributions that digitalization and digital networks have made in extending the public domain and enabling projects to preserve the digital commons. In some respects, digital information and digital networks have made the public domain more vibrant and robust, and if various digital commons initiatives attain their goals, the public domain may flourish as never before.

II

MAPPING THE PUBLIC DOMAIN AS AN AID TO UNDERSTANDING ITS PRESENT STATE IN THE DIGITAL ENVIRONMENT

The public domain has been, for the most part, an uncharted terrain. Sometimes it seems an undifferentiated blob of unnamed size and dimensions.[5] More often, discourse about the public domain focuses on one, or a small number, of its component parts or traits.[6] As a number of scholars have recognized, the public domain consists, in fact, of a vast and diverse assortment of contents.[7] The public domain is, moreover, different sizes at different times and in different countries.[8] Sometimes the public domain grows, as when patents or copyrights expire, or as in the aftermath of decisions such as *Feist Publications, Inc. v. Rural Telephone Service*, which held that uncreative compilations of facts

---

4. The idea of mapping the public domain is not original to me, but rather to Laurel Jamtgaard, formerly a Boalt student and now a practicing lawyer, who proposed to write a paper on this subject on the theory that such a map might prove fruitful in analysis of public domain issues.

5. *See, e.g.*, Edward Samuels, *The Public Domain in Copyright Law*, 41 J. COPYRIGHT SOC'Y U.S.A. 137, 137 (1993) (public domain is what remains when all forms of protected information are taken into account).

6. *See, e.g.*, Paul J. Heald & Suzanna Sherry, *Implied Limits on the Legislative Power: The Intellectual Property Clause as an Absolute Constraint on Congress*, 2000 U. ILL. L. REV. 1119, 1168-76 (2000) (arguing that the Copyright Term Extension Act is unconstitutional, as was earlier legislation restoring copyrights in foreign works that had been consigned to the public domain by U.S. formality requirements prior to 1989); Paul J. Heald, *Reviving the Rhetoric of the Public Interest: Choir Directors, Copy Machines, and New Arrangements of Public Domain Music*, 46 DUKE L.J. 241 (1996) (discussing illegitimate claims of derivative work copyrights in public domain music); Arti Rai, *Regulating Scientific Research: Intellectual Property Rights and the Norms of Science*, 94 NW. U. L. REV. 77 (1999) (expressing concern about efforts to propertize human genome data).

7. *See, e.g.*, BOYLE, *supra* note 1, at 209 n.8; Litman, *supra* note 1, at 992-95.

8. Some things are in the public domain in one country but not another. Some countries, such as the United Kingdom, allow copyright protection for laws and other government works, whereas U.S. law precludes this. *See* 17 U.S.C. §105 (2002). Some categories of intellectual creations that once were in the public domain are now subject to intellectual property rights. *Compare* 17 U.S.C. §102(a) (architectural works are listed as among the original works of authorship protected under the Copyright Act of 1976, as amended) *with* 17 U.S.C. §5 (repealed 1976) (listing protectable subject matters of copyright protection under the Copyright Act of 1909, now superceded, a list that did not include architectural works).

cannot be protected by U.S. copyright law.[9] Sometimes it shrinks, as when the European Union promulgated a directive requiring EU member states to protect the contents of databases[10] or when U.S. courts decided that business methods could be patented.[11] The public domain also has some murky areas. For example, some intellectual creations are, in theory, in the public domain, but for all practical purposes, do not really reside there.[12] Although I define the public domain as a sphere in which contents are free from intellectual property rights, there is another murky terrain near the boundaries of the public domain consisting of some intellectual creations that courts have treated as in the public domain for some, but not all, purposes.[13]

Across the border from the public domain are several categories of content that are so widely usable that, for practical purposes, they seem to be part of the public domain.[14] This includes, importantly, much content that is technically protected by copyright law but is widely available to the public, as when it is posted on publicly accessible web sites available to all comers without fee or apparent restrictions on use. Also outside the public domain in theory, but seemingly inside in effect, are such things as open source software; a penumbra of privileged uses under fair use, experimental use, and other copyright rules that permit unlicensed uses and sharing of information to take place; and standards that are licensed without payment of royalties.[15] Also at the perimeter of the public domain are works whose intellectual property rights are on the verge of expiring and, arguably, some creations that are about to be made—such as a new computer programming language or the solution to a longstanding mathematical problem—that, once they exist, will be part of the public domain. In the map below, the public domain is akin to its own nation-state. Various categories of public domain information are akin to regions of that nation. The contents of each category are akin to the cities or villages within that region that, in turn, have populations of various sizes. Some artifacts may reside in more than

9. 499 U.S. 340, 363-64 (1991).

10. Council Directive 96/9 of 11 March 1996 on the Legal Protection of Databases, 1996 O.J. (L 77), 20 [hereinafter EU Database Directive].

11. State St. Bank & Trust Co. v. Signature Fin. Servs., 149 F.3d 1368, 1375 (Fed. Cir. 1998). Policy-makers in the European Union have decided not to follow the United States in this respect.

12. A painting from the mid-nineteenth century that remains in a private collection or was destroyed in a fire is, in theory, in the public domain as a matter of copyright law, but its non-public nature or its destruction mean that it may, in fact, be there only in theory.

13. *See, e.g.*, Frederick Warne & Co. v. Book Sales, Inc., 481 F. Supp. 1191, 1196 (S.D.N.Y. 1979) (holding that illustrations from Beatrix Potter's Peter Rabbit stories were in the public domain as a matter of copyright law, but were nonetheless protected by trademark law when a competing publisher included the illustrations in its books).

14. Some commentators consequently treat some of these contiguous areas as part of the public domain. *See, e.g.*, Benkler, *supra* note 3, at 358 n.16 (treating fair uses as part of the public domain).

15. Until very recently, the World Wide Web Consortium had a policy of standardizing on patented technologies only if they were licensed on a no-royalty basis for W3C purposes. A change in the W3C policy that would allow royalty-bearing licenses has generated some controversy. *See, e.g.*, Kendall Grant Clark, *Patents, Royalties, and the Future of the Web*, O'REILLEY XML.COM, Oct. 10, 2001, *at* http://www.xml.com/pub/a/2001/10/10/patents-web-future.html.

one "town;" for example, a scientific article may contain three or four categories of public domain contents.

Mapping the public domain and contiguous terrains is useful for several reasons. First, it can help in an assessment of the likely impacts of certain developments on the public domain, such as the digitization of information and the development of global digital networks. Second, the map can be a tool for calibrating the extent to which a particular legal or policy initiative may affect the public domain, either in a positive or negative way. Some legal and policy initiatives, as we shall see, have broader and more serious potential impacts than others. Third, it can contribute to an analysis of which among the contents of the public domain are detritus (for example, grocery lists), which are gems (for example, Mozart symphonies), which are among the constitutionally core elements of the public domain (for example, scientific principles), which elements are there more by chance than design or necessity (for example, exercises), and which of the public domain's contents will be most harmed if propertized (for example, information).

FIGURE 1:
A MAP OF THE PUBLIC DOMAIN

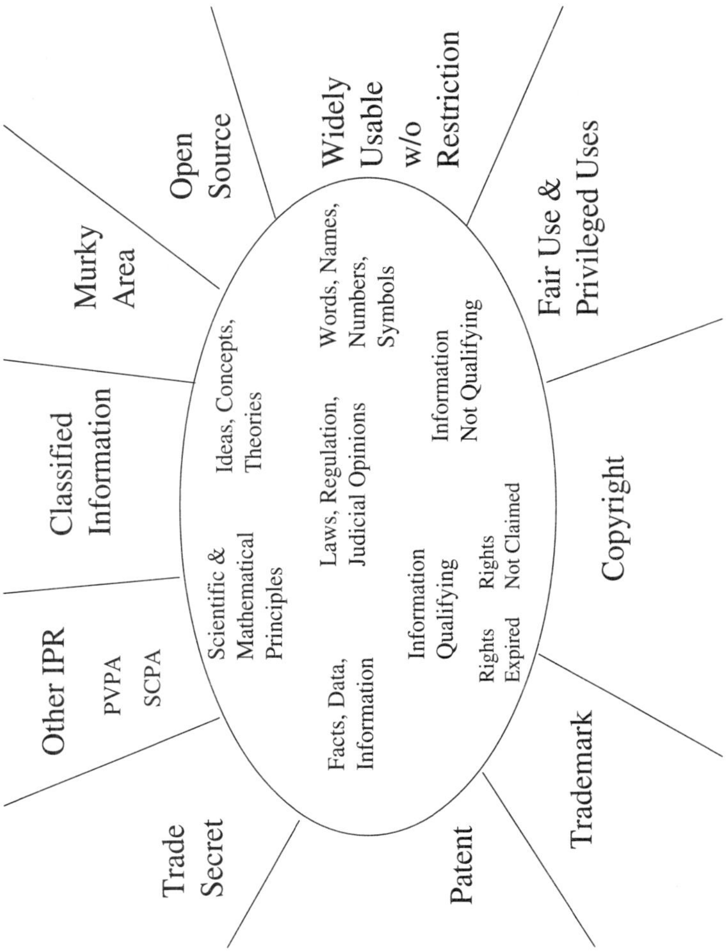

That digitization of information can have a very positive impact on the effective existence of the public domain is readily apparent. To the extent scientific data are either collected in or transposed into digital form, they can then be shared and processed more readily than if they remained in paper files in the basement of a scientist's lab.16 Global digital networks mean that scientists from around the world can share data sets and conduct experiments, leading to discoveries that will contribute to further growth of the public domain. Similarly, digitization of government information, such as bills pending before the legislature, government reports, schedules for hearings before legislative committees or administrative tribunals, and posting of this information on the Internet makes the information more widely accessible than print equivalents. This makes the public domain more effective and robust in serving that part of the public interested in such information.

Digitization of information and the existence of digital networks do not, of course, necessarily enhance the public domain. Firms may be able to attain meaningful exclusive control over digital information that is in the public domain, both in theory and in law, through technological access controls or licensing or both. The LEXIS and Westlaw databases contain hundreds of thousands of public domain judicial opinions and other legal texts in digital form that the database owners control both technologically and by licenses.[17] Do these technical controls or licenses diminish the public domain? Some would argue yes; others would argue no. Printed forms of these materials are, for the most part, still widely available without license or technical restrictions, and they may be a resource for further digitization projects having a non-proprietary character. Even those who care deeply for the continued existence of the public domain in legal information would have to admit that no firm could justify undertaking the very substantial expense of digitizing public domain legal information and building a database of these contents and software tools to enable effective use of the database without some way to recoup these expenses, as through some exercise of exclusive control over the resource. When Mead Data Central initially made its investments in digitizing judicial opinions, neither the government nor non-profit organizations had the foresight or the willingness to undertake such a project.[18] Legal scholars have greatly benefited by the existence of databases such as LEXIS and Westlaw. These scholars would be less capable of producing new works and making their own contributions to the public domain without access to these databases.

16. *See, e.g.*, NATIONAL RESEARCH COUNCIL, BITS OF POWER: ISSUES IN GLOBAL ACCESS TO SCIENTIFIC DATA 2-3 (1997).

17. Mead Data Central, a forward-looking paper company, anticipated an era in which digital information might displace paper. It started the LEXIS legal database by scanning print copies of the same cases contained in West Publishing Company's books of laws and judicial opinions to make digital source files.

18. West Publishing Company did not initially perceive the market potential for online databases of legal information. It introduced its Westlaw database in 1975, nine years after the introduction of LEXIS. *See* About Westlaw, *at* http://www.westlaw.com/about/?tf=91&tc=0 (last visited Nov. 13, 2002); About Lexis Nexis, *at* http://www.lexisnexis.com/about/default.asp (last visited Nov. 13, 2002).

Concern about restrictions imposed by proprietary databases of legal information has, moreover, generated a variety of initiatives to "free" legal information from these constraints. Courts themselves have undertaken to publish judicial opinions on court web sites. Legislatures post pending bills. Certain law schools, most prominently Cornell, have undertaken to establish non-proprietary databases of key legal information, such as Supreme Court decisions, open to all comers.[19] Some for-profit firms provide open Internet access to digitized legal information without charge in the hopes of attracting customers to their sites.[20] In these and other initiatives, digitization of the information and the availability of digital networks have been essential components of the strategy for effectively contributing to an enhancement of this aspect of the public domain.

Should the data in the LEXIS and Westlaw databases be available free on the Internet without restrictions? Perhaps so, and this is surely achievable, although not without cost. The U.S. government could clearly exercise its eminent domain power to acquire rights to make this information freely available on the Internet. But even if the political will could be mustered to do this (about as likely as Osama bin Laden's conversion to Christianity), would society be better off with a public domain LEXIS? Who would continue to invest in maintaining the database, extending it, and improving its tools? Perhaps social welfare is enhanced by a mix of digital public domain and proprietary databases of legal information, with the public domain sites providing some competition to hold in check the duopolistic tendencies of the market players and providing access to key information, such as pending bills and Supreme Court opinions, to those who cannot afford to pay database access fees.

III

THREATS TO THE PUBLIC DOMAIN IN THE DIGITAL ENVIRONMENT

Threats to the public domain come in different shapes and sizes. A relatively small, although still significant, incursion on the subset of the public domain consisting of digital information is represented by the Anti-Cybersquatting Consumer Protection Act ("ACPA").[21] ACPA extends property rights of trademark owners in the digital networked environment well beyond the bounds of trademark law.[22] Insofar as ACPA is being used to seize domain names from legitimate organizations and users, this incursion on the public domain is troublesome.[23] As compared with other initiatives, however, ACPA

19. *See, e.g.*, Legal Information Institute, *at* http://www.law.cornell.edu (last visited Nov. 13, 2002).

20. *See, e.g.*, FindLaw, *at* http://www.findlaw.com (last visited Nov. 13, 2002); Bureau of National Affairs, Inc., *at* http://www.bna.com (last visited Nov. 13, 2002).

21. Pub. L. No. 106-113, 113 Stat. 1536 (1999).

22. *See, e.g.*, Jessica Litman, *The DNS Wars: Trademarks and The Internet Domain Name System*, 4 SMALL & EMERGING BUS. L. 149, 163 (2000).

23. *See* Ford v. Great Domains.com, 177 F. Supp. 2d 635 (E.D. Mich. 2001) (Ford claimed that a domain name incorporating the word "jaguar" violated ACPA even though defendant had posted information on the domain name web site about preserving these animals).

is a relatively minor threat to the digital public domain. Its impact only extends to one subset of the most southern terrain of the public domain map.

A more substantial and differently configured threat to the digital public domain arose from Congress' enactment of the Copyright Term Extension Act ("CTEA") in 1998.[24] Strictly speaking, it was a threat when enacted, but is now a virtual dam blocking the flow of information into the public domain. It will remain so unless a challenge to its constitutionality is eventually successful.[25] The CTEA's incursion on the public domain is more substantial and more economically significant than ACPA's because it affects a larger region of the public domain, altering the legal status of hundreds of thousands of works for decades. Its principal impact may be on non-digital components of the public domain; in contrast, ACPA's impact is only in the digital domain. That the CTEA impacts the digital public domain can be seen in the thwarted plans of Eric Eldred to build a digital library of works that, but for the CTEA, would be in the public domain.[26] The CTEA's raid on the public domain has more constitutional significance than ACPA's because the constitutional provision that authorizes Congress to enact intellectual property laws requires limits on the term of copyright.[27]

Among the legal initiatives primarily aimed at digital information with major implications for the public domain are these: the Uniform Computer Information Transactions Act ("UCITA"),[28] the Collections of Information Anti-Piracy Act ("CIAA"),[29] and the Digital Millennium Copyright Act of 1998 ("DMCA")[30] in tandem with its inevitable brother legislation to mandate instal-

---

24. Pub. L. No. 105-298, 112 Stat. 2827 (1998) (codified as amended in scattered sections of 17 U.S.C. including §§101-106, 203, 301-304).

25. One legal challenge to the CTEA's constitutionality has so far been unsuccessful. *See, e.g.*, Eldred v. Reno, 239 F.3d 372 (D.C. Cir. 2001), *en banc denied sub nom.* Eldred v. Ashcroft, 255 F.3d 849 (D.C. Cir. 2001). However, one judge dissented from this decision insofar as the CTEA extended the terms of existing copyrights. *See Eldred*, 239 F.3d at 380-83. The U.S. Supreme Court has granted a petition for certiorari to hear Eldred's appeal of this decision. Eldred v. Ashcroft, 534 U.S. 1126 (2002), *and cert. amended*, 534 U.S. 1160 (2002).

26. *See Eldred*, 239 F.3d at 374. Other plaintiffs in the Eldred case were non-digital distributors of public domain works affected by the CTEA extension. *Id.*

27. U.S. CONST. art. I, §8, cl. 8 (exclusive rights may be granted only for "limited times"). The characterization of the CTEA as an instance of perpetual copyright on the installment plan derives from the work of Peter Jaszi. *See The Copyright Term Extension Act: Hearing on S.4839 Before the Senate Comm. on the Judiciary*, 100th Cong. (1995) (statement of Professor Peter Jaszi, Washington College of Law, American University). For an analysis of the constitutional deficiencies of the CTEA by one of the counsel for Eldred, see Lawrence Lessig, *Copyright's First Amendment*, 48 UCLA L. REV. 1057, 1065 (2001). *See also* Jane C. Ginsburg, et al., *Symposia: The Constitutionality of Copyright Term Extension: How Long Is Too Long?*, 18 CARDOZO ARTS & ENT. L.J. 651 (2000) (expressing various views on CTEA).

28. UNIF. COMPUTER INFO. TRANSACTIONS ACT (UCITA) (2001), *available at* http://www.law.upenn.edu/bll/ulc/ucita/ucita01.htm.

29. *See* H.R. 354, 106th Cong. (1999) (to be codified as 17 U.S.C. §§1401-1408).

30. Pub. L. No. 105-304, 112 Stat. 2860 (1998) (codified as amended in scattered sections of 17 U.S.C. including §§1201-1204).

lation of standard technical measures in digital media devices.[31] Each of these initiatives poses threats to the digital public domain that are broader in scope and scale than those posed by the CTEA. This is, in part, because of their implications not just for one region of the public domain map, but for multiple regions. Of these initiatives, only the CIAA directly offers protection to what is, under current law, public domain material. The other three mainly aim to give an extra layer of protection to intellectual creations, most of which are already protected by intellectual property law, although each affects the public domain and contiguous territories as well. Before probing each initiative in detail, it is worth pointing out that there may be synergies amongst these initiatives that multiply their effects. Further magnifying the potential effects of these legal initiatives are certain non-legal developments such as the formation of the Secure Digital Music Initiative ("SDMI") and the DVD Copy Control Association ("DVD-CCA") that aim to provide a secure technical infrastructure to avert leakage of digital works that the law alone would be unable to control.[32]

UCITA's most obvious implications for the digital public domain arise from its validation of mass-market licenses for computer information. *Pro-CD, Inc. v. Zeidenberg*[33]—a case decided, it should be said, under state commercial law rules, not under UCITA—is a widely cited example of the use of mass-market licenses to undermine the public domain in digital information.[34] ProCD manufactured and mass-marketed a CD-ROM containing white pages listings from thousands of telephone directories in digital form. ProCD could not get copyright protection for this compilation because the Supreme Court's *Feist* decision held that the white pages listings of telephone directories are in the public domain because they consist of facts that copyright law does not protect and because, as compilations, they lack sufficient originality to qualify for copyright protection.[35] ProCD put a license in the package containing the CD-ROM of telephone directory information that permitted only personal uses of the data, a restriction that Zeidenberg violated by posting the contents of ProCD's disks on an open site on the Internet. In the view of the trial judge in the *ProCD* case and of many commentators, enforcing this license restriction interfered with achieving policy objectives of copyright law.[36] The appellate court disagreed,

---

31. *See* Declan McCullagh , *New Copyright Bill Heading to DC*, WIRED NEWS, Sept. 7, 2001, (describing bill to mandate technical measures in digital devices), *at* http://www.wired.com/news/politics/ 0,1283,46655,00.html.

32. *See, e.g.*, DVD-CCA v. McLaughlin, 2000 WL 48512, *1 (Cal. Super. Ct. 2000) (describing DVD-CCA); SDMI challenge FAQ, (discussing the Secure Digital Music Initiative), *at* http://www.cs.princeton.edu/sip/sdmi/faq.html (last visited Nov. 13, 2002).

33. 86 F.3d 1447 (7th Cir. 1996).

34. *See, e.g.*, Niva Elkin-Koren, *Copyright Policy and the Limits of Freedom of Contract*, 12 BERKELEY TECH. L.J. 93, 93-98 (1997); David Nimmer et al., *The Metamorphosis of Contract into Expand*, 87 CALIF. L. REV. 17, 42-76 (1999); Maureen O'Rourke, *Copyright Preemption After the* ProCD *Case: A Market-Based Approach*, 12 BERKELEY TECH. L.J. 53, 55-57 (1997).

35. Feist Publ'ns Inc. v. Rural Tel. Serv. Co., 499 U.S. 340, 362-63 (1991).

36. *See* ProCD Inc. v. Zeidenberg, 908 F. Supp. 640, 658 (W.D. Wis. 1996); Elkin-Koren, *supra* note 34, at 63-71.

asserting that the existence of a contract between ProCD and Zeidenberg distinguished ProCD's claim from copyright.[37] Because ProCD's license only created rights as between the parties and not rights against the world, the license did not create rights equivalent to copyright.[38]

If UCITA's only impact on the public domain was to protect compilers of unoriginal data against market-destructive appropriations, there would be little reason to worry about this law. In a variety of ways, however, UCITA protects the interests of purveyors of digital information beyond—and in some respects in contradiction with—the default rules of intellectual property and other information laws. First, UCITA's willingness to enforce licenses protecting digital forms of public domain information does not depend on whether this is necessary to avert market failures. Second, to the extent that licenses are drafted to bind subsequent users, the distinction between contract rights that bind only the two parties to the transaction and property rights that bind the world erodes significantly.[39] Third, in a variety of subtle ways (for example, in presumptively enforcing confidentiality restrictions as to data that would generally be deemed "public" by virtue of its being mass-marketed), UCITA aims to stop leakages of information into the public domain.[40] Fourth, UCITA affects the penumbra of privileged uses lying adjacent to the public domain in significant ways. Under UCITA, the paradigmatic transaction is a license, not a sale.[41] This characterization of the transaction affects rights that copyright law confers on owners of copies of copyrighted content (for example, to make backup copies of software, to modify software, and to sell or otherwise redistribute one's copy of software).[42] In addition, UCITA presumes that all license terms are enforceable without regard to whether they aim to override public policy limitations on intellectual property rights.[43] For example, many software licenses restrict the right to reverse-engineer computer programs, even though

---

37. *ProCD*, 86 F.3d at 1454.

38. *Id.* Commentators have pointed out that preemption analysis can and should consider whether enforcing the state law would interfere with federal intellectual property policy. *See, e.g.*, Nimmer et al., *supra* note 34, at 40-63.

39. *See, e.g.*, Margaret Jane Radin, *Humans, Computers, and Binding Commitment*, 75 IND. L.J. 1125, 1132-33 (2000) (discussing viral contracts).

40. *See, e.g.*, Rochelle Cooper Dreyfuss, *Do You Want To Know a Trade Secret? How Article 2B Will Make Licensing Trade Secrets Easier (But Innovation More Difficult)*, 87 CALIF. L. REV. 193, 198, 241 (1999). *See also* David A. Rice, *License With Contract and Precedent: Publisher-Licensor Protection Consequences and the Rationale Offered for the Nontransferrability of Licenses Under Article 2B*, 13 BERKELEY TECH. L.J. 1239, 1248-51 (1998).

41. *See, e.g.*, Robert W. Golmulkiewicz, *The License Is the Product: Comments on the Promise of Article 2B for Software and Information Licensing*, 13 BERKELEY TECH. L.J. 891, 892-902 (1998).

42. *See* 17 U.S.C. §117. Licensing has especially important implications for libraries to the extent that the rightsholder has adopted a "single user license" policy. *See, e.g.*, NATIONAL RESEARCH COUNCIL, THE DIGITAL DILEMMA: INTELLECTUAL PROPERTY IN THE INFORMATION AGE 100-04 (2000) (discussing implications for libraries of licensing) [hereinafter DIGITAL DILEMMA]. Similarly, to the extent that existing consumer protection laws apply to sales of goods, arguably UCITA relieves its licensors from consumer protection responsibilities. *See, e.g.*, Jean Braucher, The Uniform Computer Information Transactions Act (UCITA): Objectings From the Consumer Perspective (Aug. 15, 2000) (on file with the author).

43. *See* UNIF. COMPUTER INFO. TRANSACTIONS ACT (UCITA) §105 (2001).

this activity would be acceptable under trade secrecy and copyright law as a means to get access to information that, once known, may become part of the public domain.[44] UCITA's presumption of enforceability may also apply to clauses in mass market licenses that direct the licensee not to criticize or reveal flaws in the licensed computer information,[45] which affects the legal status of many uses of information at the borders of the public domain.

There are, however, several ways in which the public interest in balanced licensing rules may be protected even if UCITA is, over time, more widely adopted than now. First, section 105 of UCITA recognizes the possibility that courts may rule some license provisions conflict with federal law or otherwise violate fundamental public policies, and insofar as they do, they may be unenforceable.[46] Courts may interpret this broadly and not enforce anti-reverse-engineering clauses or license restrictions on public domain information when there is no danger of market failure. Second, courts may invoke other legal doctrines, such as misuse of intellectual property rights and First Amendment values, to limit the enforceability of computer information licenses in appropriate cases.[47] This, too, may enable reuse of public domain information. Third, new legal doctrines may emerge in the case-law, such as "fair breach" of licenses to reach similar results under UCITA licenses as under copyright's fair use doctrine.[48] Fourth, the desire of licensors to impose unreasonable restraints on users by means of licenses may be held in check to some degree by market forces.[49]

How much comfort one should take in these checks on UCITA licenses is hard to gauge, given that UCITA essentially allows vendors of computer information to give themselves more rights than intellectual property law would and to avoid the burdens of public interest limitations.[50] Licensor restrictions are guarded, under UCITA, by a heavy presumption in favor of enforceability; this presumption can only be overturned after lengthy and expensive litigation that

---

44. *See, e.g.*, David McGowan, *Free Contracting, Fair Competition, and Article 2B: Some Reflections on Federal Competition Policy, Information Transactions, and "Aggressive Neutrality,"* 13 BERKELEY TECH. L.J. 1173, 1195-96 (1998). For more general expressions of concern about UCITA licenses and fair uses, see, for example, Charles R. McManis, *The Privatization (or Shrinkwrapping) of American Copyright Law*, 87 CALIF. L. REV. 173 (1999); Nimmer et al., *supra* note 34. *But see* Joel Rothstein Wolfson, *Contract and Copyright Are Not at War: A Reply to "The Metamorphosis of Contract into Expand,"* 87 CALIF. L. REV. 79 (1999) (arguing that Nimmer and McManis overstate the potential conflict between licenses and copyright policy).

45. *See, e.g.*, Mark A. Lemley, *Beyond Preemption: The Law and Policy of Intellectual Property Licensing*, 87 CALIF. L. REV. 111, 128-29 (1999).

46. UCITA §§105(a), (b). UCITA §105(c) defers to consumer protection laws to the extent they apply to computer information. There is, however, a question as to whether consumer protection laws, which were drafted to protect consumers in transactions involving *sales* of goods, apply to licensed information.

47. *See, e.g.*, Lemley, *supra* note 45, at 151-67.

48. *See* Jane C. Ginsburg, *Copyright Without Walls: Speculations on Literary Property in the Library of the Future*, 42 REPRESENTATIONS 53, 63 (1993).

49. *See, e.g.*, Gomulkiewicz, *supra* note 41, at 901.

50. *See, e.g.*, Julie E. Cohen, Lochner *in Cyberspace: The New Economic Orthodoxy of "Rights Management,"* 97 MICH. L. REV. 462, 464-67 (1997).

those injured by UCITA licenses may not have the means or will to undertake.[51] Many will simply be chilled from engaging in activities that would be determined legitimate had they been able to challenge a UCITA license term. Parents may blithely ignore the license term for the Adobe e-book version of *Alice in Wonderland* that forbids reading the book aloud,[52] but libraries have greater reason to worry about the potential enforceability of such a term.

In contrast to UCITA, whose scope is presently restricted to transactions in computer information,[53] legislation proposed to protect the contents of data compilations resembles the CTEA in affecting more than the digital public domain. Much of the rationale for such legislation relies, however, on the vulnerability of information in digital form to market-destructive appropriations,[54] and this legislation would certainly affect the size and scope of the digital public domain. Under current U.S. law, neither unoriginal compilations nor the data in original (and, hence, copyrightable) compilations is legally protectable unless it is a trade secret or otherwise confidential.[55] Several times in the past five years, the U.S. Congress has considered legislation to protect the contents of databases akin to measures adopted by the European Union in 1996.[56] The EU regime grants those who have invested substantial resources in making a database fifteen years of exclusive rights to control the extraction and reuse of all or substantial parts of the contents of that database.[57] Database rights are renewable upon further expenditures of resources, and substantiality is to be judged in qualitative as well as quantitative terms.[58] The most recent EU-style database bill introduced into the U.S. Congress was the CIAA.[59]

Although its sponsors characterize the CIAA as a regulation of unfair competition,[60] opponents characterize it as an intellectual property regime that is unconstitutional, bad public policy, or both.[61] The CIAA differs from the EU

51. *See* UCITA §105(b).

52. *See* Robert Menta, *Read an E-book to Your Child, Go to Jail?*, MP3.NEWSWIRE.NET, Dec. 26, 2002, *at* http://www.mp3newswire.net/stories/2000/ebook.html.

53. Drafters of this model legislation once intended it to regulate all transactions in information. *See, e.g.*, Pamela Samuelson & Kurt Opsahl, *Licensing Information in the Global Information Market: Freedom of Contract Meets Public Policy*, 21 EUR. INTELL. PROP. REV. 386, 386 (1999) (discussing the evolution of the scope of UCITA's subject matter).

54. *See, e.g.*, J.H. Reichman & Pamela Samuelson, *Intellectual Property Rights in Data?*, 50 VAND. L. REV. 51, 64-76 (1997) (discussing the rationale for sui generis database legislation).

55. *See, e.g.*, Feist Publ'ns Inc. v. Rural Tel. Serv., Inc., 499 U.S. 340, 344-45 (1991).

56. *See, e.g.* J.H. Reichman & Paul F. Uhlir, *Database Protection at the Crossroads: Recent Developments and Their Impact on Science and Technology*, 14 BERKELEY TECH. L.J. 793, 799-812 (1999) (discussing the DMCA and CIAA); Reichman & Samuelson, *supra* note 54, at 102-09 (discussing database bill).

57. EU Database Directive, art. 7, 10.

58. *Id.* art. 10.

59. H.R. 354, 106th Cong. (1999) (to be codified as 17 U.S.C. §§1401-1408); *see also supra* note 29 and accompanying text.

60. *See, e.g.*, H.R. REP. NO. 106-349 (1999).

61. Professor Benkler considers the CIAA to be an intellectual property law rather than an unfair competition law. *See, e.g.*, Yochai Benkler, *Constitutional Bounds of Database Protection: The Role of Judicial Review in the Creation and Definition of Private Rights in Information*, 15 BERKELEY TECH. L.J. 535, 575-86 (2000). Benkler concludes that the CIAA is unconstitutional. *Id.* at 586-87; *see also*

Directive in requiring proof of harm to actual or potential markets[62] and in its "reasonable use" limit on the liability of scientific and educational users for extractions and uses of data in protected compilations,[63] as well as in several exemptions such as those for news reporting, verification, and genealogical information.[64] By conferring rights on compilers to control the use or extraction of all or a substantial part of a collection of information that is the product of substantial investment,[65] however, the CIAA would substantially contract the digital public domain—and not just as to items of information, but also as to public domain works such as Shakespeare's plays, which fall within the meaning of "data" under the legislation.[66] The main reason that the CIAA has not been enacted is that organizations of scientists and a coalition of Internet-based firms, prominently including Yahoo!, recognized the serious threats that the CIAA posed to the digital public domain and mobilized against this legislation.[67] In the aftermath of the September 11 attacks on the World Trade Center and the Pentagon, Congress has had other more urgent matters to consider, but like the Terminator, the CIAA will almost certainly be back.

Although the CIAA and the EU database law pose substantial threats to the digital public domain, more narrowly crafted legislation to protect data compilations against market failures would not. H.R. 1858 is the alternative bill to the CIAA, considered during the same congressional session.[68] It forbids duplicating another firm's database and then engaging in direct competition with that firm.[69] While this bill would, of course, affect the public domain, it does so in a much narrower and more targeted way than the CIAA. Assuming there was persuasive evidence that market failures were occurring or imminent in the database industry because firms were competitively duplicating existing databases, this limitation on the reuse of public domain information would be justifiable.[70] This approach is consistent with the Supreme Court's ruling in

Malla Pollack, *The Right to Know? Delimiting Database Protection at the Juncture of the Commerce Clause, the Intellectual Property Clause, and the First Amendment*, 17 CARDOZO ARTS & ENT. L.J. 47, 49-50 (1999) (arguing that database legislation is unconstitutional). *But see* Jane C. Ginsburg, *"No Sweat?" Copyright and Other Protection of Works of Information After* Feist v. Rural Publications, 92 COLUM. L. REV. 338, 367-87 (1992) (arguing that database protection legislation would be constitutional). Whether EU-style legislation is a good idea as a matter of policy is a matter of heated debate. *Compare* Reichman & Samuelson, *supra* note 54, at 55-57 (critical of EU-style legislation) *and* Reichman & Uhlir, *supra* note 56, at 799-812 (critical of EU-style legislation) *with* Ginsburg, *supra*, at 341 (supportive of EU-style legislation).

62. H.R. 354 §1402.

63. *Id.* §1403.

64. *Id.*

65. *Id.* § 1402.

66. *Id.* § 1401. The CIAA defines "information" as "facts, data, works of authorship, or any other intangible material capable of being collected and organized in a systematic way." *Id.*

67. *See, e.g.*, Reichman & Uhlir, *supra* note 56, at 821.

68. H.R. 1858, 106th Cong. (1999).

69. *Id.* § 102.

70. In previous work, I have expressed support for narrowly drawn database protection. *See* Reichman & Samuelson, *supra* note 54, at 55-57; *see also* Benkler, *supra* note 61, at 602-03 (concluding that unfair competition legislation to protect data compilations would be constitutional); Reichman & Uhlir, *supra* note 56, at 836-37 (endorsing an unfair competition approach to database protection). In

International News Service v. Associated Press, which held that INS had engaged in unfair competition with the Associated Press ("AP") when its reporters took news from early editions of AP newspapers and published it verbatim in International News Service ("INS") papers that were in direct competition with AP papers.[71] The Supreme Court's *Feist* decision may have said that "raw facts may be copied at will,"[72] but the Court qualified this statement with a reference to its *INS v. AP* decision.[73]

The DMCA, like UCITA, principally aims to provide an extra layer of protection for commercially valuable digital information that is already protected by intellectual property law.[74] Like UCITA, the DMCA posits that private firms are free to devise regulatory regimes that deviate from the default rules of intellectual property law.[75] The principal difference between UCITA and the DMCA is that the DMCA's extra layer of protection is focused on technical measures used to protect digital information, whereas UCITA's extra layer protects licenses. Following on Lawrence Lessig's insights,[76] we might characterize the DMCA as code (law) that reinforces code (program instructions) as code (a private regulatory regime). Hacking is the act of civil disobedience (or user self-help) to which code as code is vulnerable. This is why the DMCA makes it illegal to "hack" certain technical measures and to make or distribute hacking tools.[77]

Although not principally aimed at protecting public domain works, the DMCA has significant implications for the digital public domain and for territories contiguous to the public domain. Technical measures will be effective in protecting public domain information as long as the vendor has the presence of mind to use the same technical measure to protect digital versions of both public domain and copyrighted works.[78] Technical measures will, unless pro-

---

addition, I have endorsed a short term of anti-cloning protection for industrial compilations of applied industrial know-how. Pamela Samuelson et al., *A Manifesto Concerning the Legal Protection of Computer Programs*, 94 COLUM. L. REV. 2308, 2413-18 (1994). James Boyle, one of the strongest advocates of the public domain, has also endorsed intellectual property protection for shamanic knowledge (which U.S. law would likely consider to be in the public domain) to prevent unjust enrichment. *See* BOYLE, *supra* note 1, at 128-30.

71. 248 U.S. 215 (1918). The Court's decision is persuasive as a matter of unfair competition, but has been widely criticized insofar as it relied on the existence of a "quasi-property" right in AP to stop INS's misappropriation. *See, e.g.*, Wendy J. Gordon, *On Owning Information: Intellectual Property and the Restitutionary Impulse*, 78 VA. L. REV. 149, 179-80 (1992); Pamela Samuelson, *Information as Property: Do* Ruckelshaus *and* Carpenter *Signal a Changing Direction in Intellectual Property Law?*, 38 CATH. U. L. REV. 365, 388-95 (1989).

72. Feist Publ'ns, Inc. v. Rural Tel. Serv. Co., 499 U.S. 340, 350 (1991).

73. *Id.* at 353-54.

74. *See supra* note 30 and accompanying text.

75. *See, e.g.*, Cohen, *supra* note 50, at 464-67; *see also* Tom W. Bell, *Fair Use vs. Fared Use: The Impact of Automated Rights Management on Copyright's Fair Use Doctrine*, 76 N.C. L. REV. 557, 559-60 (1998).

76. *See* LAWRENCE LESSIG, CODE AND OTHER LAWS OF CYBERSPACE 6 (2000) (discussing computer program code as a regulatory regime).

77. 17 U.S.C. § 1201.

78. The implications of the DMCA rules for the public domain have been recognized by many commentators. *See, e.g.*, Benkler, *supra* note 3, at 421; David Nimmer, *A Riff on Fair Use in the Digital*

grammed otherwise, persist after copyrights expire, thereby undermining new entrants to the digital public domain. Even if one could successfully argue that bypassing an access control used to protect a public domain work was not actionable under the DMCA's anti-hacking rule (because that provision only protects technical measures used by *copyright owners* to protect access to their works),[79] it would generally be necessary to build a tool to bypass any technical measure that controls access to public domain and copyrighted information. That tool would arguably be illegal under the DMCA because it would necessarily enable bypassing of an access control protecting copyrighted works.[80] Even Judge Lewis Kaplan, who found the application of the DMCA untroublesome as to Eric Corley's posting of circumvention software on the Internet, seemed somewhat concerned that the DMCA might be used to protect public domain works in contravention to copyright policy.[81]

The more serious and immediate concern about the DMCA is not about its implications for the public domain, but about its implications for territory contiguous to the public domain, where fair use and other privileged acts have long resided.[82] Under existing law, technical measures do not need to be designed to enable privileged uses, and few thus far deployed do so.[83] For example, the Content Scrambling System ("CSS"), the technical measure widely used to protect DVD movies, does not enable fair uses to be made; indeed, it does not even permit users to skip through commercials included on the disk.

Debates have raged in the law review literature as to whether Congress intended to preserve some room for fair uses under the DMCA and whether the DMCA is constitutional to the extent they did not so intend.[84] A substantial

---

Millennium Copyright Act, 148 U. PA. L. REV. 673, 738-40 (2000); Hannibal Travis, *Pirates of the Information Infrastructure: Blackstonian Copyright and the First Amendment*, 15 BERKELEY TECH. L.J. 777, 861 (2000).

79. 17 U.S.C. § 1201(a)(1)(A).

80. § 1201(a)(2). *See also* §1201(b)(2) (outlawing making or distributing other anti-circumvention tools). The vendor of technically protected public domain works might not have standing to complain about such a tool unless it used the same technical measure to protect works in which it did own copyrights.

81. Judge Kaplan stated:

> Moreover, the combination of such a work with a new preface or introduction might result in a claim to copyright in the entire combination. If the combination then were released on DVD and encrypted, the encryption would preclude access not only to the copyrighted new material, but also to the public domain work. As the DMCA is not yet two years old, this does not yet appear to be a problem, although it may emerge as one in the future.

Universal City Studios, Inc. v. Reimerdes, 111 F. Supp. 2d 294, 338 n.245 (S.D.N.Y. 2000), *aff'd sub nom.* Universal Studios, Inc. v. Corley, 273 F.3d 429 (2nd Cir. 2001).

82. *See, e.g.*, Julie E. Cohen, *WIPO Treaty Implementation in the United States: Will Fair Use Survive?*, 21 EUR. INTELL. PROP. REV. 236, 237-39 (1999); Pamela Samuelson, *Intellectual Property and the Digital Economy: Why the Anti-Circumvention Regulations Need To Be Revised*, 14 BERKELEY TECH. L.J. 519, 557 (1999).

83. An exception is technically protected digital audio tapes which permit first generation digital copies. *See infra* notes 89-90 and accompanying text.

84. *Compare* Samuelson, *supra* note 82, at 537-41 (fair use preserved to some degree) *and* Jane C. Ginsburg, *From Owning Copies to Experiencing Works*, *in* UNITED STATES INTELLECTUAL PROPERTY LAW (Hugh Hansen ed., forthcoming 2002) (fair use preserved to some degree; DMCA might be unconstitutional without some fair use limitations) *with* Raymond T. Nimmer, *Breaking Barriers: The*

consensus exists among scholars that without some room for fair use hacking, the DMCA would be unconstitutional.[85] Federal judges, however, may be reluctant to strike down the DMCA given the vulnerability of digital information products to uncontrolled infringements. They may be disinclined to second-guess the congressional judgment that the DMCA is necessary to the survival of the entertainment industry, exaggerated though this claim may be.

Senator Hollings has recently introduced a bill to mandate technical measures in every digital media device.[86] The assumption underlying this legislation seems to be that digital content cannot be protected effectively by software because the software's protections are too easy to hack, and the programs to bypass them, even though illegal under the DMCA, can be distributed easily via the Internet.[87] Content will not really be secure until and unless hardware systems have embedded technical protections. The Hollings bill would require all digital media devices to comply with standard technical protection measures.[88] In this respect, the Hollings bill resembles the Audio Home Recording Act ("AHRA"), which requires vendors of consumer-grade digital audio taping ("DAT") technologies to install serial copy management system ("SCMS") chips that prevent the making of perfect digital copies of digital sound recordings.[89] The AHRA represents a compromise between copyright owner and consumer interests because the SCMS chip allows consumers to make usable first generation copies of music, thereby allowing some fair uses of the music.[90] Any copies made from those copies, however, degrade in quality.

The Hollings bill does not contain a similar compromise provision, and the entertainment industry will undoubtedly resist efforts to add one. If it is enacted, the Hollings bill would have substantial implications for the public domain and contiguous terrain. Once technical protection measures are embedded in hardware, hacking to release public domain information or to enable fair or other privileged uses will become much more difficult than at present—and indeed, that would seem to be the point of making systems more secure.[91] The computer industry has successfully opposed legislation that would

---

Relation Between Contract and Intellectual Property Law, 13 BERKELEY TECH. L.J. 827, 880-88 (1998) (fair use not preserved).

85. *See, e.g.*, Ginsburg, *supra* note 48; Glynn S. Lunney, *The Death of Copyright: Digital Technology, Private Copying and the Digital Millennium Copyright Act*, 87 VA. L. REV. 813, 846-49 (2001); Neil Netanel, *Locating Copyright Within the First Amendment Skein*, 54 STAN. L. REV. 1, 37-42 (2001).

86. S. 2048, 107th Cong. (2002).

87. *See, e.g.*, DIGITAL DILEMMA, *supra* note 42, at 154-64.

88. Senate Bill 2048 would require the Federal Communications Commission to hold hearings about standard technical measures that might be installed in digital media devices and to mandate that future digital media devices install such technical measures. *See* S. 2048 § 3.

89. *See* 17 U.S.C. § 1002.

90. Sellers of DAT machines and tapes must, however, make regular payments of two percent of their sales to the U.S. Copyright Office to fund a royalty pool for compensating copyright owners for personal use copying. *See* 17 U.S.C. §§ 1003-04.

91. *See, e.g.*, Mark Stefik, *Shifting the Possible: How Trusted Systems and Digital Property Rights Challenge Us to Rethink Digital Publishing*, 12 BERKELEY TECH. L.J. 137, 144-53 (1997).

have required them to install copy-protection systems in the past,[92] so they may be allies of advocates of the digital public domain in lobbying against the Hollings bill.

More likely, at least in the short run, is scaled-back legislation applicable to consumer electronics equipment, but not (yet) to computers. This would address a key problem for the content industry: Manufacturers of consumer electronics equipment want to make products that customers will be eager to buy, and customers prefer technologies that enable them to copy and share digital content over those that lock the content down to one device. Efforts, such as the Secure Digital Music Initiative ("SDMI"), which aim to establish standards that can be built into equipment or rendering software to technically protect digital content, are not easy to bring to fruition because the content industry has very different interests than the consumer electronics industry.[93] Why waste all that time, money, and energy in a long, drawn-out negotiation with a consumer electronics industry that does not share your perspective on the need for technical protections, when generous campaign contributions and years of successful lobbying experiences provide access to a group with a long history of sympathizing with copyright industry concerns, namely the U.S. Congress? If private legislation proves unsuccessful, public legislation offers an alternative means to the desired end.

Which among these three initiatives—UCITA, the CIAA, and the DMCA/Hollings bill—poses the most serious threat to the digital public domain? Each is a serious threat in its own right, but more significant are the potential synergies among them, assuming all are enacted in the form currently proposed and are deemed constitutional. Any compilation of digital information protectable by the CIAA may also be protected by a UCITA license and by a technical protection measure capable of enforcing any restriction imposed on the digital information and legally validated by the DMCA and the CIAA. Even if the CIAA exempts "reasonable uses" from liability, such uses may be thwarted by the terms of a UCITA license or by a technical measure controlling what the user can and cannot do with the information.

As between UCITA licenses and technical measures (backed up by the DMCA), the more significant threat to the digital public domain and to reasonable uses of digital information would seem to be from technical measures. Secure systems do not allow reasonable uses to be made of protected digital information unless those uses have been authorized, whereas one can always ignore a UCITA license provision purporting to override rights to use information arising under other laws or challenge its enforceability in a legal proceeding. A person who makes reasonable uses of UCITA protected information in breach of the license can at least argue that the license term interferes with fed-

92. *See, e.g.*, News Release, Computer & Communications Industry Association, Hollywood's Copy-Control Proposal Will Harm Industry and Betray Consumers (June 4, 2002), *available at* http://www.ccianet.org/press/02/0604.php3.

93. *See supra* note 32.

eral intellectual property policy and should be preempted, is a misuse of intellectual property rights, is a fair breach of the license, or is unconscionable.[94] Ignoring a technical measure will be ineffectual because it will simply enforce the licensor's rules regardless of what the law says. A legal challenge to a technical measure that interferes with reasonable uses, given early court interpretations of the DMCA, is unlikely to succeed or be cost-effective. Some scholars have endorsed "self-help" measures by users to preserve the public domain or have argued for changes to the DMCA, making anti-circumvention protections only available to copyright owners who had escrowed keys to unlock technical measures and get access to the blocked material.[95]

Although the Internet was initially constructed as an open information environment, it is capable, as Lawrence Lessig has pointed out, of evolving into an architecture of perfect control.[96] The DMCA and the Hollings bill are elements of a legal infrastructure to support such a secure technical infrastructure. Governments and commercial entities may prefer architectures of control to architectures of openness.[97] Although the reasons for their preferences may differ, their goals may converge sufficiently to make governments and commercial entities allies in insisting on greater control over the online environment. This would diminish the digital public domain.

As between UCITA and the CIAA, it is difficult to say which would have the most harmful effects on the digital public domain. The CIAA would have a more immediate impact on this domain because it would propertize collections of digital information across the board. Analysts who have studied the CIAA's exceptions and limitations do not believe they adequately protect the public interest.[98] It is possible, of course, that courts will construe the exceptions and limitations more generously than intended in order to comport with constitutional requirements.[99] The CIAA has not yet been enacted and may evolve into a more balanced piece of legislation in response to criticisms leveled at highly protectionist versions of the bill.[100] UCITA does not directly diminish the public domain; it only presumptively validates license terms that implicate the public domain and adjacent terrain. The harm UCITA may do to the digital public

---

94. *See* sources cited *supra* notes 34, 44; J. H. Reichman & Jonathan A. Franklin, *Privately Legislated Intellectual Property Rights: Reconciling Freedom of Contract with Public Good Uses of Information*, 147 U. PA. L. REV. 875 (1999).

95. *See, e.g.*, Dan L. Burk & Julie E. Cohen, *Fair Use Infrastructure for Copyright Management Systems*, 15 HARV. J.L. & TECH. 41, 54-65 (2001); Julie E. Cohen, *Copyright and the Jurisprudence of Self-Help*, 13 BERKELEY TECH. L.J. 1089, 1137-42 (1998).

96. LESSIG, *supra* note 76, at 6-7.

97. *Id.* at 54-60. Governments may want more control over the Internet in order to stop gambling or to protect children from patently offensive materials; commercial firms may want more controls over the Internet in order to protect commercial transactions.

98. *See, e.g.*, Benkler, *supra* note 61, at 583-84; Reichman & Uhlir, *supra* note 56, at 811-12.

99. If, for example, an historian of the Vietnam War extracted and used a substantial quantum of data from a compilation of data about weaponry of that war, a court might consider the First Amendment as a limiting principle on CIAA liability.

100. *See, e.g.*, Reichman & Uhlir, *supra* note 56, at 823-28 (regarding Senator Hatch's discussion draft of database legislation).

domain is more likely to occur indirectly from the manner in which information providers license information and the extent to which they enforce license limitations. The same may be true for the DMCA. How much harm it ultimately does to the digital public domain and contiguous terrain depends in large part on how copyright owners deploy technically protected products in the marketplace and the extent to which courts limit uses (*if* they limit uses) of the DMCA against liberators of public domain information or fair users.

Threats to the digital public domain should also be gauged in terms of the statutes' likelihood of enactment and success. The CTEA constitutes the most substantial threat to the digital public domain because it has already been enacted and, thus far, has successfully blocked works from entering the public domain. The DMCA's anti-circumvention rules are also in effect, and its anti-tool rules have so far withstood constitutional challenges.[101] In the years since its initial promulgation, UCITA has been enacted in two states.[102] It has met with resistance in several state legislatures, and its future is clouded because of the controversies surrounding it. As noted above, Congress has not adopted the CIAA, although the House of Representatives passed it twice in 1998.[103] Compromise legislation may be necessary to attain enactment, and this would presumably limit the damage that the CIAA would do to the digital public domain. The Hollings bill has very little immediate chance of passage, but it is an ominous portent for the future.

As for private initiatives, DVD-CCA has, through a complex licensing arrangement, successfully ensured that all DVD players sold in the United States. and elsewhere have technical measures embedded in them. The huge success of the DVD movie market shows that the content industry's fond hope that consumers will buy technically protected content once they get used to it may have some chance of being actualized. The overwhelming majority of movies distributed on DVDs are works in copyright, not public domain works. Although the impact on the digital public domain from CSS-protected DVDs is consequently limited, impacts on fair uses are considerable. SDMI has been unsuccessful as a recording industry initiative to ensure secure content and secure players, but there is every reason to believe that the major players in the sound recording industry will move forward with distributing technically protected content. The major players are, moreover, aggressively challenging through litigation a range of technologies they perceive as threats to their interests. MP3 files of commercial sound recordings and technologies for distribut-

101. *See, e.g.*, Universal City Studios, Inc. v. Reimerdes, 111 F. Supp. 2d 294 (S.D.N.Y. 2000), *aff'd sub nom.* Universal Studios, Inc. v. Corley, 273 F.3d 249 (2d Cir. 2001); Real Networks, Inc. v. Steambox, Inc., 2000 U.S. Dist. LEXIS 1889 (W.D. Wash. 2000).

102. The states that have enacted UCITA are Virginia, VA. CODE ANN. tit. 59.1 §501.1-509.2, and Maryland, MD. CODE. ANN., tit. 22 §101-816.

103. The House version of the legislation that became the DMCA included the CIAA. However, because the Senate had not given due consideration to the CIAA or similar legislation at that point and because of non-consensus about such legislation, the Senate would not agree to the inclusion of the CIAA in the DMCA. *See* Reichman & Uhlir, *supra* note 56, at 829-30.

ing MP3 files have come dangerously close, in the industry's view, to an involuntary dedication of this digital content to the public domain.[104] While some commentators assert that efforts to use technical measures to protect mass-marketed digital content and legislation such as the DMCA will prove as futile as trying to make water not wet,[105] it remains an open and hotly contested question how technology, digital content, and the law will evolve and interact in the next decade or so.

IV

STRATEGIES FOR PRESERVING AND NURTURING THE PUBLIC DOMAIN IN THE DIGITAL ENVIRONMENT

One of the goals of this symposium is to articulate strategies for preserving and nurturing the public domain as a natural, if intangible, resource. This goal is particularly appropriate for digital information because it is so cheap and easy to collect, store, process, and make available via global digital networks. The THOMAS database of materials on legislation pending before Congress is an example of a digital public domain resource of great value to the public.[106] Other federal government web sites publish agency reports, procedures for applying for benefits, schedules of hearings, judicial opinions, rulemaking data, and the like in digital form on the Internet.[107] Numerous states have made similar resources available on open sites on the Web.[108] In addition, projects to establish digital libraries, digital repositories, knowledge conservancies, creative commons, and the like already exist, and more such initiatives will surely be undertaken in the coming years.[109] Scientists have created a variety of digital public domain resources, including libraries of reusable code and databases of scientific and technical information in digital form, which are also available on the Internet.[110] The Library of Congress has undertaken digitalization projects of historically significant parts of the Library's collection.[111] It has also convened a group to consider strategies for digital preservation of information.[112] Both initiatives have very substantial and positive implications for the digital public

104. *See, e.g.*, DIGITAL DILEMMA, *supra* note 42, at 76-94 (analyzing digital music as "intellectual property's canary in the digital coal mine").

105. *See* Bruce Schneier, *The Futility of Digital Copy Protection*, THE CRYPTOGRAM NEWSLETTER, May 15, 2001, *at* http://www.counterpane.com/crypto-gram-0105.html.

106. THOMAS: US Legislative Database, *at* http://thomas.loc.gov (last visited Nov. 13, 2002).

107. *See, e.g.*, Social Security Agency, *at* http://www.ssa.gov (last modified Nov. 12, 2002).

108. *See* Library of Congress State and Local Government Resources, *at* http://www.loc.gov/global/state/stategov.html (last modified Mar. 3, 2000); New York State Assembly, *at* http://www.assembly.state.ny.us (last visited Nov. 13, 2002).

109. *See, e.g.*, Project Gutenberg, *at* http://promo.net/pg (last modified Nov. 13, 2002).

110. *See, e.g.*, Scientific Applications on Linux, *at* http://sal.kachinatech.com (last visited Nov. 13, 2002).

111. Library of Congress Prints and Photographs Online Catalog, *at* http://lcweb.loc.gov/rr/print/catalog.html (last modified Nov. 4, 2002).

112. Library of Congress Metadata Encoding and Transmission Standard, *at* http://www.loc.gov/standards/mets (last visited Nov. 13, 2002).

domain. As much information may be lost to the public domain because it was stored in proprietary formats that are no longer readable by current generations of technologies as by legislation such as the CIAA or UCITA.

Entrepreneurial individuals have also taken advantage of the Web to make available a wide array of materials that, strictly speaking, are protected by copyright, but nonetheless are posted on open web sites with few or no restrictions on copying or distribution. This includes articles written by academics posted on their home pages,[113] pre-print archives of articles enabling scientists to share the latest learning in their fields,[114] electronic journals,[115] newsgroups,[116] web resources on the poster's favorite topic,[117] and MP3 files of music posted by bands wanting to attract new audiences.[118] Brewster Kahle has created a vast non-profit digital archive of the Internet and World Wide Web so that researchers can investigate such things as how much the Web has grown over time, what changes occur in the languages used on the Web over time, and what proportion of Web content is taken down or put up in units of time, just to name a few researchable questions.[119] A very substantial amount of high quality free content is available on the Web, although junk information is also prevalent. Even sites of profit-making entities, such as espn.com, cnn.com, and nytimes.com, post a large volume of high quality information on the Internet which are accessible by those who are willing to let cookies be planted on their hard drives or sign up as users.

Open source or "free" software is among the most interesting developments contributing to the digital public domain, even though open source software is not, strictly speaking, in the public domain.[120] Open source software contributes to the public domain because its licenses require that source code instructions be publicly available. All of the know-how embodied in the program is thus accessible. Because open source licenses encourage follow-on innovation, open source contributes to ongoing learning that further enhances the public domain. Open source software, however, is not itself in the public domain. Rather, it invokes intellectual property rights as the basis for a licensing strategy aimed at preserving the digital commons that the program's developer wished to establish for it.[121] From the standpoint of many open source developers, dedicating a

113. *See, e.g.*, Professor Alessandro Duranti, *at* http://www.sscnet.ucla.edu/anthro/faculty/duranti/publish.htm (last visited Nov. 13, 2002).

114. *See* Los Alamos Physics Preprint Server, *at* http://www.arxiv.org (last visited Nov. 13, 2002).

115. *See, e.g.*, First Monday, *at* http://www.firstmonday.dk (last visited Nov. 13, 2002).

116. *See, e.g.*, Slashdot, *at* http://slashdot.org (last visited Nov. 13, 2002).

117. *See, e.g.*, Archinect: Architectural and Urban Planning Sites, *at* http://www.archinect.com (last visited Nov. 13, 2002).

118. *See, e.g.*, Epitonic Music, *at* http://www.epitonic.com (last visited Nov. 13, 2002).

119. *See, e.g.*, The Internet Archive, *at* http://www.archive.org (last visited Nov. 13, 2002).

120. *See, e.g.*, Chris DiBona et al., *Introduction*, *in* OPEN SOURCES: VOICES FROM THE OPEN SOURCE REVOLUTION (Chris DiBona, et al. eds., 1999), *available at* http://www.oreilly.com/catalog/opensources/book/intro.html (last visited Nov. 13, 2002).

121. *See, e.g.*, Eben Moglen, *Anarchism Triumphant: Free Software and the Death of Copyright*, 4 FIRST MONDAY 8 (Aug. 2, 1999) (discussing the General Public License used by the Free Software Foundation), *at* http://firstmonday.dk/issues/issue4_8/moglen/index.html. The open source community

program to the public domain is a suboptimal strategy for achieving open source objectives because proprietary derivatives can be made of public domain programs. Those who breach the terms of an open source license by making a proprietary derivative program will be deemed infringers of the underlying intellectual property rights in the program and may be enjoined from this form of free-riding on open source development. Thus, open source licenses use property rights to preserve and maintain a commons in an existing intellectual resource.[122] While the initial subject matter of open source development was software, some efforts are being made to adapt open source licenses to other subject matters, such as digital music.[123]

As admirable as open source is as an example of a strategy for preserving and extending the digital commons, there is also value in preserving a public domain from which proprietary derivatives can be made. One of the key objections to the CTEA concerns new works that will not be created because of it. An inducement to the creation of new works from the public domain is the incentive of copyright protection for the derivative work. Writers would be less likely to adapt a public domain story into a dramatic play if the play, once written, had to be dedicated to the public domain because its genesis was a public domain work.

Concerns about risks to the public domain should not blind us to risks to investing in high- value digital information products. The marginal cost of reproducing and distributing digital information may be zero (or nearly so), but initial development costs may still be high, as may be costs of transforming digital information into marketable form and then marketing it. While some have hoped that advertising would provide a sustainable revenue stream through which digital content providers could recoup investments, this seems a less viable long-term strategy after the dot.com bust. Some commentators have proposed that firms give digital content away for free and rely on what were previously ancillary markets as their new primary markets, for example, selling support or customization services instead of software, or selling concert tickets instead of copies of digital music.[124] This strategy may be more viable for some digital content than for others. Some economists have suggested that digital

---

has mixed feelings about UCITA. On the one hand, members want mass-market licenses to be enforceable and want warranties to be disclaimable. On the other hand, open source developers depend on the ability to reverse engineer and make other unauthorized uses of other firms' software—which software licenses generally forbid. Hence, open source developers are generally opposed to enactment of UCITA.

122. Carol Rose suggests that limited common property rights may be appropriate for some types of digital information. *See* Carol M. Rose, *The Several Futures of Property: Of Cyberspace and Folk Tales, Emission Trades and Ecosystems*, 83 MINN. L. REV. 129, 181 (1998). This, in essence, is what open source licenses assert.

123. *See, e.g.*, Oscar S. Cisneros, *Expanding the Universe of Ideas*, WIRED NEWS, June 17, 1999 (discussing the open publication license), *at* http://www.wired.com/news/news/politics/story/20276.html; Campaign for Audiovisual Free Expression (CAFÉ project), *at* http://www.eff.org/cafe (last visited Nov. 13, 2002).

124. *See, e.g.*, Esther Dyson, *Intellectual Value*, WIRED, July 1995, *at* http://www.wired.com/wired/archive/3.07/dyson.html.

content providers may be able to sell different versions of their products on different terms to different customers, for example, giving away some content to create demand for one's product, but offering higher value versions for a higher price, or offering some information for free or at very low cost, but charging more to those willing to pay for earlier access to the information.[125] With a good business model, intellectual property rights may be much less important.[126] The digital information market is quite unstable right now, in part because no one is sure what business models are viable for distributing digital information via global networks. The fear, uncertainty, and doubt this has engendered among content providers may explain why they have been so intent on getting stronger legal rights. They do not exactly know what they need, but want more rights just in case an emerging business model might be based on those rights. What they don't need, they won't use.[127]

V
CONCLUSION

This article has considered a variety of ways in which the digitalization of information and the development of global digital networks have made positive contributions to the public domain. It mapped the public domain as an aid to assessing how various legal and policy initiatives threaten the digital public domain. UCITA, the CIAA, and the DMCA affect a broad swath of the digital public domain and contiguous territories, such as the realm of fair uses and, as shown above, these legislative initiatives may produce negative synergistic effects that further undermine the digital public domain.

There are several ways to avert these threats to the digital public domain. First, Congress, or in the case of UCITA, state legislatures, can become more aware of and attentive to expressions of concern about the deleterious effects these laws would have. Legislators can decide not to enact them, or to amend them to alleviate the problems they present. Second, courts can construe these laws more narrowly than they were initially drawn, strike them down as unconstitutional, or interpret them as unconstitutional unless limited by public domain and fair use principles. A key obstacle to reliance on the Constitution is that courts too often behave as though there is an intellectual property exception to the First Amendment.[128] They have been quite deferential to legislative

125. *See, e.g.*, CARL SHAPIRO & HAL VARIAN, INFORMATION RULES: A STRATEGIC GUIDE TO THE NETWORK ECONOMY 53-55 (1999); DIGITAL DILEMMA, *supra* note 42, at 176-86 (discussing various business models for digital content).

126. DIGITAL DILEMMA, *supra* note 42, at 183-84 ("One approach to IP rights in a world where digital content is difficult to control entails selecting a business model that does not require strict control.").

127. Cary Sherman, General Counsel to the Recording Industry Association of America, once offered this explanation when I asked him why the content industry was so intent on getting control over all temporary, as well as permanent, copies of digital content.

128. *See, e.g.*, Eldred v. Reno, 239 F.3d 372, 375 (D.C. Cir. 2001) (citing case-law holding that copyrights are categorically immune from challenges under the First Amendment); *but see* Mark A. Lemley & Eugene Volokh, *Freedom of Speech and Injunctions in Intellectual Property Cases*, 48 DUKE L.J. 147,

judgments, using rational basis analysis rather than intermediate scrutiny.[129] Judges sometimes act as though the limits in Article I, section 8, clause 8, both express and applied, lack meaningful substance.[130] The progress of science and the useful arts depends on information being in the public domain and available for reuse, as much as on the grant of intellectual property rights. Third, the public can refuse to accept laws that impede socially desirable uses. If people just say no to licensing and to technically protected content, the content industry, the courts, and the legislature will have to adjust.

Those who care about preserving and nurturing the public domain should pay attention to legal and policy initiatives affecting this domain, analyze their implications, assess their constitutionality, and write and speak to various audiences to raise consciousness about the negative impacts that particular initiatives may have. Some will undertake litigation to preserve the public domain and contiguous territories.[131] Others will draft testimony about pending or proposed legislation or offer alternative proposals. The rhetoric of scholarly discourse lacks the crispness of the vernacular. Legal scholars need to search for new vocabularies and metaphors to convey messages of concern. Efforts to affect policymaking will sometimes bear fruit (for example, the CIAA has not been enacted, and UCITA has encountered more difficulties than its drafters expected), but sometimes they will not (for example, DMCA and CTEA). To achieve our public interest objectives, we need not only to keep doing what we do well but also to reach beyond the communities we already inhabit to find friends and allies among those likely to be affected by initiatives that concern us. And, we need to be cheerful about it, too.

It is possible to construct a new politics of intellectual property that has regard for the public domain and fair uses.[132] To be successful, a new public-regarding politics of intellectual property must have a positive agenda of its own. It cannot just oppose whatever legislative initiatives the major content industry organizations support (although it almost certainly will need to do this as well). It should be grounded on the realization that information is not only or mainly a commodity; it is also a critically important resource and input to learning, culture, competition, innovation, and democratic discourse. Intellec-

---

150 (1999) (criticizing the frequency with which injunctions issue in intellectual property cases on First Amendment grounds).

129. *See Eldred*, 239 F.3d at 378.

130. The D.C. Circuit, for example, recently held that the preamble to Art. I, § 8, cl. 8 ("to promote the progress of science and useful arts") did not constitute a substantive limitation on Congress. *Id.* at 376-77.

131. *See, e.g.*, Paul J. Heald, *Payment Demands for Spurious Copyrights: Four Causes of Action*, 1 J. INTELL. PROP. L. 259, 261-62 (1994) (discussing legal claims that might be used to challenge spurious claims of copyright in public domain material).

132. James Boyle was the first to call for a new politics of intellectual property. *See, e.g.*, James Boyle, *A Politics of Intellectual Property: Environmentalism for the Net?*, 47 DUKE L.J. 87, 87 (1997). For my endorsement of this concept, see Pamela Samuelson, *Toward a New Politics of Intellectual Property*, 44 COMM. ACM 98 (2001). Public Knowledge is a nonprofit organization recently established to build a public-regarding politics of intellectual property. *See* Public Knowledge, *at* http://www.publicknowledge.org (last visited Nov. 13, 2002).

tual property must find a home in a broader-based information policy, and be a servant, not a master, of the information society.

***

THROUGH THE LOOKING GLASS: ALICE AND THE CONSTITUTIONAL FOUNDATIONS OF THE PUBLIC DOMAIN

YOCHAI BENKLER*

I
INTRODUCTION

A. The White Rabbit

Alice Randall, an African-American woman, was ordered by a government official not to publish her criticism of the romanticization of the Old South, at least not in the words she wanted to use. The official was not one of the many in Congress and the Administration who share a romantic view of the Confederacy. It was a federal judge in Atlanta who told Randall that she could not write her critique in the words she wanted to use—a judge enforcing copyright law. Randall is the author of a book called *The Wind Done Gone*.[1] In it, she tells a story that takes off from *Gone with the Wind*[2] from the perspective of Scarlet O'Hara's mulatto half-sister. In 2001, more than fifty years after Margaret Mitchell died, and years after the original copyright for the book would have expired under the law in effect when Mitchell wrote it, a federal district judge ordered Randall's publisher not to publish *The Wind Done Gone*. The Court of Appeals then overturned the injunction as a prior restraint.[3]

B. Off with His Head!

Dmitry Sklyarov is a Russian programmer who faced the prospect of an American jail because he wrote software that enables people to read books that they are not allowed to read. Adobe Systems convinced the government to prosecute Sklyarov because he made it possible for people to read documents that Adobe had encrypted so that they could only be read with its eBook reader program. The Digital Millennium Copyright Act ("DMCA") makes it a criminal offense to provide software that lets people read digitized books with

---

This article is also available at http://www.law.duke.edu/journals/66LCPBenkler.

* Professor of Law, New York University

1. ALICE RANDALL, THE WIND DONE GONE (2001).
2. MARGARET MITCHELL, GONE WITH THE WIND (1939).
3. This subpart describes the facts of *SunTrust Bank v. Houghton Mifflin Co.*, 268 F.3d 1257 (11th Cir. 2001).

equipment that is not licensed to decrypt them.[4] The DMCA does not exempt people who write software that readers can use to read books that they are perfectly privileged to read. It does not matter that the person who wants to read the book owns a copy of it. It does not matter that the person who wants to quote from a book or a DVD wants to do so in a manner that is permitted under copyright law, such as under the fair use doctrine. It does not even matter if the encrypted materials are in the public domain—like *Alice in Wonderland*.[5]

Adobe wanted to demonstrate how useful its eBook reader would be to publishers who wanted to distribute their books digitally. It used a digital book that it could get cheaply—*Alice in Wonderland*. The original text was in the public domain. *Alice* had already been digitized and proofread by volunteers as part of Project Gutenberg.[6] All that Adobe needed to do was take this free text, wrap it in its digital code, and *presto*—Adobe had a cheap and effective demonstration of how its technology could help copyright owners. The cover sheet of the closed edition of *Alice* is immensely instructive. It explains to the readers that they may not give, lend, quote, or print out a copy of this public domain work.[7]

C. What, Exactly, Is Your Problem?

Edward Felten is a computer scientist at Princeton. As he was preparing to publish a paper on encryption, he received a threatening letter from the Recording Industry Association of America ("RIAA"), telling him that publication of the paper constituted a violation of the DMCA.

The music industry had spent substantial sums developing encryption for digital music distribution. In order to test the system before it actually entrusted music with this wrapper, the industry issued a public challenge, inviting all cryptographers to try to break the code. Felten succeeded in doing so, but he did not continue to test his solutions because the industry required that, to continue testing, he sign a nondisclosure agreement. Felten is an academic, not a businessperson. He works to make knowledge public, not to keep it secret. He refused to sign the nondisclosure agreement and prepared to publish his findings. As he did so, he received the RIAA's threatening letter. In response, he asked a federal district court to declare that publication of his findings was not a violation of the DMCA. The RIAA suddenly realized that trying to silence academic publication of a criticism of the weakness of its

4. 17 U.S.C. § 1201 (1998).

5. LEWIS CARROLL, ALICE IN WONDERLAND (1865).

6. Project Gutenberg is an effort involving hundreds of volunteers who find books no longer covered by copyright, scan them, and proofread them so as to make them freely available on the web. *See* Project Gutenberg *at* http://www.gutenberg.net (last visited Sept. 9, 2002).

7. This subpart describes the facts of *United States v. Elcom, Ltd.*, 203 F. Supp. 2d. 1111 (N.D. Ca. 2002). *See also* Robert Menta, *Read an E-book to Your Child, Go to Jail?* MP3.NEWSWIRE.NET, Dec. 26, 2002, *at* http://www.mp3newswire.net/stories/2000/ebook.html.

approach to encryption was not the best litigation stance, and it moved to dismiss the case on the understanding that it would never *dream* of bringing suit.[8]

***

This paper does three things. First, it outlines the general framework of the relationship between two constitutional provisions—Article I, Section 8, Clause 8 and the First Amendment—and Congress's power to regulate the use of information and cultural resources through the institutional form of exclusive private rights. Second, this paper explains why it is appropriate, as a normative matter, to require close judicial scrutiny of congressional use of this particular form of regulation. Third, it identifies six specific pressure points currently bearing on this framework.

II
GENERAL FRAMEWORK

Copyright law is defined by constant tensions between exclusive private rights on the one hand and the freedom to read and express oneself as one wishes on the other hand. As a matter of economics, copyright represents a tension between the advantages of market-based production of information and cultural goods on the one hand, and the intrinsic limitations of property rights as institutional solutions to the public goods problem of information production on the other hand. As a matter of political morality, copyright supports democracy by grounding some types of expression in the market, independent of government patronage. But in doing so, copyright imposes substantial risks of harm to democracy and individual autonomy.[9]

These tensions are mediated by two constitutional provisions: Article I, Section 8, Clause 8 of the Constitution (the "Exclusive Rights Clause"),[10] and the

8. Felten v. RIAA, No. CV-01-2660 (GEB) (D.N.J. June 26, 2001) *available at* http://www.eff.org/IP/DMCA/Felten_v_RIAA/.

9. The past decade has seen a growing literature critical of exclusive private rights along these dimensions. *See* LAWRENCE LESSIG, CODE AND OTHER LAWS OF CYBERSPACE (1999); James Boyle, *A Politics of Intellectual Property: Environmentalism For the Net?*, 47 DUKE L.J. 87 (1997); Julie E. Cohen, *Examined Lives: Informational Privacy and the Subject as Object*, 52 STAN. L. REV. 1373 (2000); Rosemary J. Coombe, *Objects of Property and Subjects of Politics: Intellectual Property Laws and Democratic Dialogue*, 69 TEX. L. REV. 1853 (1991); Niva Elkin-Koren, *Cyberlaw and Social Change: A Democratic Approach to Copyright Law in Cyberspace*, 14 CARDOZO ARTS & ENT. L.J. 215 (1996); William W. Fisher, III, *Reconstructing the Fair Use Doctrine*, 101 HARV. L. REV. 1661 (1988); Jessica Litman, *Copyright Owner's Rights and User's Privileges on the Internet: Reforming Information Law in Copyright's Image*, 22 U. DAYTON L. REV. 587 (1997); Michael Madow, *Private Ownership of Public Image: Popular Culture and Publicity Rights*, 81 CAL. L. REV. 125 (1993); Eben Moglen, *Anarchism Triumphant: Free Software and the Death of Copyright*, 4 FIRST MONDAY 8 (Aug. 2, 1999) *available at* http://www.firstmonday.dk/issues/issue4_8/moglen/index.html; Pamela Samuelson, *Is Information Property?* 34 COMMUNICATIONS OF THE ACM 15 (1991); David Lange, Cyberspace and its (Dis)Contents: The Future of an Illusion (published as part of the symposium collection prepared for Yale Law School Symposium on Internet Policy Choices), *available at* http://webserver.law.yale.edu/censor/lange.htm (April 1999).

10. U.S. CONST. art. I, § 8, cl. 8. This is also known as "the Patents and Copyrights Clause" or the "Intellectual Property Clause." I think "the Exclusive Rights Clause" is better for two reasons, one

First Amendment's Speech Clause.[11] Because of physical and economic characteristics, existing information and culture are, absent law to the contrary, largely available for anyone to use as and when they please. For good reason and within the constitutional constraints imposed by the two provisions, Congress may deviate from this baseline. No one expressed this more poetically than Thomas Jefferson:

> That ideas should freely spread from one to another over the globe, for the moral and mutual instruction of man, and improvement of his condition, seems to have been peculiarly and benevolently designed by nature, when she made them, like fire, expansible over all space, without lessening their density in any point, and like the air in which we breathe, move, and have our physical being, incapable of confinement or exclusive appropriation. Inventions then cannot, in nature, be a subject of property. Society may give an exclusive right to the profits arising from them, as an encouragement to men to pursue ideas which may produce utility, but this may or may not be done, according to the will and convenience of the society, without claim or complaint from anybody.[12]

The role of the Constitution is to delimit the contours of the grant of exclusive rights and to constrain Congress's power to regulate, in pursuit of "the will and convenience of society," the use of information and cultural materials.

The Exclusive Rights Clause operates as a threshold filter on congressional attempts to create exclusive private rights in information. Uncharacteristically for Article I, much of its text is involved not in granting power, but in delimiting it. The preamble takes a specific stand on the theory underlying the American approach towards exclusive rights in information. Congress is empowered to grant exclusive rights "To promote the Progress of Science and the useful Arts." Ours is a self-consciously utilitarian, not moral, theory of such rights, consistent with the sentiments expressed in Jefferson's letters and those more generally prevalent at the time.[13] The Supreme Court too has consistently interpreted the Exclusive Rights Clause in a utilitarian way, holding that "the primary objective

---

trivial and one significant. The trivial point is that neither the historical terms-of-art "patents" and "copyrights"—well known at the time of the Constitution's drafting—nor the anachronistic term "intellectual property" are used in the clause. The clause actually refers to granting "exclusive rights." There are two functional reasons for shifting our usage to the original term from either of the more common terms. First, it is broader than the technical terms, and it implies that the clause is intended to govern all exclusive rights in information, not only those that formally are called patents or copyrights. This is clearly the correct understanding of the scope of the limitations the clause places on Congress when it enacts exclusive rights in information. Second, it is more neutral about the desirability of the rights enacted than the term "intellectual property." As we stand at the beginning of the twenty-first century, "property" has come to be seen almost universally as a beneficial institutional device to manage physical resources. By calling the cluster of regulations of information production and exchange that give private parties exclusive rights to control information "property," we endow it with an inevitability and desirability that are not justified by either economic theory or empirical evidence. It is better to use the descriptive term—exclusive rights—and subject any given set of exclusive rights to neutral inquiry as to whether these particular rights are in fact beneficial.

11. U.S. CONST., amend. I.

12. Letter from Thomas Jefferson to Isaac McPherson, *quoted in* Graham v. John Deere Co., 383 U.S. 1, 8 n.2 (1966).

13. Edward C. Walterscheid, *To Promote the Progress of Science and Useful Arts: The Background and Origin of the Intellectual Property Clause of the United States Constitution*, 2 J. INTELL. PROP. L. 1, 33-36 (1996).

of copyright is not to reward the labor of authors, but 'to promote the Progress of Science and useful Arts.'"[14]

For over a century, unanimous Supreme Court opinions have interpreted the textual framework of the Exclusive Rights Clause as imposing a set of threshold constraints on legislation it enables. A congressional law creating exclusive private rights in information must comply with these constraints to fall within the grant of Article I, Section 8, Clause 8.[15] The *Trade-mark Cases*[16] were the first instance in which the Court held that the clause imposes affirmative constraints on Congress's power to create exclusive rights, but the Court most clearly outlined the content of these constraints in *Graham v. John Deere Co.*:[17]

> The Congress in the exercise of the patent power may not overreach the restraints imposed by the stated constitutional purpose. Nor may it enlarge the patent monopoly without regard to the innovation, advancement or social benefit gained thereby. Moreover, Congress may not authorize the issuance of patents whose effects are to remove existent knowledge from the public domain, or to restrict free access to materials already available.
>
> Innovation, advancement, and things which add to the sum of useful knowledge are inherent requisites in a patent system which by constitutional command must "promote the Progress of . . . useful Arts." This is the *standard* expressed in the Constitution and it may not be ignored.[18]

This reading of the Clause—that it requires an exclusive right to encourage at least some information production and that it restrains such rights from removing or burdening free access to materials already in the public domain—is one that the Court has unanimously reaffirmed.[19]

---

14. As the Court said in *Feist Publications, Inc. v. Rural Telephone Service Co.*, 499 U.S. 340 (1991):

> It may seem unfair that much of the fruit of the compiler's labor may be used by others without compensation. As Justice Brennan has correctly observed, however, this is not "some unforeseen byproduct of a statutory scheme." Harper & Row Publishers, Inc. v. Nation Enters., 471 U.S., 539, 589 (Brennan J., dissenting). It is, rather, "the essence of copyright," *ibid.*, and a constitutional requirement. The primary objective of copyright is not to reward the labor of authors, but "to promote the Progress of Science and useful Arts." Art. I, § 8, cl. 8. . . . To this end, copyright assures authors the right to their original expression, but encourages others to build freely upon the ideas and information conveyed by a work.

Id. at 349-50.

15. *See Feist*, 499 U.S. at 346-47; Bonito Boats, Inc. v. Thunder Craft Boats, Inc., 489 U.S. 141, 146 (1989); Sears, Roebuck & Co. v. Stiffel Co., 376 U.S. 225, 230-31 (1964); Compco Corp. v. Day-Brite Lighting, Inc., 376 U.S. 234, 237-38 (1964); Trade-Mark Cases, 100 U.S. 82 (1879). For discussions of the limitations imposed by Article I, Section 8, Clause 8 of the Constitution, see Julie E. Cohen, *Copyright and the Jurisprudence of Self-Help*, 13 BERKELEY TECH. L.J. 1089, 1130-35 (1998); Theodore H. Davis, Jr., *Copying in the Shadow of the Constitution: The Rational Limits of Trade Dress Protection*, 80 MINN. L. REV. 595, 596 (1996); David L. Lange, *The Intellectual Property Clause in Contemporary Trademark Law: An Appreciation of Two Recent Essays and Some Thoughts About Why We Ought to Care*, 59 LAW & CONTEMP. PROBS. 213, 232 (1996); Malla Pollack, *The Right to Know?: Delimiting Database Protection at the Juncture of the Commerce Clause, the Intellectual Property Clause and the First Amendment*, 17 CARDOZO ARTS & ENT. L.J. 47, 50-4 (1999); Malla Pollack, *Unconstitutional Incontestability?: The Intersection of the Intellectual Property and Commerce Clauses of the Constitution: Beyond a Critique of Shakespeare Co. v. Silstar Corp.*, 18 SEATTLE U. L. REV. 259, 260 (1995).

16. 100 U.S. 82 (1879).

17. 383 U.S. 1 (1966).

18. *Id.* at 5-6 (emphasis in original).

19. *See Feist*, 499 U.S. at 346-47; *Bonito Boats*, 489 U.S. at 146.

Furthermore, this constraint is substantive, not formal. It applies whenever Congress attempts to enact exclusive rights in information, regardless of whether it formally invokes the Exclusive Rights Clause.[20] While Congress may regulate information markets under the Commerce Clause, it may not do so by creating exclusive private rights in information in a way that circumvents the substantive limitations placed on its power by the Exclusive Rights Clause. This limitation requires that regulations enacted under the commerce power be different in kind, not only in subject matter and degree, from exclusive property rights—like rights that are the subject of the Exclusive Rights Clause.[21] This does not mean, however, that every technical aspect of the Exclusive Rights Clause—like the fixation requirement—constrains Congress when it acts under the Commerce Clause. Still, plainly "the Commerce Clause cannot be used [by Congress] to eradicate a limitation placed upon Congressional power in another grant of power,"[22]—such as the Exclusive Rights Clause.

The First Amendment operates as an overlay. It provides a second level of analysis for laws that pass the initial threshold filter imposed by the Exclusive Rights Clause. This First Amendment analysis is more context-sensitive. It requires that the government justify its regulation of the use of information and cultural goods in terms that are largely understood to be the "intermediate" level of scrutiny applied in *Turner Broadcasting System v. FCC*.[23] As was the case with the must-carry rules at issue in *Turner*, copyright or similar laws are usually benign in intent. Their purpose is to enhance, rather than constrain, speech. They are, in many applications, content-neutral. First, they mark information or cultural materials for regulation on the basis of the history of their origination—the fact that they were authored. Second, the form of the regulation is usually a prohibition on use of the protected materials in a pre-stated variety of ways, absent permission of an identified party, the right holder. Not all applications of copyright law are content-neutral, however. One of the current pressures on this general framework comes from the anti-device provision of the DMCA[24]—under which a number of current cases, including the *Sklyarov*,[25] *Felten*[26], and *Reimerdes/Corely*[27] cases, are being decided. The anti-

20. *See* Yochai Benkler, *Constitutional Bounds of Database Protection*, 15 BERKLEY TECH. L.J. 535, 549 (2000). The core of the argument is that what was left of the *Sears* and *Compco* cases by *Bonito Boats* was a commitment to subject all legislation that is functionally equivalent to exclusive rights to the limitations of the Exclusive Rights Clause.

21. This difference in kind is nowhere more clearly articulated than in the differentiation provided by the Supreme Court between what kind of laws regulate commerce, and what kinds of laws are in effect exclusive private rights. *Bonito Boats*, 489 U.S. at 157-59.

22. United States v. Moghadam, 175 F.3d 1269, 1279-80 (11th Cir. 1999) (treating the fixation requirement as not central to the Exclusive Rights Clause, and holding that the anti-bootlegging statute at issue there, which did not comply with the fixation requirement but was enacted under the Commerce Clause, was valid, and implying that were there another, central requirement of the Exclusive Rights Clause, like originality, implicated, the outcome would have been different).

23. 512 U.S. 622 (1994).

24. 17 U.S.C. §1201(a).

25. 203 F. Supp. 2d 1111 (N.D. Ca. 2002).

device provision, as applied to software programmers, may better be described as taking the form of a content-based prohibition on the use of a particular professional language or code to describe acts that the government deems particularly harmful—namely, decryption of specific kinds of encryption intended to protect copyrighted materials. For the moment, I will put this problem aside. It is a thorny one, and I will return to it in the third part of this paper.

To pass muster under the *Turner* standard, the government must show the statute: (1) serves an important government interest, and (2) does so in a manner no more restrictive than is necessary.[28] To fulfill the first prong of the test, it must be shown "that the recited harms are real, not merely conjectural, and that the regulation will in fact alleviate these harms in a direct and material way."[29] The second prong requires that "the means chosen do not 'burden substantially more speech than is necessary to further the government's legitimate interests.'"[30] This does not mean that in every case the specific use by the user and the specific exclusive right claimed must be considered afresh, as demonstrated by *Harper & Row*.[31] It also does not mean that the contours of copyright law—the exclusive rights and the various detailed political deals between stakeholders—are categorically exempt from First Amendment review, as recently held by the Court of Appeals for the District of Columbia in *Eldred v. Reno*.[32] Categorical exemption is untenable. All one needs to do is imagine Congress amending the Copyright Act so that the definition of "a work" will include the sentence, "except that nothing shall be deemed a work of authorship if the author is at the time of authorship, or was within the preceding ten years, a Republican member of Congress." If the viewpoint bias makes the analogy too easy, imagine the same appellate court being confronted with a copyright law that adds to Section 107 of the Copyright Act: "Any use of a work is categorically a fair use if the copyright in the work is held, directly or indirectly, by any person who holds the copyrights in more than 10% of the works in the same market as the work used."[33] The Supreme Court in *Harper & Row* refused to create a special First Amendment defense in copyright, "[i]n view of the First Amendment's protections already embodied in the Copyright Act's distinction between copyrightable expression and uncopyrightable facts and ideas, and the latitude for scholarship and comment traditionally afforded by

26. Felten v. RIAA, No. CV-01-2660 (GEB) (D.N.J. June 26, 2001) *available at* http://www.eff.org/IP/DMCA/Felten_v_RIAA/.

27. Universal City Studios v. Reimerdes, 111 F. Supp. 2d 294 (S.D.N.Y. 2000), *aff'd sub nom.*, Universal City Studios, Inc. v. Corely, 273 F.3d 429 (2d Cir. N.Y. 2001).

28 *See Turner*, 512 U.S. at 662.

29 *Id.* at 664.

30 *Id.* at 662 (citations omitted).

31. Harper & Row, Publishers, Inc., v. Nation Enters., 471 U.S. 539 (1985).

32. 239 F.3d 372, 375-76 (D.C. Cir. 2001), *cert. granted sub nom.*, Eldred v. Ashcroft, 534 U.S. 1062, *and cert. amended*, 534 U.S. 1160 (2002).

33. Compare the holding of another panel of the same court, within weeks of *Eldred*, in *Time Warner Entertainment Co., L.P. v. FCC*, 240 F.3d 1126 (D.C. Cir. 2001), of which more will be said below.

fair use . . . ."[34] Nothing in that opinion suggests that if Congress were to abolish the idea/expression distinction, or severely constrain "the latitude for scholarship and comment traditionally afforded by fair use," that its decision to do so would be exempt from First Amendment review.

The contours of copyright law and the shape of the prohibitions must be justifiable under the *Turner* standard as a proper regulation of the use of the information or cultural materials at stake. This test is not only applicable to changes in the law but also to existing rights as they are applied to categories of cases. Whether sampling for a few seconds[35] or using part of a poster for a number of seconds in a television show[36] is or is not a fair use, at least when a category of cases is being developed in case-law, requires an analysis of whether fair use law, thus interpreted, would cohere with the First Amendment.

III

POLITICAL THEORY OF THE CONSTITUTIONAL LIMITATIONS ON EXCLUSIVE RIGHTS IN INFORMATION

What, one might ask, justifies such extensive judicial review of the creation and definition of exclusive rights in information? At some level, the answer is provided by the stories at the beginning of this paper. Alice Randall's freedom to shatter a cultural icon that she sees as profoundly offensive, in the words and means she deems most effective, is no less compelling than Paul Cohen's right to criticize the draft using his particular locution.[37] Dmitry Sklyarov's physical freedom is at stake. It has been threatened so that no one develops software that allows users and courts, rather than vendors, to decide when reading, quoting, and sharing of knowledge is privileged and fair. These freedoms, like Edward Felten's freedom to publish an academic paper, are all central to our understandings of freedom of expression. Randall, Sklyarov, and Felten provide crisp instances of the pressure that exclusive rights in information place on the freedom to read and express oneself. The next few pages explain more abstractly how one might understand the implications of exclusive private rights in information on democracy and autonomy—values at the core not only of the U.S. constitutional protection of freedom of expression, but of expressive freedom in modern liberal democracies more generally.

A. Democracy

Democracy is a concept with many conceptions. It would be irresponsible to argue that there is one well-defined set of policies that best serves democracy. Nonetheless, it is possible to outline the general direction in which strong or weak exclusive rights are likely to lead the organizational structure of infor-

34. *Harper & Row*, 471 U.S. at 560.
35. *See, e.g.*, Jarvis v. A&M Records, 827 F. Supp. 282 (D.N.J. 1993).
36. *See, e.g.*, Ringgold v. Black Entm't TV, 126 F.3d 70 (2d Cir. 1997).
37. Cohen v. California, 403 U.S. 15 (1971).

mation production and exchange. From this, one can develop a sense of whether one's conception of democracy leads to a preference for stronger or weaker protection on the basis that it serves, or disserves, democracy.

The most important effect of exclusive rights, in terms of democracy, is that they make institutional conditions more conducive for some approaches to information production than to other approaches.[38] Individuals with a commercial focus to their work and, more significantly, commercial organizations that build their business model around selling information and culture as finished goods benefit from strong protection. These rights are particularly helpful to organizations that own large inventories of existing information and cultural goods and that integrate new production with inventory management. Strong intellectual property rights are particularly harmful to organizations and individuals who produce information without intending to sell their output as a good. This includes non-profit organizations, such as universities, various public interest organizations, the government, and individuals who communicate with each other either as "amateurs" or as professionals driven by internal motivations, not by a profit motive. Less obviously, it also includes commercial organizations and individual professionals that operate on a service model that provides free access to information around which the service is rendered, rather than the sale of information as a product.

The conflict seen today regarding the scope of the public domain and the extent of exclusive private rights in information is a battle over the shape of the institutional ecology in which two very different modes of information production compete. The first mode is the increasingly industrial model of production that one sees in mass-mediated culture. Disney, AOL Time-Warner, Viacom, and News Corporation are some of the most visible examples. These are increasingly large organizations that control ever-larger inventories and integrate new production with reutilization and recycling of inventory. They aim to capture ever-larger audiences both nationally and internationally. Less well known, and quite poorly understood, is the emergence on the Internet of nonproprietary production as an increasingly important source of information and cultural materials. Over the past decade, with the widescale use of the Internet, the reach and scope of nonproprietary information production by nonprofit actors or by individuals—both amateur and professional—has expanded dramatically.

At a simple level, the Internet has made it possible for traditional non-profit social organizations to extend their reach and scope. In the past, the greatest constraints on non-profit production were the capital cost of production and the cost of communication, or distribution. The declining costs of making and distributing a high quality video or of collecting information and publishing reports exemplify the changes. These changes mean that information production on the public radio model, as well as production by other non-profit groups, can

38. *See* Yochai Benkler, *Intellectual Property and the Organization of Information Production*, 22 INT'L REV. L & EC. 81 (2002) [hereinafter Benkler, *Intellectual Property*].

become increasingly salient in the information environment. This possibility must be central to our evaluation of the implications of strong rights to democracy.

More obscure, but potentially much more radical, is the emergence of non-proprietary peer production of information and culture. Thanks to the success of open source development projects like GNU/Linux or Apache,[39] this model of production is increasingly recognized in the area of software development. It is less widely appreciated that this highly decentralized model of non-proprietary peer production is expanding into other areas of information and culture more generally.[40] Tens of thousands of volunteers are mapping Mars craters faster than images of the planet's surface are produced.[41] Almost 40,000 volunteers participate in creating the open directory project, the most comprehensive and highest quality human judgment-based directory of the Web.[42] Thousands of peer reviewers and posters make contributions and write comments on Slashdot, one of the most sophisticated peer-produced news sites.[43] Through many such groups of individuals, who come together to create and make sense of their information environment, peer-production has emerged as a serious antithesis to the industrial production model that dominated twentieth century mass media.

When we think, therefore, of how strong we want copyright or other exclusive rights to information to be, in terms of democratic theory, the most important question is: What can democratic theory tell us about the choice between commercial proprietary production, increasingly organized in large enterprises and whose products are sold as finished goods, and nonproprietary production, both peer-production and professional production on a traditional nonprofit model?

The strongest democratic justifications of highly protective copyright serve what Baker has described as the elitist conception of democracy[44] and one version of what might be thought of as a republican conception of democracy. Strong protection is least attractive when measured by its effect on liberal conceptions of democracy—whether one holds some version of a pluralist conception, or a liberal, rather than republican, discourse-centered conception of democracy.[45] Again, it is unlikely that conceptions of democracy can be

39. *See generally* GLYN MOODY, REBEL CODE: LINUX AND THE OPEN SOURCE REVOLUTION (2001).

40. For an inspired statement, see Moglen, *supra* note 9. For a pedestrian economic explanation see Yochai Benkler, *Coase's Penguin, or Linux and the Nature of the Firm*, 102 YALE L.J. 369 (2002).

41. For more information about NASA's Clickworkers experiment, see http://clickworkers.arc.nasa.gov/top (last visited Oct. 7, 2002).

42. http://dmoz.org (last visited Sept. 17, 2002).

43. http://www.slashdot.org (last visited Sept. 17, 2002).

44. C. Edwin Baker, *The Media that Citizens Need*, 147 U. PA. L. REV. 317 (1998).

45. This latter is a conception Baker called "complex democracy." *Id.* at 319. One might think of it as vaguely Habermasian, in the sense that it is discourse-centered but fundamentally liberal—centered on the participating agents—rather than communitarian, or republican, and centered on claims of the collectivity to independent weight in political morality.

described in pure uni-dimensional terms. One's position, however, on the relationship of exclusive private rights in information to democracy ought to be informed by the extent to which one considers one or another of these ideal-type conceptions of democracy as playing a greater role in one's understanding of how democracy is best conceived.

The baseline argument from democracy in favor of strong rights is that dependence on government largesse or patronage tends to require authors, media, and others to be solicitous to those who pay the piper. Exclusive rights create a basis in the market for expression so that professional writers and creators can be sustained, based not on the decisions of government officials or patrons of the arts, but on the popular support of any non-trivial segment of the consumer market for information and cultural products. Copyright also provides incentives for creators to write more and thereby enrich the information universe within which a democracy functions.[46]

There are two weaknesses to this argument for strong rights. First, markets for media products and information are rife with market failures that mean that they will not actually reflect the political views of the constituency.[47] Second, strong exclusive rights tend to commercialize, concentrate, and, to an extent, homogenize the information produced.[48] They aid information-as-goods vendors by raising the costs of, and potentially squelching, noncommercial discourse.

The argument for the importance of market-based production must therefore not only prefer market-based production to government-sponsored production. This is perhaps an easy choice for some—though, comparing network television news and magazines, whether national or local, to public television and radio should make one less than sanguine even about this claim. The argument, however, must also prefer market-based production to peer-production and independent nonprofit production. This requires the argument to take on a more explicitly elitist conception of democracy. "True" democracy—the participatory debate of all with all—is an illusion. Large companies, government officials, and other repeat players largely dominate the polity. The role of copyright is to create and sustain a large, powerful, and well-funded watchdog in this system, one enabled by market power to participate in this democracy of titans as an equal, criticizing the excesses of both government and the corporate world.[49] This conception has a good pedigree in the Press Clause focus on the fourth estate, and it is not implausible if it accurately describes the polity. The elitist argument has two primary weaknesses. First, it is unattractive to anyone who holds a more substantive, less cynical conception of democ-

46. *See* PAUL GOLDSTEIN, COPYRIGHT'S HIGHWAY: FROM GUTENBERG TO THE CELESTIAL JUKEBOX 11 (1994); Neil Weinstock Netanel, *Copyright and a Democratic Civil Society*, 106 YALE L.J. 283, 288 (1996).

47. C. Edwin Baker, *Giving the Audience What It Wants*, 58 OHIO ST. L.J. 311 (1997).

48. Benkler, *Intellectual Property*, *supra* note 38.

49. *See* Neil Weinstock Netanel, *Market Hierarchy and Copyright in our System of Free Expression*, 53 VAND. L. REV. 1879, 1919-20 (2000).

racy. If democracy means something more than an oligarchy of large market actors interacting with government bureaucrats who are watched by a large commercial press with occasional elections in which the masses select from among the elites who will run the government, then this argument in favor of strong rights is insufficient to justify a preference for strong exclusive rights in information. Second, the argument fails to consider the rise of peer production of information as a result of the economies created by low-cost computers and fast, ubiquitous network connections. The capacity of constituents to talk to each other as opposed to receiving the wisdom of those anointed by the television networks is profoundly important if one sees democracy as being about active engagement in discourse, rather than about passive selection from an exogenously-defined slate of candidates. One needs only to run a search request on Google[50] and then follow the variety of individuals and organizations making relevant information available, whether for free or for a fee, to see that a conception that focuses purely on large scale industrial production of information is too heavily committed to the twentieth century model of production by a few corporations transmitting to millions of passive consumers. Even without resorting to a more aspiring conception of democracy, it is not at all clear that thousands or millions of networked peers will not do as well or better than a few hundred professional reporters or commentators can do. An efficient system that allows individuals to report what they see, to blow the whistle, and to collect and comment on information globally, supplemented by a combination of publicly funded and advertising-supported (rather than property-based) professional media may well be superior to a more concentrated and commercial system that is occupied by a small number of media companies whose business model is based on the sale of access to their products.

This, however, raises a second line of defense for concentrated commercial production, which is rooted in a particular, nation-state focused version of a "republican" conception of democracy. Such a defense values polity-wide common discourse toward reaching a conception of the common good as the primary modality of democracy. This is only a somewhat unfair and oversimplified description of Cass Sunstein's primary complaint in *Republic.com*.[51] Sunstein warns us of the dangers of having too widely distributed an information production system—one where every person can find whatever information he or she wants and filter out everything else.[52] This, he argues, leads to a loss of common culture and with it, a loss of the possibility of a common discourse necessary for a polity to function well.[53] Moreover, Sunstein argues, individuals who interact only with like-minded people tend to reach more extreme posi-

50. http:// www.google.com (last visited Sept. 17, 2002).
51. CASS SUNSTEIN, REPUBLIC.COM (2001).
52. *Id.* at 55-56.
53. *Id.*

tions and discount counter-arguments.[54] Thus, deliberation toward the common good may be harder to achieve.

The aspect of Sunstein's argument that is most relevant to the comparison of widely distributed information production versus concentrated commercial production is his claim that "general interest intermediaries" form the common experiences and knowledge necessary for engaged discourse.[55] Sunstein's argument has a number of limitations, which are both internal to "republican" conceptions and also a function of the limitations of that conception as a description of what one would consider valuable in a democracy.

Internally, there are two important limitations to the argument based on maintaining a common culture and discourse. First, the argument assumes that the relevant political community is the same community whose contours are defined by the media market. This assumes that there are national media outlets and that the most relevant polity is the nation-state. It is not implausible, however, that the engaged polity is more important than the state within republican conceptions. If, for example, the city rather than the nation is the level at which engaged politics can occur, then some republican theorists would locate power where the political action is, rather than attempt to structure engagement so that it fits some other stated level of governance.[56] More generally, if the Internet permits engaged politics in civic groups, interest groups, and communities of interest, rather than national boundaries, then supporting that engagement at the local level should be a concern of republican democracy. In some sense, the attempts to make the Internet Corporation for Assigned Names and Numbers ("ICANN")[57] into a representative, open, deliberative Internet governance forum is the kind of thing one might imagine developing out of the a republican view of the discourse actually occurring on the Internet. It is not at all clear that a commitment to engaged politics requires burdening local discourses so as to secure the revenue streams of national media giants, on which one relies to sustain nationwide common discourse.

This leads to the second internal criticism of this republican defense of strong copyright. Relying on a set of actors to define the common agenda and culture is only acceptable if these actors are "virtuous" in the republican sense—that is, if they set the agenda and the common culture with reference to the common good. Exclusive-rights-based commercial producers are unlikely to provide such a virtuous common culture for two reasons.

First, within the republican conception, common culture only benefits a democracy if it is made of materials conducive to creating informed and engaged citizens. It is crucial to see what the large speakers are saying before one can tell whether they help or harm discourse. There are two distinct types

54. *Id.* at 76-77.

55. *Id.* at 36.

56. *See* Gerald E. Frug, *The City As a Legal Concept*, 93 HARV. L. REV. 1057, 1128 (1980).

57. ICANN is the non-profit organization that supervises the management of Internet domain names. *See* http://www.icann.org (last visited Sept. 17, 2002).

of concern in this category. First, there is what one might call the Berlusconi effect. Owners of large media that occupy center-stage in creating the common culture can capture a disproportionate share of political power and undermine, rather than serve, democracy. Whether this effect is worth the creation of "common culture" is questionable, unless one has a particularly naïve view of the benign nature of media barons. Programs like the *Jerry Springer Show*, *Baywatch*, or even cheap network television news capture the second type of difficulty. Market actors are supported by advertising and direct revenues. To gain these revenues, market actors will offer materials that the largest number of people, on a national and international level, will buy. There is no reason to think that this fare will be particularly conducive to an engaged polity; quite the contrary. Moreover, an information good is particularly valuable *as a good* requiring property protection if it is not ephemeral. Programming that is most valuable to democratic discourse—ephemeral news, analysis of current affairs—is the type of information that least benefits from exclusive rights, even when produced commercially.

Second, Sunstein's conception of the relationships of individuals to the information production and exchange system is too passive and too limited in its view of individuals as consumers in the market. He does not consider the productive, rather than the consumption, role that individuals can play. Diversity on the Internet does not exist primarily because someone decided to sell consumers something in a finely sliced market segment—the segmentation Sunstein sees as occurring and embodied in Negroponte's trope, the Daily Me.[58] Instead, the diversity exists because individuals themselves participate in developing and expressing a viewpoint. This is precisely the type of productive relationship to the information flow in one's polity that peer-production facilitates and proprietary production squelches. It is in these yeoman speakers that republican democracy thrives, and squelching their speech to maintain universal attention to synthetic discourse packaged for mass consumption is perverse.

Widely distributed and noncommercial production strategies—those best characterized by the emerging properties of peer production on the Internet—are particularly attractive from the perspective of liberal conceptions of democracy. This includes both pluralist conceptions and discourse-focused substantive conceptions that root the value of discourse in individuals rather than an independent valuation of "the common good." In this context, "pluralist" conceptions means those conceptions that accept as given the possibility that some people's interests will be fundamentally and irreconcilably opposed. They are conceptions aimed at a polity that will allow people to express their interests, fight over them politically, and implement them in law. The implementation, however, occurs subject to constraints that allow the losers in the political process sufficient freedom from coercion to remain committed to the democratic polity rather than trying to resist it.[59] Liberal discourse-oriented conceptions of

58. NICHOLAS NEGROPONTE, BEING DIGITAL (1995).
59. *See* JOHN RAWLS, POLITICAL LIBERALISM 103-04 (1993).

democracy, as opposed to republican or communitarian conceptions of democracy, largely focus on the equivalent notion that democracy entails engaged discourse by individuals. Such discourse-oriented conceptions draw the legitimacy of sovereignty from maintaining appropriate conditions to allow people to engage in fair and open discourse.[60] It differs from the pluralist conception in that it assumes the possibility of the emergence of common values through dialogue among participants and sees such discourse, rather than the clearance of pre-defined conflicting values in peaceful co-existence, as the core of democracy. Both these conceptions, however, value the possibility of discourse not only, or even primarily, on a society-wide basis but also, importantly, in smaller settings, even among like-minded people, working to clarify and develop a full conception of the values they hold as well as the ability to express these views. The capacity of individuals in small and large groups to come together to discuss their interests is central to a well-functioning democracy under both these liberal conceptions. Also, the capacity of non-proprietary production or service-based provision of the platforms over which individuals and groups "meet" to engage in dialogue and collective self-definition becomes central to the democratic enterprise. It, rather than the generation of a "common culture" to be received by individuals, becomes the most important mode of information production. An important caveat here is that if, as Sunstein claims, individuals become more polarized and less willing to listen and engage in discourse when they talk to like-minded people,[61] then this conception of discourse-centered democracy, not only the nationwide republican version, will be undermined by discourse occurring solely at the level of small groups.

The point of this discussion is not, of course, to offer an exhaustive democratic theory of communications. The point is to outline the considerations and concerns regarding democracy that can be seen as involved in decisions about stronger or weaker exclusive private rights. To the extent one values active, engaged individual participation in defining and expressing political values in a polity as central to the democratic enterprise, one should strengthen peer-based models of information production and exchange, even if this requires policies that weaken proprietary production based on a sale of goods model.

B. Autonomy

Autonomy is also a concept admitting of many conceptions, some quite vigorously opposed to others. In general, conceptions of autonomy can be divided into two camps: formal—or as Richard Fallon described them, ascriptive—and substantive.[62] "Ascriptive" refers to those conceptions that view autonomy as a capacity ascribed to human subjects as an assumption of liberal law making. As

60. *See, e.g.*, JÜRGEN HABERMAS, BETWEEN FACTS & NORMS: CONTRIBUTIONS TO A DISCOURSE THEORY OF LAW AND DEMOCRACY (1996); BRUCE A. ACKERMAN, SOCIAL JUSTICE IN ITS LIBERAL STATE (1980).

61. SUNSTEIN, *supra* note 51, at 76-77.

62. Richard H. Fallon, Jr., *Two Senses of Autonomy*, 46 STAN. L. REV. 875, 875 (1994).

Robert Post explains, the nature of "structures of social authority" will depend on whether they treat the object of regulation as autonomous individuals.[63] "From the point of view of the designer of the structure, therefore, the presence or absence of autonomy functions as an axiomatic and foundational principle."[64] Those who adhere to an ascriptive conception assume the existence of autonomy as a foundational principle, not as a proper subject for institutional manipulation. Therefore, autonomy is also "formal" in that it operates as an analytic constraint on law making, rather than substantive, or concerned with identifying and affecting the actual condition of autonomy of individuals. Substantive, or descriptive conceptions of autonomy, locate individual autonomy within the actual constraints, both internal and external, with which real human beings live. Under the substantive conception, autonomy is a capacity and a condition admitting of degree, which is partly a function of, rather than an assumption underlying, institutional structures. It functions not as a formal analytic constraint on policymaking, but as a substantive goal to be attained by policy. In this framework, achieving, preserving, and improving the autonomy of actual individuals is a proper, for some the primary, object of liberal institutional design.

Elsewhere I have attempted to offer a specific set of practical guidelines for autonomy-loving institutional design in the area of information policy that is neutral as among these competing conceptions.[65] While I derive the policy guidelines from a substantive conception of autonomy, the operative design principles are two that cannot offend even those who hold a purely ascriptive or formal conception of autonomy.

First, law or policy that systematically and drastically reduces the information available to large numbers of, or defined classes of, individuals in a society, undermines autonomy. "Reduces" has both a quantitative and a qualitative dimension. The quantitative dimension is largely irrelevant in a modern liberal state and is more relevant to describe totalitarian efforts to control people's lives by severely restricting information flows to them. The qualitative dimension is still very much relevant even in the most liberal of democracies and involves the availability of information about non-mainstream or critical life options. For an individual to be autonomous, she must play a substantial role in defining her life plan. Where the range of life options perceived is largely congruent with the range of behaviors followed by everyone else in the mainstream of her society, the opportunity to make that life her own, as opposed to simply the life she leads as part of a herd, is diminished. The presence of knowledge about and opportunity for unconventional life choices enable an individual to make any life plan her autonomously selected own.

63. Robert Post, *Meiklejohn's Mistake: Individual Autonomy and the Reform of Public Discourse*, 64 U. COLO. L. REV. 1109, 1131 (1993).

64. *Id.*

65. Yochai Benkler, *Siren Songs and Amish Children: Autonomy, Information, and Law*, 76 N.Y.U. L. REV. 23, 109-113 (2001).

Second, a law that systematically gives one person or class of people control over the information flows that make up the information environment within which others live is a law that suffers an autonomy deficit. To the extent that a law increases the opportunities for one person to manipulate the information another person receives, so as to make that other hew more closely to a life plan set by the manipulator, the law violates the autonomy of the person whose information is so manipulated.

Both of these design principles are decidedly agnostic about whether the immediate source of constraint on an individual's autonomy is a government agent. The primary focus here is on the relative role an individual plays in defining and pursuing his own life plan, irrespective of the source of constraint. Whether the manipulator is the state, or whether it is state law or corporate policy that restricts information about the range of available life options, is irrelevant from the perspective of autonomy. Some of the most fruitful discussions of autonomy have, for example, occurred with regard to the physician-patient relationship, where the government is absent. This is because autonomy is a distinctly personal and humanistic value.[66] Autonomy relates to a capacity or condition of an individual *qua* individual, not as a citizen of a state or constituent of a community. All constraints placed on that individual affect autonomy, not purely, and not always most importantly, those placed by the state. The state-centered focus of legal analysis enters only at the level of selecting for inquiry from among the many potential actions that affect autonomy. A legal or constitutional inquiry, as opposed to general moral inquiry, into autonomy is concerned with laws that affect the relative role individuals have in selecting and pursuing a life plan. But whether those laws directly restrict autonomy, or indirectly do so by, for example, placing one non-government person in the position to control the life of another, is irrelevant to the question of whether those laws restrict autonomy.

The practical implication of all this is that there is an area of overlap between the concerns of democracy—at least a wide range of liberal versions of democracy—and those of autonomy. A widely dispersed system of information production, which produces a wide range of diverse information about and representations of how life can be, serves autonomy in the first dimension just as it serves robust democratic discourse. Furthermore, large-scale commercial media that occupy most of the channels of communication and control most of the cultural raw materials from which expression is made have substantial power to shape the perception of alternative life choices available to many individuals. An Internet-like system of news and cultural production, operating with weak property rights, dissipates this power and structures the interaction of individuals with the information flows around them in a less externally controlled pattern.

66. By humanistic I mean to emphasize that it is a value that places the human being at the center of moral gravity, rather than any external supra-individual being, such as God or community.

In addition, some aspects of autonomy are directly tied to the emergence of peer-production. However, these aspects are more closely associated with a substantive, or descriptive, rather than formal or ascriptive, conception of autonomy. The emergence of peer-production as an economic—and ultimately social—transformation represents, most importantly, a change in the menu of options for productivity in the information economy. In the "atoms economy,"[67] we settled more or less on two modes of making production decisions: the market and hierarchy (whether in managerial firms or government-owned enterprise). Coase's *Nature of the Firm* explains that markets best coordinate some economic activities, while managers better organize others.[68] Accordingly, most individuals live their productive life as part of corporate organizations, with relatively limited control over how, what, or when they produce. These organizations, in turn, interact with each other through a combination of markets and hierarchy. Consumption is strictly separated from production for most people and is largely devoted to receipt of finished goods, not to creative utilization of materials to shape one's own environment. What emerges in the information economy is a model of peer-production—where individuals communicate with each other about what projects are worth pursuing, and who might want to take them up and share their products in an economy of gifts, reputation, and relationally-based rewards. Consumption and production are integrated, not separated, so that each individual is a user, rather than either purely a producer or a consumer.

From the perspective of autonomy, there are two enormously important chunks of life during which individuals can play a larger role in defining how their time is spent: production and consumption. The production dimension of autonomy occupied much of the "third way" literature that emerged in the 1980s, from Piore and Sable's *Second Industrial Divide*[69] to Unger's *False Necessity*.[70] It is mirrored on the consumption side by the shift to "user" from consumer. Because this shift is an attribute of autonomy that is not necessarily shared across conceptions of autonomy, I have not included it as a core consideration in thinking about autonomy and information policy for purposes of analyzing the liberal constitutional constraints on the creation of exclusive private rights in information and cultural materials. Yet as background, for those who do believe that autonomy is affected by how much of one's day is, and what range of activities are, more or less valuable under an individual's control, peer production should be a valued social and economic phenomenon; a phenomenon that policymakers concerned with autonomy should facilitate.

---

67. Nicholas Negraponte divided the world of business into "atoms" such as manufacturing businesses, and "bits," such as online digital-based business. *See* NICHOLAS NEGRAPONTE, BEING DIGITAL 1 (1995) *available at* http://archives.obs.us.com/obs/english/books/nn/ch01c01.htm (last visited Oct. 8, 2002).

68. Ronald Coase, *The Nature of the Firm*, 4 ECONOMICA 386 (1937).

69. MICHAEL PIORE & CHARLES SABLE, THE SECOND INDUSTRIAL DIVIDE (1982).

70. ROBERTO MANGABERIA UNGER, FALSE NECESSITY: ANTI-NECESSITARIAN SOCIAL THEORY IN THE SERVICE OF RADICAL DEMOCRACY (1987).

There are two important concerns regarding the claim that autonomy is served by weak exclusive rights that lead to decentralized information production. First, there is the information overload complaint. Wide distribution of the capacity to produce information leads to the generation of a tremendous amount of information of varying degrees of quality. An agent who constantly needs to sift through mounds of data to understand the world is left exhausted and incapable of making a decision, rather than empowered to control his own life.

There are two reasons why the concern with information overload does not suggest a retreat from the limited design principles proposed here. First, although a widely distributed information production system causes potential information overload, a concentrated information production system may still not be preferable from the perspective of autonomy. If the "filter" that reduces the amount of information available to an individual is perfectly aligned with the individual's interest in being autonomous, a concentrated system may succeed from an autonomy perspective. Unfortunately, deviations from this ideal state create a situation where the filter controls the life of the recipient. The more that the mechanism of reducing the amount of information and its organization through a relevance and accreditation algorithm is controlled by a third party with an agenda of its own, the more the price paid for reducing information by concentrating the information production function becomes unacceptable. Second, increasingly sophisticated mechanisms allow individuals to reduce the amount of information they receive without abdicating control of one's life to Berlusconi or Murdoch. An individual may utilize technical mechanisms to customize the information environment encountered according to parameters the individual sets. These are some of the same mechanisms that Sunstein decries as harming the public sphere. Furthermore, relevance and accreditation themselves are being produced on a peer-production model, as one sees in a wide range of sites, including the Open Directory Project,[71] Slashdot,[72] some aspects of Google.com,[73] Everything2.com,[74] and many others.[75] As these mechanisms for common, non-proprietary production of the relevance and accreditation function improve, individuals will be able to manage the universe of diverse information available to them without subjecting themselves to the power of others to the point of surrendering their autonomy.

Second, specifically with regard to exclusive private rights in information, there is an argument that autonomy or some conception of individual freedom actually supports, rather than criticizes, exclusive private rights. This is largely the argument underlying European moral rights. Perhaps, goes this argument, there is some "cost" in terms of autonomy from the creation of exclusive rights

---

71. *See* http://dmoz.org (last visited Sept. 17, 2002).
72. *See* http://slashdot.org (last visited Sept. 17, 2002).
73. *See* http://everything2.com (last visited Sept. 17, 2002).
74. *See* http://www.google.com (last visited Sept. 17, 2002).
75. *See* Benkler, *Intellectual Property*, *supra* note 38.

to control information and cultural materials, but there are also strong autonomy-based claims to such exclusive rights. This article is *mine* in the deep moral sense that it is an external reflection of my intellectual will and that it, in some sense, is an externalization of my persona, my identity. It is much more *me* than many physical things that belong to me, and at least on a Hegelian conception of property, I have a very strong claim to exclusive control over it as the embodiment of my will and the creation of my personality.[76]

Initially, it should be understood that such an argument can be based only on a substantive or descriptive conception of autonomy, not on a formal or ascriptive conception of autonomy. Under a formal conception, law treats individuals as having the capacity for autonomy independent of or prior to law, and designs law accordingly. Autonomy under this conception cannot be a function of the law that gives exclusive rights. People are autonomous regardless of whether you grant them such exclusive rights. Furthermore, nothing about formal recognition of individuals' capacity for autonomy requires that (a.) law prohibit some people from reading, viewing, or reworking cultural materials that (b.) they, as a practical matter, can read, view, or rework, so that (c.) other people can successfully pursue their plans to make money from selling permission to read, view, or rework.[77] An autonomy-based argument in favor of exclusive rights must therefore rely on some substantive conception of autonomy, one that sees autonomy as in some important measure a function of and dependent on the legal framework within which individuals live, rather than as an axiomatic presupposition to its design. This is not to say that such an argument is improper, in particular given that aspects of my own argument rely on a substantive conception of autonomy. But it does weaken the appeal of this argument as a criticism of autonomy-oriented policy design principles that are intentionally limited to those that can be defended on grounds neutral as between these two basic conceptions of autonomy.

Substantively, there are two types of answers to the argument from the moral claims of the author. The first, to which I will return, is that this argument is irrelevant whenever the owner of the copyright is a corporation. Works

76. For the most complete statement of the Hegelian property theory underlying intellectual property, see Justin Hughes, *The Philosophy of Intellectual Property*, 77 GEO. L.J. 287 (1988).

77. This description does not undermine the acceptability of my design principles to a formal conception of autonomy. The formal conception will not accept law designed to enhance or facilitate autonomy of persons. Indeed, it does not acknowledge the coherence of such an enterprise. A formal conception, however, has no objections to a legal design principle that constrains law from being shaped so as to limit the information flows to already autonomous individuals in a way that either limits the options they see too much, or that gives the controller of information flows power to manipulate the autonomous subject by selectively revealing and concealing information. A substantive conception of autonomy would treat such laws as "reducing" the autonomy of the agent, while a formal conception might treat them as "violating" the agent's autonomy. The congruence between these conceptions in their treatment of the policy design principles is not analytical, but practical. I am not claiming to have found a philosopher's stone; only the analysis of specific policy proposals can adopt—as a self-constraining device—a focus on finding policies that are "autonomy loving" under either conception. The reason to do so is that those policies are an area of practical agreement among autonomy lovers and can be adopted to enhance autonomy without a need to solve more or less immutable disputes about the nature of human agency.

for hire, complex multi-participant works such as films that movie studios produce, works otherwise assigned to corporations are no longer the expression of autonomy. Rather, they represent an alienation of the connection between the author and the work. It is precisely for this reason that countries with strong moral rights traditions do not recognize work-for-hire or alienation of the moral rights, as opposed to commercial exploitation rights. Treating corporations as legal persons may be a very useful legal construct for organizing human production, but that does not make corporations into agents with independent moral claims. Since in many cases the claimant is a corporate owner of rights, not an individual author, the moral claims in favor of exclusive rights are weak.

The second answer is that autonomy does not support the actual exclusive rights Americans have—which are almost completely focused on commodification and alienation. If at all, autonomy supports rights that are not recognized in the United States—inalienable rights to attribution and control over integrity of the work. The Hegelian defense of intellectual property derives from a notion that individual will expresses itself and embodies the person in things.[78] The strongest rights derived from this notion are rights to be associated with the expression and rights to maintain the expression's integrity in the form in which a person has expressed their personality. The former requirement, attribution, has to do with the sense that the value of the thing as an expression of self is in its being an expression of a particular self—its author—and not a fungible expression of human creativity as a general category. The latter requirement, integrity, has to do with respect for the thing as a unique expression of self, and it requires that the individual be able to control that expression, because its alteration, and in particular its alteration inconsistent with the will of the author, alienates the expression from the person and undermines the capacity of the person to be expressed and embodied in the intellectual creation. This is why European "moral rights" include rights of attribution and integrity that resist removal of the actual author from future control over his or her work.[79] In the United States, quite to the contrary, such practices as work-for-hire and relinquishment of authorial control are perfectly common. American exclusive rights are focused on enabling and facilitating the alienation and economic exploitation of covered works, not on giving authors inalienable rights to attribution and control over the integrity of the work. The moment of alienation is the weakest point of the Hegelian defense of property. At that point, one person parts with the thing that previously embodied his will, handing it over to the property of another, who acquires it as part of her plans to embody her will in the thing. Continued control after alienation would subject the latter to the will of the former. Hegelian intellectual property theory then has to rely on some instrumental explanation to sustain support for alienability of the

78. *See* Hughes, *supra* note 76 at 344-45.

79. *See* Michael B. Gunlicks, *A Balance of Interest: The Concordance of Copyright Law and Moral Rights in the Worldwide Economy*, 11 FORDHAM INTELL. PROP. MEDIA & ENT. J. 601, 653-54 (2001) (detailing the concept of moral rights in each of the European nations).

commodity aspects of the work, while requiring inalienability of the moral claims.

Commodification and alienation of my work—the treatment of it as a thing alienable from me and exchangeable for money through a market[80]—is an act of separation of the thing from what is uniquely mine and its instantiation in a fungible commodity. That is not to say that it is morally wrong of me to alienate my work. But when I do so, I am treating those aspects of the work that I am selling as a commodity, whose fungible remuneration is useful to me, but is not an expression of me. Certainly, when the entire right is alienated, as when an author sells all rights to the work to the publisher, what has happened is alienation, not embodiment. And where copies are sold and the right protecting the market in copies is a prohibition on selling copies, each copy is a thing that does not embody the self and which is instead a thing through which the reader is attempting to embody him or herself. Justin Hughes argued in favor of treating the right to control copying as nonetheless a personality-based right. Hughes claimed that by paying me money readers recognize my personality, while those who do not pay for copies recognize the personality embodied in the work no more than a trespasser recognizes the property of a landowner.[81] Yet a company that invests some of its excess cash in buying art based on professional advice as to what will appreciate in value is not "recognizing the personality of the artist." Additionally, fans passing bootleg tapes are expressing a complete association between the artistic expression and the artist and are expressing adoration of the artist's personality as embodied in the art. To hold otherwise is to be a "fetishist of little green paper."[82] Failure to pay for the commodity or for its utilization largely in the form in which it was commoditized is, at most, an interference with the artist's success in commoditizing her work. If commoditizing her work is her life plan, a refusal to pay for the commodity interferes with her *wellbeing* as an autonomous agent, constituted by her success in pursuing her autonomously chosen life plan.[83] But they are not interferences with the thing as an expression of her personality and are not interferences with her autonomy—her capacity to express herself in the world through the manipulation of ideas and symbolic representations. On the contrary, it is when one interjects a right to commoditize against someone else who uses materials one authored as part of the materials with which they choose to express *their* autonomous view of the world, that autonomy is offended.

A perfect example of this is open-source licensing or free software licenses. An open source license will often secure the original author's rights of attribu-

---

80. I rely here on Radin's definition. *See* MARGARET JANE RADIN, CONTESTED COMMODITIES 118-19 (1990).

81. Hughes, *supra* note 76 at 349.

82. RONALD DWORKIN, A MATTER OF PRINCIPLE 246 (1985).

83. Raz defines the wellbeing of an autonomous agent in terms of successful pursuit of an autonomously chosen life. JOSEPH RAZ, THE MORALITY OF FREEDOM 390-95 (1986).

tion and integrity,[84] while eschewing commercial exploitation rights. This type of license, therefore, is an implementation of the autonomy of the authors that largely preserves the expressive autonomy of users. The license enhances autonomy on both sides. As a result, open source licenses are directly inverse to more traditional licenses that serve the commercial exploitation interests of the original authors (but not their personality interests) while restricting the expressive autonomy of users.

Consider also the *Wind Done Gone* case.[85] There, SunTrust Bank, administrator of Margaret Mitchell's estate, sued Houghton Mifflin, the publishers of Alice Randall's book, to prevent its publication. The book told a story that clearly borrowed from Margaret Mitchell's *Gone with the Wind*. First, if SunTrust Bank were the owner of the copyright, standing in its own shoes because it had hired Margaret Mitchell and owned the copyright, it would have had commercial but not moral claims to the book. Second, assuming SunTrust Bank was simply asserting Mitchell's rights as administrator of the Mitchell estate, the claims must be considered as though they were made by Mitchell.

Imagine that Alice Randall and the bank had conducted negotiations in which the bank required Randall to pay the bank 25% of the revenues from *The Wind Done Gone* and omit any direct or implicit reference to interracial sex.[86] It is intuitively simple to see this request for payment as one for commercial exploitation of the work. It may be perfectly sensible for the author to demand payment. It may also be perfectly sensible, on a utilitarian calculus, for society to pass a law requiring Randall to either pay what the bank asks or forego use of the story. Still, it is not a violation of Mitchell's autonomy for Randall to refuse to pay. If, however, the romantic view of the Old South was a central component of Mitchell's world view, and its expression in *Gone with the Wind* is an expression of this central aspect of her self, then use of her book, through a critical prism, to expose the ubiquity of interracial sex in the Old South is something that goes to the integrity of Mitchell's work as an expression of her self. Yet it is precisely this transformative utilization of work to subvert and mock the very message of the original author that is the quintessential case of permitted fair use in U.S. copyright law. In terms of autonomy and democracy, this is not a surprising calculus. Randall's retelling of *this* story, given the central role it plays in American culture by masking what she perceives to be a central truth in her experience as an African American woman and the central role it played in her childhood in defining her alienation from American society, is central to *her* autonomy. Moreover, Mitchell's autonomy is directly pitted against the democratic commitment to airing the widest range of views

84. This is seen most expressly in the *Open Source Definition, Version 1.9 Section 4*, *available at* http://www.opensource.org/docs/definition_plain.html; *see also* GNU GPL § 2(a).

85. SunTrust Bank v. Houghton Mifflin Co., 268 F.3d 1257 (11th Cir. 2001).

86. *See* David D. Kirkpatrick, *A Writer's Tough Lesson in Birthin' a Parody*, N.Y. TIMES, April 26, 2001, at E1.

expressed in the terms that their speakers find most effective to convey their message.

C. The Court as an Institutional Counterbalance

The preceding two subparts outlined substantive support for the robust constraints Article I of the U.S. Constitution and the First Amendment impose on the creation and definition of exclusive private rights in information. At their core, Article I and the First Amendment claim that both democracy and autonomy are better served by an information production and exchange system built around a robust public domain, rather than one built around extensive regulation of the use of information and cultural materials through the creation and enforcement of exclusive private rights. This subpart discusses the institutional reason, rather than the substantive reason, to introduce close judicial scrutiny of legislation that expands exclusive private rights at the expense of the public domain.

Our legislative process demonstrates a systematic imbalance in favor of the expansion and deepening of exclusive rights to information at the expense of the public domain. The imbalance exists because the benefits of such rights are clearly seen by, and expressed by, well-defined interest holders that exist at the time the legislation is passed. In contrast, most of the social costs—which are economic, social, political, and moral—are diffuse and likely to be experienced in the future by parties not yet aware of the fact that they will be affected by the extension of rights. For example, the Estate of Margaret Mitchell knew that an extension of copyright, negotiated in the 1960s, then in the 1970s, and again in the 1990s, would increase revenues to the estate by postponing the date when the book falls into the public domain. Alice Randall, however, was too young in the 1960s or 1970s to participate in the debate. Similarly, it is unlikely Randall focused on the effect the Sonny Bono Copyright Term Extension Act of 1998 (the "Copyright Term Extension Act"),[87] would have on her book when it was under debate. Likewise, Ed Felten in his worst nightmares probably could not have imagined that his academic paper on the weaknesses of the Secure Digital Music Initiative would subject him to civil suit, and, if Dmitry Sklyarov's experience is a predictor, perhaps even criminal liability. The recording industry, however, when it was lobbying for the Digital Millennium Copyright Act had a clear sense that this legislation would enable them to sell encrypted music in a more tightly controlled fashion.

In contrast, it is never the case that the diffuse and future users will band together to expand fair use. Even if they were to band together, it is impossible that copyright owners would remain unaware of the initiative and fail to offer substantial opposition in the legislative process. The legislative process, therefore, has a systematic bias toward more extensive exclusive, private rights at the expense of the public domain. This bias explains the constitutional framework

87. Pub. L. No. 105-298 (1998).

developed by the Supreme Court over the past century whereby courts provide a filter to limit Congress's power to expand private information rights. Both the threshold inquiry of Article I, and the *Turner* standard for First Amendment review, treat expansion of rights as subject to constitutional scrutiny. In contrast, expansion of the public domain, or elimination of exclusive rights does not require the same scrutiny. Expansion removes constraints on the use of cultural materials and information, making more modes of expression available. Thus, it deregulates, rather than regulates, the use of cultural and information materials. The justification of this one-way ratchet is precisely the systematic imbalance in the other lawmaking branch—the legislature. Since too extensive a definition of rights is economically inefficient and harms both democracy and autonomy, but is directly in the interest of a powerful lobby, it is the role of courts to prevent the systematic and excessive expansion of exclusive rights by serving as a backstop against this political economy.

Moreover, it is important to underscore that it is even more justified for courts to act as a moderating force on politics in the area of intellectual property rights than in media regulation—a parallel area of regulation of information production and exchange where courts have taken a very active role. When the broadcast and cable industries battle over "must carry" rules, each industry is well represented in Congress, and all of the potentially regulated parties are at the table. Power plays and successful capture of an agency or a legislature sometimes determine the outcome of this process. Often, however, negotiated deals determine the outcome and are later challenged by actors in the negotiation who try to make their deal sweeter. Laws regulating large players whose interests are well defined and understood at the time of the regulation—like broadcast, cable, or telephone regulation—are therefore substantially less in need of judicial review from an institutional perspective. In contrast, with copyright and similar exclusive rights judges must be attentive to prevent legislatures from selling the store in the absence of the parties likely to bear the primary brunt of the regulation.

IV

PRESSURE POINTS—THE STATE OF PLAY TODAY

Thus far I have covered two issues. First, I have delineated in doctrinal terms the constitutional framework within which Congress can regulate the use of information and cultural materials through the creation and definition of exclusive private rights. In this context, Article I of the Constitution operates as a threshold constraint, requiring Congress to show in creating such rights: (1) that the exclusive control the rights grant can plausibly increase information and cultural production, (2) that the rights be given only to those who add original contributions, and (3) that the rights not prevent use of materials in the public domain. The First Amendment then requires Congress to show that any given right meets, at least, the *Turner* standard of intermediate scrutiny. In subpart III, I explain why such a vigorous system of judicial review is normatively required. My argument is that both democracy and autonomy are served by a robust public domain and harmed by exclusive rights that excessively regulate the use of information, knowledge, and cultural materials. Moreover, the political economy of legislation is such that the legislature will systematically tend to create exclusive rights beyond what is economically efficient, as well as beyond what gives proper consideration to the implications of these rights for democracy and autonomy.

This section briefly outlines six particularly salient pressure points on this constitutional framework.

A. That's Not What the Law Says at All

The description I have given of the law is declarative—as though it is an uncontroversial view of the constitutional framework that constrains Congress from regulating information and cultural production too greatly. It is not. It is a decidedly contested view, though I believe it is the best reading of the Supreme Court's precedent. It is also true, however, that the Supreme Court largely has been more solicitous of user privileges and less enamored with "intellectual property" than the lower courts. In addition, not all the lower courts have accepted the spirit of the constitutional framework delimited by the Supreme Court's jurisprudence in this area. The lower courts' rejection of the Supreme Court's view that either Article I or the First Amendment substantially constrain Congress is most completely and starkly seen in *Eldred v. Reno*.[88]

Eldred v. Reno reviews Congress' adoption of the Copyright Term Extension Act in 1998. Through this Act, Congress extended the copyright protection term from life of the author plus fifty years to life of the author plus seventy years. The Act extended the seventy-five year term of protection for works initially owned by a corporation to a ninety-five year term.[89] These extensions were retroactively applied to existing works.[90] Eric Eldred, a retired programmer who scans out-of-print books and produces online editions for free distribution, challenged the Copyright Term Extension Act because it prohibited him from scanning and making available works that would have fallen into the public domain but for the extension. The D.C. Circuit rejected Eldred's claims that the Copyright Term Extension Act violated the "limited times" constraint imposed by the Exclusive Rights Clause and the First Amendment.[91] It held that the Preamble provides no constraint on the power of Congress and that when Congress creates the limited monopolies that it is empowered to create under Article I, it is subject to rationality review.[92] The Circuit Court seemed

88. 239 F.3d 372 (D.C. Cir. 2001), *cert. granted sub nom*, Eldred v. Ashcroft, 534 U.S. 1126, *and cert. amended*, 534 U.S. 1160 (2002).

89. *Id.* at 373.

90. *Id.*

91. *See id.* at 374.

92. *Id.* at 380.

little bothered by the fact that its holding directly contradicts the Supreme Court's decision in *Graham v. John Deere Co.* In *Graham*, the Court stated:

> At the outset it must be remembered that the federal patent power stems from a specific constitutional provision which authorizes the Congress "To promote the Progress of . . . useful Arts, by securing for limited Times to . . . Inventors the exclusive Right to their . . . Discoveries." Art. I, § 8, cl. 8. . . . The Congress in the exercise of the patent power may not overreach the restraints imposed by the stated constitutional purpose.[93]

The Circuit Court brushed away this specific requirement that copyright be for "limited times." The court claimed that "limited times" included very long, but not perpetual, grants, as well as retroactive extensions of time. Its argument with regard to the First Amendment claim was the implausible argument that laws Congress calls "copyright" are "categorically immune" from First Amendment scrutiny.[94]

The Copyright Term Extension Act of 1998—although not the decision in *Eldred v. Reno*—provides an excellent ground for explaining how the two constitutional constraints should interact. First, there is the retroactive application aspect of the Act. According to *Graham*, Congress can only create exclusive rights if the new rights could plausibly stimulate creation and if they do not remove anything from the public domain.[95] The adoption of a retroactive extension for works that have already been created fails both tests set forth in *Graham*. First, retroactive extension cannot plausibly promote the progress of science and the useful arts.[96] It cannot create incentives. Margaret Mitchell will not rewrite *Gone with the Wind* in 1998 no matter how many more years of copyright protection the book receives. Similarly, new books will not be written because old books are retroactively protected for a longer period than their authors were promised when they wrote them. For any future action to be affected by retroactive extension, a current author would have to think that a project would not justify itself under the present term of copyright but would nonetheless be worth the effort if copyright were extended to an additional given term, discounted by the probability that copyright will in fact be extended in the future to that necessary length. The implausibility of this argument can readily be captured by conjuring up the image of a movie studio executive pitching a project to investors by saying, "we won't make money within the seventy-five years that copyright law currently gives us, but Congress has traditionally extended rights over time, and if Congress extends copyright to ninety-five years, we'll make a killing on this one!"

Second, once a work is created, there are aspects of it that are enclosed, and aspects of it that are in the public domain. When Margaret Mitchell wrote *Gone with the Wind* in 1936, the longest term of protection possible for the book was fifty-six years. In 1936, then, the state of the world was that the

93. Graham v. John Deere Co., 383 U.S. 1, 5-6 (1966).

94. *Eldred*, 239 F.3d at 375-76.

95. *Graham*, 383 U.S. at 6.

96. *See* William M. Landes & Richard Posner, *An Economic Analysis of Copyright Law*, 18 J. LEGAL STUD. 325, 326 (1989).

enclosed domain included the book *Gone with the Wind* for fifty-six years. The public domain included the book *Gone with the Wind* in the year 1992. This is not a word game. It is an economically accurate description of the state of the resource called *Gone with the Wind* as perceived at the time of its creation by rational economic actors. If someone were to value the rights to make a movie from the book, they would have to price the license necessary. Imagine that the price is *P*. Whether it is worth paying that price is partly a function of the cost of waiting for the expiration of the copyright—*P* discounted to present value from the date of expiration to the date of use. That calculus is likely to have little effect on a decision made in 1938, but likely to have tremendous effect on a decision made in 1991. *Gone with the Wind* is "in the public domain"—on a deferred basis—at the moment of its creation. The precise value of its presence in the public domain depends on the time remaining until expiration. To extend the term of copyright for *Gone with the Wind* after it has been created is to remove its public domain aspect from the public domain.

Where, as in the case of retroactive term extension, Congress passes a law that removes material from the public domain with no plausible claim to increase incentives for creation, the law must fail under the limitations of the Exclusive Rights Clause. The *Eldred* court's failure to discipline its rationality review by focusing on the specific elements required by Article I, Section 8, Clause 8 of the Constitution resulted in practically no review of the Copyright Term Extension Act.

But what becomes of the prospective application of the Act? Extending protection from seventy-five to ninety-five years for works that do not yet exist removes nothing from the public domain. The story of the movie executive is slightly different. Here the pitch must be, "we won't make money within the first seventy-five years, but just you wait for years seventy-six through ninety-five!" It is possible that this aspect too will not pass the "promoting progress" threshold test.[97] If, however, it does pass the threshold, the prospective applications should not pass the *Turner* standard. The extension substantially burdens present expressive interests—interests of those people like Eldred who wish to use old materials expressively. The government's legitimate goal of giving sufficient incentives to authors is only furthered very weakly, if at all, and certainly there is no evidence, empirical or theoretical, suggesting that a less restrictive means—such as life of the author plus fifty years, or a term of fifty-six or twenty-eight years, is insufficient.

Considering this background, the D.C. Circuit's decision in *Eldred v. Reno* represents a lack of understanding of the constitutional dimensions of copyright law and the role of the judiciary in ensuring that the use of information and cultural materials by everyone is regulated no more than necessary. The decision

---

97. Both Stephen G. Breyer, *The Uneasy Case for Copyright: A Study of Copyright in Books, Photocopies, and Computer Programs*, 84 HARV. L. REV. 281, 323-28 (1970), and Landes & Posner, *supra* note 96, express substantial doubts about the marginal impact of term lengths so distant into the future.

neglects the important role courts have to play as an institutional counterbalance to a systematically imbalanced and overprotective legislative process. The court entirely misses the regulatory aspects of exclusive private rights and the necessity of a significant level of judicial First Amendment scrutiny to protect against over-regulation of access to, and use of, the cultural and information environment by individuals regardless of whether under that standard, it finds the DMCA unconstitutional. Needless to say, how the Supreme Court will resolve *Eldred* will largely settle the core question of the relationship between the constitution and the line demarcating the boundary between the public and proprietary domains.

B. Neo-Lochnerism and the Moral Inversion of the First Amendment

For over a century, lawyers have been treating corporations as legal "persons." With habit, this useful legal fiction has taken on a natural aura, as though General Motors and Joe's Trucking were just like individuals for all purposes. This fiction was not particularly important from a First Amendment perspective as long as free speech law was largely occupied with working out the relationship of the First Amendment to direct censorship, as it was throughout the first two-thirds of the twentieth century. As the information economy and society have moved to center stage, the First Amendment is increasingly used to impose judicial review on all regulation of this sphere of social and economic life.

Starting with cases like *First National Bank of Boston v. Bellotti*,[98] which protected a corporation's right to speak on matters of public concern as part of public discourse, and continuing with cases like *Central Hudson Gas & Electric Corp. v. Public Service Commission of New York*,[99] which began to protect corporate speech aimed for commercial purposes, First Amendment jurisprudence has gradually shifted to treating corporate speakers engaged in any form of information production and exchange as though they were no different than individual speakers engaged in political discourse or personal expression. This is an exaggerated characterization of the law in this area that I will not defend. Rather I will use it to identify a potential source of instability in First Amendment law.

The trend towards judicial review of the regulation of how corporations make money from information production, exchange, and carriage as though the regulation was aimed at individual rights, not economic regulation, has a particularly alarming trajectory in an information economy. The normatization of this position is nowhere more starkly evident than in Chief Justice Rehnquist's joining the majority in the *United Foods* case.[100] In *Central Hudson*, it was then Justice Rehnquist who accused the Court of returning to the

98 435 U.S. 765 (1978).

99 447 U.S. 557 (1980).

100 United States Dep't of Agric. v. United Foods, Inc., 533 U.S. 405, 429 (2001).

Lochner v. New York[101] era.[102] In *United Foods*, the Chief Justice joined the Court in finding unconstitutional a regulation that required mushroom growers to contribute to a general fund to support advertising mushrooms.[103] Justice Breyer responded, "I do not believe the First Amendment seeks to limit the Government's economic regulatory choices in this way—any more than does the Due Process Clause."[104] His invocation of the specter of *Lochner* in the context of First Amendment law was the first since Justice Rehnquist used it for the same purpose two decades earlier.

The video dial tone cases starkly exemplified the implications of this First Amendment interpretation trend in an economy where information production, dissemination, and carriage are central.[105] In the early 1990s, the FCC sought to allow telephone carriers into the video delivery market, with the caveat that the telephone carriers do so as common carriers. The FCC's video dial tone order required carriers to carry video signals on a nondiscriminatory basis, just as the FCC had previously required for telephone and data signals. The appellate courts treated this imposition as a violation of the telephone companies' editorial rights—the right to determine what information they would carry over their systems.[106] This, in turn, led these courts to scrutinize the economic rationale of the common carriage requirement—which was based on the FCC's experience with the telephone carriers as providers of competitive services dependent on their platform.[107] Rejecting the economic rationale offered by the FCC, the courts overturned the video dial tone order as violating the First Amendment.[108] The Supreme Court eventually vacated the case as moot, because the passage of the Telecommunications Act of 1996[109] disposed of the video dial tone model.[110] But the problem persists.[111]

Perhaps the most extreme version of this use of the First Amendment is *Time Warner Entertainment Co.* v. *FCC*.[112] In this case, the D.C. Circuit invalidated the FCC's limits on vertical and horizontal integration of cable carriers.[113] The FCC limits were intended to maintain a sufficient number of outlets to assure that any programmer not owned by a cable operator would have access

---

101. 198 U.S. 45 (1905)
102. *Central Hudson*, 447 U.S. at 589.
103. *United Foods*, 533 U.S. at 429.
104. *Id.*
105. Chesapeake & Potomac Tel. Co. v. United States, 42 F.3d 181 (4th Cir. 1994); *see also In re* Telephone Company-Cable Television Cross-Ownership Rules, Further Notice of Proposed Rulemaking, First Report and Order and Second Further Notice of Inquiry, 7 F.C.C.R. 300, 309 (Nov. 22, 1991).
106. *See Chesapeake & Potomac*, 42 F.3d at 203.
107. *See id.* at 202-03.
108. *Id.* at 185.
109. Pub. L. No. 104-104 (1996).
110. United States v. Chesapeake & Potomac Tel. Co., 516 U.S. 415, 416 (1996).
111. *See* Comcast Cablevision, Inc. v. Broward County, 124 F. Supp. 2d 685 (S.D. Fla. 2000).
112. 240 F.3d 1126 (D.C. Cir. 2001).
113. *Id.* at 1144.

to forty percent of the viewers in the total U.S. market.[114] The FCC decided that a minimum of four competitors was required to achieve this goal. It reasoned that two competitors could collaborate, and if together they controlled more than sixty percent of the viewers, the entities would be able to prevent programmers unaffiliated with them from surviving.[115] The FCC therefore capped the total number of viewers to whom any single cable operator could offer cable services at thirty percent.[116] To the court, there was no question that this cap on the potential number of subscribers violated the cable company's First Amendment rights.[117] All that was left for the court to do was to supplant its own economic judgment that there was not a high probability of collusion between two giant competitors to shut out unaffiliated programmers for the expert agency it was reviewing. As a result, the D.C. Circuit found the FCC's regulation unconstitutional under the *Turner* standard, because the regulation was not narrowly tailored.[118]

Now, one might think that this represents a general rise in courts' solicitude towards First Amendment claims against government regulation. However, we have already seen that in *Eldred v. Reno*,[119] which was decided within weeks of *Time Warner Entertainment Co. v. FCC*,[120] another panel of the same court reached a diametrically opposed result. By holding that copyright was categorically exempt from First Amendment review, the court upheld a regulation sustained by an economic rationale that is laughable under the *Time Warner* standards. The stark difference between the two cases is instructive: the first reverses a plausible, if unpersuasive to the judges, economic theory regarding concentration and collusion, and the second affirms an impossible economic theory about the effects of retroactive extension of an already ridiculously long copyright protection period.

Clearly, one aspect of this dissonance is the fact that copyright is considered a "private rights" concern, while horizontal ownership rules are considered a "public regulation" concern. *Eldred* and *Time Warner*, however, along with other copyright cases, evidence a deeper problem of moral inversion. For example, in the *Los Angeles Times v. Free Republic*[121] case the court saw the newspapers as the First Amendment rights bearers, while the individual users who would cut and paste stories as a basis for their political commentary and discourse with their fellow forum participants represented a lesser interest. The court did not consider that the clash was between political discourse on one hand and the right to charge for online access to archival materials (already

114. *Id.* at 1137.
115. *Id.* at 1132-33.
116. *Id.*
117. *Id.* at 1129.
118. *Id.* at 1136.
119. 239 F.3d. 372 (D.C. Cir.) *en banc denied sub nom.* Eldred v. Ashcroft, 255 F.3d 849 (D.C. Cir. 2001). *cert. granted*, 534 U.S. 1126, *and cert. amended*, 534 U.S. 1160 (2002).
120. 240 F.3d. 1126 (D.C. Cir. 2001).
121. No. 98-7840, 2000 WL 1863566 (C.D.Ca. Nov. 16, 2000).

fully remunerated through advertising) on the other hand. The criminalization of noncommercial use and exchange of digitized materials that one sees with the introduction of the NET Act[122] and the DMCA similarly fails to appreciate the chilling effect on real people—like Ed Felten—of a criminal prosecution against Dmitry Sklyarov, where the interest on the other side of the equation is the protection of a business model of a recording company or a movie studio.

This trend in First Amendment law of the information economy—towards protecting corporations broadly, even at the expense of very real and immediate constraints on the expressive autonomy and democratic speech of individuals—is unstable because it represents a moral inversion of the First Amendment. The First Amendment is not a technical rule of law stating that government shall not make any law regulating information flows regardless of their source or nature. Rather, it is a constitutional provision central to the functioning of our democracy and the security of our individual autonomy.

Our democracy does not generally treat corporations as citizens. They do not vote. They cannot be elected. Their contributions to political discourse are valued instrumentally, not intrinsically. Their claims to speech rights derive from the fact that corporations sometimes act as the best vehicles to bring useful information to the attention of a democratic polity.[123] From a First Amendment perspective, that is the corporation's only role. This use may entail quite substantial rights on the part of corporations, in particular news media. In the clash, however, between instrumental reasons to protect corporate speech and instrumental reasons to restrict it, for example, to permit others to enrich democratic discourse over the telephone company's network, the calculus is ultimately instrumental and subject to fairly flexible balancing. This could be a systematic justification for a new balancing approach that Justice Breyer seems to be developing in this area—for which he has received support from Justices O'Connor and Ginsburg in some cases.[124]

Furthermore, one cannot in any coherent fashion treat corporations as the bearers of moral claims to autonomy. In some fashion or another, claims to autonomy are based either in some dignitary interest or in some respect for rational beings or will. They are, in any event, entirely unavailable as intrinsic claims for corporations or other corporate bodies.[125] Organizations or corporations can serve or defeat autonomy. Their regulation, similarly, may serve or defeat autonomy. When it does defeat autonomy, such as when a regulation requires a corporation to prevent users from receiving information they wish to

122. Pub. L. No. 105-147 (1997).

123. C. EDWIN BAKER, HUMAN LIBERTY AND FREEDOM OF SPEECH 220-21 (1989). This is the crux of Baker's focus on treating the rights of corporations as always based in what he sees as the more instrumental press clause, and not in the speech clause that he largely reserves for protection of liberty interests in expressive autonomy.

124. *See* U.S. Dep't of Agric. v. United Foods, Inc., 533 U.S. 405, 425-28 (2001); Nixon v. Shrink Missouri Gov't Pac, 528 U.S. 377, 400-03 (2000); Turner Broad. Sys., Inc. v. FCC, 520 U.S. 180, 225-28 (1997).

125. *See* MEIR DAN-COHEN, RIGHTS, PERSONS, AND ORGANIZATIONS: A LEGAL THEORY FOR BUREACRATIC SOCIETY 55-119 (1986).

use or from disseminating expressions individual users wish to disseminate, the organizations may have an autonomy-based First Amendment claim. This claim, however, is autonomy-based only derivatively, not directly. As with the case of regulation that may instrumentally limit speech in ways that limit or enhance democracy, so too regulation of corporations may do so in ways that limit or enhance the autonomy of individuals.

In any event, when the person regulated is a human being, a citizen of a democracy, a direct claimant of autonomy, that person's claims are translated into an intrinsic First Amendment claim against instrumental regulation. In contrast, corporations' claims under the same constitutional provision are weaker, pitting one instrumental claim against another. Particularly when the government regulates corporations so as to serve the real parties in interest (the constituents and individuals) in an effort to enhance speech and increase diversity in discourse, the First Amendment largely devolves into assessing the instrumental approaches to serve the same intrinsic claims. In some sense, the corporations' First Amendment claims pit a rule-utilitarian instrumental approach (it on the whole serves this desideratum to follow this rule), while the regulation tries to serve the good more directly.

The instability comes from the flow of cases that do exactly the opposite. Exclusive private rights in information, as they are increasingly applied to constrain individual use of information and cultural resources, are a form of regulation of individual expressive freedom. Very often corporations are the beneficiaries of this regulation. These regulations are subject to little or no First Amendment scrutiny. On the other hand, rules that limit business practices or corporate management in an effort to give individuals greater access to information or greater access to avenues of expression are routinely struck down.

The result is a restriction of individual expressive autonomy and democratic discourse by and among the actual constituents of democracy. The First Amendment is interpreted to permit government to restrict individuals' access to and use of information and cultural materials, but prohibits the government from aiding individuals by similarly restricting corporations. The result is a world in which both government and corporations can restrict individuals while public corrective action to increase individual freedom is constrained. This inversion is partly sustained by characterizing copyright-like laws as "private ordering" or "property laws," and media access rules as "public laws" or "regulations." Partly, this approach relies for its stability and coherence on a workmanlike attention to doctrinal moves to the exclusion of principle, but these strategies cannot be stable in the long run. The moral inversion of the First Amendment puts too much pressure on the particular form of First Amendment law that has developed for the information economy.

C. Private Ordering

The fact that the regulations in question are usually conceptualized as property or contract rights, rather than direct command and control regulations is another element that is likely to play an important role in framing the constitutional understanding of exclusive rights in information and culture. As property or contract rights, regulations partake of the aura of "private actions," an area where government action is not generally subject to constitutional review (*Shelley v. Kraemer*[126] aside). The operation of this construct, in its simplest form, is seen in the D.C. Circuit's statement in *Eldred v. Reno*, "plaintiffs lack any cognizable First Amendment right to exploit the copyrighted works of others."[127] Here the court conceptualizes the conflict as involving two private parties—one that owns a work, another that wants to use it. The First Amendment has no traction.

The simple fact that the last person triggering a prohibition on a particular use is not a government actor does not, however, render the prohibition immune to First Amendment scrutiny. Much depends, instead, on the source of power that enables the prohibition. Imagine that Congress created and auctioned off rights to prohibit Republicans from appearing on television and sold the rights to private parties. What if courts are then asked to enforce the prohibitions by the individuals? Whether a particular Republican would or would not be allowed on television would not be a government decision, but rather a decision of the private license owner. The source of prohibition, however, would be a law that discriminates against speech based on viewpoint, and thus almost without question would be struck down. Or would it? The baseline rule as to cable access requirements became privatization of the censorship decision. Nonetheless, the privatization of the decision confounds the issues. *Denver Area Educational Telecommunications Consortium*[128] is in many senses functionally similar. There, the Court in fact upheld a content-based regulation against protected speech, because the law delegated the final censorship decision to cable operators. The statute reviewed in that case[129] related to cable channels on which cable carriers were generally required to carry all programming on a nondiscriminatory basis, much as would a common carrier. The statute challenged in that case excluded from this general nondiscrimination requirement only smut that Congress disapproved of but could not, under the court's First Amendment jurisprudence, directly prohibit. While the plurality did not find private party control dispositive, it did weigh in favor of finding constitutionality.[130] As a practical matter, the Court indeed upheld a content-discriminating regulatory burden of protected speech that it would never have upheld had it not been structured as a privatization of the utility censorship act. Private party control, moreover, was the deciding factor for Justices Thomas, Rehnquist, and Scalia.[131]

126. 334 U.S. 1 (1948).
127. 239 F.3d 372, 376 (D.C. Cir. 2001).
128. Denver Area Educ. Telecomm. Consortium v. FCC, 518 U.S. 727 (1996).
129. *Id.* at 735.
130. *See id.* at 768.
131. *Id.* at 812 (Thomas, J., dissenting).

Clearly, however, cases exist where a private person can rely on, for example, property rights, to prevent someone from speaking, and can do so on a viewpoint-based or any other grounds. Indeed, such cases are regarded as the "normal" case, while situations like the company town in *Marsh v. Alabama*[132] are the exception. What is the difference between exclusive private rights in information—like copyright—and a private homeowner's request of a guest not to annoy everyone with praise for the Taliban? The point is that understanding copyright within the framework of First Amendment law does not require one to consider whether a copyright owner is more like a company town or a mall. In those cases, the owner of physical property would use a law that was not directed at speech and did not use legal power to exclude the speaker. The speaker, in reliance on the First Amendment, demanded an exception to the general property law. The court either accepted or rejected this claim. The relationship of the First Amendment to copyright is entirely different. Users are not confronted with an inability to speak, print, or play music without access to resources—like streets, parks, or transmitters—governed by a general law like property. They have the means to do so under their control. They are confronted with a legal rule—the law of copyright—that in the pursuit of the public interest prohibits them from speaking, printing, or playing music in ways that they otherwise could. The law of copyright is the only thing that stands between the user and the user's capacity to speak as she pleases. It is a public law, enacted by the legislature, to benefit public interests, that takes the form of telling many people that they are prohibited from printing certain words that they want to print or publicly perform. It may be a perfectly justifiable law, but to say that a person has no cognizable First Amendment interest in not being forbidden by law from printing something he or she wishes to print or say publicly, and can as a practical matter print or say, is implausible.

This answer depends, however, on the theory one has regarding the source of exclusive private rights in information. If one takes some form of natural rights approach—along the Lockean or Hegelian lines—then the source of the property right is pre-legal. In that case the law is simply enforcing pre-political rights, whose contours therefore are not themselves reviewable "government action." Then, the source of the prohibition that the owner places on the user is not itself a reviewable law, though obviously when the Sheriff comes to enforce the prohibition there is a government action, just as in *Shelley v. Kraemer*.[133]

If, however, one sees, as U.S. tradition and Supreme Court opinions repeatedly state, exclusive private rights in information as positive law, rooted in a utilitarian calculus, then the law creating the right is itself the "law" that Congress has made abridging the freedom of speech. The meaning of an exclusive private right in information is that Congress has identified a person who, for reasons of the general welfare, receives a right to prevent others from saying certain words. The person stymied by copyright law is just like the person with

132. 326 U.S. 501 (1946).
133. 334 U.S. 1 (1948).

the right to prevent Republicans from talking on television. The viewpoint neutrality of copyright goes to the likelihood that the law will be upheld, not to the presence of a "cognizable First Amendment interest." This does not mean that every copyright infringement case now has a case-specific First Amendment review component. It does, however, mean that where the law of exclusive private rights draws the boundaries of the right, these boundaries must be subject to First Amendment scrutiny.

While this issue is important in the copyright context, as *Eldred* indicates, the primary locus for its likely mischief is in confounding the constitutional analysis of institutional mechanisms explicitly intended to facilitate "private ordering" of access to and use of information and cultural materials, rather than to embed public policy choices. This is particularly true with the Uniform Computer Information Transactions Act ("UCITA"),[134] whose most controversial feature is the validation of mass-market licenses.

Consider a term appended to the news reports of a technology news service: "Information contained in this CNET News.com report may not be republished or redistributed without the prior written authority of CNET, Inc."[135] Under copyright law, the information contained in a report, as distinguished from the expressive form that it takes, is not the property of the reporter. There may be a very limited "hot news" exception to this general rule,[136] but certainly nothing that would encompass the broad claim of right expressed in CNET's terms.

Most courts prior to the passage of UCITA did not enforce such broad terms.[137] In refusing to enforce these provisions, some courts relied on state contract law, by finding an absence of sufficient consent[138] or an unenforceable contract of adhesion.[139] Others courts relied on preemption—stating that to the extent state contract law purported to enforce a contract that prohibited fair use or material in the public domain (like the raw information contained in a report), it was preempted by federal copyright law that chose to leave this material in the public domain.[140] While the Seventh Circuit held otherwise,[141] this was the majority position prior to UCITA. UCITA, however, obviates the state contract law bases for refusing to enforce such contracts.

A state's enactment of UCITA does not trigger direct constitutional review under Article I, although it might under the First Amendment. In *Bonito*

134. UNIF. COMPUTER INFO. TRANSACTIONS ACT (UCITA) (2001), *available at* http://www.law.penn.edu/bll/ulc/ucita/ucita.htm.

135. *See* http://news.com.com (last visited Sept. 17, 2002).

136. *See* Int'l News Serv. v. Associated Press, 248 U.S. 215 (1918); National Basketball Ass'n v. Motorola, 105 F.3d 841, 853 (2d Cir. 1997).

137. Mark A. Lemley, *Intellectual Property and Shrinkwrap Licenses*, 68 S. CAL. L. REV. 1239, 1248-53 (1995).

138. Step-Saver Data Sys., Inc. v. Wyse Tech., 939 F.2d 91, 99-100 (3d Cir. 1991).

139. Vault Corp. v. Quaid Software Ltd., 655 F. Supp. 750, 761 (E.D. La. 1987), *aff'd*, 847 F.2d 255 (5th Cir. 1988).

140. Vault Corp. v. Quaid Software Ltd., 847 F.2d 255, 270 (5th Cir. 1988).

141. *See* Hill v. Gateway 2000, Inc., 105 F.3d 1147 (7th Cir. 1997); ProCD, Inc. v. Zeidenberg, 86 F.3d 1447 (7th Cir. 1996).

Boats, Inc. v. Thunder Craft Boats, Inc., the Court specifically stated that the limitations imposed on Congress by Article I, Section 8, Clause 8 did not directly apply to the states.[142] The Court, however, also held that states could not create rights that were functionally equivalent to rights created by federal statute—like patent law—but did not serve the core policy goals of the federal law in retaining access to the information to which exclusive rights are granted. The correct analysis of UCITA, insofar as Article I is concerned, is to consider whether its blanket validation of mass-market licenses, including those that prohibit users from making uses preserved for them by the Copyright Act, is preempted by that Act, or conflicts with the requirements of Article I as implemented in the Copyright Act. In the case of UCITA, for example, validation of a shrinkwrap license that prohibits copying of public domain materials covered by the contract would be a simple example of state law enforcement of a term in a mass-market contract that could violate Article I as implemented through the Copyright Act. The Copyright Act implements access to public domain materials in a variety of ways.[143] It does so in many cases as a direct implementation of Article I's mandate not to create rights in public domain materials. When UCITA is enforced to circumvent these privileges, it does so in violation of the constitutionally embedded federal policy just as surely as the boat hull design considered in *Bonito Boats* violated federal patent policy.

Moreover, enforcement of mass-market shrinkwrap licenses to prohibit users from using information in ways permissible under copyright law is generally a suppression of speech that must be reviewed under *Turner*. That shrinkwrap license enforcement is based in contract law about speech no more insulates it from First Amendment review than the private law basis of defamation law insulates it from complying with a federally imposed, constitutional baseline. When contract law refuses to enforce contracts that are against public policy, it recognizes the irreducible public role in defining the conditions of enforceability. Just as the exclusive rights themselves are reviewable because they seek to achieve a public purpose by prohibiting certain expressive acts, so too contracts about permitted and prohibited expression call upon the state to prohibit certain speech in pursuit of public policy. The decision whether to enforce contracts for gambling, or prostitution, or assassinations under the law, was a public decision, aimed at public goals, with implications as to the enforcement of a legal form of interpersonal agreements. Similarly, the decision about whether to enforce contracts that determine whether one person will say certain things or read certain things will be enforced under the law is a public decision, implemented through public law. That public decision is subject to review under the First Amendment. Again, not every contract is subject to *de novo* review. Categories of policy decisions, however—such as whether to enforce mass-market licenses that prohibit uses of information otherwise privileged by copyright law—are subject to *de novo* review.

---

142. 489 U.S. 141, 165 (1989).

143. Jessica Litman, *The Public Domain*, 39 EMORY L.J. 965, 992-94 (1990).

The "public" character of the license is even less problematic when the "contract" is not a negotiated agreement between equal parties, but a mass-market license that is in effect a privately selected, but publicly enforced, regulation of how certain information is used by wide ranges of the population. When Congress creates a particular set of rules regulating access to information or cultural materials, it determines that the means it adopted adequately serves the goal of promoting incentives for creativity. Given the political economy of congressional legislation on exclusive private right in information, at any given moment the federally enacted baseline is likely to be more protective than optimal. This baseline, the federal law of copyright, always stands as a less restrictive alternative for attaining that goal than the terms a mass-market vendor will add to that baseline. The result is that a state law or court order that prohibits a person from using information as the user is permitted to under the Copyright Act is an overly restrictive regulation of that use. A less restrictive alternative is readily available in the form of the federal baseline.

D. Regulating the Logical Layer: Code and the Constitution

Imagine a critic of Hollywood culture—say, a feminist film critic or a fundamentalist preacher—preparing a presentation about the ills he or she sees in this culture. The most effective means of explaining and communicating this criticism would be a presentation laced with illustrations from actual films. The Copyright Act generally permits such quotations from video. The DMCA however, has created a framework that operates at the logical, or software layer, and effectively prohibits these quotations.

The DMCA prohibits anyone from circumventing a technical measure that controls access to a work.[144] It also prohibits anyone from making or distributing utilities that would help users circumvent protection measures.[145] Neither provision, at least as currently interpreted, is subject to the fair use exception, and the quotations by the feminist critic or the fundamentalist preacher would not likely fall under any exception to the DMCA. If producers encrypt cultural products, as the film industry has done with DVDs and new videocassettes, it becomes illegal under the DMCA to perform the functions at the logical layer that are necessary to quote from them.[146] A bill is presently being contemplated to force manufacturers of both the physical and logical layers of the information environment—the hard drives, computers, screens and the like, as well as software—similarly to design their wares to enforce the licensing practices of the copyright industry.[147]

---

144. 17 U.S.C. § 1201(a)(1).

145. 17 U.S.C. § 1201(a)(2).

146. Universal City Studios, Inc. v. Reimerdes, 111 F. Supp. 2d 294, 322 (S.D.N.Y. 2000), *aff'd sub nom.*, Universal City Studios, Inc. v. Corely, 273 F.3d 429 (2d Cir. N.Y. 2001) (note that this case is referred to as *Reimerdes* at the district court level and *Corely* on appeal).

147. *Security Systems Standards and Certification Act [Draft]*, *available at* http://cryptome.org/sssca.htm (Aug. 6, 2001).

Some technical protection may be necessary to preserve the viability of a commodified, copyright-based business model in cultural production. A pervasive rebuilding of both the infrastructure's physical and logical layers designed to control the way individuals interact with their cultural environment, however, undermines both individual expressive freedom and the richness of political discourse. In particular, these provisions make cultural resources less available and more expensive for the noncommodified sector—like the feminist film critic or the fundamentalist preacher—thus, threatening to impoverish an increasingly important dimension of social discourse.

Three cases that test the constitutionality of the DMCA's anti-device provision have recently been considered. These are *Corely*, *Felten*, and *Sklyarov*. *Corely* presents the most substantial First Amendment decision. *Sklyarov* arises in the context of criminalization. *Felten* is almost too easy a test, presenting the real-world example of what would otherwise be considered a "parade of horribles"-type argument.

Corely involves a suit by the eight Hollywood studios against a hacker magazine, *2600*, published by Eric Corely. The plaintiffs sought an injunction prohibiting *2600* from making available, or linking to other sites that make available, a program called "DeCSS."[148] DeCSS is a computer program that circumvents the copy protection scheme, CSS, used to control access to DVDs. CSS prevents copying or any use of DVDs unauthorized by the vendor. DeCSS was written by a fifteen-year-old Norwegian named Jon Johanson, who claims (though the district court discounted his claim) to have written it as part of an effort to create a DVD player for Linux based machines.[149] *2600* posted a copy of DeCSS on its site, together with a story about it. The industry obtained an injunction against *2600* prohibiting not only the posting of DeCSS, but also its links to other sites that post the program.[150] The court rejected the defendant's arguments that sought to interpret the DMCA to include a fair use exception, as well as the defendant's constitutional argument that if the DMCA's anti-device provision prohibited DeCSS, then the DMCA was unconstitutional.[151]

The defendant presented the Court of Appeals with both an Article I argument and two types of First Amendment arguments against the DMCA. The Article I argument was that the limitations Article I places on Congress's power to grant exclusive private rights in information require, among other things, that a law not remove materials from the public domain and that it provide protection only for limited times.[152] Encryption, however, allows a vendor to encrypt not only copyrighted materials, but also public domain materials never owned by the copyright owner and materials whose term of protection has expired.

148. *Reimerdes*, 111 F. Supp. 2d at 308-09.

149. *Id.* at 311.

150. *Id.* at 312.

151. *Id.* at 332-33.

152. Julie Cohen, *Brief of Amici IP Law Professors*, *at* http://www.eff.org/IP/Video/MPAA_DVD_cases/20010126_ny_lawprofs_amicus.html (Jan. 26, 2001).

Thus, a law that prohibits the existence of circumvention devices, even those usable to reach public domain materials, is a law that excludes these materials from the public domain, or indefinitely extends the term of protection, in violation of the constricts of Article I. Furthermore, it is law, rather than technology or private action that excludes access to the materials. This is because counter-technology (circumvention devices like DeCSS) is perfectly capable of enabling users to use the public domain materials. Therefore, only the law prohibiting these devices causes the exclusion. But, according to Article I, a law giving exclusive rights to control access to information or cultural materials may not include a right to indeterminately exclude others from either public domain or copyrighted material. If the court does not accept this argument, or some similar limitation on what Congress can indirectly achieve through regulating the logical layer of the information environment, then, the argument goes, regulations like the DMCA as a practical matter can obviate the Article I protections of the public domain.

The defendants also advanced two First Amendment arguments—one for strict scrutiny, the other for intermediate, or *Turner*-level scrutiny.[153] Accepting that the purpose of encouraging commercial proprietary production of information through creating exclusive rights is an important government interest, *Turner*-level review questions whether the specific law burdens speech too much. The internal limitations in copyright law—like the fair use exception or the privileged use of public domain materials—are constitutive mediating devices permitting copyright law to comply with the constraints of the First Amendment. The anti-device provision of the DMCA in effect eliminates these mediating devices by giving vendors of digitized materials complete, rather than limited control over materials they encrypt. The effective elimination of access to video materials for purposes of quotation, or to materials no longer covered by copyright, or to materials otherwise in the public domain imposes too heavy a burden on the speech of users, particularly in the presence of less restrictive alternatives. Less restrictive alternatives include: imposing liability for infringing uses of circumvention, requiring that access-protection devices permit statutorily defined fair uses, or allowing copy protection mechanisms that permit first-, but not second-generation copying.[154] Given the presence of less restrictive alternatives that Congress has used in similar circumstances, the DMCA imposes too great a burden and should be found to violate the First Amendment.

The district court below held that the *Turner* standard was in fact applicable but that the harms to fair users were too remote and speculative to justify finding the act unconstitutional on its face.[155] In addition, the court found that the

153. *Reimerdes*, 111 F. Supp. 2d. at 327-28.

154. *See* ACLU et al., *Brief of Amici Curiae*, *at* http://www.aclu.org/court/corley.pdf (Jan. 26, 2001); Yochai Benkler & Lawrence Lessig, *Brief of Amici*, *at* http://www.eff.org/IP/Video/MPAA_DVD_cases/20010126_ny_2profs_amicus.html (Jan. 26, 2001); *EFF Supplemental Letter Brief*, *at* http://www. eff.org/IP/Video/MPAA_DVD_cases/20010530_ny_eff_supl_brief.html (May 30, 2001).

155. *See Reimerdes*, 111 F. Supp. 2d at 327-37.

specific defendants were not fair users and could not claim therefore to invalidate the act as applied.[156] The Second Circuit Court of Appeals largely upheld the lower court's decision.[157] It, too, applied *Turner* scrutiny, and found the DMCA to be sufficiently narrowly tailored given the perceived threat to copyright holders.[158] It did not disagree with the arguments that there were less restrictive means available but held that government need not use the least restrictive means.

The lion's share of the briefs and the opinions, both at the appellate and district court level, were devoted to regulation of code as itself the regulation of speech. Following the district court, the court of appeals accepted that code was a language that computer scientists used to communicate with each other, finding that "programmers communicating ideas to one another almost inevitably communicate in code, much as musicians use notes."[159] The court further added in a footnote, "[r]einforcing the conclusion that software programs qualify as 'speech' for First Amendment purposes—even though they instruct computers—is the accelerated blurring of the line between 'source code' and conventional 'speech.' There already exist programs capable of translating English descriptions of a program into source code."[160] The court then rejected, however, the appellants' view that this speech nature of code required strict scrutiny of the DMCA.

> Unlike a blueprint or a recipe, which cannot yield any functional result without human comprehension of its content, human decision-making and human action, computer code can instantly cause a computer to accomplish tasks and instantly render the results of those tasks available throughout the world via the Internet. The only human action required to achieve these results can be as limited and instantaneous as a single click of a mouse. These realities of what code is and what its normal functions are require a First Amendment analysis that treats code as combining nonspeech and speech elements, i.e. functional and expressive elements.[161]

The court then quoted extensively from the lower court's opinion, which described how the functionality of DeCSS was to permit free and easy copying of instantaneous perfect worldwide distribution, concluding that this functionality properly affects the scope of First Amendment protection, "the capacity of a decryption program like DeCSS to accomplish unauthorized—indeed, unlawful—access to materials in which the Plaintiffs have intellectual property rights must inform and limit the scope of it First Amendment protection."[162] This logic eventually led the court to apply intermediate scrutiny, under which it found the DMCA's application to DeCSS unconstitutional.

The fundamental concern of the Second Circuit is, in my opinion, the proper one. Computer programs can indeed perform functions by being applied to

156. *See id.* at 323.
157. *Corely*, 273 F.3d at 429.
158. *Id.* at 454-55.
159. *Id.* at 448.
160. *Id.* at n.23.
161. *Id.*
162. *Id.*

machines without human cognitive intervention, in a way that instructions of how to build a bomb published in a magazine cannot. Yet if law had said that musicians may not use notes to exchange ideas about militaristic nationalism because such music incites to violence through some primal mechanism not in cognition, there would be no question that the regulation would be subject to strict scrutiny.

If, instead of copyright and computer code, the law had said one may not speak in Russian about overthrowing the U.S. government or in Arabic about Jihad, the need for strict scrutiny would have been obvious. Nothing in either the change of language or the change of topic should result in a different outcome. It is still the case that there is an identifiable group of people for whom use of a specific language is particularly helpful. It is still the case that there are particular topics the government believes are more dangerously spoken about in some languages than in others. This governmental judgment needs to be subjected to strict scrutiny. Perhaps a court today will decide that under the *Brandenburg* test, prohibiting the sale of flight manuals in Arabic is justified. Yet, in doing so a court would be required to utilize strict scrutiny, not some lesser standard. The repeated references in the Second Circuit's opinion to the threat DeCSS posed to Hollywood were inappropriate in considering the standard of review. They would only have been appropriate to consider whether the DMCA is valid under the higher standard of review.

From the perspective of First Amendment doctrine, the potential difficulty is that no regulation of computer programming can be undertaken unless it complies with the strict scrutiny standard. That is not, in principle, an implausible result. Journalists generally cannot be regulated in terms of the words they use, except under strict scrutiny. Why couldn't the same be true of computer programmers?

As the Second Circuit noted, the most important potential concern with this outcome is that a communication to a machine intended to cause it to perform a function is not a communication that triggers the First Amendment. No one would suggest that it is unconstitutional to regulate communication between a human and a urinal achieved through an infrared port or communication between a human and a remote-control car. The complicating fact with code is that the same words can be uttered, and some or even many human beings will understand them as meaningful human communications, while some machines will understand them as instructions. The difficulty is how to regulate utterances intended to "push buttons" without burdening human communications. This might mean that executing a program must be distinguished from communicating it in a humanly readable form capable of being either read by a human or run by a machine. It might mean that distribution with the intent of running, as opposed to that of communicating, should be more readily regulable. The obvious difficulty, once one presents the distinction in these terms, is the potential chilling effect on human communication. This is exemplified most clearly by David Touretsky's superb website, devoted to prodding the boundaries of this precise problem.[163] Touretsky presents various forms of describing DeCSS, some more readily machine-readable than others. He presents it, for example, in plain English and in Haiku form, as well as in a computer language for which a compiler has not yet been written. Therefore, a machine could theoretically read it, but the computer translation mechanism does not yet exist.

This kind of richly detailed argument is provocative. It does not, however, necessarily imply that software can never be regulated except under conditions that would permit the regulation of a news report. Journalists cannot have an effect on the world through their writing, except through the acts of human readers absorbing their words and opinions. Regulating the words of journalists is therefore regulating directly the human interaction that lies at the core of both the democracy and the autonomy concerns of the First Amendment. In contrast, computer scientists writing code can have an effect on the world even if no human being ever reads their work. It seems plausible that the state should be able to regulate those aspects of code distribution that are intended to operate without operating on the human cognition.

Touretsky's argument is, therefore, in large measure a well-presented, finely detailed, slippery slope argument.[164] It suggests that some cases will be easier, and others harder. Liability for sending an executable file of a virus, intended to function on the computer of a user without communicating to the user, should be relatively straightforward to understand in First Amendment terms as not implicating expressive values. In contrast, liability for publishing an academic paper that includes instructions for how to attain a certain result in computing should be treated as implicating First Amendment interests of the highest order. The presence of formal representations normally used in the discipline, which are machine-readable and sufficient to be automatically compiled into running code, should not change this characterization. This is why the *Felten* case is so compelling, and why even though it implicated the same threats as *Corely*, the court plainly would have been required to find the DMCA unconstitutional. This is probably why the recording industry ran away from the field in it and settled the case. In between there are hard cases that need to be resolved on the basis of the extent to which a regulation burdens speech among computer professionals. Thus, a law that prohibits distribution of source code (as defined functionally in the GNU General Public License ("GPL") to be the form most usable by programmers)[165] should be treated as directly burdening speech. If it treats code about different human actions differently because government treats communication in this form about this subject as more dangerous to its interests, as the DMCA anti-device provision does, it should be seen as content-based speech regulation. This is why the

163. David Touretsky, *Gallery of CSS Descramblers*, *at* http://www-2.cs.cmu.edu/~dst/DeCSS/Gallery/index.html (last modified Aug. 29, 2002). In principle, the logic of linking liability in the DeCSS case could treat this footnote as an act of trafficking (though this is unlikely).

164. *Id.*

165. GNU GPL § 3, *available at* http://www.gnu.org/copyleft/library.txt (last visited Oct. 25, 2002). The source code for a work means the preferred form of the work for making modifications to it.

DMCA, which treats uncompiled sources of code and object code alike, should have been treated as content-based speech regulation and struck down. A law that prohibits only the distribution of executable files already compiled for a known set of machines, should be seen as incidentally affecting speech, and subject to *O'Brien* review.[166] I do not pretend that this cursory discussion resolves this issue. Here I only raise this difficult question, and suggest my own intuitions about this thorny question.

E. Criminalization

The DMCA and regulation of the logical layer is also where the story of Dmitry Sklyarov enters and looms large.[167] Encryption of information and cultural materials is intimately involved in the denial of permission to read, view, or quote the encrypted materials. A legal prohibition on decryption—on taking practical steps that would allow one to read, view, or quote the information or cultural materials regardless of the prohibition—directly implicates First Amendment considerations. To impose criminal sanctions in this delicate area is to force innovators and readers to adopt wide margins around the contours of the law. The high risk of criminal liability and its chilling effect on protected activities requires courts to be especially wary of criminal provisions that burden speech. It is one thing for Alice Randall, Edward Felten or 2 Live Crew to test the bounds of the law when the consequences might be an injunction preventing publication or a damage award. It is quite another to ask them to continue to enrich our speech environment at the risk of spending years in a federal prison.

Beginning with the No Electronic Theft Act ("NET Act")[168] and later incorporated into the DMCA,[169] criminal copyright recently has greatly expanded. Prior to passage of the NET Act, only commercial pirates—those that slavishly made thousands or millions of copies of video or audiocassettes and sold them for profit—would have qualified as criminal violators of copyright. With the passage of the NET Act, criminal liability has been expanded to cover private copying and free sharing of copyrighted materials whose cumulative nominal price, irrespective of actual displaced demand, is quite low. As criminal copyright law is currently written, many individuals involved with the over tens of millions of peer-to-peer file sharing systems are felons. It is one thing when in an effort to conform social norms to their business model the recording industry labels tens of millions of individuals in a society as "pirates." It is quite another when the state brands these individuals as felons and fines or imprisons them.

---

166. *See* United States v. O'Brien, 391 U.S. 367, 376-77 (1968).
167. *See supra*, Part I.B.
168. Pub. L. No. 105-147 (1997).
169. 17 U.S.C. § 204.

Jessica Litman has offered the most plausible explanation of the criminalization phenomenon.[170] She argues that as networking makes low-cost production and exchange of information and culture easier, large-scale commercial producers are faced with a new source of competition—volunteers, people who provide information and culture for free.[171] As the universe of people who can threaten the industry has grown to encompass almost all potential customers, the plausibility of using civil actions to force individuals to buy rather than share information decreases. Suing all of one's customers is not a sustainable business model. In an effort to maintain their business model, which relies on control over information goods and their sale as products, the copyright industry has enlisted criminal enforcement. By doing so, commercial producers prevent the emergence of such a system of free exchange. In *Sklyarov*, this is illustrated by the fact that Adobe instigated the prosecution. Even though Adobe later receded in the face of the outrage of many of its customers, it does not change the fundamental fact that it instigated precisely the chain of events that it wished would occur—criminal enforcement without direct involvement by the vendor.

The changes in law, coupled with the Justice Department's current focus on enforcement of intellectual property rights,[172] have lead to a substantial increase in the likelihood of criminal enforcement. The potential stakes of using information and cultural materials have risen. Now users are required to seek a license and pay for use in many more instances than they would have only a few years ago.[173] It is still, as of this writing, a serious constitutional question whether a law like the DMCA, that prohibits Dmitry Sklyarov from writing code that has substantial noninfringing uses—such as letting users read public domain materials like *Alice in Wonderland* or quote from e-books without permission—is a valid exercise of Congress's power under Article I or is consistent with the First Amendment. Asking programmers to write the software that will make these privileged uses available, so that legal challenges can determine the constitutionality of that prohibition is difficult when the price of a mistake is imprisonment.

The Supreme Court has expressed particular concern with the chilling effect of criminal, as opposed to civil, enforcement of policy. In *Reno v. ACLU*, the Court specifically stated that "the severity of criminal sanctions may well cause speakers to remain silent rather than communicate even arguably unlawful words, ideas, and images,"[174] distinguishing it from the civil measures used to effectuate similar child-protection goals in *Denver Area Educational Telecom-*

---

170. *See* Jessica Litman, *Electronic Commerce and Free Speech*, 1 J. ETH. & INFO. TECH. 213 (1999), *available at* http://www.law.wayne.edu/litman/papers/freespeech.pdf.

171. *Id.*

172. *See DOJ Intellectual Property Policy and Programs*, *at* http://www.usdoj.gov/criminal/cybercrime/ippolicy.htm (last modified July 20, 2001).

173. *See supra* Part IV.C.

174. 521 U.S. 844, 872 (1997).

munications Consortium, Inc. v. FCC.[175] Similarly, in *FCC v. Pacifica Foundation* the court's approval of the FCC's administrative action specifically noted as one consideration that the sanction imposed was not criminal.[176]

The thoughtful critical essay that David Touretsky has published includes materials that could be interpreted as circumvention devices; providing them could be interpreted as trafficking.[177] The problem with the expansive criminalization of copyright is that Touretsky must be a braver man to bring his criticism to the public than he would need to be if the sole remedy were civil—say an injunction requiring him to remove his web page following time-wasting and costly litigation. Some brave critics will continue. Others will be chilled. Discourse, however, will undoubtedly be impoverished.

Given the tremendous expansion of rights in the past few years, and the serious arguments that these expansions have deleterious implications for free speech and are unjustified as a matter of economic theory, the heightened criminalization of copyright should present an immediate target for judicial review. The Sklyarov case presents an excellent opportunity for the judiciary to exercise its moderating power.

F. Raw Information and Information about Information

In 1991, in *Feist Publications, Inc. v. Rural Telephone Service Co.*, the Supreme Court held that raw facts in a compilation or database were not covered by the Copyright Act, and could not be protected consistent with the constraints imposed by the Exclusive Rights Clause.[178] The Court held that the creative element of the compilation—for example, its organization or selectivity—could be protected under copyright law.[179] The facts compiled, however, could not be protected.[180] Copying data from an existing compilation was therefore not "piracy"; it was not unfair or unjust; it was purposefully privileged in order to advance the goals of exclusive rights—the advancement of progress and creative uses of the data.[181]

In the years since the Court decided *Feist*, there have been repeated efforts by the larger players in the database publishing industry to pass legislation that would, as a practical matter, overturn *Feist* and create exclusive private rights in the raw data in compilations.[182] Since the Court rooted its *Feist* decision in a robust interpretation of the Exclusive Rights Clause, efforts to protect database providers eventually settled on an unfair competition law. Based in the Commerce Clause, protections under unfair competition law are free and clear of

175. 518 U.S. 727 (1996).
176. 438 U.S. 726, 747 (1978).
177. Touretsky, *supra* note 163.
178. 499 U.S. at 349-50.
179. *Id.* at 350-51; 17 U.S.C. § 103.
180. *Feist*, 499 U.S. at 351.
181. *Id.* at 349-50.
182. The Collections of Information Anti-Piracy Act (CIAA) H.R. 354, 106th Cong (1999).

the inconvenient weight of *Feist*. In reality, however, the primary law that has repeatedly been introduced walks, talks, and looks like a property right.[183] If some version of this law ultimately passes, it will present an important focal point for defining the constitutional status of raw data, under both the Exclusive Rights Clause and the First Amendment.

Even if the congressional law may be stopped, however, other avenues have recently opened to appropriate raw data. In particular, some litigants have turned to state law remedies to protect their data indirectly, by developing a trespass-to-server form of action. The primary instance of this trend is *eBay, Inc. v. Bidder's Edge, Inc.*, a suit by the leading Internet auction site against an aggregator site.[184] Aggregators collect information about what is being auctioned in multiple locations, and make them available in one place so that a user can simultaneously search eBay,[185] Yahoo,[186] and other auction sites. The eventual bidding itself is done on whatever site the item's owner chooses to make his or her item available, under whatever terms are imposed by that site. The court in *eBay* held that the automated information collection process—the process of running a computer program that continuously requests information from the server about what is listed on it, called a "spider" or a "bot"—was a trespass to chattels.[187] The injunction led to Bidder's Edge closing its doors before the Ninth Circuit had an opportunity to review the decision.[188]

Decisions like *eBay* create an exclusive private right in information under the common law. While, in principle, the information is still free of property rights, reading it mechanically, which is an absolute necessity given the volume of the information and its storage on magnetic media, can be prohibited as trespass. The practical result would be equivalent to some aspects of a federal exclusive private right in raw data, but without the mitigating attributes of any exceptions that would be directly introduced into legislation. To prevent such an eventuality, if these cases cannot be won on state common law grounds, they must be challenged either on preemption grounds—based on the copyright law—or on First Amendment grounds—using the model of *New York Times Co. v. Sullivan*.[189] The preemption approach could be similar to the model followed by the Second Circuit in *NBA v. Motorola*.[190] In *Motorola* the court restricted state misappropriation claims to narrow bounds delimited by the federal policy embedded in the Copyright Act.[191] Perhaps requiring actual proof that the bots have stopped service, or that they threaten the very existence of

183. *Id.*
184. 100 F. Supp. 2d 1058 (N.D. Cal. 2000).
185. http://www.ebay.com (last visited Sept. 17, 2002).
186. http://auctions.yahoo.com (last visited Sept. 17, 2002).
187. *Ebay*, 100 F. Supp. 2d at 1069.
188. Peg Brickley, *Now-Defunct Bidder's Edge Settles Online Dispute*, CORPORATE LEGAL TIMES, July 2001, at 70.
189. 376 U.S. 254, 266 (1964).
190. 105 F.3d 841 (2d Cir. 1997).
191. *Id.* at 850.

the service—a requirement imposed, *mutatis mutandis* in *Motorola*—would be sustainable under a First Amendment or preemption analysis.

Beyond raw data and the various ways of controlling it, a central question that will have to be addressed is the status of legal control of information about information—like linking, or other statements people make about the availability and valence of some described information. Linking—the mutual pointing of many documents to each other—is the very core idea of the World Wide Web. In a variety of cases, parties have attempted to use law to control the linking practices of others. These efforts have largely been an effort to retain control over the information about which the challenged link provides information. What is common to these cases is that they aim to create an exclusive private right to give people information about where they can find information. The linking aspect of *Reimerdes* directly raises this exclusive right argument as an interpretation of the anti-device provision of the DMCA.[192]

In *Reimerdes*, the movie industry sought and received an injunction prohibiting defendants from linking their site to places on the Internet where users could access DeCSS.[193] The district court concluded that the defendants were prohibited from telling others where copies of DeCSS were available.[194] It concluded that providing a link to an online distribution point was the virtual equivalent to giving it on a disk.[195] The court argued that a link is just another way to make the prohibited software available to users, thus violating the prohibition on trafficking in circumvention devices.[196] The district court found this analysis straightforward where the link directly began a downloading process.[197] It was not as clear-cut where a general-purpose publication, like a newspaper, linked to a broad site that discussed many issues, and included a link to a copy of the program. The court found its decision harder in instances where there was some material on the end of a link, but not much other than the prohibited circumvention software.[198] Similarly, the court found it important that the person linking had intended to facilitate circumvention by linking.[199] As a result, the court set out a sliding scale of likelihood of finding liability. The scale depended on the intent of the linking and the extent to which a link was close to, or removed from, being a download button in practice.[200] The Court of Appeals largely accepted this analysis, and, indeed, refused to hold that the test might not be even less constraining.

The difficulty with the district court's approach in *Reimerdes* is that linking is simply a statement about where information can be found. Prohibiting

192. *See* Universal Studios v. Reimerdes, 111 F. Supp. 2d 294, 339-41(S.D.N.Y. 2000)
193. *Id.* at 341.
194. *Id.*
195. *Id.* at 324.
196. *Id.*
197. *Id.* at 325.
198. *Id.*
199. *Id.* at 324-25.
200. *Id.* at 340-41.

people from telling other people where information can be found, while leaving them free to use that information as they please is very difficult to square with the First Amendment. A list of links is not fundamentally different from a newspaper listing of all the bookstores in town where pornography can be found. The "intent" factor the district court used to mitigate this effect would have allowed imposition of liability against a publication that intended to help its readers obtain pornography, but would have exempted a conservative newspaper that published the list as part of a campaign to boycott the stores. The general-purpose publication versus dedicated distribution site factor may have meant that if a publication had enough other content it would not be liable, but a person handing out handbills with the same exact list would be liable. This degree of *ex post* judicial judgment as to intent and purpose of the publication would chill speech. Perhaps, under a clear and present danger analysis, some links can indeed be prohibited. For example, a link that, without warning the person clicking, begins to download a virus without the intervention of human cognition is a fairly obvious example of a link that could be prohibited. Such a link plays a purely functional, not communicative role. If, however, you are linked to a site that has such a link, particularly with some statement—"you can find this virus here"—it is then a matter providing information, not of causing harm.

A more subtle regulation of linking occurs when parties seek either to prohibit others from linking to them or to control how others do so. The quintessential case involved a service that Microsoft offered—sidewalk.com.[201] This service provided access to, among other things, information on events in various cities. If a user wanted a ticket to an event, the sidewalk site linked that user directly to a page on ticketmaster.com where the user could buy a ticket. Ticketmaster objected to this practice, preferring instead that sidewalk.com link to its home page.[202] Linking to the Ticketmaster home page would ensure user exposure to all of the advertising and services Ticketmaster provides, rather than solely to the specific service the user sought after being referred by sidewalk.com. This case settled. Another similar case, *Ticketmaster Corp. v. Tickets.com, Inc.*, was resolved in an unpublished opinion that focused on other aspects of the case.[203]

At stake in these linking cases is who will control the context in which certain information is presented. If deep linking is prohibited, Ticketmaster will control the context. They will control the other movies or events available to be seen, their relative prominence, reviews, and similar information. The right to control linking then becomes a right to shape the meaning and relevance of one's statements for others. Although the choice between Ticketmaster and Microsoft as controllers of the context of information may seem of little norma-

---

201. *See* Michael Newman, *Ticketmaster vs. Microsoft is Bully Battle*, PITTSBURGH POST-GAZETTE, May 18, 1997, at C-3.

202. http://ticketmaster.com (last visited Sept. 17, 2002).

203. No. CV99-7654-HLH (BQRx) 2000 U.S. Dist. LEXIS 12987 (C.D. Cal. Aug. 10, 2000).

tive consequence, it is important to recognize that the right to control linking could easily apply to a local library, or church, or a neighbor.

On the Internet, there are a variety of ways that people can provide information about materials elsewhere on the Web. In doing so, they loosen someone else's control over the information—be it the government, a third party interested in limiting access to the information described, or the person offering the information described. In a series of instances we have seen people attempt to limit the ability of others to loosen their control by providing information about the specified information. These are not cases in which a person without access to information seeks affirmative access. Rather, these are cases where someone seeks the aid of law to control what others say to each other about the controlled information. Understood in these terms, the restrictive implications of these moves for free speech become clear. In turn, the need to subject them to First Amendment scrutiny is obvious.

V

CONCLUSION

Exclusive private rights in information exist in tension with individual freedom to read and express oneself. This tension is mediated by constitutional constraints placed on Congress when it enacts such rights, constitutional constraints that in practice some lower courts have relaxed.

The constraints are justified because overly strong exclusive private rights in information entail substantial costs for democracy and autonomy. The driving mechanism from both a democracy and autonomy perspective is that strong exclusive rights increase the importance of large-scale commercial producers of commodified information. This is at the expense of both nonprofit information production and the emergence of nonproprietary, peer production as core elements of our information production system. For democracy, that means that more of the available information and the channels of communication are funneled through a small number of large commercial media companies. This curtails the opportunities for a more diverse universe of content and loci of discourse. For autonomy, it means that we will have a system with substantially less information of critical and fringe possibilities, and greater opportunities for some players—the owners of media and "content"—to structure the information environment of consumers. It also means that opportunities for enhancing personal autonomy in both the productive and consumption aspects of individuals' lives—opportunities made possible by the emergence of peer production—will be more limited.

The constraints are also explained by the fact that the political economy of legislation in this field has a systematic bias towards ever-stronger exclusive rights. The beneficiaries of the rights see private and present gains from strengthening rights. Those who bear the costs are diffuse. Usually, also, the costs are to be incurred in the future, sometimes by generations not yet born or at least not yet able to foresee the effects on them. This leads to a systematic overstatement of the benefits and understatement of the costs of rights.

At present, a number of pressure points are likely to play a central role in defining the relationship between the Constitution and the institution of exclusive private rights in information. First, the framework I suggest is controversial. Whether it will end up reflecting the law will largely be determined in a number of cases currently in the courts, in particular *Eldred*.

Second, the way the First Amendment plays in this debate will be heavily affected by how First Amendment law resolves an internal tension in responding to the rise of the information economy. The First Amendment's gradual extension of rights to corporations, and of the status of speech to what are essentially the commercial operations of firms in the information economy, pushes towards a new-Lochnerism for the information economy. The simultaneous failure to protect individuals from commercial overreaching that impoverishes and controls individuals' information environment introduces a moral inversion in First Amendment law. The First Amendment has come to protect as central rights that can only be justified instrumentally. This is often at the expense of individuals who are the real bearers of intrinsic claims to freedom of speech and expression.

Third, this is an area in which the form of many of the regulations has the look and feel of private ordering, a characteristic that tends to confound First Amendment law. Nonetheless, the design of exclusive private rights should be treated as any other law whose operative characteristic is the prohibition of speech.

Fourth, how we resolve the First Amendment status of the regulation of code will be immensely important. It will determine how the logical layer of the information environment is made to comply with, or resist, enclosure of the public domain. The increasing sophistication of computers and the ease of translation from human to machine languages significantly complicates this problem.

Fifth, heightened criminalization raises the stakes of the constitutional debate. It presents one of the most important needs for immediate resolution.

Sixth, a variety of mechanisms being developed to give some people power to control the information that other people give about particular information is an area where the First Amendment has an important role to play. It should stem the expanding range of rights to control information that are intended to sustain the business model of selling information as goods.

What is up for grabs in these debates is the way that information and culture is produced in the pervasively networked society. How information is produced and used, who engages in information production and exchange, with what motives and with what degree of control over what others see and speak in society, will have significant implications for democracy and freedom. The Constitution cannot be silent or neutral in answering these questions. It places its thumb on the scales of freedom on the side of a robust democratic discourse, of diversity of antagonistic voices, and of individual expressive autonomy.

RECONCILING WHAT THE FIRST AMENDMENT FORBIDS WITH WHAT THE COPYRIGHT CLAUSE PERMITS: A SUMMARY EXPLANATION AND REVIEW

WILLIAM W. VAN ALSTYNE*

We need education in the obvious more than investigation of the obscure.

Oliver Wendell Holmes[1]

I

INTRODUCTION

At least since an early article by Professor Melvin Nimmer in the 1970s,[2] there has been some general agreement that Congress is fully *within* its proper power to enact, pursuant to the Copyright Clause of Article I,[3] an act that may nonetheless be of a kind it is *forbidden* to enact because of the restraints placed upon it by the Speech-and-Press Clause of the First Amendment.[4] But just how or why that can be so (or even that it is in fact so[5]) is not all that easy to explain. Indeed, on the face of each respective clause, the First Amendment may well quite reasonably be read to acknowledge that the Copyright Clause is a part of the *same* Constitution. And, since it is, insofar as Congress stays within *its* boundaries (that is, the "boundaries" furnished by the Copyright Clause itself), it would arguably be perverse for a court to read the First Amendment as for-

---

This article is also available at http://www.law.duke.edu/journals/66LCPVanAlstyne.

* William R. & Thomas S. Perkins Professor of Law, Duke University.

1. OLIVER WENDELL HOLMES, *Law and the Court*, *in* COLLECTED LEGAL PAPERS 291, 292-93 (1920).

2. Melville B. Nimmer, *Does Copyright Abridge the First Amendment Guarantees of Free Speech and Press?*, 17 UCLA L. REV. 1180 (1970).

3. "The Congress shall have Power . . . To promote the Progress of Science and useful Arts, by securing for limited Times to Authors and Inventors the exclusive Right to their respective Writings and Discoveries . . . ." U.S. CONST. art. I, § 8, cl. 8.

4. "Congress shall make no law . . . abridging the freedom of speech, or of the press . . . ." U.S. CONST. amend. I.

5. The Supreme Court has never held that an act of Congress adopted pursuant to the Copyright Clause was either void on its face or invalid as applied on First Amendment grounds (as distinct from being void on its face because of not being within the power actually granted by the clause). *See also* Neil W. Netanel, *Locating Copyright Within the First Amendment Skein*, 54 STAN. L. REV. 1, 3 n.8 (2001) ("Recent cases have followed the view that copyright requires *no* external First Amendment scrutiny.") (emphasis added).

bidding what the Copyright Clause declares is precisely within the authority of Congress to do.

Of course, the First Amendment is later in time. But nothing on the face of the First Amendment purports to affect the power granted to Congress pursuant to the Copyright Clause. So, again, one may say that whatever is *properly* done by Congress within the permission of the Copyright Clause ought not be said at the same time to be *forbidden* by some other part of the Constitution, at least unless that "other part" so declares, or unless its express provisions are simply incompatible with an earlier part it necessarily displaces and amends. We have already noted that the First Amendment contains no such declaration putting it at odds with the Copyright Clause. And certainly nothing on its face suggests that it in any respect "amends" (that is, displaces) that clause.[6] The First Amendment is a general admonition—namely, that Congress shall make no law abridging the freedom of speech or of the press. The Copyright Clause on the other hand is a very specific, enumerated power, expressly granting Congress discretion simply to secure to authors the exclusive right to their respective writings, albeit for limited times rather than in perpetuity. It would seem again, on this basis as well, puzzling to declare that the First Amendment may forbid something the more specifically "targeted" clause empowers Congress to do. One may well suggest that this is another clear case where the useful maxim, *expressio unius, exclusio alterius est*, appropriately applies.[7]

It happens I fully agree with those who say the First Amendment "limits" what Congress may do pursuant to the Copyright Clause, despite the preceding, introductory thoughts. Still, it has seemed to me that the obvious reason that this is so has not yet been adequately explained or expressed. It is to that end that this brief essay, and these quite summary remarks, are meant to be addressed, with suitable thanks (and apologies) to Justice Holmes.

II

THE FIRST AMENDMENT AND CONGRESSIONAL POWER

Consider the following approach to relating the First Amendment to the powers granted to Congress. We proceed in the following way—by noting that the Constitution provides that: "Congress shall make no law . . . abridging the

6. There are of course amendments that do precisely this. Compare, for example, the provision in the Seventeenth Amendment that Senators from each State shall be "elected by the people thereof," with the provision it displaces, in Article I, Section 3, that Senators from each State shall be "chosen by the Legislature thereof." Here, in the example just given, the respective provisions *are* at odds, and the later in time means to displace the original provision. In contrast, the First Amendment does not appear to be at odds, or in displacement of, the Copyright Clause (rather, it may be wholly "accepting" of that clause).

7. Here, adapting the maxim appropriately, it would stipulate that "what is *expressly* given to Congress to do, is by necessary implication excluded from the provision specifying what Congress is *forbidden* to do."

freedom of speech, or of the press . . . ."[8] Although, to be sure, we note that the Constitution also provides that: "The Congress *shall* have Power . . . To regulate Commerce with foreign Nations, and among the several States, and with the Indian Tribes . . . ."[9] As we readily agree, as well, that according to the Constitution, Congress shall *also* have Power: "To promote the Progress of Science and Useful Arts, by securing for limited Times to Authors and Inventors the exclusive Right to their respective Writings and Discoveries . . . ."[10]

So, now to start in the simplest way, with our first case. If the act of Congress is one that presumes to abridge "the freedom of speech or of the press," we agree that it is void pursuant to the prohibitory terms of the First Amendment (that is, the law is one prohibited to Congress and such a law, *being* prohibited, is to be given no force of law in the courts). If, on the other hand, the act of Congress is merely one that presumes to regulate some aspect of commerce—whether "with foreign nations," or "among the several states," or "with the Indian Tribes"—it is an act plainly authorized by the Constitution, within the grant of power expressly conferred upon Congress, and it *is* to be given the force of law in the courts. So far so good. The clauses simply speak to different kinds of laws. Nor is there any difficulty in reconciling these clauses. It is simply a matter of identifying the type of law, as fitting either under one of these clauses or under the other, and that is our essential task. It is the task, moreover, if just because, quite plainly, a law may be of *either* type ("a law prohibited" or "a law expressly authorized") but it could hardly, at least *at-one-and-the-same-time*, be *both*.[11]

The necessary rub comes, however, when the act of Congress is concededly one that *does* presume to "regulate" some aspect of commerce (among the several states), *neither more nor less*, and thus is utterly unexceptional (and unexceptionable) as *plainly* within the scope of the positive power thus conferred. But the "commerce" thus "regulated" is itself a product, say, of "*the press*" (for example, a book, a newspaper, a journal, or a leaflet), sent by freight or via some other commercial medium from one state to addresses or recipients in other states or abroad. *And* the manner in which the book (newspaper, leaflet, etc.) is "regulated" is to *forbid* its participation in that commerce, such as it is. So, now, what shall one do about that?

One easy, clean way of resolving this seeming (but perhaps *merely* "seeming") problem is to resolve it directly and simply, that is, without any "clause conflict," and to do so in just the following way: to say that there frankly is no

8. U.S. CONST. amend. I. In brief, merely to paraphrase the Amendment if just for suitable emphasis: "Congress is granted *no* power, indeed, *is hereby denied any power*, to make any law abridging the freedom of speech or of the press."

9. U.S. CONST. art. I, § 8, cl. 3 (emphasis added).

10. U.S. CONST. art. I, § 8, cl. 8.

11. Indeed, for how can it be both? For to say that it is "both" is to say that it is "authorized" but also that it is "forbidden," though each is necessarily an exclusion of the other, and thus our assertion would appear to be a mere contradiction in terms.

conflict in the case just put. Rather, the conflict was utterly in one's mind, and it was a conflict *wholly contrived.* There is no conflict, we might well say, because:

> A. The act in question *confines* itself to regulating an aspect of "commerce among the several states," no less here, in a case where it merely involves books, than in any other case (for example, a case involving steel products, pork, beef, drugs, lottery tickets or kitchen sinks); *and*
>
> B. That the commerce is, or happens to be, "commerce *in books*," rather than "commerce *in wheat*," or "commerce *in steel*," may be true—but *being* true, how does that bear upon the question? That is to say, is there *anything* to suggest that the power thus expressly given ("to regulate commerce . . . among the several states") is given *only* in respect to *some* kinds of commerce but *not* in respect to other kinds? *But what makes one imagine that that is so?* Nothing on the face of the clause so suggests. Nothing found *elsewhere* in the Constitution, moreover, appears to do so either.[12]

May one yet complain that the act is *nonetheless* "void" or unenforceable because it *is* a law made by Congress, and that *this* law, as made by Congress (and applied as it is) is one that "abridg[es] the freedom of speech, or of the press"? Yes, of course one may *say* this, but then, one may say anything one likes. Saying it, in short, does not make it so. Moreover, the assertion that this *is* just such a law, is, as such, merely what it appears to be: simply an assertion, nothing more. One may even say straightforwardly that, taken *as* an assertion, without something more to back it up, it assumes its own conclusion. It begs the very question, in that it *assumes* that "*the* freedom of the press" extends to a freedom of "marketing books in commerce among the states *even when Congress forbids it to be done*." But *does* it? Why does one suppose that this is so? Isn't this the burden for the person so asserting? And if that person cannot discharge that burden, isn't it obvious that *they have no First Amendment claim even to assert*?

And, surely, this much is plainly right. Unless the freedom of the press extends to, or includes, a freedom to engage in commercial trade (in books) across state lines, *even when Congress decides by law that it shall not be done*, we would say there is no conflict between what Congress has presumed to do on the one hand, pursuant to the power to regulate commerce among the several states, and what the First Amendment forbids on the other. So, let that be conceded as obviously correct.

---

12. "Nothing," that is, including the First Amendment as well. The First Amendment obviously does *not* declare that "Congress shall have no power to regulate commerce in books among the several states."

Yet, if that much is so, so also may the obverse be equally true. If the freedom of the press *does* so extend, then the act of Congress must *necessarily* fail, for by stipulation, that the act was conditionally, or even "*apparently* authorized" insofar as it regulates (an aspect of) "commerce among the several states," so it does not fail *merely* under the doctrine of enumerated powers,[13] it turns out *not* to be *finally* or "ultimately authorized" after all, but rather, "prohibited" instead, and prohibited because it runs afoul of the specific "prohibitory words" of the First Amendment which apply (even) in respect to every power given to Congress, whatever that power may be.

In short, and quite consistent with this *latter* view, the "enactment" of the First Amendment (that is, its proposal subsequent to ratification of the Constitution by more than two-thirds of the first Congress in 1789, and its swift ratification within two years by more than three-fourths of the states by 1791) signaled a rejection of Alexander Hamilton's advice that no point would be served by providing an express provision forbidding Congress to make any law abridging the freedom of the press.[14] Instead, the enactment of the First Amendment, rejecting Hamilton's counsel, meant expressly to put affirmative restrictions on the "enumerated" powers of Congress (for example, those of regulating commerce,[15] of taxation,[16] of spending,[17] establishing a post office,[18]

13. *See, e.g.*, Kansas v. Colorado, 206 U.S. 46, 89 (1907) ("[T]he proposition that there are legislative powers . . . not expressed in the grant of powers [to Congress], is in direct conflict with the doctrine that this is a government of enumerated powers."); United States v. Fisher, 6 U.S. (2 Cranch) 358, 396 (1805) (Marshall, C.J.) ("[U]nder a constitution conferring specific powers, the power contended for must be granted, or it cannot be exercised."); *applied in* Trade-Mark Cases, 100 U.S. 82 (1879) (Holding act of Congress providing for registration of trademarks and civil and criminal sanctions for infringers unconstitutional under the enumerated powers doctrine; the act could not be sustained under the Copyright and Patent Clauses because both clauses required some degree of creativity or invention, and many trademarks involved neither one; nor could it be sustained under the Commerce Clause because, on its face, it reached trademarks not involved in any commerce "among the several states" or "with foreign nations."). In brief, the act failed for want of any power vested in Congress pursuant to any of the enumerated powers given to Congress, whether in Article I, Section 8, or elsewhere in the Constitution.

14. *See* THE FEDERALIST NO. 84, at 513-15 (Alexander Hamilton) (Clinton Rossiter ed., 1961) ("For why declare that things shall not be done which there is no power to do? Why, for instance, should it be said that the liberty of the press shall not be restrained, when no power is given by which restrictions may be imposed?"). Then, albeit in a manner seemingly very much at odds with what he has just declared, Hamilton also went on to say: "What is the liberty of the press? Who can give it any definition which would not leave the utmost latitude for evasion? I hold it to be impracticable; and from this I infer, that its security, whatever fine declarations may be inserted in any constitution respecting it, must altogether depend on public opinion, and on the general spirit of the people and of the government. And here, after all . . . must we seek for the only solid basis of all our rights." *Id.* at 514.

15. *See, e.g.*, Reno v. ACLU, 521 U.S. 844 (1997) (holding congressional restrictions imposing special requirements for posting and accessing "patently offensive" and "indecent" material on the Internet an instrumentality of interstate and of foreign commerce, violates the First Amendment). *See also* the discussion of *Thompson v. Western States Medical Center*, 535 U.S. 357 (2002) in note 20 *infra.*

16. *See, e.g.*, (albeit in these cases, state taxes), Ark. Writers' Project, Inc. v. Ragland, 481 U.S. 221 (1987) (holding four percent gross receipts tax exempting newspapers and some other publications, but not "general interest" magazines, violates the First Amendment's guarantee of freedom of the press); Grosjean v. Am. Press Co., 297 U.S. 233 (1936) (same, re: two percent gross receipts tax from advertising revenue of publications with more than 20,000 weekly circulation).

etc.). Moreover, it did so with an expressed expectation that the courts would honor those restrictions as such in cases where, though the act of Congress *was* one otherwise clearly "within" the scope of some enumerated power, it nonetheless was not consistent with the First Amendment freedoms meant to be preserved from congressional abridgment. So, for example, Jefferson suggested that "a declaration of rights," once added as amendments to the Constitution, would "put into the hands of the judiciary" a "legal check" against Congress when popular sentiment flagged.[19] And likewise, in summing up his reasons for favoring the addition of amendments as a means of forestalling Congress from using any of its enumerated powers in any way inconsistent with respect to the rights and freedoms memorialized in these amendments, James Madison observed: "If they are incorporated into the Constitution, independent tribunals of justice will consider themselves in a peculiar manner the guardians of those rights . . . ."[20]

III

TENTATIVENESS IN THE FIRST AMENDMENT

And all of this would seem to be quite correct, and quite convincing, too. *Unless*, to be sure, just as there is a tentativeness in respect to whether, say, the power "to regulate commerce among the several states" extends to a certain thing, and Congress may not do so insofar as *that* power may be qualified in some respect by some *other* provision (for example, a provision in the First

---

17. *See, e.g.*, Legal Servs. Corp. v. Valasquez, 531 U.S. 533 (2001) (holding congressionally mandated restriction on use of grants provided pursuant to spending power for certain legal services by grantee organizations inconsistent with, and forbidden by, the First Amendment).

18. *See, e.g.*, Lamont v. Postmaster Gen., 381 U.S. 301 (1965) (holding act of Congress requiring Postmaster to intercept and detain certain mail and then destroy it unless addressee registered an affirmative request for its delivery violates the First Amendment).

19. Letter from Thomas Jefferson to James Madison (Mar. 15, 1789), *reprinted in part in* THE LIFE AND SELECTED WRITINGS OF THOMAS JEFFERSON 462, 462-64 (Adrienne Koch & William Peden eds., 1944).

20. Address by James Madison before the United States House of Representatives (June 8, 1789), *reprinted in* V THE WRITINGS OF JAMES MADISON 370, 385 (Gaillard Hunt ed., 1904). *See also* I WILLIAM BLACKSTONE, COMMENTARIES pt. 2, app. at 29 (St. George Tucker ed., 1803) ("The danger justly apprehended by those states which insisted that the federal government should possess no power, directly *or indirectly*, over the subject, was, that those who were entrusted with the administration might be forward in considering every thing as a crime against the government, which might operate to their own personal disadvantage; it was therefore made a fundamental article of the federal compact, that no such power should be exercised, or claimed by the federal government, leaving it to the state governments to exercise such jurisdiction and control over the subject, as their several constitutions and laws permit.") (emphasis added); Barron v. Baltimore, 32 U.S. (7 Pet.) 243, 250 (1833) (Marshall, C.J.) ("These amendments demanded security against the apprehended encroachments of the general government . . . ."). For merely the most recent example of the Supreme Court applying the First Amendment to strike down an act of Congress otherwise (that is, but for the First Amendment) plainly *within* its enumerated power to enact pursuant to the commerce clause, see *Thompson v. Western States Medical Center*, 535 U.S. 357 (2002) (holding void on its face a prohibition on consumer advertising of "compounded" drugs—drugs lawful for pharmacies to prepare and to sell, pursuant to a physician's prescription, albeit drugs not submitted for FDA approval pursuant to rigorous FDA testing requirements).

Amendment) so that we cannot know what the power in the Commerce Clause "finally" includes until we have determined what the First Amendment "keeps back" from its ultimate reach, *unless*, I say, *there is also a similar "tentativeness" in respect to the First Amendment itself*, a tentativeness, moreover, of just the very same sort. A "tentativeness" we cannot resolve until we look even *further* to see whether there is something some *other* clause recovers, or reserves (or "keeps back") from the First Amendment, even as we found in the First Amendment in its "keep back" provision qualifying (that is, limiting) the power given Congress to regulate commerce among the several states.

This possibility may strike us as unlikely, even as highly implausible, to be sure. For what might such an additional provision having *this* effect look like, or say?! That's a fair question. Well, perhaps it could look like—and even *say*—something very much like this:

> The Congress shall have Power To promote the Progress of Science and useful Arts, by securing for limited Times to Authors and Inventors the exclusive Right to their respective Writings and Discoveries.

And so, to the extent that Congress enacts legislation pursuant to such power as it *is* so specifically granted *within* the four corners of *this* separate, distinct, freestanding clause, it—Congress—shall surely *not* be thought to have made a law abridging "the freedom of the press." We should surely say this, for indeed, to say otherwise *would* seem now to construe the Constitution "against itself," that is, to read one clause (the First Amendment) to forbid that which another clause (the Copyright Clause) *expressly* declares is *quite all right to do*.[21] On this understanding, then, we should logically conclude, that if Congress has acted "within" this clause, it has made no law that can be said to be a law "abridging the freedom of speech, or of the press." Rather, it has merely made a law that the Constitution itself deems *compatible* with the freedom of the press, *as it takes express care so straightforwardly to declare*.

The logic of this position seems to me to be quite strong, even quite compelling, and it tends, I think, to explain why both commentators and courts still exhibit some genuine uncertainty in this particular area of constitutional law. If Congress *has* acted *within* (and not in excess) of whatever the scope of power expressly granted it by this clause, then whatever provisions securing to the authors the *exclusive* right to *their* respective writings are contained in affirmative legislation, insofar as those provisions are well grounded in the express power as granted by this clause so to enact them, this clause (implicitly) declares

21. Namely, "to do" *what*? To do this: merely by legislation to secure to "authors and inventors, the *exclusive* right to *their* respective writings and discoveries," neither more *nor less*; albeit, to be sure, to secure those exclusive rights for "limited times," rather than in perpetuity (as, without this limitation, Congress might otherwise be inclined—but is not permitted—to do).

that legislation *not* to be a law "abridging the freedom of speech, or of the press."[22]

Of course, many eminently reasonable persons may well feel that proceeding in the manner that this clause provides Congress an authority to pursue (namely, to secure "for limited Times to Authors and Inventors [an] *exclusive* Right to their respective Writings and Discoveries"), may not be as effective as proceeding by some other means, even to stimulate the production (and distribution) of "new" works. Indeed, some may feel that proceeding in this manner may actually be far less effective—and far less conducive to the public good—than proceeding in other ways. So, for example, they may reasonably believe that proceeding instead by providing for "public subsidy" of authors, artists, inventors and other creative people, without, however, granting them any subsequent "*exclusive* right" to control, charge for, or limit copies (rather, the incentive to be creative is the incentive of the subsidy thus provided—set at a level one thinks just right to do its work well), will be the better recourse. Discovery, creative work, etc., are thus "appropriately" encouraged and stimulated—and the product at once becomes released into the public domain. The system is superior by far, one may well conclude, better "balancing" incentives for creative endeavors that also promptly enrich, and become a part of, the public domain.

Such persons may well be right. And I'll grant that they may well be. Moreover, in their favor, we may note in passing that absolutely nothing in the Constitution forbids that this means of "stimulating" "new knowledge" be pursued,[23] even as we know it already is and, indeed, on a very large scale. Let it be so. Moreover let it be admitted they may even be "right" in suggesting that the

22. The D.C. Circuit Court seems to treat the matter in just this way, although it is not entirely clear. *See, e.g.*, United Video, Inc. v. FCC, 890 F.2d 1173, 1190 (D.C. Cir. 1989) (rejecting a claim that an FCC ban on broadcasters from carrying materials exclusively licensed by the copyright holder to others was subject to *some* (minimal) measure of First Amendment review, and declaring that "the [FCC] was correct to find that the rules are not subject to *such* scrutiny," evidently meaning even minimal, or weak, First Amendment scrutiny, and then explaining why in the following terms: "The Constitution grants Congress the power to secure for limited times to authors the exclusive right to their works, and *this power generally supersedes the first amendment rights of those who wish to use another's copyrighted work.*") (emphasis added); Eldred v. Reno, 239 F.3d 372, 375 (D.C. Cir. 2001), *cert. granted sub nom*, Eldred v. Ashcroft, 534 U.S. 1126, *and cert. amended*, 534 U.S. 1160 (2002) ("[W]e held in United Video that copyrights are *categorically immune from challenges under the First Amendment.*") (emphasis added). Not that they may sometimes—or even usually—prevail against challenges under the First Amendment, rather, that they are "categorically *immune*" from such challenges.

23. The relevant enumerated power is merely the spending power in Article I, Section 8, generously interpreted by the Supreme Court as conferring on Congress a virtually nonjusticiable breadth of discretion to determine for itself what grants in aid, or appropriations from tax revenues, are sufficiently consistent with providing for the "general Welfare of the United States," as to be within its authority under this clause. *See, e.g.*, THE CONSTITUTION OF THE UNITED STATES OF AMERICA, ANALYSIS AND INTERPRETATION 156 (Johnny H. Killian & George A. Costello eds., 1996) (citing *South Dakota v. Dole*, 483 U.S. 203, 207 (1987) and *Buckley v. Valeo*, 424 U.S. 1, 90-91 (1976), and quite accurately summarizing: "[G]reat deference is judicially accorded Congress' decision that a spending program advances the general welfare, and the Court has suggested that the question whether a spending program provides for the general welfare may not even be judicially noticeable.")

manner in which the Copyright Clause proceeds is not only *not* the "best" way, but may in some measure even be a "dysfunctional" way, in that it, and Congress by employing it, may miss the "proper balance" between the end (stimulation and distribution of new knowledge) and the means (vesting exclusive rights, of "monopoly" control, in the author for a rather lengthy—albeit "limited"—period of years).

But we may also properly note that if Congress wishes to agree with us, it may not merely modify and trim back the protection its sundry copyright laws now (too generously?) enact. Rather, it may repeal them in part or in whole, indeed, *repeal them all*, and then just go forward to "substitute" wholly public subsidy means of stimulating creativity, the products of which would at once "drop" into the public domain. In short, it is open to Congress even now to agree with Thomas Macaulay that vesting copyrights in the "creator-monopolist" is, or may be, in some manner of speaking, a highly undesirable "tax on knowledge,"[24] a "tax" levied in such amount as each "author" (*given* exclusive rights by statute) decides to extract for anyone's right to copy his or her work, or any part thereof, payable to himself or herself, albeit a "tax" of a sort that, in a sense, merely provides delayed compensation for the author's creative work (and contribution to the public fund of knowledge).[25] Maybe the "tax" allowed thus to be imposed (by each author or by those to whom he assigned his right to determine the conditions of copying his or her work) is "too high," maybe not. *But that is up to Congress to determine*, as it does by setting the metes and bounds of the author's "exclusive" rights, consistent with its enumerated power to do so, *as conferred by this clause*. Our objections to the manner in which it works out the calculus, however, are, at this level, merely political objections (for example, we think it succumbed to utterly false representations by various corporate copyright interests), not constitutional ones, as long as it is clear that however Congress worked things out, it nonetheless stayed *within* the "four corners" of the power confided to it by this clause.[26]

---

24. Thomas B. Macaulay, A Speech Delivered in the House of Commons (Feb. 5, 1841), *in* VIII THE LIFE AND WORKS OF LORD MACAULAY 201 (London, Longmans, Green, and Co. 1897).

25. For discussion (and references to other cases) elaborating this view, see, for example, *Harper & Row Publishers, Inc. v. Nation Enterprises*, 471 U.S. 539, 558 (1985). "[I]t should not be forgotten that the Framers intended copyright itself to be the engine of free expression. By establishing a marketable right to the use of one's expression, copyright supplies the economic incentive to create and disseminate ideas." *Id.*

26. *See, e.g.*, Gibbons v. Ogden, 22 U.S. 1, 196-97 (1824) (Marshall, C.J.) (addressing this same sort of issue as it may be raised in respect to how Congress uses is power "to regulate commerce . . . among the several states"). Marshall eschewed any role for the judiciary in second-guessing the wisdom of an act of Congress, even respecting the extremes of congressional use of its various enumerated powers:

> This power [referring in the particular instance to the power to "regulate commerce . . . among the several states"], like all others vested in Congress, is complete in itself, may be exercised to its utmost extent, and acknowledges no limitations, other than are prescribed in the constitution. . . . The wisdom and the discretion of Congress, their identity with the people, and the influence which their constituents possess at elections, are, in this, as in many other instances, as that, for example, of declaring war, the sole restraints on which they have relied,

The point remains, that if it *did* stay within those four corners of authorized law-making, its act cannot then be said to be invalid under the First Amendment. For, again, "the First Amendment provision on 'the freedom of the press' should not be interpreted or applied to forbid what the Copyright Clause itself *expressly* permits."

The question is, where is the flaw, or fundamental error, if there be one, in this reasoning?

IV

PERPETUATING UNCHECKABLE PLURALISM

Perhaps it resides in the following different, and more constrained, view of what the Copyright Clause is about—that what it is about, essentially, is pretty much just this and nothing more.

We noted already that the Constitution takes care to provide a power in Congress to "regulate commerce among the states," albeit a power all do concede is itself subject to First Amendment limitations in respect to how that power may, in turn, be used by Congress. And we know that *that* power was provided in order to enable the national legislature to establish uniform norms in respect to the commerce to which the power attaches ("commerce among the states"), in order that such commerce as this must not be left to such differing regimes as each state might presume to enact; rather, it was to be dealt with as the national legislature should feel disposed so to do.

But, at the time, neither this new and express power (to "regulate commerce among the states") nor any other proposed enumerated power would per se grant—or was seen as granting—to Congress an authority to establish a uniform rule in respect to what was patentable or not, or what was subject to copyright or not, and nationally established exclusive "ownership" rules of a like sort. And, indeed, *absent* establishing a *separate* power, *distinctly* entrusting to Congress an authority so to provide, then all such "rules" would be whatever rules (however conflicting and differing) one would find by consulting the patchwork statute books, and common law, of each particular state.[27]

The manifest undesirability of *perpetuating this uncheckable pluralism*, that is, that the extent to which an author's work could or could not lawfully at once be copied (and such copies sold by the copier) would just depend upon what each state legislature—or the common law of the state—might provide, is what "drives" (that is, *essentially accounts for*) the provision in Article I. And, in brief, the provision in the clause stands in relation to *its* particular subject, *in the same way* that the commerce power stands in relation to *its* subject in turn. It *is*

> to secure them from its abuse. They are the restraints on which the people most often rely solely, in all representative governments.

Id.

27. At least, that is, all such rules as would be beyond the reach of Congress to preempt merely by its (limited) power to regulate "commerce" among the several states.

meant to empower Congress to provide *a pre-emptive uniformity of law*, in respect to the subject embraced by the clause (and to the extent the subject is embraced by the clause), thus pre-empting what would, absent use of this power by Congress, be the varying kinds of laws controlling within each state.[28]

But note as to such laws (that is, state laws, statutory or common), we would not doubt that each, whatever *its* particular scope, and whatever *its* provisions, would be subject to full First Amendment review.[29] So, for example, supposing there were no federal copyright law in the field[30] and that, in North Carolina, the legislature provided by statute that:

> **N.C.G.S. §2001.** No one shall within 120 years of its publication, make any copy, or distribute or sell any copy, of an author's original work, in whole or in any part, absent written permission or license granted by the author, his assigns, or his heirs.

We would not doubt that the North Carolina act would be subject to full First Amendment review in an appropriate case pressing the issue. To be sure, depending upon how one might add certain features to this North Carolina

---

28. *See, e.g.*, Wheaton v. Peters, 33 U.S. (8 Pet.) 591, 681-84 (1834). The Court noted that under the Articles of Confederation, the most that Congress could do was to recommend to the several states certain measures securing to authors and publishers exclusive copyrights for "not less than fourteen years." Some states adopted variable statutes on the subject (some of which provided protection for authors who were citizens of other states only if the state of their citizenship reciprocated by providing a like protection), while other states applied varying understandings of common law rights. The Court concluded that "under the existing governments of the United States, before the adoption of the present constitution, adequate protection could not be given to authors throughout the United States, by any general law." *Id.* at 684. *See also* THE FEDERALIST No. 43, at 271-72 (James Madison) (Clinton Rossiter ed., 1961) (Madison, after quoting the proposed, separate constitutional clause on "authors and inventors," proceeds to explain it: "The utility of this power will scarcely be questioned. The copyright of authors has been solemnly adjudged, in Great Britain, to be a right of common law. The right to useful inventions seems with equal reason to belong to the inventors. The public good fully coincides in both cases with the claims of individuals. *The States cannot separately make effectual provision for either of the cases*, and most of them have anticipated the decision of this point, by laws passed at the instance of Congress.") (emphasis added); JOSEPH STORY, COMMENTARIES ON THE CONSTITUTION OF THE UNITED STATES § 558, 402-03 (Carolina Acad. Press 1987) (1883) ("It is beneficial . . . to authors and inventors, because, otherwise, they would be subjected to the varying laws and systems of the different states on this subject . . . ."). Moreover, that the commerce power was *not* regarded as per se sufficient to grant this kind of pre-emptive power to Congress, incidentally, is merely well reflected in the Supreme Court's holding later on, in the original *Trade-mark Cases*, 100 U.S. 82 (1879), holding that the act of Congress did not meet the requirements of the Copyright Clause, because a "trademark" as such may represent no original creativity at all but may merely borrow a familiar image or figure to use, to identify one's product, and neither could it alternatively be sustained under the commerce power, because it presumed to extend to trademarks identified to goods and services whether or not involved in commerce among the several states.

29. Well, strictly speaking, Fourteenth Amendment review (but "Fourteenth Amendment" review applying full First Amendment standards). *See, e.g.*, Bridges v. California, 314 U.S. 252, 268 (1941) (Black, J.) ("Not until 1925 . . . did this Court recognize in the Fourteenth Amendment the application to the states of the *same standards* of freedom of expression as, under the First Amendment, are applicable to the federal government.") (emphasis added).

30. As there might not be, indeed, if no power were given to Congress to enact such legislation (and, of course, the Commerce Clause power were itself not understood to be sufficiently far-reaching to enable Congress simply to rely upon it).

statute (for example, a long list of "exceptions," with respect to which no permission need be sought before one made copies and either sold or simply gave them away), perhaps the act could be sustained. We need not tarry to see whether that might be so.

But we have said enough to show plainly where this discussion must now carry us. The clause in Article I is meant to (and certainly does) empower Congress to preempt that North Carolina statute, indeed, to provide a uniformity of law to control, within the field of the subject thus expressly confided to its preemptive power, as both described and boundaried in the four corners of the clause setting it forth. But it does no more work than *this* work. That is, *the* power thus vested in Congress now "stands in lieu of" the swath of legislative power formerly held, severally, in the states. It is a power enabling Congress to set the norms to govern the field covered by the clause, in lieu of, or in exclusion of, different regimes within each state. Whatever each of those regimes might be (or might have been), obviously each would yet have to "answer" to the First Amendment (as applied to each state and in each state, through the Fourteenth Amendment). And so, likewise, whatever regime Congress enacts within its authority so to preempt this field from the states in such degree as it is inclined to do—and indeed is given power so to do by this clause—is itself in turn answerable to the First Amendment. And as much as this, then, is true of every part, section, word, and punctuation point of the current act as well.

The point here, then, is that just as the Commerce Clause provision "answers" Federalism questions but not First Amendment questions, *the same is exactly true in respect to the Copyright Clause as well.* When Congress acts "within" the clause (generously,[31] albeit not too generously[32] construed), that

31. "Generously" (rather than grudgingly, or narrowly), in merely the *same* manner as befits the construction of each other enumerated power provided in the Constitution, that is, *in the "federalism" understanding of the clause.* In *this* regard, the "federalism" regard, for the Court to construe the clause more grudgingly than, say, the Court has construed the Commerce Clause, or the Spending Clause, or Tax Clause, in respect to each of their respective "fields" of national legislative discretion of "enactment authority," would be wholly misplaced, and it would merely raise a fair question of its own bias were it to presume to do so (that is, in picking and choosing among clauses, reading "generously" those clauses providing authority for kinds of acts of Congress it—the Court—may think desirable to have Congress enjoy a suitable power to enact, but less generously those clauses providing authority for other kinds of acts of Congress to which the Court is somehow itself frankly opposed (and thus inclined to find no suitable power granted to Congress to enact)). Simply to provide a single example: That "motion pictures" ("movies") are regarded as within the discretion of Congress to qualify for copyright protection may certainly seem to stretch the meaning of a critical term as it appears in Article I, Section 8, in the crucial clause granting the power to benefit "authors" in respect to their "writings" (for few persons would straightforwardly and ordinarily describe a motion picture as itself a "writing"). Still, it is not remarkable, given the general understanding of the place and the purpose of the clause—any more than it is remarkable that the Supreme Court has systematically accepted "movies" as equally within the understanding of "*speech*" embraced by the First Amendment as well. *See* Kingsley Int'l Pictures Corp. v. Regents of Univ. of N.Y., 360 U.S. 684 (1959); Joseph Burstyn, Inc. v. Wilson, 343 U.S. 495 (1952). So, quaintly but sensibly, even "silent" movies may be "*writings*" on the one hand (for copyright purposes) and "*speech*" (for First Amendment purposes) on the other hand as well.

32. *See, e.g.*, Feist Publ'ns, Inc. v. Rural Tel. Serv. Co., Inc., 499 U.S. 340 (1991); Trade-Mark Cases, 100 U.S. 82 (1879) (noting *some* discernible creativity, *some* modicum of originality, must characterize a qualifying work).

puts to rest any question respecting the controlling authority of its act vis-à-vis that of some inconsistent, or incongruent state or local law. It answers the "federalism question." It answers no other question, however, any more than in a Commerce Clause case, and none arising under the First Amendment as such.

The proposition is easily tested, simply by supposing that the act Congress adopted were of the extreme sort illustrated by our hypothetical North Carolina law. Reproducing it here, as an act of Congress, may aid us to see how that is so:

> ___ **U.S.C. §2001.** No one shall within 120 years of its publication, make any copy, or distribute or sell any copy, of an author's original work, in whole or in any part, absent written permission or license granted by the author, his assigns, or his heirs.

The act "fits" snugly and well *just as it appears*, as to be clearly *within* the tight phrasing of the relevant clause in Article I. And it does so, though it provides no exceptions whatever, in particular no exceptions of "fair use" (for example, copying and republishing some part of an author's original work *without the author's permission*, in the course of producing a published, highly critical, review of the author's opus). The omission of such a "permitted" exception obviously does not put the adoption of the statute "beyond" the power of Congress to enact it (for nothing in the clause suggests that any such "exception" *need* be provided for). Plainly, just as it is, it appears to be easily within the boundaries of the authorizing constitutional clause.[33]

So much being conceded, however, it does not answer to the First Amendment in the least. When the author seeks to invoke his right, *exactly* in keeping with the terms of the act, against the person who, without his permission, presumed to copy a part of his or her work, albeit "merely" incidental to writing and publishing a critical review, the infringer will "lift up" the First Amendment as his or her "shield," rather than invoke anything *within* the act. And it is virtually beyond controversy that the First Amendment would readily shield a

33. Nor could the decision of Congress *not* to make any exception for securing the author's permission to copy and reprint "selected lines" or "paragraphs," etc., by one who seeks to use the copied portions "merely" within the body of some critical review of the author's work, be thought to be inconsistent in some way with the essential purpose of the Copyright Clause as such. To the contrary. Authorship as such would surely be *more* encouraged by assuring to each original author that *no one*, without their permission, could cull, quote, and copy selected parts of their original work as part of a critical review, the publication of which may well impair (or even destroy) the market for their work, as well as bring them into a discouraging and depressing disrepute. In brief, authorship is clearly encouraged by confiding to each author the "*exclusive* right to their respective writings," allowing each to ration downstream licensed copiers in exactly such manner as each author believes will best promote his or her work. Of course, such strengthened copyright protection could not forestall critical reviews as such, but it would nonetheless assure authors that spiteful critics could not, without their consent, presume to use *their own words* "against" them, or cull, elide, and thus (by selective quotation) misrepresent the excellence of their work by that device. So, to *that* extent, each prospective author may be encouraged and comforted by being assured, by act of Congress, that without their consent, no rival, or self-promoting critic, or other person, may make any copy, or use any copy, or publish any copy, of any part of their work, without their consent (on such terms as they, as author, deem best).

critic's use of quoted parts of an author's work, quite without the author's consent, to give both example and point to the review in concrete form, that no mere paraphrase could manage to do. Insofar as the copyright holder relied on the act of Congress, in brief, the action would fail not because the act was improperly invoked, but because it was useless to serve as a basis for suing to enjoin, or to seek damages, for the knowingly copied and republished portions of the author's work. "Useless" because the First Amendment will not permit Congress to grant to authors a true monopoly power over even their "own" works—despite the appearance on the face of the clause exactly as it appears in Article I, even when the unconsented-to uses may well destroy both the market for their work, and pretty well destroy their own repute and incentives for future authorship as well. Some may find this folly and paradox. Others, however, will understand, and celebrate it as part of the American view of the meaning of freedom of speech and of the press.[34]

V

CONCLUSION

Here, we have but tried to put the matter in some repose merely on the early question of how to regard the clause itself, as to whether it "excepts" a certain area of legislation from the First Amendment. It does not. The clause, again, is meant to put an end to one more kind of federalism question, and on that front, it deserves to be generously interpreted and applied in what it may confide to the discretion of Congress to legislate as it thinks best to do, in preemption of various regimes that might otherwise riddle the field. It "preempts" nothing within the protection of the First Amendment, however, and any feature of any portion of any act Congress has, or may in the future, provide under sanction of this clause, may always be brought into question respecting whether, on its face or as applied, it offends against the larger freedom of speech and of the press provided constitutional sanctuary in the First Amendment still unfolding in the United States.

---

34. For two excellent, contemporary examples of cases in which, were the "fair use" provisions of the current act *not* interpreted themselves to permit the infringing uses at stake, the First Amendment itself might easily have compelled the same result, see *Campbell v. Acuff-Rose Music, Inc.*, 510 U.S. 569 (1994), concerning commercial parody of Roy Orbison's "Pretty Woman," and *Hustler Magazine, Inc. v. Moral Majority, Inc.*, 796 F.2d 1148 (9th Cir. 1986), where the "infringing" party copied and distributed in excess of *700,000* copies of the particular original work (a parody cartoon), without the copyright holder's consent. *See also* 71 U.S.L.W. 3258 (Oct. 15, 2002) (reporting oral argument of Oct. 9, 2002, in Eldred v. Ashcroft, No. 01-618) ("O'Connor pointed out that the Supreme Court on several occasions has avoided the invocation of the First Amendment in copyright cases." It has indeed done just this, by managing to "interpret" the fair use provisions to deny the relief sought by the copyright holder against the infringing use.) And for a near-equivalent case, involving a state law (akin to copyright, but based on a state tort law notion of "right of publicity" for commercial gain, and a Lanham Act claim), where it is strongly arguable First Amendment *should* have protected the "copied" features of the plaintiff's persona, despite the circuit court's (majority) view, see *White v. Samsung Electronics America, Inc.*, 971 F.2d 1395 (9th Cir. 1992).

TWO RELATIONSHIPS TO A CULTURAL PUBLIC DOMAIN

NEGATIVLAND*

INTRODUCTION

It's been well over ten years since Negativland was sued by Island Records for supposed copyright infringement, trademark infringement, defamation of character and consumer fraud contained in our 1991 *U2* single. In the big wide world of the ownership of ideas, a lot has changed since then—the advent of the Internet and its worldwide empowerment of individuals through personalized interconnection, the effects of economic globalization and how it bypasses both the ideologies of local governments and the rule of their national laws, and the Digital Millennium Copyright Act with which intellectual property owners are attempting to survive as all these rugs are being pulled out from under them. There is a contemporary realization that, on one hand, the fate of all content is now in the hands of its receiving audience more than ever before, and, on the other hand, that worldwide commerce is scrambling to forge all kinds of new laws and regulations to maintain their traditional control over the fate of "their" content.

Over the last decade, Negativland has continued to be associated with these issues, sometimes because we volunteer ideas on these subjects, sometimes because we continue to make art that ends up evoking them. Other than the two lawsuits against us in the wake of the *U2* single, we've never been sued again. There have been other scares, skirmishes, and threats against us over the years, at various times from the Recording Industry Association of America, PepsiCo, Beck, Geffen Records, Philip Glass, Fat Boy Slim, the CD pressing plants we work with, and even attorneys for ax murderer David Brom. But, surprisingly, we've actually been left alone throughout the 1990s and into the 2000s as we continued to release work that appropriates from privately owned mass media, often times in much more glaring ways than anything we were ever sued over. Perhaps it's because we've been flying under the radar as "alternative" music, or perhaps that highly publicized suit, which we publicly defended as "anti-art" because we couldn't afford to defend it in court as fair use, caused others to think twice before suing us again. Or perhaps, at least these days, it's

This article is also available at http://law.duke.edu/journals/66LCPNegativland.

* The experimental music and art collective known as Negativland has been recording music/audio/collage works since 1980, producing a weekly 3-hour radio show ("Over The Edge") since 1981, hosting a World Wide Web site (http://www.negativland.com.) since 1995, and performing live on occasional tours throughout America and Europe. They are the authors of FAIR USE: THE STORY OF THE LETTER U AND THE NUMERAL 2 (1995).

because, in the wake of Napster, DSL, cable modems, file sharing, and mp3s, the music industry now has much bigger things to worry about than a bunch of underground audio artists chopping up and re-using bits of their privately owned intellectual property.

Whatever the reasons, Negativland has remained appropriatively unrepentant, and we continue to work in the same ways we always have. And, in the wake of those lawsuits, we expanded our own self-run record label, Seeland Records, to help out other artists who also "infringe" in order to collage, most notably in the compilation *Deconstructing Beck*, and in our re-release of John Oswald's historic *Plunderphonics* project, both of which, unlike most of our own work, are constructed entirely by cutting up and transforming other people's music.

We've continued to work this way because we like the sound of it. We like the results. We get inspired by what we find out there, it's simply *fun* to do, and we sense we are not alone in these perceptions. In continuing to pursue collage and found-sound as elements in our music, we have set our work out as public examples of how appropriation from our media surroundings is neither culturally harmful nor dangerous to anyone else's business. Instead, it hopefully does represent some interesting art perspectives, as well as cultural commentary and criticism which are well worth having around whether or not our work happens to be "authorized" by our subjects and sources. We consider it to be a matter of free speech.

At this late date in the proliferation of collage, we no longer see this "appropriation" approach as particularly daring, edgy or trangressive, as it once truly was. The "aesthetic" of collage (though not always the actual thing itself) has by now become a very mainstream style in music, television, and movies. We see it in mass media everywhere we look. We see it in the many web-based CD stores that now have a *Plunderphonics* category, in the frequent appropriation-based film and music festivals around the world, and in the way our own phrase "culture jamming" has been appropriated, commodified and marketed (via *Adbusters* magazine), and has entered into routine anti-corporate and anti-advertising activist lingo. We see it in the way collage and its ramifications has become a common subject in courses in film schools, law schools, art schools, and music schools. Even though it's all *still* tacitly illegal, this way of working is now nothing unusual. Observing this now generally culture-wide acceptance of collage's appropriation methodologies, one would think that sympathetic laws of allowance would also emerge to encourage the practice and assure that it is able to proceed legally. But that has not yet happened. What's wrong with this picture?

PART ONE:

FREE EXCHANGE IN THE DIGITAL DOMAIN

TWO POSITIONS

Any argument over what should or should not be considered a public domain for cultural works stems from one of two positions:

Position One: Everything created by humans is "work" that is done to gain income and which cannot continue to be done without that income. Therefore, all pieces of cultural "work" need to be compensated, usually on a per-unit basis, if we expect such work to continue. And, therefore, becoming a "user" of such work without compensating the creators for their work is a theft of the creators' rightful and necessary compensation. This position—the ethical and economic standard within our usual practice of cultural creation—stems directly from our evolution through a pre-digital, hard-copy-based world in which the supply of anything made was necessarily physical and so also supply-limited in nature. The physical supply of anything made was controlled by the maker of that thing and the units or copies of it were doled out exclusively by the maker. That condition quite naturally evoked and supported the above ethic in a material world that provided virtually no other options.

Position Two: Digital technologies of reproduction have dragged the above ethic into a virtual new world of production realities in which there is still the creation of individual "works," but once a digital copy of that work is released, it's up for grabs. Those on the receiving end of it are capable of making their own indistinguishable copies *ad infinitum* and distributing them *ad infinitum* as well. And they can do this at little cost as individuals at home using consumer technology available to anyone. In other words, we have begun to allow those on the receiving end of cultural output to put themselves in charge of the reproduction and distribution of that work if they so wish. As music makers, for instance, we are no longer in charge of our own music once it actually leaves our hands in digitized forms. We cannot control the further duplication and distribution of our music by those who receive it. This unexpected and perplexing reality has begun to encourage a different ethic and economic standard for digitized cultural work, one that those who have always ruled in Position One are oblivious to. Of course this new ethic is really nothing new at all, emerging as it does from a very old ethic, an ethic that every effort of private capitalism over the last century has sought to deflect, delay, and smother: The concept of public domain.

THE DEATH OF FOLK ART AND THE BIRTH OF THE INTERNET

It is primarily computers and the Internet that have prompted the creation of Position Two, and out of them comes a renewed interest in the free and open exchange of cultural works. This new digitally-driven ethic of free exchange emerged so easily because the *ideal* of an unhindered, wide-open, and free cultural exchange has always held a deep philosophical appeal for the receiving end of culture, and the receivers have now suddenly been given an effective technological tool to actually make this happen. The lack of any need to pay for anything in this new domain does nothing to limit its popular appeal. But deep within these unfamiliar realizations about how reality is now working remains the conundrum of how to pay for cultural production. This is the one nagging residue of practicality from Position One which Position Two does not yet have a good answer for. But interestingly enough for our human brains, on the Internet we don't appear to have a viable choice! All digitized media, particularly on the Internet, has actually turned the world of traditional copyright controls upside down, putting the general public in a distribution driver's seat that simply did not exist before. In doing so, digitally reproduced media has opened up the public's imagination to what *they* would like to do with whatever forms of culture come their way. The audience can now bypass the creator's control over sales and distribution. Once again in the history of human technology, new technology has thrown us and our society's prior "values" for a loop.

In much earlier times, prior to the corporately driven modern era of hands-off, privately owned and copyrighted cultural material, the natural human approach to our own culture was to participate in it by not only absorbing it as an individual, but also by remaking it—adding to it, removing from it, recombining it with other elements, reshaping it to our own tastes—and then redistributing the adjusted results ourselves. Virtually the whole history of human culture consisted of altering, reusing, and copying from the universal public domain in various re-imagined ways . . . until copyright came along.

SUE ME, SUE YOU

Copyright has made true folk music, for instance, illegal and impossible. It is extinct as a process. What's left are professional "singer/songwriters," each one "original," each one intending to remain legal by being lyrically and melodically distinguished from all the others, and all having little to do with any kind of true, evolving "folk" process at all. Any kind of modern folk music (as opposed to that which has already reached the legally defined "public domain") became impossible once it could be sued it out of existence. Along with this general direction in the modern parameters of creativity came complete twists in human perception itself, such as the very concept of copying (which is how this species actually got to where we are) becoming a term of disrepute, something to be avoided, an UNcreative act! So now all music, which is always chock full of copying regardless of any laws, continues under self-delusional standards of "originality" based on carefully delineated degrees of copycat provability.

Acknowledging the strengths and realities of human nature (monkey see, monkey do) has now become a disrespected practice in our commercialized culture. Nothing is allowed to incrementally evolve through various individuals.

Each individual must make a legally defined leap from another's (phony) "originality" to his or her own (phony) "originality." We wonder if the whole history of human culture would agree with the copyright lawyers and content owners who think this is a good thing for the evolution of human culture.

As for the Net, digital distribution does not remove the right to sue for copying or "unauthorized" reuses of existing work, but it does remove a great deal of practicality in actually enforcing such legal mandates. These are "crimes" committed by countless individual citizens inside countless homes, and tracking any of this criminal multiplicity is so difficult it just becomes expensively pointless. Now, we are discovering just how difficult it is for copyright's relatively short-lived repression of the public's urge for a cultural public domain to continue, as if nothing has happened. The success of Napster (over twenty-five million file-sharing users) showed that the public's desire to engage in cultural reprocessing and trading for their own purposes had not become extinct. It seems the general public will always take control of revising the destiny of cultural products which enter their sphere of possession if given the opportunity. With digital technology, they suddenly can, and so they do. But this new opportunity has also evoked a newly awakened awareness of the economics of modern culture and the encompassing of the electronic arts by commercial interests which have thus come to characterize our popular culture as a whole. These commercial interests have actually come to rule what is "important" and what is not in cultural material. Among other things, when private cultural income threatens to go out the window, some very different sorts of standards for popular "worth" may start to emerge.

SCREAMS OF INDIGNATION

The music industry, in which virtually all mainstream music is at the moment owned and controlled by five transnational corporate entities, screams that free digital exchange will kill music if left to its own home reproduction devices.[1] Well, it could possibly kill *their* kind of expense-laden music, but their self-absorbed assumption that they *are* all the music that counts is one of the reasons it is so appealing to subvert their economic grip on music by reproducing it and passing it on for free. But such an emotion, regardless of how justifiable it may be if focused, is actually vague at best and merely a general feeling about what *all* music is actually "worth" in a commercially compromised creative culture. This newly empowered free-exchange attitude does not necessarily distinguish between musical examples. So this "subversion" of profit extends equally to the small independent varieties of music, too, and thus we have a

1. It should be pointed out here that the small drop in CD sales seen over the last few years might also be attributed to the following: an economy in recession, CDs being criminally overpriced, DVDs selling for way cheaper than CDs, DVDs, web surfing and video games taking up much more of people's free time and entertainment dollars, and the widespread shift in the mainstream music biz away from releasing good albums and focusing instead only on hit singles.

potential support problem for all music, whether it's made in a corporate music factory at great expense or for very little in a home studio.

One thing that may shake out of this situation is that if payment for any and all music significantly diminishes, all the other-than-profit-motivated home studios will hang on and keep producing music a lot longer than the big, extravagant, corporate music factories will ever care to. As economies of scale come into play, the consolidation of the major record labels into fewer and fewer hands creates a gigantic economic infrastructure they simply may not be able to sustain. If their worst case downloading disaster scenario comes true, they may slowly implode under their own size and weight, breaking up into smaller companies with lower overheads.

Of course music will not disappear under these conditions any more than it did throughout most of human history, when no one was being paid to make it. Music may, though, change in nature. The notion that one could run a business or have a career based on selling thousands of round pieces of plastic is a relatively new one in human history and not written in stone. The thousands of tunes now churned out yearly by the labels as formula bids for mass popularity may become less and less worth doing because such a shotgun approach, dependent on the few-in-a-thousand that "hit" to pay for it all, is too expensive when free copies of those few hits can proliferate so easily. And whatever is done online may not provide much of a living if it never escapes an Internet format. To suggest that all this will automatically be bad for *music itself*, however, is not that easy to assume. We have become so accustomed to equating something's quality and value with the income it earns, we hardly know what to think about that something when it can't rely on this particular self-justifying link. Negativland, for example, has never made even a decent living off of music, yet we continue to make music. And we're probably not the only ones. Perhaps music at a "survival" level of self-support will not necessarily be any worse than most of the professional factory music we're getting now, supported as it is by more careless waste than you care to know about.

THE OTHER HALF OF THE GLASS

The Internet, however, finally opens up self-production as a significant alternative to the notorious corporate label intimidation that has ruled modern pop music production. For a musician, it potentially provides, at very low cost, what has always been missing before—self-distribution that can actually get beyond one's own neighborhood. A single master is now all that's needed to be a potential worldwide distributor. When manufacturing multiple hard goods is no longer the only way to distribute music, literally anyone can play. The Net's unique ability to encourage the self-control and self-ownership of one's own musical career by utterly bypassing the former only game in town—corporate labels' usurpation of control and ownership rights—is not to be dismissed just because the resulting living may be smaller. (And keep in mind that of the three billion web pages online as of this writing, only about thirty percent of them are for commercial or corporate interests. The rest are simply just *there* to share information, art, and ideas.)

This may be the main future of music on the Internet, as yet still filled with corporate hand wringing over economic collapse. The Net's motto for the future may well be "Get Small or Get Off." Optimistically, and perhaps naively, we hope that the Net will end up being characterized as a people's medium, primarily designed by and for individuals rather than yet another comfortable bed for the mass culture of corporate marketing, which has so far successfully taken over all other available mass media. Such a medium as the Net, geared to the interconnection of individuals, could also inevitably become divorced from copyright constraints, which will go on ruling the material world. The Net could become a simultaneously operating alternative, in which everything that remains is functionally in the public domain and open to anyone's reuse. This is not to assume that there will be no ways for creators to garner individual incomes in a digitized public domain, but those ways will probably be unusual in the history of making livings, perhaps including voluntary payment, and are mostly yet to be invented.

For the time being, there are still persistent and expensive efforts on the part of corporate producers of cultural content to somehow maintain the Position One economic standard for digitized media (per-unit payment) within the new Position Two functioning reality (free exchange by default). With dollar signs sparkling in their eyes, the music factories dream of charging for those millions of "unauthorized" downloads which are now happening, when, of course, any charges for them will instantly dry them up to an unknown degree. Practically none of these efforts at placing a toll on what everyone knows is an infinite and virtually expense-free supply in the digital domain has ever worked very well, and none of them has worked at all for long. And there is not much hope that they ever will, because no matter how many very smart encrypters and digital security specialists the private producers employ, the world is always much bigger. There will always be someone else out there who is just as clever and who is, by nature, opposed to a privately controlled culture of limited supply on the Net. Perhaps there will *never* be a way to make much money off of digital content on the Net. Locks are an anachronism there. All private exclusivity codes will be cracked by the vast and alternatively motivated population at large, given enough time. Why are they doing this? The Position Two ethic. How will we pay for cultural production? Nobody knows. Can business pound a square peg into a round hole? Probably not.

THE CONSUMER AS CRIMINAL

Meanwhile, all this has landed us in an era in which the traditional business of culture is in the impossible position of seeing its customer base as criminally dangerous to its business. This paranoia stems from the essence of capitalist logic—charging is good, free is bad. And not just bad—impossible! But in the realm of the Net, cultural materials—text, images, and audio—are all constantly moved around by an online audience operating under the assumption that free is good and charging is bad. Online users express this notion there because, for the first time in their lives, they actually can. And they see how the Net can apparently go on and on this way, that the essence of western civilization is perhaps not so threatened by it, that perhaps it even adds something worthwhile to it, and most significantly, that not one off-line business concern, individual or company, has yet gone out of business because of *anything* that's happening with online file-sharing.[2]

The Internet was never designed as a commercially structured medium for selling digital data. It was designed as a medium for a free, open, and decentralized exchange of information. This tenacious foundation of technology and software is proving extremely difficult to convert into various forms of toll taking. Only cultural content as apparently irresistible and indispensable as pornography has succeeded in making non-physical content pay there. There are few, if any, other economic success stories on the Net which are not offering off-line material goods as the lure.

So far, all forms of paid advertising (a major way that cultural content supports itself), have proved themselves to be largely ineffectual on the Net. Few people click through those banners. It's just a whole different kind of place, suggesting a different attitude among its users and allowing them to change their usual media expectations upon entering. It's a worldwide place that somehow suggests personal direction and individualized participation more than any other medium that has ever been available to us. No matter how flawed and imperfect, what we seek on the Net seems to be something more individually specific to us as individuals. The medium itself seems to prefer unmodulated individual expression and priorities. Homogenized, generic, conglomerized corporate intrusions into this arena automatically appear anachronistic, disruptive, and annoying. It's not so easy to just turn it into television. Logos, branding, and selling itself—all the things we now accept as characterizing our corporate culture in other media and the off-line material world—do not yet get the same free and willing pass inside Net culture. There still appears be some kind of choice there, an inherent flexibility to make of it what we will, a choice which no longer strikes us as possible in the commercially locked up brick and mortar world.

---

2. A report issued in May, 2002 by Jupiter Research confirmed their earlier research demonstrating that Napster had had a positive effect on sales of CDs:

> According to the Jupiter Consumer Survey, experienced file sharers were 75 percent more likely that the average online music fan to say that they increased their music spending levels during exposure to music on the Web. Meanwhile, users with CD-writable drives were 16 percent more likely than average to report increases, and broadband users were two percent more likely than average to report increases. Consumers with all three technologies were the most likely of all to say that they increased their purchasing—95 percent more likely than the average online music fan.

Jupiter Research, File Sharing: To Preserve Music Market Value, Look Beyond Easy Scapegoats (2002).

It is often surprising how oblivious corporate commerce is to how self-damning their own unconsidered nature appears to be when it reaches the Net. They are looking at the Net as a new and lucrative nut to be cracked, but they are doing this in the same old ways they tackled every other new medium that ever appeared. They either ignore the basic design of Net technology, which is so persistently opposed to that form and function, or they are hard at work with their well-greased representatives in Congress to legally change the basic design of the software and the hardware into something they can work with. Failure after failure has not made much of a dent in their assumptions that the Net, too, can and will be turned into another medium for commercial placement and selling products. The RIAA's attack on Napster (and by default, their attack on the twenty-five million music fans who used Napster) was an alienating public relations disaster for the music industry, a disaster that industry still seems to fail to grasp. They are still looking at the Internet as the biggest mall of all. The vast majority of users, however, hardly seem interested in more malls at all. This may be because, for the majority of users, the Internet still represents a very new expression of public domain ethics and possible procedures, a place where cost and content are not necessarily bound together. This is a way of thinking that has been denied to us in all other forms of mass media, all of which succumbed to commercial domination and sponsored purposes long ago.

ART OVER PROFIT?

Life is often a series of overlapping contradictions fighting for survival and predominance. Music on the Net has just become a new example of this evolutionary principle in action. Music might evolve (or devolve, if you prefer) into a dual life, one being its present status as private property, copyrighted and supply-controlled in the material world, and the other being a non-proprietary "vapor service" as long as it remains digitized within the confines of the Internet. From the "art over profit" perspective that is ours, this perfectly possible legal distinction would act as a form of protection against private capitalism's compulsion to change the Internet experience as we know it to suit its own marketing purposes.

Many assume that such a dual distribution of cultural material—all copyrighted in the material world and all subject to free fair use on the Net—is not a plausible option. They assume this would be a form of "competition" the material world could not economically sustain, that no one is going to pay for something here that they can get free over there. But actually, if experience is a somewhat more reliable teacher than theory, we might notice that this is exactly what is happening right now. One can download practically any music for free somewhere on the Net, yet CD sales, for year after year while this has been possible, continue to remain pretty much the same. There are many factors at work in this paradox which may actually be more than a temporary pause while download quality catches up to CD quality. The Net approaches being a functioning public domain for whatever enters it. It is accessible worldwide. The amount of material found there is inestimable, as is the total population of users who access it. The numbers involved in both amounts of content and amount of access distinguish the Internet as an unprecedented participatory phenomenon with which we have no previous "marketing" familiarity.

The key to the continuing CD sales paradox may be found in the unprecedented scale of the Net. Most music buyers will very likely always find a certain preference for hassle-free, glitch-free (in other words, computer-free), audio perfection, along with the relevant packaging which CDs or their hard copy successor will always provide. But everyone's CD budget is forever limited to what is most important to them. They purchase music they are *sure* they like, sure they want to add to a physically permanent collection. Computer-housed music, on the other hand, has all the aura and charm of disposable music. It's a way to sample unknown things with no obligation to buy, a way to try out or collect a whole lot of stuff one would never ordinarily buy in any case, and a place where a great deal of unknown music is easily checked out and deleted without losing any investment at all. Every free download whim definitely does *not* represent a "lost" sale, and in fact, the literally unconsumable plethora of available free music on the Net can and does create sales.

Free digitized music still appears to be excellent advertising and the mainstream music industry has shot itself in the foot with its aggressive moves to stop it. Even if some of the saleable variety of music is supplanted by free downloads, those downloads also produce enough sales for "permanent" music which is first discovered through all this disposable digital sampling, that it balances out to keep CD sales no significantly less than they were before the Internet came along. The amount of free music downloading going on (perhaps now in the billions) really scares the mainstream recording industry, but they seem to forget the scale of practicality involved. They only need to sell a tiny fraction of the amount of music that is downloaded to become sinfully rich anyway. So far, this digital public domain for all music exists in tandem with record stores selling the same stuff, and, surprisingly, the relationship may not be any more destructive than it is helpful to sales. When it comes to the Net, simple patience, rather than a rush to reconstitute it, is in order, as there is still much to learn about its many unpredictable effects on the outside world.

But such a dualistic reality appears unthinkable to commercial interests who remain deep in the habit of assuming that exclusive and protected ownership is the only guarantee of private profit. The Net has been no significant part of that habit yet, but business interests seem incapable of noticing the Net's more innovative suggestion that this assumption may not, in fact, be true at all, especially in terms of how this new medium increasingly interacts with and informs the whole world of copyrighted experiences that the entertainment industries already *do* profit from.

PARADOXES OF PRACTICALITY

What may be even more difficult for commerce to swallow is the ultimate realization that any alternative to the whole Internet remaining a public domain by default is bound to fail anyway. All it takes to subvert copyright constraints online is for one individual to purchase access to a work on or off the Net, and from that point on the work is potentially up for grabs on the Net for nothing. The basic functionality of this medium was beautifully designed to promote and facilitate copying and spreading, and, unless its basic nature is significantly altered (efforts are underway as we write), it will always be prone to do this well. As paranoia grows among the corporate owners of culture and content, the Net becomes all the more curiously fascinating to its largely commercially unaffiliated users precisely because it just sits there—a profound enigma in the midst of a society so otherwise firmly entrenched in capitalist formulas for success. How can this commercially unworkable anomaly be accommodated? The psychic and societal shifts these paradoxes of practicality may eventually produce among us reaches far beyond the arts. They question the value of intellectual property ownership itself, which has suddenly been turned into a revitalized question for so many since the Internet appeared.

All other previous mass media have been one way in nature and designed for passive spectatorship and sponge-like absorption. Mass media value their audiences primarily as target consumers representing demographic statistics with which they can sell advertising. Their listening/viewing audience is actually called a "market" in their own terminology. The Internet, however, still appears to be an actual medium *for* the masses—a medium for active, individual exchange and interchange, without a center of control or executive offices making decisions about its future, and where personal contribution rather than anonymous absorption is what is suggested by the technology. The difference consists of who and what is really in charge, and who and what it's really for.

WHO ARE WE, WHO ARE YOU?

A view of the world as a freely reusable public domain has long been the traditional view of artists involved in creating art responses to the world they live in. Now the Internet has reawakened this possible view of the world to the average user and the general public at large. The general public's concerns revolve not so much around the need for fair use to include fragmentary reuse and appropriation in the creation of new art works, but in the current corporate attempts to curb "personal copying" fair use allowances within the Internet. Users want to copy what they download, create copies in other formats, and transmit personal copies freely. Corporate IP owners see all this as a threat to their proprietary income and are hard at work to create all sorts of barriers to this kind of traditional fair use: If you don't pay for your copy online, it's not yours. If you do pay for your copy online, it may be "yours," but it may destroy itself in 30 days if you don't continue paying, and it sometimes can't be copied at all, even for your own reuse in another format. Such attempts at post-distribution control by content owners have had all kinds of technological problems—there seem to be ways around all anti-copy schemes so far—and these kinds of new attempts at content control are unique to Internet culture, where content owners think this new technology will actually allow such intricate post-distribution controls for the first time. But they are barking up the wrong little tree in a very large forest of quite opposite interests and abilities.

Our overall approach to these general "problems" of copying and transferring whole works freely is that it probably doesn't make much economic difference, as indeed, it has not to date. When we see convincing evidence that off-line business is being destroyed by online activity, we will reconsider. Until then, we see no need to assume that the Net, as it is now, is actually dangerous to existing off-line economic concerns, nor do we assume that corporate commerce has some indisputable right to get in there, colonize it, redirect it, become an online economic concern by any means necessary, and generally rule the roost as they have already done in TV, radio, and movies. Especially if it means changing the Net's technological architecture to do so. The fact is, *anyone* with a computer can get onto the Internet and operate there because it's rather inexpensive to do so, unlike all our other mass media in which the expense requirements to play enforce sponsorship and prohibit popular participation entirely. We are all ready for a medium for the masses that is, in this one isolated instance, not completely dominated in purpose and content by corporate commercial interests. The really interesting thing is that it is actually possible for the Net to be that and to endure. We wonder if others ever contemplate what a single worldwide medium for the masses, one of corporate non-accommodation rather than corporate subjugation, would be or become? We wonder if anyone else is interested in finding out? Optimistically, it might still be up to us, the unaffiliated users, but probably not for long. If corporate interests have their way and locks on copies are developed and file sharing is made preventable, we will all soon be customers only. And it probably won't be the same kind of decentralized Net anymore, either.

Because the Internet is new to us at the moment, seeming to thrust many new abilities at us for which we have no precedent in the history of popular reuse, it is currently the biggest and most widely perceived symbol for the popular desire to spread and exchange all culture as if it existed in a public domain. But the human urge towards a public domain is nothing new. Long before, and still continuing outside the Internet, this philosophical ideal concerning our cultural environment has been evident in the evolution of modern art. And that can form a historical basis from which to consider the desirability of all of today's forms of free cultural reuse in general.

PART TWO:

STICKY FINGERED HISTORY

GRIST FOR THE MILL

Beginning with the Industrial Revolution and extending all the way through the entire twentieth century up to this point in late high-capitalism, there has been an intertwined relationship between the co-option of our mental and physical environment by private commercial interests on one hand, and, on the other, a simultaneous awareness in the evolution of art content of this ever growing unilateral encroachment on everyone's personal and public spaces.

This awareness was not always displayed by art that was trying to point this out in particular, but much art has taken it into account, nevertheless. Some art is concerned with the social consequences of what is happening around it, other art is not, but all art tends to be affected by whatever it is seeing, no matter how unconsciously assimilated or openly displayed these perceptions may be in the work. There is a certain perceptual stance most artists have always taken in relation to their work and their environment—a perception that sees everything out there as grist for their mill. Whether they are painting a tree in a landscape or sampling someone else's music, for artists, it's just what's out there, and it's all equally usable if it "works" to make the art they want to make. It matters not who "owns" the music they sample any more than it matters who "owns" the tree they paint. Ownership has never had anything to do with creativity.

This ancient, universal artist's view of art's potential subject matter proceeded just fine for quite a while. For centuries, there were no lawsuits against landscape painters by landowners, and neither did they demand a cut of the painting's price (presently, however, Disneyland claims copyright on any photos you take inside their imagineered landscapes). Throughout the twentieth century, the world was surprised by many unforeseen new technologies which, as usual, began to produce new forms of thinking and new forms of creative activity. For instance, one technology—the ability to capture and reproduce sound electrically—began to allow those involved in creating music to think differently about what music might consist of. Electrical transcription meant that music no longer needed to be performed live to be heard. Music as an artifact frozen in time and space was almost immediately seen by composers as having recombinable possibilities. Prerecorded sounds and music began appearing in *musique concrete* performances by the second decade of the last century. At the same time that electrical invention was spreading, so were the brand-new techniques of visual collage (recombining disparate elements or imagery into a single new composition, also the founding attitude of surrealism in general).

Collage first appeared in a brand-new reproduction technology of the late-1800s called photography (another form of freezing light/time into material form which makes it capable of post-creation manipulation), parts of which could be cut up and recombined to make joke or "impossible" photo imagery.

Lots of fun. This cut-and-paste visual technique quickly spread to painting, with foreign objects beginning to be used. Lawsuits against early photography were unknown. There were also no lawsuits against the early painters who embraced collage around the turn of the twentieth century. They began to attach found material from the world around them to their canvases, sometimes including commercially produced products like candy wrappers or fragments of advertising. Still no offense taken. Musical collage, for the most part, remained in the realm of classical music up until mid-century. However, all through the endless, live-performance-only centuries of music creation, many composers had routinely included pre-existing music "quotes" within new work, which might range from familiar folk melodies to fragments borrowed from their classical predecessors or contemporary colleagues. When recorded music came along, it was no great leap for some composers to add that into their compositional concepts. Music was proceeding exactly as it always had and as it wanted to then, with hardly a hassle from those early commercial copyright laws starting to congeal over in the shadows.

In the fine art realms of creation, there was a clear appreciation that copying and appropriation was not only a tradition in art, but also seemed to be growing in relevance as the modern perceptual world around the artists of the last century fragmented into the many reproduction possibilities that electric imagery and sound began to shower civilization with. We'll skip World War I and Dada's found objects (though their effect on creating an artistic view of the world as both absurdly surreal and entirely available to become art via appropriation was profound), but hot on those heels came Surrealism's concept of *detournment*, which consisted of cleverly changing the nature of existing material to make it say or show things it never originally intended to say or show, often in the form of ironic juxtaposition and derailment of meaning. The earliest form of culture jamming. But still no lawsuits, still all relatively uncontested as long as it was fine art.

In the middle of the twentieth century, the "crassness" of Pop Art emerged in rude response to the U.S. culture's already commercially saturated consciousness, particularly the unavoidable barrage of advertising iconography filling society's public view with its insistent "taste." With Pop Art, we see the beginning of lawsuits based on the "infringement" of the private copyrights of commercial subjects which became the unwilling content of new works. Even then, such artistically constricting absurdities against art's freedom of expression were still generally seen as just that, and while the *New York Times* sued Robert Rauschenberg for an unauthorized silk-screen of one of their news photos, Campbell's Soup saw Andy Warhol's paintings of their cans as great free advertising. Which it was!

JUMPING MUSIC

About this same time in the late 1950's, collage and the use of "found" subject matter jumped over to pop music, having been apparent in classical music for some time already. This happened most notably in the form of Buchanan and Goodman's "novelty" edits consisting of fragments of then-current rock & roll hits with connecting narration which became "completed" by clips of familiar song lyrics. This was the beginning of mass-appeal collage music in the pop realm, and they were immediately threatened legally by the owners of the music they reused. It was also the beginning of music owners deciding to take this artistic appropriation business as some kind of serious economic threat and increasingly criminalizing it as commercial "theft."

But collage and the artistic attitude behind it continued to grow and spread and eventually infiltrate all forms of creativity during the last century. In fact, collage is now often considered the single most influential and, indeed, the single most defining aesthetic for the entire twentieth century. And it shows no signs of diminishing in the twenty-first. Turn on the news, it's solid collage. Watch a commercial or a music video, it's solid collage. Go see a live baseball game, with its mix of the game itself and improvisationally dropped in found audio and video clips from popular culture used to wind up the audience—that is collage as well. Every computer user in the world knows and understands the term "cut and paste." But amazingly, as this cut-and-paste "style" began to spread far and wide beyond the realm of fine art (even becoming part of people's technologically assisted attitude towards sifting through an increasingly complex world of reproduced stimuli, information, and influences in daily life), then this process in art started to get sued.

By the time collage cropped up in popular music, that kind of music was no less technically an art form than any other, but you'd never know it by its owners and operators. By the mid-twentieth century, music of the popular variety had been thoroughly harnessed by marketers of recordings as a mass commodity. Whatever artistic qualities of popular music may have been touted in the PR of those producing it, behind the scenes it was definitely a commodity game. Profit and loss, not artistic integrity, was determining success or failure. Popular recorded music became all about money, where it remains focused to this day. Thus art, which is not defined as a business, became a business in the form of popular music. And music, which is not defined as a competition, became a competition in the hands of record labels.

This anti-art trend never materialized in painting or other fine arts as it certainly has in music (although it still occasionally happens in other arts too), because the scope of intellectual activity in the fine arts world is much smarter about art and what makes it tick and sees that it's not a competition but an all-inclusive accumulation. They better understand that all art is steeped in "theft," and that art has always proceeded by copying from whatever appeals to it, including other art. Add to that the fact that fine art generally ends up as a singular, unique object (the "original" is all there is), while music ends up as endlessly mass-produced objects which can be sold again and again over time. Music, once something which could only be heard live and in person, became a repeating object—a mass marketable product regardless of how much art it might happen to contain, and forever in competition with all other such music "products."

Add to this the fact that pop music marketing was not run by the likes of artistically enlightened museum or gallery directors, but by dollar-hungry entertainment moguls, their accountants, and their lawyers, many of whom, by mid-century, were already engaged in illegally cornering distribution with payoffs and thug tactics, co-opting airplay with payola, concocting rip-off artist contracts, cooking the books for embezzlement, and actually being leaned on or infiltrated by organized crime (as documented in Fredric Dannen's book *Hit Men*, among others). So you have the *industry* of pop music becoming, amid all the art within it, a crass and opportunistic nest of thieves and scoundrels in which any artistic priorities, if understood in the first place, were quickly readjusted or cast aside in favor of the bottom line on a regular basis. In pop music, with the aid of modern copyright law, any kind of perceived copying became just another way to collect money and crush possible competition, even though no other art form in human history is more thoroughly based on copying the precedents of others than music is.

IN CREPT COLLAGE

Into this peculiar, highly competitive, proprietary obsessed "art" of popular music, eventually crept the well-respected, classically founded motivations and techniques of collage. Who knew? Cutting and editing analog tape of musical and non-musical material into new recordings was occurring throughout the 1960s and 1970s, but it was in the 1980s that all hell broke loose. The music electronics industry began marketing various digital sampling devices and computer controlled music sequencing software intended to allow musicians to easily play back the sounds of "public domain" flutes and cellos and saxophones. What the inventors of samplers never guessed would occur was that this new device also easily allowed musicians to capture and then play back bits of *any* pre-recorded music or found sound and add it to their own music. Collage, in the form of sampling others' work to make new work, began to be routinely suppressed. Pop samplers, initially emerging in rap and hip-hop, began freely plucking the grooves they wanted from the grooves of other popular music, and soon found themselves in court. By the late 1980s, lawsuits and threats of lawsuits proliferated as this particular capturing technology spread far and wide throughout music of all kinds. Musical collage and its use of "unauthorized" sound became a criminal activity. Collage music became criminal music and the natural evolution of hip-hop was stopped dead in its tracks. Copyright law became the art police.

Presently, we have a somewhat more settled situation in which sample clearance fees, rather than lawsuits, rule the economies of collage in music. But music owners continue to make great efforts to stamp out unauthorized collage in music, even going so far as to intimidate and threaten, via the RIAA, any CD pressing plants that manufacture any sort of unauthorized found-sound music.

The RIAA acknowledges the existence and idea of fair use only in its literature's footnotes, and hopes it doesn't spread.

As artistically stupid as all of this is on the face of it (trying to control what art wants to do whether it happens to be a "product" or not), it has become possible because we have established inflexible copyright mandates across all the arts which allow any and all creations to be "protected" as private, untouchable property, unavailable for any purpose other than their original purpose, including any reuse in new art by others. For artists, copyright means that other art is emphatically not allowed to be seen as part of their landscape, not as part of their usable environment, not as something that influences their creative minds. Art has become completely unavailable to any succeeding artist's use without payment and permission. One can buy it and absorb it as a consumer, but one can't do anything further with it. This withdrawal of all copyrighted art from any further creative recycling goes directly against the above stated universal and historical artists' prerogative to see the entire world around them as grist for their mill. If they see other art products as part of the public environment they materially draw from, copyright tells them they cannot.

HOW IT BEGAN AND WHAT IT BECAME

When copyright was originally instituted, it certainly began to put boundaries on the public domain, which at the time extended everywhere, but there were some valid reasons to do so. A total free-for-all public domain inevitably results in the counterfeiting and re-sale of all kinds of entire existing works. Once rampant, this form of covert income siphoning *is* theft, and it has been severely limited by being made prosecutable under copyright law, as it should be in the material world of hard goods where every copy is an expense to support. A creator should be able to reap whatever rewards accrue from what they do, and getting paid for a manufacturing investment is essential. Counterfeiting others' work for sale in the material world removes this ability, and counterfeiting hard goods in their entirety for unauthorized resale is an unarguable misuse of the concept of public domain. Good law so far, and if this was the only form of reuse that copyright law prohibited, we would have no complaint against it (trading or offering another's work for free remains another story, however, since freely exchanging work in one medium that is for sale in another medium has not yet been shown to harm anyone).

Unfortunately, copyright now goes against so much that has appeared within its reach since it was conceived that the very thing it originally proclaimed to protect—the encouragement and promotion of the useful arts and sciences—is often its target for hindering and prohibiting. Collage is now well entrenched in our array of creative possibilities, universally acclaimed and valued in the arts for over a century, yet copyright, devised to protect and encourage just such creative originality, is routinely invoked to stop it from happening. Copyright law, as presently interpreted and enforced with regard to collage, is being used by cultural property owners as anti-art law, and can economically devastate its perpetrators so as to keep them from ever trying it again.

Something has happened in human creativity which copyright law never foresaw and was never written to accommodate—the fragmentary reuse of others' art to make new art. The opportunistic minds behind pop music, in particular, were able to use copyright law to act like this proven creative form (fragmentary and transformational appropriation within new works) was no different than counterfeiting entire works. Copyright law did not distinguish such a difference and neither did they. Sampling source owners called these collaged uses piracy and sued to crush the practice because:

(1) They did not and do not understand how modern art is working.
(2) They claimed such reuses were in economic competition with their source works.
(3) They were not getting paid for the reuse.

After a while, it somehow wore into their brains that modern musicians were not going to let go of collage as a technique and that sampling was only spreading more profusely into all varieties of new music. So the best way to handle it from a business perspective was to ignore reasons (1) and (2) and concentrate on (3)—getting paid for it. That's where we stand today and here's what's still wrong with it.

Just because a recognized art form like music becomes manifested as a commercial mass commodity, it is still an *art form*, which necessarily depends on free expression. Free expression demands free access to the elements of its expression, even when those elements happen to be owned by someone else. *Especially* when they are owned by someone else. This is the free pass all art has always been given to speak its mind, and commercial interests of any kind do not negate this creative imperative. If we want this kind of art to occur at all, it goes with the territory. We don't expect a writer to get permission and make a payment in order to use any particular words. We don't require payment and permission for a painter to represent the billboard that is sitting in the middle of their landscape view. Yet we are doing exactly this in the case of music collage (even as we continue *not* to do it in other, less commercially oriented collage arts). The simple fact that an art form happens to be *worth* more in its potential income generation does not negate the principles of free expression that form its creative foundation and reason for being. Pre-existing private properties, even pre-existing art, can and do form the "alphabet" that any form of modern collage might use. The current copyright restrictions on using this alphabet constitute a prior restraint that amounts to both inhibiting the process and censorship of the creative practice itself. This should not be happening, whether or not the practice happens to be housed in a commercial product.

MORE ATTITUDE

Collage, recontextualizing familiar and recognizable elements from our common experience as it does, is often a statement involved with social awareness or social commentary. It is often expressing forms of satire, direct reference, and criticism. It is not always polite. As such, it often represents a potent form of creative free speech requiring just as much protection as any other form of free speech. The entire range of practice called collage must be considered in this way in order to protect this potential in all its forms and possibilities. It's no good to trivialize these concerns by noting how hip-hop musicians simply use a sample of another's music just because they like the riff. It is truly irrelevant! Allowing source owners to have control over that practice through payment and permission requirements also prevents another collagist from using a clip of music or some damning dialog in a critical or unflattering context which the clip's owner doesn't happen to appreciate and thus refuses to allow. This potentially stifles commentaries and criticisms of many sorts within new art. Fair use may be available to parody for this reason (as defined in the Supreme Court's 2 Live Crew case), but it is *not* available at all to satire, which can be equally unflattering to source owners, and thus, not permitted. And, by the way, do you know which is which?

"Fair use" claims for cases of sampling/collage in our courts are now a morass of tortured and irrelevant nitpicking guided by a technologically outdated law, which is wholly inappropriate to acknowledge or accommodate the practice. The creative process has lost all benefit of the doubt, and commerce decides what can and cannot be art on whims of selective prosecution. These being the rather insane laws of modern art we are stuck with, we are proud to sanely make criminal music for all to hear and judge for themselves.

PAY TO PLAY

The dangers to collage from payment and permission requirements also include the aspect of affordability. Once collage had made its presence sufficiently felt in modern music and was obviously not going away because of litigation, the music industry settled down to pursue charging everyone to do it. They all set up brand-new suites in their office buildings devoted to this intercorporate trade in music samples, and usage fees were set at what competing music corporations could pay. Purchasing a single sample can run anywhere from hundreds to many thousands of dollars, depending on what the owner arbitrarily thinks the potential sales traffic will bear. If these commercial rules of legitimacy are followed, collage becomes confined to realms in which there is a wealthy label supporting the musician's desires and a mutually lucrative trade among relatively rich and already successful music purveyors. Any independent, grass roots efforts at collage are left out of this expensive loop of sampling "legitimacy."

From our personal experience as collage music-makers who have no affiliation with the major labels, we in Negativland can assure you that we simply could not be making the style of collage music we do at all if we agreed to pay for every clip and sample we use. The cumulative price of working in the particularly densely sampled way that we do is totally prohibitive to grass roots, independent, barely surviving practitioners like us. Just one of our CDs may use a hundred or more different samples and fragments recorded off of radio, movies, TV, or records. The haphazard nature of found sound collecting from mass media often does not happen to include the owner's name and address, so we sometimes have a very practical difficulty in even knowing who actually owns the bits we recorded, perhaps recorded years before we actually get around to using them. If we do know or can find out these hundreds of separate owners, we certainly don't appreciate their simply ignoring usage requests from the likes of us (we have heard from many other independents who try that no response is a usual response). If they ever *do* get back to you, the whole process can take years. Thus, they have already successfully abrogated any release schedule you may be financially counting on, which becomes crucial when you are releasing only one record at a time as a small, independent label. And then, of course, even if we could afford to pay for all these multiple samples from all these multiple owners, and all that could be worked out on schedule, these usages must also hang on their multiple permissions granted. This is where source owners can prevent this kind of work from appearing at all if they don't happen to like the content or attitude of it. This is the final and ultimate dead end wall that copyright forces collage up against, especially in cases like ours where we are often not being flattering or ideologically supportive to the sources in our work.

Which brings us to fair use.

A Distinct Lack of Understanding

Copyright law's allowance for fair use is already established within present copyright law, requiring neither payment nor permission for making limited copies of a work for personal use, or for the partial reuse of another's work in the context of news, comment, criticism, parody, and a few other education-related things. It is the only legal acknowledgment we have that copyright controls can, indeed, equal censorship of free speech and free expression if permitted total and unrestricted reign over all possible reuses. The problem with fair use as it stands is in its interpretation with regard to *art reuses* when that art is immersed (if not sinking) in a sea of competing commercial interests, as modern music is.

Fair use, as a legal concept, occurred in the original mandate for the creation of U.S. copyright law, and preceded the modern technologies that produced and encouraged the unexpected technique of collage. The aging guidelines for determining fair use do not yet accommodate, or even acknowledge, the modern tendency to actually create new work out of old. This leap of understanding has yet to appear in any of our commercially biased lawmaking as a culture, a culture already drenched in the practice of legal and illegal collage from top to bottom. Commerce goes on seeing collage, now a century old, only as an opportunistic target from which to acquire some unearned and unexpected income via copyright mandated clearance fees. As artists, we see the indistinguishing overreach of copyright's control over almost all creative reuse to be a selective prohibition on modern art's evolution.

From an artistic point of view, it is delusional to try to paint all these new forms of fragmentary reuse and sampling as economically motivated "theft" or "piracy." These terms must be reserved for the unauthorized taking of whole works and reselling them for one's own profit. Artists who routinely appropriate, on the other hand, are not attempting to profit from the marketability of their sources at all. They are using elements, fragments, or pieces of someone else's created artifact in the creation of a new one for *artistic reasons*. Collage's reused musical elements may remain identifiable, or they may be transformed to varying degrees as they are incorporated into the new work, where they may join many other fragments, all in a new context and forming a new "whole." This becomes a new "original," neither reminiscent of nor competitive with any of the "originals" it may draw from. Direct referencing does not equal copying.

DEFINING ART AND BUSINESS

Because art is not defined as a business, yet some art like music must compete for economic survival in the marketplace, we think certain legal priorities in the *idea* of copyright should be revised to uphold certain artistic imperatives in commercial contexts. Specifically, we propose a revision of the fair use guidelines to apply to a great deal more artistic activities than they now do. This revision would throw the benefit of the doubt to reuses within collage contexts, and place the burden of proof for showing economically motivated infringement on the owner/litigator. It would no longer be what is legally known as an "affirmative defense." Ideally, when a copyright owner wished to contend an unauthorized reuse of their property, they would have to show essentially that the usage does not result in anything new beyond the original work appropriated. In other words, that the usage does nothing more than counterfeit their property, adding nothing created by the appropriator to it. If the new work, however, is judged to significantly fragment, transform, rearrange, or recompose the appropriated material within a new work, then it should be automatically seen as a valid fair use—an original attempt at new creative work, whether or not the result is successful or pleasing to the original source creators or owners. There would be a general right of free reuse in the creation of new works.

This level of free reuse in the creation of new work would cause no great or destructive economic hardship to source owners because, first, none of them are making much of a living by just sitting back and collecting fees for rare or occasional reuses of their work in collages anyway, and if they say they are, then perhaps they should be encouraged to do something new once in a while themselves! Such an expansion of fair use would let all possible music collage works through the copyright gate but still prohibit wholesale counterfeiting. Unlikely? So is the present commercial suppression of collage through payment and permission requirements!

The usual fair use interpretation that assumes only non-profit works need apply is the worst of all its myriad misperceptions. Again, just as the original supporting reasoning for copyright law stated in the first place: Are we out to support, dare we say even *encourage* new arts of collage in this world or aren't we? If we want collage to flourish without economic bias or ideological censorship, especially at the grass roots level, it must be able to support itself in the very same way all its sources do—by selling *itself*. Otherwise, it withers in poverty, not to mention lawsuits.

A DIFFERENT VALUE

All claims that collage is simply out to resell its sources are patently absurd. Anyone familiar with actual examples of collage understands that any internal snippets of familiarity present within it in no way duplicate or compete with the appeal of those original sources in their entirety. It is this fragmentary selecting and combining which creates an entirely *new* effect which is at least partially dependent on recognizing that familiar thing as part of the expression, but that reference is existing in a new context, a new whole that is more than the sum of its parts. This is a new effect that is thereafter original to the collage alone. But if there is no practical economic theft involved, if a collage and its sources are not possibly in direct economic competition with each other, exactly what *is* the fundamental objection to fragmentary free appropriation in the creation of new work?

Please consider the ungenerous and uncreative logic we are overlaying our copyrighted culture with. In this age of reproduction, so typified by recorded music everywhere and battles for the consumer consciousness of our population through the mass saturation of our environment with logos, brands, messages, ideas, and imagery, artists—not to mention others—will naturally continue to be interested in sampling material from this modern environment of both reproduced art and psychological influence-mongering. Appropriating from all these publicly available influences that we swim in as a society is desirable precisely because of how these elements express and symbolize something potently recognizable about the society from which we spring. The private owners/public spreaders of such art, artifacts, icons, messages, and ideas are enormously concerned that their "message" reaches everyone, yet they are seldom happy to see their properties in unauthorized contexts which may be antithetical to the way they wish to spin them. But their knee-jerk use of copyright restrictions to prevent any kind of public "spin" which they don't approve of on their property now amounts to the corporate censorship of such direct referencing within our culture.

The present role of the courts in this ongoing censorship, bound as they are by the law as it is written, is not helpful. Though many of us object, few of us can actually make our case for the rights of art before a judge. Unlike the basic thrust of all the rest of United States law, copyright law actually assumes that all "unauthorized" uses are illegal until proven innocent. Since any contested reuse always requires a legal "affirmative" defense, such a legal expense, even when fair use *does* apply, remains beyond the financial grasp of most accused "infringers." This financial intimidation, especially on the part of large corporate source owners, results in the vast majority of unauthorized art appropriators caving in and settling out of court, their work being consigned to oblivion, and the corporate "owner" having it all their own way, including their legal expenses paid under a claim of "damages" from collage.

So, a question to consider is this: Should those who might be borrowed from have an absolute right to prevent all such free reuses of their properties, even when the reuse is obviously part of a new and unique work? Do we want to actually put all forms of unauthorized reuse under the heading of "theft," implicating a socially valuable art form such as collage with criminal intent—a form which may be making controversial social or cultural points and cannot operate true to its vision when, regardless of whether or not it can afford the price of authorization, *prior permission is required?*

FAIR USE FOR COLLAGE

We would like to see copyright law acknowledge the logical and inalienable right of artists, not publishers or manufacturers, to determine what new art will consist of. The current corporate control over our cultural output has an ominous feel to it because it has given culture over to fewer and fewer corporate committees of taste-molders and marketers who are driven only by image-making and an overriding need to maintain an ever-rising bottom line for their shareholders. Is the admittedly pivotal role which society places on commerce really so unassailably useful when it reaches to inhibit and channel the very direction of an art form like collage, allowing it to evolve this way, but not that way? Is the role of federal law to serve the demands of private income, or to promote the public good through free cultural expression? Both?

Then the crux of the collage debate we hope to raise is this: *Why can't we do both?* Why can't we maintain for artists all reasonable forms of fair and just compensation that directly result from the work they themselves produce, while at the same time not inhibiting, preventing, or criminalizing other perfectly healthy and valuable forms of music/art, such as collage, which arise naturally out of new, enabling technology and increase our total wealth of creativity as a culture? We believe the promotion of artistic freedom should, for the first time, find a balanced representation with the purely commercial and proprietary obsessions which now dominate the purposes of our copyright laws. The minor and isolated conflicts based on commercial interference that this may entail do not measure up to the conflict with public interest which doing nothing about it maintains.

TWO RELATIONSHIPS TO A CULTURAL PUBLIC DOMAIN

In the isolated medium of the Internet, and in the suggestion of fair use for collage, we are being guided by new technologies to reacquaint ourselves with cultural urges toward a rejuvenated public domain, right here in the twenty-first century. And since we are actually *forced* to accommodate these two persistent references to the boundaries of public domain in our midst (the Internet and collage), we may begin to seriously consider what value, or lack thereof, a larger public domain might actually entail in practice. Not having a choice gives us the opportunity of finding unnoticed values that an easy and habitual dismissal never considers. The billions in private income reserved for private interests under copyright controls, or the withholding and denying of all reuses of culture in lieu of payment and permission, may not be the best rules in sight for mass enlightenment. And if an improvement in mass enlightenment is our goal, the "value" of totally privatized intellectual property may not actually outweigh the cultural value of enlarging *all* our brains in a more intellectually unconstricted environment, not to mention the enlargement of our enthusiasm for, and participation in, our own culture which will result from a broadened concept of public domain.

For years, copyright has been a nagging restraint on all forms of popular reuse concepts. We now welcome a brand new medium, the Internet, to the debate. It is an interesting new player because it significantly widens the formerly narrow and specialized artistic desire to recycle found material to the whole general public's desire to recycle anything for any reason. The Internet tends to give every user who enters it an artist's perspective on the contents there—the suggestion to copy, to edit, to cut and paste, to appropriate, to reform, to redistribute. The degree to which *the public's* ability to follow their own sense of free expression in this new, wide-open, digital no man's land might surprise us and is yet to be determined. In the broadest sense, it remains a struggle between the rights of commerce and the rights of personal creativity. The degree to which these mutually opposed interests find a reasonable balance of productive co-existence in this new domain will say much about what it is we value most as a culture.

Both the status of music on the Internet and the status of collage in music are primary signposts of how the ever latent urge to receive, perceive, use, and reuse the world around us as a *public* domain remains a vital issue for living in the twenty-first century. For most of human history, cultural creation was always intended to be a shared phenomenon, an activity attached to spiritual sustenance and spiritual confirmation between the maker and their community. Only recent human history has found it advisable to withhold virtually all such creative activity until it can be paid for. That old selflessness that infuses the human urge to communicate through art may no longer be so practical in a world in which making art has become more and more expensive, and so much of the potential subject matter for art's ancient habit of free appropriation has been legally declared off-limits. But suddenly, the Internet offers an isolated "look and feel" that rekindles the rather ancient and generous purpose behind all cultural experience—a glimpse of no fences, possibly existing for the sake of mutual connectedness, community relevance, and "free" enlightenment. Possibly, like art, existing for its own sake and no other.

"FAIREST OF THEM ALL" AND OTHER FAIRY TALES OF FAIR USE

DAVID NIMMER*

I
INTRODUCTION

Once upon a time, in a happy land, courts decided which usage constituted fair use in copyright cases, and justice prevailed throughout the realm. Then the Royal Council ("Congress") imported something from beyond the sea called "codification." Henceforward, the Council proclaimed, the law-books would spell out if usage were fair or unfair in four pellucid factors.[1] The Wisest Men of the Kingdom ("Supreme Court") declared that the result in any given case would depend on all four of the factors.[2] The Copyright Specialists ("Second Circuit") added, "[b]ecause this is not a mechanical determination, a party need not 'shut-out' her opponent on the four factor tally to prevail,"[3] to which Soothsayers embroidered that if nonetheless "she does so, victory on the fair use playing field is assured."[4] But these are only fairy tales.[5]

This article is also available at http://law.duke.edu/journals/66LCPNimmer.

* Visiting Professor, UCLA School of Law and Of Counsel, Irell & Manella LLP, Los Angeles, California.

This essay develops oral remarks delivered at the Duke Conference on the Public Domain. I thank Mark Lemley, Neil Netanel and Eugene Volokh for disagreeing with parts and Robert Kasunic for rejecting it *in toto*.

1. 17 U.S.C. § 107 (2000) embodies four factors, culled from cases decided under the Copyright Act of 1909, Pub. L. No. 60-349, 35 Stat. 1075 (repealed 1976). *See* 4 MELVILLE B. NIMMER & DAVID NIMMER, NIMMER ON COPYRIGHT § 13.05[A] (rel. no. 58, 2002).

2. As the Court noted:

> The task is not to be simplified with bright-line rules, for the statute, like the doctrine it recognizes, calls for case-by-case analysis. . . . Nor may the four statutory factors be treated in isolation, one from another. All are to be explored, and the results weighed together, in light of the purposes of copyright.

Campbell v. Acuff-Rose Music, Inc., 510 U.S. 569, 577-78 (1994).

3. Wright v. Warner Books, Inc., 953 F.2d 731, 740 (2d Cir. 1991).

4. Arica Inst., Inc. v. Palmer, 970 F.2d 1067, 1079 (2d Cir. 1992).

5. Apropos of which I must add that the Seventh Circuit long ago recognized protection for research undertaken in the tales of Hans Christian Andersen based upon original Danish sources. *See* Toksvig v. Bruce Publ'g Co., 181 F.2d 664 (7th Cir. 1950). But the Supreme Court later sang "the swan song for *Toksvig*, a case that has been long derided in any event as a judicial ugly duckling." 1 NIMMER, *supra* note 1, § 2.11[E].

II

FLOSSING AND TRANSUBSTANTIATION

David Lange's foundation paper contains language that usefully serves as the launching pad for my own analysis:

> In short, appropriation flourishes. The copyright industries concede privately that it cannot be eliminated in individual cases unless a massive effort at brainwashing should persuade an entire generation of primary school children to accept the main tenets of copyright into their personal belief systems and then to hold them there and act upon them, along with such other items of prescribed doctrine as flossing and transubstantiation.[6]

The final language struck responsive chords for me, given recent copyright cases I have handled in the domains, respectively, of *flossing* and *transubstantiation*.

A few years back, I participated in a case before the Court of Appeals for the Second Circuit, defending Colgate-Palmolive in a case that Procter & Gamble, the maker of Crest, brought against it.[7] When Colgate entered the very lucrative Chinese market, it aired a television commercial showing two eggs: one bathed in fluoride, the other not.[8] After sitting overnight, the egg removed from the fluoride is tapped, and found to be solid; the untreated egg, by contrast, cannot withstand a tap and breaks. So with your teeth, Colgate's ad demonstrated.

But Crest was not buying. In preparing for the case, I reviewed a series of toothpaste commercials going back to the 1960s. Crest had done an earlier ad for the Chilean market actualizing a similar fluoride experiment. I compared the two ads. The one did not look much like the other: one guy was wearing a serape, the other was eating with chopsticks; one commercial was narrated in Spanish, the other in Mandarin. But both did illustrate how putting an egg in fluoride protects it against decay, and why the viewer should go out and buy crate-loads of toothpaste immediately.

Procter & Gamble Co. v. Colgate-Palmolive Co. illustrates the idea–expression dichotomy in copyright law. Our client's brief argued extensively that such similarity as existed between Crest's and Colgate's advertisements lay in the unprotectable realm, and did not cross the threshold to becoming substantial similarity in expression. Our client ultimately prevailed in the Second Circuit, although on the alternative basis that Colgate independently created the particular commercial at issue, rather than copying it from Crest.[9]

The other case that comes to mind unfolded earlier this year: I litigated the copyright renewal status of *The Urantia Book*, a 2,000-plus-page occult book

---

6. David Lange & Jennifer Lange Anderson, Copyright, Fair Use and Transformative Critical Appropriation 130, 140 (presented at the Duke Conference on the Public Domain, Nov. 9, 2001) *available at* http://law.duke.edu/pd/papers/langeand.pdf.

7. Procter & Gamble Co. v. Colgate-Palmolive Co., 199 F.3d 74 (2d Cir. 1999).

8. A host of commercials were at issue in the case. Some actually used a cowrie shell instead of an egg.

9. *Colgate-Palmolive*, 199 F.3d at 78.

whose devotees believe it was authored, as the tome itself declares, in part by the Archangels of Nebadon, in part by the Corps of Superuniverse Functionaries, with interstitial amendments by the Thought Adjuster, and so on.[10] The Urantia Foundation registered the book as a composite work, a category of the Copyright Act that applies to something to which a great number of individuals contributed, such as an encyclopedia.[11] Both parties to the litigation believed *The Urantia Book* to be a composite work, because they accepted that it was written by the Archangels of the Nebadon, the Corps of Superuniverse Functionaries *et al.* But I argued to the Western District of Oklahoma that, as a secular court, its job was not to investigate the esoteric truth behind the book's revelations, but rather to look at the exoteric circumstances of its composition. Lo and behold, as it appeared in this sublunary realm, its manuscript appeared all in the handwriting of a single individual. Therefore, I concluded, *The Urantia Book* was not a composite work; ergo, it was not validly renewed. The jury found in favor of my client on that basis. The matter currently awaits resolution by the Tenth Circuit.

These cases illustrate the two poles of copyright. The *Colgate* case is one of *transubstantiation*; namely, the idea–expression dichotomy and substantial similarity. It poses the metaphysical inquiries of where an idea ends and expression begins, and how substantial an appropriation must be to infringe. The *Urantia* litigation, by contrast, concerns *flossing*; namely, how does one take the language of the Copyright Act defining "composite work" and break one's teeth on it in a concrete situation? Both problems loom large in the copyright realm.

Someone who wishes to operate a service called, let's say, My.MP3.com,[12] to which 10,000 songs will be uploaded, must actually be prepared to clear rights in 10,000 sound recordings, and separately in another 10,000 musical works,[13] for a subtotal of 20,000. And, of course, there's a reproduction right, a public distri-

10. Much previous litigation had arisen concerning the same work. *E.g.*, Urantia Found. v. Maaherra, 114 F.3d 955 (9th Cir. 1997); Urantia Found. v. Burton, 210 U.S.P.Q. 217 (W.D. Mich. 1980); Urantia Found. v. King, 194 U.S.P.Q. 171 (C.D. Cal. 1977). *See also infra* note 40. My own paean to the work is contained in David Nimmer, *Back from the Future: A Proleptic Review of the Digital Millennium Copyright Act*, 16 BERKELEY TECH. L.J. 855, 861 (2001) ("So why on Urantia did Congress need to add a specific exemption . . . ?").

11. *See* 17 U.S.C. § 304(a)(1)(B)(i) (2000).

12. Litigation targeting that service has been multiple. *E.g.*, Chambers v. Time Warner, Inc., 282 F.3d 147 (2d Cir. 2002); Teevee Toons, Inc. v. MP3.com, Inc., 134 F. Supp. 2d 546, 549 (S.D.N.Y. 2001); UMG Record'gs, Inc. v. MP3.Com, Inc., No. 00 Civ. 0472 (JSR), 2000 U.S. Dist. LEXIS 17907 (S.D.N.Y. Nov. 14, 2000); UMG Record'gs, Inc. v. MP3.Com, Inc., 109 F. Supp. 2d 223 (S.D.N.Y. 2000); UMG Record'gs, Inc. v. MP3.Com, Inc., 2000 Copr. L. Dec. ¶ 28,141 (S.D.N.Y. 2000); UMG Record'gs, Inc. v. MP3.Com, Inc., 92 F. Supp. 2d 349 (S.D.N.Y. 2000). In my estimation, the most noteworthy aspect of those multiple decisions has been their revolutionary decoupling of the magnitude of the statutory damages awards from actual damages caused or profits earned by infringement. *See* 4 MELVILLE B. NIMMER & DAVID NIMMER, NIMMER ON COPYRIGHT §14.04[E][1] (forthcoming 2003) [hereinafter NIMMER 2003].

13. *See* 17 U.S.C. § 106; 1 NIMMER, *supra* note 1, §§ 2.05, 2.10.

bution right, and a public performance right for each copyrighted work.[14] So now we're up to 60,000 potential claimants. But who's to say that only one claimant exists for each right? When jazz legend Billy Strayhorn took the "A" Train to the great hereafter, his estate was composed of one sister and eleven nieces and nephews.[15] Depending on an author's date of death relative to the births of children and grandchildren, it is easy to imagine five or ten heirs to a deceased author's estate. The count could thus reach 300,000 or 600,000 entities whose permission is needed. That's a lot of flossing! In all likelihood, it would not be possible to hire enough dentists and hygienists for the job. Nonetheless, at base, the problem is *mechanical*—if one could identify the numerous claimants and secure rights from each, the situation would be resolved.

III

FAIR USE

Other problems continue to bedevil even those who have done their homework completely. Copyright law is built on such transcendental distinctions as the idea–expression dichotomy, substantial similarity, and finally, fair use. What use is fair? Here, we enter a great divide: All three issues grew up as part of copyright doctrine through its common-law development, but in the Copyright Act of 1976, Congress attempted no categorization of either the idea–expression dichotomy or substantial similarity. As to the former, it simply defined "work[s] of authorship" to exclude "any idea, procedure, process, system, method of operation, concept, principle, or discovery,"[16] without defining those various terms.[17] As to the latter, the Act itself made no attempt to mark the threshold for when similarity becomes substantial, leaving the matter to its traditional domain of judicial explication.[18]

On the fair use front, Congress took a different tack: It synthesized prior case law developments into four statutory factors.[19] Moreover, alone among provisions of the 1976 Act, fair use has reached the Supreme Court on multiple occasions. There are now four majority opinions (and several dissents) explicating the four factors.[20] One could accordingly posit that, unique among copyright's transcendental issues, fair use has been worked through a *Summa Theologica*[21] or, if you will, Talmudic exposition followed by codification in a sort of

14. It should be noted that the public performance right for sound recordings is limited largely to interactive webcasting. *See* 2 NIMMER, *supra* note 1, § 8.22.

15. Music Sales Corp. v. Morris, 73 F. Supp. 2d 364, 366 n.2 (S.D.N.Y. 1999).

16. 17 U.S.C. § 102(b).

17. *See* 17 U.S.C. § 101 (defining numerous other terms).

18. *See* 4 NIMMER, *supra* note 1, § 13.03.

19. *See supra* note 1.

20. Campbell v. Acuff-Rose Music, Inc., 510 U.S. 569 (1994); Stewart v. Abend, 495 U.S. 207 (1990); Harper & Row, Publ'rs, Inc. v. Nation Enters., 471 U.S. 539 (1985); Sony Corp. v. Universal City Studios, Inc., 464 U.S. 417 (1984).

21. ST. THOMAS AQUINAS, SUMMA THEOLOGICA (Fathers of the English Dominican Province trans., Christian Classics, 1981) (1274). Leave it to one of the world's most original pens to conflate the SUMMA with GULLIVER'S TRAVELS. *See* Jorge Luis Borges, *A Weary Man's Utopia*, *in* COLLECTED

Mishneh Torah.[22] We should, therefore, expect fair use to have been demystified from transubstantiation to straightforward ingestion.[23]

How do the factors work out in practice? The literature reveals that judges,[24] treatise writers,[25] and other commentators[26] offer a host of different explanations for how fair use cases actually get decided, apart from the four factors. The present examination, by contrast, takes the factors at face value, seeking to test whether, as advertised, they determine the analysis.

The following chart summarizes fair use cases decided since issuance of the most recent decision of the Supreme Court quartet.[27] Each heading in the chart sets forth whether the factor in question favors fair use or cuts against it.[28] Thus, four Fairs represent the "fairest of them all," four Unfairs the weakest fair use

---

FICTIONS 461-62 (Andrew Hurley trans., 1998) ("[I]n any case, it is not the reading that matters, but the rereading.").

22. The great Maimonides took the entire corpus of the *Babylonian Talmud* (itself an elaborate explication of Biblical laws) and distilled it into fourteen volumes, called the *Mishneh Torah* ("repetition of the law") or *Yad Chazakah* ("strong hand" punning on the fact that the Hebrew word for *hand* signifies the numeral fourteen).

23. Before the 1976 Act, one could posit that confusion clouded the fair use issue. In fact, the only two times before 1976 that the Supreme Court had a 4-4 split in a copyright dispute were both fair use cases. *See* Williams & Wilkins Co. v. United States, 487 F.2d 1345 (Ct. Cl. 1973), *aff'd by an equally divided court*, 420 U.S. 376 (1975); Benny v. Loew's, Inc., 239 F.2d 532 (9th Cir. 1956), *aff'd by an equally divided court*, 356 U.S. 43 (1958).

24. Fair use may be unique among copyright doctrines in having inspired numerous Second Circuit judges to join battle on the issue not only in their judicial opinions, but also in the pages of the reviews. *See, e.g.*, Pierre N. Leval, *Commentary: Toward a Fair Use Standard*, 103 HARV. L. REV. 1105 (1990); Roger J. Miner, *Exploiting Stolen Text: Fair Use or Foul Play?*, 37 J. COPYRIGHT SOC'Y 1 (1989); Jon O. Newman, *Not the End of History: The Second Circuit Struggles with Fair Use*, 37 J. COPYRIGHT SOC'Y 12 (1989); James L. Oakes, *Copyrights and Copyremedies: Unfair Use and Injunctions*, 38 J. COPYRIGHT SOC'Y 63 (1990). As the Second Circuit itself notes about its members' scholarly contributions: "Some of these articles are highly critical of the state of the law with respect to the fair use doctrine and offer suggestions for improvement." New Era Publ'ns Int'l, ApS v. Carol Publ'g Group , 904 F.2d 152, 155 (2d Cir.), *cert. denied*, 498 U.S. 921 (1990). In that spirit, Second Circuit Judges Oakes, Leval, and Miner were among the witnesses to testify before Congress regarding an amendment to the fair use doctrine. *See* H.R. REP. NO. 102-836 (1992).

25. My own opinion is that the fourth factor is the most important. 4 NIMMER, *supra* note 1, § 13.05[A][4]. But "even if viewed as central, this factor cannot substitute for an evaluation of each of the four statutory factors." *Id.* at 13-182. To flesh out application of the fourth factor, my father proposed application of the "functional test" to determine if a given usage is fair. *See id.* § 13.05[B]. For the application of that test to the chart set forth below, see *infra* note 57.

26. *E.g.*, William W. Fisher III, *Reconstructing the Fair Use Doctrine*, 101 HARV. L. REV. 1661 (1988); Wendy Gordon, *Fair Use As Market Failure: A Structural and Economic Analysis of the* Betamax *Case and Its Predecessors*, 82 COLUM. L. REV. 1600, 1614-22 (1982); Alex Kozinski & Christopher Newman, *What's So Fair About Fair Use? The 1999 Donald C. Brace Memorial Lecture*, 46 J. COPYRIGHT SOC'Y 513 (1999); Karen Burke LeFevre, *The Tell-Tale "Heart": Determining "Fair" Use of Unpublished Texts*, 55 LAW & CONTEMP. PROBS. 153, 165 (Spring 1992); Lloyd L. Weinreb, *Fair's Fair: A Comment on the Fair Use Doctrine*, 103 HARV. L. REV. 1137 (1990).

27. The "quartet" is *Campbell*, *Stewart*, *Harper & Row*, and *Sony*. Given that *Campbell*, the most recent case, was handed down on March 7, 1994, the chart commences after that date.

28. It should be noted that Fair (or Unfair) for one of the four factors indicates that that particular factor inclines the result in that direction; by contrast, the final column in the chart tracks the court's actual conclusion as to whether the given utilization was Fair (or Unfair).

defense.[29] The column for the first fair use factor ("purpose and character of the use")[30] resuscitates[31] the label "Productive"[32] to indicate Fair when the defendant reworks the plaintiff's expression to create a new work of authorship,[33] itself capable of copyright protection,[34] and does not simply re-present the esthetics of plaintiff's work. The next column recognizes that "[t]he factor two analysis[35] provides additional protection to works that are unpublished or that are creative or fictional."[36] The next column addresses the third factor[37] by inquiring whether defendant reproduced essentially the entire copyrighted work.[38] Finally, the penultimate column addresses the fourth factor[39] by inquiring whether defendant's use deprived plaintiff of revenue that likely would have accrued absent the allegedly infringing conduct.

---

29. The situation is actually more complicated. *See infra* text accompanying note 61. Thus, the first factor alone could be isolated into four discrete subcategories, of which the above chart covers only one. *See* 4 NIMMER, *supra* note 1, § 13.05[A][1][a] – [d].

30. 17 U.S.C. § 107(1) (2000).

31. The current vogue is to use the label "transformative," deriving from Leval, *supra* note 24, at 1111. As the Supreme Court comments, citing Judge Leval quoting Justice Story, the "central purpose of this investigation [under the first fair use factor] is to see . . . whether the new work merely 'supersede[s] the objects' of the original creation (citation omitted), or instead adds something new, with a further purpose or different character, altering the first with new expression, meaning, or message; it asks, in other words, whether and to what extent the new work is 'transformative.'" Campbell v. Acuff-Rose Music, Inc., 510 U.S. at 579. I am avoiding that term here, as its application has proven less than uniform in the case law. *See* 4 NIMMER, *supra* note 1, § 13.05[A][1][b] ("Instead of such conclusory applications, one should perform the transformative inquiry on its own merits, bearing in mind that just because a given use qualifies as 'transformative' does not even mean that defendants prevail under the first factor, much less that they prevail altogether on the fair use defense.").

32. The Ninth Circuit used this standard in Universal City Studios, Inc. v. Sony Corp., 659 F.2d 963, 970 (9th Cir. 1981), *rev'd* 464 U.S. 417 (1984). Although the Supreme Court reversed, it conceded that the "distinction between 'productive' and 'unproductive' uses may be helpful in calibrating the balance, but it cannot be wholly determinative." 464 U.S. at 455 n.40. The dissent discerned productive use as a "common theme" facilitating "socially laudable purposes." *Id.* at 478-79 (Blackmun, J., dissenting). But it stopped short of declaring "that every productive use is a fair use." *Id.* at 808.

33. Another area of confusion concerns whether the defendant's usage qualifies as "productive" because the defendant produced a new work that itself transforms plaintiff's work, or alternatively reproduces plaintiff's work wholesale, albeit in the context of a greater whole that is itself copyrightable. For instance, in Case Nine treated below, a newspaper reproduced an allegedly racist allegory from a police monthly newsletter. Belmore v. City Pages, 880 F. Supp. 673, 675 (D. Minn. 1995). There is no question that defendant's newspaper, considered as a whole, is a new work of authorship. Yet, because it reproduced the allegory in its entirety, the usage is listed as non-productive.

34. For this purpose, I elide the further inquiry whether the defendant's incorporation of material from plaintiff without authorization would itself deprive defendant of copyright protection for its new creation. *See* 17 U.S.C. § 103(a) ("The subject matter of copyright . . . includes . . . derivative works, but protection for a work employing preexisting material in which copyright subsists does not extend to any part of the work in which such material has been used unlawfully.")

35. The statute simply refers to "the nature of the copyrighted work." 17 U.S.C. § 107(2).

36. Robinson v. Random House, Inc., 877 F. Supp. 830, 841 (S.D.N.Y. 1995).

37. 17 U.S.C. § 107(3) ("amount and substantiality of the portion used in relation to the copyrighted work as a whole").

38. Again raising case-specific questions, such as: Was the usage less than the plaintiff's registered work, but nonetheless the entirety of a work that is capable of living its own copyright life? The phrase, albeit arising in another context, is drawn from *Robert Stigwood Group Ltd. v. O'Reilly*, 530 F.2d 1096, 1105 (2d Cir. 1976), *cert. denied*, 429 U.S. 848 (1976).

39. 17 U.S.C. § 107(4) ("effect of the use upon the potential market for or value of the copyrighted work").

CASE			FACTORS				CONCLUSION
	CITATION	PRÉCIS	1. PRODUCTIVE	2. PUBLISHED AND FACTUAL	3. WHOLESALE	4. CAUSING LOSS OF REVENUE	FAIR USE
1.	American Geophys. Union v. Texaco Inc., 60 F.3d 913 (2d Cir. 1994)	Copying articles for research library of corporation	UNFAIR	FAIR	UNFAIR	UNFAIR	UNFAIR
2.	Marshall & Swift v. BS&A Software, 871 F. Supp. 952 (W.D. Mich. 1994)	Copying tables from *Michigan Assessor's Manual*	FAIR	FAIR	UNFAIR	FAIR	UNFAIR
3.	Sega Enters. Ltd. v. Maphia, 857 F. Supp. 679 (N.D. Cal. 1994); *modified*, 948 F. Supp. 923 (N.D. Cal. 1996)	Copying of video games to BBS to facilitate piracy	UNFAIR	UNFAIR	UNFAIR	UNFAIR	UNFAIR
4.	Robinson v. Random House, Inc., 877 F. Supp. 830 (S.D.N.Y. 1995)	Copying of material into rival book about Pan Am Airways	FAIR	FAIR	FAIR	FAIR	UNFAIR
5.	Metro-Goldwyn-Mayer, Inc. v. American Honda Motor Co., 900 F. Supp. 1287 (C.D. Cal. 1995)	Copying of elements of James Bond into fanciful car commercial	FAIR	UNFAIR	FAIR	FAIR	UNFAIR
6.	Religious Tech. Ctr. v. Netcom On-Line Commun. Servs., Inc., 923 F. Supp. 1231 (N.D. Cal. 1995)	Copying of L. Ron Hubbard writings to criticize him	UNFAIR	UNFAIR	UNFAIR	UNFAIR	UNFAIR
7.	Religious Tech. Ctr. v. Lerma, 908 F. Supp. 1362 (E.D. Va. 1995)	Copying of L. Ron Hubbard writings in *Washington Post*	FAIR	UNFAIR	FAIR	UNFAIR	FAIR
8.	Religious Tech. Ctr. v. F.A.C.T.NET, Inc., 901 F. Supp. 1519 (D. Colo. 1995)	Copying of L. Ron Hubbard writings in web postings about scientology	FAIR	UNFAIR	FAIR	UNFAIR	FAIR
9.	Belmore v. City Pages, Inc., 880 F. Supp. 673 (D. Minn. 1995)	Copying of "fable" from police newsletter to demonstrate racism	UNFAIR	UNFAIR	UNFAIR	FAIR	FAIR

CASE			FACTORS				CONCLUSION
	CITATION	PRÉCIS	1. PRODUCTIVE	2. PUBLISHED AND FACTUAL	3. WHOLESALE	4. CAUSING LOSS OF REVENUE	FAIR USE
10.	College Entrance Exam. Bd. v. Pataki, 889 F. Supp. 554 (N.D.N.Y. 1995)	Copying of standardized test pursuant to state law to foster openness	UNFAIR	UNFAIR	UNFAIR	FAIR	UNFAIR
11.	Compaq Computer Corp. v. Procom Tech., Inc., 908 F. Supp. 1409 (S.D. Tex. 1995)	Copying of warning IDs used in computer hard drives	UNFAIR	FAIR	UNFAIR	FAIR	UNFAIR
12.	Triad Sys. Corp. v. Southeastern Express Co., 64 F.3d 1330 (9th Cir. 1995)	Copying by independent service organization of software necessary to service computer	UNFAIR	FAIR	UNFAIR	FAIR	UNFAIR
13.	Monster Communs., Inc. v. Turner Broad. Sys., Inc., 935 F. Supp. 490 (S.D.N.Y. 1996)	Copying of footage about Muhammed Ali into documentary *When We Were Kings*	FAIR	UNFAIR	FAIR	FAIR	FAIR
14.	Princeton Univ. Press v. Michigan Doc. Servs., Inc., 99 F.3d 1381 (6th Cir. 1996)	Copying of "course packs" for college courses	UNFAIR	UNFAIR	UNFAIR	UNFAIR	UNFAIR
15.	Lamb v. Starks, 949 F. Supp. 753 (N.D. Cal. 1996)	Copying of "trailer" of motion picture in order to demonstrate defendant's "3-D" technology	UNFAIR	UNFAIR	UNFAIR	FAIR	UNFAIR
16.	Ringgold v. Black Entm't Telev., Inc., 126 F.3d 70 (2d Cir. 1997)	Showing *Church Picnic Story Quilt* in *ROC* TV show	FAIR	UNFAIR	UNFAIR	FAIR	UNFAIR

CASE			FACTORS				CONCLUSION
	CITATION	**PRÉCIS**	**1. PRODUCTIVE**	**2. PUBLISHED AND FACTUAL**	**3. WHOLESALE**	**4. CAUSING LOSS OF REVENUE**	**FAIR USE**
17.	Jackson v. Warner Bros., Inc., 993 F. Supp. 585 (E.D. Mich. 1997)	Showing plaintiff's lithographs of African ceremonies in *Made in America* film; when two characters kiss, they knock the lithographs sideways	FAIR	UNFAIR	UNFAIR	FAIR	FAIR
18.	Sandoval v. New Line Cinema Corp., 973 F. Supp. 409 (S.D.N.Y. 1997)	Fleeting and obscured use of photos in film *Seven*	FAIR	UNFAIR	UNFAIR	FAIR	FAIR
19.	Higgins v. Detroit Educ. Telev. Found., 4 F. Supp. 2d 701 (E.D. Mich. 1998)	Use of two barely discernable snippets of an instrumental portion of song as background music to public interest *Club Connect* episode "Stop the Fighting II"	FAIR	UNFAIR	FAIR	FAIR	FAIR
20.	Los Angeles News Serv. v. KCAL-TV Channel 9, 108 F.3d 1119 (9th Cir. 1997)	Unauthorized use of video in news program showing Reginald Denny beating	UNFAIR	FAIR	UNFAIR	UNFAIR	UNFAIR
21.	Dr. Seuss Enters., L.P. v. Penguin Books USA, Inc., 109 F.3d 1394 (9th Cir. 1997)	Reworking of Dr. Seuss anapestic tetrameter to retell O. J. Simpson double murder story	FAIR	UNFAIR	FAIR	FAIR	UNFAIR
22.	Kulik Photography v. Cochran, 975 F. Supp. 812 (E.D. Va. 1997)	Court TV broadcast photo that Johnnie Cochran had admitted into evidence at O. J. Simpson trial	UNFAIR	UNFAIR	UNFAIR	FAIR	FAIR
23.	Castle Rock Entm't v. Carol Publ'g Group, Inc., 150 F.3d 132 (2d Cir. 1998)	Publishing of quiz book called *The Seinfeld Aptitude Test*	FAIR	UNFAIR	FAIR	FAIR	UNFAIR

CASE			FACTORS				CONCLUSION
	CITATION	PRÉCIS	1. PRODUCTIVE	2. PUBLISHED AND FACTUAL	3. WHOLESALE	4. CAUSING LOSS OF REVENUE	FAIR USE
24.	Paramount Pictures Corp. v. Carol Publ'g Group, 11 F. Supp. 2d 329 (S.D.N.Y. 1998)	Publishing of fan book called *The Joy of Trek*	FAIR	UNFAIR	FAIR	FAIR	UNFAIR
25.	Toho Co. v. William Morrow & Co., 33 F. Supp. 2d 1206 (C.D. Cal. 1998)	Similar holding regarding *The Official Godzilla Compendium*	FAIR	UNFAIR	FAIR	FAIR	UNFAIR
26.	Duffy v. Penguin Books USA Inc., 4 F. Supp. 2d 268 (S.D.N.Y. 1998)	Intermediate photocopying of book setting forth "style and fashion for large sized women"	FAIR	UNFAIR	UNFAIR	FAIR	FAIR
27.	Infinity Broad. Corp. v. Kirkwood, 150 F.3d 104 (2d Cir. 1998)	Service allowing subscribers "to listen over the telephone to contemporaneous radio broadcasts in remote cities"	UNFAIR	UNFAIR	UNFAIR	FAIR	UNFAIR
28.	Lucent Info. Mgmt., Inc. v. Lucent Techs., Inc., 5 F. Supp. 2d 238 (D. Del. 1998)	Use of survey from trademark infringement case by adverse party	UNFAIR	UNFAIR	UNFAIR	FAIR	FAIR
29.	Columbia Pictures Indus., Inc. v. Miramax Films Corp., 11 F. Supp. 2d 1179 (C.D. Cal. 1998)	Poster for Michael Moore documentary showing him smirking in front of an oversized microphone, mocking famous *Men in Black* poster	FAIR	UNFAIR	FAIR	FAIR	UNFAIR
30.	Leibovitz v. Paramount Pictures Corp., 137 F.3d 109 (2d Cir. 1998)	Staging nude photo of pregnant Leslie Nielsen in place of Demi Moore, to advertise *Naked Gun*, a film "due this March"	FAIR	UNFAIR	UNFAIR	FAIR	FAIR

CASE			FACTORS				CONCLUSION
	CITATION	**PRÉCIS**	**1. PRODUCTIVE**	**2. PUBLISHED AND FACTUAL**	**3. WHOLESALE**	**4. CAUSING LOSS OF REVENUE**	**FAIR USE**
31.	Storm Impact, Inc. v. Software of the Month Club, 13 F. Supp. 2d 782 (N.D. Ill. 1998)	Distribution of free shareware outside licensed terms	UNFAIR	FAIR	UNFAIR	FAIR	UNFAIR
32.	Michaels v. Internet Entm't Group, Inc., 5 F. Supp. 2d 823 (C.D. Cal. 1998)	Unauthorized posting to Internet of a film depicting celebrities having sex	UNFAIR	UNFAIR	UNFAIR	FAIR	UNFAIR
33.	Sundeman v. Seajay Soc'y, Inc., 142 F.3d 194 (4th Cir. 1998)	Reproducing unpublished story by author of *The Yearling*	UNFAIR	UNFAIR	UNFAIR	FAIR	FAIR
34.	Richard Feiner & Co. v. H.R.I. Indus., Inc., 10 F. Supp. 2d 310 (S.D.N.Y. 1998)	Unauthorized use of colorized photo of Laurel & Hardy perched at the edge of a tall building to introduce *Hollywood Reporter*'s "Special Effects & Stunts" section	FAIR	FAIR	FAIR	FAIR	UNFAIR
35.	Nihon Keizai Shimbun, Inc. v. Comline Bus. Data, Inc., 166 F.3d 65 (2d Cir. 1999)	Selling abstracts of news articles	FAIR	FAIR	FAIR	UNFAIR	UNFAIR
36.	Lyons P'ship v. Giannoulas, 179 F.3d 384 (5th Cir. 1999)	Parody of Barney the dinosaur assaulted by The Famous Chicken at sporting event	FAIR	UNFAIR	FAIR	FAIR	FAIR
37.	DSC Communs. v. Pulse Communs., Inc., 170 F.3d 1354 (Fed. Cir. 1999)	Pulsecom created copies of software on its cards by using RBOCs' Litespan systems	FAIR	FAIR	FAIR	FAIR	UNFAIR

CASE			FACTORS				CONCLUSION
	CITATION	**PRÉCIS**	**1. PRODUCTIVE**	**2. PUBLISHED AND FACTUAL**	**3. WHOLESALE**	**4. CAUSING LOSS OF REVENUE**	**FAIR USE**
38.	Tiffany Design, Inc. v. Reno-Tahoe Specialty, Inc., 55 F. Supp. 2d 1113 (D. Nev. 1999)	Use of plaintiff's photo as starting point to produce digitally altered scene of Las Vegas strip	FAIR	FAIR	UNFAIR	FAIR	UNFAIR
39.	Ty, Inc. v. Publications Int'l, Ltd., 81 F. Supp. 2d 899 (N.D. Ill. 2000)	Book about Beanie Babies, replete with historical essay, doll-by-doll data, evaluation as to price, and recommendation as to purchase	FAIR	UNFAIR	UNFAIR	FAIR	UNFAIR
40.	Educational Testing Serv. v. Simon, 95 F. Supp. 2d 1081 (C.D. Cal. 1999)	Copying questions from standardized test for "Hot Questions" portion of test preparation course	FAIR	UNFAIR	FAIR	FAIR	UNFAIR
41.	Chicago Sch. Reform Bd. of Trs. v. Substance, Inc., 79 F. Supp. 2d 919 (N.D. Ill. 2000)	Newspaper stirs public debate about the educational value of standardized test by publishing substantial portions of it	FAIR	UNFAIR	UNFAIR	FAIR	UNFAIR
42.	Sony Computer Entm't Am., Inc. v. Bleem, LLC, 214 F.3d 1022 (9th Cir. 2000)	Reproduction of "screen shot" from Sony's copyrighted game to show superior resolution of defendant's hardware	FAIR	UNFAIR	FAIR	FAIR	FAIR
43.	Sony Computer Entm't, Inc. v. Connectix Corp., 203 F.3d 596 (9th Cir. 2000)	Reverse engineering of entire Sony PlayStation BIOS to achieve interoperability	FAIR	FAIR	UNFAIR	FAIR	FAIR

CASE			FACTORS				CONCLUSION
	CITATION	**PRÉCIS**	**1. PRODUCTIVE**	**2. PUBLISHED AND FACTUAL**	**3. WHOLESALE**	**4. CAUSING LOSS OF REVENUE**	**FAIR USE**
44.	Williams v. Columbia Broad. Sys., Inc., 57 F. Supp. 2d 961 (C.D. Cal. 1999)	Army cadets appropriated "Mr. Bill" to generate "spirit message" broadcast during Army/Navy game	FAIR	UNFAIR	UNFAIR	FAIR	FAIR
45.	Images Audio Visual Prods., Inc. v. Perini Bldg. Co., 91 F. Supp. 2d 1075 (E.D. Mich. 2000)	Party to construction arbitration introduced into evidence photographs that it commissioned but declined to pay for	UNFAIR	UNFAIR	UNFAIR	UNFAIR	UNFAIR
46.	Worldwide Church of God v. Philadelphia Church of God, Inc., 227 F.3d 1110 (9th Cir. 2000)	After reformed church withdrew *Mystery of the Ages* for theological error, breakaway church distributed it to traditional adherents	UNFAIR	UNFAIR	UNFAIR	FAIR	UNFAIR
47.	Núñez v. Caribbean Int'l News Corp., 235 F.3d 18 (1st Cir. 2000)	Newspaper published old fashion photograph depicting nude Joyce Giraud, after she was named "Miss Universe Puerto Rico"	UNFAIR	UNFAIR	UNFAIR	UNFAIR	FAIR
48.	National Ass'n of Gov't Employees/Int'l Bhd. of Police Officers v. BUCI Telev., Inc., 118 F. Supp. 2d 126 (D. Mass. 2000)	*Boston Globe* used excerpts of videotape to bolster its reportage that talk show host made veiled anti-Semitic comments	FAIR	FAIR	FAIR	FAIR	FAIR

CASE			FACTORS				CONCLUSION
	CITATION	PRÉCIS	1. PRODUCTIVE	2. PUBLISHED AND FACTUAL	3. WHOLESALE	4. CAUSING LOSS OF REVENUE	FAIR USE
49.	Davis v. The Gap, Inc., 246 F.3d 152 (2d Cir. 2001)	Advertisement for clothing store featuring model sporting plaintiff's eyeglass jewelry	FAIR	FAIR	UNFAIR	FAIR	UNFAIR
50.	UMG Recordings, Inc. v. MP3.Com, Inc., 92 F. Supp. 2d 349 (S.D.N.Y. 2000)	Company offered service "advertised as permitting subscribers to store, customize, and listen to the recordings contained on their CDs from any place where they have an internet connection."	UNFAIR	UNFAIR	UNFAIR	UNFAIR	UNFAIR
51.	Hofheinz v. AMC Prods., Inc., 147 F. Supp. 2d 127 (E.D.N.Y. 2001)	Clips from B movies used to create documentary about the impact the genre exerted on the public	FAIR	UNFAIR	FAIR	FAIR	FAIR
52.	Hofheinz v. A&E Television Networks, 146 F. Supp. 2d 442 (S.D.N.Y. 2001)	Brief snippets used of a famous actor's early film appearances in the context of a biography about his career	FAIR	UNFAIR	FAIR	FAIR	FAIR
53.	Byrne v. British Broad. Corp., 132 F. Supp. 2d 229 (S.D.N.Y. 2001)	Usage of music as background to BBC story about Irish terrorists	FAIR	UNFAIR	FAIR	FAIR	UNFAIR

CASE			FACTORS				CONCLUSION
	CITATION	PRÉCIS	1. PRODUCTIVE	2. PUBLISHED AND FACTUAL	3. WHOLESALE	4. CAUSING LOSS OF REVENUE	FAIR USE
54.	World Wrestling Fed'n Entm't, Inc. v. Bozell, 142 F. Supp. 2d 514 (S.D.N.Y. 2001)	After 14 year-old boy killed 6 year-old girl and jury rejected his “wrestling defense,” media watchdog engaged in fundraising efforts by copying portions of *SMACKDOWN!*	FAIR	UNFAIR	FAIR	FAIR	UNFAIR
55.	Fleming v. Miles, 181 F. Supp. 2d 1143 (D. Or. 2001)	Use of image from artist's portfolio	UNFAIR	UNFAIR	UNFAIR	FAIR	FAIR
56.	A&M Records, Inc. v. Napster, Inc., 239 F.3d 1004 (9th Cir. 2001)	Internet search engine provided peer-to-peer access to MP3 files	UNFAIR	UNFAIR	UNFAIR	UNFAIR	UNFAIR
57.	SunTrust Bank v. Houghton Mifflin Co., 268 F.3d 1257 (11th Cir. 2001)	Alice Randall's *The Wind Done Gone* rectifies racist underpinnings of the largest seller of all time (except *The Bible*)	FAIR	UNFAIR	FAIR	FAIR	FAIR
58.	Greenberg v. National Geo. Soc'y, 244 F.3d 1267 (11th Cir. 2001)	Morphing image in sequence highlighting a century of photographs contributed to famous magazine	FAIR	FAIR	UNFAIR	UNFAIR	UNFAIR
59.	Lucasfilm Ltd. v. Media Mkt. Group, Ltd., 182 F. Supp. 2d 897 (N.D. Cal. 2002)	Pornographic animated version of *Star Wars* entitled *Starballz*	FAIR	UNFAIR	FAIR	FAIR	FAIR
60.	Kelly v. Arriba Soft Corp., 280 F.3d 934 (9th Cir. 2002)	Internet search engine reproduced photographs in thumbnail form	UNFAIR	UNFAIR	UNFAIR	UNFAIR	FAIR

First, the obligatory disclaimers. Every column in the chart is controversial,[40] even the first one setting forth the case citation, as some cases were otherwise disposed of on appeal[41] (and even the number to the left [1, 2, 3. . .], given that not every reported case is rigorously included in the chart). The last column is especially controversial, because some district court cases merely denied summary judgment rather than reaching a final conclusion on fair use,[42] and some appellate courts remanded for further factfinding rather than make a final pronouncement of fair or unfair.[43] Despite these difficulties, every cell in the grid is assigned an entry of Fair or Unfair, as objectively as I could determine.[44]

To illustrate the chart's composition, let us begin with Case One. In *American Geophysical Union v. Texaco Inc.*,[45] a scientist named Dr. Chickering made photocopies from the *Journal of Catalysis* to support experiments he performed in his Texaco lab.[46] Because he did not write a new article based on submissions to the *Journal*, but simply made wholesale copies, his exploitation was not productive. Factor One, therefore, receives an Unfair (by itself, inclining against fair use).[47] The subject articles that Dr. Chickering copied were both published in the *Journal of Catalysis* and of a factual rather than creative nature. Factor Two receives a Fair (by itself, inclining toward fair use). The subject photo-

---

40. As an example of the difficulty, consider Cases Six to Eight concerning the writings of L. Ron Hubbard. Is the copyrighted work at issue factual? If so, the answer to Factor Two will be Fair; if not, Unfair. To a Scientologist, the answer is yes, thus indicating Fair. One could take the prophet "at [his] word and assume that [his narrative] is an unalterable fact, the product of discovery and not creativity." Arica Inst., Inc. v. Palmer, 970 F.2d 1067, 1076 (2d Cir. 1992) (addressing Oscar Ichazo's "enneagram"). Or one could adopt the stance of another court confronting copyright claims over religious writings: "If I were to declare *The Urantia Book* to be a divine revelation dictated by divine beings, I would be trampling upon someone's religious faith. If I declared the opposite, I would be trampling upon someone else's religious faith. I shall do neither." Urantia Found. v. Maaherra, 895 F. Supp. 1337, 1338 (D. Ariz. 1995). Neither of those dodges strikes me as tenable for current purposes. I have therefore called Hubbard's writings "creative." Although that label might offend devotees, it actually supports the Church of Scientology, as it helps to weigh the second factor against fair use.

41. *E.g.*, Richard Feiner & Co. v. H.R.I. Indus., Inc., 10 F. Supp. 2d 310 (S.D.N.Y. 1998), *vacated without opinion by* 182 F.3d 901 (2d Cir. 1999); Sandoval v. New Line Cinema Corp., 973 F. Supp. 409 (S.D.N.Y. 1997), *aff'd on other grounds* 147 F.3d 215 (2d Cir. 1998).

42. Even more equivocal is denying a preliminary injunction based on a failure to prove a likelihood of success at an initial stage of the proceedings, as occurred in *Lucasfilm Ltd. v. Media Market Group, Ltd.*, 182 F. Supp. 2d 897, 901 (N.D. Cal. 2002).

43. The Supreme Court did just that in *Campbell v. Acuff-Rose Music, Inc.*, 510 U.S. 569, 594 (1994).

44. Particularly vexing are cases that contain two separate fair use analyses, reaching a different alignment of factors and even a different bottom line. *See infra* note 75.

45. 60 F.3d 913 (2d Cir. 1994).

46. *Id.* at 915-16.

47. One constant lesson to be borne in mind is that every formulation in the fair use realm is capable of its own exegesis. Thus, one could define "productive" to mean "in service of a socially laudable function," in which case a Fair would go into the Factor One box. As indicated above, "productive" for current purposes means that the defendant reworked the plaintiff's expression to create a new work of authorship, itself capable of copyright protection. By that formulation, Dr. Chickering's usage fails. However, one could legitimately define the term otherwise, such that laboratory research potentially leading to a future publication, or creation of a plastic copy in case of chemical spills, deserves the label "productive."

copies were of whole articles, thereby earning an Unfair for Factor Three.[48] Finally, absent Dr. Chickering's copying activities, Texaco would have needed to enter more subscriptions to the *Journal of Catalysis* to have the desired articles in his laboratory, meaning there was actual damage to an established market.[49] Factor Four, therefore, also receives an Unfair. The court denied the fair use defense, so the final column is filled in with Unfair. In this case, three factors support the court's conclusion.

Case Two differs from Case One with respect to the entries for Factors One and Four. In *Marshall & Swift v. BS&A Software*,[50] defendant did not simply photocopy plaintiff's works; it took tables from the *Michigan Assessor's Manual* and produced its own computer Equalization Appraisal Program to automate the real estate assessment process.[51] Accordingly, the use was productive, and Factor One gets a Fair. In addition, although plaintiff claimed that it would have charged defendant $95,000 as a licensing fee to reproduce the copied materials, there is no indication from the case that an established market existed for those materials, or that plaintiff suffered actual damage in the process (that is, that defendant would have paid the fee absent the infringement, the way that Texaco presumably would have entered more subscriptions for the *Journal of Catalysis* absent photocopying in Case One). In light of the circumstances, I entered a Fair for Case Two as to Factor Four, cognizant that the situation is not altogether different from Case One, which attracted the opposite entry for this factor.[52] In this case, only one factor supports the court's conclusion.[53]

In nonscientific form,[54] this top-sixty chart attempts to determine if a mechanistic view of the four factors reveals the secret of how fair use cases get resolved. What does it reveal? I am not very adept at statistics, but I studied

48. Nonetheless, one could look at this issue differently, given that the subject photocopies did not reproduce whole issues of the *Journal of Catalysis*.

49. It has already been remarked that the columns in the chart are more limited than the actual fair use factors. In particular, Factor Four as defined in the statute is not limited to loss of revenue (the simplified form in the chart). Instead, it looks to the entire potential market for the copyrighted work. *See* 17 U.S.C. § 107(4) (2000).

50. 871 F. Supp. 952 (W.D. Mich. 1994).

51. *Id.* at 954-55.

52. Among many tough choices, Factor Four presented a disproportionate share. Consider Case Five. In *Metro-Goldwyn-Mayer, Inc. v. American Honda Motor Co.*, 900 F. Supp. 1287 (C.D. Cal. 1995), the owner of film rights to James Bond filed suit over a humorous commercial involving a suave spy, in the company of a beautiful woman, making his getaway from grotesque villains in a Honda. There is an established market for 007 movies, but it is difficult to imagine actual damage to it from a car commercial. In reality, plaintiff was apparently aggrieved because it had a product placement agreement with BMW, and the Honda commercial perhaps threatened actual damage to that relationship. *Id.* at 1301. But there was no indication that loss of revenue would result.

53. Based on a universe of only these two cases, one would conclude that the factors only have 50% reliability in predicting the ultimate resolution of the cases in which they arise. As will be seen, the aggregate tally is basically in accord with that initial estimate.

54. Not only does the chart as a whole fail to cover every reported decision since 1994, but of the cases selected, one could dispute just about every entry. Indeed, it would take little to convince me to substitute Fair for Unfair (or vice versa) in many instances. Whether my detractors will wish to champion the Mirror Chart (in which the polarity of each entry is reversed) remains to be seen.

the chart to discern correlations. Of the twenty-four cases upholding fair use, and the thirty-six cases denying its existence, the findings are as follows:

(1) The first factor corresponds to the conclusion of fair use fifty-five percent of the time;[55]

(2) The second factor corresponds to the conclusion of fair use forty-two percent of the time;

(3) The third factor corresponds to the conclusion of fair use fifty-seven percent of the time;[56]

(4) The fourth factor corresponds to the conclusion of fair use fifty percent of the time;[57]

(5) The cumulative correspondence for all four factors is slightly under fifty-one percent.[58]

Beyond elevating the first and third factors slightly, while denigrating the second, the numbers hardly tell a compelling story. The last figure is the most revealing. Basically, had Congress legislated a dartboard rather than the particular four fair use factors embodied in the Copyright Act, it appears that the upshot would be the same.

This conclusion is not to say that judges enter findings as to the four factors in support of their ultimate fair use determination only half the time. Perusal of fair use cases would reveal that the figure actually approaches ninety percent. In other words, judges who uphold fair use almost always find that three, if not four, of the factors incline in its favor; judges who deny the fair use defense almost always find that three, if not four, of the factors incline against it.[59] The difference between the chart's figure, showing virtually a dead heat, and the actual figure pushing ninety percent, stems from the malleability of the fair use factors.

---

55. Every time the final column indicates "Fair," there is a correspondence in the first column when it indicates "Fair." Every time the final column indicates "Unfair," there is a correspondence in the first column when it indicates "Unfair." Obviously, the test employed for the remaining factors is the same.

56. It is a chestnut that "generally, it may not constitute a fair use if the entire work is reproduced." Infinity Broad. Corp. v. Kirkwood, 150 F.3d 104, 109 (2d Cir 1998), quoting 4 NIMMER, *supra* note 1, § 13.05[A][3]. Yet the chart reveals that among the cases in which wholesale reproduction of the copyrighted work took place, thirty-six percent upheld the usage as fair. (In other words, even when the entry for Factor Three is Unfair, the case ultimately rules the utilization Fair in the chart's final entry thirty-six percent of the time.).

57. To test my own pet theory, I redid the chart pursuant to the functional test, by asking whether the defendant used the work for a different function not within the purview of the plaintiff's normal exploitation of the work. The result (again, as agonizing and subject to disagreement as every other attempt to fill in the chart) was to answer Fair for Cases 1, 5-10, 12, 15-18, 20, 22-27, 30, 33, 34, 36, 39-43, 47-49, 51, 52, 54, 55, and 59, and Unfair for all others. To my chagrin, that change resulted in a fifty-nine percent correspondence rate—an improvement, but hardly the silver bullet that I desired. But, as previously noted, even with the functional test, one must still analyze each of the four factors. *See supra* note 25.

58. In other words, of the 240 entries in the chart for Fair or Unfair under factors one through four, the match with the ultimate conclusion of Fair or Unfair worked out only 50.8 % of the time.

59. *See infra* text accompanying notes 63-65.

First, each column heading in the chart represents far less than the totality of the Copyright Act factor at issue.[60] It has already been noted that the first factor, for example, contains categories in addition to productive usage.[61] The third factor, to offer another example, investigates the "amount and substantiality of the portion used in relation to the copyrighted work as a whole," as compared to the chart's sole inquiry whether the usage is one hundred percent. A given utilization could be less than one hundred percent (meaning it would be listed as Fair in the chart) but still constitute substantially all of the copyrighted work quantitatively (inclining against fair use) or qualitatively (again inclining against fair use). Plenty of room exists, therefore, for courts to reach results not reflective of the reductionist approach of the chart.

Second, each factor contains wide room for subjective evaluation to come into play. In the third factor just encountered, for example, what is *qualitatively* substantial? In the first factor, what is a fair *purpose*? One could multiply the questions endlessly, without finding ready answers.

Third, even after each factor is tallied, Congress included no mechanism for weighing divergent results against each other and ultimately resolving whether any given usage is fair. What is to be done when two factors are pro and two con? When can one factor outweigh three? On those matters, the statute is mute. Courts must therefore proceed by the seat of their pants.

In the ultimate analysis, my review of the cases convinces me that the high correspondence in judicial opinions between the individual fair use factors and courts' ultimate disposition, as opposed to the absence of any meaningful correspondence in the chart, reflects an important insight into how judges actually resolve fair use cases: Courts tend first to make a judgment that the ultimate disposition is fair use or unfair use, and then align the four factors to fit that result as best they can.[62] At base, therefore, the four factors fail to drive the analysis, but rather serve as convenient pegs on which to hang antecedent conclusions.

The courts are not to blame for that state of affairs. Rather, by injecting such a high degree of subjectivity and imprecision into each factor and into their cumulative application, as canvassed above, Congress essentially foreordained that result in the 1976 Act. Thus, it is not surprising to discover, in a given case, that the district judge found each of the four factors favoring fair use, whereas the Court of Appeals, in reversing, concluded the very opposite as to each factor.[63] To quash the facile explanation that the district judge in such a case

60. The exception is Factor Two. Given that the chart combines both "published" and "factual," Factor Two actually represents a composite capturing most of the complexity of this prong of the analysis—it reflects a Fair entry only when both those subfactors favor fair use.

61. *See supra* note 29.

62. Alternatively, as courts work their way through the four factors, at some point they decide what the ultimate conclusion should be—which, in turn, molds the way that they reach resolution as to which direction each factor points.

63. *E.g.*, Fin. Info., Inc. v. Moody's Investors Serv., Inc., 751 F.2d 501 (2d Cir. 1984). That decision could be explained as straddling the Supreme Court's clarification in *Sony*. But such an excuse fails to

simply failed to understand copyright law as well as did the appellate panel of three, it suffices to note that the same phenomenon has unfolded at the Supreme Court level. In *Harper & Row, Publishers, Inc. v. Nation Enterprises*,[64] six justices analyzed each of the four factors as disfavoring fair use; three justices, in dissent, reached the opposite conclusion as to each factor.[65]

By now, we have come far enough to realize that, pious words notwithstanding, it is largely a fairy tale to conclude that the four factors determine resolution of concrete fair use cases.[66] What of the conclusion that "a party need not 'shut-out' her opponent on the four factor tally to prevail"?[67] It turns out to be a fairy tale, too. The clash of the nine justices themselves in *Harper & Row* demonstrates that jurists up to the Supreme Court level feel the need to align the factors unanimously in favor of the desired result, perceiving that any deviation could be a fatal chink in the armor.

But if there is a "shut-out," the common wisdom goes, "victory on the fair use playing field is assured."[68] Is at least that much true? The chart again belies it. One need proceed no further than Case Four before encountering unanimous Fair entries for the four factors—meaning that this case must be the "fairest of them all," yet the ultimate conclusion rejects fair use! Specifically, in *Robinson v. Random House, Inc.*,[69] the author of *American Saga: Juan Trippe and His Pan Am Empire* alleged copyright infringement via publication of *American Icarus: The Majestic Rise and Tragic Fall of Pan Am*. The latter book was a new work of authorship, and therefore productive (Factor One inclining toward fair use); the former book was both published and factual in nature (Factor Two inclining toward fair use); the latter book copied far less than the totality of the former (Factor Three inclining toward fair use); and the posture more closely matches Case Two (loss of imputed license fee that copyright owner claimed adverse party should have paid) than Case One (ready market in subscription already existed, which would have resulted in revenue had the infringing conduct not occurred). Therefore, I conclude that the former book did not cause a loss in revenue (Factor Four inclining toward fair use). In sum, all four factors of the chart show Fair, yet the court[70] determined Unfair. The situation is not an anomaly; Cases Thirty-Four and Thirty-Seven show the same

apply to the district court's finding three factors against fair use and one neutral in *New Era Publications International, ApS v. Carol Publishing Group*, 729 F. Supp. 992 (S.D.N.Y. 1990), followed by a reversal in which the Second Circuit concluded that each of the four factors inclined in favor of fair use. 904 F.2d 152 (2d Cir.), *cert. denied*, 498 U.S. 921 (1990).

64. 471 U.S. 539 (1985).

65. *See* 4 NIMMER, *supra* note 1, § 13.05[A][5].

66. *See* Campbell v. Acuff-Rose Music, Inc., 510 U.S. 569, 577-78 (1994).

67. Wright v. Warner Books, Inc., 953 F.2d 731, 740 (2d Cir. 1991).

68. Arica Inst., Inc. v. Palmer, 970 F.2d 1067, 1079 (2d Cir. 1992).

69. 877 F. Supp. 830 (S.D.N.Y. 1995).

70. Of course, the court bolstered its finding by aligning Factors One, Two, and Four against fair use. As previously noted, the chart does not track the analysis actually employed in fair use cases, as that exercise would show a 90% correspondence.

pattern.[71] This recurring equation of *Fair x 4 = Unfair* is a frightening confirmation of how deeply rooted the fairy tales have become.

What about the converse phenomenon? Case Sixty presents an exemplar. In *Kelly v. Arriba Soft Corp.*,[72] plaintiff Kelly complained that photographs on his web site had been made subject of thumbnail sketches on defendant's search engine. The engine simply presented the images as is, rather than molding them into new works of authorship, so no productive use was present (Factor One inclining against fair use); the photographs in question evinced creativity, unlike articles about catalysis or tables of Michigan property values (Factor Two inclining against fair use); the subject thumbnails reproduced the whole images (Factor Three inclining against fair use);[73] and plaintiff was at least able to present an argument that he had suffered damage to an established market (Factor Four inclining against fair use).[74] In this instance, all four entries in the chart show Unfair, yet both district court and Ninth Circuit determined Fair on fair use.[75] Again, the situation is not wholly anomalous, as Case Forty-Seven demonstrates.[76]

---

71. Another instance almost matching the same scenario is Case 53. In *Byrne v. British Broadcasting Corp.*, 132 F. Supp. 2d 229 (S.D.N.Y. 2001), the BBC used background music in a television segment on an FBI investigation of gun smuggling from Florida to Ireland. Its segment was a new work of authorship, and therefore productive; the plaintiff's song in issue was published, but not factual (therefore making Factor Two equivocal); the BBC's copying related only to a small segment, far less than the whole; and there would have been no payment for the song absent the BBC's infringing conduct. In sum, three and a half factors favored fair use, but the court denied it.

72. 280 F.3d 934 (9th Cir. 2002).

73. The salient fact about thumbnail reproductions is that they lose most digital information from the original. Therefore, from both a qualitative and quantitative perspective, much less than the whole is reproduced. Nonetheless, in filling out the chart, I put Unfair for Factor Three, inasmuch as the thumbnail sketch nominally reproduces the plaintiff's image wholesale.

74. The opinion below ventilates this aspect:

> Plaintiff argues the market for his various products has been harmed. Defendant's conduct created a possibility that some users might improperly copy and use Plaintiff's images from Defendant's site. Defendant's search engine also enabled users to "deep link" directly to the pages containing retrieved images, and thereby bypass the "front page" of the originating Web site. As a result, these users would be less likely to view all of the advertisements on the Web sites or view the Web site's entire promotional message.

Kelly v. Arriba Soft Corp., 77 F. Supp. 2d 1116, 1120-21 (C.D. Cal. 1999). One must lean very far in plaintiff's direction to accept his self-serving characterizations.

75. Actually, there were two fair use decisions in the case. The one I highlight in the chart concerns thumbnail images, which drew a long analysis from the Ninth Circuit. *See Kelly*, 280 F.3d at 940-44. Personally, I agree with that determination in favor of fair use. *See* 4 NIMMER 2003, *supra* note 12, §13.05[G]. But a separate part of the opinion treats, in more abbreviated form, defendant's claim of fair use for inline linking to full-size images. *See Kelly*, 280 F.3d at 947-48. As to that issue, the court rejected fair use, a conclusion in which I part company with the Ninth Circuit. *See* 3 NIMMER 2003, *supra* note 12, § 12B.01[A][2]. Instead of including two separate references in the chart for the same case, I encapsulated it into its primary ruling. (As of this writing, the Ninth Circuit has decided to entertain rehearing on the latter issue in *Kelly*, meaning that it still remains possible for the case's two fair use holdings to converge.)

76. In *Núñez v. Caribbean International News Corp.*, 235 F.3d 18 (1st Cir. 2000), the reproduction of a nude photograph of "Miss Universe Puerto Rico" was not productive, even though it appeared in the larger context of a newspaper, for the reason set forth in *supra* note 33. Although a photograph of the Las Vegas strip may be so pedestrian as to be essentially factual rather than imaginative (see Factor Two for Case Thirty-Eight, *Tiffany Design, Inc. v. Reno-Tahoe Specialty, Inc.*, 55 F. Supp. 2d 1113 (D. Nev. 1999)), I am presuming that the artistic decisions involved in posing Ms. Giraud nude made that

The "assured" victory when all factors incline a certain way turns out to be just another fairy tale.[77] Instead, fair use runs deeper than any mechanistic exercise can capture.[78] For that reason, it seems unlikely that anyone will develop a heuristic device for computer programs to calculate when fair use should apply—at least, at any time before machines become human.[79]

IV

THE POESIE ALBUM

It is time now to leave the cornucopia of cases in the chart, which collectively defy convenient categorization, and to focus on a single case, that might itself confound. Consider the image that a client recently brought to me, set forth on the facing page, which has never before been published.

On March 4, 1940, Nazi troops had already taken over Czechoslovakia and Poland. In Western Europe, relative calm still prevailed, albeit punctuated by infinite worry. A Jewish girl named Henny Scheerder hosted a birthday party in Amsterdam, to which she invited her friends. One was a young lady named Anne Frank. In her keepsake book (*poesie album*), Henny asked the assembled friends to each sign a page with personal memories. Young Anne affixed some stickers (presumably copyrighted by someone else, although that is not the focus here) to Henny's album, then she wrote *Beate Henny* ("Dear Henny") followed by (translating loosely from the Dutch): "It's of little worth what I can offer you—pluck roses on earth, and forget me not."

In her paper for this conference, Pamela Samuelson contrasts a grocery list, that she calls "detritus," against a "gem" like a Mozart symphony.[80] I submit

---

photograph closer to the creative side of the spectrum. In terms of loss of revenue (Factor Four), the standard used in the chart is whether defendant's usage deprived the plaintiff of revenue that likely would have accrued absent the allegedly infringing conduct. When the only allegation is that defendant's own utilization should have occasioned a royalty payment, there is no such damage (which is why Factor Four inclines toward Fair in such instances as Case Fifteen, *Lamb v. Starks*, 949 F. Supp. 753 (N.D. Cal. 1996); absent defendant's usage of the subject movie trailer to demonstrate its 3-D technology, no market for that usage would have likely arisen). In this case, by contrast, after Ms. Giraud was named "Miss Universe Puerto Rico," there could have been a market for old photographs of her, independent of defendant's exploitation, which could have been harmed by that exploitation. For that reason, Factor Four indicates Unfair.

77. One could also posit other explanations for the cases in the chart, such as: Usage in Litigation Is Always Fair (see Cases 22 and 28). But it is not always so (see Case 45). Another candidate might be: Usage for News Is Always Fair (see Cases 9, 22, 47, 48). Again, not always (see Cases 20, 35, 41, 53). What about: Capitalizing on Sex Is Always Unfair (see Case 32). Nope (see Cases 30, 47, 59). At the moment, Combating Prejudice in Plaintiff's Work Is Always Fair (see Cases 9, 48, 57) holds sway, with no contrary case. But one would have to be foolhardy in the extreme to guarantee victory on the fair use defense to a defendant in the next case in which it is combating prejudice in plaintiff's work.

78. Indeed, if one takes seriously the notion that the four factors are nonexclusive, meaning that non-enumerated factors may also be taken into account, then it must be so. *See* New Era Publ'ns Int'l, ApS v. Henry Holt and Co., 873 F.2d 576, 588 (2d Cir. 1989) (Oakes, C.J., concurring) ("I emphasize non-exclusive. . .").

79. *See* David Nimmer, *Brains and Other Paraphernalia of the Digital Age*, 10 HARV. J.L. & TECH. 1 (1996).

80. Paula Samuelson, *Mapping the Digital Public Domain: Threats and Opportunities*, 66 LAW & CONTEMP. PROBS. 147, 151 (Winter/Spring 2003). *See also* David Nimmer, *Copyright in the Dead Sea*

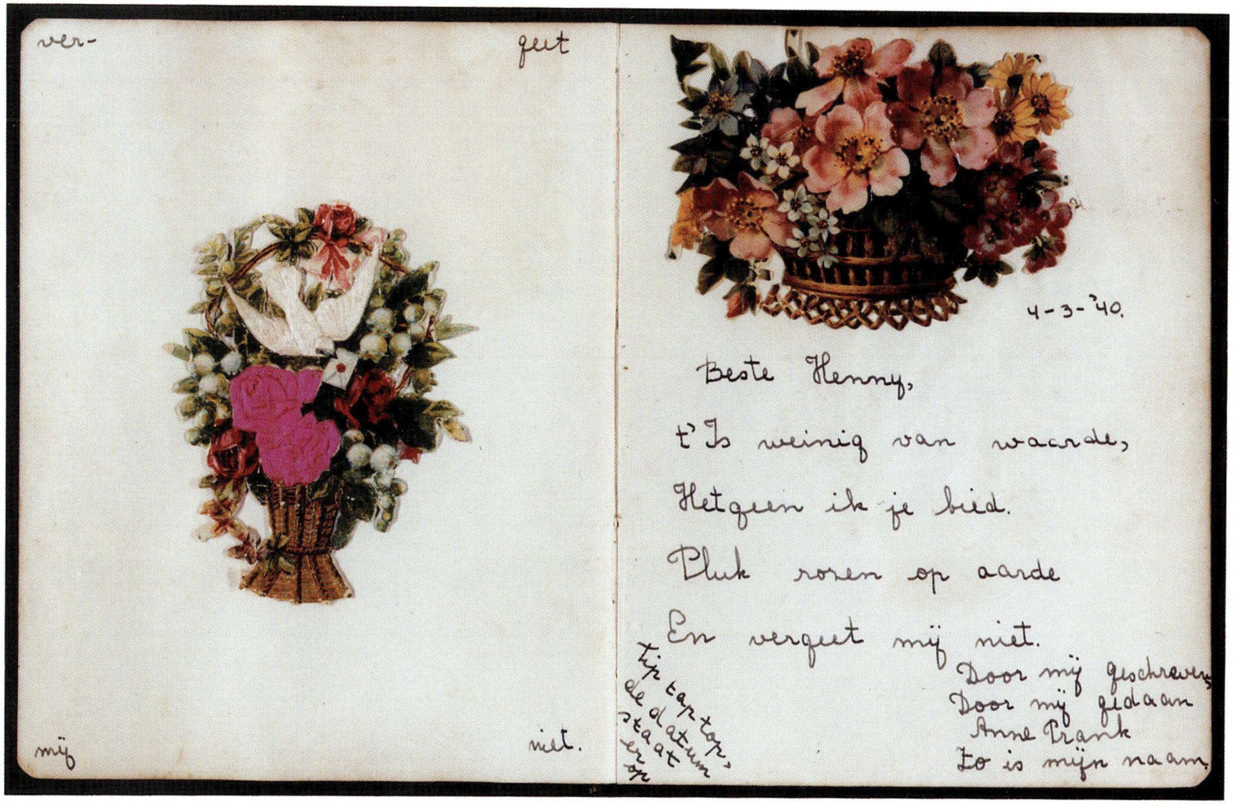

Photo courtesy the Simon Wiesenthal Center.

A poem written and signed by Anne Frank, in the *poesie album* of her classmate Henny Scheerder. Dated March 4, 1940.

that Anne Frank's words penned on March 4, 1940, challenge that dichotomy. Having left her parents that day amidst news from the east of the Nazi juggernaut (may their names be blotted out), Anne offered "nothing" but the advice to "pluck roses on earth, and forget me not." In my estimation, her short reflection offers much more than its "nothing" self-characterization—indeed, it is a little gem.

Henny survives to this day, thank G-d. Her *poesie album*, meanwhile, has come into the possession of The Simon Wiesenthal Center in Los Angeles, California, which came to me for *pro bono* copyright advice.[81] (The Center is getting full value for what it paid!) Although the Wiesenthal Center has no objection to my setting forth the image, it does not pretend to be the copyright owner. The claimant to that status is The Anne Frank Foundation in Basel, Switzerland, purportedly recipient of a grant from Anne Frank's sole survivor, her father.[82] The Foundation has not consented to the use of the work in any form.

What is the status of the exploitation planned by the Wiesenthal Center of selling postcards and posters of this image at its onsite gift shop? From the standpoint of the four fair use factors, one could posit at first blush that such a use poses an easy copyright case requiring denial of the defense. Running quickly through the four factors: the purpose of the use is fundraising and hence commercial; the nature of Anne's work is creative and unpublished; the amount to be copied is one hundred percent; and the potential market for the Swiss foundation to sell its own postcards and posters will be clobbered. Accordingly, all four factors disfavor the fair use defense.

One delightful aspect of David Lange's foundation paper[83] is its utter lack of concern for any precedent or decided case. Explicitly employing that methodology, let us run backwards through the four factors as they affect the subject page from the *poesie album.*

The fourth factor looks to the effect on the potential market. Justin Hughes, a colleague at UCLA, has developed an intriguing way of looking at the fair-use doctrine without giving undue deference to copyright owners whose terms Congress may repeatedly extend. He posits that courts should examine the effect on the market over time.[84] So, if *The Jazz Singer* from 1928 is at issue, any usage made in 2002 will leave the work unaffected from 1928-2001, and therefore can exert only a relatively limited effect on the copyright considered over its life as a whole. How does that logic apply here? Anne Frank's murder

---

Scrolls: Authorship and Originality, 38 HOUS. L. REV. 1, 41 n.155, 177 (2001) (considering copyright in laundry lists) [hereinafter Nimmer, *Dead Sea Scrolls*].

81. Since receiving the donation of the *poesie album*, the Wiesenthal Center has placed it on display at its Museum of Tolerance, located a few blocks from my home. A public display does not constitute publication. *See* 1 NIMMER, *supra* note 1, § 4.09.

82. Another potential claimant could be the Netherlands State Institute for War Documentation, recipient of all Anne Frank's papers. For simplicity, current analysis will focus on the Swiss foundation.

83. *See* Lange & Anderson, *supra* note 6.

84. Justin Hughes, *Fair Use Across Time*, 43 UCLA L. REV. (forthcoming 2003). I thank Justin for his many helpful suggestions incorporated herein.

in 1945[85] means that her work would have expired in 1995,[86] except its unpublished status gave it protection through at least December 31, 2002.[87] Congress' later extension of all terms, via the Sonny Bono Copyright Term Extension Act,[88] now protects this work through 2015.[89] No matter what my client does today, there will be no effect on the market for Anne Frank's page during at least the period from its inception in 1940 through 2003. Accordingly, the potential effect on the market (solely during its last twelve years of subsistence) is highly circumscribed, inclining Factor Four in favor of fair use.

Looked at from another perspective, The Anne Frank Foundation in Basel not only has never exploited this work, but does not even possess a single copy of it that it could exploit; the sole original is at the Wiesenthal Center. The Foundation thus has no potential market for the work which could be adversely affected. Again, Factor Four would favor fair use.[90]

Winding back to the third factor, what is the "amount and substantiality of the portion used in relation to the copyrighted work as a whole?"[91] I previously mentioned that the copying was one hundred percent (corresponding to the term "wholesale" in the chart above). But the statute does not refer to percentages; it refers to "amount." The amount of the copying in this case is precisely eighteen words (or sixteen, excluding the salutation, *Beate Henny*). That amount is minuscule. In the nonprecedential way that I am currently proceeding, this factor therefore inclines sharply in favor of fair use.

What about the second factor, looking to the nature of the work? Anne's few words were no more destined for publication than a grocery list.[92] They are, in that sense, no more dear to the copyright core than is a ransom note—something that is technically subject to copyright protection, but which was not written because of the incentive to promote the progress of science and the useful arts.[93] This factor could favor fair use as well.

---

85. Historians believe that Anne perished in the typhus epidemic at the Bergen-Belsen Concentration Camp in March 1945.

86. 17 U.S.C. § 302(a) (1976) (amended 1978).

87. 17 U.S.C. § 303(a) (1976) (amended 1978). Failure to publish the work by that date forfeited the option of extending its term until December 31, 2047. *Id.*

88. Pub. L. No. 105-298, 11 Stat. 2827 (1998).

89. *See* Yochai Benkler, *Through the Looking Glass: Alice and the Constitutional Foundations of the Public Domain*, 66 LAW & CONTEMP. PROBS. 173 (Winter/Spring 2003); Charlotte Hess & Elinor Ostrom, *Ideas, Artifacts, and Facilities: Information as a Common-Pool Resource*, 66 LAW & CONTEMP. PROBS. 111 (Winter/Spring 2003).

90. This conclusion is admittedly glib. After all, to the extent that the Center began selling postcards and posters, the Swiss Foundation would have access to something that it itself could exploit. Indeed, even if the Center only displayed the work, the Foundation could send someone to Los Angeles to view it and subsequently sketch it from memory. *See supra* note 81.

91. 17 U.S.C. § 107(3) (2000).

92. EDITOR'S NOTE: When this article was in proof prints, the Wiesenthal Center conveyed to Professor Nimmer information it had just learned about the *poesie album*, indicating that the poem might indeed have been intended for publication (and, what is more, was based on a poem authored by another). For ruminations about this latest twist, see David Lange, *Reimagining the Public Domain*, 66 LAW & CONTEMP. PROBS. 463, 482-83 (Winter/Spring 2003).

93. Leval, *supra* note 24, at 1108.

Finally, we return to the first factor. Considering the *nature* of the work, I cannot get past the fact that its author pleaded "forget me not." That request affects the *purpose* of the use, to which the first factor adverts. The Wiesenthal Center's exploitation is designed to preserve the memory of a most poignant victim of the Holocaust. To use copyright law as an instrument to suppress dissemination of her words runs afoul of both the author's purpose and the work's nature.[94] From the nonprecedential method just elaborated, the four factors unanimously favor a finding of fair use.

V

CONCLUSION

So which is it, fair use or unfair use? I firmly believe the Wiesenthal Center's potential exploitation of the *poesie album* to be fair. But the problem with the four factors is they are malleable enough to be crafted to fit either point of view.[95] Where does that leave us? The Supreme Court puts it pithily:

> Professor [Melville] Nimmer notes: Perhaps no more precise guide can be stated than Joseph McDonald's clever paraphrase of the Golden Rule: Take not from others to such an extent and in such a manner that you would be resentful if they so took from you. This equitable rule of reason permits courts to avoid rigid application of the copyright statute when, on occasion, it would stifle the very creativity which that law is designed to foster.[96]

Father knows best. Although that formulation scarcely resolves concrete cases, it provides the beginning of wisdom[97] by acknowledging that rigid application of set formulae may itself prove inexact. In the end, reliance on the four statutory factors to reach fair use decisions often seems naught but a fairy tale.

---

94. This case presents the inverse of the Dead Sea Scrolls case—there, the owner of the one physical artifact containing the historic words tried to use copyright law to keep the world out by avoiding publication; in the instant case, by contrast, the owner of that one artifact is trying to achieve wide-scale dissemination and faces a potential copyright claim in return. *See* Nimmer, *Dead Sea Scrolls*, *supra* note 80.

95. As to the Supreme Court's decisions in *Sony Corp. v. Universal City Studios, Inc.*, 464 U.S. 417, *Harper & Row, Publishers Inc. v. Nation Enterprises*, 471 U.S. 539, and *Campbell v. Acuff-Rose Music, Inc.*, 510 U.S. 569,

> The malleability of fair use emerges starkly from the fact that all three cases were overturned at each level of review, two of them by split opinions at the Supreme Court level.

4 NIMMER, *supra* note 1, § 13.05 (footnote omitted).

96. *Harper & Row*, 471 U.S. at 550 n.3(citations and quotations omitted).

97. *Cf. Proverbs* 1:7; *Psalms* 111:10.

***

BAYH-DOLE REFORM AND THE PROGRESS OF BIOMEDICINE

ARTI K. RAI* AND REBECCA S. EISENBERG**

I

INTRODUCTION

Advances in fundamental biomedical research play an important and growing role in the development of new therapeutic and diagnostic products. Although the development of pharmaceutical end products has long been a proprietary enterprise,[1] biomedical research comes from a very different tradition of open science. Within this tradition, longstanding norms call for relatively unfettered access to fundamental knowledge developed by prior researchers.[2] The tradition of open science has eroded considerably over the past quarter century as proprietary claims have reached farther upstream from end products to cover fundamental discoveries that provide the knowledge base for future product development.

One important reason for this change has been a narrowing of the conceptual gap between fundamental research and commercial application. Once largely a matter of serendipity or trial-and-error, drug discovery is now critically dependent on basic knowledge of genes, proteins, and associated biochemical pathways. The foreseeable practical payoffs of this fundamental research make it easier to obtain patents for discoveries that, in an earlier era, would have seemed too far removed from useful applications for patent protection. As these early-stage advances in human understanding have become patentable,

---

This article is also available at http://www.law.duke.edu/journals/66LCPRai.

* Assistant Professor, University of Pennsylvania Law School.

** Robert & Barbara Luciano Professor, University of Michigan Law School.

The authors would like to thank Rochelle Dreyfuss, Kristin Madison, and John Walsh for helpful comments. Earlier versions of this paper were presented at Duke University's Conference on the Public Domain and at the University of Pennsylvania Law School. The authors thank the participants of these symposia for their helpful comments.

1. Various empirical studies have underscored the critical role played by patents on end-stage pharmaceutical products. *See, e.g.*, Wesley Cohen et al., *Protecting Their Intellectual Assets: Appropriability Conditions and Why U.S. Manufacturing Firms Patent (or Not)*, NATIONAL BUREAU OF ECONOMIC RESEARCH, Working Paper No. 7552 (2000) (discussing the importance of patents relative to other mechanisms of appropriation across various industries and concluding that patents are particularly important in the pharmaceutical arena); Richard C. Levin et al., *Appropriating the Returns from Industrial Research and Development*, in 3 BROOKINGS PAPERS ON ECONOMICS ACTIVITY 783 (Martin N. Baily et al, eds., 1987).

2. Indeed, at a certain point in time, these norms may have even called for resisting proprietary claims on relatively downstream research. As discussed further below, however, this time has long past. *See infra* Part III.

new firms have emerged, raising capital to develop and market proprietary research that lies somewhere between traditional academic research and end-product drug development.

This upstream shift in patenting activity has met little resistance from the courts. In 1980, the Supreme Court held that genetically engineered microorganisms were eligible for patent protection, construing the language of the patent statute as permitting patents for "anything under the sun that is made by man."[3] Shortly thereafter, Congress created a specialized court to hear appeals in patent matters, the Court of Appeals for the Federal Circuit ("Federal Circuit").[4] The Federal Circuit has further extended the Supreme Court's expansive approach to patent eligibility[5] while relaxing the stringency of standards for patent protection, such as utility[6] and nonobviousness,[7] that might otherwise have prevented the patenting of incremental advances in upstream biomedical research. The Federal Circuit's generally supportive attitude towards patents has encouraged imaginative claiming strategies and unprecedented levels of patenting activity.

These changes in the economic structure of research and in the case law have been important factors in promoting intellectual property claims in fundamental research discoveries. Perhaps an even more significant factor, however, has been the explicit U.S. policy of allowing grantees to seek patent rights in government-sponsored research results. This policy, which was codified beginning in 1980 with passage of the Bayh-Dole Act,[8] and the Stevenson-Wydler Act,[9] has turned universities into major players in the biopharmaceutical patenting arena. The goal of these legislative initiatives was to promote widespread utilization of federally-sponsored inventions. The sponsors of the legislation believed that grantee ownership of patent rights, which would permit grantees to convey exclusive licenses to their inventions to private firms, was necessary to motivate private investors to pick up where government sponsors left off and transform new discoveries into commercial products.[10] But the leg-

---

3. Diamond v. Chakrabarty, 447 U.S. 303, 309 (1980) *quoting* SEN. REP. NO. 1979 (1952).

4. *See* Federal Courts Improvement Act of 1982, Pub. L. No. 97-164, 96 Stat. 25 (codified as amended at 28 U.S.C. §§ 41-49 (1982)).

5. *See, e.g.*, State St. Bank & Trust Co. v. Signature Fin. Group, Inc., 149 F.3d 1368 (Fed. Cir. 1998) (holding that the concrete transformation of data made a mathematical algorithm patentable).

6. *Compare* Brenner v. Manson, 383 U.S. 519, 534-5 (1966) (holding that a process patent may only be granted "where specific benefit exists in currently available form"), *with In re* Brana, 51 F.3d 1560, 1568 (Fed. Cir. 1995) (noting that "usefulness in patent law . . . in the context of pharmaceutical inventions, necessarily includes the expectation of future R&D").

7. *Compare* Graham v. John Deere Co., 383 U.S. 1 (1966) (holding that an inquiry into the obviousness of an invention is a prerequisite to patentability), *with In re* Deuel, 51 F.3d 1552, 1559 (Fed. Cir. 1995) ("A general incentive [to try] does not make obvious a particular result.").

8. Act of Dec. 12, 1980, Pub. L. No. 96-517, § 6(a), 94 Stat. 3015, 3019-28 (1980) (codified as amended at 35 U.S.C. §§ 200-212 (1994)).

9. Stevenson-Wydler Technology Innovation Act of 1980, Pub. L. No. 96-480, § 2, 94 Stat. 2311-2320 (1980) (codified as amended at 15 U.S.C. §§ 3701-3714 (2000)).

10. The Bayh-Dole Act states that its purpose is "to use the patent system to promote the *utilization* of inventions arising from federally funded research or development . . . ." 35 U.S.C. § 200 (emphasis added).

islation draws no distinction between downstream inventions that lead directly to commercial products and fundamental research discoveries that broadly enable further scientific investigation. Universities have taken the opportunity to file patent applications on basic research discoveries, such as new DNA sequences, protein structures, and disease pathways, that are primarily valuable as inputs into further research, thereby accelerating the encroachment of the patent system into what was formerly the domain of open science. Even when they do not seek patents, universities often seek to preserve their expectations for profitable payoffs by imposing restrictions on the dissemination of research materials and reagents that might generate commercial value in subsequent research.

This frenzy of proprietary claiming has coincided with unprecedented levels of both public and private investment in biopharmaceutical research and development and impressive scientific and technological accomplishments. Paradoxically, however, in the long run, it may hinder rather than accelerate biomedical research. Although intellectual property rights may sometimes be necessary to motivate private firms to develop and disseminate university-based discoveries, the trend towards assertions of intellectual property rights by universities might also impede the progress of science. The challenge lies in distinguishing discoveries that are better developed and disseminated through open access from discoveries that are better developed and disseminated under the protection of intellectual property rights. Under the Bayh-Dole Act, institutions that perform funded research enjoy largely unfettered discretion to determine when intellectual property rights are appropriate.[11] We argue, however, that it is the funding agencies that will often have a more appropriate combination of knowledge and incentives to make these determinations in furtherance of the overall public interest in research and product development. The Bayh-Dole Act should therefore be reformed to give funding agencies greater discretion to determine when to require that publicly-funded research discoveries be dedicated to the public domain.[12]

II

THE INCREASINGLY PROPRIETARY CHARACTER OF UNIVERSITY-BASED BIOMEDICAL RESEARCH

Even prior to passage of the Bayh-Dole Act of 1980, some agencies allowed universities to patent publicly-funded research discoveries.[13] In the late 1970s, when research advances in molecular biology began to offer the promise of

---

11. *See infra* notes 70-72 and accompanying text.

12. By "public domain" we mean an arena where the research is either available free of charge or at a nominal fee that covers the marginal cost of production.

13. *See* Rebecca S. Eisenberg, *Public Research and Private Development: Patents and Technology Transfer in Government-Sponsored Research*, 82 VA. L. REV. 1663, 1683 (1996). Of particular relevance to biomedical research, the Department of Health, Education and Welfare (now Health and Human Services) allowed academic institutions with established technology licensing offices to patent the results of their research. *Id.*

near-term commercial applications, grantees began to seek patents,[14] and in 1979 universities received 264 patents.[15] The patenting trend accelerated significantly, however, after the passage of the Bayh-Dole Act in 1980.[16] By 1997, the total number of patents issued annually to universities had increased to 2,436.[17] This almost ten-fold increase in university patenting was significantly greater than the two-fold increase in overall patenting during the same time period,[18] and substantially exceeded growth in university research spending.[19]

Biomedical research discoveries account for a major share of these university patents, particularly in terms of licensing revenues.[20] Moreover, the majority of this research is publicly funded: Despite the increasingly intimate involvement of industry with universities, industry actually funds only a small percentage of university-based research in the life sciences.[21] Many university-owned patents do not cover commercial end products, but rather fundamental research discoveries and research tools. For example, one recent study of Columbia University's patent portfolio indicates that more than 50% of its licensed patents represent research tools.[22]

A prominent recent example of a publicly-funded basic research discovery patented by a university is pluripotent primate embryonic stem cell lines. In the

---

14. *See* D.C. Mowery et al., *The Growth of Patenting and Licensing by U.S. Universities: An Assessment of the Effects of the Bayh-Dole Act of 1980*, 30 RES. POL'Y 99, 104 (2001).

15. *Id.*

16. *See* D.C. Mowery & A.A. Ziedonis, *Academic Patent Quality and Quantity Before and After the Bayh-Dole Act in the United States*, 31 RESEARCH POLICY 399, 414-15 (2002) (noting that the apparent decline in "importance and quality of post-1980 U.S. academic patents may have resulted from the Bayh-Dole Act's encouragement of entry into patenting by academic institutions with relatively little experience in this activity").

17. Mowery, *supra* note 14, at 104.

18. In 1979, a total of 48,854 utility patents were granted. By 1997, that number had increased to 111,983. *See* U.S. PATENT STATISTICS, CALENDAR YEARS, 1963-2000, *available at* http://www.uspto.gov/web/offices/ac/ido/oeip/taf/reports.htm#PSR.

19. Mowery et al., *supra* note 14, at 104.

20. *Id.* at 117 (noting that leading patents at the University of California, Stanford, and Columbia "are concentrated in the biomedical arena"); *see also* Annetine C. Geljins & Samuel O. Thier, *Medical Innovation and Institutional Interdependence: Rethinking University-Industry Connections*, 287 JAMA 72, 75 (2002) (observing that medical center at Columbia accounts for nearly 85% of all licensed inventions).

21. David Blumenthal et al., *Relationships Between Academic Institutions and Industry in the Life* Sciences–*An Industry Study*, 334 NEW ENG. J. MED. 368, 369 (1996) (stating that industry funds 11.7% of academic research in the life sciences and about 7% of university research in science as a whole). More generally, although overall spending on biomedical research by the private sector exceeds spending by the public sector, the public sector is still responsible for the majority of spending on basic research. According to one study, basic research represented only about 14% of all private sector pharmaceutical R&D in the 1990s. TRENDS IN FEDERAL SUPPORT OF RESEARCH AND GRADUATE EDUCATION 80 (Stephen A. Merrill, ed. 2001).

22. Geljins & Thier, *supra* note 20, at 74; *see also*, Jerry Thursby et al., Objectives, Characteristics, and Outcomes of University Licensing: A Survey of Major Universities (July 2000) (unpublished working paper, on file with authors) (concluding, based on a survey of 62 university technology transfer offices, that most licensed university technologies are "embryonic"). Some commentators define the term "research tool" more narrowly. *See, e.g.*, Michelle R. Henry et al., *DNA Patenting and Licensing* SCIENCE, August 23, 2002 at 1279 (differentiating between research tools and research targets). We use the term "research tool" broadly to include materials, data and methods that are employed in the research that leads to an end product.

1990s, the National Institute of Health ("NIH") sponsored research at the University of Wisconsin that succeeded in deriving embryonic stem cells from rhesus monkeys and macaques. The NIH-sponsored research on primates yielded a broad patent for the Wisconsin Alumni Research Foundation ("WARF"), the technology transfer arm of the University of Wisconsin. The patent covers all primate embryonic stem cell lines (which include, of course, human embryonic stem cell lines), and provides disclosure support for subsequently filed claims drawn more narrowly to human embryonic stem cell lines.[23]

Although NIH has a strong interest in ensuring widespread dissemination of broadly enabling research tools like stem cell lines for use across the broad spectrum of biomedical research, the Bayh-Dole Act seriously limits the extent to which NIH can oversee the use of intellectual property rights by its grantees. As long as the contractor is based in the United States, funding agencies such as NIH may restrict patenting only in "exceptional circumstances," when the agency determines that withholding title to the invention from the contractor will better promote the goals of the Act.[24] The statute provides an elaborate administrative procedure for challenging such determinations, with a right of appeal to the United States Claims Court.[25] The agency must also notify the Commerce Department, which has primary responsibility for administering the Bayh-Dole Act, each time it makes a determination of exceptional circumstances, and provide an analysis justifying the determination.[26] If the Secretary of Commerce determines that "any individual determination or pattern of determinations is contrary to the policies and objectives of [the Bayh-Dole Act]," the Secretary must advise the head of the agency and the Administrator of the Office of Federal Procurement Policy and recommend corrective

23. James A. Thomson, Primate Embryonic Stem Cells, U.S. Patent No. 5,843,780 (issued December 1, 1998). At the time of his original patent application, University of Wisconsin Professor James Thomson had worked with stem cells in rhesus monkeys and macaques only. Nonetheless, the patent broadly claims all primate embryonic stem cells. Several years later, when Thomson isolated human embryonic stem cells, the University of Wisconsin filed a subsidiary, or divisional, application specifically claiming the human stem cells. This divisional application was issued on March 13, 2001. James A. Thomson, Primate Embryonic Stem Cells, U.S. Patent No. 6,200,806. Because of a moratorium on federal funding for research on human embryonic stem cells, Thomson's research on human stem cells was funded not by the federal government but by Geron, a private biotechnology firm. *See* NATIONAL RESEARCH COUNCIL AND INSTITUTE OF MEDICINE, STEM CELL RESEARCH AND THE FUTURE OF REGENERATIVE MEDICINE 33 (2001). Geron agreed to provide funding in exchange for exclusive rights to six types of differentiated cells that could be derived from human stem cells. Wisconsin Alumni Research Foundation's Brief in Opposition to Geron Corporation's Fed. R. Civ. Pro. 12 (c) Motion for Judgment on the Pleadings, Wisconsin Alumni Research Foundation v. Geron, Case No. 01-C-0459-C at 2 (on file with author).

24. 35 U.S.C. § 202 (a)(i)-(ii) (2000).

25. 35 U.S.C. § 203(2); *see also* 35 U.S.C. § 202(b)(4) (providing for review of exceptional circumstances determinations under last paragraph of section 203(2)). The Commerce Department, to which Congress gave rulemaking authority under section 206 of the Bayh-Dole Act, has promulgated regulations which specify that administrative appeals must "afford the contractor the opportunity to appear with counsel, submit documentary evidence, present witnesses, and confront such persons as the agency may rely upon." 37 C.F.R. § 401.4(b)(3) (2001).

26. 35 U.S.C. § 202(b)(1).

actions.[27] Perhaps not surprisingly, NIH declarations of exceptional circumstances have been extremely rare.[28]

In addition to these cumbersome provisions for withholding grantee patent rights *ex ante* in the terms of funding agreements, the Bayh-Dole Act also permits agencies to exercise statutory "march-in rights"[29] *ex post* to compel licensing of university patents on inventions made in the course of previously funded research.[30] An agency can do so, however, only if it determines that the university (or its exclusive licensee) is not taking steps to achieve "practical application of the subject invention,"[31] or if such licensing is necessary "to alleviate public health or safety needs or requirements for public use specified by Federal regulations."[32] In contrast to the statute's more parsimonious approach toward *ex ante* restriction of patent rights in the terms of a grant, exercise of march-in rights is not subject to an overarching directive that it be "exceptional."[33] Nonetheless, the Bayh-Dole Act seriously limits the value of march-in rights as a mechanism for achieving prompt dissemination by deferring such rights from taking effect pending elaborate administrative proceedings and exhaustion of court appeals.[34] The administrative obstacles are sufficiently cumbersome that NIH has never exercised these rights.[35]

As universities have become more aggressive about claiming intellectual property rights, and as the conceptual gap between academic and industrial biomedical research has narrowed, commercial firms that might once have viewed academic researchers as benign, nonprofit benefactors of pre-market science have today come to view them instead as potential commercial rivals. An important consequence of this shift has been an increase in restrictions on the transfer of research tools, even those that are not patented. When universities supply research tools to private firms, they seek cash payments or reach-through royalties on sales of future products in return. Although cash payments are less common when private firms supply academic researchers with research tools, firms typically require the scientist and the university to sign a material

27. *Id.*

28. The single case of which we are aware involved a declaration of exceptional circumstances issued in connection with a small project on cDNA sequencing funded by the National Cancer Institute. *See* NCI Solicitation, Molecular Target Laboratories, *reprinted in* COM. BUS. DAILY, February 24, 2000, available at 2000 WL 8961813.

29. 35 U.S.C. § 203(1).

30. *Id.*

31. 35 U.S.C. § 203(1)(a), (b).

32. 35 U.S.C. § 203(1)(b)-(c).

33. 35 U.S.C. § 203.

34. 35 U.S.C. § 203(2).

35. Indeed, a 1998 General Accounting Office report on administration of the Bayh-Dole Act determined that "[a]ccording to Commerce officials, no agency has yet taken back the title to any inventions because they were not being commercialized." U.S. GENERAL ACCOUNTING OFFICE, GAO/RCED-98-06, TECHNOLOGY TRANSFER: ADMINISTRATION OF THE BAYH-DOLE BY RESEARCH UNIVERSITIES 2 (1998). *See, e.g.*, Barbara M. McGarey & Annette C. Levey, *Patents, Products and Public Health: An Analysis of the CellPro March-In Petition*, 14 BERKELEY TECH. L. J. 1095 (1999).

transfer agreement ("MTA") that may include grant-back provisions calling for an option to license patent rights to subsequent discoveries made through use of the tools.[36] MTAs from both private firms and universities also typically prohibit researchers from sharing these tools with other institutions and call for pre-publication review of research results.[37] Similar restrictions now appear in MTAs that govern purely academic exchanges of unpatented research tools *between* academic institutions. Institutional representatives balk at approving these agreements, which often leads to protracted negotiations, delays, and sometimes outright denial.[38]

III

PROPRIETARY BARRIERS TO BIOMEDICAL RESEARCH & DEVELOPMENT

For a number of reasons, these proprietary claims threaten to impede biomedical research. First, and most obviously, patents on upstream discoveries hinder subsequent research by permitting owners to charge a premium for the use of discoveries that might otherwise be more cheaply available in a competitive market or in the public domain. Protection from price competition inevitably excludes some users who would be willing to pay marginal cost, but not the higher prices that patents permit. This inherent feature of patents is particularly troubling for biomedical research, given the importance to scientific progress of work by researchers in nonprofit institutions with limited resources for paying patent premiums.

The standard retort to this argument—that without patents to permit pricing in excess of marginal cost, no one would be motivated to incur R&D expenses that were vulnerable to appropriation by free riders—is an empirical claim that is more plausible for discoveries that depend on private investment than for discoveries made with public funds. The more qualified argument for patents on government-sponsored research results—that without patents, these discoveries would languish in government and university archives, neglected by private firms as commercial non-starters—makes little sense for discoveries that can be

36. *See* Report of the NIH Working Group on Research Tools, at 4 (June 4, 1998), *at* http://www.nih.gov/news/researchtools/index.htm. One of the authors of this article (Eisenberg) chaired the Working Group that prepared this report.

37. *Id.* at 7-8.

38. Rebecca S. Eisenberg, *Bargaining Over the Transfer of Proprietary Research Tools: Is This Market Failing or Emerging?*, *in* EXPANDING THE BOUNDARIES OF INTELLECTUAL PROPERTY: INNOVATION POLICY FOR THE KNOWLEDGE SOCIETY 226 (Rochelle Dreyfuss et al. eds., 2001). A recent empirical study led by Eric Campbell indicates that 47% of geneticists who, in the preceding three years, had asked other faculty for additional data or materials regarding published research were denied such data or materials. *See* Eric G. Campbell et al., *Data Withholding in Academic Genetics: Data From a National Survey*, 287 JAMA 473, 478 (2002). This 47% figure represented a substantial increase over the 34% figure reported in a prior study conducted in the mid 1990s. The reasons cited by geneticists for denying data or materials included the need to honor the requirements of an industrial sponsor and the need to protect the commercial value of results. *Id.* at 478. The authors of the study also specifically note that academic scientists are most likely to encounter refusal when they seek access to biomaterials. The authors suggest that "it may be that material transfer agreements have become so complex and so demanding that they inhibit sharing." *Id.* at 479.

broadly disseminated right away without further private investment. Free dissemination of discoveries that are still far removed from end product development will enable follow-on research that is likely to yield additional patents on discoveries made further downstream, closer to a marketable end product. As discussed further below, these downstream patents are generally far more important in motivating private firms to develop end products than upstream patents on prior discoveries owned by a university.

Some commentators have also argued that patents rarely impose high costs on academic research because patent holders practice an informal regime of price discrimination in favor of nonprofit researchers, primarily by not enforcing their patents against such researchers for non-commercial uses.[39] But some patent holders have been more aggressive about insisting that university researchers sign license agreements,[40] especially when university researchers seek transfer of materials covered by a patent rather than simply practicing a patented invention inconspicuously in their own labs. Given that patent law offers no significant experimental use exemption from infringement liability,[41] and that the division between non-commercial and commercial research can be blurry, it may be foolhardy for nonprofit researchers to rely on the forbearance of patent holders.[42]

Upstream patents may also hinder subsequent research if they give a single entity monopoly control of basic research discoveries that enable subsequent investigation across a broad scientific territory. Because the principle constraint on the scope of patent claims is prior knowledge in the field of the invention, this concern is particularly acute for patents on early-stage discoveries that open up new research fields (such as the discovery of pluripotent embryonic stem cells), as distinguished from narrower technological applications that grow out of and build incrementally upon existing knowledge in an established field. Unconstrained by prior art, such patents may be quite broad, permitting their owners to control subsequent research across a significant range of problems. The standard response to this argument is that profit-seeking owners of pioneer patents will find it in their own best interest to disseminate path-breaking dis-

---

39. *See* John Walsh, et al., *The Patenting and Licensing of Research Tools and Biomedical Innovation*, May 5, 2002 draft at 35 (on file with authors).

40. One notable example is DuPont, a firm that has generated considerable controversy in the scientific press over the restrictive terms of its research tool licenses to academic researchers. One controversial license involved DuPont's patented cre-lox gene knockout technology. The controversy over the cre-lox technology was resolved only after NIH threatened to boycott the technology unless DuPont allowed broader use by academic licensees. *See* Memorandum of Understanding (July 1, 1998), *available at* http://ott.od.nih.gov/textonly/cre-lox.htm. More recently, DuPont has engendered controversy in the context of sub-licenses to use oncomouse technology, which DuPont controls as exclusive licensee under a patent owned by Harvard University. Eliot Marshall, *DuPont Ups Ante on Use of Harvard's OncoMouse*, SCIENCE, June 21, 2002 at 2112.

41. *See* Madey v. Duke University, 307 F.3d 1351 (Fed. Cir. 2002).

42. Reliance on forbearance may be particularly foolhardy given the availability of treble damages for willful infringement.

coveries to as many follow-on improvers as possible.[43] Unfortunately, this prediction is belied by historical examples in many industries, including the electrical lighting, radio, automobile, and aircraft industries. In these industries, holders of broad patents were unable or unwilling to grant licenses to potential competitors upon mutually agreeable terms.[44] The argument that broad upstream patents will promote coordinated licensing depends on unrealistic assumptions about the information, foresight, and goals of people who are bargaining with current or potential scientific and commercial rivals. Given imperfect information, disparate assessments of value, and the danger that pioneer patent holders will simply misappropriate the confidential research plans of follow-on researchers once they are disclosed in the course of negotiations, the transaction costs associated with such bargaining are likely to be quite high.[45]

Transaction costs mount quickly when the basic research discoveries necessary for subsequent work are owned not by one entity, but by a number of different entities.[46] Concern about an anticommons, or "patent thicket," is quite pressing in contemporary biomedical research that draws upon many prior discoveries made by different scientists in universities and private firms.[47] Exchanges of DNA sequences, laboratory animals, reagents, and data that were once subject to a normative expectation of free access are today subject to license agreements, material transfer agreements and database access agreements. These agreements need to be reviewed and renegotiated before research may proceed, imposing high transaction costs long before the research promises a likely revenue stream that would justify incurring these costs. A standard response to this concern—that market forces will motivate the emergence of patent pools and other institutions for bundling intellectual property rights, thereby reducing transaction costs and permitting the parties to realize

---

43. *See generally* Edmund Kitch, *The Nature and Function of the Patent System*, 20 J.L. & ECON. 265 (1977).

44. *See generally* Robert Merges & Richard Nelson, *On the Complex Economics of Patent Scope*, 90 COLUM. L. REV. 839, 885-91 (1990).

45. *See* Arti K. Rai, *Fostering Cumulative Innovation in the Biopharmaceutical Industry: The Role of Patents and Antitrust*, 16 BERKELEY TECH. L.J. 813, 833-34 (2001); Arti K. Rai, *Regulating Scientific Research: Intellectual Property Rights and the Norms of Science*, 94 NW. U. L. REV. 77, 125-129 (1999) (discussing difficulties in achieving licensing of upstream patents).

46. It bears mention that the problems of unduly broad patent scope and proliferation of patent rights held by multiple owners can occur simultaneously. An initial broad patent on a pioneering research discovery doesn't necessarily preclude a proliferation of upstream patents related to that discovery. To the contrary, follow-on improvers often seek and obtain patent rights within the scope of the claims of the initial broad patent. In these "blocking patents" situations, parties need to cross-license in order for further research to occur. For example, in the early years of the aircraft industry, the Wright Brothers held an initial broad patent on an aircraft stabilization system. Other companies were able, however, to secure blocking patents on improvements. Cross-licensing arrangements necessary for the production of aircraft could not be worked out until after the United States entered World War I. At that point, the Army and Navy intervened to impose cross-licensing. *See* JACOB A. VANDER MEULEN, THE POLITICS OF AIRCRAFT 19-26 (1991).

47. Eisenberg, *supra* note 38; Michael A. Heller & Rebecca S. Eisenberg, *Can Patents Deter Innovation? The Anticommons in Biomedical Research*, SCIENCE, May 1, 1998 at 698.

gains from exchange[48]—is an empirical claim that has not yet been borne out by the experience of the biomedical research community.[49] The public domain economizes on transaction costs by eliminating the need to find and bargain with patent owners, allowing research to proceed expeditiously and without the risk of bargaining breakdown.

Indeed, when stakeholders in the biopharmaceutical industry have seen the potential for an anticommons, they have reacted not by forming patent pools but, rather, by enhancing the public domain. The case of single nucleotide polymorphisms ("SNPs")[50] provides an interesting example of this strategy. Collections of SNPs occurring throughout the genome are a useful resource for scientists searching for genes involved in specific diseases.[51] SNPs also promise to be useful in developing diagnostic products to predict patient responses to drugs or other treatments.[52] In recent years, various biotechnology companies have identified and sought patents on large numbers of SNPs, provoking concern on the part of both NIH and the pharmaceutical industry about the potential for balkanization of intellectual property rights in this important resource. Paradoxically, in the Bayh-Dole era, the pharmaceutical industry has enjoyed more latitude than NIH to respond effectively to this threat by placing SNPs in the public domain. Pharmaceutical companies have joined together with the nonprofit Wellcome Trust, a U.K.-based, non-governmental partner in the public Human Genome Project that is not bound by the Bayh-Dole Act, in a consortium to sponsor a SNP-identification effort with explicit instructions to put the information in the public domain. The SNP Consortium has candidly avowed a goal of defeating patent claims to SNPs.[53] The willingness of private

48. *E.g.*, Robert P. Merges, *Contracting Into Liability Rules: Intellectual Property Rights and Collective Rights Organizations*, 84 CALIF. L. REV. 1293 (1996).

49. In a recent paper based on interviews with researchers and executives from 25 biopharmaceutical firms, as well as researchers and technology transfer officers from 6 universities, John Walsh, Ashish Arora, and Wesley Cohen argue that examples of projects actually being stopped because of anticommons difficulties are rare. John Walsh, Ashish Arora, & Wesley Cohen, *The Patenting of Research Tools and Biomedical Innovation*, draft at 15-16 (on file with author). They do note, however, that the presence of research tool patents can result in delay, costly negotiation, and even litigation. *Id.* at 31-35. The presence of these patents can also influence the choice of research project, *id.* at 21-22, particularly in cases where firms deny access to patents on biological targets. *Id.* at 28-31. Walsh and his co-authors also acknowledge that some anticommons problems have been alleviated not by traditional market responses but by shifts in the law that suggest a higher utility standard and narrower patent scope as well as by a variety of public and private efforts to enhance the public domain by thwarting the acquisition of upstream patent rights. *See id.* at 16, 46-48. Finally, the Walsh study indicates that some private firms are avoiding access difficulties by simply ignoring research tool patents and hoping that because of difficulties in detecting infringement, they won't be sued. *Id.* at 44-45. Although the study characterizes this firm behavior as a "working solution," one might question the long-term viability of a solution that is based on pervasive law-breaking that may yet trigger costly litigation when it comes to light.

50. SNPs are single base points within the genome at which the DNA sequence of individuals differs.

51. *See, e.g.*, Leslie Roberts, *SNP Mappers Confront Reality and Find it Daunting*, SCIENCE, March 17, 2000 at 1898.

52. For a discussion of SNP-based "precision" therapies, see Allen D. Roses, *Pharmacogenetics and the Practice of Medicine*, 405 NATURE 857 (2000).

53. *See* SNP Consortium website, http://snp.cshl.org/about/ (last visited Nov. 19, 2002).

firms in a patent-sensitive industry to spend money to enhance the public domain is powerful evidence of a perception that intellectual property rights in the research results could create significant barriers to subsequent research and product development.[54]

One set of responses to these problems might involve changing the patent laws to minimize the impact of patents on upstream research. One might, for example, reinvigorate the "products of nature" limitation on patent eligibility so as to exclude discoveries of DNA sequences, proteins, and biochemical mechanisms from patent protection, or to fortify the utility standard to limit the patenting of broadly enabling research tools. Another much-discussed idea is to provide an exemption from infringement liability for research, particularly non-commercial research.[55] Although such legal adjustments are worth considering, and some of them might be justified,[56] it is difficult to calibrate these changes accurately, and the consequences of overdoing it could be grave. Patents clearly matter in the biopharmaceutical industry, and undue restrictions on patent protection may deter valuable private investment. While it is possible that biopharmaceutical firms, particularly those that produce end products, would benefit in the long term from restrictions on the upstream patents that feed into drug development, many of these firms continue to insist that they need patents on their research in order to attract risk capital for further development.[57] Changes in the patent laws that exclude research tools from protection or exempt research activities from infringement liability could have a significant effect on the ability of these firms to raise funds for research. Given that overall private investment in biomedical R&D today exceeds public funding, the strong belief of private sector investors that patents are essential to their profit expectations urges caution in changing the underlying legal rules that support these investments.

54. The SNP consortium is not the only recent example of the private sector stepping forward to defend the public domain in the field of genomics. In the mid-1990s, the pharmaceutical company Merck sponsored an effort to put information about DNA fragments known as expressed sequence tags, or ESTs, into the public domain. More recently, Merck has sponsored a project to create 150 patent-free transgenic mice. Eliot Marshall, *A Deluge of Patents Creates Legal Hassles for Research*, SCIENCE, April 14, 2000, at 257. The private sector has also been collaborating with the NIH in sequencing the mouse genome and making this sequence publicly available. *Id.*

55. *See, e.g.*, Janice M. Mueller, *No "Dilettante Affair": Rethinking the Experimental Use Exception to Patent Infringement for Biomedical Research Tools*, 76 WASH. L. REV. 1 (2001); Maureen O'Rourke, Toward a Doctrine of *Fair Use in Patent Law*, 100 COLUM. L. REV. 1177 (2000); Genome Research and Diagnostic Accessibility Act of 2002, H.R. 3967, 107th Cong. 82.

56. We have begun to see some efforts in the direction of legal change. For example, the guidelines on utility issued by the PTO in 2001 exclude upstream research results from patent protection unless such research has a "specific, substantial, and credible" utility. *See* Utility Examination Guidelines, 66 Fed. Reg. 1092, 1098 (Jan. 5, 2001). In addition, various Federal Circuit decisions, and PTO guidelines implementing these decisions, indicate that the allowable scope of biotechnology claims may be relatively narrow. *See* Rai, *supra* note 45, at 840-41 (discussing decisions and PTO guidelines).

57. *See, e.g.*, John Golden, *Biotechnology, Technology Policy, and Patentability*, 50 EMORY L.J. 101, 167-72 (2001) (discussing widespread acceptance of the idea that small, capital-poor biotechnology companies need a patent portfolio to compete in the capital markets).

When research is publicly sponsored, however, the argument for strong patent rights loses much of its force. The Bayh-Dole Act does not presume that patents are necessary to motivate grantees to perform research with federal funds, but rather that patents will promote subsequent utilization and development of inventions arising from federally supported research. The reasoning that lurks behind this presumption is that patents and exclusive licenses are essential to attract the private investment necessary to develop preliminary research discoveries into commercial products. In other words, without the security of a monopoly right to protect against rent-dissipating competition, the private sector would not be interested in product development. Whatever the merits of this presumption for patents on downstream inventions such as new drugs, it makes little sense for patents on broadly enabling upstream research technologies that are ready for dissemination to researchers in both the public and private sectors and may be put to use in the laboratory without further investment in developing them as products. Such technologies represent a significant share of the patent portfolios assembled by universities under the Bayh-Dole Act.

A classic historical example of a federally-funded research technology for which exclusive rights were not necessary to achieve widespread dissemination and use is the Cohen-Boyer method for combining DNA from different organisms.[58] Many observers attribute the rapid progress of the biotechnology industry to the fact that this technology was made widely available rather than licensed exclusively to a single firm. Although this pre-Bayh-Dole technology was in fact patented, the patents were licensed nonexclusively and cheaply to encourage firms to take licenses rather than to challenge the patents. These nonexclusive licenses generated considerable revenue for the universities that owned the patents, but it is difficult to see how they did anything to enhance profitability or otherwise motivate subsequent research and product development as contemplated by the Bayh-Dole Act. If anything, the patent royalties imposed a modest tax on product development.[59] When a publicly-funded technology is licensed widely and nonexclusively the central, if not sole, function of the patent is to generate revenue for the patent owner. Although universities today may have great expectations of making money from their patent portfolios (even if these expectations have not, in most cases, thus far been fulfilled),[60] this interest played little role in the original justification for the Bayh-Dole

---

58. For a description and analysis of the licensing of the Cohen-Boyer patents, see NATIONAL RESEARCH COUNCIL, INTELLECTUAL PROPERTY RIGHTS AND RESEARCH TOOLS IN MOLECULAR BIOLOGY 40-42 (1997).

59. *Id.* at 41-42 (quoting Lita Nelsen, director of the Technology Licensing Office at the Massachusetts Institute of Technology).

60. A few schools have reaped much of the monetary gain. In 2000, the five top-grossing schools brought in $570 million from technology licensing. This represents about half of the $1.26 billion earned by all schools in that year. *See* 2000 Survey, Association of University Technology Managers (2000), *available at* http://www.autm.net/surveys/2000/summarynoe.pdf [hereinafter 2000 Survey] (last visited Jan. 22, 2003).

Act.[61] It is worth considering whether fundamental research tools that may be effectively disseminated and put to use through nonexclusive licensing should be patented at all, or whether the purposes of the Bayh-Dole Act would be better served by making them broadly available at minimal cost or in the public domain.

Of potentially greater concern, the Bayh-Dole Act does little to ensure that a university that patents such a broadly enabling technology will license the patent nonexclusively. To the contrary, Congress was careful in the terms of the Bayh-Dole Act and subsequent legislation to give universities discretion to grant exclusive licenses, consistent with its goal of using patents to motivate licensees to invest in further technology development by protecting them from competition.[62] But whether or not exclusive licensing is necessary to achieve this goal, it may be more financially attractive to universities than nonexclusive licensing. Exclusive licenses typically command higher royalties than nonexclusive licenses, and firms holding exclusive licenses are more willing to reimburse for patent costs and to provide additional grant funding to the inventor. Indeed, the available empirical data suggest that the majority of university licenses to small firms are exclusive.[63]

A prominent example of exclusive licensing on a broadly enabling research tool is the previously noted patent on primate embryonic stem cell lines held by the Wisconsin Alumni Research Foundation ("WARF").[64] Under an agreement that provided one million dollars of research support for subsequent work by the inventor, WARF granted a broad exclusive license for commercial use of six important cell types that could be derived from these cell lines to a single private firm, Geron.[65] Exclusive licenses on research tools with potentially broad applications threaten to throttle scientific progress by limiting the number of players in a developing field.

It is also unclear whether such exclusive licenses are necessary to further the Bayh-Dole Act's goal of promoting commercial product development. The farther removed university-based research discoveries are from end-product development, the more likely it is that subsequent research will generate additional patents that will be more important to the profit expectations of private investors than patents on the prior research. Indeed, patents on the many discoveries that enable product development are more likely to add to a product's costs than to enhance its profitability. Given that the long course of biophar-

61. Eisenberg, *supra* note 13, at 1698-1701.

62. Eisenberg, *supra* note 13, at 1698-99.

63. 2000 Survey, *supra* note 60 (indicating that 54% of licenses to small firms are exclusive, and 90% of licenses to startup firms are exclusive).

64. *See supra* note 23. As noted earlier, a divisional of the parent application specifically claims human embryonic stem cells.

65. As a consequence of media scrutiny, as well as pressure from NIH, WARF subsequently reversed its decision, sued Geron, and concluded an agreement to reduce the number of cell types to which Geron has an exclusive license from six to three. *See* Andrew Pollack, *University Resolves Dispute on Stem Cell Patent License*, N.Y.TIMES, Jan. 10, 2002, at C11.

maceutical product development typically generates a great many patented inventions on the road to market, Congress' fear that potential new products would never be developed if the early discoveries from which they sprang remained unpatented seems quaintly out of touch with contemporary R&D and patenting practices.

A recent example of a situation where patenting, and subsequent exclusive licensing, of a broadly enabling research discovery was not necessary for downstream development involves federally-funded research identifying a basic biochemical pathway known the NF-kB cell-signaling pathway. This research, which was done in the 1980s by scientists at Harvard, Massachusetts Institute of Technology ("MIT"), and the Whitehead Institute for Biomedical Research, led to a broad patent application claiming all drugs that worked by inhibiting NF-kb cell-signaling. Because the NF-kB pathway has been implicated in diseases ranging from cancer and osteoporosis to atherosclerosis and rheumatoid arthritis, the patent, which finally issued in 2002,[66] may cover drug treatments for all of these diseases. Indeed, the academic institutions, together with their exclusive licensee Ariad Pharmaceuticals, are now suing Eli Lilly & Co., claiming that Lilly's osteoporosis drug Evista and its sepsis drug Xigris work in a manner that infringes the NF-kB patent.[67] Ariad has also sent letters to some 50 other companies with products that work via the NF-kB pathway, asking them for royalties on present or future product sales. Obviously, the companies that are now being asked to pay royalties did not need an exclusive license from Harvard, MIT, and Whitehead to motivate them to pursue product development. The prospect of obtaining patents on their own end-product drugs was sufficient. In this case, as in many others, upstream patents issued to academic institutions serve as a tax on innovation, diluting rather than fortifying incentives for product development.[68]

For many discoveries emerging from government-sponsored research, the benefits of patenting are low relative to its costs. But some discoveries, including some important research tools and enabling technologies generated in the course of publicly-sponsored research, undoubtedly require substantial commercial investment for reliable mass-production and widespread distribution. For example, technologies and machines for DNA sequencing and analysis, initially developed in academic laboratories, have required substantial follow-on investment by private firms to turn them into reliable and commercially avail-

66. Nuclear Factors Associated With Transcriptional Regulation, Patent No. 6,410,516, issued June 25, 2002.

67. Sharon Begley & Laura Johannes, *Ariad Alleges Eli Lilly Drugs Infringe on Biomolecule Patent*, WALL ST. J., June 28, 2002, at C1.

68. Even patents on relatively downstream university-based research may be unnecessary for purposes of promoting follow-on R&D. For example, the University of Rochester's federally funded research on the cox-2 enzyme, which is responsible for the inflammation process, has yielded a patent that claims inhibitors of this enzyme. The university has filed patent infringement actions against pharmaceutical companies that make such lucrative cox-2 inhibitor products as Vioxx and Celebrex. These pharmaceutical companies clearly did not require an exclusive license from Rochester to motivate their investments in developing cox-2 inhibitors.

able laboratory equipment.[69] Patents and exclusive licenses may be crucial to motivate this sort of investment.

The policy challenge is to devise a system that distinguishes cases in which proprietary claims make sense from cases in which they do not. The complexity of biomedical research makes this a formidable task, and the public interest in getting these determinations right demands assigning this task to an appropriate decision-maker. Ideally, decisions about the dividing line between the public domain and private property should be made by institutions that are in a position to appreciate the tensions between widespread access and preservation of commercial incentives without being unduly swayed by institutional interests that diverge from the overall public interest. In the context of biomedical research, NIH may be the institution best suited for this task.

IV

THE ROLE OF NIH IN PRESERVING THE PUBLIC DOMAIN

Under the Bayh-Dole Act, determinations of what to patent are assigned in the first instance to the institution receiving federal research funds—typically a university in the case of NIH-sponsored biomedical research.[70] Universities, in turn, have delegated this task to technology transfer professionals who are charged with building patent portfolios that will bring in revenue to the university. If the university declines to pursue patent rights on a particular invention, the sponsoring agency may claim ownership.[71] If neither institution wants to patent the invention, the investigator may do so.[72] In other words, if anyone involved in the research—the grantee, the sponsor, or the investigator—thinks the invention is worth patenting, that party may prevail over anyone who believes the invention should be left in the public domain. As noted earlier, the research sponsor may vary these rules in the terms of a funding agreement only in "exceptional circumstances," and only by complying with burdensome procedural safeguards.

In 1980, these restrictions on the ability of research sponsors to depart from the pro-patent presumption of the Bayh-Dole Act doubtless seemed sensible

---

69. In the case of the major DNA sequencing technology, an automated sequencer that relies on optical scanning and four-color fluorescent technology, the California Institute of Technology owns the first major patent. This patent was exclusively licensed to, and developed for commercial use by, a private firm, Applied Biosystems. *See* NATIONAL RESEARCH COUNCIL, *supra* note 58, at 46-48.

70. In keeping with its original title—the University and Small Business Patent Procedures Act—the Bayh-Dole Act also gives small businesses the right to seek patents on the results of their federally funded research. Congress was quite taken by the "very impressive record in technological innovation" complied by small businesses, S. REP. NO. 96-480, at 1 (1979), but initially rejected proposed legislation, Science and Technology Research and Development Utilization Policy Act, S. 1215 96th Cong. (1979), that would have extended the same rights to large businesses. Large business interests were not defeated for long, however. In 1983, President Reagan extended the right to retain patent ownership to large businesses in a Memorandum, and Congress quietly endorsed this extension the next year in an inconspicuous housekeeping provision to a 1984 change in the law. Trademark Clarification Act of 1984, 15 U.S.C. § 1501 (2000); 35 U.S.C. § 210(c).

71. 35 U.S.C. § 202(c)(2).

72. 35 U.S.C. § 202(d).

enough. At that time, university patenting was the exception rather than the rule, the biotechnology industry was in its infancy, and government research sponsors, particularly NIH, had a reputation for being hostile to patents to a degree that impeded development of new products and collaborations between academic and commercial investigators.[73] The prevailing belief was that U.S. industry was missing opportunities to build upon a national advantage in university-based research because universities had no incentive to patent their discoveries and had to overcome strong bureaucratic resistance on the part of government sponsors to retain patent rights.[74] The story Congress heard was that universities cared only about scientific recognition and were indifferent to patents, that private industry needed exclusive rights under university-owned patents to make product development profitable, and that government funding agencies had to be restrained from indulging their anti-patent reflexes so that universities and private industry could join forces to develop new technologies for the benefit of the U.S. economy.

Two decades later, much has changed. NIH and universities have become active patent claimants and collaborate with private industry across the spectrum of biomedical research.[75] Universities are no longer indifferent to patents, but are eager to patent their discoveries in the hope of sharing in the bounty of future blockbuster products.[76] Public research sponsors, such as NIH, have taken to heart their mandate to promote commercial product development as well as scientific progress.[77] Product-developing firms lament patents on publicly sponsored discoveries as rent-diverting siphons as readily as they welcome them as rent-preserving protection from competition in potential product markets. Indeed, in the context of genome-related projects, the patent-sensitive pharmaceutical industry has repeatedly joined with NIH in calling for the dedication of new knowledge to the public domain.[78]

In this changed environment, the decision of Congress to divest funding agencies of any significant discretion to restrict patenting makes much less sense than it did in 1980. Indeed, because of the breadth of their missions and because of their dual roles as both patent owners who use their own patents to promote dissemination and development of new technologies and research sponsors who ultimately pay the costs that patents impose upon future research, public research sponsors are well-positioned to take into account the impact of

---

73. Eisenberg, *supra* note 13, at 1692. In addition to NIH, the Department of Defense was also perceived as resistant to giving patent rights to universities. *Id.* at 1692-93.

74. *See id.*

75. For a recent summary of products developed through NIH-funded research, see National Institutes of Health Response to the Conference Report Request for a Plan to Ensure Taxpayers' Interests are Protected (July 1, 2001), *available at* http://www.nih.gov/news/070101wyden.htm.

76. *See supra* notes 66-68 and accompanying text.

77. For example, in fiscal years 1993 to 1999, NIH executed 1,171 licenses based on NIH and FDA intramural invention portfolios. NIH royalties accounted for 70% of all federal royalties.

78. *See supra* notes 50-54 and accompanying text.

upstream patents on both future product development and future scientific research.

Research sponsors like NIH have significant advantages in making these judgments over two other institutions that might choose what should be patented—Congress or the universities themselves. If Congress attempted to specify in any detail what criteria should determine decisions about patenting publicly-sponsored research, it would doubtless be faced with rent-seeking demands from every stakeholder potentially affected by its determination. Given that Congress has generally tended to accede to such demands, at least in the context of detailed intellectual property legislation,[79] there is little reason to believe that criteria enunciated by Congress would promote the overall public interest. Moreover, Congress would be at a significant disadvantage in trying to formulate broadly applicable criteria *ex ante*, rather than making sensible choices about specific issues as they arise. By contrast, funding agencies are in a position to make case-by-case determinations and can readily modify their criteria in the face of new experiences.

As for the universities themselves, their self-interest is an imperfect proxy for the overall public interest, particularly given the large role played in university decision-making by technology transfer professionals who are not themselves academics. From a broad institutional perspective, universities both reap the rewards of the proprietary restrictions they impose on others and also pay the costs of restrictions that others impose on them. Thus, one might imagine that universities would have some interest in maintaining the public domain. The costs and benefits do not accrue, however, to the same university constituencies. The costs are largely borne by scientists who cannot get prompt access to the proprietary technologies they seek, while the gains from licensing revenues are much more salient to the technology transfer offices.

Even when universities recognize that the larger academic community might be better off sharing their research tools more freely, they face a serious collective action problem. So long as other institutions are staking out proprietary claims, no university is likely to forbear from asserting its own claims unilaterally. Traditional norms of open science may no longer be sufficient to address this collective action problem,[80] especially given that the scientists who hold the norms do not necessarily make the ultimate decisions about asserting proprietary rights.

The limited success of the 1995 Uniform Biological Materials Transfer Agreement ("UBMTA")[81] demonstrates the collective action problem. The UBMTA is a form contract designed to provide for relatively free exchange of

---

79. *See generally* Robert Patrick Merges & Glenn Harlan Reynolds, *The Proper Scope of the Copyright and Patent Power*, 37 HARV. J. ON LEGIS. 45 (2000).

80. *Cf.* ELINOR OSTROM, GOVERNING THE COMMONS (1990) (discussing the use of norms to address the specific collective action difficulty associated with conservation of common-pool resources); *see also* ERIC POSNER, LAW AND SOCIAL NORMS 22-23 (2000) (discussing norms as an alternative to law in solving problems of collective action).

81. Uniform Biological Materials Transfer Agreement, 60 Fed. Reg. 12771 (March 8, 1995).

unpatented research materials for research and educational purposes, in effect creating a limited public domain among universities. More than 100 universities, including all of the major research universities, have signed on to the UBMTA, and in so doing indicated their willingness to accept the agreement without further modification as the governing document for materials that their scientists receive from other institutions.[82] Many of these same institutions, however, have substituted their own form agreement for the UBMTA when they send materials out to other universities. These different agreements may be more restrictive than the UBMTA in their terms and need to be reviewed by institutional representatives before they are signed. Such departures from the relatively nonrestrictive form agreement are unsurprising. The university technology transfer officials who draft agreements for the transfer of research materials tend to see their primary job as bringing licensing revenue into the university.[83] Their ability to bring in license revenue may also be an important criterion by which their performance is assessed. Adherence to norms of open science is at odds with this primary mission and tempts technology transfer professionals to depart from the form whenever they think a particular material may have commercial value. The limited province of the UBMTA, which is not mandatory even for all exchanges among universities and makes no attempt to extend the principle of open access to exchanges between academic institutions and industry, opens the door for case-by-case departures that further weaken the power of the norms.

Left to their own devices, universities may be unable to take sustained collective action in favor of the public domain. For this reason, the role of NIH is crucial. On a number of occasions, NIH has been able to use hortatory strategies to convince academic institutions to act collectively to keep basic research information in the public domain. For example, leaders of the National Human Genome Research Institute ("NHGRI"), together with the Wellcome Trust and academic researchers at the major human genome mapping centers, resolved in February 1996 that "all human genomic DNA sequence information generated by centers funded for large-scale human sequencing should be freely available and in the public domain in order to encourage research and development."[84] NHGRI followed up with an April 1996 policy statement making "rapid release of data into public databases" a condition for grants for large-scale human

82. *See id.*

83. *See* Thursby et al., *supra* note 22 (finding, based on survey of 62 universities, that securing royalty and licensing fees was most important objective of technology transfer officers). Indeed, at a recent meeting of the Advisory Committee to the NIH Director, William Brody, the President of Johns Hopkins University, noted that even higher level university administrators are being pressured by their boards and by local or state government officials to develop technology transfer offices into profit centers. *See* Minutes of the Meeting of the Advisory Committee to the Director (December 7, 2000) *available at* http://www.nih.gov/about/directors/120700min.htm.

84. Eliot Marshall, *Genome Researchers Take the Pledge: Data Sharing*, SCI., April 26, 1996 at 477. This pledge, known as the "Bermuda resolution," echoed conclusions reached in earlier reports from the NIH Ad Hoc Program Advisory Committee on Complex Genomes and the National Research Council (a division of the National Academies).

genome sequencing.[85] NIH could not, however, go so far as to forbid its grantees from filing patent applications without relying on the cumbersome "exceptional circumstances" clause of the Bayh-Dole Act.[86] Rather than take this step, NIH declared that raw human genomic DNA sequence information should not be considered patentable as a matter of doctrine and policy.[87] The statement also warned that NHGRI would monitor whether grantees were patenting "large blocks of primary human genomic DNA sequence" and might invoke the "exceptional circumstances" limitation in future grants.[88] In the specific context of large-scale genome mapping, universities were willing to embrace a limited patenting norm,[89] and there was no need to invoke the "exceptional circumstances" clause.

NIH undertook a similar strategy for SNPs. Before the SNP Consortium stepped forward to put SNPs in the public domain, NIH had decided to allocate public funds for SNP identification.[90] Once again, NIH refrained from invoking the "exceptional circumstances" provision of the Bayh-Dole Act.[91] Instead, in its request for applications for SNP-related grants, NIH stressed the importance of making information about SNPs readily available to the research community and asked grant applicants to specify their plans for sharing data, materials and software.[92] NIH also specified that NIH staff would consider the adequacy of the plan for sharing and data release as one of the criteria for an award, and warned that NIH reserved the right to monitor grantee patenting activity.[93]

The hortatory efforts of NIH to constrain its grantees in pursuing intellectual property rights have not been limited to genome-related projects. A more general statement of "Principles and Guidelines for Sharing of Biomedical Research Resources," adopted by NIH in December 1999, also attempts to guide NIH grantees in the deployment of their proprietary rights. These principles state that:

> The use of patents and exclusive licenses is not the only, nor in some cases the most appropriate, means of implementing the [Bayh-Dole] Act. Where the subject inven-

---

85. NHGRI Policy Regarding Intellectual Property of Human Genomic Sequence (April 9, 1996), *available at* http://www.nhgri.nih.gov/Grant_info/Funding/Statements/RFA/intellectual_ property.html.

86. *See supra* note 24.

87. *See* NHGRI Policy, *supra* note 85.

88. *Id.*

89. Even university technology transfer offices, whose institutional culture and self-interest promote a commitment to patenting that is probably stronger than that of the research science community itself, did not challenge the policy. *See supra* note 84, at 478 (noting that key university patent officials endorsed policy). Some leading officers did, however, admit to being wary of the "bad precedent" that the April 1996 policy might set. *Id.* (quoting Lita Nelsen of MIT).

90. National Institutes of Health RFA HG-98-001, Methods for Discovering and Scoring Single Nucleotide Polymorphisms (Jan. 9, 1998), *available at* http://grants.nih.gov/grants/guide/rfn-files/RFA-HG-98-001.html.

91. *See id.*

92. *See id.*

93. *See id.*

> tion is useful primarily as a research tool, inappropriate licensing practices are likely to thwart rather than promote utilization, commercialization, and public availability.[94]

One factor that counsels in favor of wide dissemination of a particular invention is its status as "a broad, enabling invention that will be useful to many scientists, or multiple companies in developing multiple products, rather than a project or product-specific resource."[95] In addition, the Principles and Guidelines urge universities to exchange all unpatentable research tools freely, both within the academic community and with industry.[96]

The goals that NIH has sought to promote through these various hortatory statements are broadly consistent with the stated goal of the Bayh-Dole Act: "[T]o promote the utilization of inventions arising from federally supported research or development."[97] Arguably, NIH has acted outside the scope of its statutory authority, however, at least with respect to patentable inventions, leaving itself vulnerable to a potential legal challenge from a recalcitrant grantee.[98]

Consider, for example, NIH's suggestion that it would find the filing of university patents on large blocks of primary human genomic DNA sequence "problematic."[99] The only legal authority that the NIH has for restricting patenting is the "exceptional circumstances" clause of the Bayh-Dole Act.[100] Therefore, since NIH specifically chose not to rely upon the clumsy administrative procedure required by that clause, its suggestion has no legal authority whatsoever. The same holds true for NIH's general policy statement of *Principles and Guidelines for the Sharing of Biomedical Research Resources*.[101] Indeed, NIH has no authority under the Bayh-Dole Act to issue broadly applicable substantive regulations concerning the licensing of inventions (as distinguished from making specific determinations regarding march-in rights in the context of particular grants).[102] Congress specifically conferred the broader power to promulgate such regulations on the Commerce Department, not the

---

94. Department of Health and Human Services, National Institutes of Health, Principles and Guidelines for Recipients of NIH Research Grants and Contracts on Obtaining and Disseminating Biomedical Research Resources: Final Notice, 64 Fed. Reg. 72,090, 72,093 (Dec. 23, 1999).

95. *Id.* at 72,094. Other factors include whether the invention is primarily useful as a tool for discovery rather than as an FDA-approved product or component of such product and whether the resource is readily usable, without the need for private sector involvement in further development. *Id.*

96. *Id.*

97. 35 U.S.C. § 200 (2000).

98. With respect to inventions that are not patentable, NIH presumably has greater discretion in constraining proprietary activity. Because many inventions fall into a grey area with respect to patentability, however, a decision by NIH to force free exchange of unpatented material may, in the absence of other reform, simply lead some grantees to patent more aggressively. To forestall this possibility, NIH needs to be given more control over the patenting activities of grantees.

99. *See* NHGRI Policy, *supra* note 85.

100. 35 U.S.C. § 202(a)(i)-(ii).

101. *See* 64 Fed. Reg. 72,090.

102. 35 U.S.C. § 203.

funding agencies.[103] NIH's attempted departures from the Bayh-Dole Act's grant of broad discretion concerning patenting and licensing to grantee institutions would thus appear to have little legal weight.[104]

The success that NIH has enjoyed thus far in its efforts to constrain the proprietary strategies of grantees may reflect the continuing vitality of norms of free exchange, at least among a subset of academic researchers.[105] Researchers, and even their associated institutions, might voluntarily acquiesce in abiding by these norms, or at least balk at mounting an open challenge.

But there is growing evidence that NIH may require authority beyond the bully pulpit to ensure continuing compliance with these norms in the future.[106] Consider, for example, the recent controversy over the broad patent held by WARF on primate embryonic stem cells.[107] Although embryonic stem cells are precisely the type of broadly applicable enabling technology that, as a general matter, should be licensed nonexclusively in the interest of promoting future research and product development, WARF chose to license exclusively some of the most important commercial rights under the patent.[108] To be sure, the WARF case is somewhat unusual in that the exclusive licensee, Geron, provided crucial funding at a point when the federal government felt legally prohibited from funding the research necessary to move from chimpanzee and monkey cell lines to human cell lines.[109] But even if the federal government had provided all of the funding, WARF could still have decided to license the invention exclusively, at least with respect to certain fields of use, rather than to follow the Cohen-Boyer model of nonexclusive licensing. Although NIH might, in theory, exercise its march-in rights to make the invention more broadly available, these rights would be held in abeyance until all court appeals were exhausted, meanwhile delaying use of the invention in research.[110] Given this legal backdrop, it is unsurprising that recent negotiations between WARF and

---

103. 35 U.S.C. § 208 ("The Secretary of Commerce is authorized to promulgate regulations specifying the terms and conditions upon which any federally owned invention . . . may be licensed on a nonexclusive, partially exclusive, or exclusive basis.")

104. *See* United States v. Mead, 533 U.S. 218, 226-7 (2001) (noting that administrative implementation of a particular statute qualifies for "strong" deference under the *Chevron* doctrine, Chevron USA, Inc. v. Natural Resource Defense Council, Inc., 467 U.S. 837 (1984), only "when it appears that Congress delegated authority to the agency generally to make rules carrying the force of law, and that the agency interpretation claiming deference was promulgated in the exercise of that authority")

105. *See generally* Rai, *Regulating Scientific Research*, *supra* note 45.

106. *Cf. id. at* 151 (suggesting that, to the extent greater authority were needed to rein in federal grantees who violated open science norms, the Bayh-Dole Act could be amended).

107. *See* Thomson, *supra* note 23.

108. Wisconsin Alumni Research Foundation's Brief in Opposition to Geron Corporation's Fed. R. Civ. Pro. 12(c) Motion for Judgment on the Pleadings, Wisconsin Alumni Research Foundation v. Geron, Case No. 01-C-0459-C at 2 (on file with author).

109. *See* NATIONAL RESEARCH COUNCIL AND INSTITUTE OF MEDICINE, *supra* note 23.

110. 35 U.S.C. § 202(b)(1).

NIH over use of embryonic stem cell lines in research left WARF maintaining tight control over commercial applications of the technology.[111]

As patenting by universities gains momentum, the normative baseline in the academic community concerning free exchange appears to have shifted. Twenty-five years ago, universities thought long and hard before filing a patent application on such a fundamental discovery as gene-splicing, yet today they proclaim an entitlement to control and profit from commercial use of their government-sponsored inventions without apology for resulting restrictions on subsequent research and development. In this environment we expect to see increasing departures from norms that previously constrained proprietary behavior.

V

ENHANCING THE LEGAL AUTHORITY OF NIH

The time is ripe to fine-tune the Bayh-Dole Act to give funding agencies more latitude in guiding the patenting and licensing activities of their grantees. More generally, Congress should recognize that patenting and exclusive licensing are not always the best way to maximize the social value of inventions and discoveries made with federal funds. We propose two modest reforms that would further these goals.

First, the circumstances in which an agency may depart from the statutory presumption that the contractor may retain title to an invention in the terms of particular grants should be liberalized. The current "exceptional circumstances" language creates a clear presumption that the agency should exercise its power to restrain patenting only infrequently.[112] This parsimonious approach unduly constrains the authority of agencies such as NIH to use federal funding to enrich the public domain. Once the "exceptional circumstances" language is deleted, the substantive standard set forth in the current statutory language, which permits departure from the usual rule "when it is determined by the agency that restriction or elimination of the right to retain title to any subject invention will better promote the policy and objectives of this chapter,"[113] could be more freely applied to achieve the legislative goal of promoting widespread dissemination and use of research results. The current cumbersome administrative process for review of such determinations should be streamlined as well, with provision for research to proceed while the review process runs its course.[114]

111. Memorandum of Understanding Between NIH and Wicell (Sept. 5, 2001), *available at* http://www.nih.gov/news/stemcell/WicellMOU.pdf.

112. Thus, even though courts would presumably have to show *Chevron* deference to an agency finding of "exceptional circumstances," such deference would be in tension with the idea that the agency is (by definition) not supposed to find exceptional circumstances in too many cases.

113. 35 U.S.C. § 202(a)(ii).

114. To be sure, action *ex ante* may be problematic to the extent that it may sometimes be difficult to determine at the outset whether particular research is best distributed broadly or under a regime of

Second, with respect to the "march-in" right of funding agencies, the requirement that march-in authority be held in abeyance pending exhaustion of all court appeals by the government contractor should be changed. Indeed, the tolerance for protracted delays inherent in the current process is at odds with the time-sensitive nature of the interests reflected in the substantive standard, such as achieving practical application of the invention "within a reasonable time" and "alleviat[ing] health or safety needs."[115] An agency, however, should not be given march-in authority without adequate provision for judicial review. Unlike a prospective agency determination to restrict patenting at the grant stage before any invention has been made, a subsequent exercise of march-in rights disturbs settled expectations of grantees and licensees that may underlie investments. If these expectations are too readily upset by the exercise of march-in rights, industry could become wary of investing in university-based technology.

It might be argued that restoring greater authority to agencies would return us to the unhappy position that motivated Congress to pass the Bayh-Dole Act twenty-two years ago. Then, Congress acted to eliminate the uncertainty and delay associated with agency discretion over the patent rights available to contractors.[116] At least with respect to NIH, an agency that was singled out as a cause of concern in the legislative history of the Bayh-Dole Act, this danger appears quite small today. In the intervening years NIH has embraced patenting and technology transfer in furtherance of its public health mission.[117] Moreover, our proposal to give agencies greater authority would not overturn the general presumption in favor of allowing government contractors to patent inventions. It would simply permit agencies to decide that patenting is not warranted in particular cases, while streamlining procedures for making and reviewing these decisions. Greater discretion for agencies would also correct a dangerous oversimplification of how best to achieve the important policies underlying the Bayh-Dole Act by recognizing that patenting and exclusive licensing are not necessarily the best way to go.

A skeptic influenced by public choice theory might fear that our proposal would tempt agencies like NIH to use their discretion to justify an allocation of greater resources to expand their own roles.[118] NIH might invoke ostensibly public-spirited arguments for public funding as a means of promoting widespread access to research results, when in fact these arguments would cover self-

property rights. As discussed in the text, however, action *ex post* is problematic to the extent that it may disturb settled expectations of grantees and licensees.

115. 35 U.S.C. § 203(a), (b).

116. For example, the Senate report on the statute that would become the Bayh-Dole Act observed that "[p]resently, there are at least 24 different patent policies in effect in the Federal agencies. There are frequently contradictory from agency to agency (and even sometimes within the same agency) and have proven to be formidable barriers to organizations interested in participation in Government work." S. REP. NO. 96-480, at 2 (1979).

117. *See supra* note 73 and accompanying text.

118. *See, e.g.*, WILLIAM A. NISKAKEN, JR., BUREAUCRACY AND REPRESENTATIVE GOVERNMENT 114 (1971).

serving efforts to expand the scope of its own research, even in research areas where the private sector is already operating. These public-spirited arguments, however, have considerable force. When the willingness of private firms to do research depends on their ability to restrict the dissemination of research results, public funding may be essential to ensure that basic research discoveries are widely disseminated. That arguments for public funding of research in the public domain might in fact be driven by agency self-interest does not, in and of itself, detract from the soundness of the arguments.

While the public choice theorist might worry about agency self-aggrandizement, the policy analyst might be concerned that NIH does not have the expertise to make sophisticated judgments about when research should be left in the public domain. To put the point another way, although NIH scientists may have an intuition about what type of research belongs in the public domain, this intuition may not always be economically well-grounded. The intuition of scientists could, however, be supplemented by the expertise of policy analysts who specialize in innovation. NIH might employ such experts on its staff, perhaps in the Office of Technology Transfer ("OTT"), or it could include such expertise in the composition of its external advisory boards.

One might also worry that giving NIH greater discretion to mandate dedication of research results to the public domain would cause some university researchers to forsake public funding in favor of funding from industry. Given that private sector funding generally comes with very significant proprietary constraints, such defection might result in a net loss for the public domain. Although this is a reasonable concern, we do not see it as a serious threat. Unless universities act collectively to boycott federal funding in a particular research area, *some* university researchers will presumably be willing to take NIH funds to conduct their research in the public domain, limiting the attractiveness to industry of allocating private funds to the same purpose. Moreover, despite the increasingly intimate ties between universities and industry, NIH funding is not only much more extensive than private funding for university-based research, but it remains the coin of the realm for tenure, promotion, and other measures of academic success.[119] Unless that situation changes dramatically, significant defections from peer-reviewed public funding seem unlikely. Moreover, given that NIH leadership is typically drawn from the same community of scientists as university researchers,[120] the agency is unlikely to drift too far from the concerns of the community it regulates. Thus, to the extent that NIH tries to ensure compliance with open access norms, it is likely to use

---

119. As noted earlier, NIH still funds the vast majority of university-based research in the life sciences. *See supra* note 21. Moreover, of the 75 American Nobel laureates in physiology or medicine in the period from 1945-1998, 56 had either worked at NIH or were supported by NIH prior to winning the prize. *See* NIH Funds Support Nobel Laureates, at http://www.nih.gov/news/NIH-Record/11_03_98/story06.htm (last visited Jan. 22, 2003).

120. For example, the current NIH Director, Elias Zerhouni, was a professor at Johns Hopkins University. The previous NIH Director, Harold Varmus, is a Nobel-prize winning molecular biologist who now heads the Memorial Sloan-Kettering Cancer Institute.

"gentle nudging" rather than destabilizing "hard shoves."[121] Indeed, far from being destabilizing to the scientific community, NIH action could strengthen the position of university scientists who favor open access vis-à-vis those university constituencies that are less supportive of open access.

Finally, one might be concerned that funding agencies such as NIH might use their expanded discretion over patenting decisions to respond to political pressures unrelated to the legitimate goal of mediating the tension between access and product development. For example, an executive branch that was motivated to suppress controversial research might be unable to convince Congress to withhold funding for such research entirely, but could decide unilaterally to withhold patents on the research, in the hope that, absent patent protection, the research might never be developed for commercial use. This is a serious concern, particularly given the political heat surrounding many promising areas of biomedical research, such as research that involves human embryos.[122] Although we have no illusions that public sector research can be completely insulated from political controversy, we hope and expect that judicial review of agency determinations would provide a check on an agency's use of its discretion under the Bayh-Dole Act to advance agendas unrelated to research and development.

VI

CONCLUSION

As proprietary claims have proliferated in biomedical research, the costs that patents impose on R&D have become more salient. At the same time, patents on biomedical research discoveries plainly offer important social benefits in the form of motivating further private investment in product development. The presumption that patent incentives are necessary to promote research and development has less force for inventions arising from government-sponsored research than for inventions arising from purely private funding. It is therefore important that decisions about patenting the results of government-sponsored research be made on the basis of a careful balancing of the costs and benefits that they entail for future R&D. Current law entrusts these decisions to the unbridled discretion of institutions, such as universities, that receive federal funds, but these institutions are inadequately motivated to take the social costs of their proprietary claims into account in deciding what to patent. A more sensible approach would give research sponsors, such as NIH,

121. *Cf.* Dan Kahan, *Gentle Nudges vs. Hard Shoves*, 67 U. CHI. L. REV. 607 (2000) (arguing that decision-makers charged with implementing laws that seek to change social norms will be more likely to implement laws that do not represent a radical break with governing practices).

122. Similar concerns might arise for research that could be used for terrorist purposes. The Bayh-Dole Act already provides that agencies that have responsibility for national security can act to restrict or eliminate patents that affect security. 35 U.S.C. § 202 (2000). Our proposal does not alter the allocation of power with respect to that issue.

more authority to restrict patenting of publicly-funded research when such patenting is more likely to retard than promote subsequent R&D.

A CONTRACTUALLY RECONSTRUCTED RESEARCH COMMONS FOR SCIENTIFIC DATA IN A HIGHLY PROTECTIONIST INTELLECTUAL PROPERTY ENVIRONMENT

J. H. REICHMAN* AND PAUL F. UHLIR**

TABLE OF CONTENTS

This article is also available at http://www.law.duke.edu/journals/66LCPReichman.

* J. H. Reichman is Bunyan S. Womble Professor of Law, Duke University.

** Paul F. Uhlir is Director of International Scientific and Technical Information Programs at the National Academies.

The opinions expressed in this article are the authors' and not necessarily those of the National Academies.

The authors gratefully acknowledge partial support for their work on this article from the Center for the Public Domain, under Grant No. OPVT-4676, and the John D. and Catherine T. MacArthur Foundation, under Grant No. 02-73708-GEN. Any opinions, findings, and conclusions or recommendations expressed in this article are those of the authors and do not necessarily reflect the views of the supporting organizations.

Draft versions of this article were also presented at workshops sponsored by the National Research Council, Washington, D.C., Sept. 4-6, 2002, the Intellectual Property Research Institute of Australia ("IPRIA"), Melbourne, on Nov. 28, 2002, and the REGNET Social Sciences and Law Program, Australian National University, Canberra, Australia, Dec. 2, 2002. We are grateful to the participants for comments and suggestions. We also wish to thank the following individuals for their helpful comments and advice on previous drafts of this article: Peter Arzberger, Geoff Bowker, Andrew Christie, Peter Drahos, Peter Eckersley, Brett Frischmann, Janet Hope, Maureen Kelly, Steve Maurer, and William van Caenegem. Finally, we are grateful for the research support provided by Troy Petersen and Meredith Zinnani.

Portions of this article will also be appearing in National Research Council, *Proceedings of the Symposium on the Role of Scientific and Technical Data and Information in the Public Domain* (forthcoming 2003).

I

INTRODUCTION

Factual data are fundamental to the progress of science and to our preeminent system of innovation. Freedom of inquiry, the open availability of scientific data, and full disclosure of results through publication are the cornerstones of basic research, which both domestic law and the norms of public science have long upheld.[1]

The rapid advances in digital technologies and networks over the past two decades have radically altered and improved the ways that data can be produced, disseminated, managed, and used in science and in all other spheres of

1. *See* NATIONAL RESEARCH COUNCIL, BITS OF POWER: ISSUES IN GLOBAL ACCESS TO SCIENTIFIC DATA 2 (1997) [hereinafter BITS OF POWER]. Data are "facts, numbers, letters, and symbols that describe an object, idea, condition, situation, or other factors." NATIONAL RESEARCH COUNCIL, A QUESTION OF BALANCE: PRIVATE RIGHTS AND THE PUBLIC INTEREST IN SCIENTIFIC AND TECHNICAL DATABASES 15 (1999) [hereinafter A QUESTION OF BALANCE].

human endeavor.[2] As a result, these changes have given rise to a dramatic increase in the amount of data produced and have fostered unprecedented opportunities for accelerating research and creating wealth based on the exploitation of data.[3] Every aspect of the natural world, from the sub-atomic to the cosmic, all human activities, and indeed every life form, can now be observed and captured through an electronic database.[4] Whole areas of science are entirely data-driven, such as bioinformatics in molecular biology and the observational environmental sciences. All research increasingly depends on easy access to and use of data resources.[5]

Apart from the obvious technological advances that made these activities possible, much of the success of this revolution derives from the U.S. legal and policy regime that supports the open availability and unfettered use of scientific data.[6] This regime, which remains among the most open in the world,[7] has placed a premium on the broadest possible dissemination and use of scientific data produced by governmental or government-funded sources. This policy was traditionally implemented in several complementary ways: by expressly prohibiting intellectual property protection of all information produced by the federal government; by contractually reinforcing the sharing ethos of science[8] through open data terms and conditions in federal research grants and contracts;[9] by carving out a very large and robust public domain[10] for non-copyrightable data;[11]

---

2. BITS OF POWER, *supra* note 1, at 2; *see also* A QUESTION OF BALANCE, *supra* note 1, at 14-38.

3. *See generally* PAUL A. DAVID & DOMINIQUE FORAY, ECONOMIC FUNDAMENTALS OF THE KNOWLEDGE SOCIETY (Stanford Inst. for Econ. Pol'y Res., Discussion Paper No. 01-14, 2002), *available at* http://siepr.stanford.edu/papers/pdf/01-14.html (last visited Feb. 18, 2003).

4. J. H. Reichman & Paul F. Uhlir, *Database Protection at the Crossroads: Recent Developments and Their Impact on Science and Technology*, 14 BERKELEY TECH. L. J. 793, 812-13 (1999) [hereinafter Reichman & Uhlir, *Database Protection*].

5. BITS OF POWER, *supra* note 1, at 47-57.

6. *Id.* at 17.

7. *See* Peter N. Weiss & Peter Backlund, *International Information Policy in Conflict: Open and Unrestricted Access versus Government Commercialization*, *in* BORDERS IN CYBERSPACE 300, 307 (Brian Kahin & Charles Nesson eds., 1997).

8. For statutory waiver of copyright in government production, see 17 U.S.C. § 105 (2000). For the sharing ethos of science, see R.K. Merton, *The Normative Structure of Science*, *in* THE SOCIOLOGY OF SCIENCE 267-78 (R.K. Merton ed., 1973). *See also* PAUL A. DAVID, FROM KEEPING 'NATURE'S SECRETS' TO THE INSTITUTIONALIZATION OF 'OPEN SCIENCE,' 2 (Stanford Dep't of Econ., Working Paper No. 01006, 2001) [hereinafter DAVID, NATURE'S SECRETS], *available at* http://www-econ.stanford.edu/faculty/workp/swp01006.pdf (last visited Feb. 20, 2003); Michael Polanyi, *The Republic of Science: Its Political and Economic Theory*, 1 MINERVA 54, 59-79 (1962); BITS OF POWER, *supra* note 1, at 17-19, 21-22. For the environmental sciences perspective, see generally NATIONAL RESEARCH COUNCIL, ON THE FULL AND OPEN EXCHANGE OF SCIENTIFIC DATA (1995) [hereinafter FULL AND OPEN EXCHANGE] and NATIONAL RESEARCH COUNCIL, RESOLVING CONFLICTS ARISING FROM THE PRIVATIZATION OF ENVIRONMENTAL DATA 15-19 (2001) [hereinafter RESOLVING CONFLICTS], regarding scientists' views on the need for full and open access to environmental and earth science data.

9. *See infra* Part II.B.

10. We define "public domain" information as sources and types of data and information whose uses are not restricted by statutory intellectual property ("IP") laws and other legal regimes and that are accordingly available to the public for use without authorization. For analytical purposes, information in the public domain, including scientific data and information, may be divided into three major categories:

or by applying other immunities and exceptions that favor science and education to intellectual property rights that otherwise protect collections of information.[12]

A. Countervailing Trends Affecting the Production, Distribution, and Use of Scientific Data

A second and opposing trend, however, is characterized by the progressive privatization and commercialization of scientific data, and by the attendant pressures to hoard and trade them like other private commodities.[13] This trend is reinforced by the creation of new legal rights and protectionist mechanisms that are largely extrinsic to the scientific enterprise,[14] but increasingly adopted by it. These include greatly enhanced copyright protection of digital information;[15] new ways to control access to and use of digital data by contractual

---

(1) Information that is not subject to protection under exclusive IP rights.

(2) Information that qualifies as protectable subject matter under some IP regime, but that is contractually designated as unprotected (for example, is transferred or donated to a public archive or data center, or is made available directly to the public, with no rights reserved). Typically, such material consists of scientific data collections.

(3) Information that becomes available under statutorily created immunities and exceptions, which is also important in this context although it does not constitute public domain information per se.

"Open access" may be defined as proprietary information that is made openly and freely available on the Internet or through other media by the rights holder but that retains some or all of the exclusive property rights that are granted under statutory IP laws. Open access may be provided by all types of public and private sector sources. Of course, public domain information may be provided freely through open access as well. By no means is all public domain information freely available, however, even though once accessed, it may be used without restriction. This article focuses primarily on scientific and technical ("S&T") data in the public domain available through open access. *See generally* NATIONAL RESEARCH COUNCIL, PROCEEDINGS OF THE SYMPOSIUM ON THE ROLE OF SCIENTIFIC AND TECHNICAL DATA AND INFORMATION IN THE PUBLIC DOMAIN (forthcoming 2003) [hereinafter NRC SYMPOSIUM].

11. 17 U.S.C. §§ 102(a)-(b), 103(b) (2000); Feist Publ'ns, Inc. v. Rural Tel. Servs. Co., 499 U.S. 340 (1991).

12. *See, e.g.*, 17 U.S.C. § 107 (2000) (fair use); § 108 (reproductions by libraries and archives); § 109(a) (first-sale doctrine); § 110(1) (face-to-face teaching activities); § 110(2) (educational broadcasts).

13. *See, e.g.*, Rebecca S. Eisenberg, *Bargaining Over the Transfer of Proprietary Research Tools: Is this Market Failing or Emerging?*, *in* EXPANDING THE BOUNDARIES OF INTELLECTUAL PROPERTY: INNOVATION POLICY FOR THE KNOWLEDGE SOCIETY, at 223-49 (Rochelle Dreyfuss et al. eds., 2001) [hereinafter Eisenberg, *Bargaining*] (stressing delays and high transaction costs impeding transfers of university-generated biotech research tools); Walter W. Powell, *Networks of Learning in Biotechnology: Opportunities and Constraints Associated with Relational Contracting in a Knowledge-Intensive Field*, *in id.* at 251, 263-65 (stressing "sea change in the focus of basic research" in life sciences owing to commercialization by universities of basic science discoveries, increasingly under exclusive property relationships).

14. *See generally* COMMITTEE ON INTELLECTUAL PROPERTY RIGHTS AND EMERGING INFORMATION INFRASTRUCTURE, NATIONAL RESEARCH COUNCIL, THE DIGITAL DILEMMA: INTELLECTUAL PROPERTY IN THE INFORMATION AGE 96-122, 152-98 (2000) [hereinafter DIGITAL DILEMMA].

15. Digital Millennium Copyright Act of 1998 (DMCA), 17 U.S.C. §§ 1201-1203 (2000). Irrespective of the DMCA, federal appellate courts have begun to broaden copyright protection of low authorship publications. *See infra* text accompanying notes 286-87.

restrictions that are technologically enforced;[16] and the enactment of proposals for novel intellectual property rights[17] to protect collections of data.[18]

These new legal rights and mechanisms are being promoted by certain information industry conglomerates because of economic opportunities for the private exploitation of new digital information resources and as a legal reaction to a possible loss of control over certain proprietary information products in the digital environment.[19] At the same time, the new laws pose the danger of disrupting the normative customs at the foundation of public science, especially the traditional cooperative and sharing ethos, by producing both the pressures and the means to enclose the scientific commons and to greatly reduce the scope of data in the public domain.[20] Viewed dispassionately, the need to reconcile these trends in a socially productive framework has become imperative, and the goal of such a reconciliation seems clear. A positive outcome would maximize the dissemination of scientific data in a quasi-public space where access and use for research purposes was ensured, without disrupting new opportunities for commercial exploitation of scientific databases in the private sector.[21]

Perhaps a single example at the outset will help to illuminate some of these developments. Under traditional assumptions, scientific researchers would

16. *See, e.g.*, ProCD, Inc. v. Zeidenberg, 86 F.3d 1447 (7th Cir. 1996). *See generally* J. H. Reichman & Jonathan A. Franklin, *Privately Legislated Intellectual Property Rights: Reconciling Freedom of Contract with Public Good Uses of Information*, 147 U. PA. L. REV. 875 (1999); Symposium, *Intellectual Property and Contract Law for the Information Age: The Impact of Article 2B of the Uniform Commercial Code on the Future of Information and Commerce* (pts. 1 & 2) 87 CAL. L. REV. 1 (1999), 13 BERKELEY TECH. L.J. 809 (1998) [hereinafter *Intellectual Property & Contract Law*].

17. The U.S. House of Representatives' Committee on the Judiciary had introduced a series of bills modeled after Directive 96/9 of the European Parliament and the Council of 11 March 1996 on the legal protection of databases, 1996 O.J. (L 77) 2 [hereinafter E.C. Database Directive]. The most recent officially introduced version was H.R. 354, the Collections of Information Antipiracy Act (2000). *See* Reichman & Uhlir, *Database Protection*, *supra* note 4, at 824. In 1999, the House Committee on Commerce (now called the House Committee on Energy and Commerce) introduced a more narrowly drawn version of database protection legislation based on unfair competition law principles: the Consumer and Investor Access to Information Act of 1999, H.R. 1858.

18. For detailed discussion of the E.C. Database Directive as it impacts science, see Reichman & Uhlir, *Database Protection*, *supra* note 4. *See also* J. H. Reichman & Pamela Samuelson, *Intellectual Property Rights in Data?*, 50 VAND. L. REV. 51, 114-23 (1997). *See generally* Jane C. Ginsburg, *U.S. Initiatives to Protect Works of Low Authorship*, *in* EXPANDING THE BOUNDARIES OF IP, *supra* note 13, at 55, 68-72 [hereinafter Ginsburg, *U.S. Initiatives*]; J. H. Reichman, *Database Protection in a Global Economy*, 2002 REVUE INTERNATIONALE DE DROIT ECONOMIQUE 455-504 (2002) [hereinafter .Reichman, *Database Protection in a Global Economy*].

19. *See generally* DIGITAL DILEMMA, *supra* note 14, at 51-58, 61-67.

20. *See generally* PAUL A. DAVID, THE DIGITAL TECHNOLOGY BOOMERANG: NEW INTELLECTUAL PROPERTY RIGHTS THREATEN GLOBAL 'OPEN SCIENCE' (Stanford Dep't of Econ., Working Paper No. 00-006, 2000) [hereinafter DAVID, DIGITAL BOOMERANG], *available at*: http://www-econ.stanford.edu/faculty/workp/swp00016.pdf; PAUL A. DAVID, WILL BUILDING "GOOD FENCES" REALLY MAKE 'GOOD NEIGHBORS' IN SCIENCE? DIGITAL TECHNOLOGIES, COLLABORATIVE RESEARCH ON THE INTERNET AND THE EC'S PUSH FOR PROTECTION OF INTELLECTUAL PROPERTY, (Stanford Inst. for Econ. Pol'y Res., Discussion Paper No. 00-33, 2000) [hereinafter DAVID, GOOD FENCES], *available at* http://siepr.stanford.edu/papers/pdf/00-33.pdf (last visited Feb. 20, 2003).

21. For our proposals to achieve such a positive outcome, see Part IV of this article.

publish their findings together with the supporting data. Both the findings and the data would enter the public domain and become part of the scientific knowledge base. Traditional copyright principles have supported this result, as have the normative practices of the scientific community.[22] Today, however, the fact that the data are published with the article, whether in print or digital form, may tell us little or nothing about the terms of their accessibility and their use by other scientists for follow-on work, for a variety of reasons.

First, as a growing commercial or cultural phenomenon, the data may have been conditionally deposited or imperfectly revealed at the time of publication.[23] Second, recent changes to copyright law make it possible to control online access to the supporting data, even though the data as such are technically ineligible for copyright protection.[24] Third, European states have adopted a new *sui generis* database right, which allows scientists to directly control access to and reuse of aggregations of facts, whether these have been disclosed as part of their research publications or made available as a separate database.[25] Bills to enact similar legislation have been introduced in the United States.[26]

Finally, even disregarding these major changes in the underlying intellectual property regime, a combination of digital rights management technologies and standard-form contracts may enable publishers to impose limits on the redissemination and use of supporting data even after formal publication of a scientific article. This power of the "two-party" deal, which modern telecommunications technology has restored, would grow even stronger in the United States if either a strong database protection bill were enacted or a pending proposal for new and uniform contract laws regulating information products were more widely adopted at the state level.[27] If both types of laws were adopted, either the scientist or the publisher could retain maximum power to control subsequent access to and use of any compilation of scientific data (but not individual facts) otherwise disclosed to the public and previously in the public domain.

The foregoing list illustrates the very far-reaching revisions in the legal rules that have supported traditional modes of accessing and exchanging scientific data and databases. The resulting problems are further complicated by the

---

22. *See infra* text accompanying notes 78-113; BITS OF POWER, *supra* note 1, at 2 (regarding the normative practices of the scientific community); Reichman & Uhlir, *Database Protection*, *supra* note 4, at 800-02 (discussing user-friendly rules of copyright law).

23. *See, e.g.*, Ari Patrinos & Dan Drell, *The Times They Are A-Changin'*, 417 NATURE 589, 589-90 (June 6, 2002).

24. *See* Digital Millennium Copyright Act of 1998 (DMCA), 17 U.S.C. §§ 1201-1203 (2000); Ginsburg, *U.S. Initiatives*, *supra* note 18, at 61-67.

25. E.C. Database Directive, *supra* note 17.

26. *See* H.R. 354, 106th Cong. (1999) and H.R. 1858, 106th Cong. (1999). Previous versions of the Collections of Information Antipiracy Act introduced by the House Committee on the Judiciary included H.R. 2281, 105th Cong. (1998); H.R. 2652, 105th Cong. (1997), and The Database Investment and Intellectual Property Antipiracy Act of 1996, H.R. 3531, 104th Cong. (1996).

27. Reichman & Franklin, *supra* note 16, at 897-99.

changing ways in which the scientific community itself uses data and exchanges them on both a formal and informal basis.[28]

B. Formal and Informal Data Exchanges

Traditionally, in "big science" projects, in disciplines such as physics, space, and earth sciences,[29] government science agencies play the predominant, controlling role in the collection and dissemination of data from large facility instruments. The agencies themselves collect the raw data, or they fund the production of data by academia through large, highly structured, and long-term research programs. Such data are then typically managed in well-organized data centers, where they are deposited on terms of open public domain access for the worldwide scientific community. Other science agencies also sponsor and fund research that makes use of these collected inputs. The public research that emerges is disclosed through peer-reviewed publications or applied to commercial endeavors. These publications or applications will then attract exclusive intellectual property rights—copyrights, patents, or, increasingly, *sui generis* rights.

What is noteworthy about this picture is the high degree of public control over the data that flow through the system. Because the government itself collects, funds, or disseminates so much of this data, it has a great deal to say about the rules of access and use that apply. It has thus promoted open access to research data as a public good, and through its use of public grants and contracts has reinforced the sharing ethos to which the scientific community traditionally subscribed. This ethos, in turn, fits comfortably within the underlying legal infrastructure, which typically distinguished between information as inputs, not subject to intellectual property rights, and aggregates of information bundled as outputs, which do attract such rights.[30]

Of course, it would be wrong to paint too rosy a picture here or to assume that data in "big science" programs have flowed through and supported the public research system optimally and that the open access and sharing norms have been rigorously and uniformly enforced. Moreover, the areas of "small science" have never really fit within this sociological description of the data access system sketched above.[31] Small science is being performed by individual

---

28. See discussion *infra* accompanying notes 65-157 and 183-210.

29. *See generally* BIG SCIENCE: THE GROWTH OF LARGE-SCALE RESEARCH (Peter L. Galison & Bruce Hevly eds., 1994) [hereinafter BIG SCIENCE].

30. *See generally* Reichman & Franklin, *supra* note 16, at 884-88 ("The Dual Function of Information in the Networked Environment") (citing authorities).

31. *See generally* Stephen Hilgartner, *Access to Data and Intellectual Property: Scientific Exchange in Genome Research*, *in* INTELLECTUAL PROPERTY RIGHTS AND THE DISSEMINATION OF RESEARCH TOOLS IN MOLECULAR BIOLOGY: SUMMARY OF A WORKSHOP HELD AT THE NATIONAL ACADEMY OF SCIENCE, Feb. 15-16, 1996, 28-39 (1997) [hereinafter Hilgartner, *Access to Data*]; Stephen Hilgartner & Sherry I. Brandt-Rauf, *Controlling Data and Resources: Access Strategies in Molecular Genetics*, *in* INFORMATION TECHNOLOGY AND THE PRODUCTIVITY PARADOX (P.A. David & W.E. Steinmueller eds., 1998) [hereinafter Hilgartner & Brandt-Rauf, *Controlling Data*]; Sherry I. Brandt-Rauf, *The Role,*

investigators or small and autonomous research groups operating outside large, organized research programs, often with non-federal sources of funding. In these areas of science, data are generated in relatively small amounts, and single laboratories or investigators work independently. Nevertheless, the latter also find themselves dependent on the results of those other individuals in their field of inquiry, to which they have no guaranteed access. Here, the data exist in various twilight states of accessibility, depending on the extent to which they are published, discussed in papers but not revealed, or just known about because of reputation or ongoing work but kept under absolute or relative secrecy.

There are few government-controlled, public domain data centers in this type of research. The data are thus disaggregated components of an incipient network that is only as effective as the individual transactions that put it together. Openness and sharing are not ignored, but they are not necessarily dominant, either. These values must compete with strategic considerations of self-interest, secrecy, and the logic of mutually beneficial exchange.

In small science, what occurs is a delicate process of negotiation, in which data are traded as the result of informal compromises between private and public interests that are worked out on an ad hoc and continual basis. Small science thus depends on the flow of disaggregated data through many different hands, all of which collectively construct a fragile chain of semi-contractual relations in which secrecy and disclosure are pitted against a common need for access and use of these resources. In this sense, big science projects are more likely to be subject to formal data access regulations while small science research is more emblematic of informal data exchange practices.

C. The Sharing Ethos Under Stress

The picture painted herein of "big" and "small" science is overstated to clarify the basic concepts. The big science system is not free of individual strategic data transactions that are typical of the small sciences, and the latter often benefit from access to public repositories where data are freely and openly available, rather than through the ad hoc transactional process. However, the "brokered networks" typical of small science are endemic to all sciences, and access to data is everywhere becoming more dependent on negotiated transactions between private stakeholders. These outcomes are increasingly achieved at the expense of the public interest, and they may bypass the contributions to public data repositories and the sharing norms of the past.[32] Moreover, in recent years the pressures to commoditize and privatize research results have extended farther upstream in the process, which affects the government's attitude toward the creation and dissemination of its own data in support of research and other public interests.

Value, and Limits of S&T Data and Information in the Public Domain for Biomedical Research, *in* NRC SYMPOSIUM, *supra* note 10.

32. *Cf.* Powell, *supra* note 13, at 263-64 (stressing risks of undermining public science).

The pressures on access to scientific data from privatization and commercialization could, in short, be a big story even if the underlying legal infrastructure were to hold constant.[33] In reality, the massive changes in the legal regime already alluded to could have profound effects on access to and use of data in every scientific discipline, whether a part of "big" or "small" science, or even "basic" or "applied."

The biggest threat to the integrity of the system is the extension of exclusive intellectual property rights to collections of data themselves, which poses a grave threat to the continuity of all those data exchange processes that scientists in the United States have long taken for granted. Moreover, this is not a battle that science can win, in the sense that there are no legislative fixes likely to stave off the many different legislative threats to the open exchange of data in the public domain. The pressures to commoditize are in many cases becoming too great, and the legal and technical protection instruments are now too varied and refined to be thwarted by ad hoc legal and technical responses. Any legislative remedies that might provide narrow exceptions for public research and education from an increasingly high-protectionist regime cannot resolve the major obstacles to the open availability and exchange of scientific data heretofore in the public domain. Rather, precisely because these pressures on the system are becoming so great, we contend that the scientific community can and must assert greater control over the management of its own data supplies.

D. Scope and Structure of this Article

The aim of this article is to promote discussion and a greater understanding within both the scientific and legal communities of the important trends and issues noted above. Part II examines the role and value of public domain data in scientific research and maps the way it functions today. It describes the legal and policy framework for government-generated and government-funded scientific data activities, the related sociological and normative structure of the scientific enterprise in the formal and informal contexts, and some of the opportunities for the exploitation of data in public research that are inherent in digital technologies and networks.

Part III begins by looking at the shifting public–private boundaries. It then documents many of the economic and legal pressures on scientific data traditionally in the public domain and the threats these changes pose to the established norms and practices supporting open access to and use of data in research.

Finally, Part IV demonstrates how the scientific community can manage its way out of these dilemmas, but only if it is willing to come to terms with real-world commercial pressures that will require some significant compromises to preserve an acceptable balance of public and private interests. Toward this end,

---

33. *Cf.* Arti Kaur Rai, *Regulating Scientific Research: Intellectual Property Rights and the Norms of Science*, 94 NW. U. L. REV. 77, 92-94, 109-15 (1999).

we propose a dual strategy, one that contractually reinforces the public domain for data that exists within the ambit of the federal government and another that contractually reconstructs a research commons for data (and other forms of information) in academia and the private sector. We argue that excessively rigid efforts to keep scientific data free of private control will end by yielding less and less data to the public domain, whereas a contractually reconstructed commons for data, while less pure in theory, will in practice make more data more accessible for research purposes in the long run. To make this strategy work, the funding agencies, universities, and scientific organizations must agree to a basic set of ground rules, with the goal of preserving the data commons for research purposes without impeding institutional actors or single researchers from enjoying the benefits of appropriate commercialization in the private sector.

II

RESEARCH OPPORTUNITIES IN A DIGITALLY NETWORKED ENVIRONMENT SUPPORTED BY A ROBUST PUBLIC DOMAIN

The producers of scientific data can be divided into three sectors: government agencies (primarily but not exclusively federal), academic and other not-for-profit research institutions, and private sector commercial enterprises. In the past, the research activities of the first two sectors—the government agencies and the non-profits—operated largely unimpeded by the classical intellectual property system. In fact, that system indirectly supported these activities by facilitating access to a robust public domain. Regarding operations in the private sector, where the objective is to commercialize data, few and relatively weak intellectual property rights have nonetheless supported private investment in a vigorous U.S. database industry that dominates the world market.[34] At the same time, this intellectual property environment has facilitated the informal exchanges of individual scientific researchers and has not unduly impeded research at either the government or university level, except insofar as licensing contracts supported by new technological protection measures have begun to cut back on pre-existing freedom of access and use.

If the pre-existing legal regime were to remain supportive, the role and value of public domain data could potentially be magnified many times over by

34. In 1998, sixty-three percent of databases were reportedly produced in the United States. Although the domestic database industry continued to expand, its share of the global output declined from a ratio of U.S. to non-U.S. databases of about two-to-one in the 1985-1993 period, to a ratio of three-to-two in 1998. Martha E. Williams, *State of Databases Today: 1999*, *in* GALE DIRECTORY OF DATABASES (L. Kumar ed., 1998). These statistics, however, do not include large numbers of government and academic databases that are not officially registered. *See* A QUESTION OF BALANCE, *supra* note 1, at 28; *see also* Cynthia M. Bott, *Protection of Information Products: Balancing Commercial Reality and the Public Domain*, 67 U. CIN. L. REV. 237 (1998); Stephen M. Maurer, Across Two Worlds: Database Protection in the U.S. and Europe, paper prepared for Industry Canada's Conference on Intellectual Property and Innovation in the Knowledge-Based Economy 8-21 (May 23-24, 2001) [hereinafter Maurer, Across Two Worlds] (comparing the U.S. database industry with that of other countries).

the advent of digital technologies and new research tools. In reality, however, this potentially enhanced role of public domain data in science is threatened by a confluence of economic, legal, and technological pressures described in detail in Part III.

A. Government-Generated Data: A Birthright of the Public Domain

The role of government in supporting scientific progress in general,[35] and its influence on the creation and maintenance of the research commons in particular, cannot be overstated. The U.S. government produces the largest body of public domain data and information used in scientific research and education. For example, the federal government alone now spends more than forty-five billion dollars per year on its research programs,[36] with a significant percentage of that money invested in the production of primary data sources, in higher-level processed data products, statistics, and models, and in scientific and technical information ("STI"), such as government reports, technical papers, research articles, memoranda, and other such analytical material.

1. The Non-Proprietary Principle

The United States—unlike most other countries—overrides the canons of intellectual property law that could otherwise endow it with exclusive rights in government-generated collections of data or other information. To this end, the Copyright Act of 1976 prohibits the federal government from claiming protection of its publications.[37] The bulk of the data and information produced directly by the government automatically enter the public domain year after year, with no proprietary restrictions.

The federal government also provides the greatest amount of funding for the production of scientific data by the non-governmental research community, as a significant part of that forty-five billion dollar investment in public research,[38] and many of the government-funded data collections it yields also become available to the scientific community through the research commons. Government-funded data follow a different trajectory from that of data produced by the government itself, however, and discussion of that topic is deferred to the next Part.

A number of well-established reasons support the policies that promote open access to and use of government-generated data, often at no cost to the public. The government needs no legal incentive to create the information; the taxpayer has already paid once for the production of a database or report and should not pay twice; transparency of governance and democratic values would

---

35. For an excellent overview of the role of the U.S. government in the domestic research system, see DONALD E. STOKES, PASTEUR'S QUADRANT: BASIC SCIENCE AND TECHNOLOGICAL INNOVATION (1997).

36. American Association for the Advancement of Science R&D Funding Update of Mar. 14, 2002, Table 2, *at* http://www.aaas.org/spp/rd/prev03pt.htm [hereinafter AAAS R&D Funding Update].

37. 17 U.S.C. § 105 (2000).

38. AAAS R&D Funding Update, *supra* note 36.

be undermined by limiting broad dissemination and use of public data and information; citizens' First Amendment rights might be compromised; and the nation generally benefits from broad, unfettered access to and use of government databases and other public information by all citizens to promote economic, educational, and cultural values.[39] It is primarily the latter justification, which involves many positive externalities and network effects from the Internet on the conduct of research and on our national system of innovation that is this article's focus of discussion.[40]

The federal government's specific policies relating to scientific data activities date back to the advent of the era of "big science" following World War II, which established a framework for the planning and management of large-scale basic and applied research programs.[41] Most of this research was initially conducted in the physical sciences and engineering, fueled largely by the Cold War and related national defense concerns. Although a substantial portion of this research was classified, at least initially, the default rule was that the research data and information produced by the government entered the public domain. This research model yielded a succession of spectacular scientific and technological breakthroughs and well-documented socio-economic benefits.

The hallmark of big science, more recently referred to as "megascience," has been the use of large research facilities or research centers and of "facility-class" instruments, which are most usefully characterized as observational or experimental.[42] In the observational sciences, some of the most significant advances initially occurred in the space and earth sciences as offshoots of classified military and intelligence space technologies and of NASA's Apollo program. Notable examples of large observational facilities have included space

39. *See* Weiss & Backlund, *supra* note 7, at 300-05; A QUESTION OF BALANCE, *supra* note 1, at 52-58. *See generally* Henry H. Perritt, Jr., *Sources of Rights to Access Public Information*, 4 WM. & MARY BILL RTS. J. 179 (Summer 1995);

40. The policies and practices of state and local governments with regard to legal protection of their databases and other information are not as straightforward as those in the federal context. Section 105 of the 1976 Copyright Act does not expressly ban copyright claims in the works of non-federal government entities. 17 U.S.C. § 105 (2000). Some states have nonetheless enacted open records laws that prohibit protection of their government information, that encourage open dissemination to the public, and contain provisions analogous to the Freedom of Information Act ("FOIA"), 5 U.S.C. § 552 (2000). *See, e.g.*, California Public Records Act, CAL. GOV'T CODE § 6253 (Deering 2003); 5 ILL. COMP. STAT. 140/3 (2002). There is no uniformity among the states in these areas, however, and there are many exceptions that allow state and local jurisdictions to protect some types of information generated by selected agencies, even in those states that have enacted open records laws. Consequently, some state and local agencies currently protect their databases and other productions under copyright and contract laws, and these agencies would likely make use of any additional intellectual property protection that new federal or state laws might provide. Nevertheless, most of the same policy reasons that support the public domain status of federal government information apply equally well at the lower levels of government and thus should exempt information produced by state and local governments from such protection. For an overview of state practice and policy implications, see Perritt, *supra* note 39.

41. *See generally* BIG SCIENCE, *supra* note 29.

42. *See* BITS OF POWER, *supra* note 1, at 58-61; *see also* OECD, EVALUATION OF THE OECD MEGASCIENCE FORUM; REPORT OF THE EXPERT PANEL (1998), *available at* http://www.oecd.org/pdf/M000014000/M00014730.pdf (last visited Feb. 13, 2003).

science satellites for robotic solar-system exploration, ground-based astronomical telescopes, earth observation satellites, networks of terrestrial sensors for continuous global environmental observations and global change studies, and more recently, automated genome-decoding machines.[43] Major examples in the experimental sciences have included facilities for neutron beam and synchrotron radiation sources, large lasers, supercolliders for high-energy particle physics, high-field magnet laboratories, and nuclear fusion experiments.[44]

The data from many of these government research projects, especially in the last two decades, have been openly shared and archived in public repositories. Hundreds of specialized data centers have been established by the federal science agencies or at universities under government contract.[45]

Scientific data and other kinds of information generated by the governments of other nations may also end up in the public domain and become available internationally.[46] Generally, however, the quantities are considerably smaller than the information resources generated by the U.S. government, and the

---

43. BITS OF POWER, *supra* note 1, at 58-61.

44. *Id.*

45. A few well-known examples of the government's public domain data archiving and dissemination activities include the NASA Space Science Data Center, http://nssdc.gsfc.nasa.gov (last visited Feb. 18, 2003); the National Oceanic and Atmospheric Administration's ("NOAA") National Data Centers, http://www.nesdis.noaa.gov (last visited Feb. 20, 2003); the U.S. Geological Survey's Earth Resources Observation Systems ("EROS") Data Center; http:// edc.usgs.gov (last visited Feb. 18, 2003); and the National Center for Biotechnology Information at the National Institutes of Health, http://www.ncbi.nlm.nih.gov (last visited Feb. 18, 2003); among many others. There is no comprehensive list of all data centers in all areas of science and technology. However, there are over 100 federal data centers listed for global change research alone. *See* NASA's Global Change Master Directory, http://gcmd.gsfc.nasa.gov (last visited Feb. 13, 2003). It is also important to note that some of these data repositories, such as the NOAA National Data Centers, charge substantial fees for access. *See infra* notes 56-60 and accompanying text.

Scientific and technical articles, reports, and other information products generated by the federal government are also not copyrightable and available in the public domain. 17 U.S.C. § 105 (2000). Most research agencies have well-organized and extensive dissemination activities for such information, typically referred to as scientific and technical information, or "STI" (as distinct from data as such). These organizations include the National Library of Medicine, http://www.nlm.nih.gov (last visited Feb. 20, 2003); the National Agricultural Library, http://www.nal.usda.gov (last visited Feb. 18, 2003); the Defense Technical Information Center, http://www.dtic.mil (last visited Feb. 20, 2003); the Office of Scientific and Technical Information at the U.S. Department of Energy, http://www.osti.gov (last visited Feb. 18, 2003); and the NASA Scientific and Technical Information Program, http://www.sti.nasa.gov (last visited Feb. 20. 2003); among others.

Most of the STI products held by these repositories are available free of charge. Many agencies, however, also use the National Technical Information Service in the Department of Commerce, http:// www.ntis.gov/ (last visited Feb. 20, 2003), which makes additional STI available to the public for a fee. The Federal Depository Library Program provides yet another outlet for such information through its regional libraries, *at* http://www.access.gpo.gov/SU_docs/locators/findlibs (last visited Feb. 18, 2003). Finally, the National Archives and Records Administration provides permanent access to a subset of the STI resources, which it appraises and makes selectively available thirty years after their production, at http://www.archives.gov/ (last visited Feb. 18, 2003).

46. David Banisar, Freedom of Information and Access to Government Records Around the World (July 2, 2002), *at* http://www.freedominfo.org/survey.htm (last visited Feb. 13, 2003) (indicating that over forty countries now have comprehensive laws to facilitate access to state records, and another thirty are in the process of enacting such statutes). For the situation in the European Union, see the European Commission's Green Paper, Public Sector Information: A Key Resource for Europe, *annexe* 1 at 20-25 COM (1998) 585 [hereinafter Green Paper].

public-access policies are much less open than those applicable in the United States.[47] Notable examples of foreign sources of public domain data are the World Data Centers for geophysical, environmental, and space data[48] and the human genome databases in Europe and Japan.[49] However, a key issue for both the exploitation of public data resources and for cooperative research generally is the asymmetry between the United States and foreign government approaches to the public domain availability of scientific data.[50] This asymmetry has been deepened by the European Union's adoption in 1996 of an exclusive property right in non-copyrightable collections of data, as discussed in more detail in Part III.

2. Limiting Factors

Before delving into the growing pressures on the public domain, a number of countervailing polices and practices that limit free or open and unrestricted use of government-generated data and information must be noted. Important statutory exemptions to public domain access are based on national security concerns,[51] the need to protect personal privacy of human subjects in research,[52] and the need to respect confidential information.[53] These limitations on the public domain accessibility of federal government information, while often justified, must nonetheless be balanced against the rights and needs of citizens to access and use it.

Another limitation derives from the fact that government-generated data are not necessarily provided cost free. The federal policy for information dissemination, as set out in the Office of Management and Budget's ("OMB") Circular A-130, stipulates that such data should be made available at the marginal cost of dissemination—that is, the cost of fulfilling a user request.[54] That policy expressly excludes recouping the costs of production, much less making a profit.[55] In practice, the prices actually charged vary between marginal and

---

47. Weiss & Backlund, *supra* note 7, at 307; Yvette Plujimers & Peter Weiss, *Borders in Cyberspace: Conflicting Public Sector Information Policies and their Economic Impacts* (unpublished manuscript, on file with authors).

48. For a brief history of the World Data Center system and their general principles of operation, see the International Council for Science Word Data Center System, at http://www.ngdc.noaa.gov/wdc/ (last visited Feb. 13, 2003). *See also* links to the various World Data Center home pages, at http://www.ngdc.noaa. gov/wdc/gdhomepg.html (last visited Feb. 13, 2003).

49. *See* European Human Genome Database, *available at* http://www.embl-heidelberg.de (last visited Feb 13, 2003); Human Genome Database of Japan, *available at* http://www.ddbj.nig.ac.jp (last visited Feb. 13, 2003).

50. The E.C. Directive on the legal protection of databases, *supra* note 17, does not prohibit proprietary rights in government-generated data (some governments assert these rights vigorously), nor does it mandate an exception for scientific uses of protected collections of data.

51. 5 U.S.C. § 552(b)(1) (2000).

52. 5 U.S.C. § 552(b)(6).

53. 5 U.S.C. § 552(b)(4).

54. Office of Management and Budget Circular A-130, § 8a(7) ("Information Management Policy—Avoiding Improperly Restrictive Practices") (Feb. 8, 1996), *available at* http://www.whitehouse.gov/omb/circulars/a130/ a130.html.

55. *Id.* at Appendix § 4.

incremental cost pricing arrangements.[56] Charges higher than the marginal cost of dissemination can create substantial barriers to access, particularly for academic research, which may require the use of large portions or the entire contents of huge databases for modeling or data mining applications. Nevertheless, this policy differs from that of most other countries, in which governmental or quasi-governmental agencies may exploit public information at full cost recovery rates and may also invoke the protection of that information under intellectual property law.[57]

In practice, a major barrier to accessing government-generated data and information arises from the failure of agencies to disseminate or preserve them for long-term availability. As a result, a massive amount of public domain information is either hidden from public view or is irretrievably lost.[58] Although this generally tends to be less problematic for scientific information, the well-known problems of inadequate documentation and organization are particularly acute for some areas of scientific data and information, particularly in the life sciences.[59] When the problem is a simple failure to disseminate, the Freedom of Information Act ("FOIA") may sometimes provide an antidote.[60] However, the process of filing a FOIA request is time consuming and bureaucratic.

Another limitation derives from OMB Circular A-76, which bars the government from directly competing with the private sector in providing information products and services.[61] This policy substantially narrows the amount and type of information that the government can undertake to produce and disseminate. As regards science, the well-accepted view is that basic research, together with its supporting data, constitute public goods that properly fall within the sphere of government activity, although the boundary between what is considered appropriate public or private functions continues to shift in this and other respects.

Finally, the government is required to respect the proprietary rights in data and information originating from the private sector that are made available for government use or, more generally, for regulatory and other purposes, unless

---

56. In some exceptional circumstances, agencies may charge full incremental cost recovery prices. For example, 15 U.S.C. § 1534 authorizes the Secretary of Commerce to charge fair market value for the data from the NOAA National Data Centers, although lower prices are allowed to be charged to educational organizations.

57. For the pricing policies for government data in the European Union, see Green Paper, *supra* note 46. *See also* PIRA INTERNATIONAL, COMMERCIAL EXPLOITATION OF EUROPE'S PUBLIC SECTOR INFORMATION, FINAL REPORT FOR THE EUROPEAN COMMISSION, DIRECTORATE GENERAL FOR THE INFORMATION SOCIETY (2000).

58. *See generally* 1 U.S. NATIONAL COMMISSION ON LIBRARIES AND INFORMATION SCIENCE, A COMPREHENSIVE ASSESSMENT OF PUBLIC INFORMATION DISSEMINATION, FINAL REPORT (2001). In the United States, some state governments also seek copyright protection of model codes and other quasi-legislative materials. *See, e.g.*, Veek v. S. Bldg. Code Cong. Int'l, 293 F.3d 791 (5th Cir.), *cert. granted*, 123 S. Ct. 650 (2002).

59. *See* BITS OF POWER, *supra* note 1, at 70-74.

60. Freedom of Information Act (FOIA), 5 U.S.C. § 552 (2002).

61. Office of Management and Budget Circular A-76 (Aug. 8, 1983, rev. 1999), Performance of Commercial Activities, § 5(c), *available at* http://www.whitehouse.gov/omb/circulars/a076/a076.html (last visited Feb. 13, 2003).

expressly exempted.[62] To the extent that more of the production and dissemination functions of research data are shifted from the public to the private sector, this limitation becomes more potent. Moreover, this trend easily gives way to pressures to prevent reasonable commercial uses of data that firms must submit to government for regulatory purposes and can even result in back door, de facto intellectual property rights that protect scientific data.[63] By the same token, foreign governments that opt to protect and commercialize their own data may seek to restrict their open dissemination and use by the U.S. government for research and other public-interest purposes.[64]

B. Government-Funded Data: Between the Research Commons and Commercial Applications

A second major source of public domain data and information for scientific research is that which is produced in academic or other not-for-profit institutions with government and philanthropic funding. However, databases and other information goods produced in these settings become presumptively protectible under any relevant intellectual property regime unless affirmative steps are taken to place such material in the public domain. In this case, the public domain must be actively created, rather than passively conferred.

This component of the public domain results from the contractual requirements of the granting agencies in combination with long-standing norms of science. These norms aspire to implement "full and open access" to scientific data as well as the sharing of research results so as to promote new endeavors. The policy of full and open access or exchange has been defined in various U.S. government policy documents and in National Research Council ("NRC") reports in the following terms: "[D]ata and information derived from publicly funded research are [to be] made available with as few restrictions as possible, on a nondiscriminatory basis, for no more than the cost of reproduction and distribu-

---

62. *See, e.g.*, TREVOR M. COOK, THE PROTECTION OF REGULATORY DATA IN PHARMACEUTICAL AND OTHER SECTORS, Preface, 7 (2000) (stressing that concerns about the confidentiality of regulatory data, including the results of clinical trials, have mainly surfaced in the past twenty-five years). Since 1982, the United States has adopted provisions to protect regulatory data submitted to federal agencies in connection with pesticides, and it has imposed regulatory exclusivity provisions for medical data since 1984. *Id.* at 4-01. These provisions reportedly "provide a *de facto* measure of . . . data protection" to new chemical entities for five years and they give three years of protection for "data filed . . . in support of . . . chemical entities which have already been approved for use in medicines but [for] which fresh authorizations are [to be] based on new clinical investigations." *Id.* For analogous provisions that may confer even longer periods of protection in the European Union, Australia, and New Zealand, see *id.* at Preface 6-7, 3-01, 5-01.

63. *See, e.g.*, Ruckelshaus v. Monsanto Co., 467 U.S. 986, 1019-20 (1984); Bayer, Inc. v. Canada (Attorney General), [1999] F.C.A.D.J. 142. Some obligations in this regard have even been codified as international minimum standards under article 39.3 of the TRIPS Agreement. Agreement on Trade-Related Aspects of Intellectual Property Rights, April 15, 1994, 33 I.L.M. 81 [hereinafter TRIPS Agreement]. *See generally* Carlos Correa, *Public Health and International Law: Unfair Competition Under the TRIPS Agreement Article 39.3: Protection of Data Submitted for Registration of Pharmaceuticals*, 3 CHI. J. INT'L L. 69 (2002).

64. *See infra* notes 543-50 and accompanying text.

tion"[65] (that is, the marginal cost, which on the Internet is zero). This policy is promoted by different U.S. government agencies with varying degrees of success. It also applies to most government-funded or cooperative research arrangements, particularly in large, institutionalized research programs, such as "global change" studies or the human genome project, and even to smaller-scale collaborations involving individual investigators who are not otherwise affiliated with private-sector partners.[66]

Because government agencies are funding these efforts, they are in a position to reinforce the underlying norms of science by suitable contractual provisions that regulate access to data before and after publication of the research results. Basic research grants in particular attempt to ensure that government-funded data enter the upstream processes of scientific research as an input available from the public domain.[67]

In addition, the research articles published in scientific journals will themselves become subject to the balancing of public and private interests that occurs under the prevailing intellectual property regime. For example, traditional copyright principles have consigned facts, ideas, data, and findings to the public domain; there are codified exceptions for research and educational uses, and exceptions for fair uses or private use to advance research and other public-interest goals have been granted.[68]

Scientists also hold much data in their individual capacities, which will be made available on a transactional basis. In principle, the government science agencies' contractual specifications that promote eventual access to government-funded data reinforce long-standing norms of science, which are traditionally premised on open access and the sharing ethos.[69] While the real-world implementation of these norms has always been imperfect and is now subject to intense countervailing pressures that are described below, one must nonetheless emphasize, at the outset, that the government's baseline default rules and the norms of science remain mutually reinforcing with respect to data as an input into scientific research. This convergence traditionally makes it harder for scientists to violate these contractual and cultural norms with regard to access to government-funded data as upstream inputs for research purposes.

Even so, scientific data have a dual nature in the sense that they are also outputs of the scientific process, and these outputs—suitably aggregated—become inputs once again into the national system of innovation. Here,

---

65. BITS OF POWER, *supra* note 1, at 1.

66. *See* FULL AND OPEN EXCHANGE, *supra* note 8 at 2; NATIONAL SCIENCE FOUNDATION, GRANT GENERAL CONDITIONS (GC-1) #36 (2001).

67. *See, e.g.*, NATIONAL SCIENCE FOUNDATION 95-26, GRANT POLICY MANUAL § 734 (1995) [hereinafter GRANT POLICY MANUAL]; *see also infra* note 72.

68. *See supra* note 12; Thomas Dreier, *Balancing Proprietary and Public Domain Interests: Inside or Outside Proprietary Rights*, *in* EXPANDING THE BOUNDARIES OF IP, *supra* note 13, at 295, 301, 303-09. *See generally* Jaap H. Spoor, *General Aspects of Exceptions and Limitations to Copyright: General Report*, *in* THE BOUNDARIES OF COPYRIGHT—ITS PROPER LIMITATIONS AND EXCEPTIONS 27-41 (Libby Baulch et al. eds., 1997) (providing the most recent comparative survey of existing law).

69. *See supra* note 8.

however, very different government policies may apply. The non-proprietarial default rule built into government-funded data exists side-by-side with a second, posterior set of default rules that encourage research entities outside the federal system to transfer government-funded research from the public to the private sector, usually by means of intellectual property rights.[70]

It becomes necessary to look beyond the surface to gain some deeper insights into how the stated policies and rules built around government-funded data are actually implemented in academic science. In this regard, it is useful to further subdivide the producers of government-funded data into two distinct but partially overlapping categories.

In one category, the research takes place in a highly structured academic setting, with relatively clear rules set by government funding agencies that determine the rights of researchers in the production, dissemination, and use of data. Publication of the research results constitutes the primary organizing principle. Traditionally, the rules and norms that apply in this sphere, which we call the zone of formally regulated access to data, aim with varying degrees of success to achieve a bright line of demarcation between the public and private rights to the data being generated.

In the other category, individual scientists establish their own interpersonal relationships and networks with other colleagues, largely within their specialized research communities. In this category, which we call the zone of informal data exchanges, scientists may generate and hold their data subject to their own interests and to the interplay of norms, rules, and competitive strategies that may deviate considerably from the practices established within the zone of formal exchanges.

1. The Zone of Formally Regulated Access to Data

As previously noted, when federal government agencies fund research projects that include the production of scientific data in not-for-profit academic institutions, they typically stipulate a set of rights and obligations binding the agency and the principal investigator with regard to those data. For example, the grant may entitle the investigator to a period of exclusive use of the relevant data prior to publication of the research results. It may also mandate that the data sets collected under the grant become freely available for others to use following the publication of results or upon the expiration of the exclusive use period, and to this end, it may further specify that such materials should be deposited in government or university data centers or archives.[71]

70. *See, e.g.*, Rai, *supra* note 33, at 95-115; *see also* Brett Frischmann, *Innovation and Institutions: Rethinking the Economics of U.S. Science and Technology Policy*, 24 VT. L. REV. 347, 353, 395-413 (2000).

71. *See, e.g.*, National Science Foundation Office of Polar Programs, Guidelines and Award Conditions for Scientific Data (1998); National Aeronautics and Space Administration, Science Policy Guide (1996); National Science Foundation Division of Ocean Sciences 94-126, Policy for Oceanographic Data (1994).

a. Contractually Reinforcing the Sharing Ethos

Contractual requirements vary by agency and discipline and even by research programs undertaken within the same agency. Different agencies may address these issues with more or less attentiveness, and different offices within the same agency may have diverse requirements as well.[72]

---

72. Although a comprehensive assessment of specific data rights across all federal science agency grants and contracts is beyond the scope of this discussion, a brief review of some of the most common provisions is instructive.

For example, the standard clause on "Dissemination and Sharing of Research Results" in a National Science Foundation ("NSF") grant provides as follows:

> a. Investigators are expected to promptly prepare and submit for publication, with authorship that accurately reflects the contributions of those involved, all significant findings from work conducted under NSF grants. Grantees are expected to permit and encourage such publication by those actually performing that work, unless a grantee intends to publish or disseminate such findings itself.
>
> b. Investigators are expected to share with other researchers, at no more than incremental cost and within a reasonable time, the primary data, samples, physical collections and other supporting materials created or gathered in the course of work under NSF grants. Grantees are expected to encourage and facilitate such sharing. . . .
>
> c. Investigators and grantees are encouraged to share software and inventions created under the grant or otherwise make them or their products widely available and usable.
>
> d. The NSF normally allows grantees to retain principal legal rights to intellectual property developed under NSF grants to provide incentives for development and dissemination of inventions, software and publications that can enhance their usefulness, accessibility and upkeep. Such incentives do not, however, reduce the responsibility that investigators and organizations have as members of the scientific and engineering community to make results, data and collections available to other researchers.

GRANT POLICY MANUAL, *supra* note 67, at § 734.

The National Institutes of Health ("NIH") is currently developing a statement on sharing research data that:

> [E]xpects and supports the timely release and sharing of final research data from NIH-supported studies for use by other researchers. Investigators submitting an NIH application will be required to include a plan for data-sharing or to state why data-sharing is not possible. This statement will apply to extramural scientists seeking grants, cooperative agreements, and contracts as well as intramural investigators.

Release, NIH Announces Draft Statement on Sharing Research Data, (March 1, 2002) (NOTICE: NOT-OD-02-035), *available at* http://grants1.nih.gov/grants/guide/notice-files/NOT-OD-02-035.html (last visited Jan. 10, 2003).

The announcement goes on to say:

> There are many reasons to share data from NIH-supported studies. Sharing data reinforces open scientific inquiry, encourages diversity of analysis and opinion, promotes new research, makes possible the testing of new or alternative hypotheses and methods of analysis, supports studies on data collection methods and measurement, facilitates the education of new researchers, enables the exploration of topics not envisioned by the initial investigators, and permits the creation of new data sets when data from multiple sources are combined. By avoiding the duplication of expensive data collection activities, the NIH is able to support more investigators that it could if similar data had to be collected de novo by each applicant.

Id.

Similarly, NASA's Data Availability Policy states that:

> [R]eady access to data from NASA research programs and missions (via modern data archiving and communications technologies) by researchers not directly involved in the program increases the return on NASA research investments. It is therefore NASA policy that nonproprietary scientific data obtained from NASA programs and missions will be made publicly available in usable form as quickly as possible.

In general, the common thrust of these different types of clauses is to ensure that the data collected or generated by grantees will be openly shared with other researchers, at least following some specified period of exclusive use—typically ranging from six to twenty-four months—or until the time of publication of the research results based on those data.[73] This relatively brief period is intended to give the grantee sufficient time to produce, organize, document, verify, and analyze the data being used in preparation of a research article or report for scholarly publication. In many cases, the data are placed in a public archive upon publication, or at the expiration of the specified period of exclusive use and are expressly designated as free from legal protection, or they are expected to be made available directly by the researcher to anyone who requests access.

In most cases, publication of research results marks the point at which data produced by government-funded investigators should become generally available. The standard research grant requirement or norm has been that once publication occurs, it will trigger public disclosure of the supporting data. To the extent that this requirement is implemented in practice, it represents the culmination of the scientific norms of sharing.[74] From this point forward, access to the investigator's results will depend on the method chosen to make the underlying data publicly available and on the traditional legal norms—especially those of copyright law—that govern scientific works.

These organizing principles derive historically from the premise that academic researchers typically are not driven by the same motivations as their counterparts in industry. Public-interest research is not dependent on the maximization of profits and value to shareholders through the protection of proprietary rights in information. Rather, the motivations of not-for-profit scientists are predominantly rooted in intellectual curiosity, the desire to create new knowledge, peer recognition and career advancement, and the promotion of the public interest.[75] As R. Stephen Berry, the Home Secretary for the National Academy of Sciences, recently noted:

> Scientists are not, for the most part, motivated to do research to make money. If they were, they would be in different fields. The primary motivation for most research scientists is the desire for influence and impact on the thinking of others about the natu-

---

BITS OF POWER, *supra* note 1, at 80 (quoting NASA Science Policy Guide (1996)). The policy goes on to provide a list of competing factors that need to be considered in determining data rights, and presents examples of data rights that have been used, mostly variations on the length of the initial period of an investigator's proprietary use.

73. *See* BITS OF POWER, *supra* note 1, at 79. One of the recommendations of that report was that all scientists conducting publicly funded research should make their data available immediately, or following a reasonable period of time for proprietary use. *Id.* at 11.

74. *See, e.g.*, NATIONAL RESEARCH COUNCIL, COMMUNITY STANDARDS FOR SHARING PUBLICATION-RELATED DATA AND MATERIALS (2002) [hereinafter COMMUNITY STANDARDS] (discussing these norms and requirements in the biological sciences).

75. *See, e.g.*, Rebecca Eisenberg, *Proprietary Rights and the Norms of Science in Biotechnology Research*, 97 YALE L.J. 177, 178 (1987) [hereinafter Eisenberg, *Proprietary Rights*] ("The scientific community rewards those who make original contributions to the common stock of knowledge by giving them professional recognition.").

> ral world—unless the desire for their own personal understanding is even stronger. . . . The currency of the researcher is the extent to which her or his ideas influence the thinking of others. . . . What this implies is that the distribution of the results of research has an extremely high priority for any working scientists, apart from those whose work is behind proprietary walls.[76]

Science policy in the United States has long taken for granted that these values and goals are best served by the maximum availability and distribution of research results, at the lowest possible cost, with the fewest restrictions on use, and the promotion of reuse and integration of the fruits of existing results in new research. The placement of scientific and technical ("S&T") data and databases in the public domain, and the established policy of full and open access to such resources in the government and academic sectors[77] reflect these values and serve these goals.

b. Legal Rules that Support the Sharing Ethos

Assuming that the relatively standard grant rules apply and that scientific data are fully disclosed at the time of publication in the manner previously described, the intellectual property norms that traditionally came into play in the post-publication phase were, on the whole, consonant with the cultural norms of the scientific enterprise. First, data as such were not generally considered subject matter eligible for copyright protection in most jurisdictions, and the few deviant jurisdictions that thought otherwise were overruled by the 1991 Supreme Court decision in *Feist Publications, Inc. v. Rural Telephone Service Co.*[78] Furthermore, the United States has not yet adopted a *sui generis* legal regime to protect non-copyrightable collections of information as the European Union did in 1996,[79] while most claims arising under unfair competition law are forfeited with voluntary disclosure to the public.[80]

Second, the power of contracts to regulate the dissemination of publicly disclosed data was inherently weak in the pre-digital age owing to the inability of the contracting parties to sue third parties who obtained the relevant data outside of the contractual relationship.[81] It was the inherent weakness of these

---

76. R. Stephen Berry, *Is Electronic Publishing Being Used in the Best Interests of Science? The Scientists' View*, 2001 INT'L J. MOLECULAR SCI. 133, 134 (2001).

77. *See supra* notes 65, 72 and accompanying text.

78. 499 U.S. 340 (1991) (holding the factual information in the white pages of a telephone book lacked creativity and originality in selection and arrangement, and was not copyrightable). *But see* Paula Baron, *Back to the Future: Learning from the Past in the Database Debate*, 62 OHIO ST. L. J. 874 (2001); Robert C. Denicola, *Copyright in Collections of Facts: A Theory for the Protection of Nonfiction Literary Works*, 81 COLUM. L. REV. 516, 528, 539-40 (1981) (stressing need for compiler's incentives); Jane C. Ginsburg, *Creation and Commercial Value: Copyright Protection of Works of Information*, 90 COLUM. L. REV. 1865 (1990) [hereinafter Ginsburg, *Commercial Value*].

79. E.C. Database Directive, *supra* note 17.

80. *See generally* RESTATEMENT (THIRD) OF UNFAIR COMPETITION §§ 38-45 (1995) (allowing claim of misappropriation of trade secrets, but not recognizing any broader misappropriation claim rooted in copying as such). However, state law doctrines of misappropriation may nonetheless apply to wholesale duplication of databases to a still unknown extent. *See, e.g.*, Int'l News Serv. v. Assoc. Press, 248 U.S. 215 (1918); Nat'l Basketball Ass'n v. Motorola, Inc., 105 F.3d 841 (2d Cir. 1996).

81. *See* PAUL GOLDSTEIN, COPYRIGHT'S HIGHWAY: FROM GUTENBERG TO THE CELESTIAL JUKEBOX 27 (1994) (noting the lack of need for copyright protection before the printing press).

"two-party deals" to regulate generally the dissemination of intangible literary and artistic productions that gave rise to copyright and neighboring rights laws,[82] which impose an unbargained-for set of default rules upon all those who gain access to such productions.[83] If anything, the traditional use of grants and contracts in the domain of government-funded data was to implement the sharing norms of science, as shown above.[84]

Third, with regard to the data and information contained in published scientific works, the balance of public and private interests traditionally struck by U.S. copyright law was particularly favorable to second-comers and researchers in general. Collections of information distributed in hard copies, such as directories, handbooks, and other useful compilations of facts or data, are copyrightable only to the extent that they manifest a minimum quantum of original and creative authorship.[85] Typically, the requisite degree of authorship is revealed in the compiler's criteria for selecting, arranging, and documenting the data assembled in any given compilation.[86] However, the facts and data contained in a copyrightable scientific work, for example, are ineligible for protection as are any "idea, procedure, process, system, method of operation, concept, principle or discovery" it contains.[87]

Moreover, after passing the threshold of copyright law, even those "factual works" that do manifest the minimum degree of creative authorship are likely to obtain only a "thin" scope of protection at the infringement stage.[88] Because the facts and data in scientific works are not copyrightable subject matter, and only the creative selection or arrangement is protectible, a second-comer can, in principle, borrow the first-comer's disparate data while varying the organizational format. As the Supreme Court noted in *Feist*, the traditional copyright approach to scientific and other factual works thus strikes a balance between incentives to invest and free competition that tends to err on the side of second-comers.[89] In effect, by severely curtailing the first-comer's ability to control follow-on applications of factual content,[90] copyright law in this area operates as a kind of roving unfair competition law that protects the authors of scientific works mainly against wholesale duplication. In the United States, these limitations are thought to have constitutional underpinnings, in keeping with First

82. *See* Reichman & Franklin, *supra* note 16, at 897-99.

83. *See, e.g.*, Peter A. Jaszi, *Goodbye to All That—A Reluctant (and Perhaps Premature) Adieu to a Constitutionally—Grounded Discourse of Public-Interest in Copyright Law*, 29 VAND. J. TRANSNAT'L L. 595, 599-600 (1996) (stressing economic and cultural bargain between authors and users).

84. *See supra* note 72 (citing specific examples).

85. 17 U.S.C. §101 (2000) (definition of compilations); § 102(a)-(b); § 103; Feist Publ'ns, Inc. v. Rural Tel. Servs. Co., 499 U.S. 340, 345 (1991).

86. *See Feist*, 499 U.S. at 348; *see also* Warren Publ'g Inc. v. Microdos Data Corp., 52 F.3d 950, 956 (11th Cir. 1995); Bellsouth Adver. & Publ'g Corp. v. Donnelly Info. Publ'g Inc., 999 F.2d 1436, 1446 (11th Cir. 1993) (en banc); Key Publ'ns, Inc. v. Chinatown Publ'g Enter., Inc., 945 F.2d. 509, 514 (2d Cir. 1991).

87. 17 U.S.C. § 102(b); Harper & Row Publ'rs, Inc. v. Nation Enters., 471 U.S. 539 (1985).

88. *Feist*, 499 U.S. at 349.

89. *Id.* at 349-50.

90. Notwithstanding 17 U.S.C. § 103 and § 106(2), which the Supreme Court limited in this respect.

Amendment rights protecting freedom of speech and with the role of a robust public domain in democratic discourse.[91]

One of the largest categories of scientific information in the United States thus consists of ineligible collections of data or the non-copyrightable contents of otherwise copyrightable works, including databases, articles, or reference books. This category of public domain information, while highly distributed among all types of proprietary works, plays a fundamental role in supporting research and education, especially in the data-intensive sciences. However, strenuous efforts are being made to devise new forms of protection for all of this previously unprotectible subject matter, as explained in Part III of this article.

When scientific works, including compilations of data and information, do attract copyright protection, the copyright laws of most countries contain codified limitations, exceptions, or immunities that favor teaching, research, and other educational activities.[92] In European Union countries, there is a "private use" exception, which to some extent overlaps the much broader "fair use" exception in U.S. copyright law.[93] Also, in the European Union compulsory licenses may be enacted to promote public policy goals, including research and education, without depriving authors of an economic return from these uses of their works.[94] For example, some countries allow the photocopying of copyrighted journals for research purposes only in exchange for compensatory payments that are increasingly worked out with collection societies representing authors' interests in these matters.[95]

In U.S. copyright law, considerable emphasis has traditionally been placed on the fair use exception to copyright protection,[96] which permits certain uses to

---

91. *Harper & Row*, 471 U.S. at 582; *see also* Yochai Benkler, *Constitutional Bounds of Database Protection: The Role of Judicial Review in the Creation and Definition of Private Rights in Information*, 15 BERKELEY TECH. L.J. 535 (2000) [hereinafter Benkler, *Constitutional Bounds*]; Yochai Benkler, *Free as the Air to Common Use: First Amendment Constraints on Enclosure of the Public Domain*, 74 N.Y.U. L. REV. 354 (1999) [hereinafter Benkler, *Free as the Air*]; James Boyle, *Foucault in Cyberspace: Surveillance, Sovereignty, and Hardwired Censors*, 66 U. CIN. L. REV. 177 (1997); Marci A. Hamilton, *A Response to Professor Benkler*, 15 BERKELEY TECH. L. J. 605 (2000); Neil Netanel, *Locating Copyright Within the First Amendment Skein*, 54 STAN. L. REV. 1 (2001).

92. *See, e.g.*, Dreier, *supra* note 68; Sam Ricketson, *International Conventions and Treaties*, *in* BOUNDARIES OF COPYRIGHT, *supra* note 68, at 3, 5-10 (stressing recurring exceptions in national copyright laws for private study, and for "use for scientific and research purposes," in addition to provisions allowing use for teaching purposes); *see also* Ruth Okediji, *Toward an International Fair Use Doctrine*, 39 COLUM. J. TRANSNAT'L L. 75 (2000).

93. *See* Adolf Dietz, *Germany*, *in* BOUNDARIES OF COPYRIGHT, *supra* note 68, at 265, 269 (noting rights of free reproduction or other private use, sometimes subject to an obligation to remunerate, under articles 53-54(a) of German copyright law); Yves Gaubiac, *France*, *in id.* at 226, 231 (noting exception for private noncommercial use to promote private study and research under French law).

94. *See, e.g.*, Dreier, *supra* note 68; Ricketson, *supra* note 92, at 9, 14; Spoor, *supra* note 68.

95. *See, e.g.*, LUCIE M.C.R. GUIBAULT, COPYRIGHT LIMITATIONS AND CONTRACTS: AN ANALYSIS OF THE CONTRACTUAL OVERRIDABILITY OF LIMITATIONS ON COPYRIGHT 81-82 (2002) (discussing mandatory collective administration of reprography right under French copyright law); Dietz, *supra* note 93, at 269 (stressing basic permissibility of private copying and reprography even when subject to collective agreements on equitable remuneration).

96. 17 U.S.C. § 107 (2000).

be made of otherwise protected content under limited circumstances, in order to advance the public interest in certain privileged policy goals without unduly burdening the authors' incentive to create.[97] On a case-by-case basis, this doctrine may permit uses of otherwise protected expression,[98] especially for such purposes as illustration, teaching, research, verification, and news reporting.[99] However, the strength of this exception varies with judicial attitudes and from period to period, and its consistency with international intellectual property law has been called into question.[100]

Because many so-called fair uses are allowed only in the context of not-for-profit research or education, this category of "public domain uses," though relatively small, is especially important in the research context. While commentators have not typically associated fair uses and other exceptions with the "public domain,"[101] a number of traditionally practiced immunities and exceptions, including fair use, may be construed as functional equivalents of public domain uses, especially where science and education are concerned.[102]

Applications of the fair use exception tend to be controversial, however, even with regard to educational and research activities, where publishers often emphasize the harm to markets resulting from ad hoc judicial concessions to users of copyrighted materials in particular situations.[103] Recently, the federal appellate courts have tended to restrict the fair use exception when technical means to overcome market failure are shown to exist,[104] and the Digital Millennium Copyright Act ("DMCA") has severely cut back on the application of fair use to online transmissions.[105] At the same time, there is growing interest in doctrines of misuse of copyrights, which courts have used to strike down

---

97. *See, e.g.*, Julie E. Cohen, *Lochner in Cyberspace: The New Economic Orthodoxy of Rights Management*, 97 MICH. L. REV. 462, 468-80 (1998); William W. Fisher, III, *Reconstructing the Fair Use Doctrine*, 101 HARV. L. REV. 1661 (1998); Wendy J. Gordon, *Fair Use as Market Failure: A Structural and Economic Analysis of the Betamax Case and Its Predecessors*, 82 COLUM. L. REV. 1600 (1982).

98. Campbell v. Acuff-Rose Music, Inc., 510 U.S. 569 (1994); SunTrust Bank v. Houghton Mifflin Co., 268 F.3d 1257 (11th Cir. 2001) (finding at preliminary injunction stage, publisher of *The Wind Done Gone* was entitled to fair-use defense against copyright infringement claim); Williams & Wilkins Co. v. United States, 487 F.2d 1345 (Ct. Cl. 1973).

99. *See* 17 U.S.C. § 107 (preambular uses). *See generally* PAUL GOLDSTEIN, COPYRIGHT: PRINCIPLES, LAW AND PRACTICE § 10.1.5 (1996).

100. *See, e.g.*, Okediji, *supra* note 92.

101. *See, e.g.*, GOLDSTEIN, *supra* note 99, at §10.1 (noting theories of fair use sounding in "privilege," "equitable rule of reason," "market failure," and "public benefit" theories).

102. *Cf., e.g.*, *id.* at §10.2.1 (stressing cultural and social values of an educated public that follow from preambular fair uses favoring teaching, scholarship, and research).

103. 17 U.S.C. § 107(4).

104. Princeton Univ. Press v. Michigan Document Servs., 99 F.3d 1381 (6th Cir. 1996); Am. Geophysical Union v. Texaco, Inc., 60 F.3d 913 (2d Cir. 1994); *see also* Gordon, *supra* note 97.

105. 17 U.S.C. § 1201; David Nimmer, *A Riff on Fair Use in the Digital Millennium Copyright Act*, 148 U. PA. L. REV. 673 (2000); Pamela Samuelson, *Mapping the Digital Public Domain*, 66 LAW & CONTEMP. PROBS. 147 (Winter/Spring 2003); *see also* Ginsburg, *U.S. Initiatives*, *supra* note 18, at 62-67; Maureen A. O'Rourke, *Copyright Preemption After the Pro-CD Case: A Market Based Approach*, 12 BERKELEY TECH. L.J. 53 (1997).

licensing restrictions that unreasonably extend the statutory bundle of exclusive rights or that otherwise impose unreasonable restraints on trade.[106]

Finally, it should be recalled that copyrights eventually expire when the statutory period of protection ends, and the public then becomes the residual owner of all previously protected works. The basic term of copyright protection is very long, especially in the United States and the European Union, where it now lasts for the life of the author plus seventy years.[107] The United States separately protects corporate works (technically, works made for hire) for either a term of ninety-five years from first publication or 120 years from creation, whichever is shorter.[108] The relevant international minimum standard requires a term of life plus fifty years for works by human authors and at least fifty years of protection for works by corporate authors.[109]

Works whose copyrights have expired constitute an enormous body of freely available literature and information with great cultural and historical significance, and some materials in this category have obvious relevance to certain types of research, especially in the social sciences and the humanities. Even some of the "hard" sciences can derive substantial value from public domain data and information that are decades or even many centuries old. For example, the extraction of environmental information from a broad range of historical sources can help to establish climatological trends, or assist in identifying or better understanding a broad range of natural phenomena.[110] Ancient Chinese writings are expected to be useful in identifying herbal medicines for modern pharmaceutical development.[111] Proposals for more systematic and ambitious databases concerning traditional know-how and medicines are on the table,[112] although these proposals would almost invariably subject such information to new forms of intellectual property rights that would limit their availability in the public domain.[113] On the whole, because of the long lag time before entering the

---

106. *See, e.g.*, Dreier, *supra* note 68, at 311-12; Brett Frischmann & Dan Moylan, *The Evolving Common Law Doctrine of Copyright Misuse: A Unified Theory and Its Application to Software*, 15 BERKELEY TECH. L.J. 865 (2000).

107. 17 U.S.C. §§ 302, 303 (2000); Council Directive 93/98/EEC of 29 October 1993 Harmonizing the Term of Protection of Copyright and Certain Related Rights, 1993 O.J. (L 290) 9; *see also* Eldred v. Reno, 239 F.3d 372 (D.C. Cir. 2001), *cert. granted sub nom*, Eldred v. Ashcroft, 534 U.S. 1062, *and cert. amended*, 534 U.S. 1160 (2002).

108. 17 U.S.C. § 302(c).

109. TRIPS Agreement, *supra* note 63, art. 12; Berne Convention for the Protection of Literary and Artistic Works, Sept. 9, 1886 (as last revised July 24, 1971, and amended Oct. 2, 1979), 828 U.N.T.S. 221, art. 7(1) [hereinafter Berne Convention]. *See generally* J. H. Reichman, *The Duration of Copyright and the Limits of Cultural Policy*, 14 CARDOZO ARTS & ENT. L.J. 625 (1996).

110. FULL AND OPEN EXCHANGE, *supra* note 8, at 3.

111. BITS OF POWER, *supra* note 1, at 73.

112. *See, e.g.*, Graham Dutfield, *TRIPS-Related Aspects of Traditional Knowledge*, 33 CASE W. RES. J. INT'L L. 239 (2001); Traditional Knowledge, Intellectual Property and Indigenous Culture, Symposium presented at the Benjamin N. Cardozo School of Law (Feb. 21-22, 2002).

113. *See, e.g.*, William van Caenegem, *The Public Domain: Scientia Nullius?*, 2002 E.I.P.R. 324, 325, 328-30 (2002) (warning that some constructions of the public domain may be used to dispossess rights of indigenous peoples deriving from different social and cultural constructs).

public domain, most of the information in this category of lapsed protection lacks relevance to most types of state-of-the-art research.

c. Countervailing Policies: The Commercialization of Government-Funded Research

In the academic sector, the predominant norms remain those of open disclosure and the sharing of research data at the time of publication, if not before, and in many cases, this ethos also entails the placement of the data derived from federally funded research in public data centers and archives. Nevertheless, diverse policy incentives and economic pressures have increasingly induced research universities and academics to protect or commercialize their research data, rather than place them in the public domain. The costs and tuitions of higher education have far outpaced inflation, so there are direct economic needs for the universities to generate new sources of income wherever possible.[114] Perhaps most significant, the 1980 Bayh-Dole Act[115] has encouraged academics to protect and commercialize the fruits of their federally funded research,[116] especially in the potentially lucrative biomedical research area.[117]

While Bayh-Dole technically applies only to data products otherwise eligible for patent protection,[118] it supports the broader principle that universities should seek to commercialize applications of government-funded research products in general. Under Bayh-Dole, universities have moved away from policies that favor pure research, both for its own sake and as a tool for advancing higher education. As the costs of education skyrocket, and government funding fails to keep up in many areas, universities have aggressively sought to exploit commercial applications of research results, with an eye toward maximizing returns on investment.[119]

There is evidence that the Bayh-Dole Act has exerted a positive effect on technological innovation and that it has generated fruitful public–private part-

114. Regarding the steep rises in higher education costs, see NATIONAL CENTER FOR PUBLIC POLICY AND HIGHER EDUCATION, LOSING GROUND: A NATIONAL STATUS REPORT ON THE AFFORDABILITY OF AMERICAN HIGHER EDUCATION (2002), *available at* http://www.highereducation.org/reports/losing_ ground/ar.shtml/ (last visited Jan. 10, 2003).

115. Pub. L. No. 96-517, § 6(a), 94 Stat. 3015, 3019-28 (1980) (codified as amended at 35 U.S.C. §§ 200-212 (2000)).

116. "It is the policy and objective of Congress to use the patent system to promote the utilization of inventions arising from federally supported research or development . . . [and] to promote the collaboration between commercial concerns and nonprofit organizations, including universities . . . ." 35 U.S.C. § 200 (2000).

117. Arti K. Rai & Rebecca S. Eisenberg, *Bayh-Dole Reform and the Progress of Biomedicine*, 66 LAW & CONTEMP. PROBS. 289 (Winter/Spring 2003); *see also* Frischmann, *supra* note 70, at 397-413; Rai, *supra* note 33, at 95-100.

118. 35 U.S.C. § 202(a) (2000).

119. Note, however, that generating revenue for universities was not the goal of the Bayh-Dole Act. Rai & Eisenberg, *supra* note 117, at 300. Technically, the Bayh-Dole Act requires that the profits accruing to the beneficiary nonprofit organizations "be utilized for the support of scientific research or education." *See* 35 U.S.C. § 202(c)(7) (2000).

nerships for commercial exploitation of academic research.[120] At the same time, the policies promoting downstream application of university research results under Bayh-Dole have increasingly come into conflict with the policies favoring full and open access to research data and with the larger educational and public interest mission of universities.[121]

First of all, because Bayh-Dole inclines university administrations and individual academics to seek opportunities for the commercial exploitation of federally funded research, they are tempted to hoard data, to refrain from divulging them fully, and to conduct research operations under rules of secrecy and confidentiality. In doing so, they are increasingly likely to treat data collections as private goods in support of commercial exploitation of related applications under restrictive licensing agreements.[122]

A second development stemming in part from the blurring and collapse of the boundaries between basic and applied research, especially in biotechnology, is the discovery of ways to commercialize upstream aggregates of data as research tools and products.[123] This development greatly augments the potential value of some scientific databases, and raises obstacles to the dissemination and use of research data as further inputs into the research process that were seldom previously encountered.[124] In this environment, the value of the data supporting a patent application under Bayh-Dole may ultimately exceed the value of the invention being claimed, and more and more patent applications cover electronic information tools built around aggregates of data.

Similarly, the data supporting published scientific research may have potential commercial value to the originating institution and the responsible team of

---

120. Rebecca S. Eisenberg, *Public Research and Private Development: Patents and Technology Transfer in Government-Sponsored Research*, 82 VA. L. REV. 1663 (1996) [hereinafter Eisenberg, *Public Research*].

121. *See, e.g.*, Eisenberg, *Proprietary Rights*, *supra* note 75, at 180 (finding that although the patent system and the norms of science have much in common, "the conjunction may nonetheless cause delay in the dissemination of new knowledge and aggravate inherent conflict between the norms and reward structure of science"); Rebecca S. Eisenberg & Richard Nelson, *Public vs. Proprietary Science: A Fruitful Tension*, DAEDALUS, Spring 2002, at 92 ("Even if expected practical benefits make patentable outcomes likely and motivate private firms to pay for the research, public funding might still be justified to increase the open domain of commonly owned knowledge upon which scientists may draw freely in future research."); Rai, *supra* note 33, at 109-37 (stressing negative impact on public domain); *see also* Avital Bar-Shalom & Robert Cook-Deegan, *Patents and Innovation in Cancer Therapeutics: Lessons from CellPro* (2002) (unpublished study on file with authors).

122. *See, e.g.*, Rai, *supra* note 33, at 115 (finding that "both communalism and norms against secrecy have been eroded by delays in publication and restrictions on the sharing of [biotech] research materials and tools caused by concerns about intellectual property rights," but recognizing some reluctance to claim property rights in certain upstream discoveries by major research universities).

123. Rebecca Eisenberg, *Patenting Research Tools and the Law*, *in* NATIONAL RESEARCH COUNCIL, IPR AND THE DISSEMINATION OF RESEARCH TOOLS IN MOLECULAR BIOLOGY 2 (1997) [hereinafter Eisenberg, *Patenting Research Tools*] (noting that, as a result of the Bayh-Dole Act, "institutions that perform fundamental research have an incentive to patent the sorts of early stage discoveries that in an earlier era would have been dedicated to the public domain"); *see also* STOKES, *supra* note 35, at 58-59 (regarding the lessening of well-defined distinctions between "basic" and "applied" research in certain areas).

124. Obstacles include potentially high direct and transactions costs between publicly funded institutions.

investigators. This prospect, in turn, puts institutional pressures on the sharing ethos in academia, which can limit disclosure and delay the publication of research results. It can also result in decisions not to publish at all or efforts to control the supporting data even after publication.

As databases become an ever more valuable commodity on the ledgers of university technology licensing offices, the university administrations may also become increasingly ambivalent about the established policies that promote open access to government-funded data.[125] Universities and segments of the academic scientific community tend to view proposals for new statutory protection of databases with considerable interest, although they also have expressed concerns about the deleterious effects that the wrong type of protection might have on education and research.[126] In addition, as a result of increased partnerships with private-sector firms, some universities have adopted stricter institutional rules and guidelines pertaining to access, use, and distribution of research data and data products.

2. The Zone of Informal Data Exchanges

The norms and policies described above characteristically apply to big science, where well-defined federal research programs and institutional structures implement the sharing ethos, and access to public domain data is facilitated by government-controlled repositories. However, small science presents a rather different picture, one in which individual investigators and small teams working independently predominate. As noted in Part I, here there are likely to be other, non-federal sources of funding and the federal support that is available will be less prescriptive about the terms of data availability, especially with respect to pre-publication data sets. Moreover, for research involving human subjects, strong regulations protecting personal privacy add an extra layer of secrecy.[127]

In the experimental or laboratory sciences, such as chemistry or biomedical research, scientists use large databases for advancement to a much lesser extent than the observational sciences do, depending instead on the use of individual, repeatable experiments. The laboratory sciences also rely on the use of highly evaluated data sets and on published scientific literature, rather than on raw observational data. Because of the extremely specialized, labor-intensive nature of evaluated data sets, many are produced outside the government and are made available in proprietary publications or databases. Nevertheless, some public domain government sources exist for these types of data, even though they are smaller in number and volume than the sources of observa-

125. *Cf.* Eisenberg, *Bargaining*, *supra* note 13, at 235-39 (discussing universities' dilemma).

126. H.R. 354 Before the House Subcomm. on Courts and Intellectual Property, 106th Cong. (Mar. 18, 1999) (testimony of Charles Phelps on behalf of the Association of American Universities, the American Council on Education, and the National Association of State Universities of Land-Grant Colleges).

127. 5 U.S.C. § 552(a) (2000). The implementing regulations can be found at 45 C.F.R § 56 (2002).

tional data.[128]

The small science independent-investigator approach traditionally has also characterized a large area of fieldwork and studies, such as biodiversity, ecology, microbiology, soil science, and anthropology. Here, too, many individual or small-team data sets or samples are independently collected and analyzed.[129] The data from such studies generally have been heterogeneous and unstandardized, with few of the individual data holdings deposited in public data repositories or openly shared.[130]

a. Normative Conflicts

In the small science environment, individual investigators working autonomously are more driven by self-interest and a competitive spirit. They are one step removed from the top-down policies that regulate big science projects because in most cases they are not dependent on access to and participation in large public domain data repositories or other structured research programs that formally promote and enforce the sharing ethos. In this realm, scientists have much greater freedom to limit the disclosure of their data, in keeping with their private interests, at least until their research is formally published. Even then—because few institutionalized public data repositories exist—they may choose to withhold all but the minimum amount of data needed to support their published findings, or may provide no data at all.[131]

---

128. *See* BITS OF POWER, *supra* note 1, at 52. Examples of evaluated laboratory physical sciences data include the Evaluated Nuclear Structure Data File, and various materials science and chemical sciences data. *Id.* at 205-12.

129. *See generally* NATIONAL RESEARCH COUNCIL, FINDING THE FOREST IN THE TREES: THE CHALLENGE OF COMBINING DIVERSE ENVIRONMENTAL DATA (1995) [hereinafter FINDING THE FOREST].

130. *Id.*; *see also* BITS OF POWER, *supra* note 1, at 83-88. However, as discussed *infra* in the last section of Part II, the advent of pervasive distributed computing and digital networks has led to the organization of many areas of previously "small science" into "big science" types of initiatives. Notable examples include the Human Genome Project and several ecological and biodiversity programs with networked and partially centralized data resources. The U.S. Long Term Ecological Research Network ("LTER Net") now connects more than 1100 scientists and students investigating ecological processes at twenty-four research sites. Data are freely available within two to three years. *See* LTER Net, http://lternet.edu (last visited Jan. 10, 2003). The Global Biodiversity Information Facility ("GBIF"), the purpose of which is to "make the world's biodiversity data freely and universally available" through an interoperable network of biodiversity databases and information technology tools, provides another example. *See* GBIF, http://www.gbif.org/ (last visited Jan. 10, 2003).

131. In a recent national survey, "forty-seven percent of geneticists who asked other faculty for additional information, data, or materials regarding published research reported that at least [one] of their requests has been denied in the preceding [three] years. Ten percent of all post publication requests for additional information were denied. Because they were denied access to data, [twenty-eight percent] of geneticists reported that they had been unable to confirm published research. Twelve percent said that in the previous [three] years, they had denied another academician's request for data concerning published results." Eric G. Campbell, et al., *Data Withholding in Academic Genetics: Evidence from a National Survey*, 287 JAMA 473-80 (2002). For a similar situation in neuroscience research, see Peter Aldhous, *Prospect of Data Sharing Gives Brain Mappers a Headache*, 406 NATURE 445, 445-46 (2000), describing how proposals to make data sharing a mandatory requirement for publication produced a significant negative response from some members of the research community. *See generally* Jon Cohen, *Share and Share Alike Isn't Always the Rule in Science*, SCIENCE, June 21, 1995, at 1715.

This lack of structure, however, may paradoxically make single scientists more dependent on cooperative relationships with other scientists working in the same or related disciplines to expand their data supplies and integrate data that result from disparate investigations. To this end, they are prompted to voluntarily construct informal sharing arrangements with other scientists, notwithstanding the rivalry and competitive goals that divide them and despite the economic opportunities that can make such disclosures risky.[132] These arrangements give rise to collective streams of data that flow through informal networks of voluntary collaborations built from the bottom up.[133]

Data in this sphere have a different configuration from that which one is accustomed to seeing in the more formal, big science endeavors. There, the data resources are often centralized databases from which scientists will borrow bits for their research, which they may combine with other similar data resources, or with personally collected data, into individual data products. In the informal, mostly small science zone of data exchanges, however, data resemble a continuous stream or assemblage that has to be constructed from the bottom up and that flows in different directions and at different rates as informal networks evolve. These data streams consist of "chains of products" in which "increasingly refined materials and inscriptions downstream" play an important role.[134]

Individual investigators constantly take parts of data sets from others and alter or refine them in ways that suit their own needs. These value-added outputs are then exchanged with the value-adding contributions of other investigators. As Stephen Hilgartner and Sherry Brandt-Rauf describe it:

> Any end-point may become a starting point; every output may become an input. One therefore cannot assume that data somehow arrive . . . on the scene in pre-packaged units that are transferable, shareable, or publishable, or that there is some discrete point in time at which data should naturally be transferred. On the contrary, there is always more than one way of dividing a data stream into portions that may or may not be disseminated.[135]

In this process timing is crucial because many of these entities are novel or "extremely scarce" and become available only by special arrangements, if at all.[136]

---

132. *Cf.* Richard Nelson, The Market Economy, and the Republic of Science 17 (July 24, 2000) (unpublished draft, on file with authors) ("[T]he fact that most of scientific knowledge is open, and available through open channels, is extremely important. This enables there to be at any time a significant number of individuals and firms who possess and can use the scientific knowledge they need in order to compete intelligently in this evolutionary process. The 'communalism' of scientific knowledge is an important factor contributing to its productivity in downstream efforts to advance technology.").

133. *See* Stephen Hilgartner & Sherry I. Brandt-Rauf, *Data Access, Ownership, and Control: Toward Empirical Studies of Access Practices*, 15 KNOWLEDGE: CREATION, DIFFUSION, UTILIZATION 355, 355-72 (1994) [hereinafter Hilgartner & Brandt-Rauf, *Access, Ownership & Control*] (describing the "data stream" dynamics in biomedical research); *see also* Hilgartner, *Access to Data*, *supra* note 31; Hilgartner & Brandt-Rauf, *Controlling Data*, *supra* note 31.

134. Hilgartner & Brandt-Rauf, *Access, Ownership & Control*, *supra* note 133.

135. *Id.*

136. *Id.*

Of course, individuals and small groups operating in this zone may nucleate.[137] For example, "[e]nvironmental information systems frequently nucleate around informal collaborations (including volunteers) that determine useful partnerships."[138] If these collaborations continue to evolve on a sharing basis, they may give rise to more formal government research program structures that will then institutionalize the data-sharing protocols on an open access foundation.[139]

However, the sharing that occurs to produce the data streams in many areas of small science, particularly in the context of the laboratory life sciences, arises from a delicate process of barter and exchange. Here access to data is both limited and targeted, a process that is mediated by intricate inter-, intra-, and extra-laboratory negotiations.[140] In this process, autonomy and dependence foster conflicting interests. By withholding data, single scientists or laboratories temporarily promote their individual comparative advantages. At the same time, they may lose opportunities to improve their positions by gaining mediated access to others' data.[141] In making decisions and negotiating barter or exchange transactions, the scientist's trading mentality is tempered to some extent by the sharing ethos, especially as expressed in peer pressure, but he or she may be impervious at this stage, at least, to the formal institutional mechanisms that might otherwise enforce that ethos.

Accordingly, it is important to reiterate that the contents of the data streams we describe here fall largely outside the public domain that was previously described, even though the bulk of the data that function as inputs into the process have been funded by the government. Rather, because these operations are proceeding on an informal, non-organized basis (typically in a prepublication environment), the data are likely to be held under varying degrees

137. *See* Powell, *Networks of Learning*, *supra* note 13, at 265 ("In fields such as biotech, where knowledge is advancing rapidly and the sources of knowledge are widely dispersed, organizations enter into an array of relationships to gain access to different competencies and knowledge.").

138. RESOLVING CONFLICTS, *supra* note 8, at 73.

139. Indeed, this is exactly what appears to be occurring in the areas of ecological studies and biodiversity, which, until recently, were conducted by individuals or small groups in autonomous field studies in separately funded programs. The data collected in these investigations were heterogeneous, unstandardized, lacking in rigorous data management protocols, and generally not shared or made available for many years, if at all. FINDING THE FOREST, *supra* note 129, at 84-96, 100-01. With the advent of the Internet, however, many of these previously disparate and autonomous research groups have begun to share their data through formally organized networks with formal, standardized protocols. *See, e.g.*, the organizations discussed at *supra* note 130.

140. Hilgartner & Brandt-Rauf, *Access, Ownership & Control*, *supra* note 133, at 369. In contrast to open publication, Hilgartner and Brandt-Rauf suggest that access here is achieved by a variety of means, including barter; selected distribution to colleagues; patents; training; confidential sharing; purchase and sale transactions; "pre-release" to corporate sponsors; or the data is held in lab for future uses.

141. *See* Stephen Hilgartner, *Data Access Policy in Genome Research*, *in* PRIVATE SCIENCE 202-15 (Arnold Thakray ed., 1998) (giving examples of data-sharing within the Human Genome Project).

of actual secrecy, much like know-how in classical industrial property relations.[142]

The problem is that for the process of mutually beneficial exchange to work, individual investigators need access to others' published and unpublished data sets, and all the players in the relevant community find themselves in a similar position. While the pressure to cooperate is obvious and is reinforced by the norms of science, self-interest—including economic self-interest and the competitive spirit—may pull strongly in the opposite direction. The system as a whole would clearly benefit in the long term from fruitful cooperative arrangements. However, there is no guarantee that individual scientists will be willing to absorb the short-term losses to which disclosure subjects them, nor is it certain that these losses will in fact be offset by future gains from cooperation.[143] In sum, there are strong pressures to hold out or, at least, to hold back and to divulge no more than is necessary in the process of barter and exchange.

How well the process works in practice depends on a number of factors. One factor is the communications networks themselves, which may or may not provide low-cost and efficient access to the different distributed sources of data. In the pre-digital environment, it was much harder to build these collaborative networks owing to constraints of space and time, whereas the Internet now collapses these limits and provides instantaneous, low-cost opportunities to overcome previous barriers to data sharing in small-scale research.[144] A second factor is the extent to which the relevant community or sub-community respects the sharing ethos and imposes peer pressure to enforce it. A third factor is the degree to which commercial pressures from private sector partners and universities themselves distort the sharing ethos and stimulate profit-maximizing strategic behavior in academics.[145] A fourth factor is the extent to which direct personal opportunities to profit either from the economic value of the data sets, their reputational value, or a combination of both will drive each player's decisions and further undermine the cooperative ethos. Of course, many additional idiosyncratic factors that may affect personal behavior and choices will come into play as well.

There is much about this small science process that is still unknown outside the circles of discrete research collaborations or subdisciplines because its dis-

---

142. *Cf.* STEVEN P. LADAS, PATENTS, TRADEMARKS, AND RELATED RIGHTS 1616-74 (1975) ("The International Protection of Know-How").

143. *See* Eisenberg, *Patenting Research Tools*, *supra* note 123, at 7 ("Negotiating for access to research tools might present particularly difficult problems for would-be licensees who do not want to disclose the direction of their research in its early stages by requesting licenses.").

144. *See* discussion of the LTER Net and GBIF examples, *supra* note 130.

145. *See* DAVID, NATURE'S SECRETS, *supra* note 8, at 10 ("In their dual capacities the administrators of academic institutions (and the individuals who staff them) must continue to seek effective ways of mediating conflicts between the societal goals that will be served by preserving the organizational modes and norms of open scientific inquiry, on the one hand, and, on the other hand, the lure of capturing for their more immediate and private purposes a larger portion of the 'information rents'—by circumscribing free access to the new knowledge gained through the researches conducted under their auspices.").

tinctive sociology has only recently become the subject of serious scholarship, and because different scientific communities operate with different value structures and have diverse needs. In addition, one should not overstate the relative importance of this informal zone in relation to the more formal structures described above, which are particularly dominant in basic research.[146]

What can be said is that much of science depends on this zone of informal data exchanges, it processes more and more data of great economic value to industry, and the value of its data streams can be greatly increased through the use of digital networks and more refined legal tools. At the same time, an increasingly protectionist legal regime and the corresponding pressures to commercialize make the voluntary nature of these exchanges ever more precarious and subject to hoarding and holdout tendencies. An already fragile, informal process of barter and exchange that largely depends on a balance of personal self-interest and the cooperative norms of science is coming under intense economic and legal pressures that call its continued vitality into question.

b. A Different Legal Regime

A salient characteristic of the zone of informal data exchanges is the extent to which it has operated without reliance on formal legal rules. Intellectual property rights, including copyrights, have played no supporting role, although patent law—as discussed below—has increasingly cast an encroaching shadow over data transactions in which it previously played a minor part. Contractual agreements like those that regulate relations between funding entities and investigators in the formal zone have seldom been used in the informal zone. Such rules that have existed seem to derive largely from unfair competition law, and the participating scientists appear to have been much less aware of them than of the relevant norms of science, as expressed through peer pressure.

In the informal zone, scientists collaborate on a voluntary, cooperative basis to produce what amounts to an inchoate common data resource, but their access to it depends on the individual transactions they are able to negotiate. Certain uses of the data and data products that comprise this resource may be regulated by the granting agency's rules and the norms of science. Yet, until the research results are published, the investigators typically will have enjoyed a period of exclusive use conferred by the grants, and the grantees are not otherwise subject to supplementary formal rules deriving either from intellectual property rights or contractual arrangements with peers. Even after publication, the federal grants usually exhort the grantee to make the underlying data available, without imposing hard and fast obligations to do so. The granting agencies have, in any case, found it difficult to enforce even these moral obligations so long as the data remain outside a public repository and under the control of

146. These relationships exist primarily at the interface of science and technology, or where the line of demarcation between basic and applied research has collapsed. Their importance varies by type of investigation.

the principal investigator. Many other sources of research funding impose no such obligations at all. The upshot is that the scientist in the informal zone retains considerable legal discretion in determining the amount and even the conditions of disclosure, subject of course to peer pressure and his or her own need to barter for access to the cumulative data stream.

In this raw state of affairs, the cumulative collection, although potentially of much greater value than the sum of its parts, remains vulnerable to strategic manipulation in keeping with the opportunities that single scientists have to commercialize or otherwise personally exploit some or all of it. Viewed individually, these scientists will normally have made no formal commitment to promote the collective interest in an inchoate data commons, and all members of the community are wary of the opportunities for strategic behavior.

Moreover, none of the players really knows what the others actually possess, so that the totality of the emerging common resource cannot be self-consciously designed (as in, say, Linux),[147] but is overwhelmingly dependent on single decisions to collaborate and reveal—decisions that are costly and could be zero sum.[148] The vulnerability of the cumulative output to strategic behavior impedes the extent to which any given player will be willing wholeheartedly to commit his data holdings to the enterprise. Thus, risk aversion is high, and there are few if any formal legal tools to reduce it.

This is not to say that law is totally absent from this environment. To be more accurate, it is present in the form of legal rules that protect know-how and confidential information generally, as a subcategory of industrial property law. At bottom, these rules put limits on the worst forms of strategic behavior, such as espionage and deception, in case the norms of science otherwise fail to impede such activities.[149] They also provide a source of quasi-moral rights, very important to scientists, by impeding a scientist from passing off another's data contribution as his or her own.[150]

Moreover, the loose liability rules[151] that are embodied in trade secret and unfair competition law give some incentive to cooperate in informal exchanges

---

147. *See* discussion *infra* at Part IV.C.1.b.

148. *See generally* Hilgartner, *Access to Data*, *supra* note 31 (discussing zero-sum competition situations in the context of scientific practice).

149. RESTATEMENT (THIRD) OF UNFAIR COMPETITION §§ 39-45 (1995) [hereinafter RESTATEMENT UNFAIR COMPETITION].

150. Because the raw values in factual data compilations remain non-copyrightable in the United States, such information is in the public domain, free for the taking. Feist Publ'ns, Inc. v. Rural Tel. Servs. Co., 499 U.S. 340 (1991). While the source should be acknowledged as a matter of professional ethics and etiquette, there is no legal recourse for the data originator against an unacknowledged use by another scientist, except as unfair competition law allows. Such uses probably occur quite frequently, and in many cases the use is either undetectable or the originator of the data does not mind. However, unacknowledged uses sometimes erupt in a very public way. *See* Eliot Marshall, *DNA Sequencer Protests Being Scooped With His Own Data*, 295 SCIENCE 1206, 1206-07 (2002). In foreign countries, the moral rights of copyright law could be invoked. *See* Berne Convention, *supra* note 109, at art. 6 *bis*.

151. "Whenever someone may destroy the initial entitlement if he is willing to pay an objectively determined value for it, an entitlement is protected by a liability rule." Guido Calabresi & A. Douglas Melamed, *Property Rules, Liability Rules, and Inalienability: One View of the Cathedral*, 85 HARV. L. REV. 1089, 1092 (1972). Under so-called property rules (in this case, the exclusive rights of intellectual

because these rules cease to protect data that are independently discovered or revealed without improper appropriation from another. Unfair competition laws do not confer an exclusive property right, but rather a set of liability rules that impede certain market-destructive ways of depriving any individual player's data set of its value by improper means.[152] But these liability rules will not impede any other player from independently creating the same data by proper means, and if the need is great enough, this may occur. When it does, any exchange value that the original data holder may have enjoyed will be diminished or eliminated. In this sense, actual or legal secrecy confers a kind of property right—a right against improper behavior and perhaps a certain amount of lead time—but it is also a "disappearing right" that becomes vulnerable to discovery and disclosure by others.[153]

Even this incentive to cooperate, however, may be much reduced in science, as compared to technical innovation, for the reason that it may not be possible for a second scientist to independently recreate the data set in question, or it may be prohibitively expensive and inefficient to do so.[154] In such cases, the generally weak liability rules governing confidential information can produce too much protection for data held in actual secrecy because there is, in practice, virtually no functional equivalent of reverse engineering.[155] When that happens, the temptation to hoard and holdout can be high, and the corresponding costs of cooperation are similarly elevated.

While the legal weight of these liability rules should not be underestimated, they are clearly of limited value in the zone of informal data exchanges. Probably, their greatest relevance will be at the moment when commercial opportunities are most palpable and when wholesale appropriation might produce tangi-

---

property law), one cannot take the entitlement in question without prior permission of the owner. In this sense, property rules are "absolute permission rules." Robert P. Merges, *Institutions for Intellectual Property Transactions: The Case of Patent Pools*, *in* EXPANDING THE BOUNDARIES OF IP, *supra* note 13, at 123, 131 (2001) [hereinafter Merges, *Patent Pools*]. "By contrast, liability rules are best described as 'take now, pay later.' They allow for non-owners to take the entitlement without permission of the owner, so long as they adequately compensate the owner later." *Id.*

152. *See* Bonito Boats, Inc. v. Thunder Craft Boats, Inc., 489 U.S. 141, 167-68 (1989) (invalidating Florida "plug mold" statute to protect against copying of boat hull designs); Compco Corp. v. Day-Brite Lighting, Inc., 376 U.S. 234, 237-38 (1964) (state unfair competition laws not to protect unpatented lamp designs in absence of source confusion); Sears, Roebuck & Co. v. Stiffel Co., 376 U.S. 225, 231-32 (1964) (preventing use of Illinois unfair competition law to block copying of an unpatented lamp design). Whether these rules impede "copying" or wholesale appropriation as such remains an open question. *Compare* Int'l News Serv. v. Assoc. Press, 248 U.S. 215 (1918) *and* Nat'l Basketball Ass'n v. Motorola, Inc., 105 F.3d 841 (2nd Cir. 1996) *with Bonito Boats*, 489 U.S. at 141 *and* Wal-Mart Stores, Inc. v. Samara Bros., 529 U.S. 205 (2000). For the view that wholesale copying should be prohibited, see, for example, Wendy J. Gordon, *On Owning Information: Intellectual Property and the Restitutionary Impulse*, 78 VA. L. REV. 149, 165 (1992), proposing a tort of "malcompetitive copying," and Dennis S. Karjala, *Misappropriation as a Third Intellectual Property Paradigm*, 94 COLUM. L. REV. 2594, 2601-08 (1994) [hereinafter Karjala, *Misappropriation*].

153. John C. Stedman, *Trade Secrets*, 23 OHIO ST. L.J. 4, 21 (1962) (characterizing trade secret rights as "disappearing rights").

154. *See* A QUESTION OF BALANCE, *supra* note 1, at 29-30 (discussing the uniqueness of many scientific and technical databases).

155. *See generally* Pamela Samuelson & Suzanne Scotchmer, *The Law and Economics of Reverse Engineering*, 111 YALE L.J. 1575 (2002).

ble economic gains. It is precisely here, however, where the traditional rules governing confidential information may be the least potent, because they cannot usually be triggered without a showing of legal, not merely actual, secrecy, and the tenets of legal secrecy will often be too high for academic scientists to meet.[156] Absent some general norm against the wholesale appropriation of another's data production,[157] the ability of scientists cooperating in the zone of informal data exchanges to invoke rules based on unfair competition law to preserve their individual and collective patrimonies remains speculative at best.

The most salient feature of the legal infrastructure as it impinges on this zone is, therefore, the extent to which it has been largely irrelevant to the social and scientific processes underway. In other words, if the available legal mechanisms do little to support the fragile process of barter and exchange, they also create few barriers to that process. However, this situation could change radically with the introduction of new technological means for controlling digital data, new opportunities for commercial exploitation, and above all, the enactment of new intellectual property rights in non-copyrightable collections of data as discussed in Part III.

C. Private-Sector Data as a Component of the Research Commons

The private sector is both a user of public domain data and a major producer of them. The contribution of the private sector to the research commons under traditional legal rules has been under-appreciated. There is also a tendency within the academic community to overlook the needs of the private sector for access to public domain data and, accordingly, a tendency to underestimate the effects that restrictions on access to such data may have on private sector research and development ("R&D").

The private sector generates an ever-increasing amount of scientific data that are indispensable to academic research. Yet, more and more scientific data produced by academics come freighted with restrictions and conditions that arise from partnerships between academic institutions and industry. How to organize the research commons so that both academic and private firms can obtain the data they need without compromising either their public or private pursuits is a key issue for science policy and this article.[158]

1. Dissemination and Use of Scientific Data in Private Sector R&D

The private sector is a major producer of scientific data that enters the public domain under existing legal rules. Disregarding database publishers for

---

156. *See, e.g.*, David Friedman et al., *Some Economics of Trade Secret Law*, 5 J. ECON. PERSP. 61, 63-66 (1991). Of course, "passing off" another's data set as one's own would not require legal secrecy. *See* RESTATEMENT UNFAIR COMPETITION, *supra* note 149.

157. State unfair competition laws may or may not provide such a norm, depending on how courts interpret *International News Service v. Associated Press*, 248 U.S. 215 (1918). *See* Hilgartner & Brandt-Rauf, *Access, Ownership & Control*, *supra* note 133.

158. See Part IV, *infra*, for an extensive analysis of this dilemma and the authors' proposed approaches for addressing it.

a moment, private sector researchers frequently publish their findings, like academics, in which case the traditional rules of copyright law apply as previously described, and there is a corresponding duty to release at least enough non-copyrightable data as are needed to support the published results. If the research project were funded by the federal government, there would typically be further obligations to disclose or deposit the underlying data sets following publication or completion of the project. If the research leads to a patent application, then that application must also meet minimum utility and disclosure requirements.[159] If the research results are neither published nor patented and are held under actual or legal secrecy, then any resulting innovations may be reverse engineered by honest means.[160] In that case, the technical information or "know-how" derived from the process of reverse engineering should also enter the public domain.[161]

Besides generating scientific data as a by-product of their R&D activities, the private sector may affirmatively contribute data directly to the public domain for a number of different reasons. For example, companies may donate data sets accumulated over time that are of value to science, even if they no longer possess significant direct commercial value to the firm. Companies may also self-publish scientific and technical information to promote their goods and services. They increasingly may decide to put even commercially valuable technical data in the public domain to deter competitors from blocking fruitful lines of research by strategic patent applications derived from the data thus disclosed.[162]

Private sector R&D activities, of course, make use of both government-generated data and government-funded data, especially from academic research undertaken at universities. Of greater importance, however, is the vast information commons that consists of the cumulative and sequential know-how and the state-of-the-art, which the community at work on any given technical trajectory has acquired and routinely shares over time.[163] This know-how—that is, information about how to achieve commercial advantages by sub-patentable

---

159. 35 U.S.C. §§ 101, 102, 111, 112 (2000) (utility, novelty, disclosure, and enablement requirements in patent law).

160. UNIF. TRADE SECRETS ACT (USTA) § 1(4), 14 U.L.A. 449 (1985).

161. For a recent discussion, see Samuelson & Scotchmer, *supra* note 155. *See also* J. H. Reichman, *Overlapping Proprietary Rights in University-Generated Research Products: The Case of Computer Programs*, 17 COLUM.-VLA J.L. & ARTS 51, 93-98 (1992).

162. *See, e.g.*, SNP Consortium, *available at* http://snp.cshl.org (last visited Feb. 14, 2003), discussed *infra* notes 676-78; *see also* Douglas Lichtman et al., *Strategic Disclosure in the Patent System*, 53 VAND. L. REV. 2175, 2197-99, 2204-09 (2000); Rai, *supra* note 33, at 112-13 (discussing reluctance of leading research universities to patent expressed sequence tags ("ESTs") and single nucleotide poymorphisms ("SNPs"). For an explanation of SNPs, see *infra* note 676.

163. *See, e.g.*, Margaret Sharp, *Technological Trajectories and Corporate Strategies in the Diffusion of Biotechnology*, *in* TECHNOLOGY AND INNOVATION: CRUCIAL ISSUES FOR THE 1990S 93, 94-97 (Erico Deiaco, et al, eds., 1990) 221-35 (Giovanni Dosi et al. eds., 1988); Richard R. Nelson, *Intellectual Property Protection for Cumulative Systems Technology*, 94 COLUM. L. REV. 2674, 2676 (1994) (distinguishing "traditional discrete invention model" from "cumulative systems model").

technical means—is typically acquired by trial and error and shaped by investors in R&D into incremental innovation products.[164]

The information commons that underlies and pervades the realm of subpatentable innovation is a fundamental asset of a competitive economy based on constant innovation.[165] In principle, patents are not granted unless the would-be inventor exceeds the level of innovation that the community at work on a given technical trajectory would be expected to produce. Below this line of "non-obviousness,"[166] trade secret laws do not impede employees from carrying their skills and personal know-how—their personal quotient of the information commons—from one job to another. The spillover effects this produces, and the rapid interchange of information between members of the technical community it encourages, become the engine of small-scale innovation in Silicon Valley and its equivalents around the world.[167]

In recent years, however, the free flow of information between members of the engineering community at work on given technical trajectories has increasingly been slowed and disrupted by a proliferation of hybrid intellectual property rights that fall between the patent and copyright paradigms.[168] Beginning with industrial design laws and utility model laws, which date back to the nineteenth century, examples include plant breeders' rights, integrated circuit designs, and most recently, *sui generis* rights in non-copyrightable databases.[169]

---

164. J. H. Reichman, *Of Green Tulips and Legal Kudzu: Repackaging Rights in Subpatentable Innovation*, 53 VAND. L. REV. 1743, 1747-53 (2000) [hereinafter Reichman, *Of Green Tulips*]; *see also* Frischmann, *supra* note 70. This information is neither copyrightable nor patentable, but is usually kept under actual secrecy. If, instead, investors spend the money to keep their valuable know-how under legal secrecy, unfair competition law will protect it against misappropriation by improper means—such as industrial espionage—but not against reverse-engineering by honest means. The second-comer's duty to reverse-engineer the processes by which innovative sub-patentable products are made gives the investor a period of natural lead time in which to recoup investments and establish a trademark. *See* UTSA, *supra* note 160, at § 1(4); J. H. Reichman, *Legal Hybrids Between the Patent and Copyright Paradigms*, 94 COLUM. L. REV. 2432, 2511-20 (1994) [hereinafter Reichman, *Legal Hybrids*] (discussing chronic shortage of natural lead time under present-day conditions).

165. *Cf.* James Boyle, *Cruel, Mean or Lavish? Economic Analysis, Price Discrimination and Digital Intellectual Property*, 53 VAND. L. REV. 2007 (2000) (stressing benefits of competition and need for public domain inputs into the information economy) [hereinafter Boyle, *Cruel, Mean or Lavish*].

166. 35 U.S.C. § 103 (2000).

167. *See* Samuelson & Scotchmer, *supra* note 155; *see also* Rochelle Cooper Dreyfus, *Trade Secrets: How Well Should We Be Allowed to Hide Them? The Economic Espionage Act of 1996*, 9 FORDHAM INTELL. PROP. MEDIA & ENT. L.J. 1 (1998) (criticizing the federal criminal Trade Secrets Act for adverse impact on spillover effects).

168. Reichman, *Legal Hybrids*, *supra* note 164.

169. In many countries, utility model laws protect functional designs and small-scale innovations generally. *See, e.g.*, UMA SUTHERSANEN, DESIGN LAW IN EUROPE 383-93 (2000) (discussing various European utility model laws); Mark D. Janis, *Second Tier Patent Protection*, 40 HARV. INT'L L.J. 151, 155-59 (1999) (classifying and discussing classical utility model regimes). While the United States does not have a utility model law, Congress has opted to protect two sets of functional designs. *See* Vessel Hull Design Protection Act of 1998, 17 U.S.C. §§ 1301-32 (2000); Semiconductor Chip Protection Act of 1984, 17 U.S.C. §§ 901-914 (2000). Most countries, other than the United States, have enacted *sui generis* laws to protect non-functional industrial designs. *See, e.g.*, SUTHERSANEN, *supra*, at 28-54; Graeme B. Dinwoodie, *Federalized Functionalism: The Future of Design Protection in the European Union*, 24 AM. INTELL. PROP. L. ASS'N Q.J. 611 (1999); J. H. Reichman, *Design Protection in Domestic and Foreign Copyright Law: From the Berne Revision of 1948 to the Copyright Act of 1976*, 1983 DUKE

These regimes are enacted because those who invest in applications of know-how to industrial products—"incremental innovation bearing know-how on its face"—become increasingly vulnerable to second-comers who duplicate their products without expending the time and money to reverse engineer or independently create. In supplying investors with artificial lead time, however, these hybrid regimes tend to block follow-on applications and disrupt the information commons that had driven sub-patentable innovation in the past.[170] As discussed in detail in Part III, the greatest threat to this information commons and the innovation systems it supports is the new hybrid exclusive property right in non-copyrightable databases, which has been promulgated throughout Europe by the 1996 Directive on the legal protection of databases.[171] This Directive provides a new and potentially perpetual intellectual property right in exchange for mere investment, which is qualitatively different and more far-reaching in its impact on the public domain than any traditional intellectual property regime.[172]

For present purposes, it suffices to note that because relations between the private sector and universities have flourished under the influence of the Bayh-Dole Act and related legislation,[173] the private sector on the whole tends to make greater use of data generated by academic research than in the past. As these two sources of data become increasingly commingled, there is a growing conflict between the open access norms of traditional university research and the tendency of the private sector to restrict access to and use of data by means of legal secrecy and the aforementioned hybrid exclusive property rights.[174] In this connection, the European database right will not only affect the distribution of academic data itself, but will also enable the private sector to restrict access to and use of all the data within its control in ways that were not previously possible. Any efforts to organize the scientific information commons on a more rational basis must accordingly take account of the role that the private sector plays both as generator and user of scientific and technical data in research.

2. Database Publishers

One would not need to treat database publishers in a separate entry so long as they remained subject to the same legal regime applicable to academic scientists described above. Under that regime, traditional copyright rules applied

---

L. J. 1143 (1983). The United States, instead, continues to rely on design patents, 35 U.S.C. § 171 (2000). For discussion of *sui generis* database protection laws, *see infra* Part III.B.2.d.

170. *See generally* Reichman, *Of Green Tulips*, *supra* note 164, at 149-56; J. H. Reichman, *Computer Programs as Applied Scientific Know-How: Implications of Copyright Protection for Commercialized University Research*, 42 VAND. L. REV. 639, 656-69 (1989).

171. *See supra* note 17.

172. *See infra* text accompanying notes 347-73.

173. *See, e.g.*, Rai, *supra* note 33, at 110 (discussing growth of academic-industrial relationships in the past two decades).

174. *Cf.* Rai, *supra* note 33, at 110-11 ("Participants in these academic-industrial relationships often depart quite markedly from traditional research norms.").

only to the original and creative selections and arrangements of compilations of data.[175] As a result, the bulk of the data entered the public domain unless otherwise protected either by state trade secret laws, or to a still unknown extent, state unfair competition laws prohibiting the wholesale duplication of non-copyrightable databases.[176]

It is worth reiterating that the U.S. database industry has thrived in this environment in which weak protection has been the rule, and it has commanded a large share of the world database market.[177] To sustain this success, the database industry relies on the constant updating of its databases and new releases, which add value as well as business protection to previously accumulated data, and on a pronounced "niche market" effect, which makes it difficult for second-comers to enter a given market segment once the first-mover has established a solid reputation for quality. In the networked environment, investors also rely heavily on technological fences to protect their databases; electronic, standard-form license contracts for mass markets; and negotiated licenses with institutional customers to regulate access to and use of their databases.[178]

While the contractual regulation of online dissemination of databases poses serious problems for science and education overall, the underlying dimensions of the public domain are shrinking rapidly owing to new and unprecedented legislative initiatives, such as the E.C. Database Directive[179] and similar database protection proposals in the United States.[180] To glimpse the far-reaching repercussions of this type of legislation, one has only to consider its potential impact on the notion of publication as the line of demarcation between private and public ownership of scientific and technical information. Under traditional copyright law and practices, a scientist who published an article will have dedicated any supporting data that accompanied it to the public domain. If the *sui generis* database right applied, however, academics could publish their articles, and they or their publisher could still retain the legal rights to control or restrict use of the same data even after publication.[181]

How the academic community would ultimately react and adjust to this new legal situation would depend on many different factors,[182] and some of them are considered later in this article. The point for now is that the established portrait of the public domain for published collections of data is in a state of flux. The radical changes stemming from legal and technical measures tending to fence that domain make it advisable for the scientific community to consider the need to construct and manage a research commons of its own for the dissemination

175. *See supra* notes 85-91 and accompanying text.

176. *See supra* note 150 and accompanying text.

177. *See, e.g.*, Maurer, Across Two Worlds, *supra* note 34.

178. *See supra* note 34.

179. *See supra* note 17.

180. *See supra* notes 17, 26 and accompanying text.

181. In practice, scientific use would then depend to some extent on explicit exceptions or immunities built into the relevant database protection laws.

182. *See generally* Reichman & Uhlir, *Database Protection*, *supra* note 4.

of scientific and technical data and information that heretofore automatically entered the public domain.

D. Potentially Enhanced Role of Public Domain Data in a Digitally Networked Research Environment

Because science builds upon science, the production of data sets is not an end in itself, but rather the means to an end, the first step in the creation of new information, knowledge, and understanding. As part of that process, the original databases are continually refined and recombined to create new databases and new insights. Each level of processing adds value to an original or raw set of data by summarizing its contents, providing different interpretations of their meaning, or synthesizing new information products. As Nobel laureate Joshua Lederberg testified before a congressional committee considering the enactment of a new database protection bill:

> Data are the building blocks of knowledge and the seeds of discovery. They challenge us to develop new concepts, theories, and models to make sense of the patterns we see in them. They provide the quantitative basis for testing and confirming theories and for translating new discoveries into useful applications for the benefit of society. They are also the foundation of sensible public policy in our democracy. The assembled record of scientific data and resulting information is both a history of events in the natural world and a record of human accomplishment.[183]

The primary purpose of this section is to emphasize the extent to which digital technologies have revolutionized the role that data in the public domain or available under open access policies can play in the research process. To quote Lederberg once again:

> [The] recent advent of digital technologies for collecting, processing, storing, and transmitting data has led to an exponential increase in the size and number of databases created and used. A hallmark trait of modern research is to obtain and use dozens or even hundreds of databases, extracting and merging portions of each to create new databases and new sources for knowledge and innovation.[184]

As will become readily apparent, the successful implementation of these data integration functions depends to a large extent on the availability, access to, and unrestricted use of affordable data resources in the public domain.

1. Digitally Pooled Data Resources

The enhanced role that digital technologies play in government-sponsored data collection activities[185] constantly adds new dimensions to both big and small science. Increasingly powerful sensor technologies are unmasking layers of previously hidden attributes of our natural universe and documenting their essential characteristics in automated data streams. The resulting data sets

183. *Collections of Information Antipiracy Act: Hearing on H.R. 354 Before the House Comm. on the Judiciary*, 106th Cong. 189-205 (March 18, 1999) (statement of Joshua Lederberg, President, Rockefeller University, on behalf of the National Academy of Sciences, National Academy of Engineering, Institute of Medicine, and American Association for the Advancement of Science) [hereinafter *Collections Hearings*].

184. *Id.*

185. *See supra* Part II.A.1 (outlining these activities).

become "foundational" in the sense that they establish a baseline characterization of natural objects or processes that then becomes a common resource for research in that particular area. Other data sets track natural phenomena or behavior on a longitudinal basis over long time periods.

In the observational sciences, for example, space-based and ground-based sensors continue to collect vast amounts of digital data about our planet and outer space in all regions of the electromagnetic spectrum.[186] Moreover, the miniaturization of sensor technologies is making it possible to place thousands of tiny sensor arrays in different ecosystems to collect environmental data concerning physical, chemical, and biological processes.[187] This instrumenting of the environment using both remote and embedded network sensing devices makes the pervasive monitoring of the ecosphere possible, with the resulting data sets able to be archived in public data centers or made directly available in the digitally networked environment for a broad range of long-term studies and applications.

Similarly, the aforementioned large facilities in the experimental physical sciences, such as nuclear fusion, high-energy laser, and neutron-beam devices, create ever-larger amounts of data that are processed and analyzed for new discoveries and applications.[188] The data sets generated by each of these large observational and experimental facilities and related data centers have grown from gigabyte levels just a decade ago, to terabytes and, in some cases, petabytes of data currently.[189]

Formally structured big science programs also increasingly rely on the compilation of large, public domain databases composed of the contributions of hundreds of individual investigators from government, academia, and even industry, who generate data independently and then contribute their findings to government or government-funded data centers. Many of these types of arrangements are in the rapidly growing area of bioinformatics, such as molecular biology,[190] ecological,[191] and biodiversity studies,[192] as well as in numerous other areas of research. Both the centralized and distributed public domain data repositories constitute a common resource from which all researchers can borrow freely, whether for fundamental exploratory investigations or for more specifically applied problem-solving purposes.

The continuing advancement of observational sensors and experimental data production technologies, particularly in miniaturized desktop computa-

186. *See supra* note 45 and accompanying text.

187. *See* Gregory Bonito, *Emergent Sensor Technologies*, *in* SCALABLE INFORMATION NETWORKS FOR THE ENVIRONMENT (Alison Withey et al. eds., 2002).

188. *See supra* note 45 and accompanying text.

189. The data center at the high-energy physics research center, CERN, and at the U.S. Geological Survey's Earth Resources Observing Systems Data Center, which archives various land remote sensing data, are now approaching the petabyte level (petabyte = quadrillion bytes).

190. *See, e.g.*, National Center for Biotechnology Information, *supra* note 45.

191. *See* discussion of LTER Net, *supra* note 130.

192. *See* discussion of GBIF, *supra* note 130.

tional devices or portable instruments for use in fieldwork, also increasingly empowers single scientists to collect or create their own data sets in the informal, small science domain. As digital capabilities for autonomous data production improve and proliferate, an immense new supply of potentially interconnected information is being created within each discipline community, which complements the large, formally structured, public-domain foundational data sets emanating from the big science programs. Although the availability of individually created scientific information resources situated in the informal research domain remain subject to the cultural and sociological impediments described above,[193] these resources nonetheless constitute a rapidly growing corpus of potentially available inputs into the research commons.

Turning from collection to dissemination functions, the growing ability of each community to use the Internet to provide virtually universal access to all this information—assuming it remains otherwise available—has revolutionized the conduct of scientific research. U.S. researchers in all scientific and engineering areas are among the most active users of the Internet. This is hardly surprising given the primary role of the U.S. governmental and academic science and technical community in the original development and early evolution of the Internet.[194] What may be less apparent, however, is that the architecture and function of the Internet itself arose as a technological manifestation of many of the same cultural attributes that characterize the public research enterprise. The Internet was developed by publicly funded government and academic researchers as a voluntary and cooperative integration of highly distributed autonomous networks, operating in a largely self-regulated and international system, through which information could pass freely and without restrictions.[195]

These parallel attributes of the public research community and the early Internet provided a natural impetus to scientists to use digital networks immediately and pervasively to make access to their reciprocal inputs and outputs generally available.[196] All of the formally organized public scientific data repositories now make their holdings known and available through the Internet, although direct access to the full set of their archived information tends to be limited by technical or security factors.[197]

---

193. *See supra* Part II.B.2.

194. *See, e.g.*, Vinton Cerf, *How the Internet Came to Be*, *in* THE ONLINE USER'S ENCYCLOPEDIA (Bernard Adoba ed., 1993).

195. *Id.; see also* LAWRENCE LESSIG, CODE AND OTHER LAWS OF CYBERSPACE (1999) (discussing Internet architecture and its initial open design).

196. In the informal sphere, however, this reciprocity is often the product of negotiated exchanges.

197. The principal technical factor that limits direct access to large databases is insufficient bandwidth in many current Internet connections, although this is expected to change rapidly with the introduction of "grid" technology, particularly in the research community. Security-based technical protection of online databases against malicious hackers further limits direct access to the entire content and creates other inefficiencies. *See generally* NATIONAL RESEARCH COUNCIL, TRUST IN CYBERSPACE (Fred B. Schneider ed., 1999).

The opportunities for direct peer-to-peer exchanges of data, and for new distributed research collaborations on either a formal or informal basis may be an even more important development.[198] Particularly noteworthy in the context of this article is the stimulus and means that the Internet provides for increasing the flow of the inchoate data stream that characterizes the informal zone of data exchanges. By providing a direct, instantaneous, and relatively secure means to communicate and share data, digital networks potentiate unlimited opportunities for implementing the cooperative and sharing ethos that has been fundamental to the progress of science. When most of one's professional peers within and outside a given area of specialization openly post their findings on their websites or remain willing to exchange information on request, the potential for serendipitous results and synergistic advances becomes greatly increased.[199]

Moreover, these integrating benefits of the Internet are not limited to single peer-to-peer exchanges, important as they may be. Ubiquitous digital networks also make possible entirely new forms of organized peer production, from small groups working in distributed collaboratories[200] to network-wide, volunteer-based, open modes of production that may have particularly significant implications and applicability in the public science context.[201] Certainly, voluntary, collaborative peer production of data, information, and knowledge was a hallmark trait of science long before the digital era. The co-authoring of research articles, joint compilations of databases, sharing of knowledge and research results at public conferences, peer-review process for publications, and participation in large research programs over long time periods were all "peer production" activities. These norms and practices of the pre-digital era take on a heightened importance in the digitally networked environment and lead to the possibility for greatly expanded peer production opportunities ideally suited to open, public research.[202]

2. Electronic Transformation Tools

While digital data production technologies and networks allow scientists to pool and instantaneously exchange the raw materials of their research, advanced software and ever more powerful computational tools enable them to process, organize, and transform the raw data into discoveries and applications. The following highlights three notable advances in this context.

A key development is the use of new software tools to process and integrate large amounts of data to create refined data products and applications. Software enables scientists to take portions of pre-existing databases from different

198. *See* Yochai Benkler, *Coase's Penguin, or, Linux and the Nature of the Firm*, 112 YALE L.J. 369 (2002) [hereinafter Benkler, *Coase's Penguin*].

199. *See* discussion of network effects, *infra* notes 223-27 and accompanying text.

200. *See generally* NATIONAL RESEARCH COUNCIL, COLLABORATORIES: IMPROVING RESEARCH CAPABILITIES IN CHEMICAL AND BIOMEDICAL SCIENCES (1999).

201. *See* Benkler, *Coase's Penguin, supra* note 198; *see also* DAVID, GOOD FENCES, *supra* note 20, at 3-4.

202. *See* Benkler, *Coase's Penguin, supra* note 198.

sources in order to combine and reprocess them to address complex problems. A quintessential example is geographic information systems ("GIS") software, which provides the means of integrating diverse environmental and socio-economic data on geospatially referenced grids for a broad array of basic research goals and practical applications.[203]

Many of the data sources used in this process are governmental or government-funded at the federal, state, and local levels, including some of the key foundational data sets mentioned above. The U.S. Geological Survey estimates that geospatial data applications in the United States alone contribute over $3.5 trillion annually to the economy.[204] The successful utilization of GIS depends in large part on easy access to the relevant data at affordable prices and, especially, on access with few restrictions on reuse and redissemination. Conversely, data sources that are too expensive or come freighted with many user limitations can undermine or even block a research project or important application. Of course, the same issues arise in other areas of data intensive research, such as biotechnology, econometrics, or climate change studies.

Data mining techniques, also known as knowledge discovery in databases, provide the means to extract salient data from very large databases and automatically convert the extracted components into useful information or even new discoveries.[205] For example, data mining algorithms were used to discover twenty new quasars in a huge astronomical database in just a few hours of processing time. A search of the same database by a team of astronomers would have taken forty times longer to yield the same results.[206] Performing such a search and extracting those discoveries could constitute an infringement under the E.C. Database Directive.

The final technology highlighted here is grid computing, which may be defined as a "super Internet" for high-performance computing by integrating geographically and organizationally dispersed computational resources, such as CPUs, storage systems, communication systems, data sources and instruments, and the researchers themselves.[207] By providing "pervasive, dependable, consistent, and inexpensive" access to such advanced computational capabilities and resources, researchers believe that computational grids will have a transforming effect similar to the electric power grid a century ago, which would allow new

---

203. For a basic description of GIS functions, see U.S. Geological Survey, *at* http://www.usgs.gov/research/gis/title.html (last visited Feb. 14, 2003). *See also* Environmental Systems Research Institute, Inc., *at* www.gis.com/whatisgis/index.html (last visited Jan. 10, 2003).

204. FEDERAL GEOGRAPHIC DATA COMMITTEE, REPORT OF THE CIVIL IMAGERY AND REMOTE SENSING TASK FORCE ON THE VALUE OF CIVIL IMAGERY AND REMOTE SENSING 2 (October 1, 2002).

205. Definition adapted from *Introduction to Data Mining*, *available at* http://www.andypryke.com/university/dm_docs/dm_intro.html (last visited Jan. 10, 2003) (listing a variety of background resources on this technology).

206. *See* Usama Fayyad, *Industrial Keynote Address: Data Mining and Databases*, *in* DATA FOR SCIENCE AND SOCIETY: THE SECOND NATIONAL CONFERENCE ON SCIENTIFIC AND TECHNICAL DATA (2000), *available at* http://books.nap.edu/html/codata_ 2nd/ch15.html (last visited Feb. 14, 2003).

207. Definition adapted from *What is a Grid?*, *available at* http://www.aei.mpg.de/~manuela/Gridweb/info/grid.html (last visited Jan. 10, 2003).

classes of applications to emerge.[208] An example of an initial project using grid technology is the European Union's "Data Grid." This initiative is expected to "enable next generation scientific exploration which requires intensive computation and analysis of shared large-scale databases, millions of Gigabytes, across widely distributed scientific communities."[209] The selected applications areas include high-energy physics, biomedical research, and satellite earth observations.[210]

Taken together, the new digital technologies discussed above, as well as numerous others omitted for reasons of brevity, enable scientists to perform the following quantitatively and qualitatively new functions:

- Collect and create unprecedented and ever increasing amounts and types of raw data about all natural objects and phenomena;
- Collapse the space and time in which data and information can be made available;
- Facilitate entirely new forms of distributed research collaboration and information production; and
- Interpret and transform the raw data into unlimited new configurations of information and knowledge.

However, the successful implementation of all these functions remains heavily dependent on the continued existence of a robust public domain and related open access policies and practices to realize the promise of new research and innovation tools.

III

SCIENTIFIC DATA AS A PRIVATE GOOD: PRESSURES ON THE PUBLIC DOMAIN AND THEIR IMPLICATIONS

The map described in the preceding pages suggests the extent to which the vast reservoir of accumulated public domain data feeds into the scientific research infrastructure and the system of innovation to which it gives rise. It has often been pointed out that government-supported research plays a primary role in making this system of innovation the most productive in the world. However, the indispensable role of public domain data in nourishing this system, while generally taken for granted, is less clearly understood or appreciated, and new possibilities for further potentiating this role in the digital environment constitute another "endless frontier." These matters require more attention lest growing pressures to fence the scientific commons lead to unforeseen and unintended consequences that could seriously disrupt the national system of innovation as a whole.

---

208. THE GRID: BLUEPRINT FOR A NEW COMPUTING INFRASTRUCTURE xvii (Ian Foster & Carl Kesselman eds., 1999). *See also* Ian Foster's web site, *at* http://www-fp.mcs.anl.gov/~foster (last visited Feb. 14, 2003) (listing numerous Grid technology resource documents).

209. E.U. Data Grid Project, *at* http://web.datagrid.cnr.it (last visited Jan. 10, 2003).

210. Learn More about DataGrid, http://web.datagrid.cnr.it/LearnMore/index.jsp (last visited Jan. 10, 2003).

A. Shifting the Public–Private Boundaries

The prominent role that public domain data have played in fueling American science and innovation is partly explained by the economic literature concerning public goods. Public goods, unlike private goods, are characterized by their *nonrival* and *nonexcludable* properties.[211] The former means that it costs nothing to provide the good to another person once someone has produced it, that is, it tends to have zero marginal cost. The latter means that once such a good has been produced, the producer cannot exclude others from benefiting from it. Typical examples of public goods that fully satisfy both criteria are national defense and the operation of lighthouses.

The problem that public goods pose is that however important their production may be for the political body as a whole, they will attract insufficient or suboptimal private investment because investors cannot deter free-riding second-comers or otherwise fully recoup the return from their investments.[212] Governments typically respond to this problem by making the investments that the private sector cannot or should not be expected to provide, such as funding public health and safety objectives, or the national defense.[213] Often these public initiatives will generate substantial additional private investment and supplementary social benefits as the private sector finds ways to convert upstream public investments in public goods into downstream commercial products and services that do generate appropriable returns.[214]

From this perspective science itself, especially basic science, resembles a public good, which private enterprise could not adequately support.[215] For example, research on tropical diseases, climate change, and astrophysics falls into the category of global public goods, as do large fundamental research facilities, such as space science spacecraft missions and high-energy particle accelerators for physics experiments, for which high up-front costs and noncommercial or uncertain applications make public investment the only feasible alternative. These public investments, in turn, contribute to the "knowledge infrastructure" required for efficient R&D directed at exploitable commercial innovations.[216]

---

211. Inge Kaul et al., *Defining Global Public Goods*, *in* GLOBAL PUBLIC GOODS: INTERNATIONAL COOPERATION IN THE 21ST CENTURY (Kaul et al. eds., 1999).

212. *See generally* ROBERT COOTER & THOMAS ULEN, LAW AND ECONOMICS 108-18 (3d ed. 2000).

213. RESOLVING CONFLICTS, *supra* note 8, at 23 ("Most government functions are carried out by the public sector either because of an overriding public interest in the outcome, or because the potential for high risk or low payoff makes the task unattractive to the private sector.").

214. *See, e.g.*, Frischmann, *supra* note 70, at 357-60 (stressing tension between maximizing consumption of public goods and constraining consumption to maximize market-based efficiency).

215. Michael Callon, *Is Science a Public Good?*, 19 SCI. TECH. & HUM. VALUES 395, 400 (1994) ("The qualification of science as a quasi-public good rather than as a full-fledged public good derives essentially from the fact that it is to a certain degree appropriable—whereas in standard theory a true public good has to be completely inappropriable.").

216. Paul David, *The Political Economy of Public Science*, *in* THE REGULATION OF SCIENCE AND TECHNOLOGY 38 (Helen Lawton Smith ed., 2001) [hereinafter David, *Political Economy*]. According to a recent study, some seventy-three percent of all patents granted in the United States during the

Notable examples include Internet communications protocols, the global positioning system, and computer simulation methods for the visualization of molecular structures.[217]

As Paul David and Michael Callon have reminded us,[218] there are good reasons for protecting many scientific endeavors from competitive market forces that cannot efficiently allocate resources for the production and distribution of pure public goods.[219] Because industry and business tend to under-invest in scientific production, government takes up the slack either by intervening directly or by providing incentives to the private sector to overcome market failure, in the form of legal monopolies falling within the domestic and international intellectual property systems.

To appreciate the full implications of the map drawn in Part II, moreover, it is important to establish that scientific and technical data also manifest the properties of "quasi public goods" that economists associate with science as a whole. Information, facts, and ideas, once divulged, cost nothing to propagate and become difficult to keep from others. Thus, the government intervenes to promote potential long-term economic and social benefits because the data produced from basic scientific research are often too commercially risky to be developed by the private sector.[220]

Even when scientific data emerge from applied science, where partial appropriability and foreseeable returns attract private investment, they may present public good properties that justify government support. For example, governments invest in providing advanced weather data largely because of the need to ensure public safety and the protection of the nation's economic assets. However, by electing to provide such data without intellectual property protection, either free or at no more than the marginal cost of dissemination, the U.S. government goes beyond its mission of protecting the safety of its citizens and their property to providing the raw material for a dynamic value-adding private sector. As scholars have noted:

> As a result of this concept of public/private partnership, the U.S. boasts a robust private meteorology industry with revenues in excess of $500 million annually, and a rapidly growing weather risk management industry with risk management instruments approaching a value of $8 billion. The authors believe that the relatively small size of

---

1990s cited government or government-funded research. Francis Narin et al., *The Increasing Linkage Between U.S. Technology and Public Science*, 26 RES. POL'Y 317 (1997).

217. "Much more critical over the long run than 'spin-offs' from basic science programmes are their cumulative indirect effects in raising the rate of return on private investment proprietary R&D performed by business firms." David, *Political* Economy, *supra* note 216, at 39.

218. *Id.* at 35; Callon, *supra* note 215.

219. David, *Political Economy*, *supra* note 216, at 36 ("[T]he findings of scientific research, being new knowledge, would be seriously undervalued were they sold directly through perfectly competitive markets.").

220. "Under U.S. policy, most federal government data are in the public domain and cannot be copyrighted. By making data easy and inexpensive to obtain, the U.S. government seeks to promote science, create a more informed public, and foster the development of a thriving commercial information industry." RESOLVING CONFLICTS, *supra* note 8, at 24.

these sectors in the E.U. is primarily due to the restrictive data policies of a number of governments and their national meteorological services.[221]

Appropriate public sector investment in the production of scientific data benefits from what economists call "positive externalities" and "network effects." A positive externality occurs when one party confers benefits on another without the latter having to fully compensate the former.[222] Basic research, together with the creation and dissemination of scientific databases, especially in their raw form, may have no immediate economic applications or market, but they can lead subsequently to unanticipated or serendipitous advances and whole new spheres of innovation and commerce. Such activities provide prime examples of positive externalities that direct government support can greatly promote and that may not be undertaken at all without such support.

The other important concept here is that of a network effect, which arises when the value of using a particular type of product depends on the number of users.[223] Examples of products with high positive feedback from network effects include telephones and fax machines, if there are many users rather than only a few.[224] Perhaps the quintessential product with positive network effects is the Internet. From this perspective, scientific databases or other collections of information can add considerably more value to society and the economy if they are openly available on the Internet (assuming that production remains feasible in the absence of appropriability, as would occur with government funding).[225]

Scientists were the pioneers of the Internet revolution and have become some of the most prolific users of the medium for accessing, disseminating, and using data.[226] When data are provided as a public good via the Internet, unencumbered by proprietary rights, the positive externalities from network effects can be especially high. They become even greater to the extent that the data are prepared and presented in a way that makes them available and usable to a broader range of non-expert users outside the scientific community.

As Joseph Stiglitz and his colleagues point out:

> The shift toward an economy in which information is central rather than peripheral may thus have fundamental implications for the appropriate role of government. In

---

221. Plujimers & Weiss, *supra* note 47, at 7 (citing authorities).

222. An externality may be defined as the action of one entity affecting the well-being of another, without appropriate compensation. A negative externality is the imposition of additional costs by entity A (for example, through the deleterious effects of pollution created by A) on entity B, without A's having to pay for those costs. Conversely, a positive externality confers benefits (innovation) from A to B without full compensation to A. JOSEPH E. STIGLITZ ET AL., COMPUTER & COMMITTEE INDUSTRIAL ASSOCIATION, THE ROLE OF GOVERNMENT IN A DIGITAL AGE 33 (2000).

223. *Id.* at 42.

224. S. J. Liebowitz & Stephen E. Margolis, *Network Externality: An Uncommon Tragedy*, J. ECON. PERSP., Spring 1994, at 133, 133-36 (giving further examples of network effects).

225. *See* Benkler, *Coase's Penguin*, *supra* note 198; *cf.* Mark A. Lemley & David McGowan, *Legal Implications of Network Economic Effects*, 86 CAL. L. REV. 479 (regarding the question of adequate incentives in peer production projects).

226. *See supra* notes 194-95 and accompanying text.

particular, the public good nature of production, along with the presence of network externalities and winner-take-all markets, may remove the automatic preference for private rather than public production. In addition, the high fixed costs and low marginal costs of producing information and the impact of network externalities are both associated with significant dangers of limited competition.[227]

These economic characteristics associated with the transmission of digital scientific data on the Internet provide a strong argument for many of the activities previously described, which are undertaken within the public domain by government agencies or by non-governmental entities receiving government support.

At the same time, attention to the economic literature suggests the importance of ascertaining the limits of public good analysis lest government compete with or otherwise undermine activities that the private sector could carry out more efficiently.[228] Scientific data, like much of science itself, are not a pure public good to the extent that they can be bundled and embodied in physical artifacts that make them appropriable to a certain degree.[229] Information can come in two forms: codified knowledge and incorporated knowledge. The former may be expressed in a standardized and compact form, so as to permit easy, low-cost transmission, verification, storage, and reproduction. The latter, by contrast, is inscribed in some machine.[230]

From this perspective, scientific data and information are both inputs into the national system of innovation and outputs of that system, and intellectual property rights tend to regulate the flow of private sector investments into downstream applications of research data.[231] How this balance of public and private interests worked out in the past was largely reflected in the map of public domain data depicted in Part II. Whatever imperfections that map brings to light, its most salient feature is that the balance of interests it reflects underlies the world's most productive and successful system of innovation.[232]

However, that inherently dynamic and shifting balance of interests has come under intense pressure in recent years for a number of different reasons. The "convergence technologies" that greatly improve access to information also afford "technological means of inhibiting access in ways that were never before practical."[233] Global competition has induced governments in developed countries to strengthen existing intellectual property rights, enact new and more

227. STIGLITZ ET AL., *supra* note 222, at 44.

228. *See supra* Part II.A.2. (discussing the limits on competition with the private sector by the federal government).

229. *See, e.g.*, Callon, *supra* note 215, at 398 (stressing that pure public goods are completely inappropriable).

230. *Id.* at 397.

231. *See* David C. Mowery & Nathan Rosenberg, *The U.S. National System of Innovation*, *in* NATIONAL SYSTEMS OF INNOVATION—A COMPARATIVE ANALYSIS 29-75 (Richard R. Nelson ed. 1993); Reichman & Franklin, *supra* note 16, at 884-86 (discussing dual function of information in the networked environment).

232. *See* Mowery & Rosenberg, *supra* note 231, at 47-54, 59-64.

233. DAVID, DIGITAL BOOMERANG, *supra* note 20, at 10; *see also* Reichman & Franklin, *supra* note 16, at 897-99 (restored power of the "two-party" deal in digital environment).

powerful rights not previously experimented with, and to press for high levels of harmonized protection at the international level.[234] Of particular importance in the United States are efforts by government "to cut expenditures by transferring to the private sector a range of data production and information distribution activities that formerly were publicly provided."[235] The end result has been the collapse of the established lines of demarcation between public and private interests that were codified in the classical patent and copyright paradigms,[236] and the enclosure and transformation of "larger and larger portions of the public data 'commons' . . . into private monopolies."[237]

The question this raises is the extent to which the functions of public domain data on which science and innovation have traditionally relied, as illustrated above, may be compromised by ill-conceived initiatives to stimulate investment for short-term private gain without sufficient attention to the long-term needs of both science and innovation, as well as the broader society. To this end, the remainder of this Part of the article will summarize the economic and legal assaults on the research commons that have recently occurred, and examine some of the implications of those pressures on the ability of the commons to continue to perform both its traditional and potentially enhanced functions in the digitally networked environment.

B. Pressures on the Research Commons

The digital revolution has made investors acutely aware of the heightened value that collections of data and information may acquire in the new information economy.[238] Attention has logically focused on the incentive and protective structures for generating and disseminating digital information products, especially online. Although most of the legal and economic initiatives have been focused on—and driven by—the entertainment sector, software producers, and large publishing concerns, there is growing interest in the possibility that commoditization of even public sector and public domain data could stimulate substantial investments by providing new means of recovering the costs of production.[239] Moreover, investors have increasingly understood the economic

---

234. *See, e.g.*, KEITH E. MASKUS, INTELLECTUAL PROPERTY RIGHTS IN THE GLOBAL ECONOMY 1-14, 15-85 (2000); Peter Drahos, *Developing Countries and International Intellectual Property Standard-Setting*, 5 J. WORLD INTELL. PROP. 765, 769-83 (2002).

235. DAVID, DIGITAL BOOMERANG, *supra* note 20, at 8.

236. J. H. Reichman, *Charting the Collapse of the Patent-Copyright Dichotomy*, 13 CARDOZO ARTS & ENT. L.J. 475 (1993).

237. DAVID, DIGITAL BOOMERANG, *supra* note 20, at 11.

238. *See, e.g.*, Maurer, Across Two Worlds, *supra* note 34.

239. *See, e.g.*, *The Collections Of Information Antipriracy Act and the Vessel Hull Design Protection Act : Hearing on H.R. 2652 Before the Subcommittee on Courts and Intellectual Property of the House Comm. on the Judiciary* 105th Cong. (1997) (testimony by Laura d'Andrea Tyson) [hereinafter *Information Antipiracy Hearings*]. This testimony was based on a research project funded by Reed-Elsevier, Inc., and The Thomson Corp., completed Sept. 5, 1997. *See also* G. M. Hunsucker, *The European Database Directive: Regional Stepping Stone to an International Model*, 7 FORDHAM INTELL. PROP. MEDIA & ENT. L.J. 697 (1997); YALE M. BRAUNSTEIN, ECONOMIC IMPACTS OF DATABASE PROTECTION IN DEVELOPING COUNTRIES AND COUNTRIES IN TRANSITION (W.I.P.O. Standing

potential that awaits those who capture and market data and information as raw materials or inputs into the upstream stages of the innovation process.[240]

What follows focuses first on pressures to commoditize data in the public sector and then on legal and technological measures that endow database producers with new proprietary rights and novel means of exploiting the facts and data that copyright law had traditionally left in the public domain. These pressures arise both within the research community itself and from forces extraneous to it. How that community responds to these pressures over time will determine the future metes and bounds of the information commons that supports scientific endeavors.

If, as we have reason to fear, current trends will greatly diminish the amount of data available from the public domain, this decrease could initially compromise the scientific community's ability to fully exploit the promise of the digital revolution. Moreover, if these pressures continue unabated and become institutionalized at the international level,[241] they could disrupt the flow of upstream data to both basic and applied science and undermine the ability of academia and the private sector to convert cumulative data streams into innovative products and services.

The pressures discussed below also pose serious conflicts between the norms of public science and the norms of private industry. We contend that failure to resolve these conflicts and properly balance the interests at stake in preserving an effective information commons could eventually undermine the national system of innovation.[242]

1. Commoditization of Data in Public Science

During the last ten years, there has been a marked tendency to shift the production of science-relevant databases from the public to the private sector. This development occurred against the background of a broader trend in which the government's share of overall funding for research and development vis-à-vis that of the private sector has decreased from a high of sixty-seven percent in the 1960s to twenty-six percent in 2000.[243] Furthermore, since the passage of the Bayh-Dole Act in 1980, the results of federally funded research at universities have increasingly been commercialized either by public–private partnerships

---

Committee on Copyright and Related Rights, #SCCR/7/2, 2002), *available at* http://www.wipo.int/eng/meetings/2002/sccr/pdf/sccr7_2.pdf (last visited Jan. 10, 2003).

240. There were, of course, always concerns about incentives to produce basic data and information as raw materials of the innovation process, especially in light of perceived gaps in intellectual property law that seemed to leave databases in limbo. *See, e.g.*, Denicola, *supra* note 78.

241. *See* J. H. Reichman, *Database Protection in a Global Economy*, *supra* note 18, 485-500 (managing transnational database protection without harmonization).

242. *Cf.* Mowery & Rosenberg, *supra* note 231, at 47-51, 53-56, 62-64 (describing the interplay of public-private interests in the U.S. system of innovation); Richard R. Nelson & Nathan Rosenberg, *Technical Innovation and National Systems*, *in* NATIONAL INNOVATION SYSTEMS, *supra* note 231, at 3, 5-9 (stressing the extent to which science and technology are intertwined).

243. Industry and Agency Concerns over Intellectual Property Rights, Testimony before the Subcomm. on Technology and Procurement Policy, House Comm. on Government Reform, 107th Cong. (May 10, 2002) (testimony of Jack L. Brock, Jr., United States General Accounting Office).

with industry or directly by the universities themselves.[244] Industry support of university research has increased in certain sectors, such as medical research, even as the federally funded share of university research support has declined.[245]

a. Reducing the Scope of Government-Generated Data

The budgetary pressures on the government are both structural and political in nature. On the whole, mandated entitlements in the federal budget, such as Medicare and Medicaid, are politically impossible to reduce, and as their costs mount, the money available for other discretionary programs, including federally sponsored research, has shrunk as a percentage of total expenditures.

This structural limitation is compounded by the rapidly rising costs of state-of-the-art research, including some researcher salaries, scientific equipment, and major facilities. With specific regard to the information infrastructure, researchers typically earmark the lion's share of expenses to computing and communications equipment, with the remainder devoted to managing, preserving, and disseminating the public domain data and information that results from basic research and other federal data collection activities. The government's scientific and technical data and information services are thus the last to be funded and are almost always the first to suffer cutbacks.

For example, the National Oceanic and Atmospheric Administration's ("NOAA") budget for its National Data Centers remained flat and actually decreased in real dollars between 1980 and 1994, while its data holdings increased exponentially and the overall agency budget doubled (mostly to pay for new environmental satellites and a ground-based weather radar system that are producing the exponential data increases).[246] Information managers at most other science agencies have complained about reductions in funding for both their data management and scientific and technical information budgets.[247]

These chronic budgetary shortfalls for managing and disseminating public domain scientific data and information have been accompanied by recurring

244. *See, e.g.*, Nelson, *supra* note 132; Rai, *supra* note 33, at 110-11; *see also* Mowery & Rosenberg, *supra* note 231, at 53 (stressing that closer ties between industry and universities restored a linkage that had been weakened in the 1950s and 1960s).

245. The percentage of university medical research funded by the federal government decreased from approximately seventy-five percent in 1976 to approximately sixty-four percent in 1997. Between 1992 and 1999, the percent of industry funding in the same research sector increased from just under seven percent to just under eight percent. Hamilton Moses III, Academic Relationships with Industry, Presentation to the Government, University, Industry Research Roundtable (Mar. 28, 2001) (on file with authors).

246. *See* BITS OF POWER, *supra* note 1, at 62. This trend has continued for NOAA up to the present time. However, in 1996, Congress authorized NOAA to charge fair market value for its data and to institute a two-tiered pricing system with discounts for educational organizations that place their orders for data online. *See supra* note 56. Since then, revenues from data sales have decreased about six percent per year. NATIONAL OCEANIC & ATMOSPHERIC ADMINISTRATION, U.S. DEPARTMENT OF COMMERCE, THE NATION'S ENVIRONMENTAL DATA: TREASURES AT RISK 35-36 (2001).

247. Interviews with STI managers in the U.S. Geological Survey, the Department of Agriculture, the Department of Energy, and the Department of Defense (2002).

political pressures on the scientific agencies to privatize their outputs.[248] Until recently, for example, the common practice of the environmental and space science agencies was to procure data collection systems, such as observational satellites or ground-based sensor systems, from private companies. Such procurements were typically made under cost-plus contracts and pursuant to government specifications based on consensus scientific requirements recommended by the research community.[249] Private contractors would build and deliver the data collection systems, which the agencies would then operate pursuant to their mission. All data from the system would belong to the government and would enter the public domain.

Today, however, industry has successfully pursued a strategy of providing an independent supply of the government's needs for data and information products rather than building and delivering data collection systems for government agencies to operate.[250] This solution leaves the control and ownership of the resulting data in the hands of the company and allows it to license them to the government and to anyone else willing to pay. Because of this new-found role of the government agency as cash cow, there has recently been a great deal of pressure on the science agencies, particularly from Congress, to stop collecting or disseminating data in-house and to obtain them from the private sector instead.

This approach previously resulted in at least one well-documented fiasco, namely, the privatization of the NASA–NOAA Landsat earth remote sensing program in 1985, which seriously undermined basic and applied research in environmental remote sensing in the United States for the better part of a decade.[251] More recently, the Commercial Space Act of 1998 directed the National Aeronautics and Space Administration ("NASA") to purchase space and earth science data collection and dissemination services from the private sector and to treat data as commercial commodities under federal procurement regulations.[252] The meteorological data value-adding industry has directed similar lobbying pressures at NOAA.[253] The photogrammetric industry has likewise

---

248. In other countries, notably those in the European Union, it has been a longstanding policy and practice to commercialize data right from the public source. *See generally* Green Paper, *supra* note 46; Plujimers & Weiss, *supra* note 47.

249. The various discipline boards and committees of the National Academies are requested by the federal science agencies periodically to provide research strategies for specific discipline or research program areas. *See, e.g.*, NATIONAL RESEARCH COUNCIL, ASTRONOMY AND ASTROPHYSICS IN THE NEW MILLENIUM (2001); NATIONAL RESEARCH COUNCIL, RESEARCH STRATEGIES FOR THE U.S. GLOBAL CHANGE RESEARCH PROGRAM (1990), *available at* http://www.nap.edu (last visited Jan. 10 2003).

250. *See, e.g.*, Management Association for Private Photogrammetric Surveyors ("MAPPS"), Licensing Data, Licensing People, summary proceedings of November 2000 conference, *available at* http://www.mapps.org/library.asp (last visited Jan. 10, 2003) [hereinafter MAPPS Conference].

251. For a discussion of the adverse effects that the privatization of the Landsat program had on basic research, see BITS OF POWER, *supra* note 1, at 121-24.

252. Commercial Space Act of 1998, Pub. L. No. 105-303, §§ 107(a), 107(b), 112 Stat. 2843, 2853 (1998).

253. *See, e.g.*, *Hearing Before the House Science Comm., Subcomm. on Energy and the Environment,* 105th Cong. (1997) (statement of Michael S. Leavitt, President, Weather Services Corp., on behalf of

indicated a desire to expand the licensing of data products to the U.S. Geological Survey and to other federal agencies.[254]

Efforts have also been made by various industry groups to limit the online information dissemination services of several federal science and technology agencies. In the cases of the patent database of the U.S. Patent and Trademark Office, the PubMed Central database of peer-reviewed life science journal literature (provided on a free and unrestricted basis by the NIH National Library of Medicine), and certain types of weather information disseminated by the National Weather Service, such efforts have proved unsuccessful to date. However, publisher groups did succeed in terminating the Department of Energy's *PubScience* web portal for physical science information.[255]

b. Commercial Exploitation of Academic Research

Turning to government-funded research activities, the trend of greatest concern for purposes of this article is the progressive incorporation of data and data products into the commercialization process that is already underway in academia. The original purpose of the Bayh-Dole Act and related legislation was primarily to enable universities to obtain patents on applications of research results.[256] More recently, this activity has expanded to securing both patents and copyrights in computer programs. Now, databases used in molecular biology have themselves become sources of patentable inventions, and the potential commercial value of these databases as research tools has attracted considerable attention and controversy.[257]

These and other databases are increasingly the subject of licensing agreements prepared by university technology transfer offices, which may be prone to treat databases like other objects of material transfer agreements.[258] The

---

the Commercial Weather Services Association); *Contracting Out and Privitization Opportunities in NOAA: Hearing Before the Senate Governmental Affairs Comm., Subcomm. on Oversight Government Management and the Dist. of Columbia*, 105th Cong. (1997) (statement of Joel Myers, President, AccuWeather, Inc.).

254. MAPPS Conference, *supra* note 250.

255. *Goodbye, PubScience, We Hardly Knew Ye: Free DOE Database Goes Dark*, LIBR. J. ACAD. NEWSWIRE, Nov. 12, 2002. It should also be noted that this lobbying effort was supported vigorously in 2001 by the American Chemical Society, a major scientific society publisher.

256. Eisenberg, *Public Research*, *supra* note 120, at 1665.

257. *See, e.g.*, DAVID & FORAY, *supra* note 3, at 16-17 ("[C]ooperatively assembled bioinformatic databases are permitting researchers to make important discoveries in the course of 'unplanned journeys through information space.' If that space becomes filled by a thicket of property rights, then those voyages of discovery will become more expensive to undertake . . . and the rate of expansion of the knowledge base is likely to slow."); Powell, *supra* note 13, at 254-55, 263-65, ("But what is striking is how actively universities and firms are seeking to privatize new information" in biotechnology and related fields.).

258. Empirical research has shown a growing acceptance by universities of confidentiality, nondisclosure, and other restraints on open research as a result of increasing private-sector partnerships. *See* W.M. Cohen et al., *Industry and the Academy: Uneasy Partners in the Cause of Technological Advance*, *in* CHALLENGES TO RESEARCH UNIVERSITIES (R. Noll ed., 1998). University technology transfer offices operate on a commercial business model and view other universities as competitors. *See* Jerry G. Thursby & Marie C. Thursby, *Who is Selling the Ivory Tower? Sources of Growth in University Licensing*, 48 MGMT. SCI. 90, 90 (2002) (indicating that there has been a dramatic increase in technol-

default rules that such licensing agreements tend to favor are exclusive arrangements under onerous terms and conditions that include restrictions on use, and even grant-back and reach-through clauses claiming interests in future applications.[259]

Moreover, there is a growing awareness in academic circles generally that data and data products may be of considerable commercial value, and individual researchers have become correspondingly more wary of making them as available as before.[260] This trend, together with the pressures on government agencies described above, could pose serious problems for the research community's ability to access and use needed data resources under any circumstances.[261] In reality, these problems could become much greater as the new legal and technological fencing measures discussed below become more broadly implemented.

2. Intellectual Property, E-Contracts, and Technological Fences

Part II of this article showed that traditional copyright law was friendly to science, education, and innovation by dint of its refusal to protect either facts or ideas as eligible subject matter; by limiting the scope of protection for compilations and other factual works to the stylistic expression of facts and ideas; by carving out express exceptions and immunities for teaching, research, and libraries; and by recognizing a catch-all, fall-back fair use exception for nonprofit research and other endeavors that advanced the public interest in the diffusion of facts and ideas at relatively little expense to authors. Reinforcing these policies were judge-made and partially codified exceptions for functionally dictated components of literary works, which take the form of non-protectible methods, principles, processes, and discoveries.[262] On the whole, these principles tended to render facts and data as such ineligible for copyright protection and allow researchers to access and use facts and data otherwise embodied in protectible works of authorship without undue legal impediments.

In contrast, recent legal developments in intellectual property and contracts law have radically changed the pre-existing regime. These and other related developments now make it possible to assert and enforce proprietarial claims to virtually all the factual matter that previously entered the public domain the moment it was disclosed.

---

ogy transfer through licensing by universities as they attempt to appropriate returns from faculty research); *cf.* Rai, *supra* note 33, at 113-15 (noting failure of post-1995 efforts to develop uniform rules on biological materials transfer agreements to govern universities and private companies, and tendency of universities to depart significantly in practice from 1995 inter-university agreement).

259. *See* Stephen M. Maurer, Promoting and Disseminating Knowledge: The Public/Private Interface, paper prepared for the National Research Council's Symposium on the Role of Scientific and Technical Data and Information in the Public Domain 39-41 (Sept. 5-6, 2002), *available at* http://www7.nationalacademies.org/biso/Maurer_background_paper.html (last visited Jan. 10, 2002) (noting that approximately half of all university licensing agreements are on an exclusive basis) [hereinafter Maurer, Promoting and Disseminating Knowledge].

260. *See, e.g.*, Campbell et al., *supra* note 131. *See* discussion *supra* Part II.B.1.c.

261. *See, e.g.*, Powell, *supra* note 13, at 264-66.

262. *See supra* notes 11-13 and accompanying text; Part II.B.1.b.

Some of the earliest changes were intended to bring U.S. copyright law into line with long-standing norms of protection recognized in the Berne Convention. For example, the principle of automatic copyright protection, the abolition of technical forfeiture due to lack of formal prerequisites, such as notice, and the provision of a basic term of protection lasting for the life of the creator plus fifty years were all measures adopted in the pre-digital era for this reason.[263]

Beginning in the 1980s, however, the United States took the lead in reshaping the Berne Convention to accommodate computer programs, which many commentators and governments had preferred to view as "electronic information tools"[264] subject to more pro-competitive industrial property laws, including patents, unfair competition and hybrid (or *sui generis*) forms of protection.[265] By the 1990s, a coalition of content providers concerned about the online copying of movies, music, and software in the new digital environment had persuaded the U.S. government to press for still more far-reaching changes of international copyright and related laws.[266] These efforts led to the codification of universal copyright norms in the TRIPS Agreement of 1994[267] and to two 1996 World Intellectual Property Organization ("WIPO") treaties on copyrights and related rights in cyberspace,[268] which endowed authors with a bevy of new exclusive rights tailor-made for online transmissions, and which imposed unprecedented obligations on participating governments to prohibit electronic equipment capable of circumventing these rights.[269] All of these new norms and obligations, ostensibly adopted to discourage market-destructive copying of literary and artistic works, then became domestic law,[270] often with no regard for their impact on science, and sometimes with deliberate disregard of measures adopted to safeguard science and education at the international level.[271]

---

263. *See* 17 U.S.C. §§ 102(a), 302, 401(a) (2000) (as amended).

264. *See* J. H. Reichman, *Electronic Information Tools: The Outer Edge of World Intellectual Property Law*, 24 INT'L REV. INDUS. PROP. & COPYRIGHT L. 446 (1993) [hereinafter Reichman, *Electonic Information Tools*].

265. *See, e.g.*, Pamela Samuelson et al., *A Manifesto Concerning the Legal Protection of Computer Programs*, 94 COLUM. L. REV. 2308 (1994).

266. *See generally* PETER DRAHOS & JOHN BRAITHWAITE, INFORMATION FEUDALISM 107-48 (2002); Gail Evans, *Intellectual Property as a Trade Issue—The Making of the Agreement on Trade-Related Aspects of Intellectual Property Rights*, 18 WORLD COMPETITION L. & ECON. REV. 137 (1994).

267. TRIPS Agreement, *supra* note 63, arts. 9-14.

268. World Intellectual Property Organization ("WIPO") Copyright Treaty, Dec. 20, 1996, 36 I.L.M. 65 (1996); WIPO Performances and Phonograms Treaty, S. TREATY DOC. NO. 105-17, 36 I.L.M. 76. (1996).

269. *See generally* Pamela Samuelson, *The U.S. Digital Agenda at WIPO*, 37 VA. J. INT'L L. 369 (1997).

270. *See, e.g.*, The Digital Millennium Copyright Act ("DMCA"), 17 U.S.C. § 1201 (2000); Council Directive 2001/29 of the European Parliament and of the Council of 22 May 2001 on the harmonisation of certain aspects of copyright and related rights in the information society, 2001 O.J. (L 167) 10 [hereinafter E.C. Directive on Copyright in the Information Society].

271. The DMCA declined to enact concessions on users' rights that the WIPO Diplomatic Conference and WIPO Copyright Treaty of 1996 had authorized. *See also* Samuelson, *U.S. Digital Agenda*, *supra* note 269.

At the same time, and as part of the same overall movement, the coalition of content providers that had captured Congress' attention took aim at two closely related areas in which much more than market-destructive copying was actually at stake. The first of these was to validate the uncertain status of standard-form electronic contracts used to regulate online dissemination of works in digital form.[272] Because traditional contract and sales laws can be interpreted in ways that limit the kinds of terms that can be imposed through "shrink-wrap" or "click-on" licenses, and the one-sidedness of the resulting "adhesion contracts,"[273] the coalition pushing the high-protectionist digital agenda has sponsored a new uniform law, the Uniform Computer Information Transactions Act ("UCITA")[274] to validate such contracts in the form they desire, and it has lobbied state legislatures to adopt it.[275]

The last major component of the high-protectionists' digital agenda was an attempt by some of the largest database companies to obtain a *sui generis* exclusive property right in non-copyrightable collections of information, even though facts and data had hitherto been off-limits even to international copyright law as reformed under the TRIPS Agreement of 1994.[276] These efforts culminated in the European Community's Directive on the Legal Protection of Databases adopted in 1996;[277] in a proposed WIPO treaty on the international protection of databases built on the same model, which was barely defeated at the WIPO Diplomatic Conference in December of 1996;[278] and in a series of database protection bills that have been introduced in the U.S. Congress that attempt to enact similar measures into U.S. law.[279]

Most of the developments outlined above resulted from efforts that were not undertaken with science in mind, although publishers who profit from distributing commercialized scientific products promoted some of the changes that appear most threatening for scientific research, especially database protection

272. *See* Raymond T. Nimmer, *Breaking Barriers: The Relation Between Contract and Intellectual Property*, 13 BERKELEY TECH. L.J. 827, 904-08 (1998).

273. *See, e.g.*, Mark A. Lemley, *Beyond Preemption: the Law and Policy of Intellectual Property Licensing*, 87 CAL. L. REV. 111 (1999) [hereinafter Lemley, *Beyond Preemption*]; Charles R. McManis, *The Privatization or "Shrink-Wrapping" of American Copyright Law*, 87 CAL. L. REV. 173 (1999).

274. UNIF. COMPUTER INFO. TRANSACTIONS ACT ("UCITA") (2001), *available at* http://www.ucitaonline.com/ (last visited May 13, 2002) (now adopted in Maryland and Virginia).

275. *See generally Intellectual Property & Contract Law*, *supra* note 16.

276. *See* TRIPS Agreement, *supra* note 63, at art. 10.2.

277. E.C. Database Directive, *supra* note 17.

278. *See* Draft Treaty on Intellectual Property Rights in Respect of Databases, WIPO doc. CRNR/DC/6 (1996), *available at* http://www.wipo.int/eng/diplconf/pdf/6dc_e.pdf; Draft Recommendation, WIPO doc. CRNR/DC/88 (1996), *available at http://www.wipo.int/eng/diplconf/distrib/pdf/88dc.pdf*. The U.S. Patent and Trademark Office and the U.S. Trade Representative initially supported this treaty, together with the Commission of the European Communities. The U.S. position changed following a series of high-level meetings of federal government officials in October and November of 1996, largely in response to a letter from the three presidents of the National Academies to Mickey Kantor, Secretary of Commerce (Oct. 9, 1996) (on file with authors) (expressing serious reservations about the potential effects of such a treaty on scientific research and noting the complete absence of any interagency consultations about this matter or any other public discussion). *See generally* Reichman & Samuelson, *supra* note 18, at 97-113.

279. *See supra* note 17.

laws. The following sections show that all these measures—whatever their ostensible purpose—have the cumulative effect of shrinking the research commons.

We will first briefly note the impact of selected developments in both federal statutory copyright law and in contract laws at the state level. We then discuss current proposals to confer strong exclusive property rights on non-copyrightable collections of data, which constitute the clearest and most overt assault on the public domain that has fueled both scientific endeavors and technological innovation in the past.

a. Expanding Copyright Protection of Factual Compilations: The Revolt Against *Feist*

The quest for a new legal regime to protect databases was triggered in part by the U.S. Supreme Court's 1991 decision in *Feist Publications, Inc. v. Rural Telephone Service Co.*,[280] which denied copyright protection to the white pages of a telephone directory. As discussed in Part II, that decision reaffirmed the principle that facts and data as such are ineligible for copyright protection as "original and creative works of authorship."[281] It also limited the scope of copyright protection to any original elements of selection and arrangement that otherwise meet the test of eligibility. Second-comers who developed their own criteria of selection and arrangement could in principle use prior data to make follow-on products without running afoul of the copyright owner's strong exclusive right to prepare derivative works.[282] Taken together, these propositions supported the customary and traditional practices of the scientific community and facilitated access to and use of research data.

In recent years, however, judicial concerns about the compilers' inability to appropriate the returns from their investments have induced federal appellate courts to broaden copyright protection of low authorship compilations in ways that significantly deform both the spirit and the letter of *Feist*.[283] At the eligibility stage, so little in the way of original selection and arrangement is now required that the only print media still certain to be excluded from protection

280. 499 U.S. 340, 349-51, 359-60 (1991).

281. 17 U.S.C. §§ 102(a), 102(b), 103 (2000). See discussion of *Feist supra* at text accompanying notes 88-89. *See also* Key Publ'ns, Inc. v. Chinatown, Today Publ'g Enter., Inc., 945 F.2d 509, 514 (2d Cir. 1991) ("thin" copyright doctrine).

282. 17 U.S.C. §§ 101, 102, 103, 106(2) (2000); *Feist*, 499 U.S. at 354 (stressing adverse effects on free flow of information by creating "monopol[ies] in public domain materials"); *see also* Jane C. Ginsburg, *No "Sweat?" Copyright and Other Protection of Works of Information After* Feist v. Rural Telephone, 92 COLUM. L. REV. 338, 339 (1992) [hereinafter Ginsburg, *"No Sweat?"*]; Jessica Litman, *After Feist*, 17 U. DAYTON L. REV. 607, 609 (1992).

283. *See, e.g.*, CDN, Inc., v. Kapes, 197 F.3d 1256, 1259-60 (9th Cir. 1999); CCC Info. Servs., Inc. v. Maclean Hunter Mkt. Reports, Inc., 44 F.3d 61, 65 (2d Cir. 1994) (stressing low threshold of eligibility); *cf.* Am. Dental Ass'n v. Delta Dental Plans Ass'n, 126 F.3d 977 (7th Cir. 1997) (taxonomies of dental procedures not excluded subject matter); Justin Hughes, Created Facts – or the Occasional Protection of Ideas, Names and Facts in Copyright Law (forthcoming 2003, on file with authors).

are the white pages of telephone directories.[284]

More tellingly, the courts have increasingly perceived the eligibility criteria of selection and arrangement as pervading the data themselves, in order to restrain second-comers from using pre-existing data sets to perform operations that are functionally equivalent to those of an initial compiler.[285] In the Second Circuit, for example, a competitor could not assess used car values by the same technical means employed in a first-comer's copyrightable compilation, even if those means turned out to be particularly efficient, and even if the second-comer combined the protected valuations with those of another rating system in an averaged set of values.[286] Similarly, the Ninth Circuit prevented even the use of a small amount of data from a copyrighted compilation that was essential to achieving a functional result.[287]

Copyright law provides a very long term of protection, and it generally endows authors with strong rights to control follow-on applications of the protectible contents of their works.[288] Stretching copyright law to cover algorithms and aggregates of facts (and even so-called "soft" or subjective ideas), as these recent decisions have done, conflates the idea-expression dichotomy and indirectly extends protection to facts as such.[289]

Opponents of *sui generis* database protection in the United States cite these and other cases as evidence that no *sui generis* database protection law is needed.[290] In reality, these cases suggest that, in the absence of a suitable minimalist regime of database protection to alleviate the risk of market failure without impoverishing the public domain,[291] courts tend to convert copyright law into a roving unfair competition law that can protect both factual and functional matter, including algorithms, for very long periods of time and that could create formidable barriers to entry. This tendency, however, ignores the historical

---

284. *See, e.g.*, Warren Publ'g Inc. v. Microdos Data Corp., 115 F.3d 1509, 1518-19 (11th Cir. 1997) (en banc); Bellsouth Adver. & Publ'g Corp. v. Donnelley Info. Publ'g, Inc., 999 F.2d 1436, 1446 (11th Cir. 1993) (en banc).

285. *See, e.g.*, Ginsburg, *U.S. Initiatives*, *supra* note 18, at 57-61 (explaining protection of subjective criteria of selection and arrangement as distinct from objective criteria, as set out *in CCC Info. Servs*, 44 F.3d at 71); *see also* Dennis S. Karjala, *Copyright in Electronic Maps*, 35 JURIMETRICS J. 395, 408-11 (1995).

286. *CCC Info. Servs.*, 44 F.3d at 71-74. *But see* Baker v. Selden, 101 U.S. 99 (1879) (denying copyright protection to functional aspects of literary works).

287. *CDN, Inc.*, 197 F.3d at 1256. *See generally* Hughes, *supra* note 283.

288. 17 U.S.C. §§ 102(a), 103, 106(2), 302-304 (2000); Eldred v. Reno, 239 F.3d 372 (D.C. Cir. 2001), *cert. granted sub nom*, Eldred v. Ashcroft, 534 U.S. 1062, *and cert. amended*, 534 U.S. 1160 (2002); *see also* Mark A. Lemley, *The Economics of Improvement in Intellectual Property Law*, 75 TEX. L. REV. 989 (1997) [hereinafter Lemley, *Improvement*].

289. *See, e.g.*, Alan L. Durham, Note, *Speaking of the World: Fact, Opinion and the Originality Standard of Copyright*, 33 ARIZ. ST. L.J. 791, 838-42 (2001).

290. *See supra* note 20; *see also* Johathan Band & Makoto Kono, *The Database Protection Debate in the 106th Congress*, 62 OHIO ST. L.J. 869 (2001).

291. *See* Reichman & Samuelson, *supra* note 18, at 137-150 (proposing minimalist regimes of database protection).

limits of copyright protection in defiance of well-established Supreme Court precedent,[292] and ultimately jeopardizes access to the research commons.

b. The DMCA: An Exclusive Right to Access Minimally Copyrightable Compilations of Data?

With regard to copyrightable compilations of data distributed online, amendments to the Copyright Act of 1976, known as the Digital Millennium Copyright Act of 1998 ("DMCA"),[293] may have greatly reduced the traditional safeguards surrounding research uses of factual works. Technically, section 1201(a) establishes a right to prevent the direct circumvention of any electronic fencing devices that a content provider may have employed to control access to a copyrighted work.[294] Section 1201(b) then perfects the scheme by exposing manufacturers and suppliers of equipment capable of circumventing electronic fencing devices to liability for copyright infringement when such equipment can be used to violate the exclusive rights traditionally held by copyright owners.[295]

In enacting these provisions, Congress seems to have detached the prohibition against gaining unauthorized direct access to electronically fenced works under section 1201(a) from the balance of public and private interests otherwise established in the Copyright Act of 1976.[296] As Professor Jane Ginsburg interprets this provision, a violation of section 1201(a) is not an "infringement of copyright" because it attracts a separate set of distinct remedies set out in section 1203,[297] and because it constitutes "a new violation" for which those remedies are provided.[298] On this reading, unlawful access is not subject to the traditional defenses and immunities of the copyright law, and one is "not . . . permitted to circumvent the access controls, even to perform acts that are lawful under the Copyright Act,"[299] including presumably the user's right to extract unprotectible facts and ideas or to invoke the fair use defense.[300] On the

---

292. *Baker*, 101 U.S. at 99; J. H. Reichman, *Computer Programs as Applied Scientific Know-How: Implications of Copyright Protection for Commercialized University Research*, 42 VAND. L. REV. 639, 693-94, n.288 (1989) [hereinafter Reichman, *Computer Programs*] (on the deeper meaning of *Baker*).

293. Pub. L. No. 105-304, 112 Stat. 2860 (1998) (codified at 17 U.S.C. § 1201 (2000)).

294. "No person shall circumvent a technological measure that effectively controls access to a work protected under this title." 17 U.S.C. § 1201(a) (2000).

295. 17 U.S.C. § 1201(b).

> Manufacture and distribution of post-access circumvention devices and services are prohibited only if they are "primarily designed" or have "only limited commercially significant purpose or use other than" to circumvent "protection afforded by a technological measure that effectively protects a right of a copyright owner under this title in a work or a portion thereof" or if they are marked "as circumvention devices."

Ginsburg, *U.S. Initiatives*, *supra* note 18, at 65 (interpreting 17 U.S.C. § 1201(b)(1)(A)-(C)).

296. *See* Ginsburg, *U.S. Initiatives*, *supra* note 18, at 62-65

297. 17 U.S.C. § 1203 (2000).

298. Ginsburg, *U.S. Initiatives*, *supra* note 18, at 63-64.

299. *Id.* at 62.

300. *See id.* at 62-64. It remains possible that a court could interpret around these provisions to reach a fair use defense in such a case, even though section 1201(c) seems to restrict that defense to post-access uses. *See* 17 U.S.C. § 1201(c); Ginsburg, *U.S. Initiatives*, *supra* note 18, at 63-64. Obstructing access to non-copyrightable components might also attract the misuse defense in appropriate circumstances. *Cf.* Frischmann & Moylan, *supra* note 106.

contrary, "Congress may in effect have extended copyright to cover 'use' of works of authorship, including minimally original databases . . . because 'access' is a prerequisite to 'use,' [and] by controlling the former, the copyright owner may well end up preventing or conditioning the latter."[301]

While the precise contours of these provisions remain to be worked out in future judicial decisions,[302] they could potentiate the ability of both publishers and scientists to protect online collections of data that were heretofore unprotectible in print media. If, for example, a database provider combined the non-copyrightable collection of data with a nominally copyrightable component, such as an analytical explanation of how the data were compiled, the "fig leaf" copyrightable component might suffice to trigger the "no direct access" provisions of section 1201(a).[303] In that event, later scientific researchers could not circumvent the electronic fence in order to extract or use the non-copyrightable data, even for nonprofit scientific research, because section 1201(a) does not recognize the normal exceptions to copyright protection that would allow such use and scientific research is not one of the few very limited exceptions that were codified in section 1201(d)-(j).[304]

Later researchers would thus have to acquire lawful access to the electronically fenced database under section 1201(a) and then attempt to extract the non-copyrightable data for nonprofit research purposes under section 1201(b) which does, in principle, recognize the traditional users' defenses as well as the privileges and immunities codified in sections 107-122 of the Copyright Act of 1976.[305] Even here, however, later scientists could discover that the technical devices they had used to extract non-protectible data from minimally copyrightable databases independently violated section 1201(b) of the DMCA

---

301. Ginsburg, *U.S. Initiatives*, *supra* note 18, at 63.

302. For the moment, they have withstood attack on constitutional grounds. *See, e.g.*, A&M Records, Inc. v. Napster, Inc., 239 F.3d 1004, 1014-18 (9th Cir. 2001). *See generally* DIGITAL DILEMMA, *supra* note 14; JESSICA LITMAN, DIGITAL COPYRIGHT: PROTECTING INTELLECTUAL PROPERTY ON THE INTERNET (2001); Pamela Samuelson & Randall Davis, *The Digital Dilemma: A Perspective on Intellectual Property in the Information Age*, *available at* http://www.sims.berkeley.edu/~pam/papers/digdilsyn.pdf (last visited Nov. 15, 2002).

303. *See* Ginsburg, *U.S. Initiatives*, *supra* note 18, at 63 (finding that "the copyrightable fig leaf a database producer affixes to an otherwise unprotectible work could, as a practical matter, obscure the public domain nakedness of the compiled information").

304. *See* 17 U.S.C. § 1201(d)-(j) (2000). *But see* discussion *supra* note 300. In principle, scientific bodies could petition for an exemption from § 1201(a) as adversely affected users, or they could seek to argue that non-infringing uses of copyrightable databases should fall within a class of adversely affected uses, but the Copyright Office has so far resisted this approach. *See* 17 U.S.C. § 1201(a)(1)(C), (D); Ginsburg, *U.S. Initiatives*, *supra* note 18, at 64 nn.40, 41.

305. Ginsburg, *U.S. Initiatives*, *supra* note 18, at 65-67. Assuming that the end-user cannot circumvent the electronic fence without recourse to some technical device, much would depend on the extent to which any such device could readily be used for infringing as well as non-infringing uses.

> Section 1201(b) thus seems to lead to an impasse: it is permissible to circumvent anticopying controls in order to make noninfringing use, but the software or device needed to engage in the circumvention cannot be disseminated because it can all too easily be put to infringing use.

Id. at 66-67 (exploring the possibility of requiring content providers to identify nonprotectible components).

because those devices were otherwise capable of substantial infringing uses.[306] In practice, moreover, the posterior scientists' theoretical opportunity to extract non-copyrightable data by technical devices that did not violate section 1201(b) could already have been compromised by the electronic contracts these scientists will have accepted in order to gain lawful access to the online database in the first place to avoid the crushing power of section 1201(a). In that event, the scientists would almost certainly have waived any user rights they had retained under section 1201(b), unless the electronic contracts themselves became unenforceable on one ground or another, as discussed below.[307]

In effect, the DMCA allows copyright owners to surround their collections of data with technological fences and electronic identity marks buttressed by encryption and other digital controls that force would-be users to enter the system through an electronic gateway.[308] To pass through the gateway, users must accede to non-negotiable electronic contracts, which impose the copyright owner's terms and conditions without regard to the traditional defenses and statutory immunities of copyright law.[309]

The DMCA indirectly recognized the potential conflict between proprietors and users of ineligible material, such as facts and data, that section 1201(a) of the statute could thus trigger, and it empowered the Copyright Office, which reports to the Librarian of Congress, to exempt categories of users whose activities might be adversely affected.[310] While representatives of the educational and library communities petitioned for relief on various grounds, including the need of researchers to access and use non-copyrightable facts and ideas transmitted online, the authorities have so far declined to act.[311]

It is too soon to know how far owners of copyrightable compilations can push this so-called "right of access"[312] at the expense of research, competition, and free speech without incurring resistance based on the misuse doctrine of copyright law, the public policy and unconscionability doctrines of state contract laws, and First Amendment concerns that have in the past limited copyright protection of factual works.[313] For the foreseeable future, nonetheless, the

---

306. *See* 17 U.S.C. § 1201(b)(c).

307. *See* Reichman & Franklin, *supra* note 16.

308. Cohen, *Lochner in Cyberspace*, *supra* note 97; *see also* 17 U.S.C. § 1202 (prohibiting removal of copyright management information).

309. *See, e.g.*, McManis, *supra* note 273. *See generally* GUIBAULT, *supra* note 95, at 291-304. Attempts to bypass these electronic barriers in the name of pre-existing legal defenses then constitute either a violation of the access right under section 1201(a), which could impede third parties from raising even the well-established traditional defenses to an action for infringement, or an independent basis for infringement under § 1201(b). *See supra* notes 296-301, 306 and accompanying text.

310. 17 U.S.C. § 1201(a)(1)(C)-(D).

311. *See supra* note 304; *Exemption to Prohibition on Circumvention of Copyright Protection Systems for Access Control Technologies*, 37 C.F.R § 201 (2000);.

312. *See* Robert A. Kreiss, *Accessibility and Commercialization in Copyright Theory*, 43 U.C.L.A. L. REV. 1, 32-34 (1995) (discussing thesis that copyrighted works should be accessible).

313. Lemley, *Beyond Preemption*, *supra* note 273; Reichman & Franklin, *supra* note 16, at 929-53 (proposing and applying doctrine of "public interest unconscionability" as functional equivalent of misuse doctrine).

DMCA empowers owners of copyrightable collections of facts to contractually limit online access to the pre-existing public domain in ways that contrast drastically with the traditional availability of factual contents in printed works.

c. One-Sided Electronic Licensing Contracts

Data published in print media traditionally entered the public domain under the classical intellectual property regime described above. Further ensuring that result is an ancillary copyright doctrine, known as "exhaustion" or "first sale doctrine," which limits the authors' powers to control the uses that third parties can make of copyrighted literary works distributed to the public in hard copies.[314]

Under this doctrine, the copyright owner may extract a profit from the first sale of the copy embodying an original and protectible compilation of data, but cannot prevent a purchaser from reselling that physical copy or from using it in any way the latter deems fit, say, for research purposes, unless such uses amount to infringing reproductions, adaptations, or performances of the expressive components of the copyrighted compilation.[315] In effect, copyright law not only made it difficult to protect compilations of data as such, but it denied authors any exclusive right to control the use of a protected work once it had been distributed to the public in hard copies.[316]

The first sale doctrine thus complements and perfects the other science-friendly provisions described above, unless individual scientists, libraries, or scientific entities were to contractually waive their rights to use copies of purchased works in the manner described. Such contractual waivers always remain theoretically possible, and publishers have increasingly pressed them upon the scientific and educational communities in the online environment for reasons discussed below.

Nevertheless, it was not generally feasible to impose such waivers against scientists who bought scientific works distributed to the public in hard copies, and even when attempts to do so were made, such contracts could not bind subsequent purchasers of the copies in question. The upshot was that, precisely because authors and publishers could not rely on contractual agreements, they depended on the default rules of copyright law, which are binding against the world. These default rules, in turn, impose legislatively enacted "contracts," which balance public and private interests by, for example, defining the uses that libraries can make of their copies,[317] immunizing certain protected uses for

314. 17 U.S.C. § 109(a) (2000); *see also* § 117 (allowing owner of copyrighted computer program to use it on any computer).

315. *See* 17 U.S.C. § 106 (delineating exclusive rights to reproduce, adapt, publicly perform, distribute, and display copyrighted works, but conferring no exlcusive right to use); § 109(a) (defining right of owner to dispose of physical copy of protected work); Ralph S. Brown, *Eligibility for Copyright Protection: A Search for Principled Standards*, 70 MINN. L. REV. 579, 588-89 (1985) (stressing importance of denial of exclusive use).

316. *Accord* Ginsburg, *U.S. Initiatives*, *supra* note 18, at 63.

317. 17 U.S.C. § 108.

educational purposes,[318] and further allowing a set of fair uses that scientists and other researchers can invoke.[319]

i. Restoring the Power of the "Two-Party" Deal

Against this background, online delivery of both copyrightable and non-copyrightable productions possesses the inherent capabilities of changing the pre-existing relationship between authors and readers or between content providers and users. As previously discussed, by placing a collection of minimally copyrightable data online and surrounding it with technological fencing devices, publishers can condition access to the database on the would-be user's acquiescing to the terms and conditions of the former's "click-on," standard-form, non-negotiable contract (known as a contract of adhesion).[320] To this end, highly restrictive digital rights management technologies ("DRM") are being developed that include hardware and software based "trusted systems," online database access controls, and increasingly effective forms of encryption.[321]

The power to control online access that digital rights management technologies confers is, moreover, conceptually and empirically independent of statutory intellectual property rights, which makes it of capital importance for the theses discussed in this article. It means that even if a given compilation of data lacked any copyrightable "fig leaf" whatsoever, so that it could not trigger the so-called "access right" that section 1201(a) of the DMCA otherwise provides,[322] the electronic contract accepted at the gateway to the provider's electronic fence may itself enable him to control all the uses of the non-copyrightable data, which would technically enter the public domain. So long as third parties cannot feasibly acquire the data in question except by individually accepting the online provider's "click-on" licensing restrictions, online delivery can solve most of the problems that the printing press created for authors by enabling them contractually to restrict the use of productions made available to the public, whether copyrightable or not, and in this sense it restores the "power of the two-party

318. *See* 17 U.S.C. § 110(1), (2).

319. 17 U.S.C. § 107; Campbell v. Acuff-Rose Music, Inc., 510 U.S. 569, 573-96 (1994); Harper & Row Publ's, Inc. v. Nation Enters., 471 U.S. 539, 569 (1985).

320. *See, e.g.*, 17 U.S.C. §§ 1201(a), 1202; McManis, *supra* note 273; *see also* GUIBAULT, *supra* note 95, at 3.

321. *See, e.g.*, Julie E. Cohen, *A Right to Read Anonymously: A Closer Look at "Copyright Management" in Cyberspace*, 28 CONN. L. REV. 981, 983-89 (1996) (discussing technologies that copyright owners may employ to monitor and control access to information); Jessica Litman, *The Exclusive Right to Read*, 13 CARDOZO ARTS & ENT. L.J. 29 (1994); Mark Stefik, *Shifting the Possible: How Trusted Systems and Digital Property Rights Challenge Us to Rethink Digital Publishing*, 12 BERKELEY TECH. L.J. 137 (1997); *see also* PETER ECKERSLEY, VIRTUAL MARKETS FOR VIRTUAL GOODS: AN ALTERNATIVE CONCEPTION OF DIGITAL COPYRIGHT, Intell. Prop. Res. Inst. of Australia Working Paper (2002), *available at* http://www.cs.mu.oz.au/~pde/writing/virtualmarkets.pdf; Dan L. Burk & Julie Cohen, *Fair Use Infrastructure for Copyright Management Systems*, 15 HARV. J.L. & TECH. 41-83 (2001); Pamela Samuelson, *Intellectual Property and the Digital Economy: Why the Anti-Circumvention Regulations Need to be Revised*, 14 BERKELEY TECH. L.J. 519 (1999).

322. The presence of some original copyrightable expression remains a necessary prerequisite to triggering the technical protection measures of the DMCA, which to that extent remain copyright dependent. *See* 17 U.S.C. §§ 102(a)(b), 103 (2000); Ginsburg, *U.S. Initiatives*, *supra* note 18, at 63.

deal" that publishers lost in the sixteenth century.[323]

Because electronic contracts are enforceable in state courts, they provide private rights of action that tend to either substitute for or override statutory intellectual property rights. Electronic contracts become substitutes for intellectual property rights to the extent that they make it infeasible for third parties to obtain publicly disclosed but electronically fenced data without incurring contractual liability for damages. They may override statutory intellectual property rights by, for example, forbidding the uses that libraries could otherwise make of a scientific work under federal copyright law, or by prohibiting follow-on applications or the reverse engineering of a computer program that both federal copyright law and state trade secret law would otherwise permit.[324]

To the extent that those who draft electronic contracts are allowed to impose terms and conditions that ignore the goals and policies of the federal intellectual property system, they could establish "privately legislated intellectual property rights" unencumbered by concessions to the public interest.[325] By the same token, a privately generated database protected by technical devices and electronic adhesion contracts is subject to no federally imposed duration clause and accordingly will never lapse into the public domain.

ii. The Proposed Uniform Computerized Information Transactions Act ("UCITA")

Whether state courts should enforce electronic contracts—especially the non-negotiable, standard-form "click-on" and "shrink-wrap" contracts—remains an open and controversial question.[326] Besides technical obstacles to formation sounding in general contracts law, commentators argue that courts may deem such contracts unenforceable under the public policy defense of state contracts law, under the preemption doctrine that supports the integrity of the federal intellectual property system, or under some combination of the two.[327] In this regard, the doctrine of unconscionability, spawned by the Uniform Commercial Code,[328] could be expanded to encompass a concept of "public interest unconscionability," which in effect would endow state courts with a

323. *See* Reichman & Franklin, *supra* note 16, at 897-99.

324. *See, e.g.*, Rochelle Cooper Dreyfuss, *Do You Want to Know a Trade Secret? How Article 2B Will Make Licensing Trade Secrets Easier (But Innovation More Difficult)*, 87 CAL. L. REV. 191 (1999). *But see, e.g.*, 17 U.S.C. § 301 (2000); Dennis S. Karjala, *Federal Preemption of Shrinkwrap and On-Line Licenses*, 22 U. DAYTON L. REV. 511 (1997); David A. Rice, *Public Goods, Private Contract and Public Policy: Federal Preemption of Software License Prohibitions Against Reverse Engineering*, 53 U. PITT. L. REV. 543 (1992).

325. *See generally* Reichman & Franklin, *supra* note 16, at 929-53 (proposing misuse of contracts doctrine to regulate privately legislated intellectual property rights that disrupt the public-private balance of the federal system without reasonable economic justification).

326. *See, e.g.*, Hill v. Gateway 2000, Inc., 105 F.3d 1147, 1148 (7th Cir. 1997), *cert. denied*, 522 U.S. 808 (1997); ProCD v. Zeidenberg, 86 F.3d 1447 (7th Cir. 1996). *But see* Alexander M. Meiklejohn, *Castles in the Air: Blanket Assent and the Revision of Article 2*, 51 WASH. & LEE L. REV. 599, 603 (1994).

327. *See generally Intellectual Property and Contract Law*, *supra* note 16

328. U.C.C. § 2-302 (2002).

"misuse of contracts" concept to parallel and dovetail with the doctrines of "misuse of intellectual property rights."[329]

In practice, however, courts appear reluctant to exercise such powers even when their right to do so is clear. The most recent line of cases, led by the Seventh Circuit's opinion in *Pro-CD v. Zeidenberg*,[330] has tended to validate electronic contracts of adhesion in the name of "freedom of contract." In this same vein, the National Council of Commissioners for Uniform State Law ("NCCUSL") has proposed a Uniform Computer Information Transactions Act ("UCITA"), which, if state legislatures enacted it, would broadly validate such contracts and largely immunize them from legal challenge.[331]

For example, UCITA permits vendors of information products to define virtually every transaction as a "license" rather than a "sale," and it tolerates perpetual licenses.[332] It could thus override the first-sale doctrine of copyright law and any analogous doctrine that might be embodied in the proposed database protection laws discussed below.

The proposed uniform law would then proceed to broadly validate mass market "click-on" and "shrink-wrap" licenses that impose all the provisions vendors could hope for, with little regard for the interests of scientific and educational users, or the public in general.[333] It would permit vendors to add further, non-negotiated conditions to the perpetual licensing agreement even after the product had been paid for, and in case of dispute, it would permit vendors to block recalcitrant "licensees" who too vigorously complained about either the product or the terms and conditions that accompany it from further accessing or using the information it made available.[334]

A detailed analysis of UCITA's provisions is beyond the scope of this study. Suffice it to say, however, that its less-than-transparent drafting process so favored the interests of sellers of software and other information products at the expense of consumers and users generally that a coalition of sixteen state attorneys general vigorously opposed its adoption, and the American Law Institute withdrew its co-sponsorship of the original project. Nonetheless, two states—Maryland and Virginia—have adopted non-uniform versions of

329. *See* Reichman & Franklin, *supra* note 16, at 927-37 ("Validating Non-negotiable Terms that Respect the Balance of Public and Private Interests"); *see also* Niva Elkin-Koren, *A Public-Regarding Approach to Contracting Over Copyright*, in EXPANDING THE BOUNDARIES OF IP, *supra* note 13, at 191-222.

330. 86 F.3d at 1447; *Intellectual Property and Contract Law*, *supra* note 16.

331. UNIF. COMPUTER INFO. TRANSACTIONS ACT (UCITA) (2001), *available at* http://www.ucitaonline.com/ (last visited Feb. 14, 2003). At the time of this writing, the NCCUSL had just completed some revisions to UCITA that reportedly address some of the most excessive features of the proposed act that heavily favor the rights of vendors over licensees. Nonetheless, the American Bar Association has refused to endorse it.

332. UCITA § 308.

333. UCITA § 209. *See generally* Reichman & Franklin, *supra* note 16, at 938-65.

334. *See, e.g.*, Julie E. Cohen, *Copyright and the Jurisprudence of Self-Help*, 13 BERKELEY TECH. L. J. 1089 (1998).

UCITA,[335] and major software and information industry firms continue to lobby assiduously for its enactment by other state legislatures.

If present trends continue unabated, privately generated information products delivered online—including databases and computer software—may be kept under a kind of perpetual, mass market trade secret protection, subject to no reverse engineering efforts or public-interest uses that are not expressly sanctioned by licensing agreements. Contractual rights of this kind, backed by a one-sided regulatory framework, such as UCITA, could conceivably produce an even higher level of protection than that available from some future federal database right subject to statutory public-interest exceptions. The most powerful proprietary cocktail of all, however, would probably emerge from a combination of a strong federal database right with UCITA-backed contracts of adhesion.

d. New Exclusive Property Rights in Non-Copyrightable Collections of Data

The challenge of protecting commercially valuable collections of information that fail to meet the technical eligibility requirements of copyright law poses a hard problem that has existed in one form or another for two centuries,[336] and at least three different approaches have emerged over time.[337] One solution would allow a domestic copyright law to accommodate low authorship literary productions, with some adjustments to the bundle of rights at the margins.[338] A second approach, adopted in the Nordic countries, would enact a short term *sui generis* regime, built on a distinctly copyright-like model that would protect catalogues, directories, and tables of data against wholesale duplication, without conferring on proprietors any exclusive adaptation right like that afforded to authors of true literary and artistic works.[339] A third approach, experimented with at different times and to varying degrees in different countries, including the United States, would protect compilers of information against wholesale duplication of their products under different theories rooted in the misappropriation branch of unfair competition law.[340]

---

335. Robert A. Hillman & Jeffrey J. Rachlinski, *Standard-Form Contracting in the Electronic Age*, 77 N.Y.U. L. REV. 429, 491 n.314 (2002).

336. *See, e.g.*, Ginsburg, *U.S. Initiatives*, *supra* note 18, at 55.

337. This section is based on J. H. Reichman, *Database Protection in a Global Economy*, *supra* note 18, at 455, 459-84.

338. *See, e.g.*, Desktop Mktg Sys. Pty. Ltd. v. Telstra Corp. Ltd. (2002) 192 A.L.R. 433 (Austl.) (holding that white pages of telephone directory qualify for copyright protection under "sweat of the brow" theory). *See generally* Baron, *supra* note 78; Denicola, *supra* note 78; Ginsburg, *"No Sweat?"*, *supra* note 282; Ginsburg, *Commercial Value*, *supra* note 78.

339. *See, e.g.*, Gunnar W. G. Karnell, *The Nordic Catalogue Rule*, *in* PROTECTING WORKS OF FACT 67 (Egbert J. Dommering & P. Bernt Hugenholtz eds., 1991).

340. Int'l News Serv., Inc. v. Assoc. Press, 248 U.S. 215 (1918); Nat'l Basketball Ass'n v. Motorola Inc., 105 F.3d 841 (2d Cir. 1997); Jane C. Ginsburg, *Copyright, Common Law and Sui Generis Protection of Databases in the United States and Abroad*, 66 U. CIN. L. REV. 151 (1997); *see also* Gordon, *supra* note 152; Jason R. Boyarski, *The Heist of* Feist*: Protection for Collections of Information and the Possible Federalization of "Hot News,"* 21 CARDOZO L. REV. 871 (1999); Brian F. Fitzgeral, *Protecting*

What changed in the 1990s was the convergence of digital and telecommunications networks, which potentiated the role of electronic databases in the information economy generally, and which made scientific databases in particular into agents of technological innovation whose economic potential may eventually outstrip that accruing from the patent system.[341] Notwithstanding the robust appearance of the present day database industry under free market conditions,[342] analysts asked whether inadequate investment in complex digital databases would not inevitably hinder that industry's long-term growth prospects if free-riding second-comers could rapidly appropriate the contents of successful new products without contributing to their costs of development and maintenance over time. In other words, if copyright, contract law, DRM technologies, residual unfair competition laws, and various protective business practices inadequately filled a gap in the law, then regulatory action to enhance investment might be justified.[343] This utilitarian rationale, however, raised new and still largely unaddressed questions about the unintended social costs likely to ensue if intellectual property rights were injudiciously bestowed upon the raw materials of the information economy in general and on the building blocks of scientific research in particular.[344]

Any serious effort to find an appropriate *sui generis* solution to the question of database protection should have engendered an investigation of the comparative economic advantages and disadvantages of regimes based on exclusive property rights as distinct from regimes based on unfair competition laws and other forms of liability rules.[345] This investigation should also have taken account of larger questions about the varying impacts of different legal regimes on freedom of speech and the conditions of democratic discourse, which, in the United States at least, are of primary constitutional importance.[346] Instead, the Commission of the European Community cut the inquiry short by adopting the

Informational Products (Including Databases) Through Unjust Enrichment Law: An Australian Perspective, 1998 E.I.P.R. 244 (1998).

341. *See, e.g.*, Reichman & Uhlir, *Database Protection*, *supra* note 4; *cf.* Reichman, *Electronic Information Tools*, *supra* note 264. The emergence of digitally networked environments has generated a host of new value-added services and products, and appreciably increased the importance of this segment of the database market. David Fewer, *Constitutionalizing Copyright: Freedom of Expression and the Limits of Copyright in Canada*, 55 U. TORONTO FAC. L. REV. 175 (1997); *see also* Hunsucker, *supra* note 239.

342. *See* Fewer, *supra* note 341 (case of Canada); Maurer, Across Two Worlds, *supra* note 34. *See generally* A QUESTION OF BALANCE, *supra* note 1.

343. *See, e.g.*, Hunsucker, *supra* note 239; *Information Antipiracy Hearings*, *supra* note 239.

344. *See* BITS OF POWER, *supra* note 1; Reichman & Samuelson, *supra* note 18, at 113-37.

345. *See* Reichman, *Of Green Tulips*, *supra* note 164; *supra* note 151 (defining liability rules).

346. For example, the constitutional foundations of United States copyright law have always rested on a clear and sharp distinction between facts and ideas that were freely available to all and the author's expression of facts and ideas, which could not be copied. 17 U.S.C. § 102(b) (2000). Allowing exclusive property rights to cover aggregates of data and information that had been previously unprotectible must sooner or later pose fundamental constitutional questions for countries that take freedom of speech seriously, questions that a creative use of liability rules might altogether avoid. *See generally* Benkler, *Constitutional Bounds*, *supra* note 91; Hamilton, *supra* note 91; Paul J. Heald, *The Extraction/Duplication Dichotomy: Constitutional Line-Drawing in the Database Debate*, 62 OHIO ST. L.J. 933 (2001).

Directive on the Legal Protection of Databases in 1996.[347] This Directive requires all E.U. member countries (and affiliated states) to pass laws that confer a hybrid exclusive property right on publishers who make substantial investments in non-copyrightable compilations of facts and information.[348]

i. The E.C. Database Directive in Brief

The hybrid exclusive right that the European Commission ultimately crafted in its Directive on the Legal Protection of Databases does not resemble any pre-existing intellectual property regime. It protects any collection of data, information, or other materials that is arranged in a systematic or methodological way, provided that it is individually accessible by electronic or other means.[349] To become eligible for protection, the database producer must demonstrate a "substantial investment," as measured in either qualitative or quantitative terms,[350] which leaves the courts to develop this criterion with little guidance from the legislative history.[351] The drafters explicitly recognized that the qualifying investment may consist of no more than simply verifying or maintaining the database.[352]

In return for this investment, the compiler obtains exclusive rights to extract or reutilize all or a substantial part of the contents of the protected database.[353] The exclusive extraction right pertains to any transfer in any form of all or a substantial part of the contents of a protected database;[354] the exclusive reutilization right, by contrast, covers only the making available to the public of all or a substantial part of the same database, typically by incorporation of those data into another database.[355] In every case, the first-comer obtains an exclusive right to control uses of collected data as such, as well as a powerful adaptation (or derivative work) right along the lines that copyright law bestows on "original works of authorship,"[356] even though such a right is alien to the protection of investment under existing unfair competition laws.[357] In a recent interpretation of this provision, a United Kingdom court vigorously enforced this right to control follow-on applications of an original database against a value-adding sec-

347. E.C. Database Directive, *supra* note 17.

348. *Id.* at arts. 1(2), 7(1).

349. *Id.* at art. 1(2).

350. *Id.* at art. 7(1).

351. The Recitals, and some implementing laws, state that the "substantial investment" may entail financial, material, or human resources. *See, e.g., id.*, Recital 40; *see also* Ginsburg, *U.S. Initiatives*, *supra* note 18, at 69 n.55.

352. E.C. Database Directive, *supra* note 17, at art. 7(1).

353. *Id.* at arts. 7(1)-(2).

354. *Id.* at art. 7(2)(a). For example, any transfer of all or a substantial part of a paper or disc will trigger this clause. "Indeed, extraction also occurs if the user simply downloads a 'substantial part' . . . to 'RAM' to view on a screen since 'extraction' . . . shall mean the permanent *or temporary* transfer." Ginsburg, *U.S. Initiatives*, *supra* note 18, at 69.

355. E.C. Database Directive, *supra* note 17, at art. 7(2)(b).

356. *See, e.g.*, 17 U.S.C. §§ 101 ("derivative works"), 103, 106(2).

357. *See* Reichman & Samuelson, *supra* note 18, at 137-51.

ond-comer.[358] It took this position even though the proprietor was the sole source of the data in question and there was no feasible way to generate them by independent means.[359]

The Directive contains no provision expressly regulating the collections of information that member governments themselves produce. This lacuna leaves European governments that generate data free to exercise either copyrights[360] or *sui generis* rights in their own productions in keeping with their respective domestic policies. This result contrasts sharply with the situation in the United States, where the government cannot claim intellectual property rights in the data it generates and must normally make such data available to the public for no more than a cost-of-delivery fee.[361]

The Directive provides no mandatory public-interest exceptions comparable to those recognized under domestic and international copyright laws. An optional, but ambiguous, exception concerning "illustrations for teaching or scientific research" applies to extractions but not reutilization.[362] This provision would prevent a nonprofit scientist from incorporating an extract taken from a protected database into a new and different compilation.[363]

The Directive's *sui generis* regime exempts from liability anyone who extracts or reuses an insubstantial part of a protected database, and this exception may not be overridden by contract.[364] However, such a user bears the risk of accurately drawing the line between a substantial and an insubstantial part, and any repeated or systematic uses of even an insubstantial part will forfeit this exemption.[365] Judicial interpretation has so far taken a restrictive view of this exemption, and one cannot effectively make unauthorized extractions or uses of an insubstantial part of any protected database without serious risk of triggering an action for infringement.[366]

Qualifying databases are nominally protected for a fifteen-year period.[367] In reality, each new substantial investment in a protected database, such as the

---

358. British Horseracing Bd. Ltd. v. William Hill Org. Ltd., 2001 E.W.C.A. Civ. 1268 (Eng. C.A.).

359. *Id.*

360. *See* E.C. Database Directive, *supra* note 17, at ch. I, arts. 1-6; Berne Convention, *supra* note 109, at art. 2(4) (leaving this to discretion of governments).

361. 17 U.S.C. § 105 (2000).

362. E.C. Database Directive, *supra* note 17, at arts. 9, 9(b). This exception requires attribution and must not exceed an amount "justified by the noncommercial purpose to be achieved"); *see also id.* at art. 9(a) (broader exception for private use extractions from hard copies).

363. *See, e.g.*, Reichman & Uhlir, *Database Protection*, *supra* note 4, at 803; *accord* Ginsburg, *U.S. Initiatives*, *supra* note 18, at 69-70. This provision may be open to a more flexible interpretation, and some member countries, notably the Nordic countries, have implemented a broader version. Other countries, notably France, Italy, and Greece, have simply ignored this exception altogether, which defeats the Commission's supposed concerns to promote uniform law.

364. E.C. Database Directive, *supra* note 17, at arts. 8(1), 15.

365. *Id.*, arts. 7(2), 7(5), 8(1).

366. P. Bernt Hugenholtz, The New Database Right: Early Case Law from Europe, paper presented at the Ninth Annual Conference on International Intellectual Property Law and Policy, Fordham University School of Law, New York (Apr. 19-20, 2001), *available at* http://www.inir.nl/medewerkers/hugenholtz.htm; *see also* Reichman & Samuelson, *supra* note 18, at 87-95.

367. E.C. Database Directive, *supra* note 17, at art. 10(1).

provision of updates, can re-qualify that database *as a whole* for a new term of protection.[368] In this and other respects, the scope of the *sui generis* adaptation right exceeds that of copyright law, which attaches only to the new matter added to an underlying, pre-existing work and expires at a time certain.[369]

Finally, the Directive carries no national treatment requirement into its *sui generis* component. Foreign database producers become eligible only if their countries of origin provide a similar form of protection or if they set up operations within the European Union.[370] Non-qualifying foreign producers, however, may nonetheless seek protection for their databases under residual domestic copyright and unfair competition laws, where available.[371]

The E.C.'s Directive on the Legal Protection of Databases thus broke radically with the historical limits of intellectual property protection in at least three ways. First, it overtly and expressly confers an exclusive property right on the fruits of investment as such, without predicating the grant of protection on any predetermined level of creative contribution to the public domain. Next, it confers this new exclusive property right on aggregates of information as such, which had heretofore been considered as unprotectible raw material or basic inputs available to creators operating under all other pre-existing intellectual property rights. Finally, it potentially confers the new exclusive property right in perpetuity, with no concomitant requirement that the public ultimately acquire ownership of the object of protection at the end of a specified period.[372] The Directive thus effectively abolishes the very concept of a public domain that had historically justified the grant of temporary exclusive rights in intangible creations.[373]

368. *Id.* at art. 10(3).

369. *See* 17 U.S.C. §§ 103, 302 (2000); Reichman & Samuelson, *supra* note 18, at 84-90.

370. E.C. Database Directive, *supra* note 17, at art. 11, Recital 56.

371. *Id.* at art. 13. Copyright protection is independent of *sui generis* protection, but the two regimes may apply cumulatively.

372. In this and other respects, the E.C. Database Directive broke with the history of intellectual property law by allowing a property rule—as distinct from a liability rule—to last in perpetuity. Trademarks may last in perpetuity, but they do not protect innovation or investments as such, only the signs and symbols that enable consumers to distinguish one producer's goods from another's. William Landes & Richard A. Posner, *Trademark Law: An Economic Perspective*, 30 J.L. ECON. 265 (1987). Trademarks are thus not legal monopolies, and because they protect only against acts that yield a likelihood of confusion, there are historical questions about their status as "property" at all.

These historical debates in turn reflect confusion about the fundamental distinction between exclusive property rights and liability rules, which have a different economic logic. *See* discussion *supra* at note 151. Trademarks are property in the sense that proprietors obtain legally enforceable entitlements, but that entitlement is only to avoid deceiving or confusing consumers by the adoption of similar identifying symbols. While the property-like status of marks has been strengthened against dilution in recent years, a trademark confers no rights in the underlying products of innovation or investment as such, which anyone remains free to copy and sell under a different mark.

373. Reichman & Samuelson, *supra* note 18. *See generally* James Boyle, *The Second Enclosure Movement and the Construction of the Public Domain*, 66 LAW & CONTEMP. PROBS. 33 (Winter/Spring 2003) [hereinafter Boyle, *Second Enclosure Movement*]; David Lange, *Recognizing the Public Domain*, 44 LAW & CONTEMP. PROBS. 147 (Autumn 1981); Jessica Litman, *The Public Domain*, 39 EMORY L.J. 965 (1990). *But see* van Caenegem, *supra* note 113, at 324, 328-30.

ii. The Database Protection Controversy in the United States

The situation in the United States differs markedly from that which preceded the adoption of the European Commission's Directive on the Legal Protection of Databases. In general, the legislative process in the United States has become relatively transparent. Since the first legislative proposal, modeled on the E.C. Directive, was introduced by the House Committee on the Judiciary in May of 1996,[374] this transparency has generated a spirited and often high-level public debate.[375] Very little progress toward a compromise solution had been reached as of the time of writing, however, which is hardly surprising given the intensity of the opposing views, the methodological distance that divides them, and the political clout of the opposing camps.[376]

We are accordingly left with the two basic proposals that were still on the table at the end of the last legislative session, which ended in an impasse. These proposals, as refined during that session, represent the baseline positions that each coalition carried into the current round of negotiations. One bill, H.R. 354, as revised in January of 2000,[377] embodies the proponents' last set of proposals for a *sui generis* regime built on an exclusive property rights model (although some effort has been made to conceal that solution behind a facade that evokes unfair competition law). The other bill, H.R. 1858, sets out the opponents' views of a so-called minimalist misappropriation regime as it stood on the eve of the current round of negotiations.[378]

(a) The exclusive rights model. The proposals embodied in H.R. 354 attempt to achieve levels of protection comparable to those of the E.C. Directive by means that are more congenial to the legal traditions of the United States.[379] The changes introduced in that bill softened some of the most controversial provisions at the margins, while maintaining the overall integrity of a strongly protectionist regime.[380]

The bill in this form continued to define "collections of information" very

---

374. H.R. 3531, 104th Cong. (1996). For details, see Reichman & Samuelson, *supra* note 18, at 102-09.

375. *See* J. H. Reichman, *Database Protection in a Global Economy*, *supra* note 18 at 467-70. For developments in the period between 1996 and 1999, see Reichman & Uhlir, *Database Protection*, *supra* note 4, at 821-28.

376. Nevertheless, at the beginning of the last series of negotiations between the stakeholder groups in March 2001, the two committee chairmen vowed to draft a compromise bill if the interested parties themselves failed to agree. *See* Transcript of Press Conference of Rep. Billy Tauzin and Rep. James Sensenbrenner, March 29, 2001, *available at* http://www.techlawjournal.com/cong107/database/20010329.

377. *See* H.R. 354, 106th Cong. (1999). This bill was subject to proposed amendments on Jan. 11, 2000, which, however, were not formally submitted as an amended proposal. The summary in the text sometimes reflects changes that were introduced in publicly disclosed proposals for amendments.

378. *See* H.R. 1858, 106th Cong. (1999).

379. *See generally* Amanda Perkins, *United States Still No Closer to Database Legislation*, 2000 E.I.P.R. 366; Band & Kono, *supra* note 290; Roger L Zissu, *Protection for Facts and Databases in the New World Order*, 1998 J. COPYRIGHT SOC'Y U.S.A. 271 (1998).

380. Many of these changes came under pressure from agents of the past Administration seeking to engender a compromise.

broadly as "information . . . collected and . . . organized for the purpose of bringing discrete items of information together in one place or through one source so that persons may access them."[381] Like the E.C. Directive, the bill then casts eligibility in terms of an "investment of substantial monetary or other resources" in the gathering, organizing or maintaining of a "collection of information."[382] It confers two exclusive rights on the investor: first, a right to make all or a substantial part of a protected collection "available to others;" and, second, a right "to extract all or a substantial part to make available to others." Here the term "others" is manifestly broader than "public" in ways that remain to be clarified.[383]

H.R. 354 then superimposed an additional criterion of liability on both exclusive rights that is not present in the E.C. Directive. This is the requirement that, to trigger liability for infringement, any unauthorized act of "making available to others" or "extraction" for that purpose must cause "material harm to the market" of the qualifying investor "for a product or service that incorporates that collection of information and is offered or intended to be offered in commerce." The crux of liability under the bill thus derives from a "material harm to markets" test that is meant to cloud the copyright-like nature of the bill[384] and shroud it in different terminology.[385]

Here a number of concessions were made to the opponents' concerns in the last public iteration of the bill on Jan. 11, 2000, some of them real, others nominal in effect. The addition of "material" to the market harm test,[386] may, for example, address complaints that proponents viewed one lost sale as constituting actionable harm to the market.

At the same time, the revised bill contained convoluted and tortuous definitions of "market" that the previous Administration hoped would reduce the scope of protection in the case of follow-on applications.[387] On closer inspec-

381. H.R. 354, 106th Cong. §1401(1) (1999). Here the overlap with copyright law is so palpable that it is hard to conceive of any copyrightable assemblage of words, numbers, facts, or information that would not also qualify as a potentially protectible collection of information.

382. *Id.* at §1402(a).

383. However, the second right represents a concession to the past Administration in that it foregoes the general *right to control private use* that appeared in previous versions. This concession thus *reduces* the scope of protection to a point more in line with the E.C.'s reutilization right, and it does not impede personal use by one who lawfully acquires access to the database. *See id.* at §1402(a).

384. Because the Supreme Court insists that "originality" is a constitutional requirement for copyright protection, it "has arguably stripped Congress of power . . . to enact a copyright-like statute for non-original databases." Ginsburg, *U.S. Initiatives*, *supra* note 18, at 73-74.

385. *See* H.R. 354, 106th Cong. § 1402(a) (1999). As originally deposited, H.R. 354 spoke of "material harm to the primary market or a related market" of the investor. *Id.* The analysis in the text is based on the more refined but unpublished proposals of January 11, 2000. In fact, a "harm to markets" test is lifted bodily from section 107(4) of the Copyright Act of 1976, and it reflects the better view of what U.S. copyright law is all about. *See* J. H. Reichman, *Goldstein on Copyright Law: A Realist's Approach to a Technological Age*, 43 STAN. L. REV. 943 (1991) (reviewing PAUL GOLDSTEIN, COPYRIGHT: PRINCIPLES, LAW AND PRACTICE (1990)).

386. H.R. 354 § 1402(a).

387. "Market" is thus supposed to assimilate "all markets" in which a protected investor "derives or reasonably expects to derive substantial revenue, directly or indirectly," as well as all markets in which that investor "has taken demonstrable steps discernable to the public, to offer in commerce within a

tion, however, these definitions provide a static picture of a moving target that amounts to a mostly illusory limitation on the investor's broad adaptation right.[388] Notwithstanding these so-called concessions, the bill effectively assigns most follow-on applications to any initial investor whose dynamic operations expand the range of potentially protectible matter with every update, ad infinitum.

The bill then introduced a "reasonable use" exception that was intended to benefit the nonprofit user communities, especially researchers and educators,[389] and that conveys a sense of similarity to the fair use exception in copyright law.[390] Once again, these benefits become largely illusory on closer analysis, because under the proposed bill, the very facts, data, and information that copyright law excludes have themselves become the objects of protection, and there are no other significant exceptions. Hence, virtually every customary or traditional use of facts or data compiled by others that copyright law would presumably have allowed scientists, researchers, or other nonprofit entities to make in the past now becomes a prima facie instance of infringement under H.R. 354. These users would, in effect, either have to license such uses or be prepared to seek judicial relief for "reasonableness" on a continuing basis. Because university administrators dislike litigation and are risk averse by nature, and this provision puts the burden of showing reasonableness on them, there is reason to expect a chilling effect on customary uses by these institutions of data heretofore in the public domain.[391]

---

short period of time a product or service" from which he expected to derive substantial revenue. H.R. 354 §§ 1401(3)(A), (B) (with additional proviso added Jan. 11, 2000).

388. In principle, only actual, likely, or planned markets are protected under this scheme, which creates a narrow opening for a value-adding competitor who arrives on the scene with an unlikely or unplanned application. Even here, however, the definitions ignore the prospects that the initial investor will continue to expand the range of projected investments over time and thus convert all the tests to moving targets that constantly expand his potential claims to protected market segments.

In practice, moreover, database proprietors would be well-advised to plan for any market segments they can remotely foresee over time and to craft their business models in broadly worded terms accordingly. Should a competitor discover a surprise market niche to slip into all the same, the initial proprietor's most likely strategy would be to surround the competitor with applications of its own, to limit the competitor's field of expansion and to extract cross-licenses wherever possible.

389. H.R. 354 § 1403(2).

390. In copyright law, there is a thicket of exclusions and exceptions that must be worked through before anyone can infringe. In particular, one cannot infringe for a taking of unprotectible facts or ideas, and even a taking of protectible expression may be excused by codified exceptions for, say, teaching or research. The "fair use" exception comes into play only as a last resort, to excuse marginal takings by an alleged infringer that advance the public interest at a small cost to the proprietor. *See* 17 U.S.C. §§ 102(b), 107-122 (2000).

391. *Cf.* Ginsburg, *U.S. Initiatives*, *supra* note 18, at 69; Reichman & Uhlir, *Database Protection*, *supra* note 4, at 812-20, 825-29. A further provision then completes the sense of circularity by expressly exempting any nonprofit educational, scientific, and research use that "does not materially harm the market" as previously defined. *See* H.R. 354 § 1403(b). Since any use that does not materially harm the market remains unactionable to begin with, this "concession" adds nothing but window dressing. However, another vaguely worded exception seems to recognize at least a possibility that certain "fully transformative uses" might nonetheless escape liability, but this ambiguous proposal defies interpretation in its present form and remains to be clarified.

The bill recognized an "independent creation" norm, which presumably exempts any database, however similar to an existing database, that was not the fruit of "copying."[392] This provision codifies a fundamental norm of copyright law, and the European Commission made much of a similar norm in justifying its own regulatory scheme. In reality, this "independent creation" principle produces unintended and socially deleterious consequences when transposed to the database milieu precisely because many of the most complex and important databases are inherently incapable of independent regeneration. Sometimes the database cannot be reconstituted because the underlying phenomena are one-time events, as often occurs in the observational sciences.[393] In other instances, key components of a complex database can no longer be reconstituted with certainty at a later date. Any independently regenerated database suffering from these defects would necessarily contain gaps that made it inherently less reliable than its predecessor.

These problems point to a more general phenomenon that affects competition in large or complex databases. Even when, in principle, such databases could be reconstituted from scratch, the high cost of doing so—as compared with the add-on costs of existing producers—will tend to make the second-comer's costs so high as to constitute a barrier to entry. Meanwhile, the first-comer's comparative advantage from already owning a large collection that is too costly to reconstitute will only grow more formidable over time, an economic reality that progressively strengthens the barriers to entry and tends to reinforce (and, indeed, to explain) the predominance of sole-source data suppliers in the marketplace.[394]

Government-generated data remained excluded, in principle, from protection, in keeping with current U.S. practice,[395] which differs from E.U. practice in this important respect. However, there is considerable controversy surrounding the degree of protection to be afforded government-generated data that subsequently become embodied in value-adding, privately funded databases.[396] All parties agree that a private, value-adding compiler should obtain whatever degree of protection is elsewhere provided, notwithstanding the incorporation of government-generated data, assuming that this transaction entails a "substantial investment."[397] The issue concerns the rights and abilities of third parties to continue to access the original, government-generated data sets. The propo-

---

392. H.R. 354 § 1403(c).

393. *See* Reichman & Uhlir, *Database Protection*, *supra* note 4, at 807-08.

394. *See* Benkler, *Free as the Air*, *supra* note 91. As more and more segments of industry come to appreciate the market power that major database producers could acquire under the proposed legislation, one after another has petitioned the subcommittee for special relief. Thus, H.R. 354, which grew to some thirty pages in length, singled out various special interests that benefit, to varying degrees, from special exemptions from liability. At the time of writing the list of those entitled to such immunities included news reporting organizations; churches that depend on genealogical information, notably the Mormons; online service providers; and certain online stockbrokers. *See* H.R. 354 § 1403(e)(f)(i).

395. *See* H.R. 354 § 1404.

396. *See, e.g.*, Weiss & Backlund, *supra* note 7, at 300, 303.

397. For the view that it may not, see Ginsburg, *U.S. Initiatives*, *supra* note 18, at 70.

nents of H.R. 354 have been little inclined to accept measures seeking to preserve access to the original data sets, despite pressures in this direction.[398]

H.R. 354 imposed no restrictions whatsoever on licensing agreements, including agreements that might overrule the few exceptions otherwise allowed by the bill.[399] Despite constant remonstrations from opponents about the need to regulate licensing in a variety of circumstances—and especially with respect to sole-source providers[400]—the bill itself does not budge in this direction. On the contrary, new provisions added to H.R. 354 in 2000 would set up measures that prohibit tampering with encryption devices ("anti-circumvention measures") and electronically embedded "watermarks" in a manner that parallels the provisions adopted for online transmissions of copyrighted works under the DMCA.[401] Because these provisions would effectively secure the database against unauthorized access (and so tend to create an additional "exclusive right of access" without expressly so declaring),[402] they would only add to the database owner's market power to dictate contractual terms and conditions without regard to the public interest. These powers are further magnified by the imposition of criminal sanctions in addition to strong civil remedies for infringement.[403]

The one major concession that was made to the opponents' constitutional arguments concerns the question of duration. As previously noted, the E.C. Directive allows for perpetual protection of the whole database so long as any part of it is updated or maintained by virtue of a new and substantial investment, and the proponents' early proposals in the United States echoed this provision.[404] However, the U.S. Constitution clearly prescribes some limited term of duration for intellectual property rights,[405] and the proponents have finally bowed to pressures from many directions by limiting the term of duration to fifteen years.[406]

Any update to an existing database would then qualify for a new term of fifteen years, but this protection would apply, at least in principle, only to the matter added in the update. In practice, however, the inability to clearly separate old from new matter in complex databases, coupled with ambiguous language concerning the scope of protection against harm to "likely, expected,

398. *See* A QUESTION OF BALANCE, *supra* note 1, at 102-05.

399. H.R. 354 § 1404(e).

400. For a recent discussion, see Ginsburg, *U.S. Initiatives*, *supra* note 18, at 76.

401. *Cf.* Digital Millennium Copyright Act (DMCA), Pub. L. No. 105-304, § 103, 112 Stat. 2860, 2863 (1998) (codified at 17 U.S.C. §§ 512, 1201, 1205). For a discussion of the DMCA, see *supra* notes 286-287 and accompanying text.

402. *See, e.g.*, Ginsburg, *U.S. Initiatives*, *supra* note 18, at 63-68; Jane C. Ginsburg, *Copyright and Control Over New Technologies of Dissemination*, 101 COLUM. L. REV. 1613 (2001).

403. *See* H.R. 354 §§ 1406-1407.

404. *See* H.R. 3534 and H.R. 2652; Reichman & Samuelson, *supra* note 18, at 103-09 (citing authorities).

405. U.S. Const., art. I, § 8, cl. 8; Eldred v. Reno, 239 F.3d 372 (D.C. Cir. 2001), *cert. granted sub nom*, Eldred v. Ashcroft, 534 U.S. 1126, *and cert. amended*, 534 U.S. 1160 (2002).

406. *See* H.R. 354 § 1409(i).

or planned" market segments,[407] may still leave a loophole for an indefinite term of duration.[408]

(b) The unfair competition model. The opponents' bill, the Consumer and Investor Access to Information Act of 1999, H.R. 1858, was introduced by the House Commerce Committee in 1999, as a sign of good faith,[409] in response to critics' claims that the opponents' coalition sought only to block the adoption of any database protection law.[410] H.R. 1858 begins with a definition of databases that is not appreciably narrower than that of H.R. 354, except for an express exclusion of traditional literary works that "tell a story, communicate a message," and the like.[411] In other words, it attempts to draw a clearer line of demarcation between the proposed database regime and copyright law, to reduce overlap or cumulative protection as might occur under H.R. 354.

The operative protective language in H.R. 1858 appeared short and direct, but it relied on a series of contingent definitions that muddy the true scope of protection. Thus, the bill would prohibit anyone from selling or distributing to the public a database that is (1) "a duplicate of another database . . . collected and organized by another person or entity," *and* (2) "is sold or distributed in commerce in competition with that other database."[412] The bill then defines a prohibited duplicate as a database that is "substantially the same as such other database, as a result of the extraction of information from such other database."[413]

Here, in other words, liability attached only for a wholesale duplication of a pre-existing database that resulted in a substantially identical end product. However, this basic misappropriation approach becomes further subject to both expansionist and limiting thrusts. Expanding the potential for liability is a proviso added to the definition of a protectible database that treats "any discrete sections [of a protected database] containing a large number of discrete items of information" as a separably identifiable database entitled to protection in its own right.[414] The bill would thus codify a surprisingly broad prohibition of

407. *Id.*

408. *Cf.* Ginsburg, *U.S. Initiatives*, *supra* note 18, at 76 (proposing measures to close this loophole).

409. *See* H.R. 1858, 106th Cong. (1999); *see also* H.R. REP. NO. 106-350, PART I (1999); Perkins, *supra* note 379.

410. This may be true of some, but not all, members of that coalition. Both scientists and universities, for example, although allied with the opponents' coalition for strategic reasons, prefer a minimalist approach because they want some protection against unauthorized commercial applications of their data without hindering access to data for public research activities. Over time, pressures for some form of database protection have built up to the point where the minimalist alternative bill has become a serious basis of negotiation, even though, in our view, it remains poorly crafted and contains numerous ambiguities.

411. *See* H.R. 1858 § 101(1).

412. *See id.* § 102.

413. *See id.* § 101(2).

414. *See id.* § 101(1)(B).

follow-on applications that make use of discrete segments of pre-existing databases,[415] subject to the limitations set out below.

A second protectionist thrust resulted from the lack of any duration clause whatsoever, with the prohibition against wholesale duplication—subject to limitations set out below—*conceivably lasting forever*. This perpetual threat of liability would attach to wholesale duplication of even a discrete segment of a pre-existing database, if the other criteria for liability were met.

These powerfully protective provisions, put into H.R. 1858 at an early stage to weaken support for H.R. 354, were offset to some degree by other express limitations on liability and by a codified set of misuse standards to help regulate licensing. To understand these further limitations, one should recall that liability even for wholesale duplication of all, or a discrete segment, of a protected database does not attach unless the unauthorized copy is sold or distributed in commerce and "in competition with" the protected database.[416] The term "in competition with," when used in connection with a sale or distribution to the public, is then defined to mean that the unauthorized duplication "displaces substantial sales or licenses likely to accrue from the original database" *and* "significantly threatens . . . [the first-comer's] opportunity to recover a reasonable return on the investment" in the duplicated database.[417] Both prongs must be met before liability will attach.

It follows that even a wholesale duplication that was not commercially exploited or did not substantially decrease expected revenues (as might occur from, for example, nonprofit scientific research activities) could presumably escape liability in appropriate circumstances. Similarly, a follow-on commercial product that made use of data from a protected database might escape liability if it were sold in a distant market segment or required substantial independent investment.

H.R. 1858 then further reduced the potential scope of liability by imposing a set of well-defined exceptions and limiting enforcement to actions brought by the Federal Trade Commission ("FTC").[418] There are express exceptions comparable to those under H.R. 354 for news reporting, law enforcement activities,

---

415. The Clinton Administration expressed reservations about this de facto derivative work right, which is built into a regime that lasts forever. Communication with Professor Justin Hughes (Oct. 17, 2001) (on file with authors). At that time, Professor Hughes worked at the U.S. Patent and Trademark Office and was the principal coordinator of the Administration's submission of opinions regarding the database protection bills introduced in Congress.

416. *See* H.R. 1858 § 102.

417. *Id.* § 101(5).

418. *See id.* § 107. The provision that conditions liability for infringement on an official FTC action was a tactical expedient devised to provide the House Commerce Committee with some basis for asserting concurrent jurisdiction over database legislation, along with that of the House Judiciary Committee's Subcommittee on Courts and Intellectual Property. Most observers believe that the absence of any private right of action in H.R. 1858 as it stands constitutes a fatal flaw that would have to be removed in any final compromise decision to adopt an unfair competition approach. Some supporters consider FTC supervision a necessary safeguard, especially in view of the First Amendment tensions that any database protection law is certain to generate in the United States.

intelligence agencies, online stockbrokers, and online service providers.[419] There is also an express exception for nonprofit scientific, educational, or research activities,[420] in case any such uses were thought to escape other definitions that limit liability to unauthorized uses in competition with the first-comer. Still other provisions clarify that the protection of government-generated data or of legal materials in value-adding embodiments remains contingent upon arrangements that facilitate continued public access to the original data sets or materials.[421] A blanket exclusion of protection for "any individual idea, fact, procedure, system, method of operation, concept, principle or discovery" wisely attempts to provide a line of demarcation with patent law and to ward off unintended protectionist consequences in this direction.[422]

Another important set of safeguards emerged from the drafters' real concerns about potential misuses of even this so-called "minimalist" form of protection. These concerns are expressed in a provision that expressly denies liability in any case where the protected party "misuses the protection" that H.R. 1858 affords. A related provision then elaborates a detailed list of standards that courts could use as guidelines to determine whether an instance of misuse had occurred.[423] These guidelines or standards would greatly clarify the line between acceptable and unacceptable licensing conditions, and if enacted, they could make a major contribution to the doctrine of misuse as applied to the licensing of other intellectual property rights as well.[424]

In summary, the underlying purpose of H.R. 1858 was to prohibit wholesale duplication of a database as a form of unfair competition. It thus set out to create a minimalist liability rule that prohibits market-destructive conduct rather than to enact an exclusive property right as such,[425] and in this sense, initially posed a strong contrast to H.R. 354. Over time, however, different iterations of the bill, designed to win supporters away from H.R. 354, have made H.R. 1858 surprisingly protectionist—especially in view of its de facto derivative work right.[426]

419. H.R. 1858 §§ 103(b), 103(c), 104(b), 104(e), 106(a).

420. *See id.* § 103(d).

421. *See id.* §§ 101(b), 104(f). There are also express exclusions of telecommunications carriers' subscription lists (for example, telephone directories) and of securities market data. *Id.* § 104(g). However, the bill proposes an amendment to the Securities Exchange Act of 1934 that would prohibit the misappropriation of "real-time" stock market information. *Id.* § 201.

422. *See id.* § 104(d).

423. *Id.* §§ 106(b), 106(b)(1-6). *See infra* note 540.

424. These provisions could particularly assist judicial regulation of shrink-wrap and click-on licenses affecting online distribution of software and other electronic information tools. *See generally* Reichman & Franklin, *supra* note 16, at 929-60.

425. For early proposals to this effect, see Reichman & Samuelson, *supra* note 18, at 139-45. For a definition of liability rules, see *supra* note 151.

426. The realities of the bargaining process are such that concessions made to the high-protectionist camp at an earlier stage, for whatever tactical reasons, are unlikely to be withdrawn later.

C. Implications for Science: Disintegration of the Research Commons?

Part II of this study described some of the potentially limitless possibilities for research and innovation that might ensue from using digital technologies to exploit scientific data available from the public domain as it was traditionally constituted. However, these prospects dim the moment we consider the ramifications for science of the economic, legal, and technological assaults on the public domain currently under way. This section explores some of the likely negative effects that these trends could have on science and innovation unless science policy directly addresses these risks.

1. Restricting Access to and Use of Scientific Data

In the interests of clarity, we outline the implications of present trends on a sectoral basis, in keeping with the functional map of public domain data flows indicated above. We begin with the government's role as primary producer of such data and then consider the implications of present trends for academia and the private sector.

a. In Government

If a basic trend is the shifting of more data production and dissemination activities from government to the private sector, one should recognize at the outset that the social benefits of such a shift can exceed its costs under the right set of circumstances. In principle, private database producers may sometimes operate more efficiently and attain qualitatively better results than government agencies. Positive effects are especially likely when markets have formed, competition occurs, and the public interest, including the needs of the research community that was previously served by the government, continues to be satisfied.

There are also numerous drawbacks associated with this trend, however, which require careful consideration.[427] To begin with, a private data supplier will seldom be in a position to produce the same quantity and range of data as a government agency, charge prices that users can afford, and still make a profit. In other words, a government agency has typically taken on the task of data production and dissemination precisely because the social need for such data outweighs the market opportunities for these activities. Social costs from privatization begin to rise if the profit motive induces a private supplier to unduly reduce the quantity and range of data produced or made available.

For example, a private data producer typically markets refined data products to end users in relatively small quantities, whereas basic research, particularly in the observational sciences, often requires raw or less commercially

427. *See, e.g.*, DAVID, DIGITAL BOOMERANG, *supra* note 20, at 2 ("We really do not know how much further the current rush toward privatization of scientific and technological knowledge can go before it starts to seriously undermine the inherited structure of fragile conventions and institutions that support cooperative research activities, thereby setting in motion the contraction of the global domain of scientific inquiry.").

refined data in voluminous quantities. On the whole, overzealous privatization of the government's data production capabilities poses real risks for both science and innovation because the private sector simply cannot duplicate the government's public good functions and still make a profit.[428]

Unless the private sector can demonstrably produce and distribute much the same data more effectively and with higher quality standards than a government agency, privatization may become little more than a sham transaction. The would-be entrepreneur merely appropriates a government function and then licenses data back to a captive market at much higher prices and with greatly increased restrictions on access and use. In the absence of market-induced competition, there is a very high risk of trading one monopolist with favorable policies toward science and the broader society—the government—for another monopolist driven entirely by profit and the restrictions made necessary by this motive.

Absent a sham transaction, one cannot say *a priori* that any given privatization project necessarily results in a net social loss. The outcome will depend on the contracts the agency stipulates and the steps it is willing to take to ensure continued access to data for research purposes on reasonable terms and conditions. In contrast to buying data collection services, the licensing of data and information products from the private sector raises serious questions about the type of controls the private sector places on the redistribution and uses of such data and information the government can subsequently undertake. If the terms of the license are onerous to the government, and access, use, and redistribution are substantially restricted—as they almost always are—neither the agency nor the taxpayer is well served. This is particularly true in cases where the data that need to be collected are for a basic research function or serve a key statutory mission of the agency.

A classic example of what can go wrong was the privatization of the Landsat earth remote sensing program in the mid-1980s. Following the legislatively mandated transfer of this program to EOSAT Co., the price per scene rose more than 1000%, and significant restrictions were imposed, even on research uses. Use by both government and academic scientists fell sharply, and recent studies have shown the extent to which both basic and applied research in environmental remote sensing was set back.[429] This experiment also failed in com-

428. *See* Stephen Maurer, *Raw Knowledge: Protecting Technical Databases for Science and Industry*, *in* NATIONAL RESEARCH COUNCIL, COMMITTEE FOR A STUDY ON PROMOTING ACCESS TO SCIENTIFIC AND TECHNICAL DATA FOR THE PUBLIC INTEREST, PROCEEDINGS OF THE WORKSHOP ON PROMOTING ACCESS TO SCIENTIFIC AND TECHNICAL DATA FOR THE PUBLIC INTEREST: AN ASSESSMENT OF POLICY OPTIONS (Jan. 14-15, 1999), *available at* http://www.nap.edu/html/ proceedings_sci_tech/appC.html (last visited Feb. 14, 2003). ("Since public databases do not generate the revenues needed to pay license fees, statutory protection imposes substantial (albeit inadvertent) pressures to privatize.").

429. *See* BITS OF POWER, *supra* note 1, at 121-24.

mercial terms, as EOSAT Co. became unable to continue operations after several years.[430]

Several lessons can be drawn from this and similar undertakings. One is that before a transfer to the private sector occurs, objective criteria demonstrating net social gains from the transaction should be met. Recent studies have identified such criteria, and when they are met, good reasons to privatize would exist.[431] Even when objective criteria justify a transfer of data production from the public to the private sector, government agencies should not abdicate their contractual responsibility to ensure access for research purposes on favorable terms and conditions, as will be discussed further in the final Part of this article.

We concede that, if the government lacks resources to generate data for a public research function in the first place, obtaining it from a willing producer is better than nothing.[432] Where, however, a choice exists, the wrong decision can impose high opportunity costs on the scientific community and the broader society. We also assume the government intends to continue its policy of not commercializing its own data output—unlike the European Union and most other countries—in view of the positive externalities this has generated in the past.

b. In Academia

The legal and technological pressures identified above will also affect the uses that are made of government-funded data in academic and other nonprofit institutions. These pressures will intensify the tensions that already exist between the sharing norms of science and the need to restrict access to data in pursuit of increased commercial opportunities.

Although the enhanced opportunities for commercial exploitation that new intellectual property rights and related developments make possible are clear, they will affect the normative behavior of the scientific community gradually and unevenly. Academics are already conflicted in this emerging new environment, and these conflicts are likely to grow.[433] As researchers, they need continued access to a scientific commons on acceptable terms, and they are expected to contribute to it in return. As members of academic institutions, however, they are increasingly under pressure to transfer research results to the private sector for gain, and they themselves may want to profit from the new commercial opportunities.[434]

---

430. The government then reassumed control of this program, but a new privatizing proposal is under consideration. *See* Landsat Data Continuity Mission, *at* http://ldcm.usgs.gov/ (last updated Jan. 24, 2003).

431. *See* BITS OF POWER, *supra* note 1, at 116-24; RESOLVING CONFLICTS, *supra* note 8, at 82-87.

432. *But see* Stephen Maurer & Suzanne Scotchmer, *Database Protection: Is It Broken and Should We Fix It?*, SCIENCE, May 14, 1999, at 1129 (noting that funding agencies are notoriously reluctant to pay for intellectual property licenses).

433. *See generally* Rai, *supra* note 33, at 109-15 (describing normative changes in academia after Bayh-Dole and countervailing efforts to redress the balance).

434. *See* Powell, *supra* note 13.

The government itself fuels these conflicts through the potentially contradictory policies that underlie its funding of research. One message reminds scientists of their duties to share and disclose data, in keeping with the traditional norms of science. The other, more recent message urges them to transfer the fruits of their research to the private sector or otherwise exploit the intellectual property protection their research may attract.[435]

At the moment, these conflicts are strongest where the line between basic and applied science has collapsed and commercial opportunities inhere in most projects.[436] Obvious examples are biotechnology and computer science. There, progress frequently occurs through accretions of know-how, obtained by trial and error, and theoretical explanations may follow, rather than precede, practical applications.[437] Decisions about the use of intellectual property rights and licensing contracts to exploit applications thus rebound in unexpected ways against the possibilities of further research.

In the future, the enactment of a powerful intellectual property right in collections of data might be expected to push these tensions into other areas where the lines between basic and applied research remain somewhat clearer and the pressures to commercialize research results have been less noticeable thus far. In exploring the implications of these developments for academic research, we continue to focus attention on the two distinct but overlapping research domains previously characterized as "formal" and "informal."

i. The Formal Zone

In what we call the formal sector, science is conducted within structured research programs that establish guidelines for the production and dissemination of data. Typically, data are released to the public in connection with the publication of research results.[438] Data may also be disclosed in connection with patent applications and supporting documentation. One should recall that, even without regard to the mounting legal and technological pressures, there are strong economic pressures that already limit the amount of data investigators are inclined to release at publication or in patent applications. There are growing delays in releasing those data as researchers consider commercialization options, and more of the data that are released come freighted with various restrictions.[439]

---

435. *See, e.g.*, Rai, *supra* note 33, at 112 (noting that the initial impetus to commercialize and corresponding "norm change has . . . been tempered by some attention to the traditional values of research science").

436. *See* Eisenberg, *Public Research*, *supra* note 120, at 1726 ("[A]s university patenting and private funding of university research increase, the time-honored distinction between 'basic' and 'applied' research is becoming ever more difficult to maintain, particularly in fields that are of significant commercial interest.").

437. *See, e.g.*, Reichman, *Computer Programs*, *supra* note 292. *See generally* Reichman, *Legal Hybrids*, *supra* note 164.

438. *See supra* note 72 and accompanying text.

439. *Id.*; *see also* David Blumenthal et al., *Witholding Research Results in Academic Life Sciences: Evidence from a National Survey of Faculty*, 92 JAMA 1224 (1997); Rai, *supra* note 33, at 110-11.

The enactment of a hybrid intellectual property right in collections of data, such as the E.C. Directive, would introduce a disruptive new element into an already troubled academic environment. Suddenly, such a right would make it possible to publish academic research for credit and reputation while retaining ownership and control of the underlying data, which would no longer automatically lapse into the public domain. By the same token, disclosure of research results for the purpose of filing patent applications, while continuing to count as novelty-defeating prior art in the public domain,[440] would not displace the inventor's right to control the underlying data that support the application. Because patent law has been encroaching progressively on collections of data that scientists previously regarded as falling within the public domain,[441] the database right itself—depending on how it was structured—could become more valuable than patent protection.

To some extent, this development tends to erase some of the preexisting distinctions between the "formal" and "informal" domains. In both domains, access to data might increasingly have to be secured by means of brokered, negotiated transactions, and this outcome is rife with implications.[442] For present purposes, it seems clear that any database protection law, coupled with the other legal and technological measures discussed above, will further undermine the sharing ethos and encourage the formation of a strategic, self-interested trading mentality that already predominates in the informal domain.

These pressures will necessarily tend to blur and dilute the importance of publication as the line of demarcation between a period of exclusive use in relative secrecy and ultimate dedication of data to the public. Once databases attract an exclusive property right valid against the world, the legal duty of scientists publishing research results to disclose or release the underlying data could depend on codified exceptions permitting use for verification and certain "reasonable" nonprofit research and educational purposes.[443] Of course, this new default rule would ultimately have to be reconciled in practice with the disclosure obligations of the federal funding agencies. The point is that the new default rule would nonetheless place even published data outside of the public domain, and much academic research is not federally funded or funded in ways that waive such disclosure requirements.

The role of academic journal publishers in this new legal environment also warrants consideration. At present, scientists tend to assign their copyrights to publishers on an exclusive basis, and many of these journals now produce electronic versions—sometimes exclusive of a print version. These practices

440. 35 U.S.C. § 102 (2000).

441. *See, e.g.*, Eisenberg, *Public Research*, *supra* note 120 (stressing the changing interpretation of boundaries of intellectual property law); Eisenberg, *Bargaining*, *supra* note 13; Rai, *supra* note 33.

442. "Scientists report having to wait months or even years to carry out experiments, while their insitutions attempt to negotiate the terms of 'Material Transfer Agreements,' . . . database access agreements, and patent license agreements." Eisenberg, *Bargaining*, *supra* note 13, at 225.

443. *See supra* notes 334-36 and accompanying text. We assume some such provision would necessarily be incorporated into any U.S. database law that Congress may adopt.

already complicate matters because, as shown above, the data that traditional copyright law puts into the public domain may be fenced to a still unknown extent by the technological measures that the DMCA reinforces. If, in addition, a database law is enacted, any data that the scientist assigns to the publisher with the article would become subject to the new statutory regime. The publisher would then be in a position to control subsequent uses of the data and to make them available online under a subscription or pay-per-use plan with additional restrictions on extraction or reuse.

Even if individual scientists are willing and able to resist the demands for exclusive assignment of both their copyrights and any new database rights, the fact remains that publication of the article in a journal would no longer automatically release the data into the public domain. On the contrary, and unless the scientist waived the new default rule, even the data revealed in the publication itself would remain subject to his or her exclusive right of extraction and reuse—at least as formulated under the E.C. database protection directive.[444]

With or without a new statutory database right in the United States, scientists appear certain to come under increasing pressure to retain data for commercial exploitation. The research universities are already deeply committed to maximizing income from patentable inventions under Bayh-Dole, with varying degrees of success, and they will logically extend these practices and procedures to the commercialization of databases as valuable research tools.[445] A key question is whether they will make the commercialized data available for academic research on reasonable terms and conditions.[446]

As with government-generated data, university efforts to commercially exploit their databases could produce net social gains under the right set of circumstances. Besides the incentive to generate new and more refined data products that an intellectual property right might confer, greater efforts could be made to enhance the quality and utility of selected databases than might otherwise be the case. Absent such incentives, many scientists may not take pains to organize and document their data for easy use by others, particularly those outside their immediate disciplines, and may not refine their data beyond the level needed to support their own research needs and related publication objectives. Legal incentives might thus stimulate the production of more refined databases, especially where markets for such products had formed.

At the same time, these new commercial opportunities would tempt university administrators and academics to attenuate or modify the sharing and open access norms of science and to circumvent obligations in this regard that federal

---

444. These exclusive rights would then remain subject to any exceptions for scientific use incorporated into the database protection right. These exceptions were negligible in the E.C. Database Directive, *supra* note 17, and efforts to obtain significantly broader exceptions in the U.S. proposals have not succeeded so far. *See* Reichman & Uhlir, *Database Protection*, *supra* note 4, at 825-27.

445. This process is already underway, even in the absence of any database protection right. *See, e.g.*, Powell, *supra* note 13, at 254-55, 263-65; Eisenberg, *Bargaining*, *supra* note 13, at 224-26.

446. "University technology transfer professionals report that agreements presented for the transfer of research tools impose increasingly onerous terms." Eisenberg, *Bargaining*, *supra* note 13, at 225.

agencies had established.[447] Were this to occur, the unintended harm to research could greatly exceed that we are accustomed to experiencing with regard to patented inventions under Bayh-Dole[448] because the licensing of academic databases, reinforced by a codified intellectual property right, would limit the quantity and quality of data heretofore available from the public domain.

From a qualitative perspective in particular, the data produced at universities has typically been more refined or highly processed than government data and are developed with particular research objectives or applications in mind.[449] Moreover, many of these data-intensive research activities require access to and use of multiple sources of data.[450] What has been changing is the evident commercial value of this type of refined, upstream research byproduct that makes databases both outputs as well as inputs at a much earlier stage of the research process in many areas of science. This raises serious doubts about their continued availability on acceptable terms or whether they will even be made available to other researchers at all.

Present university licensing practices with regard to material transfer agreements ("MTAs") in the biotechnology sector do not bode well in this regard. These contracts are not drafted by scientists with the needs of the larger scientific community in mind. Recent surveys of these practices show that university technology licensing offices resort to exclusive licenses that impose onerous terms and conditions, including aggressive grant-back or reach-through clauses that attempt to secure a share of the return from follow-on applications developed with the aid of the licensed technologies.[451] While anecdotal and some empirical research suggests that these offices have showed a certain willingness to negotiate reasonable terms in specific instances, the legal and economic literature foresees growing anticommons effects and ever-higher transac-

447. *Cf.* Rai, *supra* note 33, at 109-11 (stressing that commercial involvement in academic research has already "undermined norms governing the sharing of research materials and tools").

448. *See, e.g.*, Eisenberg, *Public Research*, *supra* note 120, at 1667 ("[B]y providing incentives to patent and restricting access to discoveries made in institutions that have traditionally been the principal performers of basic research, [Bayh-Dole] threatens to impoverish the public domain of research science that has long been an important resource for researchers in both the public and private sectors.").

449. *See* Nelson, *supra* note 132, at 16 ("By far the lion's share of modern scientific research, including research done at universities, is in fields where a practical application is central in the definitions of a field. In today's world science is useful to inventing, not so much because of Serendipity, but because much of modern scientific research is designed exactly to help clear the path for technological progress.").

450. *See Collections Hearings*, *supra* note 183.

451. *See, e.g.*, Eisenberg, *Bargaining*, *supra* note 13, at 225 (stressing onerous terms and limitations and overwhelming "burden of reviewing and renegotiating each of a rapidly growing number of agreements for what used to be routine exchanges among scientists. "); Rai, *supra* note 33, at 111 (noting that many MTAs require researchers to assign or license intellectual property rights to discoveries made in the course of using the research tools, while others "prohibit sharing tools with other researchers or sending them to other institutions").

tion costs.[452] There are also enormous opportunity costs for research that will prove difficult or impossible to document.

There is no reason to expect that, left to their own devices, the university technology licensing offices dealing on a case-by-case basis would demonstrate any greater concern for the research needs of the larger community with respect to databases than they have with respect to MTAs. In fact, many university databases could become more valuable than the corresponding patent portfolios over time, owing to their cumulative nature, the potential ability to control updates under the proposed new intellectual property right, and the existing ability to control online dissemination and use by electronic contracts. As the need to exploit such databases upstream becomes more pronounced, with corresponding palpable commercial payoffs, university administrators could logically become less willing to make commercially valuable data available, even to colleagues, in the absence of corresponding benefits.

If these predictions prove even partly accurate, we should then expect to see the formation of university "database pools" and cross-licensing agreements, like the "patent pools" of today,[453] which can achieve some positive synergies through cooperation.[454] However, the evidence shows that such pools are very difficult to form when the value of upstream research products defies easy measurement and the relevant players in a given industry have very different agendas, as would occur when federal agencies, academic institutions, and different types of private companies are all involved.[455] Moreover, there are far

452. *See, e.g.*, Michael A. Heller & Rebecca S. Eisenberg, *Can Patents Deter Innovation? The Anti-commons in Biomedical Research*, SCIENCE, May 1, 1998, at 698. *But see* J. Walsh, et al., *Research Tool Patenting and Licensing and Biomedical Innovation*, *in* W. COHEN & S. MERRILL, PATENTS AND THE KNOWLEDGE BASED ECONOMY (forthcoming 2003) (finding no hard evidence of anticommons effects in downstream patents, but emerging problems affecting research in upstream patents).

453. Describing Patent pools, Professor Rai says:

> Patent pools typically function by extending membership to those firms in a given industry that agree to assign or license their individual patent rights to the pool. In simple pools, membership gives each party the right to royalty-free licensing of all patents in the pool. In more sophisticated pools, members who use a particular patent pay the pool a set fee that reflects the economic significance of the patent; similarly royalties accumulated by the pool are divided according to the perceived significance of the technology put in by the parties.

Rai, *supra* note 33, at 129.

454. *See, e.g.*, Eisenberg, *Bargaining*, *supra* note 13, at 227-28 ("Collaborative research that pools research capabilities and funds from different institutions in the public and private sectors is increasingly common, not only in the life sciences but across all fields of research."); Gregory Graff & David Zilberman, *Towards an Intellectual Property Clearinghouse for Ag-Biotechnology*, 3-2001 IP STRATEGY TODAY 1, 9 (2001) ("[A]n intellectual property 'clearinghouse' might be a most effective way to reduce market inefficiencies that hinder the exchange of privately deemed knowledge, allowing researchers to obtain the freedom-to-operate status necessary to commercialize . . . research."); Merges, *Patent Pools*, *supra* note 151, at 123, 155-56. *See generally* Robert P. Merges, *Contracting Into Liability Rules: Intellectual Property Rights and Collective Rights Organizations*, 84 CAL. L. REV. 1293 (1996) [hereinafter Merges, *Contracting into Liability Rules*].

455. Rai, *supra* note 33, at 133. Professor Rai, focusing on the example of prospective biotech patent pools, points out that the relevant academic institutions and federal agencies might logically want to make marketable end products "widely available nonexclusively on a low or no-royalty basis," while "the private companies focused exclusively on upstream research might believe in more selective licensing at a higher royalty." *Id.*

greater risks that such pools lead to collusive, anti-competitive behavior, to the erection of formidable barriers to entry, and to discrimination, which in this case could adversely affect lower-tier universities that possessed few tradable assets.[456]

At present, the primary bulwarks against such a breakdown of the sharing ethos are the formal requirements of the federal funding agencies, which in many cases continue to require that data from the research projects they fund be transferred at some point to public repositories or made available upon request. To avoid these negative results, the agencies would have to strengthen these requirements—and their enforcement—and adapt them to the emerging high-protectionist intellectual property environment. We elaborate further on this topic in Part IV. The point for now is that, absent express overrides that universities voluntarily adopt or that funding agencies impose in their research grants and contracts, the new default rules of ownership and control would automatically take effect if Congress enacts a database protection law, and they could become general practice even without such a law as the result of routine, unregulated database licensing practices.

These new default rules of ownership and control could gradually undermine and dissolve the pre-existing norm that scientists publish and release their data to the public. No well-meaning resolution to the contrary by scientific bodies will, by itself, avert this outcome.

ii. The Informal Zone

In the informal zone, researchers are not yet ready to publish or are working independently on small science projects beyond the formal controls and requirements of a federal research program mandating open access or public deposit. If the research project is federally funded, the investigator is still operating in the pre-publication phase, in which he enjoys a period of exclusive use that typically lasts from six months to two years, depending on the grant. Any formal obligations to disclose data that derive from the grant do not yet apply, and data exchanges in this phase depend on self-interest, competitive advantages, and the sharing ethos. In addition, much of the research falling within the informal zone is funded by state governments, foundations, and the universities themselves, all of which leave more discretion in these matters to researchers, as well as by private companies, who normally require secrecy.

Our concerns about the effects of the new legal and technological pressures on the formal academic zone apply with even greater force to the informal zone where the impetus to commercialize data will encounter fewer regulatory constraints. The changing mores likely to undermine disclosure and open access in the formal zone would make it harder to organize cooperative networks in the

456. *See, e.g.*, Rai, *supra* note 33, at 130-35 (stressing ability of pools to withhold access to those that lack important technology to contribute or that will not pay large licensing fees). *See generally* H. HOVENKAMP, M.D. JANIS, & M.A. LEMLEY, IP AND ANTITRUST §§ 34.3, 34.4 (2002).

less structured and more unruly informal domain.[457]

This loss of cooperative incentives would prove troublesome even if the informal zone were to remain stable in the face of these pressures. In reality, such pressures—and especially a new intellectual property right in databases—will seriously destabilize the informal zone as depicted in recent sociological studies. As the new default rules make themselves felt, researchers operating in the informal zone will become aware that they own property interests in their data collections over and above any stipulated obligation to publish. In other words, a self-conscious assertion of property rights—and the corresponding proprietary mentality—will displace the softer, more inchoate legal norms that otherwise protect confidential information in ways that scientists in the informal domain typically know little about.

At present, researchers in the informal zone tend to accommodate requests to share data in response to community norms, peer pressure, the expectation of reciprocity, and other factors shaped by perceived self-interest. Under a strong database protection regime, researchers will logically begin to view such transactions as requests to waive or relinquish exclusive property rights, whose potential value is not easily measured or foreseen.[458] This outlook would tend to make researchers more reluctant to dilute their rights and more inclined to hoard data, demand up-front short term benefits as a quid pro quo, and even to insist on their own versions of the reach-through and grant-back clauses that are already routinely used by university technology licensing offices. As university administrators become increasingly aware of the commercial possibilities inherent in database protection, they may restrict their academics' freedom to informally exchange data with colleagues and require university approval—lest such exchanges damage their potential commercial interests.[459] Moreover, private partners that support university research will insist that statutory property rights in data be fully respected, and more and more private partners may become involved in the commercialization of data produced by academics.[460]

At the very least, the informal data exchanges of the past, which were already hampered by various forms of personal strategic considerations, seem likely to become more formal and complicated, with higher transaction costs and real risks of encountering holdouts, thickets of overlapping rights, and anti-

457. *See* Hilgartner, *Access to Data*, *supra* note 31, at 9 (noting that IP protection will make collaboration more difficult); Rebecca S. Eisenberg, *Patents and the Progress of Science: Exclusive Rights and Experimental Use*, 56 U. CHI. L. REV. 1017, 1061 (1989); Rai, *supra* note 33, at 129-35 (documenting difficulties of organizing collective exchange norms to address transaction costs).

458. On the difficulties of evaluation, see Rai, *supra* note 33, at 125-27.

459. *See, e.g.*, Powell, *supra* note 13, at 264-65 (stressing the extent to which universities are "seeking to privitize new information" and fearing erection of "costly toll booths").

460. *Cf.* Rai, *supra* note 33, at 182-83 (finding that since Bayh-Dole and related legal developments in the 1980s and 1990s, industry now funds "a non-trivial percentage of academic research in the life sciences," some of these relationships "resemble commercial joint ventures," and participants "often depart quite markedly from traditional research norms").

commons effects.[461] To be sure, the advent of an exclusive property right in non-copyrightable databases might facilitate some transactions that could not have occurred in the past, owing to legal uncertainty.[462] It may also stimulate new types of transactions by reinforcing the trading mentality and encouraging parties to seek deals based on their data assets, although such incentives and potential benefits are far better suited to private sector activities than to the academic milieu. On the whole, however, the outcome is likely to be increased obstacles to the construction of informal academic networks of data exchanges, with a corresponding reduction in the flow of the data streams discussed in Part II.[463] Individual researchers will be strongly tempted to hold out or bargain to impasse, at the expense of scientific cooperation.[464]

Examples of such phenomena are already observable. In academia, one promising initiative to organize a common database of human mutations data on a quasi-commercial basis, while maintaining broad community access, failed for a variety of anticommons effects, and the contributing entities ultimately bargained to impasse.[465]

If the residual force of the sharing ethos in the informal sector started to break down under these pressures, the process of disintegration would encounter fewer bulwarks protecting the public domain than in the formal sector. Scientists operating in the informal zone are, by definition, less constrained by formal federal data access requirements, and they are often closer to industry. Indeed, the more the cooperative spirit dissipates, the more likely it becomes that the commercial ethos of the private sector will fill the vacuum and pervade the informal domain.

These tendencies would predictably become more pronounced over time, as more scientists become aware of the new possibilities to retain ownership and control of data, even after publication of research results. Indeed, one would logically expect that strategic behavior in the informal zone would increasingly be geared to efforts to maximize advantages from post-publication opportunities. Should this occur, academics themselves would exert pressure on the fed-

461. *See, e.g.*, Heller & Eisenberg, *supra* note 452; Powell, *supra* note 13, at 264; *cf.* Carl Shapiro, *Navigating the Patent Thicket: Cross Licenses, Patent Pools, and Standard Setting*, 1 INNOVATION POL. & ECON. 119 (2001).

462. *But see* Mowery & Rosenberg, *supra* note 231, at 49 (finding that, in "biotechnology, continuing uncertainty over the strength and breadth of intellectual property protection may have discouraged litigation").

463. *See, e.g.*, Powell, *supra* note 13, at 266 (fearing "turf wars, with rival networks of partners looking to delay, deter, and defend themselves against competitors and poachers rather than advancing both their efforts and those of the overall field").

464. *See, e.g.*, *id.* at 265 (stressing risk of "disputes, duplication, and discord"); *cf.* Rai, *supra* note 33, at 127-29 (stressing risk of holdups in biotechnology because patentee seeks to appropriate much of the value of the improvements).

465. *See* Stephen M. Maurer, Inside the Anticommons: Academic Scientists' Struggle to Commercialize Human Mutations Data, 1999-2001, paper given at the Franco-American Conference on the Economics, Law, and History of Intellectual Property Rights, Haas School of Business, University of California at Berkeley, Oct. 5-6, 2001 [hereinafter Maurer, Inside the Anticommons].

eral system and their universities to fall in line with the needs of commercial partners.

One can thus project a kind of cascading effect if a strong database protection right were enacted and the scientific community failed to take steps to preserve and reinforce the research commons. On this view, today's formal zone, built around the release of data into the public domain at publication, would begin to resemble the informal zone, as sociologists have recently portrayed it,[466] while that same informal zone would look more and more like the private sector. Under these circumstances, one cannot necessarily assume the open access policies currently supporting the formal sector would continue in force, in which case even basic research could be adversely affected—as occurred in the United Kingdom in the 1980s through 1990s.[467]

What the new equilibrium—resulting from the conflict between these privatizing and commercializing pressures on the one hand and the traditional norms of public science on the other—will look like cannot be predicted with any degree of certainty. In a previous article, however, we outlined the cumulative negative effects such tendencies would likely have on scientific endeavor. For the sake of brevity, they are recalled here in summary form:

(1) Less effective domestic and international scientific collaboration, with serious impediments to the use, reuse, and transformation of factual data that are the building blocks of research;

(2) Increased transaction costs driven by the need to enforce the new legal restrictions on data obtained from different sources, and the implementation of new administrative guidelines concerning institutional acquisitions and uses of databases, and associated legal fees;

(3) Monopoly pricing of data and anti-competitive practices by entities that acquire market power, or by first-entrants into niche markets that predominate in many research areas; and

(4) Less data intensive research and opportunity costs.[468]

What could well be the greatest casualty of all are the new opportunities that digital networks provide to create virtual information commons within and across discipline-specific communities built around optimal access to and exchange of scientific data. To the extent that public science becomes dominated by brokered intellectual property transactions, the resulting combination of high transaction costs, unbridled self-interest, and anticommons effects could defeat the fragile cooperative arrangements needed to create and maintain such

466. *See generally* Hilgartner & Brandt-Rauf, *Controlling Data*, *supra* note 31.

467. *See, e.g.*, P.J. Runei, *Energy R&D in the United Kingdom*, BATTELLE, Mar. 2000, at 7 (paper prepared for the U.S. Department of Energy under contract DE-AC06-76RLO 1830) (citing government statistics showing that the U.K. government has downsized its support for R&D over the past two decades and that the British government has acknowledged that this policy has not worked well and that the "country's R&D had reached a critical level of ill health and a condition that threatens future economic growth and international competitiveness").

468. Reichman & Uhlir, *Database Protection*, *supra* note 4, at 812-21.

virtual information commons and the distributed research opportunities they make possible.

In industry. Proponents of a strong database protection law claim it is needed to stimulate investment in more databases than would otherwise become available.[469] However, there is no credible evidence that the market for databases has been under-supplied or under-invested in the United States, even though the share of U.S. commercial databases in the world market has declined somewhat in the last ten years.[470] On the contrary, the European Union's production since the enactment of the Directive, which reportedly showed an initial short-term spike, has subsequently remained stable.[471]

The emergence of digitally networked environments "has generated a host of new value-added services and products, and appreciably increased the importance of this segment of the database market."[472] In a previous article, Professors Reichman and Samuelson explained why digital technology would cause the market for value-added database products to flourish in the near future,[473] and their predictions have held up over time. The database industry as a whole, and its value-adding components, have in fact flourished, despite constant allegations of market failure.[474]

It remains, of course, logical to consider whether that industry's long-term growth prospects would suffer in the absence of additional legal protection against free-riding expropriations from databases that were costly to develop and maintain. In so doing, however, one must discount the availability and effectiveness of self-help measures,[475] and the relative social costs of removing vast quantities of technological information from the public domain, which have functioned as basic inputs of the knowledge economy.[476] At the very least, these and other considerations should focus attention on the choice of legal instru-

469. *See, e.g.*, E.C. Database Directive, *supra* note 17, Recitals 6-12; Maurer, Across Two Worlds, *supra* note 34 (critically evaluating this thesis); *Information Antipiracy Hearings*, *supra* note 239; BRAUNSTEIN, *supra* note 239; *see also* Hunsucker, *supra* note 239.

470. Maurer, Across Two Worlds, *supra* note 34, at 11.

471. *Id.* at 35-40.

472. Fewer, *supra* note 341, at 177.

473. First, "digital technologies facilitate the disaggregation of value-added functions" and permit new forms of data aggregation and presentation that were unavailable in print media. Reichman & Samuelson, *supra* note 18, at 125. Second, "digital technologies foster new functions, such as reformatting, filtering, and hot-linking, which have no counterparts in print media." *Id.*

474. *See* Fewer, *supra* note 341 (finding no evidence of market failure in Canada); Maurer, Across Two Worlds, *supra* note 34, at 11. *See generally* A QUESTION OF BALANCE, *supra* note 1.

475. For example, electronic fencing through encryption devices, coupled with tagging or watermarking of data, make it possible for online database providers to impose standardized contractual restrictions on all would-be users. *See* A QUESTION OF BALANCE, *supra* note 1, at 68-69; Kenneth W. Dam, *Self-Help in the Digital Jungle*, *in* EXPANDING THE BOUNDARIES OF IP, *supra* note 13, at 103, 107-10, 117-19.

476. *See, e.g.*, Boyle, *Second Enclosure Movement*, *supra* note 373.

ments to remedy any perceived market failure, and on the relative social costs and benefits of different approaches.[477]

For present purposes, it suffices to emphasize that any de facto exclusive property right in the non-copyrightable contents of databases would automatically empty the public domain of most of the factual matter the *Feist*[478] decision had consigned to that domain in 1991. While government-generated data would probably remain available to the public under domestic (but not foreign) law,[479] all non-governmental databases would become presumptively proprietary, whether made available online or in hard copies. Access to, and use of, such data for research purposes would depend on negotiated licenses or on any research exceptions to the proprietary rights that happened to be adopted in the end.[480] Depending on the type and strength of the database protection law ultimately adopted, there are good reasons to fear that barriers to entry could be high, unlicensed follow-on applications could be stifled, and sole-source providers would likely predominate.[481]

While industry would thus contribute significantly less aggregate data to the public domain than in the past,[482] its ability to bank on these same proprietary rights might induce the private sector to disclose certain kinds of data previously kept secret, especially to potential partners in the universities. Much would depend on the willingness and ability of the academic community to accommodate the private sector's needs to restrict access to or use of data made available for nonprofit research pursuits[483] and to deny access or use to would-be competitors.

To the extent that a more protectionist database regime would facilitate more public-private partnerships with universities, the social benefits likely to ensue from such interaction would have to be weighed against the risks that the norms of industry would increasingly pervade academia and foster pressure for less public disclosure of data, in potential conflict with the norms of science. At the very least, industry usually insists on confidentiality in joint projects, and would further want any end product to benefit from any new database protec-

---

477. Critics argue that, given the power of self-help remedies in the digital environment, contract and unfair competition law would suffice to close any regulatory gaps that were likely to ensue in the short or medium term, without further encumbering access to the public domain. *See e.g.*, Bott, *supra* note 34; Reichman & Samuelson, *supra* note 18, at 137-50.

478. Feist Publ'ns, Inc. v. Rural Tel. Servs. Co., 449 U.S. 340 (1991).

479. All previous versions of database protection legislation introduced in Congress have exempted both federal and state collections of information from the scope of protection.

480. *See* Reichman & Uhlir, *Database Protection*, *supra* note 4, at 822-28; *supra* notes 362-363, 389-391, 420, and accompanying text.

481. *See generally* Reichman & Uhlir, *Database Protection*, *supra* note 4, at 813-21.

482. This is clear under the E.C. Database Directive, where duration is potentially limitless in time. *See* E.C. Database Directive, *supra* note 17. Where duration is limited, long-term gains of public domain data are at least conceivable, at the expense of short and medium-term losses. *See, e.g.*, van Caenegem, *supra* note 113, at 325.

483. *Cf.* Rai, *supra* note 33, at 111 ("Companies that license . . . [biotech] materials and tools to academic researchers often force researchers to sign material transfer agreements (MTAs) that tightly restrict the researchers' use of these materials.").

tion right that Congress ultimately enacted.[484] To parry these and other anticipated negative developments, concerted efforts to accommodate and protect the research goals of government funding agencies, university administrations, and academic scientists would have to be made. Detailed proposals to this effect are set out in Part IV.

Major repercussions from database protection would also be felt in those sectors of the economy where subpatentable innovation depends on the constant exchange of technical information and know-how among the members of engineering communities working on given technical trajectories.[485] As shown above, this vibrant component of the innovation economy currently depends on liability rules that protect confidential information and on a robust public domain in which members of the technical community exchange sub-patentable know-how and information that automatically enters the public domain with disclosure or independent creation.[486] The advent of a strong exclusive database right that displaced the existing pro-competitive liability rules could hamper these exchanges, reduce spillover effects, hinder value-adding innovation, and elevate the costs of R&D, all of which could slow the pace of sub-patentable innovation generally.

2. Broader Implications for the Innovation System

Much of the economic literature that so far has addressed the topic of database protection tends unconsciously to assume the premises that ultimately yield the authors' expected conclusions. Because most economists uncritically equate "property rights" with "exclusive rights," and because the risk of market failure inherent in public goods is often efficiently overcome with "property rights," these studies usually end where they began: by endorsing property rights and taking the view that stronger is better.[487] Such studies beg the important questions that a deeper knowledge of intellectual property law might raise, namely, what level and mode of protection would produce the greatest amount of investment with the most acceptable degree of social costs.[488]

a. Underestimating the Potential Social Costs

In this connection, a codified, federal unfair competition law, based on the misappropriation rationale, could constitute a minimalist response to a poten-

---

484. *Id.* at 111 (noticing that corporate sponsors of research demand secrecy); *cf.* Nelson, *supra* note 132, at 33 ("Discussions with industry executives suggest that, until recently, industry often gave research a *de facto* research exemption. However, now they often are very reluctant to do so. In many cases they see university researchers as direct competitors to their own research efforts aimed to achieve a practical result which is patentable. And they feel themselves burdened by the requirement to take out licenses to use university research results that are patented, and see no reason why they shouldn't make the same demands on universities.").

485. *Cf.* Reichman, *Of Green Tulips*, *supra* note 164; Samuelson & Scotchmer, *supra* note 155.

486. *See supra* notes 163-167 and accompanying text.

487. *See, e.g.*, *Information Antipiracy Hearings*, *supra* note 239; BRAUNSTEIN, *supra* note 239. For trenchant criticism of this approach, see Boyle, *Cruel, Mean or Lavish*, *supra* note 165.

488. *See, e.g.*, Rochelle C. Dreyfuss, *Information Products: A Challenge to Intellectual Property Theory*, 20 N.Y.U. J. INT'L L. & POL. 897 (1988).

tial gap in the law whose true dimensions remain unknown. It could also provide the uniform model needed for proper administration of the national system of innovation and for negotiating an international arrangement.[489] Moreover, a growing number of innovative proposals rooted in liability rules[490] have been put on the table in recent years, in addition to the better-known proposals for a more traditional unfair competition approach.[491]

Most economists engaged in this topic, however, have so far ignored these and other proposals largely because their economic models and premises either do not allow them to take liability rules into account or incline them to postulate their inherent inferiority to exclusive rights. [492] In so doing, they fail to devote any serious attention to the social costs that critics of such rights—including strong database protection—continue to fear. As a result, formal economic analysis has so far taught us very little about how to craft an alternative protective regime so as to avoid market failure without erecting barriers to entry and impoverishing the public domain.

The most fundamental question these economists largely ignore is the extent to which any exclusive property right might *a priori* constitute the wrong kind of solution for a legal regime that aims to protect investment in large-scale aggregates of data as such.[493] Consider, for example, the interactions that might occur once the line between patentable inventions and the new intellectual property right in data began to blur. In the past, patent disclosures entered the public

---

489. *See, e.g.*, Reichman, *Database Protection in a Global Economy*, *supra* note 18, at 493-96 (discussing a model international treaty based on the repression of wholesale duplication of databases under a menu of legal options); Zissu, *supra* note 379.

490. *See* definition of liability rules *supra* note 151.

491. For example, Wendy Gordon has proposed a tort of "malcompetitive copying" that would rest on specific economic criteria. Gordon, *On Owning Information*, *supra* note 152; *see also* Karjala, *Misappropriation*, *supra* note 152. William Kingston has proposed a new type of liability regime that would transform intellectual property protection from a duration-based calculus of rights to an accounting-based calculus of rights based on multiples of R&D costs. William Kingston, *Unlocking the Potential of Intellectual Property*, paper presented to Swedish International Symposium on Economics, Law and Intellectual Property, Gotheberg 4 (June 26-30, 2000); *see also* WILLIAM KINGSTON, THE DIRECT PROTECTION OF INNOVATION 1-124 (William Kingston ed., 1987). J. H. Reichman and Pamela Samuelson have elsewhere proposed a "compensatory liability" regime that would allow second-comers freely to extract data from a protected database to develop value-adding follow-on products, so long as adequate compensation was paid under an "automatic license" (not a compulsory license) for a specified period of time. *See* Reichman & Samuelson, *supra* note 18, at 145-51; *see also* Reichman, *Of Green Tulips*, *supra* note 164.

492. *See, e.g.*, Robert P. Merges, *Of Property Rules, Coase, and Intellectual Property*, 94 COLUM. L. REV. 2655 (1994); Merges, *Contracting Into Liability Rules*, *supra* note 454. On this view, even the new transactional economic theories, which do worry about the use of intellectual property rights after they are granted, are miraculously advanced by a total dependence on exclusive rights, despite the need for patent pools and other institutions of dubious social value, to attenuate anticommons and other anticompetitive effects. *See, e.g.*, Merges, *Patent Pools*, *supra* note 151, at 124-32.

493. *Cf.* Yochai Benkler, *A Political Economy of the Public Domain: Markets in Information Goods Versus the Marketplace of Ideas*, *in* EXPANDING THE BOUNDARIES OF IP, *supra* note 13, at 267, 269-74. One would, indeed, expect or prefer economic analysis to focus on the comparative advantages and disadvantages of using either exclusive property rights or liability rules to address the underlying risks of market failure. *See, e.g.*, Calabresi & Melamed, *supra* note 151.

sector immediately after the patent issued.[494] Patented inventions expressed in claims approved by the patent office expired after twenty years,[495] and any relevant sub-patentable know-how remained subject to reverse engineering by "proper means" under the liability rules that protect trade secrets.[496]

If a strong database right were eventually enacted, however, the ability of a second-comer to practice the claims to a patented invention that nominally expired could in fact depend on his or her gaining access to underlying data in a database that the patent holder, or his assignees, continued to hold under the database right. Even if the original data supporting the claims also lapsed under the database right,[497] the patent holder could attempt to generate new data to surround the original patent claims in order to make the second-comer's exercise of follow-on improvements more difficult.[498]

If the initial patent claims were narrowly drawn, in keeping with present day approaches to many biotech, software, and business method patents,[499] the patentee's independent rights in data might enable him or her to project an aura surrounding these narrow claims that would actually magnify the exclusionary power of the resulting patents. Conversely, when broad patent claims were allowed, as has allegedly occurred with respect to some biotech research tools,[500] there are already well-known risks of impeding follow-on applications and blocking progress.[501] An exclusive property right in data could further magnify these risks. It would expose second-comers to further allegations of unlawfully using data from databases that surround and integrate these claims and thus reinforce the social disutilities already associated with broad patent claims.

Moreover, even as regards sub-patentable innovation, once the aggregates of information that constitute an entrepreneur's technical know-how were reduced to data embodied in a protectible database, the resulting proprietary

494. If the patent failed to issue, the traditional U.S. rule preserved trade secrecy. 35 U.S.C. § 122(a) (2000). However, the virtually universal practice is to publish the contents of patent applications after eighteen months, and U.S. law has begun to conform to this practice in recent years. *See* 35 U.S.C. §§ 122(b)(1)(A), 122(b)(2).

495. 35 U.S.C. §§ 112, 154(2).

496. UNIF. TRADE SECRETS ACT (UTSA), §1(4), comment, 14 U.L.A. 449 (1985) ("Proper means include . . . [d]iscovery by 'reverse engineering' . . . .").

497. As must occur in the United States, but not in the European Union.

498. In this event, the database right would generate some of the problems currently associated with so-called "blocking patents." *See, e.g.*, Robert Merges, *Intellectual Property Rights and Bargaining Breakdown: The Case of Blocking Patents*, 62 TENN. L. REV. 75 (1994) [hereinafter Merges, *Blocking Patents*].

499. *See, e.g.*, Diamond v. Diehr, 450 U.S. 175 (1981); Diamond v. Chakrabarty, 447 U.S. 303 (1980); State St. Bank & Trust Co. v. Signature Fin. Group, 149 F.3d 1368 (Fed. Cir. 1998).

500. *See, e.g.*, Rai, *supra* note 33, at 104 (stating that "[m]any . . . [expressed sequence tag ("EST")] applications are notable for the broad scope of their patent claims: the applications claim not only the EST but also the full genre of which it is a part and future uses of the gene") (citing Christopher Anderson, *A New Model for Gene Patents*, 260 SCIENCE 23 (1993)). Some companies have reportedly filed patent applications on hundreds or thousands of ESTs. Rai, *supra*, at 104.

501. *See generally* Eisenberg, *Bargaining*, *supra* note 13, at 225-26, 231-47; Heller & Eisenberg, *supra* note 452; Rai, *supra* note 33, at 126; Lemley, *Improvement*, *supra* note 288, at 1053-54; Merges, *Blocking Patents*, *supra* note 498.

rights could make it much harder or more costly for third parties to obtain that know-how by reverse engineering.[502] Similarly, the database right could be used to discourage efforts to work around patents or to add value to either patented inventions or sub-patentable innovations.[503] Over time, if the cumulative database rights extended into related fields of innovation, they could become the "wheel" that actually governed the "spokes," and in this sense, acquire more value—and impose more anti-competitive effects—than a given firm's patent portfolio.

One could thus conceive of an interlocking web of data rights that enabled a proprietor with strategic patents and copyrights to surround and control a spectrum of knowledge in given fields. On this scenario, the database proprietors could agglomerate the prior art into a kind of expanding arctic shelf of privatized information, with ever lower costs for aggregators, ever higher costs for users in the absence of competition, and ever higher barriers to entry. In such a case, antitrust laws might provide the only form of relief, and that is always a cumbersome and uncertain course of action.[504]

It is not that these negative synergies are certain to occur, but rather that these potential social costs must be weighed against any social benefits thought to derive from a strong exclusive property right in collections of data. Because the social costs of striking the wrong balance are manifestly so high, and the uncertainties attendant upon database protection are so great, the most credible economic advice has been that of Maurer and Scotchmer, who advise against taking any premature action that might make the end result far worse than the predicament from which we started.[505]

b. A Market-Breaking Approach

While the E.U. authorities proclaim the success of their Directive,[506] the evidence is inconclusive and at most supports a finding that the Directive has, as yet, failed to produce the harmful long-term consequences that critics expect.[507] The list of critics who predict such consequences has grown, however, and the longer the *sui generis* database law is implemented in practice, the more likely its socially harmful, over-protectionist consequences will become evident.

---

502. *Cf.* Samuelson & Scotchmer, *supra* note 155.

503. *Cf.* Reichman, *Of Green Tulips*, *supra* note 164.

504. *See, e.g.*, Arti K. Rai, *Fostering Cumulative Innovation in the Biopharmaceutical Industry: The Role of Patents and Antitrust*, 16 BERKELEY TECH. L.J. 813 (2001); Hanns Ullrich, *Intellectual Property, Access to Information, and Antitrust: Harmony, Disharmony, and International Harmonization*, *in* EXPANDING THE BOUNDARIES OF IP, *supra* note 13, 35, 381-98. "Too much or too easy reliance on antitrust relief will never solve deficiencies that the intellectual property system is likely to show." *Id.* at 383.

505. Maurer & Scotchmer, *supra* note 432.

506. *See* Maurer, Across Two Worlds, *supra* note 34.

507. This section is based on Reichman, *Database Protection in a Global Economy*, *supra* note 18, at 482-84.

To see why critics in the United States and elsewhere[508] harbor deep concerns about the long-term consequences of the E.U.'s approach, it suffices to grasp how radical a change it would introduce into the U.S. system of innovation and to consider how great the risks of such change really are. Traditionally, United States intellectual property law did not protect investment as such—a tradition that still has constitutional underpinnings.[509] At the same time, the national system of innovation depends on enormous, upstream flows of mostly government-generated or government-funded scientific and technical information, which everyone is free to use,[510] and on free competition with respect to downstream information goods.

The domestic intellectual property laws protected downstream bundles of information in two situations only: copyrightable works of art and literature, and patentable inventions. However, the following conditions apply in both cases:

(1) These regimes require palpably significant creative contributions based on free inputs of information and ideas.

(2) They presuppose a flow of unprotected information and data upstream.

(3) They presuppose free competition with regard to the products of mere investment that are neither copyrightable nor patentable.[511]

As previously observed, the E.C.'s Database Directive changes this approach, as would the parallel proposal, H.R. 354, to enact strong database rights in the United States. Specifically, these *sui generis* regimes confer a strong and, in the European Union, potentially perpetual exclusive property right on the fruits of mere investment, without requiring any creative contribution. They also convert data and information—the previously unprotectible raw materials and basic inputs of the modern information economy—into the subject matter of this new exclusive property right.

The *sui generis* database regimes would thus effectuate a radical change in the economic nature and role of intellectual property rights ("IPRs"). Until now, the economic function of IPRs was to make markets possible where previously there existed a risk of market failure due to the public good nature of intangible creations. Exclusive rights make embodiments of intangible public goods artificially appropriable, create markets for those embodiments, and make it possible to exchange payment for access to these creations.[512]

---

508. For a recent discussion, see MARK DAVISON, LEGAL PROTECTION OF DATABASES (forthcoming 2003), which is highly critical of the E.C. Directive. Davison is Associate Professor of Law, Monash University, Australia.

509. *See, e.g.*, Wal-Mart Stores, Inc. v. Samara Bros., 529 U.S. 205 (2000); Bonito Boats, Inc. v. Thunder Craft Boats Inc., 489 U.S. 141 (1989); Compco Corp. v. Day-Brite Lighting, Inc., 376 U.S. 234 (1964); Sears, Roebuck & Co. v. Stiffel Co., 376 U.S. 225 (1964); Kellogg Co. v. Nat'l Biscuit Co., 305 U.S. 111 (1938) (rejecting Int'l News Serv. v. Assoc. Press, 248 U.S. 215 (1918)).

510. *See* A QUESTION OF BALANCE, *supra* note 1, at 4-8, 9, 52-58; Mowery & Rosenberg, *supra* note 231, at 40-48, 55-61.

511. *See* Reichman & Uhlir, *Database Protection*, *supra* note 4, at 832-38.

512. *See, e.g.*, COOTER & ULEN, *supra* note 212, at 108-09, 126-35.

In contrast, an exclusive IPR in the contents of databases *breaks* existing markets for downstream aggregates of information that were formed around inputs of information largely available from the public domain. It conditions the very existence of all traditional markets for intellectual goods on:

(1) The willingness of information suppliers to supply at all (they can hold out or refuse to deal);

(2) The willingness of suppliers not to charge excessive or monopoly prices (i.e., more than downstream aggregators can afford to pay in view of their own risk management assessment); and

(3) The willingness and ability of suppliers to pool their respective chunks of information in contractually constructed cooperative ventures.

This last constraint is perhaps the most telling of all. In effect, the *sui generis* database regimes create new and potentially serious barriers to entry to all existing markets for intellectual goods owing to the multiplicity of new owners of upstream information in whom they invest exclusive rights—any one of whom can hold out and all of whom can impose onerous transaction costs (analogous to the problem of expressed sequence tags ("ESTs") and single nucleotide polymorphisms ("SNPs") in patent law).[513] This thicket of rights fosters anticommons effects,[514] and the database laws appear to be ideal generators of this phenomenon.

In short, under the new *sui generis* database regimes, there is a built-in risk that too many owners of information inputs will impose too many costs and conditions on all the information processes we now take for granted in the information economy. At best, the costs of R&D activities seem likely to rise across the entire economy, well in excess of benefits, owing to the potential stranglehold of data suppliers on raw materials. This stranglehold will increase with market power if many databases are owned by sole-source providers. Over time, the comparative advantage from owning a large, complex database will tend progressively to elevate barriers to entry.[515]

The potential social gains of a strong database law cannot justify incurring these risks of disrupting or deforming the national system of innovation. It hardly seems logical to break up all existing markets for intellectual goods just to cure an alleged market failure for investments in a single type of intellectual good, that is non-copyrightable collections of information. At present, the United States dominates this market, and there is no credible empirical evidence of market failure that could not be cured by more traditional means.[516]

---

513. *See, e.g.*, Rai, *supra* note 33, at 125-28.

514. *See* Heller & Eisenberg, *supra* note 452.

515. *Accord* Benkler *Constitutional Bounds*, *supra* note 91. All nonprofit activities will be especially hard hit. Over time, lost opportunity costs in neglected R&D projects owing to these balkanized inputs could become staggering, and many forms of innovation may stagnate as a result. Even so, it will not be easy to document these lost opportunity costs, although the past experience of science in this regard will be repeated across the whole information economy. For details, see Reichman & Uhlir, *Database Protection*, *supra* note 4, at 812-20.

516. *See, e.g.*, Fewer, *supra* note 341; Maurer, Across Two Worlds, *supra* note 34.

The foregoing analysis reinforces the hypothesis that an exclusive property right is the wrong way to address the problem of legal protection for electronic databases, and it reconfirms the desirability of considering a modern liability rule that could avoid market failure without impoverishing the public domain.[517] Supporters of strong database protection laws (and strong contractual regimes to reinforce them) believe that the benefits of private property rights are without limit, and that more is always better.[518] They expect that these powerful legal incentives will attract huge resources to the production of electronic information tools.[519]

In contrast, critics fear that an exclusive property right in non-copyrightable collections of data, coupled with the proprietors' unlimited power to impose electronic adhesion contracts in the course of online delivery, will compromise the operation of the national system of innovation, which depends on the free flow of upstream data and information. In place of the explosive production of new databases that proponents envision, opponents of a strong database right predict a steep rise in the cost of information across the global information economy and a progressive balkanization or feudalization of that economy,[520] in which fewer knowledge goods may be produced as more tithes have to be paid to more and more information conglomerates along the way.[521] In the critics' view, the information economy most likely to emerge from an exclusive property right in data will resemble models already familiar from the Middle Ages, when goods flowing down the Rhine River or moving from Milan to Genoa were subject to dozens, if not hundreds, of gatekeepers demanding tribute.

IV

A CONTRACTUALLY RECONSTRUCTED RESEARCH COMMONS FOR SCIENCE AND INNOVATION

The foregoing exposition has described the growing efforts underway to privatize and commercialize scientific and technical information that was heretofore freely available from the public domain or on an open access basis. If these pressures continue unabated, they will result in the disruption of long-established scientific research practices and in the loss of new research opportunities that digital networks and related technologies make possible. We do not expect these negative synergies to occur all at once, however, but rather to manifest

517. For details, see Reichman & Samuelson, *supra* note 18, 145-51.

518. *See, e.g.*, Raymond Nimmer, *Breaking Barriers: The Relation Between Contract and Intellectual Property Law*, 13 BERKELEY TECH. L.J. (1998); Maureen A. O'Rourke, *Property Rights and Competition on the Internet: In Search of an Appropriate Analogy*, 16 BERKELEY TECH. L. J. 561 (2001).

519. *See* E.C. Database Directive, *supra* note 17, Recitals 6-12; *Information Antipiracy Hearings*, *supra* note 239; Braunstein, *supra* note 239.

520. *Cf.* DRAHOS & BRAITHWAITE, *supra* note 266, at 1-3 (stressing the risks of raising the costs of borrowing ideas and information so high that they "will progressively choke innovation," and warning that "[m]ost businesses will be losers, not winners").

521. *Accord* Maurer, Across Two Worlds, *supra* note 34; Maurer & Scotchmer, *supra* note 432; Benkler, *Constitutional Bounds*, *supra* note 91.

themselves incrementally, and the opportunity costs they are certain to engender will be difficult to discern.

Particularly problematic is the uncertainty regarding the specific type of database protection that Congress may enact and any exceptions favoring scientific research and education that such a law might contain.[522] As we have tried to demonstrate, moreover, the economic pressures to privatize and commercialize upstream data resources will continue to grow in any event.[523] Legal means of implementing these pressures already exist, regardless of the adoption of a *sui generis* database right.[524] Therefore, given enough economic pressure, that which could be done to promote strategic gains will likely be done by some combination of legal and technical means.

If one accepts this premise, then the enactment of some future database law could make it easier to impose restrictions on access to and use of scientific data than at present, but the absence of a database law or the enactment of a lower protectionist version of it would not necessarily avoid the imposition of similar restrictions by other means. In such an environment, the existing elements of risk or threat to the sharing norms of public science can only increase unless the scientific community adopts countervailing measures.

We accordingly foresee a transitional period in which the negative trends identified above will challenge the cooperative traditions of science and the public institutions that have reinforced those traditions in the past, with uncertain results. In this period, a new equilibrium will emerge as the scientific community becomes progressively more conflicted about their private interests and their communal needs for data and technical information as a public resource. This transitional period will provide a window of opportunity that should be used to analyze the potential effects of a shrinking public domain and to take steps to preserve the functional integrity of the research commons.

A. The Challenge to Science: Formulating a Response to the Legal and Economic Pressures

The trends described above could elicit one of two types of responses. One is essentially reactive, in which the scientific community adjusts to the pressures as best it can without organizing a response to the increasing encroachment of a commercial ethos upon its upstream data resources. The other would require science policy to address the challenge by formulating a strategy that would enable the scientific community to take charge of its basic data supply and manage the resulting research commons in ways that preserved its public good functions without impeding socially beneficial commercial opportunities.

Under the first alternative, the research community can join the enclosure movement and profit from it.[525] Thus, both universities and independent labora-

522. *See* discussion *supra* at Part III.B.2.d.(ii).
523. *See* discussion *supra* at Part III.B.1.
524. *See* discussion *supra* at Part III.B.2.a-c.
525. *Cf.* Boyle, *Second Enclosure Movement*, *supra* note 373.

tories or investigators that already transfer publicly funded technology to the private sector can also profit from the licensing of databases. In that case, data flows supporting public science will have to be constructed deal-by-deal with all the transaction costs this entails and with the further risk of bargaining to impasse.[526] The ability of researchers to access and aggregate the information they need to produce discoveries and innovations may be compromised both by the shrinking dimensions of the public domain and by the demise of the sharing ethos in the nonprofit community, as these same universities and research centers increasingly see each other as competitors rather than partners in a common venture.[527] Carried to an extreme, this competition of research entities against one another, conducted by their respective legal offices, could obstruct and disrupt the scientific data commons.

To avoid these outcomes, the other option is for the scientific community to take its own data management problems in hand. The idea is to reinforce and recreate, by voluntary means, a public space in which the traditional sharing ethos can be preserved and insulated from the commoditizing trends identified above.[528] In approaching this option, the community's primary assets are the formal structures that support federally funded data and the ability of federal funding agencies to regulate the terms on which data are disseminated and used. The first programmatic response would look to the strengthening of existing institutional, cultural, and contractual mechanisms that already support the research commons, with a view to better addressing the new threats to the public domain identified above. The second logical response is collectively to react to new information laws and related economic and technical pressures by negotiating contractual agreements between stakeholders to preserve and enhance the research commons.[529]

As matters stand, the U.S. government generates a vast public domain for its own data through creative use of three instruments: intellectual property rights, contracts, and new technologies of communication and delivery. By long tradition, the federal government has used these instruments differently from the rest of the world. It waives its property rights in government-generated information, it contractually mandates that such information should be provided at the marginal cost of dissemination, and it has been a major proponent

526. *Cf.* Eisenberg, *Bargaining*, *supra* note 13, at 231-47.

527. *See, e.g.*, Powell, *supra* note 13, at 266 (predicting turf wars between rival networks of partners).

528. *Cf., e.g.*, Rai, *supra* note 33, at 144-51 (advocating norms-based approach to preserving use of biotech inventions for research purposes). What unites, or should unite, all these communities is a common understanding of the historical function of the public domain and a common need to preserve that function despite the drive for commoditization. *See, e.g.*, Powell, *supra* note 13, at 265-66. Although legislators and entrepreneurs may take time to understand the threat that a shrinking public domain poses for the national system of innovation, the one group that is best positioned to appreciate that threat is the nonprofit research sector, whose dependence on the public domain remains a matter of everyday practice and vital concern. This sector is also the best positioned to take steps to respond to the threat by appropriate voluntary collective action.

529. *Cf.* UNIF. BIOLOGICAL MATERIALS TRANSFER AGREEMENT (UBMTA) (1995), *available at* http://www.autm.net/UBMTA/intro.html (last visited Jan. 18, 2003); Rai, *supra* note 33, at 113, nn.201-04 (discussing UBMTA).

and user of the Internet to make its information as widely available as possible. In other words, the U.S. government has deliberately made use of existing intellectual property rights, contracts, and technologies to construct a research commons for the flow of scientific data as a public good. The unique combination of these instruments is a key aspect of the success of our national research enterprise.[530]

Now that the research commons has come under attack, the challenge is not only to strengthen a demonstrably successful system at the governmental level, but also to extend and adapt this methodology to the changing university environment and to the new digitally networked research environment. In other words, universities, not-for-profit research institutes, and academic investigators, all of whom depend on the sharing of data, will have to stipulate their own treaties or contractual arrangements to ensure unimpeded access to, and unrestricted use of, commonly needed raw materials in a public or quasi-public space, even though many such institutions or actors may separately engage in transfers of information for economic gain.[531] This initiative, in turn, will require the federal government as the primary funder—acting through the science agencies—to join with the universities and scientific bodies in an effort to develop suitable contractual templates that could be used to regulate or influence the research commons.

Implementing our ideas would require nuanced solutions tailor-made to the needs of government, academia, and industry in general and to the specific exigencies of different scientific disciplines. The following sections describe our proposals for preserving and promoting the open availability of government-generated scientific data, and of government-funded and private-sector scientific data, respectively. We do not, however, develop detailed proposals for separate disciplines and sub-disciplines here, as these would require additional research and analysis.

B. Proposals for the Government Sector

To preserve and maintain the traditional public domain functions of government-generated data, the United States will have to adjust its existing policies and practices to take account of new information regimes and the growing pressures for privatization. At the same time, government agencies will have to find ways of coping with bilateral data exchanges with other countries whose governments choose to exercise intellectual property rights in their own data collections.

530. Mowery & Rosenberg, *supra* note 231, at 62 (stressing the interaction of federal and private R&D expentitures).

531. Our proposals go well beyond a "clearinghouse" approach to conflicting proprietary rights, which some have suggested. *See* discussion *supra* note 454. A clearinghouse does not deal with the positive externalities that could accrue from organizing worldwide flows of scientific data online, which is the real opportunity at stake.

1. Adjusting Domestic Policies and Practice

We do not mean to imply a need to totally reinvent or reorganize the existing universe in which scientific data are disseminated and exchanged. The opposite is true. As we have explained, a vast public domain for the diffusion of scientific data—especially government-generated data—exists and continues to operate, and much government-funded data emerging from the academic communities continues to be disseminated through well-established mechanisms.[532]

Facilities for the curation and distribution of government-generated data are well organized in a number of research areas. They are governed by long-established protocols that maintain the function of a public domain, and in most cases ensure open access (either free or at marginal cost) and unrestricted use of the relevant data collections. These collections are housed in bricks-and-mortar data repositories, many of which are operated directly by the government, such as the NASA National Space Science Data Center.[533] Other repositories are funded by the government to carry out similar functions, such as the archives of the Hubble Space Telescope Science Institute at Johns Hopkins University.[534]

Under existing protocols, most government-operated or government-funded data repositories do not allow conditional deposits that look to commercial exploitation of the data in question. Anyone who uses the data deposited in these holdings can commercially exploit their own versions and applications of them without needing any authorization from the government. However, no such uses, including costly value-adding uses, can remove the original data from the public repositories. In this sense, the value-adding investor obtains no exclusive rights in the original data, but is allowed to protect the creativity and investment in the derived information products.

The ability of these government institutions to make their data holdings broadly available to all potential users, both scientific and other, has been greatly increased by direct online delivery. However, this potential is undermined by a perennial and growing shortage of government funds for such activities, by technical and administrative difficulties that impede long-term preservation of the exponentially increasing amounts of data to be deposited, and by pressures to commoditize data, which are reducing the scope of government activity and tend to discourage academic investigators from making unconditional deposits of even government-funded data to these repositories.[535]

The long-term health of the scientific enterprise depends on the continued operation of these public data repositories and on the reversal of the negative trends identified earlier in this article. Here, the object is to preserve and enhance the functions that government data repositories have always played,

---

532. *See* discussion *supra* at Parts II.A and II.B.

533. *See* NASA National Space Science Data Center, *at* http://nssdc.gsfc.nasa.gov/ (last visited Jan. 10, 2003).

534. *See* Space Telescope Science Institute, *at* http://www.stsci.edu/ (last visited Jan. 10, 2003).

535. *See* discussion *supra* at Parts III.B.1.

notwithstanding the mounting pressures to commoditize even government-generated data.

Implementing any recommendations concerning government-generated data will, of course, require adequate funding, and this remains a major problem. In most cases, however, it is not the big allocations needed to collect or create data that are lacking; it is the relatively small but crucial amounts to properly manage, disseminate, and archive data already collected that are chronically insufficient. These shortsighted practices deprive taxpayers of the long-term fruits of their investments in the scientific enterprise. Science policy must give higher priority to formulating workable measures to redress this imbalance than it has in the past.

Policy-makers should also react to the pressures to privatize government-generated research data by devising objective criteria for ascertaining when and how privatization truly benefits the public interest. At times, privatization will advance the public interest because the private sector can generate particular data sets more efficiently or because other considerations justify this approach. Very often, however, the opposite will be true, especially when the costs of generating the data are high in relation to known, short-term payoffs. Two recent National Research Council studies have attempted to formulate specific criteria for evaluating proposed privatization initiatives concerning scientific data.[536] The science agencies should make the formulation of such criteria for different areas of research a top agenda item. In so doing, the agencies also need to analyze the results of past privatization initiatives with a view to assessing their relative costs and benefits.

Once the validity of any given privatization proposal has been determined by appropriate evaluative criteria, the next crucial step is to build appropriate,

---

536. The BITS OF POWER report set forth the following conditions for privatization of the scientific data distribution function:

- Can the distribution of data be separated easily from their generation?
- Is the scientific data set used by others beyond the research community?
- Is the potential market large enough to support several data distributors?
- Is it easy to discriminate prices or differentiate products between scientific users and other users? If this is possible, can low prices be mandated contractually for government-funded data for scientific users?
- Is it costly to separate the distribution of data to scientists from their distribution to other users, such as commercial users?

"If all of these questions can be answered 'yes,' then privatizing the distribution of scientific data should be an option to be considered." BITS OF POWER, *supra* note 1, at 120-21.

Concerning the privatization of government data collection and product development functions in the environmental research context, a more recent National Research Council report recommended the following:

> Before transferring government data collection and product development to private-sector organizations, the U.S. government should ensure that the following conditions will be satisfied: (1) avoidance of market conditions that will give any firms significant monopoly power; (2) preservation of full and open access to core data products; (3) assurance that a supply of high-quality information will continue to exist; and (4) minimized disruption to ongoing uses and applications.

RESOLVING CONFLICTS, *supra* note 8, at 87.

public-interest contractual templates into that deal, to ensure the continued operation of a research commons. The public research function is too important to be left as an afterthought. It must figure prominently in the planning stage of every legitimate privatization initiative precisely because the data would previously have been generated at public expense for a public purpose. After all, the process of privatization aims to shift the commercial risks and opportunities of data production or dissemination to private enterprise under specified conditions that promote efficiency and economic growth. However, that process should not pin the functions of the research enterprise to the success of any given commercial venture; it must not allow such ventures to otherwise compromise these functions by charging unreasonable prices or imposing contractual conditions unduly restricting public, scientific uses of the data in question.

There are two situations in which model contractual templates, developed through inter-agency consultations, could play a critical role. One is where data collection and dissemination activities previously conducted by a government entity are transferred to a private entity. The other is where the government licenses data collected by a private entity for public research purposes.[537] In both cases, the underlying contractual templates should implement the following research-friendly legal guidelines:

(1) A general obligation not to legally or technically hinder access to the data in question for nonprofit scientific research and educational purposes;

(2) A further obligation not to hinder or restrict the reuse of data lawfully obtained in the furtherance of nonprofit scientific research activities;[538] and

(3) An obligation to make data available for nonprofit research and educational purposes on fair and reasonable terms and conditions, subject to impartial review and arbitration of the rates and terms actually applied, in order to avoid research disasters such as the Landsat deal in the 1980s.[539]

When the public data collection activity is transferred to the private sector, care must be taken to ensure that the private entity exercises any underlying intellectual property rights, especially some future database right, in a manner consistent with the public interest—including the interests of science. To this end, a model contractual template should also include a comprehensive misuse provision like that embodied in H.R. 1858.[540]

537. *See, e.g.*, Commercial Space Act of 1998, Pub. L. No. 105-303, 112 Stat. 2843 (Oct. 28, 1998) (codified at 42 U.S.C. § 14701).

538. Moreover, even in those cases where government data are made available for private sector uses without any express transfer or contractual arrangements, agencies must give greater consideration to the need to preserve access to the original public data sets and avoid their de facto capture by a private entity.

539. *See supra* note 251 and accompanying text.

540. H.R. 1858 § 106(b), "Limitations on Liability," provides as follows:

The larger principle is that, in managing its own public research data activities, the government can and should develop its own database law in a way that promotes science without unduly impeding commerce. This principle is not new; the government already has a workable information regime, as described in Part II. However, the government will need to adapt that regime to the pressures arising from the new high-protectionist legal environment to ensure that its agencies are consistently applying rational and harmonized public-interest principles. Otherwise, the traditional public domain functions of government-generated data could be severely compromised, an outcome that would violate the government's fiduciary responsibilities to taxpayers and raise conflicts of interest and questions concerning sham transactions.

2. Bridging the Gap with Foreign Law

The federal government will also have to continue to develop policies and procedures for dealing with data generated by foreign governments that commercialize their data and exploit all available intellectual property rights. Because international agreements concerning the exchange of scientific and technical information normally rely on national treatment clauses,[541] negotiated arrangements may be needed to bridge the differences between high and low-protectionist jurisdictions that could complicate international scientific cooperation.[542]

Ideally, arrangements with foreign governments should enable the United States to continue to waive intellectual property rights in government-generated data distributed abroad while requiring foreign governments similarly to waive intellectual property rights in government data disseminated in the United

---

(b) MISUSE—A person or entity shall not be liable for a violation of section 102 if the person or entity benefiting from the protection afforded a database under section 102 misuses the protection. In determining whether a person or entity has misused the protection afforded under this title, the following factors, among others, shall be considered:

(1) the extent to which the ability of persons or entities to engage in the permitted acts under this title has been frustrated by contractual arrangements or technological measures;

(2) the extent to which information contained in a database that is the sole source of the information contained therein is made available through licensing or sale on reasonable terms and conditions;

(3) the extent to which the license or sale of information contained in a database protected under this title has been conditioned on the acquisition or license of any other product or service, or on the performance of any action, not directly related to the license or sale;

(4) the extent to which access to information necessary for research, competition, or innovation purposes have been prevented;

(5) the extent to which the manner of asserting rights granted under this title constitutes a barrier to entry into the relevant database market; and

(6) the extent to which the judicially developed doctrines of misuse in other areas of the law may appropriately be extended to the case or controversy.

H.R. 1858; *see also* Dreier, *supra* note 68, at 295, 311-12; Ullrich, *supra* note 504.

541. *See, e.g.*, Agreement on Scientific and Technological Cooperation, U.S.-Vietnam, Nov. 17, 2000, cl. 2.2.

542. Reichman, *Database Protection in a Global Economy*, *supra* note 18, at 485-500.

States. Such a result would preserve the pure public domain approach to government-generated data that has long been official U.S. policy. However, European governments accustomed to commercializing their data reportedly have resisted this approach,[543] presumably because they fear re-exports of the data back into their own more protected markets, or because they do not want to concede preferences to foreign users that they deny their own citizens. Requiring foreign governments to subscribe to the U.S. concept of an unconditional public domain for government-generated data may thus result in those governments disclosing considerably less data than they might under a two-tiered structure that conditionally allowed access to such data for nonprofit scientific and educational purposes while restricting its availability to the private sector.

While the U.S. tradition is squarely opposed to restricted uses of government-generated data, many European (and other) governments have subscribed to a different tradition.[544] The E.C. Database Directive represents a powerful new thrust in that direction. It is worth reiterating that this Directive enables governments to exercise strong and potentially perpetual exclusive rights in *publicly* generated databases, without any mandated obligation to recognize public-interest exceptions.[545]

Some fifty countries either belonging to the European Union or having affiliated status are expected to adopt that model, and we believe that E.U. trade negotiators are seeking to impose it on other countries as part of regional trade agreements. If the United States fails to adopt a different, less protectionist database regime, founded on true unfair competition principles, the pressures for other countries to follow the E.U. model will become very great. Moreover, even if the United States adopts a significantly less protectionist database law, there will be pressures on the United States to protect data generated by foreign governments and made available to U.S. data centers despite the "no conditional deposit" rules that bind many of these centers. The United States, of course, will not be able to prevent foreign governments from commercially exploiting their public data in territories governed by the E.C. Database Directive. On the contrary, the fact that governments in the European Union themselves saw this Directive as a source of considerable income most likely disposed them favorably toward it, and this fatal attraction seems to be spreading.[546]

For these reasons, and despite the general undesirability of a two-tiered structure in the public sector, the United States must seek to persuade foreign governments that choose to exercise crown rights (both copyrights and *sui gene-*

---

543. Interview with Glenn Tallia, counsel for the National Oceanic and Atmospheric Administration, in Silver Spring, Md. (Aug. 20, 2000).

544. For an overview of the public information regimes of the E.U. member states, see Green Paper, *supra* note 46, at Annexe 1.

545. *See* discussion *supra* at Part III.B.2.d.i.

546. For example, the Republic of Korea is currently considering the adoption of a new *sui generis* database protection statute modeled on the E.C. Database Directive.

ris rights) under the E.C. Database Directive or its analogues to at least implement a conditional domain in their own countries, with a view to maximizing access for nonprofit research, educational, and other public-interest purposes.[547] Obviously, the better result would be for the E.U. governments to renounce crown rights in public information altogether and to adopt the public domain policy of the U.S. government. Some efforts in this direction are in fact under way, but the outcome is highly uncertain.[548] The overriding need to construct cooperative, worldwide open-data exchanges in support of public research and for addressing global problems—including environmental degradation, health, and the alleviation of poverty—provides a powerful mandate to achieve this result.

At the same time, there is a real danger that the European Union will continue to press intergovernmental organizations, as they have the World Meteorological Organization, to adopt two-tiered systems that deviate from established U.S. norms.[549] The European Union may also be expected to press U.S. government agencies to conditionally protect the European Union's data in intergovernmental exchanges and thus, in effect, to institute a two-tiered approach for some purposes at U.S. data centers otherwise operating on a pure public domain basis. Similarly, the European Union may seek to persuade the U.S. government to retreat from its full and open data exchange policy in international scientific research programs.

These divergent pressures indicate that the rules applicable to intergovernmental exchanges of data may need to be revisited in the emerging high-protectionist legal environment. Senior representatives of the U.S. scientific community will have to make their voices heard in any such negotiations and argue the case for an international, open and cooperative public science regime to the greatest extent possible.[550]

C. Proposals for the Academic Sector

In putting forward our proposals concerning the preservation of a research commons for government-funded data, it is useful to follow the distinction between a zone of formally regulated data exchanges and a zone of informal data exchanges drawn earlier in this article. Consistent with our analysis in Part

547. *See, e.g.*, Commission Proposal for a Council Directive on Public Access to Environmental Information, 2000 O.J. (C 337) 402; *see also* Commission Proposal for a Council Directive on the Reuse and Commercial Exploitation of Public Sector Documents, 2002 O.J. (C 227) 207.

548. *Id.*

549. For a discussion of the Eurpopean Union's efforts for the World Meteorological Organization ("WMO") to adopt a two-tiered data distribution system, see Weiss & Backlund, *supra* note 7. For a statement of the two-tiered data policy that replaced the previous policy of full and open exchange at the WMO, see WORLD METEOROLOGICAL ORGANIZATION, EXCHANGING METEOROLOGICAL DATA: GUIDELINES ON RELATIONSHIPS IN COMMERCIAL METEOROLOGICAL ACTIVITIES (1996), *available at* http://www.wmo.ch/web/pla/WMO837.pdf (last visited Jan. 10, 2003).

550. This topic is under discussion already at the OECD. *See* Background Information on the Activities of the OECD Follow-up Group on Issues of Access to Publicly Funded Research Data, *at* http:/dataaccess.ucsd.edu/ (last visited Jan. 18, 2003).

II, we emphasize that the ability of government funding agencies to influence data exchange practices will be much greater in the formal than the informal zone.

1. Formally Regulated Data Exchanges

When no significant proprietary interests come into play, the optimal solution for government-generated data and data produced by government-funded research is a formally structured archival data center also supported by government. As discussed earlier, many such data centers have already been formed around large-facility research projects.[551] Building on the opportunities afforded by digital networks, it has now become possible to extend this time-tested model to highly distributed research operations conducted by groups of academics in different countries.

The traditional model entails a bricks-and-mortar centralized facility into which researchers deposit their data unconditionally. Besides academics, contributors may include government and even private sector scientists, but in all cases the true public domain status of any data deposited is usually maintained. Examples include the National Center for Biotechnology Information ("NCBI"),[552] which is directly operated by the National Institutes of Health, and the National Center for Atmospheric Research ("NCAR"),[553] which is operated by a university consortium and funded primarily by the National Science Foundation ("NSF").

A second, more recent model, enabled by improved Internet capabilities, also envisions a centralized administrative entity, but this entity governs a network of highly distributed smaller data repositories, sometimes referred to as "nodes."[554] Taken together, the nodes constitute a virtual archive whose relatively small central office oversees agreed technical, operational, and legal standards to which all member nodes adhere.[555] Examples of such a decentralized network, which operate on a public domain basis, are the NASA Distributed Active Archive Centers under the Earth Observing System program[556] and the NSF-funded Long Term Ecological Research Network.[557]

---

551. *See supra* Part II.A.

552. *See* discussion *supra* note 45.

553. *See* National Center for Atmospheric Research, *at* http://www.ncar.ucar.edu/ncar/ (last visited Jan. 18, 2003).

554. Many networks of such distributed data nodes now exist. *See, e.g.*, *supra* note 130; *see also* Planetary Data System, *at* http://pds.jpl.nasa.gov/ (last visited Jan. 17, 2003).

555. *See* NATIONAL RESEARCH COUNCIL, PRESERVING SCIENTIFIC DATA ON OUR PHYSICAL UNIVERSE: A NEW STRATEGY FOR ARCHIVING THE NATION'S SCIENTIFIC INFORMATION RESOURCES 47-57 (1995) [hereinafter PRESERVING SCIENTIFIC DATA]; *see also supra* note 130.

556. *See* NASA's Earth Observing System, http://eospso.gsfc.nasa.gov/ (last visited Jan. 17, 2003); NASA Distributed Active Archive Data Center Alliance, *at* http://nasadaacs.eos.nasa.gov/ (last visited Feb. 3, 2003).

557. *See* LTER Net, *supra* note 130.

These virtual archives, known as "federated" data management systems,[558] extend the benefits and practices of a centralized bricks-and-mortar repository to the outlying districts and suburbs of the scientific enterprise. They help to reconcile practice with theory in the sense that the investigators—most of whom are funded by government anyway—are encouraged to deposit their data in such networked facilities. The very existence of these formally constituted networks thus helps to ensure that the resulting data are effectively made available to the scientific community as a whole, which means that the social benefits of public funding are more perfectly captured and the sharing ethos is more fully implemented.

At the same time, some of the existing "networks of nodes" have already adopted the practice of providing conditional availability of their data: a feature of considerable importance for our proposals. By conditional availability we mean that the members of the network have agreed to make their data available for public science purposes on mutually acceptable terms, but they also permit suppliers to restrict uses of their data for other purposes, typically with a view to preserving their commercial opportunities.[559]

The networked systems thus provide prospective suppliers with a mix of options to accommodate deposits ranging from true public domain status to fully proprietary data that has been made available subject to rules the member nodes have adopted. The element of flexibility that conditional deposits afford makes these federated data management systems particularly responsive to the realities of present day university research in areas of scientific investigation where commercial opportunities abound.

a. Basic Recommendations

Our first proposition is that the government funding agencies should encourage unconditional deposits of research data, to the fullest extent possible, into both centralized repositories and decentralized network structures. The obvious principle here is that, because the data in question are government-funded, improved methods should be devised for capturing the social benefits of public funding, lest commercial temptations produce a kind of de facto free-riding at the taxpayers' expense.[560]

When unconditional deposits occur in a true public domain environment removed from proprietary concerns, the legal mechanisms to implement these expanded data centers need not be complicated. Single researchers or small

558. PRESERVING SCIENTIFIC DATA, *supra* note 555, at 51-52 (describing the elements of a federated management structure).

559. An example of an international network that operates on the basis of conditional deposits is the Global Biodiversity Information Network ("GBIF"), headquartered in Denmark, which is substantially supported by U.S. government funding. *See* GBIF, *supra* note 130.

560. We use the term "free-riding" to suggest that privatization should not deprive the public of the full benefits that it paid for. At the same time, we recognize that entrepreneurs also pay taxes on their profits. *Cf.* Stephen Berry, Promoting Access to and Use of Not-for-Profit Sector Scientific and Technical Data—An Assessment of Legal and Policy Options, panel discussion at NRC Workshop, *supra* note 428, at Chapter 13.

research teams could contribute their data to centers serving their specific disciplines, with no strings attached other than measures to ensure attribution and professional recognition.[561] Alternatively, as newly integrated scientific communities organize themselves, they could seek government help in establishing new data centers or nodes that would accept unrestricted deposits on their behalf.[562] Private companies could also contribute to a true public domain model or organize their own variants of such a model; these practices should be encouraged as a matter of public policy.

If the unrestricted data were deposited in federal government sponsored repositories, existing federal information law and associated protocols would define the public access rights.[563] The maintenance of public-interest data centers in academia, however, is problematic without government support. These data centers can become partly or fully self-supporting through some appropriate fee structures,[564] but resort to a fee structure based on payments of more than the marginal cost of delivery quickly begins to defeat the public good and positive externality attributes of the system, even absent further use restrictions.

Leaving aside the funding issue, the deeper question that this first proposal raises is how the universities and other nonprofit research entities will resolve the potential conflict between the pressure to disclose and deposit their government-funded data and the valuable proprietary interests that are increasingly likely to surface in a high-protectionist intellectual property environment.[565] One cannot ignore the risk that the viability and effectiveness of these centers could be undermined to the extent that the beneficiaries of government funding can resist pressure to further implement the sharing ethos and even to decline to deposit their research data because of their commercial interests.

Despite their educational missions and nonprofit status, universities and individual academics are both increasingly prone to regard their databases as targets of opportunity for commercialization.[566] This tendency will become more pronounced as more of the financial burden inherent in the generation and management of scientific data is shouldered by the universities themselves

561. Academics are particularly concerned about receiving suitable attribution and recognition for their data-related activities. *See, e.g.*, Eisenberg, *Proprietary Rights*, *supra* note 75, at 178. There is also evidence that one reason open-source software systems have succeeded is that they confer reputational (and other non-monetary) benefits on their participants. *See, e.g.*, Josh Lerner & Jean Tirole, *Some Simple Economics of Open Source*, 50 J. INDUS. ECON. 197 (2002).

562. We note in this connection that many academics have self-organized mini-"data centers" through their websites with public domain functions, limited only by their technical and financial capabilities. Groups of academics can similarly construct more ambitious mini-centers, which become less elaborate versions of the government data model.

563. If, however, data centers are formed outside the scope of direct government control, the organizers and managers may need to reconstruct the public domain through general public use licenses to emulate the protocols that govern deposits of data in more traditional government-operated centers. *See* discussion *infra* Part IV.C.2.

564. *See, e.g.*, *infra* notes 599-601 and accompanying text (discussing Swiss-PROT).

565. *Cf.* Rai, *supra* note 33, at 94-115.

566. *See, e.g.*, Powell, *supra* note 13, at 265 ("[W]hat is striking is how actively universities and firms are seeking to privatize new information," not to profit from innovations, but because they "hope instead to profit from the supply of information or data analysis.").

or by cooperative research arrangements with the private sector. In this context, the universities are likely to envision split uses of their data and will prefer to make them available on restricted conditions. They will logically distinguish between uses of data for basic research purposes by other nonprofit institutions and purely commercial applications.[567] Even this apparently clear-cut distinction might break down, moreover, if universities treat databases whose principal user base is other nonprofit research institutions as commercial research tools.

The point is that the universities may not want to deposit data in designated repositories, even with government support, unless the repositories can accommodate these interests, and the repositories could compromise their public research functions if they are held hostage to too many demands of this kind. The same potential situation exists for individual databases made available by universities (as opposed to their contributions to larger, multi-source repositories). This state of affairs will accordingly require still more creative initiatives to parry the economic and legal pressures on universities and academic researchers to withhold data.

With these factors in mind, our second major proposal is to establish a zone of conditionally available data in order to reconstruct and artificially preserve functional equivalents of a public domain. This strategy entails using property rights and contracts to reinforce the sharing norms of science in the nonprofit, trans-institutional dimension, without unduly disrupting the commercial interests of those entities that choose to operate in the private dimension.

To this end, the universities and nonprofit research institutions that depend on the sharing ethos, together with the government science funding agencies, should consider stipulating to suitable "treaties" and other contractual arrangements to ensure unimpeded access to commonly needed raw materials in a public or quasi-public space.[568] From this perspective, one can envision the accumulation of shared scientific data as a community asset held in a contractually reconstructed research commons to which all researchers have access for purposes of public scientific pursuits.

One can further imagine that this public research commons exists in an ever-expanding "horizontal dimension," as contrasted with the commercial operations of the same data suppliers in what we shall call the "vertical" or private dimension. The object of the exercise would be to persuade the government, as primary funder, to join with universities and scientific bodies in an effort to develop suitable contractual templates that could be used to regulate the research commons. These templates would ensure that data held in the quasi-public or horizontal dimension would remain accessible for scientific purposes and could not be removed or otherwise appropriated to the private or vertical

567. *Cf.* Eisenberg, *Bargaining*, *supra* note 13, at 242-43 (describing emergence of de facto two-tiered market in which scientists exchange research tools directly on minimal obligations, while technology transfer offices haggle over proprietary exchanges and delay research).

568. *Cf.* James Boyle, *A Politics of Intellectual Property: Environmentalism for the Net*, 47 DUKE L.J. 87 (1997); Rai, *supra* note 33, at 152 (advocating "concerted public and private action centered around existing norms to preserve the public domain").

dimension. At the same time, these contractual arrangements would expressly contemplate the possibilities for commercial exploitation of the relevant data in the private or vertical dimension, and they would clarify the depositor's rights in that regard and ensure that the exercise of those rights did not impede or disrupt access to the horizontal space for research purposes.

b. Ancillary Considerations

In fashioning these proposals, we are aware that considerable thought has recently been given to the construction of voluntary social structures to support the production of large, complex information projects.[569] Particularly relevant in this regard are the open source software movement that has collectively developed and managed the GNU/Linux Operating System[570] and the Creative Commons organization,[571] which seeks to encourage authors and artists to conditionally dedicate some or all of their exclusive rights to the public domain. In both these pioneering movements, agreed contractual templates have been experimentally developed to reverse or constrain the exclusionary effects of strong intellectual property rights.

The open source model adopted by the software research and related communities relies on existing legal regulatory regimes to create a social space devoted to producing freely available and modifiable code.[572] Under the GNU/Linux operating system, components of the cooperatively elaborated structure are protected by intellectual property rights, in this case copyrights, and by licensing agreements, but these legal mechanisms are used to enforce the sharing norms of the open source community.[573] Standard-form licensing agreements are formulated "to use contractual terms and property rights to create social conditions in which software is produced on a model of openness

569. *See, e.g.*, Benkler, *Coase's Penguin*, *supra* note 198; David McGowan, *Legal Implications of Open-Source Software*, 2001 U. ILL. L. REV. 241, 245 (2001); *see also* LAWRENCE LESSIG, THE FUTURE OF IDEAS: THE FATE OF THE COMMONS IN A CONNECTED WORLD (2001); Dan Burk, *Open Source Genomics*, 8 B.U. J. SCI. & TECH. L. 254 (2002).

570. *See, e.g.*, McGowan, *supra* note 569. The Open Source Movement is also known as the Free Software Movement. On this terminology, see SAM WILLIAMS, FREE AS IN FREEDOM: RICHARD STALLMAN'S CRUSADE FOR FREE SOFTWARE, Ch. 11 (2002), *available at* http://www.oreilly.co/openbook/freedom/ch11.html (last visited Dec. 15, 2002); *see also* Free Software Foundation, Why 'Free Software' is Better than 'Open Source', *at* http://www.gnu.org/philosophy/free-software-for-freedom.html (last visited Jan. 10, 2002).

571. *See* Creative Commons, *at* http://www.creative commons.org/ (last visited Jan. 18, 2003).

572. McGowan, *supra* note 569, at 244.

573. Under the Free Software approach, the archtypical "copyleft license" is the GPL or GNU Public License, by which the copyright owner grants the user the right to copy, modify and distribute the licensed software without having to get permission or pay any license fee to the owner. "[I]f you distribute copies of such a program, whether gratis or for a fee, you must give the recipients all the rights that you have." GNU GPL, *available at* http://www.gnu.org/licenses/gpl.html (last modified July 15, 2001). According to Janet Hope, a Ph D. candidate at the Australian National University, open source was intended as a market stategy to make the "free sofware" concepts attractive to people in the business community. Janet Hope, *Open Source Biotechnology*, paper presented to the workshop on Science, Intellectual Property and Open Domains, REGNET, Intellectual Property Institute of Australia, Canberra, Australia (Dec. 2, 2002).

rather than exclusion."[574] Under these licenses, "code may be freely copied, modified, and distributed," but only if the modifications (derivative works) are distributed under these terms as well.[575] Property rights are "held in reserve to discipline possible violations of community norms."[576] The end result, as Professor McGowan recently observed, is not a true commons, but resembles a commons because of the "low cost of copying and using code combined with . . . broad grants of the relevant licenses."[577]

For present purposes, the most relevant lesson to be drawn from the open source model is the possibility for participants in networks of nodes or other data sharing arrangements to dedicate holdings protected by IPRs to the relevant scientific community itself, which would hold the collective asset in a kind of trust to which all members of the community have access. In effect, the members of such a community would use any exclusive rights granted by intellectual property laws to exclude exclusivity itself. While the collective asset—in this case, typically, a database—and its components could be routinely made available for commercial applications,[578] subject to additional terms and conditions that would have to be negotiated, the general public licenses supporting the collective asset would prevent any users from appropriating either the entire asset or its components from the quasi-public or horizontal space in which it was collectively managed for public research purposes.

The second model of particular interest, the Creative Commons, facilitates public access to copyrighted literary and artistic works by devising a set of standard-form contractual templates any author can digitally adopt.[579] Once adopted, these contractual grants permit anyone to make certain uses of the

---

574. McGowan, *supra* note 569, at 243. The movement makes some effort to downplay their reliance on technical rules of contract law as such. *See, e.g.*, Eben Moglen, *Enforcing the GPL*, LINUXUSER & DEVELOPER, Sept./Oct. 2001, at 66.

575. McGowan, *supra* note 569, at 242.

576. *Id.* at 244.

577. *Id.*

578. Open source software makes money for developers in two principal ways. First, all innovations made after the initial release are automatically available to the original developers at no cost, which can be equivalent to having an enormous, unpaid R&D department. Hope, *supra* note 573. The second type of income stream comes from providing service and support, "which is always a large part of the market in any high tech industry." *Id.*

579. The Creative Commons offers four standard templates:

> Attribution. You let others copy, distribute, display, and perform your copyrighted work—and derivative works based upon it—but only if they give you credit. . . .
>
> Noncommercial. You let others copy, distribute, display and perform your work—and derivative works based upon it—but for noncommercial purposes only. . . .
>
> No Derivative Works. You let others copy, distribute, display and perform only verbatim copies of your work, not derivative works based upon it. . . .
>
> Share Alike. You allow others to distribute derivative works only under a license identical to the license that governs your work.

Licenses Explained, *available at* http://www.creativecommons.org/learn/licenses (last visited Jan. 18, 2003).

The service also offers to help people dedicate their work to the pure public domain, with "no rights reserved," although it is not provided as one of the four standard options. *See* Creative Commons, *supra* note 571.

protected works, which are then digitally encoded, so that the search engines of would-be users can register them and thus facilitate the uses in question.[580] This technique seems particularly relevant to the goal of linking highly distributed data holders in virtual archives by digital means, as is further discussed below.[581]

Although neither of these models were developed with the needs of public science in mind, both provide helpful examples of how universities, federal funding agencies, and scientific bodies might contractually reconstruct a research commons for scientific data that could withstand the legal, economic, and technological pressures on the public domain identified in this article. In what follows, we draw on these and other sources to propose the contractual regulation of government-funded data in two specific situations: (1) when government-funded, university-generated data are licensed to the private sector, and (2) when such data are made available to other universities for research purposes.

c. Licensing Government-Funded Data to the Private Sector

In approaching this topic, one must consider that the production of scientific databases in academia is not always dominated by activities funded by the federal government. It may also entail funding by universities themselves, foundations, and the private sector. While funding from these non-government sources seems likely to grow in the future, especially if Congress adopts a database protection right, the government's role in funding academic data production will nonetheless remain a major factor, at least in the near term (though its role will vary from project to project). As discussed in Part II, this presence gives the federal funding agencies unique opportunities to influence the data-sharing policies of its beneficiary institutions.[582]

Ideally, funders and universities would agree on the need to maintain the functions of a public domain to the fullest extent possible, to provide open access to data for nonprofit research activities, and to encourage efficient technological applications of available data. At the same time, technological applications and other opportunities for commercial exploitation of certain types of databases will push the universities to enter into private contractual transactions that, if left totally unregulated, could adversely affect the availability of the relevant data for public research purposes.[583] The reconciliation of the conflict between enhancing the public research interests and freedom of contract will require carefully formulated policies and institutional adjustments.[584]

580. *Id.*

581. *See* discussion *infra* at Part IV.C.2.

582. *See* discussion *supra* Part II.B.1.a.

583. *See, e.g.*, Eisenberg, *Bargaining*, *supra* note 13, at 229 ("Institutions tend to be high-minded about the importance of unfettered access to the research tools that they want to acquire from others, but no insitution is willing to share freely the materials and discoveries from which they derive significant competitive advantage.").

584. *Cf.* Dan L. Burk, *Lex Genetica: The Law and Ethics of Programming Biological Code*, 4 ETHICS & INFO. TECH. 109, 109-11, 113-18 (2002).

Assuming the existence of sufficient funds, the maximum availability of academic data for research purposes is assured if those data have been deposited in the public data centers.[585] To the extent that agencies successfully encourage academics and their universities to deposit government-funded data into either old or new repositories established for this purpose, the research-friendly policies of these centers should automatically apply. As long as these policies are not themselves watered down by commercial and proprietary considerations, they should generally immunize the research function from conflicts deriving from private transactions.[586]

However, the universities or their academics may very well balk at contributing commercially valuable data to these repositories unless they retain some degree of autonomy to negotiate the terms of their private transactions and impose restrictions on the uses of the data deposited for commercial purposes. This raises two important questions. The first concerns the willingness of data centers themselves—whether of the bricks-and-mortar variety or networks of nodes—to accept conditional deposits that impose restrictions on use for certain purposes in the first place. The second question, closely tied to the first, concerns the extent to which federal funding agencies should further seek to define and influence the relations between universities and the private sector to protect the public research function—especially when the data in question have not been deposited in an appropriate repository or when they have been so deposited but the repository permits conditional deposits.

i. Key Questions

Regarding the first of these questions, we previously observed that the emerging network of nodes model is more likely to accommodate conditional deposits or availability than are the traditional centralized data centers.[587] Nevertheless, the practice remains controversial in scientific circles in that it deviates from the traditional norm of full and open access. For present purposes, we simply state our view that the possibilities for maximizing access to scientific data for public nonprofit research will not be fully realized in a highly protectionist legal and economic environment unless the scientific community agrees to experiment with suitably regulated conditional deposits.[588]

The second question, concerning the need to regulate the interface between universities and the private sector with regard to government-funded data, acquires important contextual nuances when viewed in the light of the policies and practices that currently surround the Bayh-Dole Act and related legislation. The Bayh-Dole Act encourages universities to transfer the fruits of federally

585. See, for example, the data centers mentioned in *supra* note 45.

586. Moreover, there are likely to be significant positive externalities when private companies can freely use the public research data. *See, e.g.*, Powell, *supra* note 13, at 263-65.

587. *See supra* Part IV.C.1.

588. *Cf.* Patrinos & Drell, *supra* note 23, at 11.

funded research to the private sector by means of the patent system.[589] In a somewhat similar vein, federal research grants and contracts allow researchers to retain copyrights in their published research results. By extension, the same philosophy could apply to databases produced with federal funding, especially if Congress were to adopt a *sui generis* database protection right, with incalculably negative results unless steps were taken to reconcile the goals of Bayh-Dole with the dual nature of data as both an input and an output of scientific research and of the larger system of technological innovation.[590]

It would also be a mistake for the science policy establishment to wait for the enactment of database legislation before considering the implications of blindly applying the spirit of Bayh-Dole to any database law that Congress might adopt. Because databases differ significantly from either patented inventions or copyrighted research results, policy-makers should anticipate the advent of some database legislation and address the problems it may cause for science—particularly with regard to government-funded data. Special consideration must be given to how the power to control uses of scientific data after publication would be exercised once a database protection law was enacted.

We do not mean to question the underlying philosophy or premises of Bayh-Dole,[591] which has produced socially beneficial results. Its very success, however, has generated unintended consequences and raised new questions that require careful consideration.[592] In advocating a program for a contractually reconstructed research commons, one of our explicit goals is, indeed, to ensure that academics and their universities benefit from new opportunities to exploit research data in an industrial context. This goal reflects the policies behind Bayh-Dole.[593] At the same time, it would hardly be consistent with the spirit of Bayh-Dole to allow the commercial partners of academic institutions to dictate the terms on which government-funded data are made available for purposes of nonprofit scientific research.

On the contrary, a real opportunity exists for government funding agencies and universities to develop agreed contractual templates that would apply to commercial users of government-funded data in general. In effect, the public scientific community would thus develop a database protection scheme of its own that would override the less research-friendly provisions of any *sui generis*

---

589. Even without a database right, Bayh-Dole prods universities to exploit data as part of the transfer of technology to the private sector. *See also* Rai, *supra* note 33, at 97, 109-15.

590. Of course, Bayh-Dole does not, and need not, apply to database protection rights as such. *See* 35 U.S.C. § 200 (2000) (limiting policy to use of the patent system). But universities would still remain unrestricted owners or assignees of government-funded databases, who could make their own rules, while Bayh-Dole already accustoms them to the commercial exploitation of their intellectual property rights. *See, e.g.*, Eisenberg, *Bargaining*, *supra* note 13; Powell, *supra* note 13, at 255 (stressing the new role of universities as both creators and retailers of intellectual property).

591. 35 U.S.C. § 200 (2000) ("Policy and Objectives").

592. *See* Eisenberg, *Public Research, supra* note 120; Bar-Shalom & Cook-Deegan, *supra* note 121; *see also* Rai & Eisenberg, *supra* note 117.

593. 35 U.S.C. § 200 (listing, *inter alia*, the goal "to promote colatoration between commercial concerns and nonprofit organizations, including universities").

regime that Congress might adopt. In so doing, the scientific community could also significantly influence the data-licensing policies and practices of the private sector, before that sector ends up influencing the data-licensing practices of university technology transfer offices.[594]

ii. Value-Adding Uses and Management Costs

If one takes this proposal seriously, a capital point of departure would be to address the problem of follow-on applications, which has greatly perturbed the debate about database protection in general. The critical role of data as input into the information economy weighs heavily against endowing database proprietors with an exclusive right to control follow-on applications. This principle becomes doubly persuasive when the government itself has defrayed the costs of generating the data in question, in which case an exclusive right to control value-added applications takes on a cast of reverse free-riding.[595]

One solution is to allow second-comers to extract and use data from any given collection freely for bona fide value-adding purposes in exchange for adequate compensation of the initial investor based on an expressly limited range of royalty options.[596] If the rules developed by universities and funding agencies imposed this kind of "compensatory liability" regime on follow-on applications of government-funded academic data, in lieu of any statutorily created exclusive right, there is reason to believe it could significantly advance both technological development and the larger public interest in access to scientific data.[597]

Universities and funding agencies could also adopt clauses similar to those proposed above in the context of government-generated data,[598] including a general prohibition against legally or technically hindering access to any database built around government-funded data for purposes of nonprofit scientific research. Clauses that prohibit private partners from hindering the reuse of data in the construction of new databases to address new scientific research objectives seem particularly important, as are clauses requiring private partners to license their commercial products on fair and reasonable terms and conditions. Also desirable are clauses forbidding misuse of any underlying IPRs and establishing guidelines that courts should apply in evaluating specific claims of misuse.

Moreover, when considering relations with the private sector, attention should be given to the high cost of managing and archiving data holdings for scientific purposes and the possibilities of defraying some of this cost through

---

594. *Cf.* Rai, *supra* note 33, at 114 (reporting instances in which the "[r]esidual norms of academic research may even have had some influence on the conduct of [biotech] industry actors").

595. In the sense that it makes the public pay twice for some of the social benefits that public funding was designed to cover.

596. *Cf.* Reichman, *Of Green Tulips*, *supra* note 164; Reichman & Uhlir, *Database Protection*, *supra* note 4; Reichman, *Database Protection in a Global Economy*, *supra* note 18, 462-63, 479-80.

597. *Cf.* Powell, *supra* note 13, at 264 (fearing exclusive license mentality that, if applied to Cohen-Boyer patent on recombinant DNA technology, would have retarded progress in biotechnology).

598. *See supra* Part II.B.1.

commercial exploitation. While government support ought to increase, especially as the potential gains from a horizontal e-commons become better understood, the cost of data management will also increase with the success of the system. For this reason, universities may want to levy charges against users in the private sector or the vertical dimension, in order to help defray the cost of administering operations in the horizontal domain and to make this overall approach more economically feasible.

One controversial example of an attempt to supplement the data management costs of a government-funded database is provided by the Swiss-PROT Protein Knowledgebase, a university-administered entity that collects and curates data concerning protein sequences contributed by academic and corporate researchers from various countries.[599] The highly specialized data in this collection are reviewed, annotated, and made available online under a conditional arrangement that operates largely on an honor system.[600] While nonprofit uses are allowed gratis, uses by private firms are licensed on an annual subscription fee basis that differentiates by the size of the corporate user (and, presumably, its ability to pay). Payments are made directly to the Swiss-PROT management entity and, reportedly, there has been minimum evasion of the rules thus far.[601]

Another interesting example is the ultimately unsuccessful attempt to negotiate a public-private partnership to manage a Human Mutations Database, which would have integrated university-generated data from around the world concerning genomic mutations into a single, openly available database.[602] The motivating idea was that a private firm, Incyte, would put up the funds to organize the database and make the data openly available to all users online, on the condition that all of the relevant data would have been channeled through Incyte alone and not its competitors. Incyte expected to gain lead time advantages from early access to the data and also to benefit from traffic-building effects on its website, but there was to be no fee charged for use of the mutations data as such. In the end, however, it proved impossible to coordinate the disparate interests of the participating entities, and the project was aborted before its feasibility could be tested.[603]

In evaluating these experiments, one may view the so-called open access system adopted by Swiss-PROT with a degree of skepticism. First of all, the relevant user community is so small and tightly knit, and so accurately monitored by tracking the electronic footprints of those who access the database, that non-compliance would pose unacceptable costs in loss of reputation, peer pressure, and possible denial of privileges. Second, the administrators are able

599. *See* Swiss-PROT, *at* http://www.ebi.ac.uk/swissprot/ (last visited Dec. 4, 2002).

600. *See* http://www.ebi.ac.uk/swissprot/information/information.html (last visited Dec. 4, 2002).

601. Reported through an informal discussion at a European Science Foundation, Funding Agencies Workshop on Public Domain of Digital Research Data, Strasbourg, France, Oct. 15, 2002.

602. Maurer, Inside the Anticommons, *supra* note 465.

603. *Id.*

tacitly to rely on the default rules, valid against the world, that derive from the E.C. Database Directive, which effectively holds every user who fails to comply with the posted conditions of access, extraction, and reuse liable for infringement.

Swiss-PROT nonetheless exemplifies one potential use of an agreed contractual template, and it anticipates techniques the Creative Commons initiative has recently further refined. It illustrates that, even in the presence of a high-protectionist intellectual property regime, contractual templates can be fashioned to promote the research commons without unduly obstructing commercial opportunities (although there are questions about Swiss-PROT's specific practices in this regard).[604]

The Swiss-PROT example also supports an otherwise intuitive inference that, under certain conditions, an intellectual property right in collections of data can encourage—rather than discourage—disclosure for scientific purposes by reducing the risk of free-riding appropriations. This comes as no surprise to the authors of this article, given that we have elsewhere advocated the adoption of a minimalist database protection regime, sounding in unfair competition law (liability rules) rather than in exclusive property rights.[605] A database protection statute based on true unfair competition principles could close any demonstrable gaps in existing law with acceptable social costs and would provide a moderate, alternative model for other countries to consider.[606] It should be clear, however, that the stronger the underlying intellectual property right, the more necessary it becomes to devise suitable contractual templates regulating relations between universities and the private sector (and inter-university relations themselves), with a view to ensuring the smooth operation of a contractually reconstructed research commons.

Moreover, complexities and coordination problems are likely to arise when the data in question are of interest to a much broader and more heterogeneous non-expert user base than in the two examples above. In this situation, more refined contractual templates could reduce both friction and transaction costs due to strategic behavior, by, for example, differentiating categories of users who may be denied access for specified lead time intervals; regulating the timing of competing or derivative publications; prospecting the possibilities of strategic cross-licenses for certain purposes; and even ensuring that grant-back, reach-through, and other clauses, sometimes appropriate in the private sector,

---

604. It should be noted that Swiss-PROT's default provision for nonprofit users was not to modify the database for any purpose, unless expressly allowed for "a valid scientific or technical reason" depending on "how the information will be presented and distributed." Maurer, Promoting and Disseminating Knowledge, *supra* note 259, at 47. This was a scientifically serious limitation. The NCBI, which previously incorporated Swiss-PROT data into its own "Reference Sequence" and "Predicted Genes" databases, stopped doing so when Swiss-PROT added this encumbrance and eventually replaced the Swiss-PROT data with data from other sources. *Id.*

605. *See generally* Reichman & Uhlir, *Database Protection*, *supra* note 4; Reichman & Samuelson, *supra* note 18.

606. *See generally* Reichman, *Database Protection in a Global Economy*, *supra* note 18, at 493-96.

are not allowed to disrupt public research.[607] However, the more complicated the situation becomes and the greater the degree of coordination required, the more likely worthwhile pooling initiatives will never get off the ground—as occurred with the human mutations database project itself.[608]

In addition, if such a project were successfully launched and the data in question became potentially of value to a broad user base, a further enforcement problem might arise due to the potential for leakage of data, supplied at preferential prices, to research users in ways that could damage the interests of users in the vertical dimension. It will be recalled that, on the horizontal plane, the option to charge for research uses (when otherwise unavoidable) is intended to entail a corresponding burden to positively discriminate in favor of science and its research goals.[609] This need for price discrimination favoring research uses correspondingly requires that the difficult problem of leakage be addressed. Any solution here would certainly benefit from congressional enactment of a minimalist database protection right.[610]

When administrative complexities appear particularly daunting, the better solution may be for participating entities to deposit their data with a designated, external administrative agency or service charged with the tasks of negotiating, formulating, and implementing the general public licenses or agreed contractual templates. These operations should remain subject to the guidance, governance, and oversight of the participating universities, government funding agencies, and other affected institutions. We also envision the need for mediation, arbitration, and dispute settlement facilities, which could be appropriately located within any oversight group that might be established.[611]

Finally, care must be taken to reduce friction between the scientific data commons as we envision it and universities' patenting practices under the Bayh-Dole Act. For example, any agreed contractual templates might have to allow for deferred release of data, even into repositories operating as a true public domain, at least for the duration of the one-year novelty grace period during which relevant patent applications based on the data could be filed.[612] Other

---

607. *Cf.* Eisenberg, *Bargaining*, *supra* note 13, at 226-31 (evidencing disruptive effects of such clauses at present in regard to biotech research tools).

608. *See, e.g.*, Rai, *supra* note 34, at 129-35; Maurer, Inside the Anticommons, *supra* note 465.

609. This practice is, of course, further restrained to the extent that the U.S. government provides the bulk of the data in the true public domain, which intrinsically restricts the amount of data available for providers who seek to opt into the conditional domain, with price-discriminated operations, along the horizontal research plane in addition to commercial operations at full rates along the vertical axis. *See supra* Part II.A.1.

610. The leakage problem might require administrators of a scientific e-commons to adopt and apply "access management systems" even though strong "digital rights management techniques" would be inappropriate in the interests of implementing and enforcing the community's norms. Institutional users are unlikely to disregard contractual access terms. *See* Peter Eckersley et al., *Neuroscience Data and Tool Sharing: A Legal and Policy Framework for Neuroinformatics*, 1 NEUROINFORMATICS 8-10 (forthcoming 2003).

611. *Cf. id.* at 10-11 (discussing a collection society model for similar purposes). A logical organizational locus for such operations would be the professional scientific societies working within the framework of the American Association for the Advancement of Science.

612. *See* 35 U.S.C. § 102 (2000); *see also* 35 U.S.C. § 111(b) (provisional patent applications).

measures to synchronize the operations of the e-commons with the ability of universities to commercialize their holdings under Bayh-Dole would have to be identified and carefully addressed. We also note that there is an interface between our proposals for an e-commons for science and antitrust law,[613] which would at least require consultation with the FTC and might also require enabling legislation. A detailed analysis of these issues lies beyond the scope of this article.

In sum, to successfully regulate relations between universities and the private sector in the United States, where most of the scientific data in question are government-funded (if not government-generated), considerable thought must be given to devising suitable contractual templates that universities could use when licensing such data to the private sector. These templates, which should aim to promote the smooth operation of a research commons and facilitate general research and development uses of data as inputs into technological development, could themselves constitute a model database regime that optimally balances public and private interests in ways that any federally enacted law might not. To succeed, however, these templates must be acceptable to the universities, the funding agencies, the broader scientific community, and the specific disciplinary sub-communities—all of whom must eventually weigh in to ensure that academics themselves observe the norms that they would thus have collectively implemented.

In so doing, the participating institutions could avoid a race to the bottom in which single universities might otherwise trade away more restrictions on open access and research to attract more and better deals from the private sector. Unless science itself takes steps of this kind, there is a serious risk that, under the impetus of Bayh-Dole, the private sector will gradually impose its own database rules on all government-funded data products developed with their university partners.[614]

d. Inter-University Licensing of Scientific Data

Whatever the merits of our proposals for regulating transfers of scientific data from universities to the private sector, the need for science policy to regulate inter-university transfers of such data seems irrefutable. In this context, most of the data is generated for public scientific purposes and at public expense, and the progress of science depends on continued access to, and further applications of, such data. Not to construct a research commons that could withstand the pressures to privatize government-funded data at the inter-university level would thus amount to an indefensible abdication of the public trust by encumbering nonprofit research with high transaction and exclusion costs.[615]

613. *Cf.* Dreier, *supra* note 68, at 311-12; Ullrich, *supra* note 504, at 367-98.

614. *Cf.* Rai, *supra* note 33, at 111-12 (reporting instances in which this has occurred regarding biotech patents).

615. *See, e.g.*, Eisenberg, *Bargaining*, *supra* note 13, at 234 ("When progress in research depends on the relatively unfettered flow of low value exchanges of information and materials among scientists, a

All the same, implementing this task poses very difficult problems that are likely to exacerbate the conflicts of interests between the open and cooperative norms of science and the quest for additional funding sources we previously identified.[616]

i. Policy Considerations

One may note at the outset that these conflicts of interest are rooted in the Bayh-Dole approach to the transfer of technology itself. This legislative framework stimulates universities to protect federally funded research results through intellectual property rights and to license those rights to the private sector for commercial applications. If Congress enacted a strong database-protection law, it could extend Bayh-Dole to this new intellectual property right. In such a case, Bayh-Dole would simply pass the relevant exclusive rights to extract and reutilize collected data straight through the existing system to the same universities and academic researchers who now patent their research results and would thus end up owning all the government-funded data they had generated. Even without such legislation, nothing impedes the universities from commercially exploiting protected databases in the spirit of Bayh-Dole, subject to any exceptions or immunities favoring research that a database law may have codified.

Moreover, the Bayh-Dole legislation makes no corresponding provision for beneficiary universities to give differential and more favorable treatment to other universities when licensing patented research products. On the contrary, there is evidence that in transactions concerning patented biotech research tools, at least, universities have viewed each other's scientists as a target market, in the exploitation of which they have virtually the same commercial interests as private producers of similar tools for scientific research.[617] Inter-university deals have accordingly been constructed on a case-by-case basis, often with considerable difficulty, by technology transfer offices normally striving to maximize all their commercial opportunities.[618]

Without any agreed restraints on how universities are to deal with collections of data in which they had acquired statutorily conferred ownership and exclusive exploitation rights, their technology transfer offices could simply treat databases like patented inventions—despite the immensely greater impact this could have on both basic and applied research. In this milieu, reliance on good faith accommodations hammered out by the respective technology transfer offices[619] would, at best, make inter-university exchanges resemble the complicated transactions that already characterize relations between highly distributed

proliferation of intellectual property claims . . . may impose transaction costs that consume the gains from exchange.").

616. *See* discussion *supra* Part III.B.1.b.

617. *See* Eisenberg, *Public Research*, *supra* note 120; Rai & Eisenberg, *supra* note 117 at 297-99. *But see id.* at 300-06 (countervailing efforts to preserve benefits of research commons).

618. *See, e.g.*, Eisenberg, *Bargaining*, *supra* note 13, at 228-48.

619. *See* COHEN & MERRILL, *supra* note 452.

laboratories and research teams in the zone of informal exchanges of scientific data.[620] All the vices of that zone would soon be imported into the more formal zone of inter-university relationships. At worst, this would precipitate a race to the bottom as universities tried to maximize their returns from these rights, in which case some technology transfer offices could be expected to contractually override any modest research exceptions a future database law might have codified.[621]

At the same time, the Bayh-Dole legislative framework may itself suggest an antidote for resolving these potential conflicts of interest, or, at least, a sound point of departure for addressing them. The Act explicitly recognizes that the public interest in certain patented inventions may outweigh the benefits usually anticipated from private exploitation under exclusive property rights. In such cases, it authorizes the government to impose a compulsory license or otherwise exercise "march-in" rights and take control of the invention it has paid to produce.[622] In fact, these public-interest adjustments have never successfully been exercised in practice,[623] and on the one known occasion when they were invoked, the government encountered stiff and questionable resistance from a major university.[624]

Nevertheless, the principle (if not the actual practice) behind these provisions presents a platform on which universities and federal funding agencies can build their own mutually acceptable arrangements to promote their common interest in full and open access to government-funded collections of data. Our goal, indeed, is to persuade them to address this challenge now, before a database protection law is enacted, by examining how to ensure the smooth and relatively frictionless exchange of scientific data between academic institutions, regardless of any exclusive property right they may eventually acquire and notwithstanding any other commercial undertakings with the private sector they may pursue. Absent such a proactive approach, we fear a slow unraveling of the traditional sharing norms in the inter-university context and an inevitable race to the bottom.

ii. Structuring Inter-University Data Exchanges

Because the issues under consideration here pertain to uses of government-funded data produced by academics for university-sponsored programs, one looks to full and open access as the optimal guiding principle and to the sharing

---

620. *See* discussion *supra* Part II.B.2.

621. At present, there are no such proposed exceptions of any real value in the pending U.S. exclusive rights model. *See supra* Part III.B.2. Even if this were to change, that model allows database producers to override such exceptions by contract, and the usual status of sole-source provider on many scientific niche markets provides the market power to do so.

622. 35 U.S.C. § 203 (2000); *see, e.g.*, Frischmann, *supra* note 70, at 402-03.

623. In the private sector, the use of "march-in rights" could raise the specter of uncertainty and hamper investment. But this risk is of secondary importance in the inter-university environment.

624. In the case of CellPro, Johns Hopkins University successfully opposed a competitor licensee's request for a compulsory license that would have brought an effective cancer diagnosis tool to the market years ahead of its own patented invention. *See* Bar-Shalom & Cook-Deegan, *supra* note 121.

norms of science as the foundation of any arrangement governing inter-university licensing of data. On this approach, the government-funded data collections held by universities would be viewed as a single common resource for inter-university research purposes. The operational goal would be to nurture and extend this common resource within a horizontally linked administrative framework that facilitated every university's public research functions, without unduly disrupting commercial relations with the private sector that some departments of some universities will undertake in the vertical dimension.

To achieve this goal, universities, funding agencies, and interested scientific bodies would have to negotiate an acceptable legal and administrative framework, analogous to a multilateral pact, that would govern the common resource and provide day-to-day logistical support. Ideally, the participating universities or their designated agents would operate as trustees for the horizontally constructed common resource, much as the Free Software Foundation does with the GNU system.[625] In this capacity, the trustees would assume responsibility for ensuring access to the holdings on the agreed terms and for restraining deviant uses that violate those terms or otherwise undermine the integrity of the commons. The full weight of the federal granting structure could then be made to support these efforts by mandating compliance with agreed terms and directly or indirectly imposing sanctions for non-compliance.

Alternatively, a less formal administrative structure could be built around a set of agreed contractual templates regulating access to government-funded data collections for public research purposes. On this approach, the participating universities would retain greater autonomy, there would be less need for a fully fleshed out multilateral pact, and the monitoring and other transaction costs might be reduced. The Swiss-PROT arrangement discussed earlier[626] provides some elements of an approach that could be adapted in a highly protectionist environment to promote certain inter-university data exchanges along these lines.

In a less than perfect world, however, there are formidable obstacles standing in the way of a negotiated commons project, over and above inertia, that would have to be removed. Initially, the very concept of an e-commons needs to be sold to skeptical elements of the scientific community whose services are indispensable to its development. Academic institutions, science funders, the research community, and other interested parties must then successfully negotiate and stipulate the pacts needed to establish it, as well as the legal framework to implement it. Transaction costs would need to be monitored closely and, whenever possible, reduced throughout the development phases.

Once the research universities became wholeheartedly committed to the idea of a regime that guaranteed them universal access to, and shared use of,

625. *See* Eben Moglen, Why the FSF Gets Copyright Assignments from Contributors, *at* http://www.gnu.org/licenses/why-assign.html (last visited Aug. 10, 2002); *see also supra* notes 572-581 and accompanying text.

626. *See supra* notes 599-601, 604-606 and accompanying text.

the government-funded data that they had collectively generated, these organizational problems might seem relatively minor. The difficulties of winning such a commitment, however, cannot be over-estimated in a world where university administrators are already conflicted about the efforts of their technology transfer offices to exploit commercially valuable databases in the genomic sciences and other disciplines with significant potential for commercial development. The prospect that Congress will eventually adopt a hybrid intellectual property right in collections of data could make these same administrators reluctant to lock their institutions into a kind of voluntary pool of any resulting exclusive property rights, even for public scientific research purposes.[627]

Conceptually, the problems inherent in organizing a pool of intellectual property rights so as to preserve access to, and use of, a common resource have become much better understood than in the past—owing to the experience gained from both the open-source software movement and the new Creative Commons initiative.[628] These projects demonstrate that there are few, if any, technical obstacles that cannot be overcome by adroitly directing relevant exclusive rights and standard-form contracts to public, rather than private, purposes.

The deeper problem is persuading university administrators that they stand to gain more from open access to each others' databases in a horizontally organized research commons than they stand to lose from licensing data to each other under more restrictive, case-by-case transactions. The more that "the nature of the rivalry between . . . [universities] would shift from cooperative competition to turf wars, with rival networks of partners looking to delay, deter, and defend themselves against competitors,"[629] the more they could make research data artificially scarce for them all. While we believe they stand to gain more from open access, following the implications of that conviction could amount to an act of faith, albeit one that resonates with the established norms of science and the primary mission of universities.

To the extent that universities may have to be sold on the benefits of an e-commons for data, with a view to rationalizing and modifying their disparate licensing policies, this project would require statesmanship, especially on the part of the leading research universities. It may also require pressure from the major government funders and standard-setting initiatives by scientific subcommunities. Funding agencies, in particular, must be prepared to discipline would-be holdouts and to discourage other forms of deviant strategic behavior that could undermine the cohesiveness of those institutions willing to pool their resources.[630]

---

627 *Cf.* Rai, *supra* note 33, at 113 n.204 (noting failure to negotiate an improved version of the Uniform Biological Materials Transfer Agreement of 1995 and major deviations from that Agreement in inter-university transactions).

628 *See supra* notes 571-579 and accompanying text.

629. Powell, *supra* note 13, at 266.

630. Account will have to be taken as well of the universities' patenting interests, which will need to be suitably accommodated.

Assuming a sufficient degree of organizational momentum, there remains the thorny problem of establishing the terms and conditions under which participating universities could contribute their data to a horizontally organized research commons. The bulk of the departments and sub-disciplines involved would almost certainly prefer a bright-line rule that required all deposits of government-funded data to be made without conditions and subject to no restrictions on use. This preference follows from the fact that most science departments currently see no realistic prospects for licensing basic research data, even to the private sector, and have not yet experienced the proprietary temptations of exclusive ownership that a *sui generis* intellectual property right in non-copyrightable databases might eventually confer.

At the same time, such a bright-line rule could utterly deter those sub-disciplines that already license data on commercial terms to either the private or public sectors, or that contemplate doing so in the near future. These sub-disciplines would not readily forego these opportunities and would, on the contrary, insist that any multilateral negotiations to establish a horizontal commons devise contractual templates that protected their commercial interests in the vertical dimension. If, moreover, Congress enacts a de facto exclusive property right in collections of data, it would probably deter other components of the scientific community, who might become unwilling to forego either the prospective commercial opportunities or other strategic advantages such rights might make possible.

A bright-line rule requiring unconditional deposits in all cases could thus defeat the goal of linking all university generators of government-funded data in a single, horizontally organized research commons. At the same time, the goal of universality could, paradoxically, require negotiators seeking to establish the system to deviate from the norm of full and open access by allowing a second type of conditional deposit of data into the horizontal domain by those disciplines or departments that are unwilling to jeopardize present or future commercial opportunities.

iii. Resolving the Paradox of Conditional Deposits

Science policy in the United States has long disfavored a two-tiered system for the distribution of government-funded data.[631] Under such a system, database proprietors envision split (or two-tier) uses of commercially valuable data and will only make them available on conditions that govern the different types of uses they have expressly permitted. In practice, there is growing evidence that, with regard to the exchange of biotechnology research tools, at least, university scientists "appear . . . to be creating a two-tiered market."[632]

Formalized, split-level arrangements typically distinguish between relatively

631. Such two-tiered systems for government or academic data distribution have been favored and promoted by the scientific community in the E.U., but these initiatives have been strongly opposed by U.S. science agencies and academics. *See, e.g.*, FULL AND OPEN EXCHANGE, *supra* note 8.

632. Eisenberg, *Bargaining*, *supra* note 13, at 242 (comparing the "free exchange tier" with the "proprietary tier" in the emerging two-tiered market in the exchange of research tools).

unrestricted uses for basic research purposes by nonprofit entities and more restricted uses for commercial applications by private firms that license data from scientific entities.[633] The latter conditions may range from a simple menu of price-discriminated payment options to more complicated provisions that regulate certain data extractions, seek grant-backs of follow-on applications by second-comers, or impose reach-through clauses seeking legal or equitable rights in subsequent products.[634] In some cases, moreover, the distinction between profit and nonprofit uses of scientific data becomes blurred, and the two categories may overlap, which adds to the cost and complications of administration.[635] For example, universities may treat some databases as commercial research tools and impose a price discrimination policy that provides access to the research community at a lower cost than to for-profit entities.[636]

We recognize that a decision to allow participating universities to make conditional deposits of government-funded data to a collectively managed research consortium represents a second-best solution: one that conflicts with the goal of establishing a true public domain based on the premise of full and open access to all users. The allowance of restrictions on use breaks up the continuity of data flows across the public sector and necessitates administrative measures and transaction costs to monitor and enforce differentiated uses. It also entails measures to prevent unacceptable leakage between the horizontal and vertical planes, and may result in charges for public-interest uses that exceed the marginal cost of delivery, even in the horizontal plane.

We nonetheless doubt that a drive for totally unconditional deposits of government-funded data could succeed in the face of mounting worldwide pressure to commoditize scientific data,[637] and we fear that excessive reliance on the

---

633. *Cf.* UNIF. BIOLOGICAL MATERIALS TRANSFER AGREEMENT (UBMTA) (1995), *available at* http://www.autm.net/UBMTA/intro.html (last visited Jan. 18, 2003) (allowing academic recipients of biological materials to use them, for noncommercial teaching and research purposes without having to negotiate a licensing agreement).

634. *Cf., e.g.*, Eisenberg, *Patenting Research Tools* , *supra* note 123; Eckersley et al., *supra* note 610; Frischmann, *supra* note 70; Rai, *supra* note 34, at 113 n.204.

635. The importance of this distinction diminishes to the extent that any data provider—whether operating in industry or academia—actually accepts the conditions that contractually regulate the research commons. That is a major objective of our proposals.

636. This approach becomes likely when there is a private sector partner. *Cf.* Rai, *supra* note 34, at 111. Scientific data can also be made available in a "conditional public domain" through complicated three-way funding arrangements typically initiated by government science agencies under Cooperative Research and Development Agreements ("CRADAs"). Complications in this instance arise from tensions between the government's continued interest in promoting public access and the legislative policies embodied in the Bayh-Dole Act, which encourage commoditization of government-funded research results. Even here, however, the fact that the government's financial contribution to the project may predominate gives it the clout to impose conditions favorable to public-interest research uses. At present, this power is not sufficienctly utilized. *Cf.* Bar-Shalom & Cook-Deegan, *supra* note 121; Rai & Eisenberg, *Bayh-Dole*, *supra* note 117, at 297-300. But a major purpose of establishing a solid legal framework for conditional deposits would be to provide standard-form licenses that clearly reinforce and implement favorable public-interest terms and conditions, without unduly compromising the relevant commercial interests.

637. European governments have already embarked on a policy of commercial exploitation of publicly generated data and even insist on conditional deposits in various governmental scientific organizations and cooperative research activities. Some academic scientific communities have recently tried to

orthodox position would, in the end, undermine—rather than save—the sharing ethos.[638] Even if one disregards the prospects for strengthened intellectual property protection of non-copyrightable databases, too many universities have already begun to perceive the potential financial benefits they might reap from commercial exploitation of genomic databases in particular and biotech-related databases in general. Their reluctance to contribute such data to a research commons that allowed private firms freely to appropriate that same data could not easily be overcome.[639]

Even if a consortium of universities were to formally consent to such an unconditional arrangement, their technology transfer offices might soon be demanding an exceptional status for any databases that contained components produced without government funds.[640] They could persuasively argue that private funds for most jointly created data products could decrease or even dry up if both customers and competitors could readily obtain the bulk of the data from the public domain. Once it became clear that an admixture of privately funded data could elicit the right to deposit data in a research commons on conditions that protected commercial exploitation of the databases in question, academics with an eye to cost recovery and profit maximization would logically make persistent efforts to qualify for this treatment. They would thus seek more private investment for this purpose or obtain the university's own funds for the project. Either way, there would be a perverse incentive to privatize more data than ever if the only legitimate way to avoid dedicating it all to the public domain was to show that some of it had been privatized.

In other words, if the quasi-public research space accommodated only unconditional deposits of data, it could foster an insuperable holdout problem as participating universities found ways to detach and isolate their commercially valuable databases from such a system. In these circumstances, a failure to obtain a best-case scenario premised on full and open access would quickly degenerate into a worst-case scenario, characterized by growing gaps in the communally accessible collection and an unraveling of the sharing ethos that

---

commercialize biotechnology databases of considerable public research value on a two-tiered basis, *see, e.g.*, Maurer, Across Two Worlds, *supra* note 34, while others have succeeded with controversial results, *see* the discussion of the Swiss-PROT at *supra* notes 599-606 and accompanying text. The reality is that U.S. universities intend to commercialize some of their data and support minimalist legislation to this end.

638. While we sympathize with the philosophy behind this position, our six years of focused study on issues concerning the legal protection of databases compels us to consider the realities of a growing trend toward two-tiered distributive activities to determine whether such activities can be operated in a manner that preserves the benefits of a public domain, notwithstanding the mounting pressures for commoditization. *See* Reichman & Samuelson, *supra* note 18; Reichman & Uhlir, *Database Protection*, *supra* note 4.

639. Adoption of a database protection law would then magnify this reluctance and encourage the respective technology transfer offices to find more ways to commercially exploit more of the government-funded data products that were subsequently invested with proprietary rights. If the Bayh-Dole philosophy is factored into this equation, the prospects for persuading the universities both to agree and actually enforce a true public-domain model for all government-funded databases appear dim indeed. *Cf.* Rai, *supra* note 33, at 109-11 (describing impact of Bayh-Dole on prior research norms).

640. *Cf. id.* at 110-11 (describing growth of joint ventures and impact on MTAs).

would require case-by-case construction of inter-university data flows, and could sometimes culminate in bargaining to impasse.[641]

In our estimation, the worst-case scenario is so bad, and the pressure to commoditize could become so great in the presence of a strong database right, that steps must be taken to ensure universal participation in a contractually reconstructed research commons from the outset by judiciously allowing conditional deposits of government-funded data on standard terms and conditions to which all stakeholders have previously agreed. Indeed, the goal is to develop negotiated contractual templates that clearly reinforce and implement terms and conditions favorable to public research without unduly compromising the ability of the consortium's member universities to undertake commercial relations with the private sector.

At stake in this process is not just a few thousand patentable inventions, but, rather, every government-funded data product that has potential commercial value to other universities as a research tool or educational device. Sound data management policies thus point to a second- best solution that would preserve the integrity of the inter-university commons by disallowing the principal ground on which concerted holdout actions might take root, by ensuring that only research-friendly terms and conditions applied in both the horizontal and vertical dimensions,[642] and by making it too costly for any institution to deviate from the agreed regulatory framework governing the two-tiered regime.

Those who object to this proposal will argue that it unduly undermines the full and open access principle by tempting more and more university departments or sub-disciplines to opt for conditional deposits than would otherwise have been the case. On this view, once a negotiated two-tiered model was set in place, universities would come under intense pressure to avoid the true public domain or open access option even when there was no need to do so.

However, a universal and functionally effective inter-university research commons simply cannot be constructed with a bright-line, true public domain rule applied across the board for the reasons we have previously set out. A bright-line rule also carries with it the well-recognized difficulty of distinguishing for-profit from not-for-profit research activities when single laboratories increasingly engage in both. In contrast, a regime based on conditional deposits overcomes this problem by allowing a scientific entity to contribute to and benefit from the data commons so long as it respects the agreed norms bearing on that arrangement. In this respect, a normative accommodation will have displaced legal distinctions that cannot feasibly be enforced.[643]

641. *See, e.g.*, Powell, *supra* note 13, at 266 (predicting "disputes, duplication, and discord" in analagous situations).

642. Data managed by a consortium would presumably also be subject to its agreed contractual templates regulating the licensing of government-funded data to the private sector. *See* discussion *supra*, at Part IV.C.1.c..

643. *Cf.* Rai, *supra* note 33 (expressing preference for normative solutions).

Moreover, the very contractual templates that make the construction of such a commons feasible in a two-tiered system should also mitigate its social costs. Even if conditional deposits are allowed, many sub-disciplines will continue to have no commercial prospects and no need to invoke the contractual templates that regulate them. When this is the case, peer pressure reinforced by the funding agencies should make it difficult, if not impractical, for members of those communities to opt out of the traditional practice of making data available unconditionally.[644]

When, instead, given communities find themselves forced to deal with serious commercial pressures, the negotiated contractual solutions that enable them to make data conditionally available for public research purposes should also tend to preserve and implement the norms of science. In particular, the applicable contractual templates should immunize deposited data from the vagaries of case-by-case transactions under the aegis of university technology transfer offices[645] and should also limit the kinds of restrictions private-sector partners might otherwise seek to impose on universities.

At the end of the day, a set of agreed contractual templates permitting conditional deposits in the interest of a horizontally linked research commons would provide a tool universities could use with more or less wisdom. If used wisely, this tool should ensure that more data are made available to a contractually reconstructed research commons than would be possible if member universities could not protect the interests of their commercial partners. This same tool may also provide incentives for the private sector to work with universities to produce better data products than the latter alone could generate with their limited funds.

iv. Other Hard Problems

Allowing universities to deposit government-funded data into a contractually reconstructed research commons, on conditions designed to protect their commercial relations with the private sector, solves two difficult problems. First, it avoids the risk that large quantities of government-funded data would remain outside the system on the ground that they had been commingled with privately funded components. Second, it ensures that any negotiated contractual templates the research consortium adopts to govern its horizontal space will apply to all the data holdings within its jurisdiction, including databases to which the private sector had contributed. However, it does not automatically determine the precise conditions that the agreed contractual templates should apply to inter-university licensing of data within their collective jurisdiction. In the process of defining these conditions, moreover, those who negotiated the

644. *Cf. id.* at 112 ("Major research universities have sought to maintain certain aspects of traditional scientific norms even while embracing the development-promoting aspects of property rights.") (citing examples).

645. *See, e.g.*, Eisenberg, *Bargaining*, *supra* note 13, at 243 (stressing the extent to which technology transfer professionals "become ever more wary of free exchange and more assiduous about restricting its domain").

multilateral pact between universities, federal funders, and scientific bodies needed to launch the consortium would have to resolve a number of contentious issues.

The guiding principle that should apply to inter-university licensing of data available from the quasi-public space is that depositors may not impose any conditions that impede the customary and traditional uses of scientific data for nonprofit research purposes. A logical corollary is that they should affirmatively adopt the measures that may prove necessary to extend and apply this principle to the online environment.[646] Because the data under discussion are government-funded for academic purposes to begin with, the open access and sharing norms of science should then color any specific implementing templates that regulate access and use.

(a) Access. With regard to access, the customary mode of implementing these norms would be to make data available to other nonprofit institutions at no more than the marginal cost of delivery. In the online environment, these marginal costs are essentially zero. This represents the preferred option whenever the costs of maintaining the data collection are defrayed by public subsidy or by non-exclusive licenses to private firms in the vertical dimension.

If, however, the policy of free or marginally priced access appears unable to sustain the cost of managing a given project at the inter-university level, an incremental pricing structure may become unavoidable. The options for such a pricing structure range from a formula allowing partial incremental cost recovery when a project is partially subsidized to a formula providing full cost recovery when this is necessary to keep the data collection alive.[647] Examples of subcommunities that have found it necessary to rely on the second option are largely in the laboratory physical sciences.[648]

The prices charged other nonprofit users to access data in the research commons should never exceed the full incremental cost of managing the collective holdings. This premise follows from the fact that the initial cost of collecting or creating the data was defrayed by the government or some combination of sources (including private sources) that normally subscribe to the open access principle.

When, however, private firms have defrayed a substantial part of the cost of generating the database in question, there are few, if any, standard solutions.

646. *Cf.* WIPO Copyright Treaty, *supra* note 268, at art. 10; Agreed Statement Concerning art. 10, WIPO.doc.CRNR/DC/96 (Dec. 20, 1996).

647. This may be accomplished through a paying inter-university consortium, such as the Inter-University Consortium for Political and Social Research ("ICPSR") at the University of Michigan, or by means of more ad hoc cost-recovery methods. Institutional membership dues for the year 2002 ranged from $2,000 per year for institutions in developing countries to $15,000 per year for full membership status by large U.S. institutions. *See* Inter-University Consortium for Political and Social Research, http://www.icpsr.umich.edu/ (last visited Jan. 18, 2003).

648. Databases operated on a cost recovery basis may be found primarily in the areas of ceramic, pharmaceutical, chemical, and metallurgical research, as well as in state-of-the-art manufacturing operations. Telephone Interview with Prof. Robert L. Snyder, Ohio St. Univ. (Aug. 30, 2002).

Occasionally, even a private partner might view the collective holdings as a valuable resource for its own pursuits, to which it agrees to contribute on an eleemosynary basis.[649] In the more typical cases, the private partner is likely to view the research community as the target market for a database it paid to create and from which it must derive its expected profits.[650]

In that event, the collection of additional revenues from private sector access charges should depend entirely on freedom of contract, while a likely demand that public research users pay access charges that exceed data management costs would pose a hard question. On the one hand, as beneficiaries of government funding, the universities should forego profits from charges levied to access their partly publicly funded databases for public research purposes. On the other hand, a private partner will not readily forego such profits, especially if it had invested in the project precisely because of its potential commercial value as a research tool.[651] If the university shared these profits with its private partner, this practice would deviate from the basic principle governing inter-university access generally, and would encourage other universities to seek private partners for this purpose, which in turn would yield both social costs and benefits.

In these cases, care must be taken to avoid adopting policies that would discourage either the formation of public-private partnerships for the development of socially beneficial data products or the inclusion of such products in a horizontal, quasi-public research space. At the same time, there is a potential loophole here that would allow universities to deviate from the general rules applicable to that space if the private partner could impose market-driven access rights for nonprofit research purposes, and its partner university shared in those profits.

We know of no standard formula for resolving this problem. If the database is also of interest to the private sector, price discrimination and product differentiation are the preferred techniques for reducing access charges levied for public research. In any event, the trustees that manage the inter-university system should monitor and evaluate these charges, and their power to challenge unreasonable or excessive demands would become especially important in the absence of any alternative or competing source of supply.[652]

This strategy, however, begs the question of whether and to what extent the universities should be allowed to retain their share of the profits from access

649. *Cf.* Rai, *supra* note 33, at 114 (discussing case of Celera's refraining from claiming certain intellectual property rights in the genome).

650. *Cf. id.* at 111, 141 (documenting restrictive conditions imposed upon researchers under MTAs arising from joint ventures between universities and private firms).

651. *See, e.g.*, Eisenberg, *Bargaining*, *supra* note 13, at 229 ("When one research institution's research tool is another firm's end product, it is difficult to agree upon a universe of materials that should be exchanged on standardized terms.").

652. Because the data in question are partly government-funded by definition, a reasonable terms and conditions clause should automatically apply.

charges levied against public research users.[653] As matters stand, this is an issue that can only be addressed by the relevant discipline communities themselves, in the absence of some general norm that would not pose insuperable administrative burdens to implement.

(b) Use. Once access to databases available to the research commons has legitimately been gained, further restrictions on uses of the relevant data should be kept to a minimum. In principle, contractual restrictions on reuse of publicly funded data for nonprofit research purposes should not be permitted. This principle need not impede the use of conditions that require attribution or credit from researchers who make use of such data,[654] and it can also be reconciled with provisions that defer access by certain users for specified periods of time or impose restrictions on competing publications for a certain period of time.[655]

This ideal principle runs into trouble, however, when confronted with the difficult problem posed by commercially valuable follow-on applications derived from databases made available to the research commons. It is one thing to posit that the academic beneficiaries of publicly funded research should be limited to the recovery of costs through access charges and should not be entitled to additional claims for follow-on uses by other nonprofit researchers. Quite different situations arise when the funding is public, but a private firm has invested its own resources to develop a follow-on application for commercial pursuits or when the initial data-generating project entailed a mix of private and public funds and the product subsequently gives rise to a commercially valuable follow-on application. These hard cases become even harder if the follow-on product primarily derives its commercial value from being a research tool universities themselves need to acquire.

Assuming, as we do, that a primary objective of any negotiated solution is to avoid gaps in the data made available for public research purposes in the horizontal domain, there is an obvious need for agreed contractual templates that would respect and preserve the commercial interests in the vertical plane identified above. This goal directly conflicts, however, with the most idealistic option set out above, which is to freely allow all follow-on applications based on data made available to the research commons, regardless of the commercial prospects or purposes and without any compensatory obligation beyond access charges (if any).

This option would represent a true public domain approach to government-funded data and would fit within the traditional legal framework applied in the past to collections of data. However, it might be expected to discourage public-private partnerships formed to exploit follow-on applications of publicly funded

653 If these charges were administered by trustees or designated agents, they could be redistributed in the form of grants. *Cf.* Eckersley et al., *supra* note 610, at 10.

654. *See, e.g.*, discussion of the Creative Commons templates, *supra* note 579.

655. *Cf.* Patrinos & Drell, *supra* note 23.

databases, contrary to the philosophy behind the Bayh-Dole Act, although this risk is tempered by the fact that all would-be competitors who invested in such follow-on applications would find themselves on equal footing in this respect. This option would certainly discourage public-private partnerships formed to produce scientific databases from making them available to the commons if that decision automatically deprived them of any rights to follow-on applications.

A second option is to leave the problem of commercially valuable follow-on applications to freedom of contract, in which case universities and their private partners could license whom they please and exclude the rest. This solution is consistent with proposals to enact a de facto exclusive property right in non-copyrightable databases and with the philosophy behind Bayh-Dole. It would also alleviate disincentives to make databases derived from a mix of public and private funds available to the nonprofit research community.

However, this second option would relegate the problem of follow-on applications to the universities' technology transfer offices once again, which might be tempted routinely to impose the kind of grant-back and reach-through clauses that are already said to generate anticommons effects in biotechnology[656] and are inconsistent with the dual nature of data as both inputs and outputs of innovation. Just as a true public domain approach tends unintentionally to impoverish the commons we seek to construct, so too a true laissez-faire approach undermines the effectiveness of that same commons and triggers a race to the bottom, as universities seek private partners solely for the purpose of occupying a privileged position with respect to follow-on applications.

A third option is freely to allow follow-on applications of databases made available to the research commons for commercial purposes while requiring their producers to pay reasonable compensation for such uses under a predetermined menu that fixes a range of royalties for a specified period of time.[657] For maximum effect, a corollary "no holdout" provision should obligate all universities engaged in public-private database initiatives to make the resulting databases available to the research commons under this compensatory liability framework.

This approach would enable investors in public-private database initiatives to make their data available for public research purposes without depriving them of revenue flows from follow-on applications needed to cover the costs of R & D or the opportunities to turn a profit. At the same time, it would avoid impeding access to the data for either commercial or noncommercial purposes, in which aspect it would mimic a true public domain and create no barriers to entry.[658] Moreover, a compensatory liability approach would implement the

---

656. *See, e.g.*, Rai, *supra* note 33 at 149.

657. For details, see discussion of compensatory liability approach in Reichman, *Of Green Tulips*, *supra* note 164. *See also* Reichman, *Legal Hybrids*, *supra* note 164; Reichman & Samuelson, *supra* note 18, at 145-51.

658. Transaction costs can be kept low by means of standard-form deals administered by the managers of the system. *See* Eckersley et al., *supra* note 610, at 10-11 (proposing collective licensing organization for analogous purposes).

policies behind the Bayh-Dole Act without the overkill that occurs when publicly funded research results are subjected to exclusive property rights that impoverish the public domain and create barriers to entry to boot.

These, or other, options would require further study and analysis as part of the larger process of reconstructing the research commons we propose. It should be clear, moreover, that any solutions adopted at the outset must be viewed as experimental and subject to review in light of actual results.

2. Informal Data Exchanges

As constituted at the present time, the zone of informal data exchange is populated by single researchers or laboratories or by small teams of associated researchers whose work is typically expected to lead to future publications. Because this zone operates largely in a pre-publication environment, the constraints of government funders on uses of data are relatively less prescriptive, and a considerable amount of the data being produced may not be funded by federal agencies at all. If funding is provided by other nonprofit sources or by state governments, the end results still pertain to public science and its ultimate disclosure norms, but the controls are not standardized. To the extent that private sector funding is also involved, even the norms of public science may not apply.

Quantitatively, the amount of scientific data held in this informal zone appears large. Despite the relative degree of invisibility that pre-publication status confers, these holdings are also of immense qualitative importance for cutting-edge research endeavors. Although these data may not be as well prepared as those released for broad, open use in conjunction with a publication, they typically reflect the most recent findings.

Moreover, this informal sector seems destined to grow even more important in the near future as it increasingly absorbs scientific data that were not released at publication as well as data researchers continue to compile after publication. If Congress were to adopt a strong intellectual property right in non-copyrightable databases, this informal zone could expand further to include all the published data covered by an exclusive property right that had not otherwise been dedicated to the public domain.

As previously discussed, actual secrecy is taken for granted in this zone, and disclosure depends on individually brokered transactions often based on reciprocity or some quid pro quo.[659] These fragile data streams, which have always been tenuous due to personal and strategic considerations, have increasingly broken down owing to denials of access and to a trading mentality steeped in commercial concerns that is displacing the sharing ethos.

Our previous analysis showed that, left to themselves, the legal and economic pressures operating in the informal zone are likely to further reduce disclosures over time and make the informal data exchange process resemble that

659. *See supra* notes 482-484 and accompanying text.

of the private sector.[660] That trend, in turn, undermines the new opportunities to link even highly distributed data holdings in virtual archives or to experiment with new forms of collaborative research on a distributed, autonomous basis, as digital networks have recently made possible. The positive synergies expected from organized peer-to-peer file sharing on an open access basis cannot be realized if researchers decline to make data available at all out of a fear of sacrificing new-found commercial opportunities or other strategic advantages. Nor will these new opportunities fully develop if those who are nominally willing to make data available impose onerous licensing terms and conditions—reinforced by intellectual property rights—that multiply transaction costs, unduly restrict the range of scientific uses permitted, or otherwise embroil those uses in anticommons effects.

Here, the immediate goal of science policy should be to reduce the technical, legal, and institutional obstacles that impede electronic peer-to-peer file exchange and to generally facilitate exchanges of data on the most open terms possible across a horizontal or quasi-public space. At the same time, the measures adopted to implement this policy must avoid compromising or inhibiting the interests of individual participants who seek commercial application of their research results in a private or vertical sphere of operations. This two-pronged approach could stabilize the status quo and reinvigorate the flagging cooperative ethos in the zone of informal data exchange, as more individual researchers and small communities experience the benefits of electronically linked access to virtual archives and discover the productive gains likely to flow from collaborative, interdisciplinary, and cross-sectoral uses.

From an institutional perspective, however, organizing and implementing such a two-pronged approach to data exchange in the informal zone presents certain difficulties not encountered in the formal zone of inter-university relations. Here, the playing field is much broader, the players are more autonomous and unruly, and the power of federal funders directly to impose top-down regulations has traditionally been weak or under-utilized. The moral authority of these funders nonetheless remains strong, and peer pressure in support of the sharing ethos would become more effective if a consensus developed that the two-pronged approach we envision actually yields tangible benefits at acceptable costs.

Much therefore depends on short-term, bottom-up initiatives that rely on individual decisions to opt for standardized, research-friendly licensing agreements in place of the defensive, ad hoc transactions that currently hinder the flow of data streams in this sector. The solution is to provide individual researchers with a toolkit for constructing prefabricated exchange transactions on community-approved terms and conditions. The toolkit would contain a menu of standard-form contractual templates that individual researchers could use to license data, and the templates adopted would be posted online to facilitate

660. *See supra* Part III.C.1.a.ii (discussing the effects of a highly protectionist regime on informal data exchanges).

electronic access to networks of nodes.[661] These templates would cover a variety of situations and offer a range of ad hoc choices, all aimed at maximizing disclosure in both digital and non-digital mediums for public research purposes.

For this endeavor to succeed, however, the templates in question would clearly need to allow participating researchers and their communities to make data available on conditions that expressly preclude licensees from unauthorized commercial uses or follow-on applications. While this suggests the need to deviate from true public domain principles once again, one should remember that, in the informal zone as it stands today and is likely to develop, secrecy and denial of access are already well-established, countervailing practices. One can hardly argue that permitting conditional availability would undermine the norms of science in this zone, given the inability of those norms to adequately defend the interests of public research in unrestricted flows of data at the present time.

The object is, rather, to invigorate those sharing norms by reconciling them with the commercial needs and opportunities of the researchers operating in the informal zone, in order to elicit more overall benefits for public science under a second-best arrangement than could be expected to emerge from brokered individual transactions in a high-protectionist legal environment. This strategy requires a judicious resort to conditionality that would make it possible to forge digitally networked links between individual data suppliers and that would let their data flow across those links into a quasi-public space relatively free of restrictions on access and use for commercial purposes.

Given the large number of players and the disparity of interests at stake, a logical starting premise is that only a small number of standard contractual templates seems likely to win the support of the general scientific community, at least initially. A true public domain option should, of course, be available for all willing to use it. For the rest, a limited menu of conditional public domain provisions, such as those offered by the Creative Commons, should suffice.[662] Clauses that delay certain uses for a specified period, or that delay competing publications based on, or derived from, a particular database for a specified period of time should also pass muster, so long as they remain consistent with the practices of the relevant scientific sub-community. In the absence of any underlying intellectual property right, an additional clause reserving all other rights and excluding unauthorized commercial uses and applications would complete the limited, "copyleft" concept. We believe that even a small number of standard contractual templates that facilitate access to and use of scientific data for public research purposes could exert a disproportionately large impact on the increasingly open, collaborative work in the networked environment.

In the scientific milieu, however, difficult problems of leakage and enforcement could also arise. To address these problems, the scientific community,

661 *See* Creative Commons, *supra* note 571 and accompanying text.

662 *See* discussion *supra*, note 579.

perhaps under the auspices of the American Association for the Advancement of Science, would need to consider developing institutional machinery capable of assisting individual researchers who feared that their data had been used in ways that violated the terms and conditions of the standard-form licensing agreements they elected to employ.

More complex or refined contractual templates are also feasible, but their use should normally depend less on individual choice and more on the consensus approval of discipline-specific communities. Moreover, in the informal zone, efforts to influence the terms and conditions applicable to private-sector uses seem much less likely to succeed than similar efforts in the inter-university context.[663]

Attempts to over-regulate the zone of informal data exchange should generally be avoided at this stage, lest they stir up unwarranted controversy and deter the more ambitious efforts to regulate inter-university transactions described above. The success of those efforts in the zone of formal data exchanges should greatly reinforce the norms of science generally. It would also exert considerable indirect pressure on those operating in the informal zone to respect those norms and emulate at least the spirit of any agreed contractual templates that had proved their merit in that context.

The more that universities succeed in amalgamating their government-funded holdings into an effective, virtual archive or repository, the more pressure that would bring to bear on individual researchers, research teams, and small communities to similarly make their data available in more formally constituted repositories. As a body of practice develops in both the formal and informal zones, the most successful approaches and standards will become broadly adopted, and the desire to obtain the greater benefits likely to flow from more formalized arrangements should grow.[664]

Meanwhile, efforts to regulate the zone of informal data exchanges should be viewed as an opportunity to strengthen the norms of science and to facilitate the creation of virtual networked archives electronically linking disparate and highly distributed data-holders. The overall objective should be to generate more disclosure than would otherwise have been possible if all the players exercised their proprietary rights in total disregard of the need for a functioning research commons for nonprofit scientific pursuits. If successful, these modest efforts in the informal zone could alleviate some of the most disturbing erosions of the sharing ethos that have already occurred, and could encourage federal funding agencies to take a more active role in regulating broader uses of research data. A successful application of "copyleft" techniques to the informal zone of academic research could also serve as a model for encouraging disclosure for public research purposes of more data generated in the private sector.

663. It seems unlikely, for example, that any standard grant-back or reach-through clauses for commercial applications of databases could serve the varied interests of the different communities operating in the informal zone.

664. *See supra* note 133 and accompanying text.

D. Proposals for the Private Sector

Scientific data produced by the private sector are logically subject to any and all of the proprietary rights that may become available, as surveyed earlier in this article.[665] Here, the policy behind a contractually reconstructed research commons is not to defend the norms of science so much as to persuade the private sector of the benefits it stands to gain from sharing its own data with the scientific community for public research purposes. The goal is thus to promote voluntary contributions that might not otherwise be made to the true public domain or to the conditional domain for public research purposes on favorable terms and conditions.[666]

From the perspective of public-interest research, of course, corporate contributions of otherwise proprietary data to a true public domain is the preferred option. While the copyright paradigm reflected in the Supreme Court's *Feist* decision presumably made the factual contents of commercially valuable compilations published in hard copy available for such purposes,[667] some federal appellate courts have lately rebelled against *Feist* and made it harder for second-comers to separate non-copyrightable facts and information from the elements of original selection and arrangement that still attract copyright protection.[668]

Online access to non-copyrightable facts and data is further restricted by the stronger regime that prohibits tampering with technological fences that was embodied in the DMCA,[669] although the full impact of these provisions on scientific pursuits remains to be seen. Meanwhile, many commercial database publishers may be expected to continue to lobby hard for a strong database protection law on the E.U. model that would limit unauthorized extraction or reuse of the non-copyrightable contents of factual compilations, and it appears likely that Congress will seek to enact a database protection statute in 2004.[670]

In contrast to the research-friendly legal rules under the print paradigm, all the factual data and non-copyrightable information collected in proprietary databases are increasingly unlikely to enter the public domain and will instead come freighted with the restricted licensing agreements, digital rights management technologies, and *sui generis* intellectual property rights that characterize a high-protectionist legal environment. Under such a regime, open access and unrestricted use become possible only if private-sector database compilers donate their data to public repositories or contractually agree to waive proprie-

665. See discussion *supra*, Parts II.C, III.B.2.

666. *Cf.* Rebecca S. Eisenberg, *Intellectual Property at the Public-Private Divide: The Case of Large-Scale cDNA Sequencing*, 3 U. CHI. L. SCH. ROUNDTABLE 557, 559 (1996); Rai, *supra* note 33, at 134 (discussing Merck & Co.'s practice of putting into the public domain the results of an EST identification project it sponsored at Washington University).

667. *See supra* notes 78, 85-89 and accompanying text.

668. *See supra* notes 283-287 and accompanying text.

669. *See* discussion *supra*, Part III.B.2.b.

670. *See supra* note 376.

tary restrictions on controls that would otherwise impede access and use for public research purposes.[671]

Some examples of both donated and contractually stipulated public domain data collections from the private sector already exist. In the first category, for instance, three major energy companies recently donated large collections of proprietary rock samples to the University of Texas at Austin.[672] The samples and related data are managed as a public research resource by the University. The companies also donated land, buildings, equipment, and additional funds to provide the physical infrastructure and a partial endowment for operating expenses, while retaining no proprietary interest in the donated materials.[673]

An example of the second type of arrangement is the SNP Consortium Ltd., a nonprofit foundation created by thirteen pharmaceutical and information technology companies and Wellcome Trust, whose stated purpose is to provide genomic data to the public domain.[674] The motivation for this apparent corporate largess was to save substantial money by pooling resources and to prevent any other private sector entity from capturing the data or otherwise encumbering access to them.[675] The Consortium partners have found this approach to be very successful. Instead of spending $250 million to identify 150,000 single nucleotide polymorphisms ("SNPs"),[676] as was originally estimated by one of the partners, the shared project cost amounted to $44 million and yielded almost 1.8 million SNPs—all freely available to researchers on the open website.[677] Two other projects are now being planned by the SNP Consortium partners using the same public domain model—a protein structures consortium and a public DNA database in the United Kingdom, the latter in collaboration with the Department of Health and the Medical Research Council.[678]

Although pure public domain models initiated by industry will no doubt continue to be the exception rather than the rule, the availability of data on a conditional public domain basis, or at least on preferential terms and conditions to the not-for-profit research community, should enjoy far broader acceptance and ought to be promoted. Certainly, the existence of contractual templates,

---

671. This will also depend to a large extent on the exceptions for nonprofit research built into the database protection law itself.

672. *See* Shirley Dutton, *Corporate Donations of Geophysical Data*, *in* NRC SYMPOSIUM, *supra* note 10; *see also* NATIONAL RESEARCH COUNCIL, GEOSCIENCE COLLECTIONS AND DATA: NATIONAL RESOURCES IN PERIL, (2002) at 25 (detailing no examples of transfer from corporate-owned repositories to state geological surveys).

673. Dutton, *supra* note 672.

674. *See* SNP Consortium *at* http://snp.cshl.org/ (last updated Feb. 5, 2003).

675. Michael Morgan, *The SNP Consortium*, *in* NRC SYMPOSIUM, *supra* note 10.

676. Single nucleotide polymorphisms are common DNA sequence variations among individuals. Although approximately 99.9% of the three billion nucleotides in each person are identical, there are nonetheless three million differences in the remaining 0.1% that are distributed throughout the three billion nucleotides. By identifying and mapping out these differences, it then becomes possible to correlate them with human susceptibility to disease (for example, diabetes or cancer) and their responsiveness to various drug therapies. *See* Morgan, *supra* note 675.

677. *Id.*

678. *Id.*

along the lines being developed by the Creative Commons, could help to encourage private sector entities to make conditional deposits of data for relatively unrestricted access and use by public-interest researchers.[679] Indeed, some enlightened CEOs have acknowledged the benefits that derive from enriching the contents of an information commons that all researchers can use for further innovation,[680] and worldwide efforts to compile databases of traditional knowledge gleaned from indigenous populations point in the same direction.[681]

Scientific publications by private sector scientists provide another valuable source of research data. However, these scientists labor under increasing pressures either to limit such publications altogether or to insist that publishers allow supporting data to be made available only on conditions that aim to preserve their commercial value.[682] Although many academics in the scientific community oppose this practice,[683] it is exactly what would proliferate if private sector scientists held exclusive property rights in the data that allowed them to retain control even after publication. This sobering observation might induce the scientific community to reconsider the need to allow private sector scientists to modify the bright-line disclosure rules otherwise applied to public sector scientists, in order to encourage them to disclose more of their data for nonprofit research purposes.

Even when companies remain unwilling to make their data available to nonprofit researchers on a conditional public domain basis, there is ample experience with price discrimination and product differentiation measures favorable to academics.[684] To the extent that the public research community does not constitute the primary market segment of the commercial data producer, either of these approaches would help promote access and use by noncommercial researchers without undue risks to the data vendor's bottom line. The conditions under which such arrangements might be considered acceptable by commercial data producers will vary according to discipline area and type of data product, but it is in the interest of the public research community to identify such producers in each discipline and sub-discipline and to negotiate favorable access and use agreements on a mutually acceptable basis.

The terms and conditions acceptable to private firms that do opt to deposit data into a public access commons arrangement might be fairly restrictive in their allowable uses, as compared with the conditions applicable under the

---

679. *See supra* note 579.

680. *See* Edward Shonsey, Biotechnology: An Idea Before Its Time?, Presentation at The University of Minnesota Conference on Governing GMOs: Developing Policy in the Face of Scientific & Public Debate, (Feb. 1, 2001), *available at* http://www.lifesci.consortium.umn.edu/conferences/gmosconf/ (last visited Jan. 18, 2003).

681. *See, e.g.*, Dutfield, *supra* note 114; Traditional Knowledge, Intellectual Property and Indigenous Culture, Symposium presented at the Benjamin N. Cardozo School of Law (Feb. 21-22, 2002). *But see* van Caenegem, *supra* note 113, at 328-30 (stressing risks of dispossessing indigenous claims to knowledge).

682. *See generally* COMMUNITY STANDARDS, *supra* note 74.

683. *Id.* (views of the biological sciences community).

684. *See, e.g.*, BITS OF POWER, *supra* note 1, at 124-25.

standard-form templates that researchers themselves would normally adopt. Nevertheless, the goal of securing greater access to privately generated data with fewer restrictions justifies this approach because it would make data available to the research community that would otherwise be subject to commercial terms and conditions in a less research-friendly environment.

Finally, the importance of regulating the interface between university-generated data and private sector applications was treated at length above, with a view to ensuring that the universities' eagerness to participate in commercial endeavors did not compromise access to, and use of, federally funded data for public research purposes.[685] Here, in contrast, it is worth stressing the benefits that can accrue from data transfers to the private sector whenever a framework for reducing the social costs of such transfers has been worked out to the satisfaction of both the research universities and the public funding sources. These arrangements are especially important if the exploitation, or applications of, any given database by the private sector would not otherwise occur in a nonproprietary environment.

Price discrimination and product differentiation can also facilitate socially beneficial interactions between the private sector and universities. For example, companies might consider licensing certain data to commercial customers on an exclusive-use basis for a limited period of time, after which the data in question would be licensed on preferential terms to nonprofit users or even revert to an open access status. This strategy might work successfully in the case of certain environmental data, in which most commercially valuable applications are produced in real time or near-real time and can then be made available at lower cost and with fewer restrictions for retrospective research that is less time dependent.[686] Such an approach might not work in other research areas, such as biotechnology, however, in which a delay in access may not be an acceptable tradeoff or that delay is too long to preserve competitive research values.[687]

Especially serious problems seem likely to arise when the public research community becomes the target market for the commercial data supplier, and there is a resulting tension between freedom of contract and the needs and capabilities of the nonprofit research sector. In principle, one expects that a supplier will not price itself out of the market. In practice, some science publishers have adopted exorbitant pricing strategies that do limit scientists' abilities to access and use their products.

If a database protection law is enacted and sole-source science publishers control databases of major importance to scientific sub-communities, access and use will increasingly depend on any exceptions and immunities favoring

685. *See* discussion *supra*, Part IV.C.i.c.

686. See, for example, the Sea Wide Field Sensor example in the NASA data purchase program, at http://seawifs.gsfc.nasa.gov/SEAWIFS.html (last visited Jan. 18, 2003).

687. The trend in industry may in fact lie in the direction of less flexibility and accommodation to nonprofit research interests. *See* Nelson, *supra* note 132.

research that are built into the law, and on any misuse provisions requiring database licensors to adopt reasonable terms and conditions. If and when these problems become acute, as may well happen, the science community will have to consider appropriate actions including both collective bargaining arrangements (to the extent permitted by antitrust laws) and concerted efforts to independently develop alternative sources of supply for public research purposes.

V

CONCLUSION

The importance of public domain data for scientific research is so taken for granted that it becomes difficult to identify the precise boundaries of that domain, to describe its operations, and especially to evaluate the normative and legal infrastructure that supports those operations. At the outset of this article, we undertook to map the public domain for scientific data as it actually functions today, with a view to addressing two new challenges. One is the advent of digital networks, which is transforming the traditional modes of exchanging scientific data and could considerably magnify the payoffs that science (and industry) derive from a policy of full and open access to public research data. The other is an array of economic, legal, and technical pressures that threaten to impede or disrupt the continued operations of that same public domain for scientific data as it was traditionally constituted.

Our investigation reveals that the policy of open access to public research data rests on a surprisingly fragile foundation in both the legal and normative sense. As scientists and universities increasingly aspire to commercialize their research products (partly in response to the Bayh-Dole Act and related legislation), their willingness to exchange data, along with other research tools, has begun to suffer. There is evidence that informal exchanges of data in some fields, such as biomedical research, have become severely compromised, while inter-university exchanges are subject to high transaction costs, delay, and a growing risk of anticommons effects. As relations between universities and industry become more intense, the ability of the industrial partners to impose restrictions on the open availability of research data also increases and could pose a formidable obstacle in the future.

In this already delicate situation, the advent of strong new intellectual property rights in databases could have disproportionately adverse effects on the operations of the public domain for scientific data. A database protection law would remove data from their traditional public domain status under copyright law. It could invest scientists and universities with exclusive property rights in collections of data—including government-funded databases—that would survive both the publication of research results in scientific journals and the disclosure of such results in patent applications. Database rights, when added to other economic and technical pressures, could thus become the hub of an enclosure process that progressively fences off the public domain for scientific data and undermines its functions. This process could greatly reduce the flow of data as a basic input into both scientific research and the national system of innovation.

We have argued that science policy should take steps now to address these challenges to ward off the threat of undue enclosure and to exploit of the potential benefits of digitally linked data resources. We focused particular attention on government-funded data because of its overall importance to the scientific enterprise and because it already benefits from a regulatory structure that could be appropriately adjusted and strengthened to preserve crucial public domain functions even in a highly protectionist intellectual property environment. We suggest that science policy should treat data produced with government funds as a collective resource for research purposes. Government agencies, research universities, and scientific bodies should accordingly negotiate and develop a regulatory framework to preserve the functions of a research commons by contractual means that constrain private rights to serve the public interest.

It is not necessary for this purpose that universities forego their growing opportunities to participate in commercial applications of research results. It is necessary, however, to curb the ability of their industrial partners to restrict the flow of data as a collective research resource. It is even more necessary to develop a strong legal and normative infrastructure that would preserve open access to, and use of, the data generated by participating universities for public research purposes. However, this outcome can only be achieved by realistic contractual arrangements that also preserve the participants' ability to license data to the private sector while ensuring that scientists can access and use the same data on reasonable terms and conditions.

We believe that science policy stands at a critical threshold. If nothing is done to address the challenges we identify, the unraveling of the sharing ethos that already characterizes what we have termed the zone of informal data exchanges between individual scientists will spread to universities, and a trading mentality will further contaminate inter-university exchanges of data.

If, instead, science policy takes timely action to address these problems, the benefits could be spectacular, given the new opportunities for scientific collaboration that digital networks make possible. If government-funded data at the university level do enter a contractually reconstructed research commons along the lines we advocate, it would put considerable pressure on single scientists and laboratories to conform their own data exchange practices to the broader normative and regulatory ethos by means of suitable contractual templates. The formulation of these templates could, in turn, make it possible to link up the highly distributed databases of cutting-edge disciplines into "networks of nodes." On this scenario, the research commons—instead of shrinking and becoming increasingly dysfunctional—could yield positive externalities and network effects that exceeded anything that the scientific community had previously experienced.

REIMAGINING THE PUBLIC DOMAIN

DAVID LANGE*

In a paper included among this collection of works from the Duke Law School's Conference on the Public Domain, James Boyle kindly credits an early essay of mine, *Recognizing the Public Domain*,[1] with having contributed initially to the contemporary study of the subject.[2] Boyle quotes a passage from that essay in which I suggested that "recognition of new intellectual property interests should be offset today by equally deliberate recognition of individual rights in the public domain . . . . Each [intellectual property] right ought to be marked off clearly against the public domain."[3]

"But what does this *mean*?" Boyle asks. "What is the nature of these 'individual rights in the public domain?' Who holds them? Indeed, what *is* the public domain?"

These are fair questions. I cannot respond to them fully, for the fact is that I have never tried to define the public domain, not even for myself.[4] Boyle's paper gains a portion of its power and its appeal from his own contemplation of these questions, but in the end I think he would agree that even he has succeeded only in approaching a number of definitions.

In its usage to date, the term "public domain" is elastic and inexact. A definition can be but one of many definitions, each surely a function of perspective and agenda, more or less as Boyle suggests. His own perspective, one in which he sees the expansion of intellectual property rights as "a second enclosure movement" reminiscent of the English land enclosure movement of the Nineteenth Century, is intriguing. From this perspective, the public domain is perhaps most usefully seen as a commons, set off against the fences that delimit the interests of individual rights holders. I have no important quarrel with this perspective, and indeed think it enormously useful for many purposes—among

---

This article is also available at http://www.law.duke.edu/journals/66LCPLange.

* Professor of Law, Duke University.

Portions of this essay draw upon earlier works and presentations by the author. Special thanks to N. Gregson Davis, Chair of the Department of Classical Studies at Duke University, for creative assistance and advice in bringing Latin into the service of this work. Thanks to Jennifer Anderson, James Boyle, Rosemary Coombe, Elizabeth Corley, Wendy Gordon, Neil Netanel, David Nimmer, Jed Rubenfeld and Lois Wasoff for ideas, suggestions, reactions, comments, and criticism.

1. David Lange, *Recognizing the Public Domain*, 44 LAW & CONTEMP. PROBS. 147 (Autumn 1981) [hereinafter Lange, *Recognizing the Public Domain*].

2. James Boyle, *The Second Enclosure Movement and the Construction of the Public Domain*, 66 LAW & CONTEMP. PROBS. 33, 59 (Winter/Spring 2003). Jamie also kindly acknowledges me as a friend and colleague, an acknowledgment I warmly reciprocate.

3. Lange, *Recognizing the Public Domain*, *supra* note 1, at 147-50.

4. A more comprehensive effort at definition will be reflected in a book by Jennifer Anderson and me (*Reading the Public Domain*), now under contract with The Stanford University Press and due for delivery in 2004. The copyright in that book will be held by The Stanford Press.

them, for the purposes of imagining a "politics of the commons" while addressing common interests in cyberspace, two important areas of inquiry in which Boyle's own scholarly agenda particularly lies.[5]

But this public domain is not my public domain. More precisely, it is not the public domain that matters to me most. And I have thought that perhaps it would be appropriate to say a bit more fully what I had in mind when I wrote my essay some twenty years ago. This is, I think, only the second occasion when I have attempted to do so publicly,[6] and it will certainly be the first in which I try in addition to bring my thinking from that time into some degree of harmony with my thinking today. Not that such an exercise will matter to posterity. But Boyle does raise the question of meaning in general, and I suppose that I, like others, am free to respond to the question in particular.

I

Sometime late in the middle nineteen-seventies a graduate of the Duke Law School, Edward Rubin[7], then a distinguished practitioner in Los Angeles specializing in motion picture transaction law, invited me to join him and a number of others in organizing what became the American Bar Association's Forum Committee on the Entertainment and Sports Industries. In 1979, the Forum Committee gave its inaugural symposium on issues affecting entertainment law. The symposium was held in Beverly Hills, and to me fell the task of preparing a lecture on the then still new (or new-ish) subject of publicity rights. Two cases were pending in the California court system at the time: one brought by heirs of Bela Lugosi[8], the other by the heirs of Rudolph Guglielmi[9], better known to the public as Rudolph Valentino, whose fevered kisses in *The Sheik* had quickened the pulse of more than one otherwise suitably composed young woman of the nineteen-twenties. I had just begun to teach at the Law School when these cases first appeared in 1971 or so; the subject matter interested me from the perspective of both intellectual property and tort law. I looked forward to the Beverly Hills lecture as an opportunity to think aloud about the several questions then still at large in the publicity field, among them, most importantly (or so I thought at the time), the question of post-death succession.[10]

---

5. *See* Boyle, *supra* note 2. Jamie's work is always more textured and sophisticated than a brief account of it can accommodate. But as I intend neither a critical response to, nor an adequate appreciation of, this excellent essay I shall count upon the reader to be forewarned, and Jamie to be forgiving, of such lapses as I may be guilty of in my attempt to summarize it here.

6. The first (and, at most, partial) occasion was my Donald Brace Memorial Lecture to the Copyright Society of America in 1992. That lecture was subsequently published as David Lange, *Copyright and the Constitution in the Age of Intellectual Property*, 1 J. INTELL. PROP. L. 119 (1993). The narrative in this part of my present essay draws upon events partially recalled and described in the Brace Lecture, though I did not truly attempt there what I intend to try here.

7. Class of 1936.

8. Lugosi v. Universal Pictures, 172 U.S.P.Q. 541 (Cal. App. Super. 1972), *rev'd*, 70 Cal. App. 3d 552 (1977), *aff'd*, 25 Cal. 3d 813 (1979).

9. Guglielmi v. Spelling-Goldberg Prods., 25 Cal. 3d 860 (1979).

10. I shall not detail the underlying issues in these cases. They were finally resolved at the end of 1979 when the California Supreme Court held that publicity rights did not descend as such in Califor-

But when the hour for my lecture at last arrived, and I had scarcely begun to speak, I was confronted by a barrage of challenging questions, angry and distressed in tone and nature, the gist of which was that this new right of publicity threatened the questioners' ability to create new works. I could see why. Among the members of my audience, in addition to the lawyers whose presence I had expected, were screenwriters from the Hollywood community, to whom publicity was not just an intriguing new interest the law might or might not appropriately choose to recognize in one fashion or another, but rather an expansion of private rights in intellectual property that would correspondingly diminish the writers' ability to borrow freely from lives whose dramatic value could mean the difference between a salable script and just another bootless Pitch From Hell. In effect, or so it seemed, the law of publicity was dispossessing individual creators in order to benefit the interests of celebrities, or, even more remarkable, their estates and heirs, since many of the celebrities themselves were long since dead.

I confronted an epiphany in the course of that lecture, one whose dimensions were not clear to me, but whose power to grip my imagination and to excite my passions I could neither deny nor resist. Though it would take another two years to translate these emotions and the resulting insights into a published essay, I knew that I would never again confront intellectual property without thinking about its capacity to encroach upon the public domain—and about the costs to the creative imagination of that encroachment—in a new and far darker way than I had done before.

I say "the public domain," and here I must acknowledge the first transformation in my thinking as I confronted what had happened in LA:

Like others at the time I suppose I had thought of the public domain mainly as whatever was left over after intellectual property had finished satisfying its appetite.[11] Now I saw that the public domain demanded recognition as an affirmative entity, conferring its own protection (which I imagined as in the

---

nia. That holding has since been supplanted by statute. For an article summarizing the publicity rights questions at the time (and particularly the question of descendibility), see Peter L. Felcher & Edward L. Rubin, *Privacy, Publicity, and the Portrayal of Real People by the Media*, 88 YALE L.J. 1577 (1979). For a more recent (and approving) appraisal of publicity rights, see Roberta Rosenthal Kwall, *Fame*, 73 IND. L.J. 1 (1997).

11. I am uncertain as to the origins of the "feeding" metaphor. I believe it to be in rather common use today, but was it then? I do not think so. At the time, I noted that:

> Remarkably little direct attention has been paid to the public domain in recent years; there seem to have been no extended treatments of the subject in its own terms . . . . The prevailing view probably was expressed by the writer who observed that "as the phrase 'in the public domain' has generally been used in the cases, it is much less an empirical datum than simply the reflection of an ultimate legal conclusion." Stern, *A Reexamination of Preemption of State Trade Secret Law After Kewanee*, 42 GEO. WASH. L. REV. 927, 967 n.184 (1974). Compare Krasilovsky, *Observations on Public Domain*, 14 BULL. CR. SOC. 205, 205 (1967) ("Public domain in the fields of literature, drama, music and art is the other side of the coin of copyright. It is best defined in negative terms. It lacks the private property element granted under copyright in that there is no legal right to exclude others from enjoying it and is 'free as the air to common use.'").

Lange, *Recognizing the Public Domain*, *supra* note 1, at 150-53 n.20.

nature of rights) upon individual creators; this would be necessary if creativity itself was to survive the tendency toward expansionism that seemed to be burgeoning everywhere among the intellectual property doctrines. In that sense, my perspective was the perspective of creative artists (in Hollywood and elsewhere), to whom intellectual property was not necessarily an incentive or an inducement or an encouragement to create, but rather always a potential impediment to creativity, and on occasion a real and powerful disincentive to the very activity intellectual property was meant to bring about. An opposing concept was required, a concept to be set in affirmative opposition to intellectual property. Of course one might invent a term to fit that need, but it seemed to me that existing terminology would do nicely. As I envisioned my project, the public domain would be pressed into service beyond its accustomed role. No longer a lesser neighborhood on the wrong side of the tracks, it would serve as a recognizable place of refuge for creative endeavor in its own right.

An atavistic restlessness was companion to my thoughts. I remember particularly that scenes from *Singin' in the Rain* flooded my imagination as I reflected on what it means to be creative—a meaning I thought perfectly captured in Gene Kelly and Cyd Charisse's transcendent production number from that film, *Gotta Dance!* And here was a subtle point: I was concerned not merely with the very public, formal, organized creativity of Hollywood (though certainly that had brought me to this work); what moved me no less was a concern for those who, like the character Kelly portrayed in that sequence, might be driven by pure need toward transient episodes of creative expression neither intended nor likely to find any public outlet.

I would say then, first, in response to Boyle's inquiry after meaning, that for me recognizing the public domain began as a rather straightforward appropriation of perfectly ordinary terminology as part of a larger exercise in iconoclasm intended to transform that terminology in the course of a new service. I was interested at the outset in gaining recognition for a different sort of public domain. The public domain I had in mind would become a place of sanctuary for individual creative expression, a sanctuary conferring affirmative protection against the forces of private appropriation that threatened such expression. Recognition for that sanctuary was the challenge. Meaning would follow. I supposed that definitions could wait.

II

The work I hoped for in those early days was not quite the work I produced in the end. Something of the passion survived in what I finally published, perhaps: Boyle suggests that my essay reflected indignation, and "eloquently sarcastic ridicule" of the widespread expansionism of that time. But the particular concerns for creativity that prompted me to write in the first place were actually somewhat muted by the structure I ultimately settled upon for the work. Where

Jessica Litman[12] later wrote directly about the relationship between creativity and the public domain, for example, my own concerns for that relationship I left mainly to others to express, in quoted passages dispersed among a number of other issues I decided to address as part of my strategy for encouraging the wider recognition of the public domain I sought.

Thanks to the heartfelt eloquence of these additional voices, creativity remained a central concern in the essay. One such *cri de coeur* (written by California practitioner Anthony Liebig, and prompted by litigation between Nancy Sinatra and the Fifth Dimension) was powerful then and remains so now, not merely as an observation on the issues raised in a long-forgotten case, but more generally as a living commentary upon the impediments to creativity engendered by encroachments upon the public domain:

> From the standpoint of performers . . . the right to perform in the popular genre or style is essential. Freedom of a performer to earn a living by adopting—either consciously or because he is "influenced" or simply "with it"—current modes and styles which may be widely or even uniformly demanded is, indeed, imperative. How else can he support himself and develop? *Any* limitation upon absolute freedom of performance—while it might result in short-lived bonanzas for one or two performers—would self-evidently be stultifying to performers as a class.
>
> Just how stultifying becomes clear when one considers the predictable volume of litigation and threatened litigation which would follow from any such limitation coupled with the equally predictable inconsistency of result. After several hundred years copyright infringement, which involves only comparison of dimensional self-described works, is still a mystery . . . . We could hardly expect the courts to set parameters and fashion workable, understandable standards of comparison in "imitation" cases in this century! In the meantime, what about the performers and artists and their disseminators who wish to go about their business unhindered?
>
> . . .
>
> From the standpoint of the audience, society at large, and cultural growth, encroachment on the freedom of performance would be destructive both qualitatively and quantitatively. Consider any artist, musician, or performer of any era and ponder what his *oeuvre* would have amounted to had he been precluded from utilizing the brush techniques, color principles, scales, meters, cadences, sounds, moods and methods—in short, the styles—of those who had gone before. Would the classical periods of music and painting have been limited to but one producer each? Would Presley have been foreclosed as an imitator or would he have had the right to foreclose those who came after him? Would the lost generation of American writers have wasted itself in litigation to determine who "got with it" first? Indeed, could there have been a Renaissance? Would we have had a Brahms, a Rubens, a Steinbeck? Or, for that matter, a Sinatra or Fifth Dimension?[13]

Here, indeed, was passion in the service of indignation.

For my own part, I began the essay with some attention to a central problem in intellectual property, namely, the problem of defining the boundaries of a property interest embodied in an intangible *res*. I turned then to what I had begun to see as a kind of metastasis in the law, particularly in the developing law of publicity, but no less so in the laws of trademark dilution and unfair

12. Jessica Litman, *The Public Domain*, 39 EMORY L.J. 965 (1990).

13. Anthony Liebig, *Style and Performance*, 17 BULL. COPR. SOC'Y 40, 46-7 (1969).

competition (of the misappropriation variety), both of which latter doctrines had troubled me before. I passed over lightly both copyright and patent law on the (then plausible but now quite clearly erroneous) assumption that these well-established areas of intellectual property law were essentially stabilized in their relationship to the public domain by internal doctrinal mechanisms designed to avoid undue encroachments. I turned finally to a section of the essay in which I offered some suggestions meant to secure greater functional recognition for the public domain, suggestions aimed mainly at courts, though as it turned out within a year or so after publication, susceptible to adoption by Congress as well.[14] Along the way I invited comparison between the public domains in intellectual property and in public lands. And I concluded with an allusion to the buffalo now vanished from the American prairie, an allusion that, frankly, I have sometimes wished since I could alter or withdraw.

It is of course idle to dwell upon such second thoughts as the ones I have hinted at here. Motivation and strategy often diverge, in the work of a scholar no less than in the work of an artist. I will acknowledge, however, that my motivation for writing now is in part to readdress, more directly, the concerns for creativity that drove me then, and to suggest in passing at least a partial, personal answer to the questions Boyle raises.

Not that I had neglected these questions altogether: the twentieth footnote to *Recognizing the Public Domain* reveals how quickly I succumbed to an examination of the public domain considerably less sanguine than I initially had in mind. Indeed, as I began to research the issues, and then to write, I found myself asking questions of the very sort that Boyle has asked: What was the public domain? How had it been understood? Was there a theory worthy of the name? Could abiding definitions be sensed in the cases or in the literature? And so on.[15] I shall spare the reader an extended exegesis of the numerous and diverse works considered in this very long note; they are faded now, as is my essay.[16] Definitions I left for others. But as for theory—theory as I understand theory; that is, an exercise in intellectual accounting that ordinarily precedes definitions —I did record that, in the course of my passage through the insights I had gathered from among these works and from my own reflections, a tentative theory actually had begun to suggest itself. It was unnecessary to my purpose to pursue the theory at length in that essay, though, and potentially a dis-

---

14. *See* Robert W. Kastenmeier & Michael J. Remington, *The Semiconductor Chip Protection Act of 1984: A Swamp or Firm Ground*, 70 MINN. L. REV. 417, 440-42 (1985) (acknowledging "the Lange test" as a benchmark for new legislation). Of course, that was then, and only briefly: *sic transit gloria mundi.*

15. *Compare* Lange, *Recognizing the Public Domain*, *supra* note 1, at 150-53 n.20 and accompanying text, *with* Boyle, *supra* note 2, at 59.

16. Lange, *Recognizing the Public Domain*, *supra* note 1, at 150-53 n.20. It is worth noting, though, that even a cursory glance at the materials cited in this note and in the remainder of the article reveals how many of the issues we discuss today, as if new, had been anticipated then. *See, e.g.*, Kenneth E. Kulzick & Amy D. Hogue, *Chilled Bird: Freedom of Expression in the Eighties*, 14 LOY. L.A. L. REV. 57, 77-78 (1980) (suggesting that the burden of proof be shifted from defendant to plaintiff in cases involving fair use).

traction. My ambition was affirmative recognition for the public domain *simpliciter*, and my medium a polemic in the guise of a scholarly essay. Constrained by that goal and that form, I was candid in not attending to the nicer questions of definition and theory. These matters I consigned to a few glancing passages in the text and to another footnote toward the end of the piece. In truth, questions of this sort have begun to be attended to quite widely in the decades since. Boyle's paper and the Conference on the Public Domain itself are testament enough to that.

But what was the theory I laid to one side? Essentially this: that an adequate comprehension of the public domain might actually have to begin with a considerably more radical and dramatic reimagining of intellectual property than I professed to see as necessary earlier in the essay, a reimagining that would marry concepts in unfair competition after *Sears* [17] and *Compco*[18] with intimate moral rights, so as ultimately to make room for the sanctuary I had initially envisioned. I had begun by supposing that rights in proprietors and rights in the public domain could stand more or less on equal footing as parties *inter pares* to a property-based regime. But as I worked my way through the piece I began to doubt whether this was so. By the time I reached the last of the half dozen suggestions I offered for action, I had come to think that the problem with intellectual property was in the nature of property itself—not merely in the boundary-fixing difficulties with which I had begun the piece, but rather in the far more central ability of proprietors to exclude others from their works in plenary fashion, and to demand compensation for trespass where no damage necessarily might follow.

I do not mean to claim too much in the way of insight through hindsight. Certainly I did not piece my thoughts together in quite the way I mean to do here. This is representative of what I did say:

> I have meant to convey two principal objections to the new thrust of the law. One is that it tends to reward a species of claim which almost always lacks definition and frequently lacks either a substantial showing of entitlement or any realistic evidence of a taking. The other is that the very momentum of these expanding claims tends to blur, and then displace, important individual and collective rights in the public domain . . . . [C]ourts ought to indulge at least a presumption against new claims. . . . [I]n cases in which it appears sensible to recognize new (or doubtful) intellectual property claims, it will be appropriate for the court to explain what is not covered by the grant as well. An explicit reservation of the public domain in these circumstances must be seen as a part of the court's obligation to be clear about the holding . . . . Inevitably, the work of defining the public domain . . . will follow and, we can hope, a more appropriate balance will be restored to the field of intellectual property[19] . . . . It may be that the key to defining the scope of the public domain in a satisfactory way is to be found in a comparison of the natural law (or "moral") basis of intellectual property with the more specific, occasional need to define and provide for certain economic or commercial interests not necessarily limited to authors and not necessarily the products of authorship . . . . [A]s often as possible, courts ought to divert claims away from intellectual property theory and into such adjacent areas of law as the original form of

17. Sears, Roebuck & Co. v. Stiffel Co., 376 U.S. 225, 230-31 (1964).
18. Compco Corp. v. Day-Brite Lighting, Inc., 376 U.S. 234, 237-38 (1964)
19. Lange, *Recognizing the Public Domain*, *supra* note 1, at 171-177 (citations omitted).

> unfair competition, contracts or, perhaps, some species of moral rights. There can be little damage to the public domain in requiring precautions designed to prevent genuine deception or confusion; *Sears* and *Compco* would have permitted as much. Nor does there seem to be any legitimate objection to moral rights requirements such as attribution of authorship, although rights against distortion, truncation, mutilation and the like are obviously another matter[20] . . . . Meanwhile, courts must be sensitive to the taking too trivial to be actionable as well as the taking which produces apportionable profits. In doubtful cases . . . the defendant ought always to prevail.[21]

A shift in proprietary rights away from property to what today would no doubt be termed a "liability" regime[22] (and by implication a corresponding withdrawal from the ready availability of injunctive relief, and perhaps a move toward compulsory licenses on a much wider basis[23]); a presumption against new proprietary interests, with doubtful cases always to be resolved in favor of the doubt; an increased concern for classic unfair competition concepts (confusion as opposed to misappropriation), with corresponding reliance upon disclaimers and the like as alternatives to exclusion; a frank embrace of the intimate aspects of moral rights, including the rights to acknowledgment and attribution, but with no provision at all for concerns grounded in appropriation; with a diminution in damage awards in trivial cases, accompanied by an equitable apportionment of profits—and meanwhile, beyond and above all these radical re-configurations of the proprietary rights regimes, a corresponding re-conceptualization of the public domain itself, but now a public domain enlarged in standing so as to render presumptively paramount the rights it would confer as against the reduced proprietary rights it would constrain: These were the essay's implicit strategies for realizing the creative sanctuary I envisioned. In this way the public domain itself could become a place of refuge for creative expression, a place of individual no less than collective entitlement, dimensioned both physically and conceptually, and sanctioned by law. In short, the public domain would be a place like home, where, when you go there, they have to take you in and let you dance.

This is close to what I might have said in answer to Boyle's questions on the basis of what I wrote twenty years ago, had I thought to say more than I did.

III

But it is not quite what I would say today.

---

20. *Id.* at 177 n.137.

21. *Id.* at 174.

22. *Cf.* Boyle, *supra* note 2, at 62-69. This term has come into vogue—when, how and why, exactly, I do not know. I distrust it intensely in that it seems to imply a compensable "wrong" in appropriation, a notion that I reject entirely.

23. I suggested as much (albeit with reservations and some hedging) in testimony before Congress in 1984, in connection with hearings on the Record Rental Amendment. *See* Audio and Video First Sale Doctrine: Hearings on H.R. 1027, H.R. 1029, and S. 32 Before the Subcomm. on Courts, Civil Liberties and the Administration of Justice of the House Comm. of the Judiciary, 98th Congress, 1st & 2d Sess. 2 (1983-1984), at 723 (statement of Professor Lange, *cited in* Kastenmeier & Remington, *supra* note 14, at 440. Today I might choose another way to express the thought, for this reason: compulsory licensing may appear to perpetuate the primacy of intellectual property in a scheme of things where I would rather see the public domain at the epicenter and intellectual property as an exception.

In the first place, I am more skeptical about the utility in efforts to reform intellectual property doctrines than I was when I wrote that essay. Note that I do not say "skeptical of the prospects for reform." Unlikely though I know some students of the field believe it to be, I actually suppose that intellectual property is susceptible to reform, not merely through action by courts, as seemed sensible twenty years ago, but through direct political action in the Congress and legislatures of the states. Consider copyright, for example.

The Copyright Society's FACE Initiative,[24] which proposes a direct appeal by copyright proprietors and their representatives to primary and secondary school students across the country, suggests to me that the agendas of the principal copyright industries (the recording and motion picture industries foremost among them, in company with publishers) are more imperiled than they are generally understood to be by outsiders. Houston's Raymond Nimmer has said that copyright cannot survive unless it is accorded widespread acquiescence by the citizenry.[25] I think his insight is acutely perceptive and absolutely correct, for a reason that I also understand him to endorse: Never before has copyright so directly confronted individuals in their private lives. Copyright is omnipresent. But what has to be understood as well is that copyright is also correspondingly over-extended. Absent a wide and no less individual acquiescence, copyright simply may not survive its encounter with the populace at large. It is in part this insight, I suppose, that animates the Copyright Society in its FACE Initiative.

I confess to reservations about this initiative for reasons beyond the parochial concerns of copyright. I think it fundamentally wrong to insist that children internalize the proprietary and moral values of the copyright system. I fear the encroachment upon the formation and growth of creativity that these values represent when they are not suitably constrained—as we cannot count upon them to be in our time. We should be haunted, for example, by the familiar story of Helen Keller, a child (her world so unimaginably circumscribed) whose early efforts at creative self-expression were damaged irreparably by harsh accusations of plagiarism, accusations leveled against her by a mentor from whom she had reason to expect more in the way of empathy and judgment than he proved capable of mustering.[26] He proved, indeed, to be a

---

24. *See* Friends of Active Copyright Education Web Site, *at* http://www.face-copyright.org/ (last visited February 10, 2003). The initiative is aimed directly and primarily at children and is meant to teach them about copyright values, especially as an antidote to peer-to-peer file sharing.

25. *Cf.* David L. Lange, *The Intellectual Property Clause in Contemporary Trademark Law: An Appreciation of Two Recent Essays and Some Thoughts About Why We Ought to Care*, 59 LAW & CONTEMP. PROBS. 213, 224 n.53 (Spring 1996).

26. Keller wrote a story (*The Frost King*) which she gave to her mentor, a man named Michael Anagnos, the director of the Perkins Institution for the Blind in Boston which Keller attended. Anagnos published the story as evidence of Keller's accomplishments, only to discover later that it appeared to have been taken, nearly verbatim, from an earlier story published by a woman named Margaret Canby. Anagnos brought charges of plagiarism against Keller. She was formally exonerated after a hearing, essentially on the ground that whatever she had done was unconscious or unknowing. But the accusation and inquiry scarred her; she said later that she never wrote comfortably again. This episode (something of a *cause célèbre* a century ago, and one addressed in Keller's autobiography as well as in

monster, not a mentor, and his assaults proved destructive to the creative efforts of his imprisoned ward for the balance of her life. But then, apart from the extremity of his appalling judgment and consequent cruelty, how was he unlike any other man or woman who believes in the moral or intellectual or legal sanctity of exclusive rights in expression?[27] The case is extreme, to be sure. But the lesson within it should be central to us all. Children do not come naturally to understand that it is wrong to appropriate creative expression—for the good and sufficient reason, I would argue, that it is not naturally wrong. Creativity and appropriation are inseparable, as inseparable as creativity and memory, and in my judgment they should remain so, at whatever cost may follow to whatever other belief systems (including copyright) may thus be obliged to stand aside.

But let us lay these broader issues to one side. I know the members of the Copyright Society to be well-intentioned. There are no monsters among them—only decent and honorable professionals, as committed to their views as I am to mine.[28] The point remains: Copyright is vulnerable. The FACE Initiative may backfire.

A contest for the hearts and minds of a public is always in doubt unless whatever is at issue makes common sense. And here I think is copyright's dilemma in the matter of the FACE Initiative: Copyright probably does not make common sense in the private lives of individuals.[29] Imagine the member-

---

standard biographies of her life) is usefully discussed in Jim Swan, *Touching Words: Helen Keller, Plagiarism, Authorship*, *in* THE CONSTRUCTION OF AUTHORSHIP: TEXTUAL APPROPRIATION IN LAW AND LITERATURE 57 (Martha Woodmansee & Peter Jaszi, eds., 1994). Swan's account of the incident is textured and intriguing, but even he does not appear to see the accusations against Keller as the straightforward assault upon her creativity that I do. In my view, it simply does not matter that she may have "known" the earlier work: if she considered the work she "created" to be hers, then I would say it was, never mind its provenance. This is what I understand to be implicit in the perfectly ordinary concept of creativity called "making a find." *See* Richard Schiff, *Making a Find: An Argument for Creativity, Not Originality*, STRUCTURALIST REV., Spring 1984, at 59.

27. Keller's tormentors were moved by concerns for academic integrity, not copyright. I do acknowledge this difference, but it does not alter my point here. Protests to the contrary notwithstanding, plagiarism charges in the academy typically spring from, and are driven by, the same misguided sense of ownership of expression that in copyright leads to claims of proprietary rights. When that is not so— when, in other words, the academy's investment in protection is grounded in genuine concerns for provenance, rather than entitlement on the part of the putative "author" and a concomitant concern for enhancement of the author's reputation—the charges should be muted and the remedy essentially one of attribution or acknowledgment. Appropriation is then a matter of legitimate concern only to the extent that these markers of provenance are deliberately withheld, and only when the withholding is essentially in furtherance of a genuine purpose to defraud or mislead. That can happen, but usually the fault, if there is one, is in ignorance, haste, carelessness, misjudgment or indifference—and even these are appropriately judged as venial, not mortal, sins. *Cf.* Judith Hughes, *The Fuzzy Side of Intellectual Dishonesty: Placing Academic Honesty in an Epistemological Context* (2002), *at* http://www.cade-aced.ca/icdepapers/hughes.htm (last visited Feb. 10, 2003). Meanwhile, it is perfectly clear that Keller had no idea she had done anything wrong at all.

28. This is not a pro forma disclaimer. I only recently completed a term as a member of the Board of Trustees of the Society. I number many members of the Society among my closest and most valued professional acquaintances and personal friends.

29. I am sometimes asked whether I think there is any place for copyright at all in the general system of freedom for creativity I favor. The short answer is that I do. In commercial settings, for example, copyright can play a perfectly appropriate role if suitably constrained. Under the 1909 Act, copyright was essentially so constrained; as Boyle points out, one had to work hard to infringe. *See* Boyle, *supra* note 2, at 40. Advances in technology make the restraint of the 1909 Act a matter for nos-

ship of the Parent-Teacher Associations of all the schools on the FACE Initiative hit list suddenly encouraged and even obliged to pay close and heretofore unaccustomed attention to copyright. What then? Now fully aware for the first time of the potential for present limitations on their children's education that copyright actually presupposes,[30] are millions of parents and thousands of teachers likely to smile politely and join hands in support of the motion picture and recording and publishing industries' agenda? I think not. Not merely because the copyright industries say their agendas are fair and just; not merely because economists promise that things will work out for the better, one fine tomorrow; not even if "it's the law"—not, in short, if it means that kids today do without access to information and materials presently at hand and readily available but for copyright. The agenda is politics, not property, not fairness, not justice, not economics or law. The potential for a present backlash at the ballot box is obvious and inescapable, perhaps unanswerable. If that backlash happens, copyright reform will follow.

In the end, I am simply not persuaded that reform will suffice. Not if the goal is my goal, which is still to secure maximum freedom for the creative imagination. There is some slippage in terminology here, to be sure. Perhaps what I have in mind today can fairly be thought of as reform. But I think it may come closer to revolution. And if that revolution is to happen I suspect it will have to happen on the public domain's watch.

And let me speak here, again briefly in passing, to what I think of as one of the least useful or persuasive notions to have sprung up in response to the growing recognition of the public domain. Professor Samuels and some others have suggested that no matter how we may struggle, in the end the public domain is whatever intellectual property is not.[31] Conceptually, this can be so only if one cannot envision the public domain as having an affirmative existence of its own. But that exercise does not require much, whether in the way of conceptual thinking or envisioning. Imagine an African veldt where lions and jack-

talgia today; that regime probably could not be reinstituted as such. To be suitably constrained today, copyright ideally would have to be converted into some version of an "opt-in" system—perhaps like the Writers' and Producers' Guilds in the motion picture industry; or perhaps like the commons of the General Public License described in Boyle's article, which, as he quite correctly observes, is an alternative system of protection. *See id.* at 44-45. While copyright remains as it is under the 1976 Act, however, the best protection against its encroachments into private lives is a separate and paramount public domain, from within which creativity can be promoted and defended.

30. What limitations? Take these as commonplace examples of a considerably wider field: (1) limits on photocopying, resulting in limits on "coursepaks"; (2) limits on the availability of musical compositions, sound recordings, motion pictures and audiovisual aids in the classroom and beyond; and (3) limits on internet access resulting from encoded content protected by the Digital Millennium Copyright Act of 1998, Pub. L. No. 105-304, 112 Stat. 2860. These limits remain substantial even after the passage of the TEACH Act, which was meant to address some issues affecting education. Technology, Education and Copyright Harmonization Act of 2002, Pub. L. No. 107-273, § 13301, 116 Stat. 1758, 1910-13. All of these limitations adversely affect the ability of students to engage in the fullest use of copyrighted works for educational purposes. Not one of them has ever been vetted widely among the parents or teachers of school-age children.

31. Edward Samuels, *The Public Domain in Copyright Law*, 41 J. COPR. SOC'Y U.S.A. 137 (1993); *see* Boyle, *supra* note 2, at 71-73.

als and gazelles dwell in uneasy symbiosis while the merciless sun shines down dispassionately upon them. There is symbiosis among them, yes, yet it requires only this much (read: "a small pinch of") imagination to understand these inhabitants of the veldt as separate animals. Indeed, the function of taxonomy is to enable us to draw these singularly useful, but also elementary, distinctions. You have to be a lion- or jackal-lover of truly limited imagination or unlimited commitment to argue that gazelles are to be understood as no more than whatever is left over after their adversaries have finished feeding. For my own part, I am not much interested in reforming the predators and scavengers among us. My project is to recognize gazelles as gazelles—and not merely to recognize them, but to give them the means with which to defend themselves against their natural enemies.

Intellectual property can go on being intellectual property, reformed or otherwise. Meanwhile, the public domain certainly can and should be envisioned as a thing apart, and strengthened accordingly.

What is needed then, in my view, is an additional reimagining of the public domain we have come to recognize. As James Boyle observes, the recurring metaphor for the public domain today is mainly that of place: a wilderness, a commons, a sanctuary, a home. These metaphors appear to follow from the term "public domain" itself. In some settings, this is undoubtedly a useful way to think. But from the perspective of creativity I think it no longer quite suffices, if it ever did.

A better metaphor than place, I think, is status. Imagine the public domain as a status that arises from the exercise of the creative imagination, thus to confer entitlements, privileges and immunities in the service of that exercise; a status independently and affirmatively recognized in law, sometimes collective in nature and sometimes individual, but omnipresent, portable and defining; and a status meanwhile paramount to whatever inconsistent status may be conferred upon a work of authorship (or its author) from time to time, whether that work is protected as intellectual property, or is included within a so-called liability regime, or is otherwise provided for. One could imagine this sort of public domain more particularly still, so as to include tenets peculiar to setting or need, while suggesting the sources from which such a public domain might derive.[32] But in this essay I will merely suggest its nature, and even that somewhat indirectly—first, briefly, by way of simile supported by example; then, at slightly greater length, through an analogy drawn from an appealing article in

32. Of course, one must eventually state plainly how such a public domain might be made a reality. The ultimate sources of law, as I suppose them to be, are essentially four in number: a happy but unlikely evolution in the main tenets of the relevant positive law; the First Amendment; the Intellectual Property Clause; and an international convention, perhaps grounded in human rights. None of these is to play any real role in this essay. But I am at work (with my Duke colleague Jeff Powell) on a book on the First Amendment in which we do address these issues somewhat directly. That book, *No Law: Intellectual Property in the Absolute Image of the First Amendment*, is under contract with the Stanford University Press, and is scheduled for completion within the coming year.

the contemporary literature, and finally, through an example of how a public domain so configured might actually work in practice.

Let us envision the public domain as if it were a status like citizenship, but a "citizenship" arising from the exercise of creative imagination rather than as a concomitant of birth.[33] It is surely no challenge to identify creativity and imagination with citizenship in a more conventional sense. This is indeed consistent with a perfectly ordinary understanding of citizenship, now well established in American life and by no means original with us. The Roman historian Tacitus, writing of the reigns of the Emperor Nerva and Trajan, observed: "Such was the happiness of the times that men could think as they pleased and speak as they thought."[34] Justice Brandeis appropriated that insight (without attribution) in *Whitney v. California*, in which he identified thinking and speaking as principal objects of First Amendment protection.[35] Here, then, is an idea powerful enough to transcend its origins: happiness as a function of thinking and speaking freely, and each of these as an attribute of desirable citizenship. I suggest in turn that thinking of the public domain as conferring a status akin to citizenship—but now a citizenship of the creative imagination—is little more than a step away from civic republicanism toward a clearer understanding of the recognition and protection that exercises of creativity require and should beget.

For make no mistake: It is protection, not merely recognition or definition, that we need. A concept like citizenship can serve usefully here, as it has for thousands of years.

Consider, for example, the Apostle Paul's claim upon citizenship in this account drawn from the Book of Acts. Paul, born Saul of Tarsus in Silesia, a Jew but also a Roman and now an apostate, is preaching the Gospel of Christ in Jerusalem Temple, to the intense displeasure of the devout, and the resulting discomfort of Claudius Lysias, Chief Captain of the Roman Guard, whose task it is to maintain order in this important but beleaguered outpost of the Empire:

> And as they cried out, and cast off their clothes, and threw dust into the air,
>
> The chief captain commanded him to be brought into the castle, and bade that he should be examined by scourging; that he might know wherefore they cried so against him.

---

33. Though I am unaware of any suggestion quite like this, I mean to make no claim of originality here, and will cheerfully accept the representations of anyone who does claim it. In some part I imagine the idea occurred to me as a result of John Perry Barlow's interesting suggestions for a "citizenship of the net," a notion now very commonly expressed in the term "netizens" – though in truth I am actually not much interested in the net as a special province of concern. And I may have been influenced by the concepts developed in Jed Rubenfeld's recent essay, *The Freedom of Imagination: Copyright's Constitutionality*, which was published last year in the YALE LAW JOURNAL, and which I had the pleasure of reading while it was still in manuscript. *See infra* note 37, and accompanying text. In any event, whatever the genesis of the idea may be, I do think it apt, and have merely tried to develop it here as an alternative to place.

34. 1 TACITUS, THE HISTORIES, § 1 (A.D. 109). I have employed this cite in a number of earlier essays.

35. 274 U.S. 357, 375 (1927).

> And as they bound him with thongs, Paul said unto the centurion that stood by, Is it lawful for you to scourge a man that is a Roman, and uncondemned?
>
> When the centurion heard that, he went and told the chief captain, saying, Take heed what thou doest: for this man is a Roman.
>
> Then the chief captain came, and said unto him, Tell me, art thou a Roman? He said, Yea.
>
> And the chief captain answered, With a great sum obtained I this freedom. And Paul said, But I was free born.
>
> Then straightway they departed from him which should have examined him: and the chief captain also was afraid, after he knew that he was a Roman, and because he had bound him.[36]

Civis Romanus Sum: As in this example, and like the model originally proposed above, citizenship is a status independently and affirmatively recognized in law. It confers entitlements, privileges and immunities, sometimes collective in nature and sometimes individual. It is omnipresent, portable and defining. Above all, it is capable of achieving paramountcy vis-à-vis rights, obligations or constraints otherwise imposed by law. I do not say that the public domain is exactly equivalent to citizenship. I do say that it might profitably take on these attributes of citizenship in securing protection for exercises of the creative imagination against the claims otherwise to be made under rights now sounding in intellectual property or its successors.

A similar suggestion can be seen in a recent essay by Jed Rubenfeld,[37] who argues that the First Amendment should be read to protect what he calls "the freedom of imagination." The analogy is plain. I envision a public domain configured so as to offer attributes akin to the status of citizenship in the service of creative imagination. Rubenfeld envisions attributes of citizenship itself in that service, particularly in the form of the First Amendment. One must not go too far. These are not quite the same thoughts. I am interested in the public domain as an affirmative source of entitlements capable of deployment, as, when and where required, against the encroachments upon the creative imagination threatened by intellectual property. He is interested in the First Amendment, but supposes that, were it read as it ought to be, some such encroachments would necessarily be curtailed.[38] He is not primarily interested in developing his ideas as an exercise in fashioning public policy for intellectual property.[39] (For that matter, properly understood, neither am I.) His project is the First Amendment. Mine is the public domain. Taking these differences fully into account, however, I am still much drawn to the parallels his argument affords.

---

36. *Acts* 22:23-29 (King James).

37. Jed Rubenfeld, *The Freedom of Imagination: Copyright's Constitutionality*, 112 YALE L.J. 1 (2002).

38. *Cf. id.* at 13.

39. *Id.* at 58.

To begin with, he relies upon an exercise of the imagination to invoke First Amendment protection. I would rely on a similar exercise to invoke the protection of the public domain.

Rubenfeld's explicit inclusion of the imagination as the central focus of his essay offers a neat resolution to a troublesome problem in envisioning the reach and scope of the public domain. This problem has been to bring within reach of the public domain and its protection those kinds of appropriations that are creative but do not necessarily result in any form of public expression, or that may result in no expression of any kind. Reading is a classic example; Rubenfeld treats reading as an exercise of the imagination and thus a central object of protection within the First Amendment.[40] I suppose that Justice Brandeis' inclusion of "thinking" as a First Amendment value is close to the "imagination" that Rubenfeld includes, and for some purposes may even be slightly the better (more capacious) term, but there appears to be something useful in the more focused connotations of "imagination" in this setting, where "creativity" and "expression" already take on the color of terms of art.

To be sure, there is never any certainty in this term or that. Imagination is distinct from action in Rubenfeld's view: "The freedom of imagination demands that people be free to exercise their imagination. It is not a freedom to do what one imagines."[41] Violence, intentional misrepresentation ("knowingly denying that an exercise of imagination is an exercise of imagination" [42]), misinformation—these are among the arguable exercises of the imagination that are not within the freedom Rubenfeld envisions. And piracy: "When copyright law bars simple piracy, it does not punish infringers for exercising their imagination. It punishes them for failing to exercise their imagination—for failing to add any new imaginative content to the copied material."[43]

I suppose that peer-to-peer file sharing (à la Napster, for example) would not qualify as an exercise of imagination under the test Rubenfeld himself has in mind here. And what about appropriation artists like Damian Loeb,[44] or Negativland,[45] or Sherrie Levine?[46] Would they be protected? Rubenfeld's analysis is additionally complex at this point because he would actually approach the First Amendment question in cases like these from within the matrix of copyright principles that have evolved from the derivative works right.[47] Thus, "not just any change in the original work should suffice to evade the copyright holder's reproduction right. Trivial or obvious modifications, or changes that involve no substantially new act of imagination, especially if intro-

40. *See id.* at 34-35.

41. *Id.* at 42.

42. *Id.* at 45.

43. *Id.* at 48.

44. *See* http://www.damianloeb.com/ (last visited Feb. 10, 2003).

45. *See* http://www.negativland.com/ (last visited Feb. 10, 2003); Negativland, *Two Relationships to a Cultural Public Domain*, 66 LAW & CONTEMP. PROBS. 239 (Winter/Spring 2003).

46. *See* http://www.crownpoint.com/html/levine.html (last visited Feb. 10, 2003).

47. Rubenfeld, *supra* note 37, at 49-60.

duced to evade the reproduction right, should not qualify. At bottom, the judge is called on to decide whether the old has been reimagined—whether the allegedly infringing new work is in fact new."[48] Appropriation artists might or might not make the grade if this is to be the approach. Negativland probably would, its madcap thefts surely creative and imaginative under the strictest scrutiny.[49] Loeb might, since in his work appropriation is mixed with elements of substantial originality.[50] Levine is another matter. As I understand Rubenfeld, he would not extend the freedom of imagination to appropriation artists whose art appears objectively to consist of appropriation *simpliciter*, unmediated by additional affirmative acts of imagination.[51] If Levine is that kind of artist (a question Rubenfeld does not consider and one I need not resolve here), then she is beyond the reach of the freedom of imagination.[52]

I expect I would apply Rubenfeld's standard less restrictively than he. I think file-sharing involves substantial exercises of the imagination: the kids who do it are producing music for themselves. And Levine's art (as I understand it) appeals to me no less than the collage work of Negativland and Loeb. But then, should Rubenfeld and I differ, so what? He can hardly be faulted for interpreting his own project in a way I do not entirely agree with. The great value in his work is the vision itself, a vision which places imagination at the center of First Amendment protection. In this vision I can and do concur entirely—though in the end I continue to think that the public domain, configured as suggested here, may offer the advantage of a somewhat more specific and reliable protection.[53] I shall conclude this essay with an elaboration upon how that public domain might work in practice.

Consider copyright's fair use doctrine. Under the proposal I have advanced here, that doctrine should now be seen as an affirmative aspect of the public domain at large, rather than as a mere affirmative defense to an allegation of

---

48. *Id.* at 55.

49. *See* Negativland, FAIR USE: THE STORY OF THE LETTER U AND THE NUMERAL 2 (1995).

50. *See supra* note 44.

51. *See* Rubenfeld, *supra* note 37, at 48.

52. The reader can judge: see *supra* note 46.

53. The real difficulty with the First Amendment as a source for an expansive vision of the public domain is that the Amendment has been so closely circumscribed by Supreme Court cases since the early 1970s as to rob it of vitality, a constraining circumstance with which even the best scholars can contend only up to a point. *See, e.g.*, Yochai Benkler, *Free as the Air to Common Use: First Amendment Constraints on the Enclosure of the Public Domain*, 74 N.Y.U. L. REV. 354 (1999); Neil Weinstock Netanel, *Locating Copyright Within the First Amendment Skein*, 54 STAN. L. REV. 1 (2001). In these and many other articles first rate scholars are obliged to pick their way among doctrines that are fundamentally at odds with a decent concern for creativity. Of course, this is in no sense a failing on their part; to the contrary, their scholarship may appear to be the more elegant and heroic for their efforts. Rubenfeld's article deals with this problem no less elegantly or heroically than have others, but in the end he cannot altogether escape the confining matrix of the Court's cases either. If the First Amendment is to serve, then it too will have to be addressed in terms of its baseline deficiencies in interpretation, an undertaking primary among the tasks my colleague Jeff Powell and I have taken up in drafting the manuscript for our book. *See supra* note 32.

copyright infringement.[54] So viewed, fair use would not be limited in the protection it confers merely to those instances in which copyright infringement is alleged. It would extend as well, and as fully, to species of infringement recognized under other doctrines, including the right of publicity, trademarks, misappropriation in unfair competition, trade secrets, ideas, and even patents. An agenda of this sort would require years to realize, of course, and more space and time than I have to describe it now. But limited even to a setting in which the adversary is copyright, one can reimagine fair use as an aspect of the public domain rather than of copyright itself, and envision a role for fair use well beyond the one it now plays in that field.

In a work-in-progress Jennifer Anderson and I offered at the Law School's Public Domain Conference last year, we sketched in a vision of fair use for what we called "transformative appropriations."[55] We have decided to continue working on our model rather than publish it among the collection of papers in this symposium. But for the sake of example I will offer excerpts from our working draft, edited to reflect the reconfigured public domain I have suggested here in action. Transformation, in the fashion proposed by Judge Leval,[56] is no longer at the center of our model. Instead, fair use is invoked by any creative act, including (thanks to Rubenfeld's suggestion) an exercise of the creative imagination. The consequence of that invocation is an investiture of rights conceptually akin to the rights invoked by a claim of citizenship:

> Creative appropriation would be presumptively privileged in every instance, without primary concern either for exploitation adversely affecting the economic value of an antecedent work or for the reputation or sensibilities of its author or proprietor – though in appropriate cases an equitable provision for sharing the proceeds of such exploitations would follow, as would suitable provisions for disclaimers, acknowledgments, attribution and the like. The exclusive rights of authors under copyright,

54. In the text, notes, and citations immediately following, I will cut blindly across vast swaths of prior writing by scholars, some whose works I know, and no doubt others whose publications have escaped my notice. I particularly acknowledge Professor Patterson (whose many writings in the field have set an example for anyone who ventures into this area of the law), as well as his occasional writing partner Professor Joyce; Professor Gordon (whose seminal essay on fair use as market failure has helped shape all following debate in the field); Judge Leval (whose proposal with respect to transformative works has had great effect in the field); Professor Fisher (whose own much longer work on fair use in some sense set the stage for Judge Leval's later work); Professor Weinreb (whose vision of fair use as "fair" I have thought especially attractive); Professor Netanel (whose work I always read with great respect and interest); Judge Birch (whose opinion in *SunTrust Bank v. Houghton-Mifflin Co.* reflects a deeper appreciation of fair use than is common among judges); Judge Kosinski (whose views on appropriation and apportionment I think interesting, if not entirely persuasive); and David Nimmer (whose writing on fair use, as on everything else, is truly remarkable). In a different sort of essay I would feel constrained to gather additional representative citations, so that the intellectual provenance of the things said by me here would be both manifest and thorough. On this occasion, however, when my purpose frankly is to present a straightforward polemic rather than conventional scholarship, I shall beg the reader's indulgence, and content myself with acknowledging that most of what I propose has probably been anticipated elsewhere, whether or not it has been assembled in quite the same way.

55. *See* David Lange & Jennifer Lange Anderson, *Copyright, Fair Use and Transformative Critical Appropriation* (2001), *available at* http://www.law.duke.edu/pd/papers/langeand.pdf (last visited Feb. 10, 2003). The introduction included here has been added since the work was posted. This work remains a work in progress, and is accordingly incomplete.

56. *See* Pierre N. Leval, *Commentary: Toward a Fair Use Standard*, 103 HARV. L. REV. 1105 (1990); Pierre N. Leval, *Nimmer Lecture: Fair Use Rescued*, 44 UCLA L. REV. 1449 (1997).

> including rights in derivative works, would be subordinated accordingly, but would remain otherwise unaffected.[57]

No revision to the Copyright Act would be required, in our view. Section 107 already supports (we would say commands) a reading that makes its provisions superior to the provisions of section 106.[58]

And how far would this carry us toward our goal of affirmative protection for creative appropriation?

> If we presuppose the necessary creative exercise in connection with the appropriation, then rarely, if ever, should fair use be withheld merely on account of either functional or aesthetic equivalency between the two works. It may be that a secondary work appears to add nothing at all to the creative offices already reflected in an antecedent work; and in that case perhaps it would be appropriate to inquire further into the justification for fair use. While such a scenario can be envisioned in theory, it is exceedingly unlikely to be encountered in practice, absent the boldest forms of appropriation through the simplest forms of copying, followed by publication to persons already identically addressed by the proprietor of the antecedent work. And even in that case, an identical creative exercise in the second work, fairly judged to have prompted that appropriation (whether or not independently), would justify the claim of fair use nonetheless. Should Lauren Greenfield take up painting, for example, the fact that she may produce works of the sort that Damian Loeb produces does not mean that Loeb's independent conceptions would not continue to be privileged. Indeed, it is entirely possible, under the analysis we propose, that Loeb and Greenfield might each identically counter-appropriate the other's expression, so as to produce works indistinguishable from each other, each claiming fair use in his or her respective appropriation. Weird as this may seem in the imagining, it is but a corollary to Hand's own contemplation as to the unobjectionable replicability of Keats' "Ode To A Grecian Urn": copyright always presupposes the possibility of works identical in expression, yet independently conceived.
>
> From the perspective of mere identity or functional equivalency, then, fair use would be withheld only when no creative exercise could be discerned in the second work at all. Straightforward piracy would continue to be forbidden, of course, and might even be regulated more closely in the absence of any lingering concern for fair use. But piracy could not effectively be urged in a transaction merely because the second work, if licensed, would amount to a derivative work. Under this analysis, to the contrary, the question of derivative work status is of no greater consequence than would follow

---

57. Lange & Anderson, *supra* note 55. The idea of apportionment of profits is by no means new, and it has seemed just, as opposed to a kind of winner-take-all outcome in fair use. It is a useful way to accommodate the fourth factor under Section 107 of the Copyright Act. 17 U.S.C. § 107(4) (2000) ("the effect of the use upon the potential market for or value of the copyrighted work"). I contemplated apportionment in passing in *Recognizing the Public Domain*, *supra* note 1, at 174, although there I considered it primarily in conceptual terms, rather than in the immediate context of fair use. Among its recent proponents are Professors Netanel and Rubenfeld, as well as Judge Kosinski, who suggested it in the course of his Brace Memorial Lecture. But I have had some second thoughts about whether this idea is in fact as useful or as fair as it seems. Specifically, I wonder whether it does not unwisely entangle the legitimacy of creative appropriation with the wholly separate (and essentially adventitious) question of profits and revenue streams. I shall not try to work this out in a footnote, but do want to record my reservation about the issue. (It is one of the reasons Jennifer Anderson and I have temporarily withdrawn our fair use essay from publication.)

58. The texts of the two sections suggest as much on their face: 17 U.S.C. § 106 is "subject to sections 107 through 122"; 17 U.S.C. § 107 applies "notwithstanding the provisions of sections 106 and 106A." In SunTrust Bank v. Houghton Mifflin Co., 268 F.3d 1257, 1260 n.3 (11th Cir. 2001), Judge Birch suggested that fair use, properly understood, is an affirmative right, not an affirmative defense. *See also* Kulzick & Hogue, *supra* note 16.

were the second work a simple copy. If an exercise of the creative imagination invokes fair use, then the exclusive rights must gracefully step aside pro tanto.[59]

Ah, but then: "straightforward piracy?" I can hear James Boyle asking, "What does *that* mean?"

It means an appropriation unmotivated by any creative exercise, including an exercise of the creative imagination. And how do we know when we are in the presence of such an exercise? There is no escaping: we must decide. In Rubenfeld's approach to this issue, he establishes what seem to me to be categories of conduct leading one to conclude that imagination is at work or not.[60] The bright lines that result I have already suggested may be more restrictive than the fair use model I have just outlined is meant to be. In my view, the decision ought to be grounded in fact-finding affected by law: The decision of a trial judge should be reviewable in plenary fashion by a court of appeal. The presumption should be fair use.[61]

And what of the most extreme cases? In private correspondence, initiated by David Nimmer and joined in by Neil Netanel, Jed Rubenfeld and me, we have asked that question of each other, having Rubenfeld's article in mind. Consider, as we have, a hypothetical (somewhat distorted from the original put by Jorge Borges) in which Cervantes' *Don Quixote* is "recreated" word for word by a later "author" to the pleasurable reception of those who have not read it before because, until its recreation, it had seemed merely an antique.[62] Is this an exercise of the imagination? I think it fair to say the members of our ad hoc discussion group are of mixed minds about the matter. But I would say it all depends on what the putative junior creator has in mind. Appropriation is creative, I think, and therefore qualifies as an exercise of the creative imagination, when we see in it the qualities or attributes we recognize in conceptual art of any kind.[63] And if the answer to the question is debatable or in doubt, then the junior creator should prevail as against all efforts by a senior party to forbid the appropriation, for the cardinal rule of good citizenship under the protective

---

59. Lange & Anderson, *supra* note 55, at 151.

60. *See* Rubenfeld, *supra* note 37, at 48-49.

61. In my view the availability of such a presumption is a necessary prerequisite to any adequate theory of the public domain. Indeed, that is essentially where this essay begins. *See* text accompanying *supra* notes 1 & 2.

62. *Cf.* David Nimmer, *Copyright in the Dead Sea Scrolls: Authorship and Originality*, 38 HOUS. L. REV. 1, 41 n.154 (2001). This article is a masterwork, nothing less, and cannot be adequately acknowledged in less extravagant terms. But do note, gentle reader, that Nimmer is addressing conceptual subtleties and nuances well beyond the single issue—imagining protection for creativity as a function of the public domain—that mainly engages me here. Read Nimmer for the sheer pleasure of the experience; and then see whether you can ever feel quite the same about the plausibility in Learned Hand's spin (in Sheldon v. Metro-Goldwyn Pictures Corp., 81 F.2d 49 (1936)) on Keats' "Ode on a Grecian Urn." If you can, you may be ready for a conservator, as Nimmer suggests, but you are also probably ready for creativity as I see it. The two propositions are in no part inconsistent.

63. *See* Schiff, *supra* note 26. Even this splendidly satisfying conception of creativity may not go as far as one might like. "Making a find" is creative, as Schiff says; I would argue that even the "find" may be creative, if motivated in play. *See* David Lange, *At Play in the Fields of the Word: Copyright and the Construction of Authorship in the Post-Literate Millennium*, 55 LAW & CONTEMP. PROBS. 139 (Spring 1992) [hereinafter Lange, *At Play*].

reach of the public domain is that doubtful cases ought always to be resolved in favor of appropriation.

Certainly, appropriation of a very ordinary sort can amount to an exercise of the creative imagination. In his provocative essay on fair use included among the papers in this symposium,[64] David Nimmer publishes for the first time the contents of a poem written by Anne Frank in 1940 to a friend whose birthday party in Amsterdam young Anne attended, perhaps for the last time. "Dear Henny," Anne Frank wrote on that occasion, "Pluck roses on earth, and forget me not."[65] The words are haunting now, poignant, simple, terribly sweet and sad. They call to us from across the years with a power they surely could not have possessed when first they were penned. Yet I would have said they were unmistakably creative then. Who today would deny that they are imagination exemplified?

But I am obliged to report—on the authority of David Nimmer himself, who discovered what I am about to relate after his own article had gone to press—that these words also appear to have been appropriated verbatim from an anthology of poems widely available in The Netherlands at the time. The poet who wrote them was named Snelders. His work appears to have been composed in 1895, and might plausibly have remained under copyright in 1940.[66]

Was Anne Frank a creator on the occasion when she wrote her note to Henny? I have said I think so, and my opinion remains unchanged.

But was she an author? Perhaps not, in the conventional understanding of that term in copyright. Was she a plagiarist, a pirate, a thief? No decent person would lay such a charge against her memory. She was just a young girl, barely ten years old, a friend writing to a friend on the occasion of a celebration. Presupposing copyright, was this fair use? Yes, surely then—and even now, under the tedious and inexact standards of our time. But I submit that these are the wrong questions, and not merely for obvious reasons of decency. The questions are wrong because, coming as they do from within the matrix of copyright, they are motivated by the wrong priorities and the wrong concerns.

It is wrong to challenge school children with responsibility for copyright. Wrong for copyright to intrude into private lives. Wrong to measure creativity by the standards of copyright. Wrong to lay impediments (moral, intellectual, legal) before exercises of the imagination, whether great or small. Wrong, in short, to rob us of this vital aspect of our citizenship: the right to think as we please and to speak as we think.

We must learn to reimagine the public domain. We must learn to ask questions from within the province of that new status, a status like citizenship, measured by creativity and the imagination, and invoked by an exercise of

---

64. David Nimmer, *"Fairest of Them All" and Other Fairy Tales of Fair Use*, 66 LAW & CONTEMP. PROBS. 263 (Winter/Spring 2003).

65. *Id.* at 284-85.

66. E-mail from David Nimmer (Nov. 21, 2002) (on file with author).

either. For then Anne Frank's answer to the question of entitlement will be our common answer: *Civis musarum sum.*

James Boyle is right, of course. There are many public domains. Perhaps we must recognize them all. But for myself and others like me, I want the public domain, however it may be defined, to secure these elemental aspirations which I believe innate in human kind: to think and to imagine, to remember and appropriate, to play and to create.[67] It will be enough if recognizing the public domain brings us to that end.

67. *See* Lange, *At Play*, *supra* note 63.

***

Notes

Notes

Notes

Notes

Notes

Notes

Notes

Notes